ROUTLEDGE LIBRARY EDITIONS: EMPLOYMENT AND UNEMPLOYMENT

Volume 9

EQUAL EMPLOYMENT OPPORTUNITY AND AFFIRMATIVE ACTION

EQUAL EMPLOYMENT OPPORTUNITY AND AFFIRMATIVE ACTION
A Sourcebook

FLOYD D. WEATHERSPOON

LONDON AND NEW YORK

First published in 1985 by Garland Publishing, Inc.

This edition first published in 2019
by Routledge
2 Park Square, Milton Park, Abingdon, Oxon OX14 4RN

and by Routledge
52 Vanderbilt Avenue, New York, NY 10017

Routledge is an imprint of the Taylor & Francis Group, an informa business

British Library Cataloguing in Publication Data
A catalogue record for this book is available from the British Library

ISBN: 978-1-138-38855-0 (Set)
ISBN: 978-0-429-02498-6 (Set) (ebk)
ISBN: 978-0-367-02741-4 (Volume 9) (hbk)
ISBN: 978-0-367-02747-6 (Volume 9) (pbk)
ISBN: 978-0-429-39804-9 (Volume 9) (ebk)

Publisher's Note
The publisher has gone to great lengths to ensure the quality of this reprint but points out that some imperfections in the original copies may be apparent.

Disclaimer
The publisher has made every effort to trace copyright holders and would welcome correspondence from those they have been unable to trace.

equal employment opportunity and affirmative action a sourcebook

Floyd D. Weatherspoon

Garland Publishing Inc. • New York & London
1985

Library of Congress Cataloging-in-Publication Data

Weatherspoon, Floyd D., 1951–
   Equal employment opportunity and affirmative
action.

   (Public affairs and administration series ; 12)
(Garland reference library of social science ; v. 164)
   Includes indexes.
   1. Discrimination in employment—Law and legislation
—United States—Bibliography.   2. Affirmative action
programs—Law and legislation—United States—Bibliogra-
phy.   I. Title. II. Series. III. Series: Garland
reference library of social science ; v. 164.
KF3464.A1W43   1985   344.73'01133   82-49157
ISBN 0-8240-9158-2 (alk. paper) 347.3041133

Cover design by Bonnie Goldsmith

Printed on acid-free, 250-year-life paper
Manufactured in the United States of America

contents

series foreword

The twentieth century has seen public administration come of age as a field and practice. This decade, in fact, marks the one hundredth anniversary of the profession. As a result of the dramatic growth in government, and the accompanying information explosion, many individuals—managers, academicians and their students, researchers—in organizations feel that they do not have ready access to important information. In an increasingly complex world, more and more people need published material to help solve problems.

The scope of the field and the lack of a comprehensive information system has frustrated users, disseminators, and generators of knowledge in public administration. While there have been some initiatives in recent years, the documentation and control of the literature have been generally neglected. Indeed, major gaps in the development of the literature, the bibliographic structure of the discipline, have evolved.

Garland Publishing, Inc., has inaugurated the present series as an authoritative guide to information sources in public administration. It seeks to consolidate the gains made in the growth and maturation of the profession.

The Series consists of three tiers:

1. core volumes keyed to the major subfields in public administration such as personnel management, public budgeting, and intergovernmental relations;
2. bibliographies focusing on substantive areas of administration such as community health; and
3. titles on topical issues in the profession.

Each book will be compiled by one or more specialists in the area. The authors—practitioners and scholars—are selected in open competition from across the country. They design their work to include an introductory essay, a wide variety of bibliographic materials, and, where appropriate, an information resource section. Thus each contribution in the collection provides a systematic basis for managers and researchers to make informed judgments in the course of their work.

Since no single volume can adequately encompass such a broad, interdisciplinary subject, the Series is intended as a continuous project that will incorporate new bodies of literature as needed. The titles in preparation represent the initial building blocks in an operating information system for public affairs and administration. As an open-ended endeavor, it is hoped that not only will the Series serve to summarize knowledge in the field but also will contribute to its advancement.

This collection of book-length bibliographies is the product of considerable collaboration on the part of many people. Special appreciation is extended to the editors and staff of Garland Publishing, Inc., to the individual contributors in the Public Affairs and Administration Series, and to the anonymous reviewers of each of the volumes. Inquiries should be made to the Series Editor:

James S. Bowman
Tallahassee

preface

In this remarkable book, the author has compiled a large collection of resource material that will be of benefit to the student as well as the practitioner of equal employment and affirmative action (EEO/AA). Since the passage of Title VII of the Civil Rights Act of 1964, a substantial body of law has developed interpreting the Act and the various amendments relating to it. This book includes a broad scope of information on EEO/AA from its infancy and progresses through its rapidly changing and developing stages. Indeed, this book will be an invaluable asset in easily acquiring and supplementing one's basic knowledge as well as providing a general overview of the subject area.

Our extensive, decentralized system of compiling and disseminating information often deters a thorough and comprehensive coverage of a subject. However, this book will greatly enhance our ability to expediently obtain concise information covering numerous aspects of EEO/AA from expansive and diverse sources.

Shirley A. Richardson, Attorney
Louisville, Kentucky

introduction

This bibliography lists articles and treatises on equal employment opportunity and affirmative action that were written and/
or published after the passage of the Civil Rights Act of 1964
through 1984. During the past twenty years, a plethora of
material has been written and published on equal employment
opportunity and affirmative action (EEO/AA). Of course, it
would have been impossible to include every publication on this
subject in this bibliography. Nonetheless, it contains more than
1,100 entries, most of which are annotated. These entries
represent a sampling of material on virtually every aspect of
EEO/AA, providing the user with a beginning point for researching any topic on EEO/AA.

Before explaining the organization of the bibliography, a historical review of the development of EEO/AA laws and regulations will provide an understanding of when and why various
EEO/AA laws and regulations were promulgated and the impact
of them. This synopsis will assist the user in not only understanding the organization of the material in the bibliography but,
just as important, why there has been a need for EEO/AA
during the past twenty years and why it continues today.

Title VII

The legislative history of the Civil Rights Act of 1964 reveals
that during the 1960s, American blacks and other protected
class individuals (i.e., women and various minority groups) were
denied employment opportunities because of their race, color,
sex, religion, and national origin. As a result, minorities and
women received lower wages and their rate of unemployment
was higher than the country's overall rate of unemployment. In

an effort to curtail employment discrimination, Congress enacted Title VII of the Civil Rights Act in 1964. This Act made it unlawful for those employers covered by Title VII:

(1) to fail or refuse to hire or discharge any individual, or otherwise to discriminate against any individual with respect to his compensation, terms, conditions, or privileges of employment, because of such individual's race, color, religion, sex, or national origin; or

(2) to limit, segregate, or classify his employees or applicants for employment in any way which would deprive or tend to deprive any individual of employment opportunities or otherwise adversely affect his status as an employee, because of such individual's race, color, religion, sex, or national origin.

Under Title VII, the Equal Employment Opportunity Commission (EEOC) was created and designated with the primary responsibility of administering Title VII through conciliation and negotiation. The EEOC was also directed to provide technical assistance to organizations covered by Title VII. Employers with fifteen or more employees were covered by the Act, excluding public sector employers. Originally, the EEOC was given limited powers and could not directly bring lawsuits to enforce Title VII. Lawsuits had to be brought by the complaining party or by the Justice Department. In 1972, the EEOC was given greater enforcement powers and public sector employees and agencies were brought under the jurisdiction of Title VII of the Act. During the past twenty years, the EEOC has been instrumental in amending Title VII and issuing guidelines that prohibit discriminatory practices in employment.

Bases of Discrimination Under Title VII

Race Discrimination

The Civil Rights Act of 1964 was primarily enacted to eradicate racial prejudices and oppression that black Americans faced in three major areas: employment, housing, and public accommodation. Specifically, Title VII of the Civil Rights Act prohibited employment discrimination, as noted, on the bases of race, color, sex, religion, and national origin.

Since Title VII's enactment, race and color complaints have dominated the type of employment charges filed by individuals. This volume of race discrimination complaints is due to the prevalence of discrimination in the labor market. Some scholars have described the labor market in America as being segmented into dual markets. One market for black workers and another for white workers, with the black market having low paying, less-desirable and dead-end jobs.[1] As blacks sought to move into primary or non-traditional jobs, they were denied such opportunity because of their race and color. Even today, 20 years after the Civil Rights Act, blacks are still largely segregated in jobs designated in the black labor market. Where blacks have been able to cross over to the white labor markets, they have been introduced to different cultures and values that cause frustration, alienation, and stress.

The first landmark case where race discrimination was raised was rendered by the U.S. Supreme Court in the *Griggs v. Duke Power*, 401 U.S. 424 (1971). There, the Court held that tests or other hiring practices that discriminated against protected class individuals were discriminatory and discriminatory intent on the part of employers need not be proved by the complaining party. It was sufficient to show that a personnel practice or policy had an adverse impact on protected class individuals. During the years following the *Griggs* decision, the Supreme Court issued a series of major decisions filed under Title VII on the basis of race.[2]

Despite the significant impact that Title VII and other regulations have had on racial biases and attitudes in employment practices, racial prejudices are still common. Minorities continue to have a higher unemployment rate than non-minorities and minority workers continue to be placed in low-paying, dead-end jobs.

Sex Discrimination

It is difficult to pinpoint exactly when the movement for equal employment opportunity for women began. However, it would be safe to say that during the past 20 years there have been various periods when women workers have vocalized their discontent with their status and treatment in the workplace. They have demanded equal pay for equal work, promotional opportunities, non-traditional jobs, pregnancy benefits, an end to sexual harassment in the work environment, and most recently, equal pay for jobs of comparable worth.

In 1964, sex discrimination was prohibited by Title VII. The prohibition can be best described as a tag-along with that against race discrimination. The legislative history documents the familiar story of how a representative from the South proposed that sex discrimination be included as a basis of discrimination; the intent was to defeat the Civil Rights Act of 1964. Nevertheless, to most people's surprise, the Act passed. In 1968, as an afterthought, sex as a basis of discrimination also was added to Executive Order 11246.

The development of laws prohibiting sex and race discrimination has been parallel, not only in regard to legislative history but also in the way the courts have developed theories of discrimination. Women and blacks have shared, sometimes unknowingly, a common goal: the eradication of employment discrimination. Women and blacks have typically been stereotyped, received less pay and benefits, denied access to non-traditional jobs and upward mobility. Because of the similarity in unfair treatment, the struggle for equity in employment has at times been a joint effort on the part of women and blacks.

In recent years, a number of scholars have determined that white females have benefitted more from Title VII than blacks.[3] Government statistics do indicate that white females have been hired and promoted in almost every job category at a higher rate than blacks.[4] However, white females have not gained the employment status that white males have obtained. Generally, white females, as well as minorities are segregated into the low-paying—low-status jobs when compared with white males.

Pregnancy Discrimination

As women increasingly entered the workforce, new forms of sex discrimination became apparent. It became necessary for Title VII to be amended to prohibit these forms of discrimination. One of the first amendments to Title VII in the area of sex discrimination was the Pregnancy Discrimination Act of 1978. This amendment was in response to the Supreme Court's decision in *General Electric Co. v. Gilbert*, 429 U.S. 125 (1976), which held that the exclusion of pregnancy benefits from an employer's disability plan was not sex discrimination. The Act required that "women affected by pregnancy, childbirth, or related medical condition shall be treated the same for all employment-related purposes . . . as other persons not so affected but similar in their ability or inability to work." Since the passage of the Act, most employers have accepted the fact that pregnancy is a short-term disability and should be treated as such. However, the present controversy in this area centers around how much pregnancy leave should be granted and in which position the female worker should be placed when returning from pregnancy leave.[5] These issues have not been settled by the courts.

Sexual Harassment

As the pregnancy discrimination issue was being resolved, Congress was addressing an even more complex problem facing women workers: sexual harassment. During 1979, Congress held public hearings to determine the extent of sexual harassment. The hearings revealed that sexual harassment was widespread in the federal workplace. Thereafter, Congress instructed the Merit Systems Protection Board to conduct a survey of federal workers "to determine the degree and nature of sexual harassment" in the workplace.

In 1980, the Board presented a summary of their preliminary findings to a Congressional subcommittee. The preliminary finding indicated that 42 percent of the persons surveyed had been sexually harassed on the job.

The same year, the EEOC approved final guidelines on prohibiting sexual harassment in the workforce. The guidelines defined sexual harassment and set forth an employer's responsibility in correcting sexual harassment. The guidelines also recognized sexual harassment as a form of sex discrimination and, therefore, a violation of Title VII.

These actions on the part of the federal government were the impetus behind practically every public and private employer to issue policy statements defining and prohibiting sexual harassment. Further, a majority of states passed legislation and issued executive orders prohibiting sexual harassment. This chain of events was also a result of female workers taking the position that sexual harassment need not be a term and condition of employment.

During the last seven years, courts have also, on a regular basis, held that sexual harassment was a violation of Title VII of the 1964 Civil Rights Act.[6] However, the courts have not totally agreed on what theory to use when concluding that an employer was liable for sexual harassment on the job.[7]

Comparable Worth

The Equal Pay Act of 1963 failed to have any significant impact on the wage disparity between women and men. Women workers still earn approximately 59 cents for each dollar men workers earn and are segregated into devalued or low-paying jobs.[8] However, the Equal Pay Act was not intended to end the disparity in wages between women and men when women are segregated in low-paying jobs. The Equal Pay Act is only applicable where men and women workers' skills, effort, responsibility, and working conditions are substantially the same.

During the early 1980s, the women's movement responded to the continued problem of men earning higher wages than women for jobs that were of equal value to the employer by proposing the concept of comparable worth. A number of studies conducted by research organizations, the federal government, and various scholars defined the concept of comparable worth, presented the pros and cons of the theory, and projected the impact of comparable worth on eradicating wage disparity between the sexes.[9] The major consensus reached by the various studies found that women workers were segregated in sex-stereotyped occupations that were low paying and low status, women workers earned substantially less than men, and that the present methods of job evaluation were outdated.

One of the first hurdles proponents of comparable worth were faced with was whether comparable worth claims could be successfully raised under Title VII or were they limited to standards mandated by the Equal Pay Act, i.e., the jobs had to be substantially the same. The issue was brought before the Supreme Court in *County of Washington v. Gunther*, 452 U.S. 161 (1981). The Court held that sex-based wage suits brought under Title VII were not limited to the equal work standard of the Equal Pay Act. Although the *Gunther* decision did not address all of the issues associated with comparable worth, it left the door open for future litigation involving comparable worth claims under Title VII.

The next major case was *AFSCME v. State of Washington*, 242 Daily Lab. Rep. (Dec. 15, 1983). The district court found that the State of Washington intentionally paid less wages to workers in predominately female jobs. The Court concluded that the pay system was discriminatory.

Since the *Gunther* and *State of Washington* decisions, similar allegations of sex-wage discrimination have been filed in other courts, and there has been a substantial increase in the number of charges filed with the EEOC related to the comparable worth theory.[10]

With growing public interest in comparable worth, the increase in the number of related charges filed with the EEOC, recent court decisions, labor and governmental support, and growing pressure from women's organizations, both state and Federal governments have attempted to respond by proposing bills and resolutions.[11] Further activity in this area will undoubtedly progress until the issues of job segregation and wage discrimination are resolved.[12]

National Origin Discrimination

The prohibition against national origin discrimination is also covered by Title VII. However, Title VII does not define the term national origin. The EEOC issued guidelines in 1970, which were later amended in 1980. These guidelines defined national origin in this manner:

> The Commission defines national origin discrimination broadly as

including, but not limited to, the denial of equal employment opportunity because of an individual's, or his ancestor's place of origin; or
because an individual has the physical, cultural or linguistic characteristics of a national origin group.

This broad definition has allowed discrimination complaints
to be filed in all types of employment practices, e.g., hiring,
termination, promotion, discipline, and so forth. However, the
courts have not been as liberal in finding national origin discrimination. For example, one of the leading cases has been the Fifth
Circuit's decision in *Garcia v. Gloor*, 618 F.2d 264 (5th Cir.
1980). In *Gloor*, the employer, Gloor Lumber & Supply Co.,
prohibited a bilingual employee from speaking Spanish on the job
unless the employee was communicating with a Spanish-speak-
ing customer. The Fifth Circuit held that, in this situation, the
"speak only English" rule was not national origin discrimination.
The Court indicated that a bilingual employee was not privileged
"to use the language of personal preference."

Generally, the majority of national origin complaints have
been concentrated in three areas of employment. First, employment practices which require employees to speak only English; second, a requirement of a minimum height and weight;
and third, harassment on the job.[13]

The number of national origin discrimination charges filed
will undoubtedly increase during the second half of the 1980s,
as the Hispanic population continues to grow. Presently, the
Hispanic population is the fastest growing minority segment of
the American population. It is projected that the Hispanic population may outgrow the black population before the end of the
1980s. This growth will have a significant impact as more
Hispanics enter the workforce. Specially designed EEO and
affirmative action programs will be necessary, if not required.

Religious Discrimination

The prohibition against religious discrimination in employment practices is covered under Title VII. Approximately one
year after Title VII became effective, the EEOC issued guidelines on religious discrimination. The EEOC stated that employers had an obligation to accommodate employees' religious be-

liefs unless it would be a serious inconvenience to business operation. In 1967, the EEOC revised the guidelines and stated that employers were obligated to reasonably accommodate employees' religious beliefs unless it created an "undue hardship."

In 1972, Congress amended Title VII to include the accommodation requirements that the EEOC had included in their guidelines. The basic issue in religious accommodation complaints is to what extent an employer is obligated under Title VII to accommodate an employee whose religious beliefs prohibit working on a particular day of the week. The Supreme Court addressed this issue in *TWA v. Hardison*, 432 U.S. 63 (1977). The Court held that an employer's obligation to make reasonable accommodations for an employee's religious beliefs does not include denying other employee's rights under a valid seniority system. As a result of the *Hardison* decision, the EEOC conducted hearings on religious discrimination to determine the impact. Subsequently, the EEOC amended its guidelines to further clarify employers' obligations to accommodate employees' religious practices. The guidelines also defined the term "undue hardship" and explained how employers could comply with the guidelines and the *Hardison* decision at the same time.

Impact of Title VII

It has been two decades since Congress enacted the Civil Rights Act of 1964. A review of civil rights activities during the past two decades overwhelmingly shows that the Act has been the impetus for achieving some parity among the races and sexes in this country. Moreover, Title VII has been the primary moving force behind efforts to eradicate employment discrimination in America.

Since the passage of Title VII "things just haven't been the same" in the way personnel practices and procedures are implemented. Title VII and affirmative action regulations caused the expansion and creation of new personnel jargon. Such terms as adverse impact, preferential treatment, applicant flow, *prima facie* case, SMSA, goals and timetables are now common terms in the fields of personnel and labor relations. In addition, new job classifications such as EEO specialist and affirmative action officer are a part of every major public and private organizational structure.

Title VII mandated equal employment opportunities in all areas of personnel. As a result, Title VII caused a dramatic change and modification in the way employees were recruited, interviewed, hired, promoted, terminated, tested, and so forth.

Even with the significant impact that Title VII has had on employment discrimination it has not achieved its purpose to the fullest. J. LeVonne Chambers, President, Legal Defense Fund, NAACP, recently described its impact in this manner:

> Title VII has had a significant impact upon the barriers to equal employment opportunity, although Title VII has not, by any measure, accomplished all that is required to end the effects and practices of discrimination. It was not inevitable that Title VII would have a significant impact. Moreover, the impact of Title VII appears to be lessening, and the outlook for continued progress towards assuring equal opportunity is bleaker now than at anytime since 1971.[14]

Affirmative Action

Aside from Title VII's impact on employment discrimination, affirmative action programming has greatly affected the employment of women, blacks, handicapped individuals, and other protected classes. On the one hand, many employers voluntarily took affirmative steps to correct discriminatory practices that violated Title VII. On the other hand, many employers took affirmative action steps as part of a conciliation agreement. The major impetus behind affirmative action has been Executive Order 11246 and EEOC encouragement for employers to voluntarily take affirmative action.

Approximately one year after Congress enacted the Civil Rights Act of 1964, Executive Order 11246 was issued by President Johnson. The purpose of the Order was similar to Title VII: to improve the economic and social status of protected class individuals, e.g., minorities and women. The Order required government contractors and subcontractors to take affirmative action to ensure that applicants and employees were not discriminated against.

Contractors and subcontractors having 50 or more employees and $50,000 in contracts are required to prepare a written affirmative action plan.[15] The Secretary of Labor has the responsibility for administering the Order and has delegated this responsibility to the Office of Federal Contract Compliance Program (OFCCP).

The Order states that an affirmative action plan should "include, but not be limited to the following: employment, upgrading, demotion, or transfer; rate of pay or other forms of compensation, and selections for training, including apprenticeship." In addition to taking affirmative action, contractors were prohibited from discriminating on the bases of race, creed, color, and national origin. In 1967, it was amended to also prohibit federal contractors from discriminating on the basis of sex. Where governmental contractors fail to comply, sanctions are authorized. Even though sanctions are authorized they have seldom been used by the OFCCP (except during the Carter Administration).

Between 1965 and 1973, government contractors "made a good faith effort" to employ minorities and women. However, in some cases "good faith effort" resulted in quotas and minorities and women being hired as "tokens" to meet affirmative action requirements.

During 1973, a change in attitude toward affirmative action was beginning. Affirmative action programs were being contested and questioned by non-minorities. One of the first court cases to question how far an affirmative action program could go legitimately was *DeFunis v. The University of Washington Law School*, 416 U.S. 312 (1974). The law school's affirmative action plan for minority recruitment guaranteed the placement of minorities in the law school. DeFunis challenged the constitutionality of the program. When the case finally reached the U.S. Supreme Court, the Court refused to hear the case because it was determined that the issue was moot, since DeFunis had entered law school.

Even though the Supreme Court refused to decide the issue, public support of affirmative action began to diminish as more law suits over the issue of affirmative action and reverse discrimination were filed.

In 1978, the U.S. Supreme Court issued the decision in *University of California Regents v. Bakke*, 438 U.S. 265 (1978), which was the first landmark decision in the area of affirmative action. In *Bakke*, a special affirmative action admission program of the University of California at Davis Medical School was challenged. The special admission program set aside a certain number of seats for minorities. Bakke, a white male was denied admission to the medical school even though his exam scores were higher than the minorities admitted to the school. Bakke alleged that he had been discriminated against on the basis of race in violation of the Equal Protection Clause of the 14th Amendment and Title VI of the Civil Rights Act of 1964. The Supreme Court in a narrow decision held that the special program was unconstitutional but race could be taken into account in admission programs; however, race could not be the only criteria for admission.

Even after the *Bakke* decision and a continued weakening of support from the public for affirmative action, the federal government continued to press government contractors to implement affirmative action programs. Some contractors under threat of being debarred from contracting with the federal government developed affirmative action programs which included preferential treatment clauses. The Kaiser Aluminum Company, in particular, set out with the union, the United Steel Workers, to incorporate an affirmative action program in their collective bargaining agreement. The affirmative action provision required that a ratio of one white to one black employee be selected into a training program until the number of blacks reflected the number of blacks in the surrounding local area where the plant was located.

In 1979, Brian Weber, a white employee at Kaiser Aluminum brought suit challenging the affirmative action program after he wasn't selected in the training program. Weber alleged that the affirmative action provision violated Title VII. The Supreme Court held that Kaiser's affirmative action was legal and permissible under the law and did not violate Title VII, even if some qualified whites were disadvantaged. The Court failed to provide employers with clear guidelines on what specifically entails a permissible affirmative action plan.

More than five years have passed since the Supreme Court issued the *Bakke* and *Weber* decisions, yet the issues of affirmative action, preferential treatment, and reverse discrimination are still misunderstood theories and are just as controversial as ever. Most recently, the Supreme Court wrestled with the legality of an affirmative action program which was in conflict with a bona fide seniority system. Specifically, in *Memphis Fire Department, et al. v. Stotts*, 81 L.Ed. 483 (1984), the issue was whether a court-ordered affirmative action program would take precedence over a seniority system when making layoffs. In *Stotts*, the City of Memphis Fire Department was under a consent decree to increase the number of blacks in the fire department by 35 percent. When the city was faced with laying off fire department employees, black employees who were hired under the consent decree were being retained while white employees with more seniority were being laid off. The Supreme Court held that the affirmative action plan could not take precedence over a legitimate seniority system.

Three major factors explain why the issue of reverse discrimination is still viable and why affirmative action programs are being contested. First, the Reagan Administration has been an active opponent of affirmative action. For example, the Justice Department filed an amicus brief in the *Memphis Fire Department v. Stotts* case on the side of the white firefighters contesting provisions of the affirmative action plan. In the Memphis case, the lower federal court had imposed quotas for the hiring of minorities. The Justice Department supports the *Stotts* decision and contends the decision will go far in limiting affirmative action programs.

The second factor influencing the issue of reverse discrimination has been the Supreme Court's decisions on affirmative action. In 1978, as noted previously, the Supreme Court issued the *Bakke* decision which left the issue of preferential treatment unsettled. In 1979, the Supreme Court issued the *Weber* decision but failed to provide clear guidance on how far employers could go in giving preferential treatment to minorities in employment actions.

The third factor that has kept the issue of reverse discrimination viable has been the poor economic state of the country. During times of prosperity, the public was more willing to allow minorities and protected groups to receive preferential treatment. The general feeling was that minorities and women had been deprived of equal employment opportunities and there were enough jobs available to give minorities and women preferential treatment in obtaining employment or promotions. Non-minorities felt that if they did not get one promotion because of affirmative action, they would get the next promotion because their employer only needed to hire "one" to meet their affirmative action goals.

During recessionary years, promotional opportunities were limited, and if one were passed over for a promotion or hiring, there probably would not be another position available in the near future. Moreover, if the recession caused layoffs, budget deficits, or hiring freezes, the hint that a protected-class individual received a position as a result of affirmative action would cause ill-feelings on the part of some non-minority employees. Consequently, the employee would file a reverse discrimination claim against the employer.

The future of affirmative action in employment is unclear. Critics claim that the *Stotts* decision further weakens affirmative-action requirements. Conversely, supporters of affirmative action argue that the *Stotts* decision was a narrow decision and did not substantially impact affirmative action.[16] Supporters also insist that a majority of employers still have and are implementing affirmative action programs in their organizations.[17] Both sides of the issue do agree that the future of affirmative action depends heavily on whether President Reagan has an opportunity to appoint new Supreme Court justices. Both sides believe that President Reagan will most definitely appoint conservatives who may outlaw all affirmative action programs that give any type of preference to protected groups.

Other Prohibited Forms of Discrimination

Handicap Discrimination

Handicap discrimination is not a basis for a cause of action under Title VII; however, a majority of states have laws and regulations which prohibit handicap discrimination. Moreover, federal contractors and subcontractors who receive a contract in excess of $2,500 are required to include an affirmative action clause in the contract whereby they agree to take affirmative action to employ and advance qualified handicapped workers. This requirement is mandated by Section 503 of the Rehabilitation Act of 1973. Further, contractors or subcontractors who receive contracts in excess of $50,000 are required to develop a written affirmative action program. Section 504 of the Act prohibits discrimination on the basis of handicap in any program receiving Federal funds or assistance. Congressional intent in enacting the Act was, in part, to make employment opportunities more accessible to handicapped workers.

The primary issues in handicap discrimination charges usually center around what is a "qualified handicap" and whether a "qualified handicap" individual can be accommodated. The Rehabilitation Act defines a handicapped individual in this manner:

> (a) an individual who has a physical or mental impairment which substantially limits one or more of such person's major life activities; (b) has a record of such an impairment; or is regarded as having such an impairment.

The leading court decision on the issue of "qualified handicap" is *Southeastern Community College v. Davis*, 442 U.S. 397 (1979). The Supreme Court held that Section 504 of the Rehabilitation Act did not require an organization to ignore a handicapped individual's disabilities or to make substantial modifications in their program to allow the individual to participate in the organization's programs. The decision indicates that participants in a federal program must still meet the basic requirements for entrance into the program regardless of their handicap.

Handicapped individuals who have been successful in obtaining meaningful employment are still faced with attitudinal barriers on the job. Jennifer S. MacLeod, a leading social psychologist describes the present situation of handicapped workers in this manner:

> In the world of work, handicapped people face a social environment in which they are stereotyped and often not treated as individual human beings but as expensive, inconvenient nuisances and unwelcome reminders of everyone's vulnerability to serious birth defects, illness, or accident. These attitudinal patterns create serious barriers for handicapped people—barriers that add immeasurably to the problem caused directly by their handicap.[18]

The Equal Pay Act of 1963

The Civil Rights Act of 1964 was not the first legislation enacted by Congress to prohibit discrimination in employment. In 1963, Congress enacted the Equal Pay Act which prohibited discriminatory wages between men and women who were performing substantially similar work which required similar efforts, skills, and responsibility. The Act permits a differential in wages in situations where the employer has a merit pay system, a seniority system, a system which measures earnings by quantity or quality of production, or any other factor than the individual's sex.

The enforcement of the Equal Pay Act was the responsibility of the Department of Labor until 1979. Under President Carter's Reorganization Plan No. 1 of 1978, enforcement of the Equal Pay Act was transferred to the EEOC.

Since the enactment of the law, the Department of Labor and the EEOC have conducted compliance investigations and have processed individual complaints which has resulted in millions of dollars being paid to female workers. However, in spite of these efforts, female workers still earn considerably less than men.

Age Discrimination

With a high rate of unemployment among older workers, Congress was compelled to address the problem of age discrimination. Congress' response to eradicating age discrimination was the enactment of the Age Discrimination in Employment Act of 1963 (ADEA). The ADEA protected employment applicants and employees between the ages of 40 and 65 from adverse employment action because of their age. The ADEA also prohibited an employer from discriminating among individuals who were in the protected class group. Individuals filing charges under the ADEA are primarily white males.

The Act was amended in 1974 to provide coverage for federal employees. The Act was again amended in 1978 to expand coverage to individuals up to the age of 70, with some exceptions, e.g., high-level executives. In 1979, the EEOC was designated as the responsible agency to enforce the ADEA; prior to 1979, the Secretary of Labor had this responsibility.

During the 1980s, the number of charges and complaints filed with the EEOC and in court on the basis of age has increased substantially. This surge in the number of charges and complaints filed has resulted in inconsistencies in the interpretation of the ADEA on the part of the courts. As in other areas of employment discrimination, additional direction is needed by the Supreme Court to clarify employers' responsibility under the ADEA.[19]

Summary

Despite the significant impact that Title VII, affirmative action, court decisions, and various other laws and regulations have had, employment discrimination is still prevalent within our society. This is reflected in the high unemployment among minorities, the wage gap between men and women, the wage gap between minorities and non-minorities, the number of minorities and women in management positions, continued employment barriers that handicapped workers face, and the surge in age discrimination complaints.

The process of achieving equal employment opportunties for all individuals has been and will continue to be a long, entangled, and sometimes a puzzling journey. The successful completion of this journey will depend on the attitude of Congress, the President, the courts, enforcement agencies, and most importantly, the American people.

Scope, Coverage, and Organization of Bibliography

Sources

Manual literature searches were emphasized, except for a computerized search at Ohio State University. Resources were utilized at the University of Tennessee, Ohio State University, University of Michigan, Howard University Law School, the Library of Congress, and the Equal Employment Opportunity Commission in Washington, D.C. Further, materials were included from conferences and workshops and from smaller-scale literature searches conducted at numerous libraries around the country.

Coverage

At the outset, guidelines were established to determine which items would be cited and which entries would be annotated. As research progressed, these guidelines were modified to ensure that certain topics were fully represented. For example, having only originally proposed 500 entries, this was later expanded to more than 1100 entries. It was extremely difficult to bring the research to a conclusion. Even when I finally concluded the bibliographic sections, I felt compelled to include footnotes in this introduction to recently published material.

One of the first guidelines established and maintained throughout was to include only material published or/and written between 1964 and 1984. Title VII was enacted by Congress in 1964. The span of twenty years gives the user a full understanding of the development of EEO and affirmative action.

Another decision was to include material from every source available. This would include published material as well as unpublished material, as noted above. Dissertations, as well as articles from popular magazines, law journals, and professional journals were examined. This cross section of material should be helpful not only to attorneys, personnel administrators, EEO and affirmative action managers, social scientists, and college professors, but also to the undergraduate student who is writing his or her first term paper on EEO/AA or the law student researching material for a law review article.

The next guideline established was to give preference to materials published by the federal government and materials published in legal, personnel, and labor journals. This was based on the fact that the federal government enacted Title VII and affirmative action regulations. Moreover, the courts and the federal government have enforced and interpreted Title VII and affirmative action regulations. Lastly, personnel and labor professionals have had the monumental responsibility of implementing EEO and affirmative action programs.

The decision as to which entries to annotate was based on whether the title of the entry was clearly descriptive of the content. For example, entry 53 provides information on Title VII, the Equal Pay Act, Executive Order 11246, the Age Discrimination Act, and the Civil Rights Acts of 1866 and 1871; however, its title would not alert the user that these topics were discussed without an annotation. This entry, as well as others, was cross-referenced into other sections of the bibliography under the respective subject.

In addition to cross-references, a subject index and author index are provided for accessibility to other entries. The resource section and the appendix will also be helpful in locating other EEO and affirmative action resources.

Organization

The entries are divided into three major sections: Equal Employment Opportunity, Affirmative Action, and Litigation. Entries listed under the EEO section are primarily concerned with Title VII and other laws and regulations which prohibit some form of employment discrimination.

The beginning EEO entries cover a wide variety of general topics, with a major emphasis on Title VII's legislative history, coverage, purpose, impact, application, and enforcement. Thereafter, entries related to each of the bases of discrimination under Title VII are cited, e.g., race, religion, sex, and national origin. Because of the various forms of sex discrimination, a sub-section on distinct forms of sex discrimination is included, e.g., pregnancy discrimination, sexual harassment, equal pay, and comparable worth.

As the EEO entries progress, citations on the other laws and regulations are discussed. Their coverage, legislative histories, and enforcement efforts are discussed. The remaining entries in the EEO section focus on employment practices which are discriminatory and/or have an adverse impact on protected classes. Employment practices include recruitment, interviewing, selections, seniority, training, preferential treatment, and testing.

The second section concentrates on affirmative action programs. These entries are concerned with planning and implementing an affirmative action program within the guidelines of the law, specifically, Executive Order 11246, court decisions, and the EEOC's guidelines on affirmative action. Many other entries refer to materials that outline the major components of an affirmative action program, such as, goals and timetables, recruitment and training programs, and utilization analysis. The entries under this section will also direct the user to materials on specialized affirmative action programs for women, handicapped employees, minorities, federal contractors and universities and colleges. From there, citations are included which speak to the continuing controversy of whether affirmative action programs have had an impact on the employment of women and minorities.

The last section focuses on the litigation of EEO and affirmative action programs. The bulk of this section cites references to the *Griggs*, *Bakke*, and *Weber* decisions. Entries on litigating cases under Title VII, remedies, discovery, and peculiar problems in employment discrimination cases are also included.

Conclusion

The goal of this bibliography is to provide a major resource guide on EEO/AA for scholars, students, attorneys, and professionals working in personnel, EEO/AA, and labor relations. It is hoped that this book will provide the user with a clear picture of the development, progress, and future of EEO/AA. Since there are many more unsettled and controversial EEO/AA issues still alive, the need for research continues. This book should be a beginning point.[20]

Acknowledgments

I wish to express my sincere thanks to Shirley A. Richardson, Attorney, Louisville, Kentucky; Douglas J. Haynes, Attorney, Columbus, Ohio; Scarlett T. Wilson, Attorney, Chattanooga, Tennessee; and Steffuni Andrews, EEO Officer, Dayton, Ohio, for their unyielding support and assistance in reviewing the drafts of the manuscript. I am also indebted to Louise Scott for typing and retyping the many drafts of the manuscript. Special thanks goes to my wife, Stephanie, and my daughter, Autumn, for their patience and understanding for the many days and nights I was away from home researching and writing this book. Lastly, I would like to thank Professor James S. Bowman of Florida State University and Julia Johnson of Garland Publishing for not giving up on me after I missed deadline after deadline.

Notes

1. For an extensive discussion of racism in the labor market see Item 101, Chapter 1 in the text.
2. See list of selected Supreme Court cases on race discrimination in the Resource Section.
3. Kathleen Sylvester, "Women Gaining, Blacks Fall Back," *The National Law Journal*, 6 (May 21, 1984), p. 1.
4. See Item 99.
5. Michael W. Sculnick, "Update on Pregnancy Leave," *Employment Relations Today*, 11 (Winter 1984–85), pp. 351–353.
6. See list of selected cases on sexual harassment in the Resource Section.
7. Note, "Sexual Harassment Claims of Abusive Work Environment Under Title VII," *Harvard Law Review*, 97 (1984), p. 1449.
8. U.S. Department of Labor, Bureau of Labor Statistics, Report No. 673, "The Female/Male Earnings Gap" (September 1982), p. 2.
9. U.S. Commission on Civil Rights, *Comparable Worth: Issues for*

the 80s, Vol. I, June 6—7, 1984 (Washington D.C.: Government Printing Office, 1984).

10. The California State Employee Association has filed a suit against the state of California which is similar to the *AFSCME v. State of Washington* suit. See *CSEA v. State of California*, N.D. Calif. (84—7275 MHP).

11. Gary Siniscalco and Cynthia L. Remmers, "Nonjudicial Developments in Comparable Worth," *Employee Relations Law Journal*, 10 (Autumn 1984), 222—240.

12. For an extensive discussion on comparable worth, see Neil E. Reichenberg, ed., "Special Issue: Comparable Worth," *Public Personnel Management*, 12 (No. 4, 1983), 325—444; Helen Remick, ed., *Comparable Worth and Wage Discrimination: Technical Possibilities and Political Realities* (Philadelphia, PA : Temple University Press, 1984); Daphne Greenwood, "The Institutional Inadequacy of the Market in Determining Comparable Worth: Implications for Value Theory," *Journal of Economic Issues* XVIII (June 1984), 457—464; Robert P. Joyce, "Equal Pay, Equal Opportunity, Comparable Worth," *Popular Government*, 49 (Spring 1984), 1—8; Thomas A. Mahoney, "Approaches to the Definition of Comparable Worth," *Academy of Management Review* 8 (No. 1), 14—22; Elaine Johansen," Managing the Revolution: The Case for Comparable Worth," *Review of Public Personnel Administration*, 4 (Spring 1984), 14—27.

13. Helen LaVan, "Employment Discrimination Against Hispanics: A Survey of Litigated Cases," *Employment Relations Today*, 10 (Winter 1983—84), 414—424.

14. Julius Chambers, "Title VII at Twenty: Twenty Years of Commitment to Ending Discrimination Is Not Sufficient to Eradicate the Legacy of More Than 300 Years of Oppression." American Bar Association, Section of Labor and Employment Law, Spring meeting, May 3—4, 1984, 12 pp.

15. In 1983, the Reagan Administration proposed changing the requirement for a written affirmative action plan to be only applicable to contractors and subcontractors who had 100 or more employees and $100,000 in contracts or subcontracts. Presently, the proposal is still pending.

16. One author indicated that the *Stotts* decision is very ambiguous and will further complicate the issue of affirmative action. See Douglas F. Seaver, "The *Stotts* Decision: Is it the Death Knell for Seniority Systems?" *Employee Relations Law Journal*, 10 (Winter 1984—85), pp. 497—504. Another author indicated that the impact "has been generally overstated." See Michael R. Zeller, "The Supreme Court's 1983—84 EEO Decisions," *Employment Relations Today*, 11 (Autumn 1984), 232. Also see U.S. Commission on Civil Rights, *Toward an Understanding of Stotts* (Washington, D.C.: Government Printing Office, 1984).

17. Anthony Neely, "Government Role in Rooting Out, Remedying Discrimination Is Shifting," *National Journal* (September 22, 1984),
pp. 1772–1775.
18. Jennifer S. Macleod, "Integrating Handicapped People into the
Workforce," *Employment Relations Today*, 11 (Autumn 1984),
262.
19. Recently, the Supreme Court invalidated an airline policy of denying retirement-age pilots the opportunity to transfer to flight
engineer positions. See *TWA v. Thurston*, Supreme Court No.
83–1325 (January 8, 1985). Also see *Whittlesey v. Union Car-
bide Corp.*, 567 F. Supp. 1320 (S.D., N.Y. 1983), which involved a
high-level official who was forced to retire.
20. At this writing, two major developments in EEO/AA were announced. First, the U.S. Commission on Civil Rights issued a draft
report which recommended "that federal civil rights enforcement
agencies and Congress reject the concept of comparable worth."
See U.S. Commission on Civil Rights, "News Release," April 11,
1985, p. 1. Secondly, the U.S. Supreme Court recently agreed to
review a lower court decision which upheld a voluntary affirmative
action plan involving teachers in Jackson, Michigan. The plan allowed some minority employees to be retained over some senior
white employees during a layoff. See *Wygant v. Jackson Board of
Education*, 84–1340.

ABBREVIATIONS

A/A	Affirmative Action
BFOQ	Bona Fide Occupational Qualification
DOL	Department of Labor
EEO	Equal Employment Opportunity
EEOC	Equal Employment Opportunity Commission
EPA	Equal Pay Act
HEW	Health, Education, and Welfare
OFCCP	Office of Federal Contract Compliance Program
SMSA	Standard Metropolitan Statistical Area
TITLE VII	Civil Rights Acts of 1964
USC	United States Code

Equal Employment
Opportunity
and
Affirmative Action

1. EQUAL EMPLOYMENT OPPORTUNITY

TITLE VII OF THE CIVIL RIGHTS ACT OF 1964 AND RELATED TOPICS

1. American Bar Association, Section of Labor Relations Law.
    PROCEEDINGS OF THE THIRD ABA NATIONAL INSTITUTE ON EQUAL
    EMPLOYMENT LAW. New Orleans, LA.: ABA Press, 1978.
    261 pp.

    A collection of speeches and papers on EEO laws presented
    at the third American Bar Association National Institute
    Proceeding. Includes discussions on age discrimination,
    equal pay, employing the handicapped, the Bakke decision,
    seniority systems, and the use of statistics to prove Title
    VII cases.

2. Anderson, Howard J. and Michael D. Levin-Epstein. PRIMER OF
    EQUAL EMPLOYMENT OPPORTUNITY. Washington, D.C.: The
    Bureau of National Affairs, Inc., 1982. 131 pp.

    Provides an easy reading approach to understanding various
    equal employment opportunity legislation and regulations,
    including their coverage and application. Briefly explains
    employment practices that may violate the law and outlines
    enforcement powers of the Equal Employment Opportunity
    Commission and the courts.

3. "Are Blacks, Women, and Hispanics Getting 'More Than Their
    Fair Share'?" EMPLOYMENT RELATIONS TODAY, 10 (Spring
    1983), 93-95.

    Reports on a study by the U.S. Civil Rights Commission,
    entitled Unemployment and Underemployment Among Blacks, His-
    panics, and Women. Summarizes the study's findings on the
    causes and rate of unemployment and underemployment among
    protected class individuals. Indicates that the report finds
    that EEO laws have not given minorities and women an ". . .
    unfair advantage in the job market. . . ."

4. Arvey, Richard D. FAIRNESS IN SELECTING EMPLOYEES. Reading,
    MA.: Addison-Wesley Publishing Company, 1979. 273 pp.

    Begins with a brief historical background of Title VII and
    other Federal civil rights laws, regulations, and court
    cases. Explains basic principles of statistics, test valida-
    tion, and their applicability to personnel testing. Reviews

major court decisions on test practices and concludes that
courts have focused almost entirely on "differential validity." Discusses and illustrates various concepts and models
of testing, e.g., "Thorndike's Quota Model" and "Cleary
Model of Test Fairness." Discusses the possibility that
tests are biased against females, older employees and the
handicapped. States that employers are using tests less
and depending more on the interviewing process, which ". . .
is particularly vulnerable to subjective biases, prejudices,
and stereotypes on the part of interviewers. . . ." Outlines
techniques in preventing discrimination during the interviewing process.

5. Bartholet, Elizabeth. "Application of Title VII to Jobs in
    High Places." HARVARD LAW REVIEW, 95 (March 1982), 947-
    1027.

    Contends that Title VII principles and standards have been
    vigorously applied by courts to prohibit employment discrimi-
    nation among employers who employ blue collar workers, yet
    courts are reluctant to apply the same principles and stand-
    ards among employers who employ employees in higher level
    jobs, e.g., teachers, lawyers, and managers. Argues that
    the same standards and principles should be applied in both
    situations.

6. Becker, Gary S. THE ECONOMICS OF DISCRIMINATION. 2d ed.
    Chicago, IL.: University of Chicago Press, 1971. 167 pp.

    Gives an empirical analysis of the causes and affects of
    discrimination on the economical status of minorities in the
    labor market.

7. Belton, Robert. "Title VII of the Civil Rights Act of 1964:
    A Decade of Private Enforcement and Judicial Development."
    SAINT LOUIS UNIVERSITY LAW JOURNAL, 20 (1976), 219-307.

    Traces the development of Title VII and the enforcement
    efforts of the EEOC and the judicial system to prohibit
    employment discrimination in the private sector.

8. Bennett, Barry J. and Ellen Siegler Bennett. "Labor Law
    Meets Title VII: Remedies for Discrimination in Employ-
    ment." CONNECTICUT LAW REVIEW, 6 (Fall 1973), 66-85.

    Compares Title VII remedies and procedures for processing a
    discrimination complaint with traditional labor law forums of
    processing complaint, e.g., arbitration, the National Labor
    Relations Board, and the Labor Management Relations Act of
    1947. Concludes that remedies are available for correcting
    discrimination under the other labor law forums but "Title

VII is the preferable remedial vehicle for most victims of
discrimination."

9. Bennett, Joel P. and Alice L. Covington. "Changes Needed in
    the Federal Employment Discrimination Laws." HOWARD LAW
    JOURNAL, 25 (No. 2, 1982), 273-293.

    Examines ". . . Title VII's venue and remedy provisions,
    interest assessment on backpay awards for federal employees,
    and problems involved in attorneys' fee awards under Title
    VII, and the Civil Rights Attorney Fees Award Act." Recom-
    mends that there be changes made in the judicial interpreta-
    tion of the above provisions to reflect the legislative
    intent of Title VII. Suggests that plaintiffs in Title VII
    cases be given a choice of venue, interim awards, interest
    on attorney's fees, allowed compensatory and punitive
    damages, and that federal employees be allowed to receive
    interest on backpay awards.

*   Bennett, Michael J. "Labor Law - Sex Discrimination - Equal
    Pay for Equal Work Standard Not Necessary for Title VII
    Sex-Based Wage Discrimination Claims. County of Washington
    v. Gunther, 101 S. Ct. 2242 (1981)." See Item 419.

10. Berg, Richard K. "Equal Employment Opportunity Under the
    Civil Rights Act of 1964." BOOKLYN LAW REVIEW, 31 (1964-
    1965), 62-97.

    A comprehensive discussion of the Civil Rights Act of 1964.
    Reviews the legislative history, coverage, effective date,
    prohibited practices, enforcement, complaint procedure, in-
    vestigation, and recordkeeping provisions. Sees deficiencies
    in the enforcement procedures, but concludes that remedies
    provided for under the Act are valuable.

*   Bernstein, John H. "Title VII - Religious Discrimination -
    Employer's Duty to 'Reasonably Accommodate' Employee's
    Religious Practices - Hardison v. Trans World Airlines,
    Inc." See Item 155.

*   Bird, Roger A. "Title VII and the Pregnant Employee." See
    Item 256.

11. Blumrosen, Alfred W. "The Crossroads for Equal Employment
    Opportunity: Incisive Administration or Indecisive Bureau-
    cracy?" NOTRE DAME LAWYER, 49 (October 1973), 46-62.

12. Brady, Robert L. LAW FOR PERSONNEL MANAGERS: HOW TO HIRE
    THE PEOPLE YOU NEED WITHOUT DISCRIMINATING. Hartford, CT.:
    Bureau of Law and Business, 1979. 87 pp.

A handbook for personnel managers to follow in making personnel selections within the law. Covers all aspects of
employment discrimination laws, including developing an
affirmative action program. Includes easily readable charts
that outline such topics as discriminatory practices, applicability of fair employment laws, EEO/affirmative action
postings, help wanted advertising, pre-employment inquiries,
testing and recordkeeping, and sample forms for setting up
and monitoring an affirmative action program.

13. Bralove, Mary. "Running Scared, Costly Lawsuits Spur Companies to Step Up Effort to End Bias." WALL STREET JOUR-
NAL, 184 (August 2, 1974), 1.

14. Brooks, Roy L. "Use of the Civil Rights Act of 1866 and 1871
to Redress Employment Discrimination." CORNELL LAW REVIEW,
62 (January 1977), 258-288.

States that the Civil Rights Acts of 1866 and 1871, principally sections 1981, 1983, and 1985(3) of Title 42 of the
U.S. Code may be used to bring employment discrimination
suits. Compares Title VII of the Civil Rights Act of 1964
with the 1866 and 1871 Civil Rights Acts. Traces the legislative history of the Acts and provides a summary of procedural limitations under each Act.

15. Bureau of National Affairs, Inc. THE CIVIL RIGHTS ACT OF
1964. Washington, D.C., 1964. 424 pp.

Explains the legislative history, coverage, prohibitions,
and affects of Title VII, Title II, and Title VI of the Civil
ights Act of 1964 on discrimination in employment practices,
public accommodation, and federal assistance.

16. _____. "EEO In Public Safety Agencies - A BNA Special
Report." GOVERNMENT EMPLOYEE RELATIONS REPORT. Washington, D.C., GERR No. 976 - Part II, August 30, 1982. 81 pp.

Suggests that EEO implementation in public safety agencies
is more controversial than in other organizations. Discusses
the enforcement policy of EEO in the public sector during the
Reagan administration, specifically the U.S. Department of
Justice. Provides information on the most recent legal development related to EEO in public safety agencies, including
an analysis of Teal v. Connecticut and Burdine v. Texas
Department of Community Affairs. Briefly analyzes the impact
of EEO regulations on public safety agencies in selected
cities, e.g., Atlanta, Chicago, New York, etc. Includes the
text of the New Hampshire State Police and Nassau County, New
York consent decrees.

17. Burstein, Paul and Margo W. MacLeod. "Prohibiting Employment
    Discrimination: Ideas and Politics in the Congressional
    Debate Over Equal Employment Opportunity Legislation."
    AMERICAN JOURNAL OF SOCIOLOGY, 86 (November 1980), 512-533.

18. Carey, William A. and Others. "Employment Discrimination,
    Panel Discussion." BUSINESS LAWYER, 29 (January 1974),
    577-614.

    A panel discussion with representatives from the EEOC, the
    Civil Rights Division of the Justice Department, Lawyer's
    Referral Committee, and Counsel for Civil Rights in the De-
    partment of Labor. Each speaker summarizes their respective
    agency's efforts in combating employment discrimination. The
    overall consensus of the panel is that the prevalent form of
    discrimination is in employment practices and policies that
    adversely affect protected class individuals.

*   Carroll, John L. and Stephen C. Whicker. "Civil Rights -
    Religious Discrimination in Private Employment Under Title
    VII of the Civil Rights Act of 1964." See Item 157.

*   Cassibry, John F. "Title VII: Sex Discrimination and the
    BFOQ." See Item 197.

*   Chenoweth, William A. "Is Title VII's Reasonable Accommoda-
    tions Requirement a Law - 'Respecting an Establishment of
    Religion.'" See Item 159.

19. "Comments, Developments in the Law - Employment Discrimina-
    tion and Title VII of the Civil Rights Act of 1964." HAR-
    VARD LAW REVIEW, 84 (March 1971), 1109-1316.

    An extensive study of Title VII of the Civil Rights Act
    of 1964. Examines the standard established by the Act in
    hiring, firing, and promotions. Focuses on issues such as
    testing, recruitment, and seniority systems. Explains the
    "meaning of sex discrimination" and BFOQ. Sets forth pro-
    cedures for processing a complaint and remedies available
    under Title VII. Concludes with an explanation of federal
    affirmative action requirements.

20. "Comments, Enforcement of Fair Employment Under the Civil
    Rights Act of 1964." UNIVERSITY OF CHICAGO LAW REVIEW,
    32 (Spring 1965), 430-470.

    Briefly discusses the legislative history of the Act.
    Focuses on the limited powers of the EEOC to enforce the Act
    and on the problems of concurrent jurisdiction between the
    EEOC and state and local agencies. Maintains that the

success of Title VII depends on the discretionary powers of
the Attorney General to enforce the Act. Concludes by discussing the problems in proving a case of discrimination in
court.

*   "Comments, Teamsters, Evans, and Title VII: Will Women be
         the Ultimate Losers?" See Item 702.

21.   Commerce Clearing House, Inc. FAIR EMPLOYMENT PRACTICES
       UNDER THE CIVIL RIGHTS ACT OF 1964, Chicago, IL., 1964.
       24 pp.

       Explains the coverage, complaint processing procedures,
       court action, and remedies under the Civil Rights Act of
       1964. Written immediately after the passage of the Act.

22.   _____. FAIR EMPLOYMENT PRACTICES UNDER FEDERAL LAW.
       Chicago, IL., 1966.

       "Designed to inform employers, employment agencies, and
       labor unions how they can comply with Title VII and other
       federal laws, executive orders, and regulations concerning
       discrimination in employment." Gives a concise explanation
       of Title VII, its coverage, investigative procedures, and
       recordkeeping requirements. Full text of Title VII, Execu-
       tive Order 11246, and the Equal Pay Act are included.

23.   Cooksey, Frank Cloud. "The Role of Law in Equal Employment
       Opportunity." BOSTON COLLEGE INDUSTRIAL COMMERCIAL LAW
       REVIEW, 7 (Spring 1966), 417-430.

       Analyzes the role of Title VII in eliminating employment
       discrimination. Focuses on the complaint procedure, juris-
       dictional definitions, basis of sex discrimination, and
       recordkeeping requirements under the Act.

24.   Curry, Theodore H. "A Common-Sense Management Approach to
       Employee Selection and EEO Compliance for the Smaller
       Employer." PERSONNEL ADMINISTRATOR, 26 (April 1981),
       35-38.

       Summarizes major provisions of Title VII and the Uniform
       Selection Guidelines. Recommends "common-sense rules" be
       followed in complying with the law, e.g., selection require-
       ments should be job-related and necessary. Maintains that
       selection devices should ". . . screen out as many people as
       possible with inexpensive tools before moving to more expen-
       sive ones" and when exams are used, they ". . . should be
       utilized late in the selection process, when few employees
       are involved."

25. Czarnecki, Edgar R., ed. EQUAL EMPLOYMENT AND UNIONS.
    Iowa City, IA.: Center for Labor and Management, College
    of Business Administration, The University of Iowa, 1974.
    42 pp.

    A collection of speeches on the union's responsibility to
    prohibit and eliminate discriminatory employment practices in
    the workforce. Discusses the union contract, federal laws
    and regulations that prohibit unions from discriminating
    against members, and the operation of the Iowa Civil Rights
    Commission.

26. Dean, John P. "Title VII and Public Employers: Did Con-
    gress Exceed Its Power." COLUMBIA LAW REVIEW, 78 (March
    1978), 372-408.

    Concludes that passage of Title VII legislation was a valid
    exercise of Congress, which can be upheld under the Commerce
    Clause and the Fourteenth Amendment of the U.S. Constitution.

27. Durling, Bette Bardeen. "Retaliation: A Misunderstood Form
    of Employment Discrimination." PERSONNEL JOURNAL, 60
    (July 1981), 555-558.

    Asserts that employers lack a clear understanding of the
    retaliation provisions of the Civil Rights Act of 1964.
    Maintains that "[t]o understand the retaliation provisions,
    it is important to recognize that two different kinds of
    retaliation are prohibited: first, discrimination against a
    person who has opposed an unlawful employment practice, and
    second, discrimination against a person who has participated
    in a discrimination proceeding." States that an employee who
    has participated in an EEO complaint should not be watched
    on the job any closer than other employees; nor should their
    terms and conditions of employment be different. Concludes
    that courts have not made the issue of retaliation any
    clearer for employers since they have applied four different
    standards in determining retaliation.

28. Dwyer, Robert A. and Alfred A. Strandgard. A MANAGER'S GUIDE
    TO EEO IN THE FEDERAL GOVERNMENT, Washington, D.C.: Gov-
    ernment Printing Office, 1975.

    Provides a brief and concise explanation to manager in the
    federal government about what EEO and affirmative action
    plans are and why they are needed. Explains what employment
    discrimination entails; why complaints are filed; and how the
    number of complaints can be reduced.

29. Edelsberg, Herman. "Title VII of the Civil Rights Act -
    The First Year." PROCEEDINGS OF NEW YORK UNIVERSITY -
    NINETEENTH ANNUAL CONFERENCE ON LABOR. Edited by Thomas
    G.S. Christensen. New York: Matthew Bender, 1967, pp.
    287-296.

    Reviews the impact that Title VII had on equal employment
    opportunity during the first years of operation. Discusses
    the ". . . trust and scope of Title VII, number of charges
    filed, the EEOC procedures, remedies, seniority systems,
    pension and retirement plans." States that more money, staff
    and enforcement powers are needed to further fight against
    job discrimination.

30. Edinburgh, Janis Roney. "Title VII and the Continuing Vio-
    lations Theory: A Return to Congressional Intent."
    FORDHAM LAW REVIEW, 47 (1979), 894-912.

    Traces the history of the continuing violation theory and
    its present day use. Argues that the use of continuing vio-
    lation ". . . should be limited to cases involving actual
    discrimination against the plaintiff within 180 days of his
    EEOC filing." Recommends that the time period for filing an
    EEO complaint be extended to one year. Believes an extension
    period would eliminate the confusion around what is a con-
    tinuing violation.

31. Edwards, Harry T. "Arbitration as an Alternative in Equal
    Employment Disputes." ARBITRATION JOURNAL, 33 (December
    1978), 22-27.

    Proposes that arbitration be used to resolve "relatively
    simple" employment discrimination cases. Presents a "two
    track system" which only allows arbitration in employment
    discrimination cases when ". . . the claimant alleges a vio-
    lation of both the collective bargaining agreement and Title
    VII law."

*   _____. "Sex Discrimination Under Title VII: Some
          Unresolved Issues." See Item 203.

*   _____ and Joel Kaplan. "Religious Discrimination and
          the Rule of Arbitration Under Title VII. See Item 162.

32. "EEO Pervades Personnel Management." EEO TODAY, 5 (Summer
    1978), 89-100.

    Indicates that the function of EEO has increasingly become
    an integral part of "all aspects of personnel management" and
    has expanded into the other personnel functions such as pen-
    sions and benefits, compensation, safety and health, and
    productivity.

33. Executive Enterprises Publication Co. SOLVING EEO PROBLEMS: A GUIDE TO EEO LAW AND PRACTICE. New York, 1980. 240 pp.

   A collection of twenty-five EEO articles which were written between 1976 and 1979. The articles were published in EEO Today. Includes discussions on handicapped discrimination, the Weber decision, age discrimination, affirmative action, OFCCP compliance, comparable pay, sexual harassment, testing, and the Uniform Guidelines on Employee Selection Procedures.

34. _____. UNDERSTANDING EEO - THE SUPERVISOR'S CASE BOOK. New York, 1975. 31 pp.

   Contends that an organization may be liable under various Federal EEO laws and regulations for discriminatory conduct of their supervisors and managers. Informs managers and supervisors how to avoid discrimination complaints. Includes case studies, a glossary of EEO terms, and an EEO quiz.

35. Farrell, Michael. "Proposed EEOC Regulations." PERSONNEL ADMINISTRATOR, 23 (November 1978), 51-60.

   Contends that the EEOC has gone beyond their authority in proposing backpay immunity in reverse discrimination cases as a means of circumventing the Fifth Circuit decision in Weber v. Kaiser Aluminum Corp. Outlines the Court's decision in Weber and the EEOC's proposed guidelines on affirmative action. Recommends that the EEOC delay the final approval of the affirmative action regulations until the Supreme Court reviews the Weber case. Also recommends that employers be very cautious in administering affirmative action programs that call for race conscious personnel decisions.

*   Fear, Richard A. and James F. Ross. Jobs, Dollars, and EEO - How To Hire More Productive Entry-Level Workers. See Item 832.

36. Feville, Peter and David LeWin. "Equal Employment Opportunity Bargaining." INDUSTRIAL RELATIONS, 20 (Fall 1981), 322-334.

   Analyzes the equal employment opportunity bargaining (EEOB) process which involves the EEOC's efforts to conciliate and settle EEO complaints in lieu of litigation. Presents the similarities and differences between the EEOB process and traditional collective bargaining methods.

37. Finneran, Hugh M. "Title VII and Restrictions on Employment of Fertile Women." LABOR LAW JOURNAL, 31 (April 1980), 223-231.

Focuses on restrictions placed on the hiring and placement
of female workers to prevent reproductive hazards. Recommends that an employer's legal counsel review the implication
of Title VII of the Civil Rights Act of 1964 on such restrictions. States that any restriction on employment opportunities of women ". . . without any scientific data is a per se
violation of Title VII." An employer may also violate the
principles of disparate impact as set forth in the Supreme
Court decision of Griggs v. Duke Power Co. Briefly discusses
the theories on bona fide occupational qualification and
business necessity as defenses to claims of sex discrimination. Concludes that during 1980 there will be a significant
increase in the number of class actions involving the issue
of restrictions on the placement of women due to reproductive
hazards.

*   Finzen, Bruce A. "Civil Rights Law--Fair Employment Testing
         and Title VII of the Civil Rights Act of 1964." See Item
         644.

38.   Fleisman, Stanley and Sam Rosenwein. THE NEW CIVIL RIGHTS
         ACT: WHAT IT MEANS TO YOU. Los Angeles, CA.: Blackstone
         Book Company, 1964. 191 pp.

         Explains the Civil Rights Act of 1964 in layman terms and
         discusses each Title of the Act, including Title VII. Inclu-
         des President Lyndon B. Johnson's statement to the nation
         when signing the Act into law and the full text of the Act.

39.   Freiberg, Robert., ed. THE MANAGER'S GUIE TO EQUAL EMPLOY-
         MENT OPPORTUNITY. New York: Executive Enterprises Publi-
         cations Co., Inc., 1977. 203 pp.

         A collection of twelve articles on various EEO and affirma-
         tive action issues, e.g., systemic discrimination, lawful
         interviewing, equal pay, affirmative action for handicapped,
         and age discrimination. Designed to assist managers in meet-
         ing their organization's goals and at the same time complying
         with EEO laws and regulations. Contains a comprehensive
         glossary of EEO terms, various EEO complaint forms, the full
         text of Title VII, and Executive Order 11246.

*   Gitt, Cynthia E. and Marjorie Gelb. "Beyond the Equal Pay
         Act: Expanding Wage Differential Protections Under Title
         VII." See Item 403.

40.   Goldman, Roger L. "The Next Ten Years: Title VII Confronts
         the Constitution." SAINT LOUIS UNIVERSITY LAW JOURNAL, 20
         (1976), 308-345.

Gives a brief explanation of how to prove a Title VII violation and the remedies available under the Act. Reviews a
series of Title VII issues, e.g., seniority, pregnancy, and
preferential treatment. Seeks to determine whether the
resolution of these issues will conflict with constitutional
principles and standards. Advises the court on what course
to take when there is a conflict between a Title VII remedy
and a constitutional standard.

* Gould, William B. "Employment Security, Seniority and Race:
  The Rule of Title VII of the Civil Rights Act of 1964."
  See Item 707.

* Greenberger, Marcia. "The Effectiveness of Federal Laws
  Prohibiting Sex Discrimination in Employment in the United
  States." See Item 210.

41. Guzzardi, Walter, Jr. "The Right Way to Strive for Equal-
    ity." FORTUNE, 103 (March 9, 1981), 98.

    Traces the civil rights movement in America from the six-
    ties to the eighties. Discusses the economic gap between
    whites and blacks, racial quotas in education, governmental
    efforts to eliminate discrimination in employment and hous-
    ing, and the growth of ghettos in America. Recommends that
    affirmative action programs be re-evaluated to determine
    whether they are still needed. Suggests that affirmative
    action programs be dismantled because they have achieved
    what they were established to accomplish.

* Handler, Solomon Z. "Title VII and the Sabbath Observer."
  See Item 165.

42. Harrison, Edward L. "Winning the EEO Game." MANAGEMENT
    WORLD, 9 (May 1980), 12.

43. Hartman, Gerald S. "Management Personnel Practices: The
    Do's and Don'ts of EEO Compliance." EEO TODAY, 7 (Winter
    1980-81), 313-331.

    Discusses common problems an employer will face when com-
    plying with various EEO and affirmative action laws. Areas
    of law discussed include: recruitment and hiring, selection
    criteria, employment testing, training, promotion and trans-
    fer, wages and benefits, the Equal Pay Act, working condi-
    tions, discipline and discharge, the Age Discrimination Act,
    Executive Orders 11246 and 11375, Rehabilitation Act of
    1973, and the Vietnam Era Veterans Re-adjustment Act of 1974.

Recommends that employers conduct a self-evaluation of personnel policies and practices within the organization to
ensure that EEO laws and regulations are not being violated.

44.   Harvard Business Review. EQUAL OPPORTUNITY IN BUSINESS.
      Boston, MA., 1975.

      A collection of articles published by Harvard Business
      Review between 1970 and 1975 on equal employment opportuni-
      ties for minorities and women.

45.   Hiestand, Dale L. ECONOMIC GROWTH AND EMPLOYMENT OPPORTUNI-
      TIES FOR MINORITIES. New York: Columbia University Press,
      1964. 127 pp.

46.   Hudson, William T. and Walter D. Broadnax. "Equal Employment
      Opportunity as Public Policy." PUBLIC PERSONNEL MANAGE-
      MENT, 11 (Fall 1982), 268-276.

      Briefly traces the development of EEO/AA laws and regula-
      tions during the past 20 years, including an assessment of
      EEO/AA during the Reagan Administration. Concludes that
      " . . . we are [presently] witnessing a major reversal in
      the EEO policies of the past 20 years . . . the elusive goal
      'to establish justice' is no longer in the forefront of the
      National agenda and we are diminished as a people because of
      it."

47.   Hunter, James M. and Milton C. Branch. "Equal Employment
      Opportunities: Administrative Procedures and Judicial
      Developments Under Title VII of the Civil Rights Act of
      1964 and the Equal Employment Act of 1972." HOWARD LAW
      JOURNAL, 18 (1975), 543-582.

      Summarizes the basic elements of Title VII of the Civil
      Rights Act, the Equal Employment Opportunity Act of 1972,
      and the EEOC's complaint processing system. Includes dis-
      cussions on seniority and promotion, testing, sex discrimi-
      nation, and affirmative action under Title VII. Examines
      special litigation problems arising under Title VII, e.g.,
      Section 760 and 707, class actions, duplicity and interven-
      tion by the EEOC.

48.   Jacobs, Rogers B. "Employment Discrimination and Continuing
      Violations: An Update of Ricks and Recent Decisions."
      LABOR LAW JOURNAL, 33 (October 1982), 684-689.

      Analyzes the Supreme Court decisions in Delaware State
      College v. Ricks and Chardon v. Fernandez. In both cases,
      the Court held that the statute of limitations in a Title
      VII complaint begins to run at the time the complainant

receives notice of termination and not from the time of the
effective date of termination. Concludes that the court
decisions may have a detrimental affect on federal court
decisions regarding continuing violation issues.

49. Kahn, Robert L.; R.P. Gurin; and A.I. Baar. DISCRIMINATION
     WITHOUT PREJUDICE: A STUDY OF PROMOTION PRACTICES IN
     INDUSTRY. Ann Arbor, MI.: University of Michigan Insti-
     tute for Social Research Survey Research Center, November
     1964. 45 pp.

50. Kandel, William L. "Introduction to EEO Laws and Regula-
     tions." THE MANAGER'S GUIDE TO EQUAL EMPLOYMENT OPPORTU-
     NITY. Edited by Robert Freiberg. New York: Executive
     Enterprises Publications Co., Inc., 1977, pp. 1-20.

     Presents a historical view of EEO laws and regulations and
     their impact on ending employment discrimination. Begins
     with the 1960s up to the Supreme Court decision in DeFunis v.
     Odegaard.

51. Kovarsky, Irving. DISCRIMINATION IN EMPLOYMENT. Iowa City,
     IA.: Center for Labor and Management, College of Business
     Administration, University of Iowa, 1976. 240 pp.

     Gives a historical discussion on the "roots of discrimina-
     tion" and traces the development of federal laws and regula-
     tions prohibiting employment discrimination.

52. Kramer, George R. "Title VII on Campus: Judicial Review of
     University Employment Decisions." COLUMBIA LAW REVIEW, 82
     (October 1982), 1206-1235.

     Reviews various judicial decisions to determine what stand-
     ard is used by courts when applying Title VII principles to
     university employment decisions. Indicates that since Title
     VII was extended to cover universities in 1972, courts have
     used various approaches to applying Title VII principles and
     standards to cases involving universities.

53. Larson, E. Richard. SUE YOUR BOSS-RIGHTS AND REMEDIES FOR
     EMPLOYMENT DISCRIMINATION. New York: Farrar, Straus,
     Giroux, 1981. 325 pp.

     Advises persons who are victims of employment discrimina-
     tion that they may take action under seven major federal
     laws which prohibit employment discrimination. Explains the
     rights and remedies available under Title VII of the Civil
     Rights Act of 1964, the Equal Pay Act, the Revenue Sharing
     Act, Executive Order 11246, Age Discrimination Act, and the

Civil Rights Acts of 1866 and 1871 for persons who have been discriminated against.

54. Leap, Terry L.; William H. Holley, Jr.; and Hubert S. Feild. "Equal Employment Opportunity and its Implications for Personnel Practices in the 1980s." LABOR LAW JOURNAL, 31 (November 1980), 669-682.

States that personnel practices have not been the same since the passage of Title VII of the Civil Rights Act of 1964 and that the implications of Title VII on personnel practices is continuously expanding. Predicts that during the 1980s the number of EEO cases will increase; EEO legislation will increase at all levels of government; employment rights of women, handicapped and older employees will continue to increase; more EEO complaints on higher level selections will occur; and "equal pay for work of comparable value" will be at issue. Suggests that personnel administrators become knowledgeable of "the myriad of employment laws" and that they continuously monitor personnel policies and practices to ensure compliance with EEO laws.

55. Ledvinka, James. FEDERAL REGULATION OF PERSONNEL AND HUMAN RESOURCE MANAGEMENT. Boston, MA.: Kent Publishing Company, 1982. 274 pp.

Discusses federal regulations related to personnel and human resources, e.g., EEO, job health and safety, and employee benefits. Includes chapters on basic EEO principles, sex discrimination, EEO classification, proof of EEO cases, and affirmative action. Addresses controversial issues such as whether EEO legislation has worked and whether preferential treatment is legal.

*   Levin, Noel A. and Mark E. Brossman. "Sexual Harassment on the Job: Title VII and EEOC to the Rescue." See Item 332.

*   Levine, Marvin J. "The Conflict Between Negotiated Seniority Provisions and Title VII of the Civil Rights Act of 1964: Recent Developments. See Item 714.

56. Levy, Leonard W. TOWARD EQUAL OPPORTUNITY IN EMPLOYMENT: THE ROLE OF STATE AND LOCAL GOVERNMENT. New York: DA CAPO Press, 1971.

A collection of essays presented at a conference during 1964 at the State University of New York at Buffalo concerning equal employment opportunities. Focuses on the plight of the "Negro" in attempting to obtain fair employment opportunities. Discusses the administrative and enforcement provisions of the State's fair employment practice commission and recommends various means of achieving equal employment opportunities.

57. Loevi, Francis J., Jr. "The Union Role in Federal EEO Programs." PUBLIC PERSONNEL MANAGEMENT, 2 (May-June 1973), 162-166.

58. Lopatka, Kenneth T. "A 1977 Primer on the Federal Regulation of Employment Discrimination." UNIVERSITY OF ILLINOIS LAW FORUM, 1977 (No. 1), 69-168.

Provides an overview on the status of employment discrimination law. Includes discussions on "the meaning of discrimination," disparate impact, statistical proof, business necessity, testing, sex discrimination, religious discrimination, federal civil rights statutes, affirmative action, and "preferential remedies."

59. "The Mandate of Title VII of the Civil Rights Act of 1964: To Treat Women As Individuals." GEORGETOWN LAW JOURNAL, 59 (October 1970), 221-239.

Discusses the coverage and prohibition of sex discrimination under Title VII and the Equal Employment Opportunity Commission's enforcement responsibilities. States that an exception to Title VII, as it relates to sex discrimination, is where sex is a bona fide occupational qualification (BFOQ). Maintains that a BFOQ permits an employer to discriminate on the basis of sex; however, the BFOQ exception is interpreted narrowly by the courts. Analyzes major court decisions related to sex discrimination, e.g., Phillips v. Martin Marietta.

*   Mansfield, Anthony R. "Sex Discrimination in Employment Under Title VII of the Civil Rights Act of 1964." See Item 218.

*   Margolin, Bessie. "Equal Pay and Equal Employment Opportunities for Women." See Item 405.

60. Marshall, Ray. "Equal Employment Opportunities: Problems and Prospects." LABOR LAW JOURNAL, 16 (August 1965), 453-468.

Provides statistical data on minority employment in occupational groups between 1940-1962. Reviews data on minority employment in federal employment and employment with Federal contractors. Discusses the problem of black unemployment, and the lack of educational opportunities and training for blacks. Briefly discusses affirmative action, the Civil

Rights Act, and preferential treatment. Believes that the
Civil Rights Act of 1964 will be more effective in the South
than elsewhere since fair employment laws are already available in other states. Predicts that "Negroes" will have a
better chance of obtaining equal job opportunities, full
employment, and economic growth at work.

61. McCarthy, Martha. DISCRIMINATION IN PUBLIC EMPLOYMENT: THE
    EVOLVING LAW. Topeka, KS.: National Organization on Legal
    Problems of Education, 1983. 61 pp.

    Finds that public employees are protected by the Constitu-
    tion and various Federal statues against employment discrimi-
    nation. Focuses on discrimination based on race, sex,
    national origin, religion, handicap, and age. Advises public
    employers on how to avoid liability when making employment
    decisions.

62. McCullough, Kenneth J. SELECTING EMPLOYEES SAFELY UNDER THE
    LAW. Englewood Cliffs, N.J.: Prentice Hall, 1981. 392
    pp.

    "Describes what is illegal in employment practices to help
    managers and personnel administrators avoid discrimination
    battles." Covers such topics as recruiting, hiring, inter-
    viewing, discipline, discharge, reductions, transfers, and
    standards for terms and conditions of employment. In addi-
    tion to a discussion on basic principles of selection, the
    author covers more complicated topics such as the uniform
    guidelines, validation, handling claims of discrimination,
    recordkeeping, and the OFCCP compliance review.

*   McCully, Carol L. "The Continuing Validity of Seniority
    Systems Under Title VII: Sharing the Burden of Discrimi-
    nation." See Item 715.

63. McLanahan, Bruce. "Unions, Collective Bargaining Agreements,
    and Equal Opportunity Laws." THE MANAGER'S GUIDE TO EQUAL
    EMPLOYMENT OPPORTUNITY. Edited by Robert Freiberg, New
    York: Executive Enterprises Publications Co., Inc., 1977,
    pp. 97-104.

    States that a collective bargaining agreement may not be a
    legitimate defense to an EEO complaint against an employer.
    Discusses common provisions of collective bargaining agree-
    ments which may be held to be discriminatory, e.g., depart-
    mental seniority and union referral systems.

64. McSpedon, Joseph H. "Standards to Avoid Employer Retaliation
    Charges." LABOR LAW JOURNAL, 33 (January 1982), 36-45.

Primarily focuses on the retaliation provisions of Title
VII of the Civil Rights Act of 1964. Section 704(a) of the
Act prohibits an employer from discriminating against an
employee or applicant who opposes a discriminatory practice
and/or participates in any manner in the investigation of
such practice. Indicates that the standard used to determine
whether retaliation exist is set forth in the Supreme Court
case of <u>McDonnell Douglas Corp. v. Green</u>. Suggests standards
for employers to follow as a means of preventing retaliation
charges, which includes developing "an effective disciplinary
system." Briefly discusses the retaliation provision in the
Fair Labor Standard Act, the Equal Pay Act, the Age Discrimination in Employment Act, the Occupational Safety and Health
Act, and the National Labor Relations Act.

65. Meltzer, Bernard D. "Labor Arbitration and Overlapping and
     Conflicting Remedies for Employment Discrimination."
     UNIVERSITY OF CHICAGO LAW REVIEW, 39 (Fall 1971), 30-50.

     Recognizes that there are an array of laws and regulations
     that prohibit employment discrimination, e.g., Title VII,
     Executive Orders, the Fair Labor Standard Act, the Constitu-
     tion, etc. Contends that employment discrimination regula-
     tions and laws sometime overlap and conflict with labor-
     management agreements. Concentrates on ". . . the inter-
     action of arbitration and the remedies provided by Title VII
     of the Civil Rights Act of 1964. . . ." Concludes that des-
     pite the overlap of arbitration and Title VII, arbitrators
     have been able to find discrimination in arbitration cases,
     and very few ". . . arbitration awards have been challenged
     in Title VII proceedings."

66. Meyers, Victoria J. "Title VII Class Actions: Promises and
     Pitfalls." LOYOLA UNIVERSITY OF CHICAGO LAW JOURNAL, 8
     (Summer 1977), 767-788.

     Sees Title VII class action suits as a helpful tool for
     eliminating some of the burden placed on aggrieved employees
     to bring individual discrimination complaints. States that
     class action suits under Title VII allow an individual to
     bring a suit for all individuals similarly situated, i.e.,
     other individuals discriminated against in violation of Title
     VII. Explains the technical requirements of Rule 23 of the
     Federal Rules of Civil Procedure, which must be met to bring
     a class action.

67. Miller, Richard B. CIVIL RIGHTS AND YOUR EMPLOYMENT PRAC-
     TICES. Swarthmore, PA.: Personnel Journal, Inc., 1965.
     39 pp.

     Advises employers on legal requirements under Title VII
     to hire and promote "Negroes." Explains the coverage, ad-
     ministrative procedures, effective date, and enforcement

provisions of Title VII. Provides recruitment sources for
locating and hiring minorities.

*   Miller, Robert Stevens, Jr. "Sex Discrimination and Title
        VII of the Civil Rights Act of 1964." See Item 221.

68.   Milligan, David T. "Remedies Available to a Victim of Em-
        ployment Discrimination. OHIO STATE LAW JOURNAL, 29
        (Spring 1968), 456-493.

        Explains and evaluates remedies available to employees and
        job applicants who are victims of employment discrimination.
        Concentrates on the procedures and remedies available under
        Ohio Fair Employment Practices Law. Sees Ohio Fair Employ-
        ment Practices Law as the most advanced of other state fair
        employment laws. Briefly discusses prohibitions and coverage
        of Title VII of the Civil Rights Act of 1964, the National
        Labor Relations Board, Executive Orders, and the Fourteenth
        Amendment. Outlines the class action suit of Ethridge v.
        Rhodes in which a suit was brought to enjoin construction of
        buildings on the Ohio State campus until qualified "Negroes"
        were employed on the construction project.

*   Modjeska, Lee. HANDLING EMPLOYMENT DISCRIMINATION CASES.
        See Item 1055.

69.   Mood, Lester E. Coping with Anti-Discrimination Laws.
        ADMINISTRATIVE MANAGEMENT, 41 (July 1980), 31-33.

*   Murray, Pauli and Mary O. Eastwood. "Jane Crow and the Law:
        Sex Discrimination and Title VII." See Item 223.

70.   National Association of Attorneys General, Committee on the
        Office of Attorney General. EQUAL EMPLOYMENT OPPORTUNITY:
        AN OVERVIEW OF LEGAL ISSUES. Raleigh, N.C., July, 1976.
        87 pp.

        Reports on the status and development of equal employment
        opportunity laws, regulations, and court decisions. Topics
        include Title VII of the Civil Rights Act of 1964, the 1972
        Amendments, veterans' preference, EEOC regulations, and
        Supreme Court decisions.

*   National Employment Law Project. LEGAL SERVICES MANUAL FOR
        TITLE VII LITIGATION. See Item 1056.

71. Nelson, Jack E. EQUAL EMPLOYMENT OPPORTUNITY IN TRUCKING:
    AN INDUSTRY AT THE CROSSROADS. Washington, D.C.: Govern-
    ment Printing Office, 1971. 78 pp.

    Despite the passage of Title VII of the Civil Rights Act of
    1964, the trucking industry still discriminates against
    minorities and women in employment practices. Presents sta-
    tistical evidence to support that minorities and women are
    underutilized and that systemic discrimination exist in the
    trucking industry. Summarizes efforts made by federal en-
    forcement agencies to enforce Title VII requirements in the
    trucking industry. Recommends steps the federal government
    should take to increase the number of minorities and women
    hired and promoted within the trucking industry.

*   Neuberger, Thomas, Stephen. "Sex as a Bona Fide Occupational
    Qualification Under Title VII." See Item 224.

72. "The New Bias on Hiring Rules." BUSINESS WEEK, (May 25,
    1981), 123.

73. Noble, A.A. "Civil Rights - An Analysis of Section 1983 and
    Title VII: A Comparative Strategy." TRIAL LAWYER'S GUIDE,
    23 (Spring 1979), 49-86.

    Examines comparative strategies under the Civil Rights Act
    of 1871, 42 USC 1983, and Title VII of the Civil Rights Act
    of 1964. Discusses the exhaustion of administrative reme-
    dies, statutes of limitation, burden of proof, damages, and
    attorney's fees. Concludes that both Acts are complex and
    attorneys will find it difficult to advise their clients on
    discrimination issues due to the complexity of the Acts and
    "conflicting and ambiguous decisions."

74. "Note, Applicability of Federal Antidiscrimination Legislation
    to the Selection of a Law Partner." MICHIGAN LAW REVIEW,
    76 (December 1977), 282-323.

    Concludes that Title VII is applicable in situations where
    individuals are not selected as law partners due to their
    race, sex, religion, etc.

75. "Note, Continuing Violations of Title VII: A Suggested
    Approach." MINNESOTA LAW REVIEW, 63 (November 1978),
    119-150.

    Explains what a continuing violation entails and analyzes
    the Court's interpretation of a continuing violation in
    United Airlines, Inc. v. Evans. Points out how the continu-
    ing violation can cause an "undue prejudice to employers."
    Suggests ways how the continuing violation doctrine can be
    changed to ensure a more equitable application.

*   "Note, Civil Rights - Religious Discrimination in Employ-
      ment - Title VII of the Civil Rights Act Requires Reason-
      able Accommodation of Employee's Religious Belief by Em-
      ployer Despite Conflicting Lawful Agency Shop Provision."
      See Item 168.

*   "Note, Civil Rights - Religious Discrimination in Employment
      - Title VII Standards of 'Reasonable Accommodation' and
      'Undue Hardship' are Constitutional, But Recent Cases Il-
      lustrate Judicial Overzealousness in Enforcement." See
      Item 169.

76.   Oganovic, Nicholas J. "The Logic of Equal Opportunity."
      PUBLIC PERSONNEL REVIEW, 32 (July 1971), 153-157.

77.   Panken, Peter, M. "Statutes and Orders Prohibiting Discrimi-
      nation in Employment." RESOURCE MATERIAL: LABOR AND
      EMPLOYMENT LAW. Edited by Peter M. Panken. Philadelphia,
      PA.: American Law Institute--American Bar Association
      Committee on Continuing Professional Education, 1984,
      pp. 1-13.

      Outlines the major provisions of Federal and State laws
      that prohibit employment discrimination, e.g., Civil Rights
      Act of 1964, the Age Discrimination Act, the Civil Rights
      Acts of 1866, 1870, and 1871.

78.   Perry, Lowell W. "The Mandate and Impact of Title VII."
      LABOR LAW JOURNAL, 26 (December 1975), 743-749.

      The Chairman of the EEOC discusses the progress that has
      been made with the enforcement of Title VII. Cites Griggs v.
      Duke Power as an example of the kind of impact Title VII has
      on the enforcement of discrimination laws. Reveals that the
      agency is going to focus more on systemic discrimination.

79.   Player, Mack A. FEDERAL LAW OF EMPLOYMENT DISCRIMINATION
      IN A NUTSHELL. St. Paul, MN.: West Publishing Co., 1976.
      336 pp.

      Gives a concise summary of federal laws that prohibit dis-
      crimination in employment. Concentrates on Title VII, the
      Equal Pay Act, the Constitution, and the Age Discrimination
      in Employment Act. Analyzes major Supreme Court decisions
      related to EEO, e.g., McDonnell Douglas and Griggs. Out-
      lines and interpret permissible testing and seniority pro-
      cedures under the law.

80. Portwood, James D. and Karen S. Koziara. "In Search of Equal
    Employment Opportunity: New Interpretations of Title VII."
    LABOR LAW JOURNAL, 30 (June 1979), 353-360.

    Because Title VII of the Civil Rights Act of 1964 failed to
    give clear "policy statements" and "definition of goals," the
    Equal Employment Opportunity Commission and the courts have
    been forced to define what employment actions by employers
    violate Title VII. The Supreme Court decision in Griggs v.
    Duke Power provided interpretative guidelines to Title VII.
    Analyzes the Supreme Court's decision in Griggs and other
    Supreme Court decisions, including Washington v. Davis,
    General Electric v. Gilbert, and U.S. v. South Carolina.
    Concludes that Supreme Court decisions have narrowed the
    scope of Title VII and made it more difficult to prove dis-
    crimination.

81. Pospisil, Vivian C. "Winding Through the Equal Opportunity
    Maze." INDUSTRY WEEK, 183 (October 7, 1974), 40.

82. Powers, Thompson, ed. EQUAL EMPLOYMENT OPPORTUNITY: COMPLI-
    ANCE AND AFFIRMATIVE ACTION. New York: National Associa-
    tion of Manufacturers, 1969. 123 pp.

    Contains more than 350 questions asked of officials at the
    EEOC and the Justice Department concerning federal enforce-
    ment of equal employment opportunity laws and regulations.
    Major topic headings include: complaints under Title VII,
    the Federal Contract Compliance program, seniority systems,
    testing, sex discrimination, and affirmative action programs.

83. Prentice-Hall, Inc. THE CIVIL RIGHTS LAW AND YOUR BUSINESS.
    Englewood Cliffs, N.J., 1980. 43 pp.

    Provides practical information for employers to use to
    comply with Title VII of the Civil Rights Act. Gives a
    straightforward, easy reading interpretation of other civil
    rights laws and includes a checklist for employers to use
    when assessing their company's employment practices.

84. _____. EQUAL EMPLOYMENT OPPORTUNITY COMPLIANCE MANUAL
    VOL. 1 & 2: Englewood Cliffs, N.J., 1979.

    A loose leaf reference book on EEO and affirmative action.
    The material is updated periodically on new developments.
    Covers all aspects of EEO law and affirmative action. Sec-
    tion topics include: "Planning your EEO programs, Human
    Resources Planning - Hiring, Upgrading, Discipline-Grievances
    - Termination, Pay and Benefits." Includes sample affirma-
    tive action plans, EEO settlements, and compliance procedure
    forms.

85. Rachlin, Carl. "Title VII: Limitations and Qualifications."
    BOSTON COLLEGE AND COMMERCIAL LAW REVIEW, 7 (Spring 1966),
    473-494.

    Discusses the exceptions and qualifications under Title VII
    which may result in further employment discrimination for
    minorities. Focuses specifically on the following provisions
    in Title VII: definition of employer, bona fide occupational
    qualification, bona fide seniority systems, merit systems,
    work in different locations, professionally developed ability
    test, state employers, and communist party membership.

86. Rasnic, Carol D. "Defending Employment Discrimination
    Charges Under Title VII." CASE AND COMMENT, 88 (January-
    February 1983), 47-52.

    Analyzes the Supreme Court's decision in Texas Dept. of
    Community Affairs v. Burdine, which ". . . held that an
    employer is not required by law to hire a female or minority
    job applicant whose objective job qualifications are equal
    to those of a white male applicant." The Court also held
    that an employer does not have to ". . . persuade the trial
    court by a preponderance of the evidence that legitimate
    nondiscriminatory reasons existed . . ." for his action after
    the plaintiff has established a prima facie case.

87. Reynolds, William Bradford. "The Justice Department's
    Enforcement of Title VII." LABOR LAW JOURNAL, 34 (May
    1983), 259-265.

    The Assistant Attorney General of the Department of Jus-
    tice's Civil Rights Division during the Reagan administra-
    tion outlines the division's policy on affirmative action.
    Focuses on the Justice Department's position in the Boston
    firefighters and police cases, and the New Orleans Police
    case. States that the department opposes ". . . court-
    ordered or court-sanctioned racial preferences for nonvictims
    of discrimination. . . ." Argues against the use of prefer-
    ential treatment and quotas in employment practices.

88. Rosen, Sanford Jay. "Division of Authority Under Title VII
    of the Civil Rights Act of 1964: A Preliminary Study in
    Federal-State Interagency Relations." George Washington
    Law Review, 34 (June 1966), 846-892.

    Concentrates on the enforcement scheme of Title VII between
    federal, state, and local agencies. Discusses 706 agencies'
    responsibilities in processing complaints that have been
    deferred by the EEOC and the "interrelationship" between
    Federal agencies when enforcing fair employment practices.

89. Rosenbloom, David H. FEDERAL EQUAL EMPLOYMENT OPPORTUNITY:
     POLITICS AND PUBLIC PERSONNEL ADMINISTRATION. New York:
     Praeger Publishers, 1977. 184 pp.

     Describes the extent and impact that politics and bureau-
     cratic policies have on the formation and implementation of
     affirmative action and EEO in the federal government.

90. Ross, John J., ed. EQUAL EMPLOYMENT OPPORTUNITIES COMPLI-
     ANCE. New York: Practicing Law Institute, 1972. 176 pp.

     A collection of articles on employment discrimination.
     Includes topics on Title VII, affirmative action, sex and
     age discrimination, types of discrimination, and federal
     regulations prohibiting employment discrimination.

*   Roth, Allan F. "Civil Rights: Sex Discrimination in Employ-
     ment Under the Civil Rights Act of 1964." See Item 234.

*   Rowe, Benjamin T. and S. Dagnal Rowe. "Employment Testing
     and Title VII of the Civil Rights Act of 1964: After
     Albemarle Paper Co. v. Moody." See Item 1066.

91. Rutherglent, George. "Title VII Class Action." UNIVERSITY
     OF CHICAGO LAW REVIEW, 47 (Summer 1980), 688-741.

     Gives an in-depth discussion of the development of class
     action suits under Title VII and rule 23 of the Federal Rules
     of Civil Procedure. Recommends that ". . . the presumption
     in favor of certification of Title VII class actions . . . be
     discarded."

92. Safren, Miriam A. "Title VII and Employee Selection Tech-
     niques." PERSONNEL, 50 (January-February 1973), 26-35.

93. Sale, Barbara. "Remedies for Nonminority Employees Under
     Title VII." THE GEORGE WASHINGTON LAW REVIEW, 46 (January
     1978), 251-272.

     Focuses primarily on ". . . whether a court ordered 'or
     otherwise prompted' affirmative action plan is a defense to
     a claim by a nonminority that such a plan has discriminated
     against him." Reviews various court ordered remedies for
     unlawful discrimination under Title VII. Recommends that
     employers not only compensate the employee who was discrimi-
     nated against but also the nonminority ". . . who never suf-
     fered discrimination but who must relinquish rights and
     expectations so that discriminatees may assume their rightful
     place." Written prior to the Weber decision.

94. Salipante, Paul F., Jr. and John D. Aram. "A System for
     Individual Equity in Equal Employment Opportunity."
     MONTHLY LABOR REVIEW, 102 (April 1979), 46-67.

95. Schrader, Thomas C. "Title VII: An Overview of Some Common
     Employer Pitfalls." CLEVELAND STATE LAW REVIEW, 23 (Spring
     1974), 245-261.

     Outlines the coverage and prohibition against employment
     discrimination under Title VII. Includes discussions on the
     EEOC, the Ohio Civil Rights Commission, and backpay remedies.
     Indicates that "employment pitfalls" may be found on employ-
     ment applications, in testing and screening procedures,
     advertising, pregnancy leave policies, and in garnishment
     procedures. Advises employers to become familiar with em-
     ployment practices that are prohibited under Title VII.

*   Schupp, Robert W.; Joyce Windham; and Scott Draughn. "Sexual
     Harassment Under Title VII: The Legal Status." See Item
     362.

96. Shaeffer, Ruth Gilbert. NONDISCRIMINATION IN EMPLOYMENT-AND
     BEYOND. New York: Conference Board, Inc., 1980. 125 pp.

     Gives an overview of federal laws and regulations that
     prohibit employment discrimination. Focuses on the Equal Pay
     Act of 1963, Title VII, the Age Discrimination in Employment
     Act of 1967, affirmative action regulations administered by
     the OFCCP, and the Civil Rights Act of 1866, 1870, and 1871.

97. Shanor, Gloria J. and Charles A. Shanor. "Employment Dis-
     crimination." MERCER LAW REVIEW, 33 (Summer 1982),
     1119-1146.

98. Sherman, Herbert L., Jr. "Union's Duty of Fair Representa-
     tion and the Civil Rights Act of 1964." MINNESOTA LAW
     REVIEW, 49 (1965), 771-820.

     Claims that there is an overlap and possible conflict in
     the administration of the Railway Labor Act (RLA), the Na-
     tional Labor Relations Act (NLRA), and Title VII. Focuses
     on the National Labor Relations Board's (NLRB) provisions
     that prohibit the union from breaching its responsibility
     of fair representation and Title VII's provisions which pro-
     hibit unions from discriminating among members. Believes
     that any conflict between the statutes can be avoided by
     allowing laws established by the RLA and the NLRA prior to
     passage of Title VII to stay intact; however, ". . . the NLRB
     should not be permitted to grant affirmative relief under its
     unfair labor practices jurisdiction for breach of a union's

duty of fair representation based on discrimination covered
by Title VII of the Civil Rights Act."

99. Simmons, Judy. "Struggle for the Executive Suite: Blacks
     vs. White Women." BLACK ENTERPRISE, 11 (September 1980),
     24-27.

     Reviews employment statistics compiled by the Equal Employ-
     ment Opportunity Commission (EEOC) on the number of blacks
     and white women employed by corporations. Determines that
     white women are being hired at a higher rate in corporations.
     Concludes that white women have benefited more from Title VII
     of the Civil Rights Act than blacks, even though Title VII
     was intended to assist blacks.

100. Smith, Arthur B., Jr. "The Law and Equal Employment Oppor-
      tunity: What's Past Should Not Be Prologue." INDUSTRIAL
      AND LABOR RELATIONS REVIEW, 33 (July 1980), 493-505.

      Recapitulates past efforts by courts and administrative
      agencies to ensure affirmative action and equal employment
      opportunity in the work force. Concludes that there has been
      a "constant change" in EEO laws and regulations which has
      resulted in unclear policy and procedure. "Argues that the
      overlapping and conflicting regulations, inconsistent re-
      sults, and general confusion produced by the past encounters
      between the law and discriminatory employment practices
      should not be the model for future development of policy."

101. _____; Charles B. Craver; and Leroy D. Clark. EMPLOY-
      MENT DISCRIMINATION LAW. Charlottesville, VA., 1982.
      1041 pp.

      Written as a textbook for teaching purposes or as a refer-
      ence guide to Equal Employment Opportunity (EEO) and affirma-
      tive action (AA). Discusses all aspects of EEO/AA. Major
      topic heads include: employment discrimination and the labor
      market, state regulations, conflicting and overlapping
      federal laws, resolving EEO claims, discrimination in employ-
      ment practices, affirmative action, and remedies.

102. Sobel, Lester A. JOB BIAS. New York: Facts on File, Inc.,
      1976. 190 pp.

      Gives a chronological listing of events related to job dis-
      crimination in America from the end of the 1960s to 1976.
      Includes illustrations, graphs, and tables on the employment
      status of minorities and women during this period.

103. Spain, Jayne B. "The Battle Against Discrimination." JOUR-
      NAL OF HOME ECONOMICS, 65 (January 1973), 16-19.

104. Stone, Morris and Earl R. Baderschneider, eds. ARBITRATION
      OF DISCRIMINATION GRIEVANCES: A CASE BOOK: New York:
      American Arbitration Association, 1974. 335 pp.

      Analyzes employment discrimination decisions of labor arbi-
      trators. Includes a brief summary of the facts, discussions
      and findings, contract provisions, and awards for each deci-
      sion. Presents cases in the area of seniority, affirmative
      action, sex discrimination, BFOQ, and "personnel practices
      in the integrated workforce." Written in a case book format.

*   Suberlak, Raymond J. "Title VII: An Employer's View of
      Religious Discrimination Since the 1972 Amendment." See
      Item 172.

105. Sullivan, Charles A.; Michael J. Zimmer; and Richard F.
      Richards. FEDERAL STATUTORY LAW OF EMPLOYMENT DISCRIMI-
      NATION. New York: Bobbs - Merrill Company, Inc., 1980.
      874 pp.

      A comprehensive study of Title VII, the Equal Pay Act of
      1963, the Age Discrimination in Employment Act, and the anti-
      discrimination sections of the National Labor Relations Act.
      Discusses coverage, exemptions, remedies, settlements and
      consent decrees under each Act. Gives an overview of affir-
      mative action and reverse discrimination principles.

106. Tillery, Stephen M. "Post-Judgment Relief for Lost Wages
      Under Title VII." SAINT LOUIS UNIVERSITY LAW JOURNAL, 20
      (1976), 409-419.

      Analyzes the backpay award provision of Title VII. Strong-
      ly believes that victims of discrimination should receive
      backpay until they are placed in the employment position they
      would have received had they not been discriminated against.

107. Tuthill, Mary. "The Job Ahead on Equal Employment Regu-
      lations." NATION'S BUSINESS, 70 (July 1982), 53-55.

*   Underwood, Osta. "Legislation and Litigation: Impact on
      Working Women." See Item 238.

*   University of Richmond Law Review Association. "Civil Rights
      Act and Professionally Developed Ability Tests -- Griggs v.
      Duke Power Co." See Item 1087.

108. U.S. Commission on Civil Rights. AMERICAN INDIANS CIVIL
      RIGHTS HANDBOOK. Washington, D.C.: Government Printing
      Office, September, 1980. 71 pp.

Summarizes the rights and privileges of American Indians under Federal laws and regulations. Includes chapters on voting rights, fair housing, fair treatment in court and from policemen, and equal employment opportunity. Briefly discusses the process in filing an EEO complaint, Federal laws which prohibit discrimination, tribal agencies, and Indian job preference.

109. _____. CIVIL RIGHTS OF AMERICAN INDIANS. Washington, D.C.: Government Printing Office, 1972. 12 pp.

Briefly outlines the rights of American Indians as guaranteed by the Federal government and the Constitution. Includes information on employment discrimination, as well as sections on the 1st, 8th, and 14th amendments to the Constitution.

110. _____. EQUAL EMPLOYMENT OPPORTUNITY UNDER FEDERAL LAW. Washington, D.C.: Government Printing Office, March 1966. 10 pp.

Outlines federal equal employment laws and regulations that are administered by the EEOC, the Department of Labor, the U.S. Civil Service Commission, the National Labor Relations Board, and the Division of State Merit Systems of the Department of Health, Education, and Welfare. Includes a listing of State Fair Employment Commissions.

111. _____. EXTENDING EQUAL EMPLOYMENT OPPORTUNITY LAW TO CONGRESS. Washington, D.C.: Government Printing Office, 1980. 37 pp.

Explores the possibility of extending Title VII to cover staff members of Congress, congressional committees, and legislative support units. Presently, employees of Congress are exempt from Federal equal employment opportunity laws. Offers recommendations to Congress on how they can, by statute, extend coverage within the guidelines of the Constitution.

112. _____. JOBS & CIVIL RIGHTS. Washington, D.C.: Government Printing Office, 1969. 318 pp.

Describes the purpose and mission of the Civil Rights Act of 1964, Executive Order 11246, and equal employment opportunity regulations in federal manpower programs. Focuses specifically on the federal government's process of implementing equal employment through the above federal laws and regulations. Includes discussions on the operation of the EEOC, the U.S. Attorney General's Office, and OFCCP.

113. _____. NONREFERRAL UNIONS AND EQUAL EMPLOYMENT
      OPPORTUNITY. Washington, D.C.: Government Printing
      Office, March 1982. 116 pp.

      Focuses on twelve of the largest private nonreferral unions
      and their impact on minorities and women employment oppor-
      tunities. The first part of the report examines whether the
      union's leadership reflects minority and women participation;
      whether the union reviews employers' selection procedures to
      ensure that adverse impact does not exist; and whether the
      international union has shown any initiatives in improving
      EEO opportunities for minorities and women. The second part
      of the report discusses adverse impact in selection proce-
      dures, seniority systems, employment qualifications, and the
      union's duty of fair representation.

*   U.S. Commission on Civil Rights. STATEMENT ON AFFIRMATIVE
      ACTION FOR EQUAL EMPLOYMENT OPPORTUNITIES. See Item 990.

114. U.S. Department of Justice, Law Enforcement Assistance Ad-
      ministration, Office of Civil Rights Compliance. EQUAL
      EMPLOYMENT OPPORTUNITY PROGRAM DEVELOPMENT MANUAL. Wash-
      ington, D.C.: Government Printing Office, 1974. 248 pp.

      Provides guidelines, techniques, and procedures on comply-
      ing with Federal EEO laws and regulations for criminal jus-
      tice agencies who receive funds from the Law Enforcement
      Assistance Administration.

115. U.S. Equal Employment Opportunity Commission. EQUAL EMPLOY-
      MENT OPPORTUNITY IS GOOD BUSINESS. Washington, D.C.:
      Government Printing Office, 1966. 15 pp.

      A brief and concise pamphlet on how EEO can be cost effec-
      tive for businesses, e.g., lower job turnover, wider job
      market, and increased production. Outlines what employers
      can do to achieve EEO within their organization.

116. _____. FIRST ANNUAL DIGEST OF LEGAL INTERPRETATIONS,
      July 2, 1965 through July 1, 1966. Washington, D.C.:
      Government Printing Office, July 1, 1966. 49 pp.

      Responds to letters of inquiries addressed to the Commis-
      sion from the public on Title VII. Gives the citation to
      the "Opinion Letter" and a brief statement summarizing the
      opinion. Includes sections on jurisdiction; discrimination
      based on race, color, religion, sex, national origin; pre-
      employment inquiries; EEO posters; and the EEO complaint
      processing system.

117. _____. HEARING . . . ON UTILIZATION OF MINORITY AND
WOMEN WORKERS IN THE PUBLIC UTILITIES INDUSTRY. Washington, D.C.: Government Printing Office, 1971. 559 pp.

Comprises hearing proceedings before the EEOC on the status
of minorities and women in public utilities. Includes testimony from major utility companies on their affirmative action
efforts to recruit and hire minorities and women. Also includes testimony from federal agency officials on compliance
procedures to monitor and enforce discrimination laws and
regulations in the gas and electrical utility industries.

118. _____. HELP WANTED . . . OR IS IT? Washington,
D.C.: Government Printing Office, 1968. 15 pp.

Summarizes and analyzes the results of a hearing conducted
in New York on discrimination in the white collar employment
market. Includes testimony from twenty-five major employers
in New York City on the progress and problems of hiring
minorities and women in white collar jobs. Explains how
minorities and women are excluded from certain jobs and
discusses methods of removing employment barriers in order
to hire disadvantaged individuals.

119. _____. JOB DISCRIMINATION-LAWS AND RULES YOU SHOULD
KNOW. Washington, D.C.: Government Printing Office, 1975.
91 pp.

Includes the full text of Title VII of the Civil Rights
Act of 1964 and the 1972 amendment, Chapter XIV -- Equal
Employment Opportunity Commission and Executive Orders
11246 and 11375.

120. _____. JOB DISCRIMINATION-LAWS AND RULES YOU SHOULD
KNOW. Washington, D.C.: Government Printing Office 1979.

A comprehensive guide to laws, rules, and regulations administered and enforced by the EEOC. Explains that since the
President's Reorganization Plan in 1978, the EEOC enforcement
responsibilities have expanded greatly. Includes the full
text of the EEOC guidelines on sex, religion, and national
origin discrimination.

121. _____. LAWS ADMINISTERED BY EEOC. Washington, D.C.:
Government Printing Office, January 1981.

Focuses on laws and regulations administered by the EEOC.
Includes the full text of Title VII, EEOC Guidelines, Age
Discrimination in Employment Act, the Equal Pay Act, and
various agreements between the EEOC and other Federal
agencies on EEO and affirmative action.

122. _____. LEGISLATIVE HISTORY OF TITLES VII AND XI OF
     CIVIL RIGHTS ACT OF 1964. Washington, D.C.: Government
     Printing Office, 1968.

     Outlines the historical and legislative background of Title
     VII and XI of the Civil Rights Act of 1964. Includes the
     full text of both titles, congressional reports, debates,
     and tabulation of amendments adopted and rejected.

123. _____. PROMISE VERSUS PERFORMANCE: THE STATUS OF
     EQUAL EMPLOYMENT OPPORTUNITY IN THE NATION'S GAS AND ELEC-
     TRIC UTILITIES. Washington, D.C.: Government Printing
     Office, June 1972. 168 pp.

     Reports on a three-day hearing in 1971 on employment prac-
     tices in the gas and electric utility industries. The pur-
     pose of the hearing was to explore advances made by some
     companies in providing EEO and the technique used. Seeks to
     determine why some companies are having difficulty employing
     and promoting minorities and women.

124. _____. WHAT EMPLOYERS, UNIONS AND EMPLOYMENT AGENCIES
     SHOULD KNOW ABOUT EQUAL EMPLOYMENT OPPORTUNITY. Washing-
     ton, D.C.: Government Printing Office, June 1977. 7 pp.

     Briefly outlines what Title VII covers and what happens
     after a charge of discrimination is filed with the EEOC.

125. Vaas, Francis J. "Title VII: Legislative History." BOSTON
     COLLEGE INDUSTRIAL AND COMMERCIAL LAW REVIEW, 7 (Spring
     1966), 431-458.

     Traces the legislative history of Title VII. Includes
     discussions on subcommittee hearings, amendments, House and
     Senate actions, and other bills proposed on Civil Rights.

126. Veerhusen, Katrina. "The Proliferation of Employment Dis-
     crimination Statutory Protections: An Overview." LOYOLA
     UNIVERSITY OF CHICAGO LAW JOURNAL, 8 (Summer 1977), 934-
     959.

     "Examines the coverage, prohibitions, procedures, and reme-
     dies of major employment discrimination statutes." Includes
     discussions on Title VII of the Civil Rights Act of 1964,
     Section 1981 of the Civil Rights Act of 1866, The National
     Labor Relations Act, the Equal Pay Act of 1963, and the Age
     Discrimination in Employment Act of 1967.

127. Veil, Fred W. "Title VII of the Civil Rights Act of 1964 --
     Educational and Testing Requirements Invalid Unless Job-
     Related." Duquesne Law Review, 10 (Winter 1971), 270-279.

Reviews the Court's decision in <u>Griggs v. Duke Power Company</u>, and concludes that the Court held screening devices such as tests, which disproportionately screen out "Negro" applicants, and are not job related, violate Title VII of the Civil Rights Act of 1964.

128. "Ways to Fight Job Bias." CHANGING TIMES, November 1978, 45-57.

Briefly outlines Title VII of the Civil Rights Act of 1964, the Equal Pay Act of 1963, and the Age Discrimination in Employment Act. Explains that discrimination is rarely obvious and must be proved by showing differential treatment of protected class individuals. Advises persons who feel they have been discriminated against to contact the Equal Employment Opportunity Commission (EEOC) or their local Fair Employment Practices Office.

129. White, Richard C. "An Overview of Title VII." ALI-ABA COURSE MATERIAL JOURNAL, 3 (October 1978), 113-121.

Designed as training course material on major provisions of Title VII. Written in a straightforward easy reading format. Explains the coverage, prohibitions, exemptions, complaint procedure, and conciliation and settlement provisions.

130. Wrong, Elaine Gale. The Social Responsibility of Arbitrators in Title VII Disputes. LABOR LAW JOURNAL, 32 (September 1981), 621-626.

Contends that arbitrators have failed in their responsibility to incorporate discrimination laws and regulations into their decisions, e.g., the Civil Rights Act of 1964. Believes that arbitrators are reluctant to take discriminatory grievances because they are not competent to determine whether the labor-management contract is violating the Civil Rights Act of 1964.

RACE DISCRIMINATION

131. Alexander, Richard D. THE MANAGEMENT OF RACIAL INTEGRATION IN BUSINESS: A SPECIAL REPORT TO MANAGEMENT. New York: McGraw-Hill, 1964. 147 pp.

132. "Arrest Records, Hiring Policies and Racial Discrimination." IOWA LAW REVIEW, 57 (December 1971), 506-529.

Examines Title VII, court decisions, EEOC guidelines, and the fourteenth amendment to determine what protection is afforded minority applicants who are denied employment due

to having an arrest record without a conviction. Sees the
intent of Congress in enacting Title VII as an effort ". . .
to prohibit a wide range of activities which adversely affect
minority employment opportunities." Contends that the practice of using arrest records to bar employment has an adverse
impact on minority applicants. Finds that the EEOC, the
courts, and the fourteenth amendment have established standards that prohibit employment practices that adversely affect
minority employment. Concludes that employers must demonstrate that the practice of using arrest records as a means
of barring employment is based on a legitimate business
necessity.

133. Blumrosen, Alfred W. BLACK EMPLOYMENT AND THE LAW. New
      Brunswick, N.J.: Rutgers University Press, 1971. 416 pp.

      Believes that racial discrimination in employment can be
      eliminated from society and suggest approaches to achieve
      such a goal. Discusses discrimination in seniority and
      recruitment systems, and the Civil Rights Act of 1964.

134. Davis, George and Glegg Watson. BLACK LIFE IN CORPORATE
      AMERICA - SWIMMING IN THE MAINSTREAM. Garden City, New
      York: Anchor Press/Doubleday, 1982. 204 pp.

      Analyzes 160 interviews taken of black and white corporate
      managers concerning their social interaction and adaptation
      to one another's cultures and values. Relays the frustra-
      tions, alienations and stresses that black managers must deal
      with to survive in a corporate setting.

135. Donegan, Charles E. and Jerry Hunter. "Notes, Current Racial
      Legal Developments." HOWARD LAW JOURNAL, 12 (Summer 1966),
      299-318.

      Discusses significant developments in the area of race
      relations and civil rights. Written approximately one
      year after the effective date of Title VII. Indicates that
      Title VII has ". . . no enforcement provision [and that] the
      EEOC relies on conference, conciliation and persuasion to
      accomplish its objectives." Also includes discussions on
      discrimination in schools, federally assisted programs,
      voting, criminal prosecution, jury selection, and housing.

136. Doriot, George F. THE MANAGEMENT OF RACIAL INTEGRATION IN
      BUSINESS. New York: McGraw-Hill Book Co., 1964.

      A study on employment problems that occur when integrating
      "Negroes" in the business industry. Written prior to the
      effective date of the Civil Rights Act of 1964. Interviews
      "National Negro Leaders, government officials and executives

of approximately sixty-five business organizations." Discusses problems in desegregated facilities, preferential
treatment, recruitment, and selection criteria, e.g., testing
and interviewing. Concludes that "Negroes" will not wait
another fifty years for businesses to integrate. Believes
that businesses don't understand the full magnitude of the
"Negro" protest and unless businesses take progressive action
to end segregation, "Negroes" will continue to demonstrate
and boycott.

137. Edwards, Harry T. "Race Discrimintion in Employment: What
      Price Equality?" UNIVERSITY OF ILLINOIS LAW FORUM, 1976
      (No. 2), 572-626.

      Gives a historical view of race discrimination in America
      and the present economic status of blacks in the workforce.
      Indicates ". . . that blacks still fall disproportionately
      low on the scales of income and occupational status, and
      that they still suffer the worst effect from unemployment."
      Insists that some form of "preferential treatment" is needed
      to eliminate the effect of past employment discrimination.
      Indicates that during a recession, seniority systems ("last
      hired, first fired") will have an adverse impact on minori-
      ties who were recently hired as a result of affirmative
      action.

138. Ferman, Louis A. THE NEGRO AND EQUAL EMPLOYMENT OPPORTUNITY:
      A REVIEW OF MANAGEMENT EXPERIENCES IN TWENTY COMPANIES.
      2d ed. New York: F.A. Praeger, 1966. 189 pp.

139. Fernandez, John P. RACISM AND SEXISM IN CORPORATE LIFE.
      Lexington, MA.: Lexington Books, 1981. 360 pp.

      Presents the results of a study on the "effect of employ-
      ment policies and practices" on the employment of managers,
      and on the attitudes and perceptions of managers who work
      in a corporate environment. Analyzes the impact that racism
      and sexism have on the attitudes and perception of whites,
      females, and minority managers, (Native Americans, Asian,
      Hispanic, and Black Americans). Summarizes the study's find-
      ings on the attitudes and perceptions that managers have on
      advancement, job relocation, employee and supervisor working
      relationships, job satisfactions, performance and training
      within the corporate structure. Explains why and how each
      group arrived at their perpections. Includes topics on "Who
      is Benefiting Most From EEO/AAP?", "Do EEO/AAP Targets Hurt
      Minority Advancement?", and "Are Female Managers Better
      Bosses than Male Managers?" Discusses the present status
      of minorities and women in corporations. Projects that
      corporations will have problems in the future with their
      workforce because of differences in values, attitudes
      and perceptions of minority, white, and female workers.

Provides some alternatives and remedies to head off further
conflicts within the work environment.

140. Friedman, Edward D. "Racial Problems and Labor Relations:
      The Civil Rights Act." PROCEEDINGS OF NEW YORK UNIVERSITY
      EIGHTEENTH ANNUAL CONFERENCE ON LABOR. Edited by Thomas
      G.S. Christensen. New York: BNA, Inc., 1966, 367-380.

      Briefly discusses the historical background of Title VII.
      Explains the issue of public rights and private litigation
      under the Act. States that the Attorney General was given
      the power to bring a law suit where a "pattern and practice"
      of discrimination exist and at the same time, a private citi-
      zen has the right to bring a civil action for discrimination.

*   Gould, William B. "Employment Security, Seniority and Race:
      The Rule of Title VII of the Civil Rights Act of 1964. See
      Item 707.

141. Klare, Karl E. "The Quest for Industrial Democracy and the
      Struggle Against Racism: Perspectives from Labor Law and
      Civil Rights Law." OREGON LAW REVIEW, 61 (No. 2 1982),
      157-200.

*   McManis, Charles R. "Racial Discrimination in Government
      Employment: A Problem of Remedies for Unclean Federal
      Hands." See Item 607.

142. Norgren, Paul H. and Samuel E. Hill. TOWARD FAIR EMPLOYMENT.
      New York: Columbia University Press, 1964. 296 pp.

      Despite efforts by a number of governmental agencies,
      employment discrimination still exists for "Negroes." Exam-
      ines employment practices that have an adverse affect on the
      hiring and promotion of "Negroes," e.g., recruitment, train-
      ing and exclusion. Recommends that existing State Fair Em-
      ployment Practice laws be revised to more effectively elimi-
      nate employment discrimination, and that a federal law be
      implemented to supplement existing state laws.

143. Peck, Cornelius J. "Remedies for Racial Discrimination in
      Employment: A Comparative Evaluation of Forums."
      WASHINGTON LAW REVIEW, 46 (No. 3, 1971), 455-495.

      Analyzes the different forums for filing an employment
      discrimination complaint, e.g., Title VII, Civil Rights Act
      of 1866, OFCCP, National Labor Relations Act, and various
      state statues.

144. Roth, Mark D. "The Relationship Between Title VII and the
      NLRA: Getting our Acts Together in Race Discrimination
      Cases." VILLANOVA LAW REVIEW, 23 (November 1977), 68-99.

      Identifies possible areas of conflict in remedies provided
      by the Civil Rights Act of 1964 and the National Labor Rela-
      tions Act in race discrimination cases. Contends that the
      judicial system has encouraged complainants to pursue reme-
      dies under both Acts concurrently. Believes that courts have
      failed to clarify the relationship between the two Acts in
      handling such cases. Seeks to reconcile the differences
      between the two Acts. Suggests guidelines to regulate which
      race cases are handled by the EEOC and which ones by the
      National Labor Relations Board.

145. Samuel, Krislov. THE NEGRO IN FEDERAL EMPLOYMENT: THE QUEST
      FOR EQUAL OPPORTUNITY. Minneapolis, MN.: University of
      Minnesota Press, 1967.

146. Schmidt, Charles T., Jr. "Title VII: Coverage and Com-
      ments." BOSTON COLLEGE INDUSTRIAL AND COMMERCIAL LAW
      REVIEW, 7 (Spring 1966), 459-472.

      Asserts that ". . . this Title is wholly inadequate to meet
      even the minimum demands of the Negro, being ill-conceived in
      scope, coverage, administration, and enforcement." Believes
      that Title VII should have focused directly on the needs of
      the "Negro," e.g., job opportunities. Feels that sex dis-
      crimination should not have been included in the Title, and
      that the EEOC should have been given authority to issue cease
      and desist orders. Recommends that "quotas" be established
      by the federal government for the placement of "Negroes" in
      the workforce to "preserve the National welfare." As an
      alternative to quotas, suggests that the federal government
      encourage private industry and union, through tax incen-
      tives, to train "Negroes" for employment. Warns that Title
      VII is not enough to alter the "collision course"--"social
      disaster" we are headed for.

147. Sovern, Michael I. LEGAL RESTRAINTS ON RACIAL DISCRIMINATION
      IN EMPLOYMENT. New York: The Twentieth Century Fund,
      1966. 270 pp.

      Defines the problems of "American Negroes," e.g., unemploy-
      ment, employment discrimination, and inferior education.
      Briefly discusses the beginning struggles for employment
      opportunities for "American Negroes." Discusses state and
      federal civil rights legislation, and provides "a few per-
      spectives" on remedying discrimination. Written a year
      after the Civil Rights Act became effective.

148. _____. RACIAL DISCRIMINATION IN EMPLOYMENT. 2d ed.
     American Casebook Series. St. Paul, Minn.: West Publish-
     ing Co., 1973, pp. 839-1003.

     This pamphlet is chapter four of a textbook entitled Cases
     and Materials on Law and Poverty. Discusses Title VII, EEO
     case laws, discrimination in seniority systems, testing and
     EEOC guidelines.

149. Stewart, Shirley E. "Comment, The Myth of Reverse Race
     Discrimination: A Historical Perspective." CLEVELAND
     STATE LAW REVIEW, 23 (Spring 1974), 319-336.

     Gives a historical view of race discrimination in employ-
     ment. Advocates the eradication of employment discrimination
     "as soon as possible." Indicates that non-minorities have
     benefited from race discrimination and the taking away of
     this benefit today does not mean non-minorities are now being
     discriminated against.

150. "A Symposium: Equal Employment Opportunity: Comparative
     Community Experience." INDUSTRIAL RELATIONS, A JOURNAL OF
     ECONOMY AND SOCIETY, 9 (May 1970), 277-355.

     A collection of articles on equal employment opportunity
     and the employment status of "Negroes" in Chicago, New York
     City, Memphis, Boston, and Los Angeles.

151. U.S. Commission on Civil Rights. EQUAL EMPLOYMENT OPPORTU-
     NITY UNDER FEDERAL LAW. Washington, D.C.: Government
     Printing Office, 1971. 27 pp.

     Summarizes federal laws and regulations that prohibit dis-
     crimination on the bases of race, religion, sex, or national
     origin in private and public employment. Includes discus-
     sions on Title VII, Executive Order 11246, the National Labor
     Relations Act, Title VI of the Civil Rights Act of 1964, and
     general guidelines on filing an EEO complaint.

152. Williams, James D. THE STATE OF BLACK AMERICA - 1983. New
     York: National Urban League, Inc., 1983. 340 pp.

     A collection of essays which give an assessment on the
     status of blacks in America. Includes topics on the demo-
     graphics of blacks, the economic status of blacks, blacks in
     businesses, blacks in the military, blacks in white educa-
     tional institutions, the political status of blacks, and the
     mental health status of blacks. Gives recommendations on how
     the status of blacks in America can be improved.

153. Williams, Walter E. THE STATE AGAINST BLACKS. New York:
      McGraw-Hill Book Company, 1982. 183 pp.

      Contends ". . . that racial bigotry and discrimination is
      neither a complete nor a satisfactory explanation for the
      current condition of many blacks in America." Believes that
      ". . . many Federal, state, and local laws that regulate
      economic activity . . ." prevent blacks from entering various
      occupations and owning and operating businesses. Focuses
      specifically on occupations and businesses that restrict the
      access for blacks to enter, e.g., the taxicab, railroad, and
      trucking industries.

                    RELIGIOUS DISCRIMINATION

154. Beard, James L. "The Constitutionality of an Employer's Duty
      to Accommodate Religious Beliefs and Practices." CHICAGO-
      KENT LAW REVIEW, 56 (No. 1, 1980), 635-669.

      Views the 1972 amendment to the Equal Employment Opportu-
      nity Act, which requires employers to reasonably accommodate
      employees when their religious beliefs conflict with the
      employer's personnel policy, as conflicting with the Estab-
      lishment Clause of the Constitution. Traces the statutory
      development of religious discrimination and reasonable accom-
      modation guidelines, and analyzes related Supreme Court
      opinions.

155. Bernstein, John H. "Title VII - Religious Discrimination -
      Employer's Duty to 'Reasonably Accommodate' Employee's
      Religious Practices - Hardison v. Trans World Airlines,
      Inc." CREIGHTON LAW REVIEW, 9 (June 1976), 795-816.

      Outlines the Eighth Circuit's opinion in the Hardison case,
      which held that the employer did not reasonably attempt to
      accommodate the employee. Traces the development of statu-
      tory and regulatory guidelines on religious discrimination,
      and the reasonable accommodation rule. Summarizes a series
      of court decisions related to religious discrimination, and
      analyzes the decisions' impact on collective bargaining
      agreements.

156. Blackburn, John D. and Kathryn P. Sheehan. "Recent Develop-
      ments In Religious Discrimination: The EEOC's Proposed
      Guidelines." LABOR LAW JOURNAL, 31 (June 1980), 335-339.

      Believes the EEOC's proposed guidelines on religious dis-
      crimination go beyond the Supreme Court's interpretation of
      reasonable accommodation law as set forth in Trans World
      Airlines v. Hardison.

157. Carroll, John L. and Stephen C. Whicker. "Civil Rights--
      Religious Discrimination in Private Employment Under Title
      VII of the Civil Rights Act of 1964." CUMBERLAND-SAMFORD
      LAW REVIEW, 3 (Fall 1972), 497-507.

      Gives a brief account of the 1972 amendment to the Civil
      Rights Act of 1964 which in part redefined the term religion.
      Reviews EEOC and judicial decisions on religious discrimi-
      nation complaints. Concludes that the amendment, the EEOC
      guidelines on religion, and EEOC and judicial decisions have
      eliminated some confusion over the issue of religion dis-
      crimination. Believes that further clarification is needed
      on the terms "reasonable accommodation" and "undue hardship."

158. "Case Study: EEO and Religious Discrimination." EEO REVIEW,
      (February 1983), 2-3.

      Presents a case study on a religious discrimination com-
      plaint. Provides comments and suggestions to managers and
      supervisors on how to effectively deal with EEO complaints
      in this area of law.

159. Chenoweth, William A. "Is Title VII's Reasonable Accommoda-
      tions Requirement A Law 'Respecting an Establishment of
      Religion.'" NOTRE DAME LAWYER, 51 (February 1976), 481-
      491.

      Seeks to determine whether the EEOC's guidelines on reli-
      gious discrimination and Congress' 1972 Amendment to the
      Civil Rights Act of 1964 create an "excessive entanglements"
      between the government and religion which in turn violate the
      Establishment Clause of the Constitution. Concludes that
      reasonable accommodation requirements do not create an "ex-
      cessive entanglement," however, they do have the effect of
      allowing religious workers to have special benefits.

160. Covino, John A. "Religious Discrimination in Employment:
      Striking the Delicate Balance." DICKINSON LAW REVIEW, 80
      (Summer 1976), 717-746.

      Addresses the issue of whether the reasonable accommodation
      rule violates the intent of Title VII and the Establishment
      Clause of the U.S. Constitution. States that the U.S. Su-
      preme Court is faced with deciding these issues in Cummins
      v. Parker Seal Co. Recommends that the Supreme Court upholds
      the EEOC's rules on reasonable accommodation.

161. Dadakis, John D. and Thomas M. Russo. "Religious Discrimi-
      nation In Employment: The 1972 Amendment--A Perspective."
      FORDHAM URBAN LAW JOURNAL, 3 (Winter 1975), 327-345.

162. Edwards, Harry T. and Joel Kaplan. "Religious Discrimination
      and the Role of Arbitration Under Title VII. MICHIGAN LAW
      REVIEW, 69 (March 1971), 599-654.

163. "EEOC's Revised Religious Discrimination Guidelines." EEO
      REVIEW, (April 1981), 6-7.

      Provides a summary and brief analysis of the guidelines for
      managers and supervisors who are involved in making personnel
      decisions. Discusses the issue of reasonable accommodation,
      undue hardship, and selection practices and procedures.

164. Englard, Rubin. "Religious Observance and Discrimination in
      Employment." SYRACUSE LAW REVIEW, 22 (1971), 1019-1046.

165. Handler, Solomon Z. "Title VII and The Sabbath Observer."
      HOFSTRA LAW REVIEW, 5 (Summer 1977), 911-928.

      Attempts to clarify the coverage of religious discrimi-
      nation under Title VII, the EEOC guidelines, and the 1972
      Amendments to Title VII. Addresses the issue of reasonable
      accommodation, undue hardship, and the claim that reason-
      able accommodation violates the Establishment Clause of the
      U.S. Constitution. Summarizes major court decisions related
      to religious discrimination and the issue of reasonable
      accommodation.

166. Hollow, Charles J. and Thomas L. Bright. "Avoiding Reli-
      gious Discrimination in the Workplace." PERSONNEL JOURNAL,
      61 (August 1982), 590-594.

      Contends that under the EEOC's guidelines on discrimina-
      tion because of religion, it will be more difficult for an
      employer to demonstrate undue hardship. States that ". . .
      the guidelines may be satisfied when proof is provided show-
      ing that a requested religious accommodation necessitates the
      employer either to commit a violation of a bonafide seniority
      clause in a collective bargaining contract or causes an em-
      ployer to incur more than 'de minimis cost.'" Provides sug-
      gestions to employers on how to comply with the law.

*   Institute of Industrial Relations, University of California,
      Los Angeles. 1980 REPORT - EQUAL EMPLOYMENT OPPORTUNITY
      AND AFFIRMATIVE ACTION - THE ROOTS GROW DEEPER. See Item
      929.

167. Norwood, John M. "But I Can't Work on Saturdays." PERSONNEL
      ADMINISTRATOR, 25 (January 1980), 25-30.

Discusses the Supreme Court's decision in <u>TWA v. Hardison</u> and other lower court decisions that speak to the issue of religious discrimination and reasonable accommodation. Concludes that Title VII ". . . requires employers to make reasonable efforts to accommodate the religious needs of its employees short of undue hardship." Concludes that the <u>Hardison</u> decision indicate that reasonable efforts should not violate the union agreement and the cost of accommodation should be reasonable.

168.   "Note, Civil Rights - Religious Discrimination In Employment-Title VII of the Civil Rights Act Requires Reasonable Accommodation of Employee Religious Belief by Employer Despite Conflicting Lawful Agency Shop Provision." BRIGHAM YOUNG UNIVERSITY LAW REVIEW, 1977 (No. 1), 152-169.

Gives a historical summary of the ". . . conflict between the free exercise of religion and labor's right to organize and establish union security provisions . . ." Discusses the Fifth Circuit's decision in <u>Cooper v. General Dynamics</u>, which held that Title VII protects employees whose religious beliefs (Seventh-day Adventists) prevent them from joining a union. The Fifth Circuit remanded the case back to the District Court to determine whether the employee could be reasonably accommodated without creating an undue hardship on the employer and the union.

169.   "Note, Civil Rights - Religious Discrimination In Employment-Title VII Standards of 'Reasonable Accommodation' and 'Undue Hardship' Are Constitutional, But Recent Cases Illustrate Judicial Overzealousness In Enforcement." TEXAS LAW REVIEW, 54 (March 1976), 616-641.

170.   "Note, Constitutional Law - Religious Discrimination In Employment-Title VII of the Civil Rights Act of 1964 and the FCC Non-Discrimination Regulations. BRIGHAM YOUNG UNIVERSITY LAW REVIEW, 1975 (No. 1), 195-211.

Analyzes the Court of Appeals for the District of Columbia's opinion in <u>King's Garden, Inc. v. FCC</u>. The Court affirmed the FCC's decision that King's Garden, a religious organization, could not discriminate on the basis of religion when selecting employees to work at a radio station. The only exception would be for ". . . those persons hired to espouse a particular religious philosophy over the air . . ." The Court further held that the FCC regulations did not violate the 1972 amendments to the Civil Rights Act nor the First Amendment to the Constitution.

171.   Pfeffer, Leo. "Workers' Sabbath: Religious Belief and Employment. CIVIL LIBERTIES REVIEW, 4 (November-December 1977).

Criticizes the Supreme Court's decision in <u>Trans World Airlines v. Hardison</u>, which held that TWA was not in violation of the law when they terminated an employee for refusing to work on Saturday. Analyzes the decision and prior court decisions related to religious discrimination.

172. Suberlak, Raymond J. "Title VII: An Employer's View of Religious Discrimination Since the 1972 Amendment." LOYOLA UNIVERSITY OF CHICAGO LAW JOURNAL, 7 (Winter 1976), 97-117.

Discusses the prohibition of religious discrimination under Title VII and by the Equal Employment Opportunity Act of 1972. Reviews the ". . . conflict between an employer's work schedule and an employee's exercise of his religious beliefs or practices." Examines the courts' interpretation of Title VII, as amended and the issue of reasonable accommodation. Believes that courts have not clearly defined how far an employer is required to go to reasonably accommodate an employee due to his religious beliefs.

173. U.S. Commission on Civil Rights. RELIGION DISCRIMINATION: A NEGLECTED ISSUE. Washington, D.C.: Government Printing Office, April 1979. 541 pp.

A collection of speeches and papers presented at a two-day consultation on religious discrimination. A major purpose of the consultation was to determine the status of religious discrimination in employment and to decide what steps the Commission needed to take in exploring the issues further.

174. _____. RELIGION IN THE CONSTITUTION, A DELICATE BALANCE. Washington, D.C.: Government Printing Office, September, 1983. 79 pp.

Includes a chapter on the problem of "Religious Discrimination in Employment." Discusses the prohibition of religious discrimination under Title VII, the Supreme Court decision in <u>Trans World Airlines v. Hardison</u>, religious organizations, the EEOC Guidelines, and Constitutional issues.

175. U.S. Equal Employment Opportunity Commission. HEARING . . . ON RELIGIOUS ACCOMMODATION. Washington, D.C.: Government Printing Office, 1979. 649 pp.

Includes comments from employers and religious groups relative to the issue of accommodating the religious needs of employees on the job. The Commission seeks to establish guidelines on accommodating employees due to their religious beliefs. The hearings were held as a result of the U.S. Supreme Court's decision in <u>TWA v. Hardison</u>, which held that

employers have an obligation ". . . to accommodate the reasonable religious needs of employees where such accommodation can be made without undue hardship on the employer's
business."

176. Vantine, James G., Jr. "Labor Law - Religious Discrimina-
     tion-- Accommodation of Refusal to Pay Dues in an Agency
     Shop Because of Religious Beliefs." WAYNE LAW REVIEW, 23
     (March 1977), 1171-1185.

     Discusses the Fifth Circuit's opinion in Cooper v. General
     Dynamics, which held that employers and unions must accommo-
     date employees who were Seventh Day Adventists and would not
     pay union dues because of their religious belief. The court
     stated that the employer had to show that accommodating the
     employees would create an "undue hardship."

                    NATIONAL ORIGIN DISCRIMINATION

177. Allegretti, Joseph G. "National Origin Discrimination and
     the Ethnic Employee." EMPLOYEE RELATIONS LAW JOURNAL, 6
     (Spring 1981), 544-560.

*   "Are Blacks, Women, and Hispanics Getting 'More Than Their
     Fair Share'?" See Item 3.

178. "Case Study: EEO and National Origin Discrimination." EEO
     REVIEW, (March 1982), 2-3.

     Presents a case study on a national origin discrimination
     complaint. Provides comments and suggestions to managers and
     supervisors on how to effectively deal with EEO complaints in
     this area of the law.

179. Davis, Dwight J. "Garcia v. Gloor: Mutable Characteristics
     Rationale Extended to National Origin Discrimination."
     MERCER LAW REVIEW, 32 (1981), 1275-1283.

     Analyzes the Fifth Circuit Court of Appeals' decision in
     Garcia v. Gloor, which held that ". . . employers' policy
     requiring employees to speak only English while at work did
     not violate the Civil Rights Act of 1964 prohibition against
     national origin discrimination." Disagrees with the court's
     rationale and believes that the decision is not in line with
     the Griggs' decision.

180. Greenlaw, Paul S. and John P. Kohl. "National Origin Dis-
     crimination and the New EEOC Guidelines." PERSONNEL
     JOURNAL, 60 (August 1981), 634-636.

Analyzes the impact of the guidelines on personnel practices. Indicates that the guidelines expand the definition
of national origin, thus extending the coverage. For example, the guidelines do not require an individual to have
citizenship to be covered. The guidelines require employers
to show business necessity when ". . . employers selection
procedures have adverse impact upon a national origin group
. . ." Believes employers will find it difficult to establish a business necessity under the "speak only English"
provision. Discusses the harassment provision and outlines
procedures for employers to effectively deal with national
origin harassment. Concludes that the guidelines are consistent with other EEOC guidelines and should be easy for
employers to understand.

181. Hollow, Charles J. and Thomas L. Bright. "National Origin
      Harassment in the Workplace: Recent Guideline Development
      from the EEOC." EMPLOYEE RELATIONS LAW JOURNAL, 8 (Autumn
      1982), 282-293.

182. La Van, Helen. "Employment Discrimination against Hispanics:
      A Survey of Litigated Cases." EMPLOYMENT RELATIONS, 4
      (Winter 1983-84), 414-424.

      Indicates that the Hispanic population in the United States
      is growing at a rapid rate, and may even surpass the black
      population in the near future. Identifies particular prob-
      lems that Hispanic workers face in the work environment,
      e.g., physical and English requirements. Predicts that the
      issue of national origin discrimination will become increas-
      ingly at issue as more Hispanics enter the workforce. Sur-
      veys and analyzes employment discrimination cases between
      1978 and 1983 involving ethnic groups to determine similar
      case characteristics and the court's disposition.

183. National Commission for Employment Policy. HISPANICS AND
      JOBS: BARRIERS TO PROGRESS. Washington, D.C.: Government
      Printing Office, September 1982. 86 pp.

      Reports on employment barriers that Hispanics face when
      attempting to enter the job market. Identifies the ". . .
      lack of proficiency in English, low levels of formal school-
      ing, and discrimination . . ." as three major barriers they
      face. Provides statistical data on Hispanics' wages and
      occupational distribution in the labor market. Outlines
      governmental actions to reduce employment barriers for His-
      panics to successfully enter the labor market.

184. Ornati, Oscar A. "Arbitrators and National Origin Discrimi-
      nation." ARBITRATION JOURNAL, 36 (June 1981), 30-34.

Reviews major provisions of the EEOC's guidelines on
national origin discrimination and related Supreme Court
rulings and arbitration decisions. Believes that because of
the guidelines, there will be an increase in the number of
national origin discrimination charges. Sees arbitrators as
having no difficulty in deciding such charges. Briefly
explains how some employers are preventing and correcting
national origin discrimination in the workforce.

185. _____ and Margaret J. Eisen. "Are you Complying with
      EEOC's New Rules on National Origin Discrimination?" PER-
      SONNEL, 58 (March-April 1981), 12-20.

      Explains that the new guidelines are more specific and are
      designed to assist employers in understanding which personnel
      practices constitute discrimination based on national origin.
      Reviews the guidelines' definition of national origin dis-
      crimination, citizenship requirements, selection procedures,
      speak-English only rules, and harassment. Outlines positive
      steps employers can take to eliminate personnel practices
      that result in national origin discrimination.

186. Reiter, Michael. "Compensating for Race or National Origin
      in Employment Testing." LOYOLA UNIVERSITY OF CHICAGO LAW
      JOURNAL, (Summer 1977), 687-721.

*   Sahlein, Stephen. THE AFFIRMATIVE ACTION HANDBOOK. See Item
      970.

187. U.S. Equal Employment Opportunity Commission. "Fact Sheet,
      Discrimination Because of National Origin." Mimeographed.
      Washington, D.C., December 1981.

      Defines the basis of national origin discrimination, and
      briefly discusses the "speak-English only" rule and filing a
      national origin discrimination charge.

188. _____. SPANISH SURNAMED AMERICAN EMPLOYMENT IN THE
      SOUTHWEST. Washington, D.C.: Government Printing Office,
      1980. 247 pp.

      Studies employment patterns of spanish surnamed Americans
      who reside in the southwestern part of the United States.
      Finds that this minority group is "underrepresented and
      underutilized in the labor force."

SEX DISCRIMINATION

189. Abramson, Joan. OLD BOYS, NEW WOMEN: THE POLITICS OF SEX
      DISCRIMINATION. New York: Praeger Publishers, 1979.
      255 pp.

      Analyzes the extent of sex discrimination in employment.
      Uses a case study approach in discussing the issue. Includes
      topics on filing sex discrimination complaints, EEO laws and
      regulations, the effectiveness of EEO enforcement agencies,
      the misuse of EEO statistics, and sexual harassment.

190. American Society for Public Administration. THE RIGHT WORD:
      GUIDELINES FOR AVOIDING SEX-BIASED LANGUAGE. Washington,
      D.C., 1979.

      Alerts public administrators to sex-role stereotyping and
      sexist language used in written and oral communication. Pro-
      vides alternative terms and titles to avoid sexist language.

191. Babcock, Barbara Allen; Ann E. Freedman; Eleanor Holmes
      Norton; and Susan C. Ross. SEX DISCRIMINATION AND THE
      LAW, CAUSES AND REMEDIES. Boston, MA.: Little Brown and
      Co., 1975. 1092 pp.

      Written as a law school textbook. Discusses the constitu-
      tional rights of women and various other social and economic
      rights, e.g., the Equal Rights Amendment. Chapter two dis-
      cusses sex discrimination under Title VII, the Equal Pay
      Act, and Executive Order 11246. Selected topics include:
      recruitment, hiring and promotion of women, pregnancy dis-
      crimination, discriminatory seniority systems, the use of
      statistics to prove a sex discrimination complaint, and sex
      discrimination within unions.

192. Berger, Ralph S. "The Courts and the Equal Employment Oppor-
      tunity Commission View Sex Discrimination Against Males.
      INDUSTRIAL AND LABOR RELATIONS FORUM, 10 (March 1974),
      15-33.

193. Blumberg, Grace. "De Facto and De Jure Sex Discrimination
      Under the Equal Protection Clause: A Reconsideration of
      the Veterans' Preference in Public Employment." BUFFALO
      LAW REVIEW, 26 (Fall-Winter 1976-77), 1-82.

      An extensive discussion on veterans' preference in public
      employment as it relates to the Equal Protection Clause of
      the Fourteenth Amendment and fair practices laws. Attempts
      to rationalize the Supreme Court's decisions in Griggs v.
      Duke Power and Washington v. Davis with sex discrimination.

Discusses the standard of review to be applied when determining whether veterans' preference is discriminatory, i.e.,
should the "strict scrutiny" or the "rational basis test"
be used. Finds that veterans' preference would be sex discrimination when applying Title VII standards. Believes
that veterans' preference would not survive a review under
the "strict scrutiny" test but would survive a review under
a "rational basis test."

*   Blumrosen, Ruth G. "Wage Discrimination, Job Segregation,
        and Title VII of the Civil Rights Act of 1964." See Item
        398.

194.   Brown, William H., III. "Sex Discrimination, It Isn't Funny,
        It is Illegal, and the Battle Has Just Begun." GOOD GOV-
        ERNMENT, 88 (Winter 1971), 18-21.

        Reports that sex discrimination in employment practices
        is a serious problem. States that during 1971 more than
        5000 sex discrimination charges were filed with the EEOC.
        Describes the various myths and discriminatory stereotype
        attitudes directed at women workers. Briefly discusses the
        status of women in the federal workforce and federal efforts
        to ensure EEO for women workers.

195.   Bryant, Willa C. "Discrimination Against Women in General:
        Black Southern Women in Particular." CIVIL RIGHTS DIGEST,
        4 (Summer 1971), 10-11.

        Explains that traditional stereotypical attitudes have been
        directed at women in America throughout the history of the
        country. Indicates that the basic stereotypical attitude
        directed at women is that women are inferior to men. Reveals
        that black women not only have to combat stereotypical myths
        directed at them because they are women, but also because
        they are black. Recommends that black women in the South
        strive toward the elimination of race discrimination first
        and foremost, before they campaign for the elimination of
        sex discrimination.

196.   "Case Study: EEO and Sex Discrimination." EEO REVIEW,
        (April 1983), 2-3.

        Presents a case study on a sex discrimination complaint.
        Provides comments and suggestions to managers and supervisors
        on how to effectively deal with EEO complaints in this area
        of the law.

197.   Cassibry, John F. "Title VII: Sex Discrimination and the
        BFOQ." LOUISIANA LAW REVIEW, 34 (Spring 1974), 590-596.

198. Cates, Judith N. "Sex and Salary." AMERICAN PSYCHOLOGIST,
      28 (October 1973), 929.

199. Chamallas, Martha. "Exploring the 'Entire Spectrum' of Dis-
      parate Treatment Under Title VII: Rules Governing Predomi-
      nantly Female Jobs." UNIVERSITY OF ILLINOIS LAW REVIEW,
      1984 (No. 1), 1-51.

200. Clynch, Edward J. and Carol A. Gaudin. "Sex in the Ship-
      yards: An Assessment of Affirmative Action Policy."
      PUBLIC ADMINISTRATION REVIEW, 42 (March/April 1982), 114-
      121.

      Assesses the impact of affirmative action enforcement by
      the federal government to hire females in the shipyard indus-
      try. Indicates that the overall results of the study support
      that federal efforts to increase the number of females in the
      shipyards have been positive.

201. DeGooyer, Janice. "Women, Worker, and Age Discrimination."
      GRADUATE WOMEN, 76 (September-October 1982), 21-23.

      Asserts that women workers may find themselves victims of
      both sex dicrimination and age discrimination, "unless the
      society changes its current emphasis on youth." Discusses
      barriers that women workers over 40 face when seeking employ-
      ment. Suggests remedies on how to remove these barriers,
      which in turn will end sex and age discrimination.

202. Dowding, Nancy E. "The Greatest Minority of All." CIVIL
      RIGHTS DIGEST, 4 (Summer 1971), 2-7.

      Asserts that there are more women in America than men but
      women are treated as minorities or worse. Believes that
      women continue to be victims of employment discrimination.
      As an example of employment discrimination, cites that women
      earn only 40% of wages that men earn. Outlines what women
      organizations are doing to confront and curtail sex discrimi-
      nation in employment. Recommends specific actions that indi-
      vidual women can take to support the movement of equality for
      women.

203. Edwards, Harry T. "Sex Discrimination Under Title VII:
      Some Unresolved Issues." LABOR LAW JOURNAL, 24 (July
      1973), 411-423.

      Contends that even after passage of Title VII and other
      federal regulations there are still a number of unresolved
      issues related to ". . . the BFOQ exception, the idea of
      customer preferences, the issue of societal standards of
      morality, fringe benefit plans, and maternity leave . . . ."

Examines the unsolved issues in the above areas and related judicial decisions.

204. Farley, Jennie. ACADEMIC WOMEN AND EMPLOYMENT DISCRIMINA-
      TION: A CRITICAL ANNOTATED BIBLIOGRAPHY. Ithaca, N.Y.:
      ILR Publications, New York State School of Industrial and
      Labor Relations, Cornell University, 1982.

      Focuses on articles, books, reports, and papers related to
      sex discrimination in higher education. Includes a summary
      of fifty cases where women filed discrimination suits against
      their employer (educational institutions) between 1971 and
      1981.

205. Ferguson, Jacqueline and Laura Garrison. "Covert Sexism in
      the Workplace." EQUAL OPPORTUNITY FORUM, 7 (October 1979),
      18.

      Covert sexism in employment may take three specific forms:
      "demeaning tactics," "work overload," and "inappropriate
      assignments and special projects." Recommends various op-
      tions for women to follow when coping with sexism, e.g.,
      ignoring the situation, transferring, and filing a complaint.
      Predicts that every working woman will be exposed to sexism
      in employment.

*   Finneran, Hugh M. "Title VII and Restrictions on Employment
      of Fertile Women." See Item 37.

206. Fiscbach, Donald F. "Union Liability for Sex Discrimina-
      tion." HASTINGS LAW JOURNAL, 23 (November 1971), 295-310.

207. Flanders, Dwight P. and Peggy E. Anderson. "Sex Discrimina-
      tion In Employment: Theory and Practice." INDUSTRIAL AND
      LABOR RELATIONS REVIEW, 26 (April 1973), 938-955.

208. Fretz, C.F. and Joanne Hayman. "Progress for Women-Men Are
      Still More Equal." HARVARD BUSINESS REVIEW, 51 (September-
      October 1973), 133-142.

      Examines why there are still attitudinal and cultural bias
      directed at women managers. Reports on a survey of 20 busi-
      ness organizations to determine how affirmative action and
      EEO programs are working to provide females with employment
      opportunities. Provides suggestions and recommendations to
      employers on how to improve their programs.

209. Godbe, Mary L. "Sex as a Bona Fide Occupational Qualifi-
      cation." UTAH LAW REVIEW, 20 (September 1968), 395-405.

210. Greenberger, Marcia. "The Effectiveness of Federal Laws
      Prohibiting Sex Discrimination in Employment in the United
      States." EQUAL EMPLOYMENT POLICY FOR WOMEN. Edited by
      Ronnie Steinberg Ratner. Philadelphia, PA: Temple
      University Press, 1980, pp. 108-128.

      Evaluates the effectiveness of Title VII of the Civil
      Rights Act of 1964, the Equal Pay Act of 1963, and Executive
      Order 11246 on prohibiting sex discrimination in employment.
      Sees deficiencies in present civil rights laws and regula-
      tions and suggest that each of them be strengthened by courts
      or congress to further eradicate sex discrimination.

211. Hallam, Charlotte B. "Legal Tools To Fight Sex Discrimi-
      nation." LABOR LAW JOURNAL, 24 (December 1973), 803-809.

212. Hauck, Vern E. "Burdine: Sex Discrimination, Promotion, and
      Arbitration." LABOR LAW JOURNAL, 33 (July 1982), 434-441.

213. Hoffman, Carl and John S. Reed. "Sex Discrimination? The
      XYZ Affair." PUBLIC INTEREST, (Winter 1981), 21-39.

*   Institute of Industrial Relations, University of California,
      Los Angeles. 1980 REPORT - EQUAL EMPLOYMENT OPPORTUNITY
      AND AFFIRMATIVE ACTION - THE ROOTS GROW DEEPER. See Item
      929.

*   Jablin, Fredric M. "Use of Discrimination Questions in
      Screening Interviews." See Item 838.

214. Kay, Herma H. SEX-BASED DISCRIMINATION: TEXT, CASES AND
      MATERIALS. 2nd ed. St. Paul, MI.: West Publishing Co.,
      1981. 1045 pp.

      Includes a chapter on "Women and Employment" that discusses
      Title VII, the Equal Pay Act, Executive Order 11246, the
      union and employment discrimination, constitutional limita-
      tion on employment discrimination and leading sex discrimina-
      tion cases.

215. Landau, Eliot and Kermit L. Dunahoo. "Sex Discrimination In
      Employment: A Survey of State and Federal Remedies."
      DRAKE LAW REVIEW, 20 (June 1971), 417-527.

      A synthesis of recent developments in "constitutional,
      statutory, case and administrative law" related to sex dis-
      crimination. Covers topics on Title VII, the Equal Pay Act,
      Executive Orders, pre-employment selections, working condi-
      tions, classifications, and fringe benefits. Concludes that
      thus far, the various laws and regulations related to sex

discrimination have made a substantial impact on combating
sex discrimination in employment.

216. Lloyd, Cynthia B., ed. SEX DISCRIMINATION AND THE DIVISION
      OF LABOR. New York: Columbia University Press, 1975.
      431 pp.

      A collection of essays from economists on the economical
      status of women in the labor market and the impact of sex
      discrimination and job segregation on their mobility.

217. _____ and Beth T. Niemi. THE ECONOMICS OF SEX
      DIFFERENTIALS. New York: Columbia University Press, 1979.
      355 pp.

      Examines the economic status of women in the labor force
      and presents empirical data on their earnings, training, edu-
      cation, and participation in the labor force. Chapter five
      focuses specifically on wage discrimination and chapter six
      focuses on laws and policies that affect wage differentials
      among the sexes.

218. Mansfield, Anthony R. "Sex Discrimination in Employment
      Under Title VII of the Civil Rights Act of 1964." VANDER-
      BILT LAW REVIEW, 21 (May 1968), 484-501.

219. Margolin, Bessie. "Management-Union Confrontation 1972 New
      Frontiers: Who Discriminates Against Women?" PROCEEDINGS
      OF NEW YORK UNIVERSITY TWENTY-FIFTH ANNUAL CONFERENCE ON
      LABOR. New York: Matthew Bender, 1973, pp. 205-224.

      Asserts that even after eight years since the passage of
      the Equal Pay Act and Title VII "[i]t is difficult to find
      any appreciable number of companies - or unions - which do
      not engage in sex discrimination in some form or other."
      Projects that since the passage of the 1972 Amendments, which
      in part give the EEOC the power to bring law suits, the EEOC
      will give special attention to sex and race discrimination
      complaints. Advises employers and unions to immediately take
      corrective measures to eliminate any practices under the
      union contract that perpetuate employment discrimination.

220. Meacham, Colquitt L. "Sex Discrimination in Employment-The
      Law: Where It Is and Where It's Going." CONTEMPORARY
      PROBLEMS IN PERSONNEL. Edited by W. Clay Hammer and
      Frank L. Schmidt. rev. ed. Chicago, IL.: St. Clair Press,
      1979, pp. 134-141.

      Reviews legislation, federal guidelines, and administrative
      and judicial decisions related to sex discrimination. Con-
      cludes that sex discrimination still exist, but it is mostly

subtle in nature and finds that ". . . most women still work
in low-paying, low status jobs."

221. Miller, Robert Stevens, Jr. "Sex Discrimination and Title
     VII of the Civil Rights Act of 1964." MINNESOTA LAW
     REVIEW, 51 (1967), 877-897.

222. Mott, Mary. "Women Workers Achieve Major Milestone In Fight
     Against Job Discrimination." TODAY'S SECRETARY, 71 (Febru-
     ary 1969), 34.

223. Murray, Pauli and Mary O. Eastwood. "Jane Crow and the Law:
     Sex Discrimination and Title VII. GEORGE WASHINGTON LAW
     REVIEW, 34 (December 1965), 232-256.

     Parallels sex discrimination with race discrimination.
     States that had sex discrimination not been added to Title
     VII, "Negro women" would have found it difficult in proving
     discrimination based on race or sex. Explains how sex may be
     used as a bona fide occupational qualification on a limited
     basis. Briefly discusses the Equal Pay Act. Believes that
     even with the passage of Title VII, the status of women in
     employment will not change drastically.

224. Neuberger, Thomas, Stephen. "Sex as a Bona Fide Occupational
     Qualification Under Title VII." LABOR LAW JOURNAL, 29
     (July 1978), 425-429.

     Analyzes the Supreme Court's decision in Dothard v. Rawlin-
     son, which held that the employer was justified in not hiring
     a female as a prison guard. The court's decision was based
     on Section 703(e) of the Civil Rights Act of 1964. Believes
     that the decision was narrow and the burden of proof in
     cases where an employer attempts to argue sex as a BFOQ is
     extremely heavy.

225. "Note, Classification on the Basis of Sex and the 1964 Civil
     Rights Act." IOWA LAW REVIEW, 50 (Spring 1965), 778-798.

*   Oaxaca, Ronald. "Sex Discrimination in Wages." DISCRIMINA-
     TION IN LABOR MARKETS. See Item 408.

226. Osterman, Paul. "Sex Discrimination In Professional Employ-
     ment: A Case Study." INDUSTRIAL AND LABOR RELATIONS
     REVIEW, 32 (July 1979), 451-464.

     Analyzes salary data on over 700 professional employees in
     metropolitan publishing firms. "Finds that the sex differen-
     tial in earnings within clusters of similar jobs is much

greater if marriage and children variables are excluded: Men
receive a large 'payoff' from being married and from having
children, but some do not."

227. Pepper, William F. and Florynce R. Kennedy. SEX DISCRIMINA-
      TION IN EMPLOYMENT. Charlottesville, VA.: Michie Company,
      1981. 327 pp.

      A guide for practitioners, researchers, and students on
      litigating sex discrimination cases. Gives a comprehensive
      analysis on the status of women prior to and after the pass-
      age of Title VII. Outlines the legislative history, cover-
      age, remedies, and other major provisions of the Act. Dis-
      cusses the various forms of sex discrimination in employment,
      e.g., sexual harassment, seniority, fringe benefits, promo-
      tions, etc. Includes twenty-four forms that are used when
      litigating a sex discrimination case.

228. Petersen, Gary G. and Linda Bryant. "Eliminating Sex Dis-
      crimination--Who Must Act?" PERSONNEL JOURNAL, 51 (August
      1972), 587-591.

229. Quinn, Jane Bryant. "A Woman's Place." NEWSWEEK, 93 (Febru-
      ary 26, 1979), 73.

230. Rogge, O. John. "Equal Rights for Women." HOWARD LAW JOUR-
      NAL, 21 (1977), 327-420.

      Presents an in-depth discussion on the plight of women to
      achieve equal rights in a selected number of areas. Section
      IV of the article focuses on women rights under Title VII and
      the Equal Pay Act.

231. Rosen, Benson and Thomas H. Jerdee. "Sex Stereotyping in the
      Executive Suite." HARVARD BUSINESS REVIEW, (March-April
      1974), 33.

      Results of a survey conducted on sexual biases of Harvard
      Business Review subscribers. Indicates that sexual biases
      are still unconsciously considered by managers when making
      personnel decisions. Concludes that the responses illustrate
      that ". . . there is greater organizational concern for the
      careers of men than there is for those of women, and there
      is a degree of skepticism about women's abilities to balance
      work and family demands."

232. Ross, Diane and Maggi Popkin. BARGAINING FOR EQUALITY. San
      Francisco, CA.: Women's Labor Project, 1981. 144 pp.

Discusses employment problems women face in the workplace
and suggests "legal and collective bargaining solutions" to
correcting the problem. Includes discussions on federal discrimination laws, women participation in the union contract,
sexual harassment, dual roles of women, affirmative action,
and job segregation. Concludes with a list of addresses of
organizations that can assist women in fighting sex discrimination in the workplace.

233. Ross, Susan C. THE RIGHTS OF WOMEN. Washington, D.C.:
      American Civil Liberties Union, Inc., 1973. 384 pp.

      Seeks to advise women of their rights under various laws
      and regulations. Includes a chapter on employment discrimi-
      nation that discusses Title VII, the Equal Pay Act, and
      Executive Orders. Written in a question and answer format.

234. Roth, Allan E. "Civil Rights: Sex Discrimination In Employ-
      ment Under the Civil Rights Act of 1964." OHIO STATE LAW
      JOURNAL, 32 (Fall 1971), 923-933.

      Provides a summary of the Supreme Court's decision in
      Phillips v. Martin Marietta Corp. The Court held that Title
      VII was violated when an employer had one hiring policy for
      female workers and another hiring policy for males.

235. Steckman, Elizabeth K. "I Charged the Government with Sex
      Discrimination." GRADUATE WOMAN, 75 (January-February
      1981), 8-10.

      Shares the experience of filing a sex discrimination com-
      plaint which was filed by the author against the Federal
      government a decade ago. Admits that the process was painful
      and costly. Believes that her complaint ". . . made it
      easier for women to be recognized for their merits. . . ."

236. Strum, Philippa. "Women at Work: Is Discrimination Real?"
      GRADUATE WOMAN, 75 (March-April 1981), 12-15.

      Finds that women are entering the workforce at a dramatic
      pace, and are gaining work experience and seniority. Reveals
      that a number of studies indicate that there is a major wage
      gap between men and women. Cites a study conducted by the
      State University of New York which not only found a wage
      gap between men and women, but also concluded that the prob-
      lem is ". . . so deeply rooted that even nondiscriminatory
      personnel procedures may not work; worse, they may perpetuate
      inequities."

237. "Supervising Women: How to Avoid Sex Discrimination in a
      Mixed Workforce." EEO REVIEW, (May 1978), 6-8.

Advises supervisors and managers of "discretionary areas of
supervision" that are prone to lead to sex discrimination
charges, if not handled properly. Presents case studies
involving sex discrimination charges and the EEOC's finding.

238. Underwood, Osta. "Legislation and Litigation: Impact on
      Working Women." AFFIRMATIVE ACTION FOR WOMEN: A PRACTICAL
      GUIDE FOR WOMEN AND MANAGEMENT. Reading, MA.: Addison-
      Wesley Publishing Company, 1977, pp. 39-70.

      Raises three key questions on the subject of working women:
      (1) "How do new laws and government regulations affect em-
      ployers and working women? (2) What can employers do in
      response to these regulations? (3) What can working women
      do who feel discriminated against?" Includes discussions
      on the Fair Labor Standards Act, the Equal Pay Act of 1963,
      Title VII, and Executive Order 11246. Suggests that employ-
      ers not wait until a complaint is filed but should develop
      an affirmative action program to eliminate discriminatory
      employment practices.

239. University of California at Los Angeles, University Extension
      and Other. SEX DISCRIMINATION IN EMPLOYMENT PRACTICES.
      Los Angeles, CA., September 19, 1968.

      Reports on the extent of sex discrimination in employment
      and on the federal government's efforts to eliminate sex
      discrimination in the workforce. Provides a step by step
      guide for developing and implementing an affirmative action
      program to eliminate sex discrimination in employment.

240. U.S. Civil Service Commission. "Women in State and Local
      Governments." EEO FOR STATE AND LOCAL GOVERNMENTS. Wash-
      ington, D.C.: Government Printing Office, Issue No. 1.
      4 pp.

      Gives a brief report on sex discrimination in employment
      and suggest that employers can prevent sex discrimination by
      developing affirmative action programs for women.

241. U.S. Commission on Civil Rights. A GUIDE TO FEDERAL LAWS AND
      REGULATIONS PROHIBITING SEX DISCRIMINATION. Washington,
      D.C.: Government Printing Office, July 1976. 189 pp.

      Provides a practical guide on individual rights under
      various Civil Right laws and regulations that prohibit sex
      discrimination and a guide on the agencies that enforce the
      laws.

242. U.S. Department of Labor, Office of the Secretary, Women's
      Bureau. EQUAL EMPLOYMENT OPPORTUNITY FOR WOMEN: U.S.
      POLICIES. Washington, D.C.: Government Printing Office,
      1982. 38 pp.

      Summarizes the federal enforcement system's efforts to
      provide equal employment opportunity. Gives a brief history
      of each federal enforcement agency's responsibility to moni-
      tor and prohibit discrimination, e.g., the EEOC, Women's
      Bureau, and the OFCCP. Discusses employment factors that
      prohibit and repress the full utilization of women in the
      workforce. Contains statistical data on women in the labor
      market and in various occupational fields. Concludes that
      minority women lag behind white women in most socio-economic
      areas, and women as a whole are still segregated in specific
      occupations.

243. _____. THE NATIVE AMERICAN WOMEN AND EQUAL OPPORTU-
      NITY:. HOW TO GET AHEAD IN THE FEDERAL GOVERNMENT. Wash-
      ington, D.C.: Government Printing Office, 1979. pp. 81.

      Reviews the current status of Native American women and
      concludes that "[n]ative American women are among the lowest
      paid workers in our economy." Advises Native American women
      how to improve their employment status, including information
      on EEO and the complaint process within the federal govern-
      ment.

244. _____. A WORKING WOMAN'S GUIDE TO HER JOB RIGHTS.
      Washington, D.C.: Government Printing Office, 1978. 32
      pp.

      Cites statistics that support that the number of women in
      the labor force increased by 41% between 1967 and 1977.
      States that many of the jobs held by women are low-paying and
      in some cases women are paid less than men for the same job.
      Summarizes federal laws and regulations that have had an
      impact on the rights of women workers, e.g. Title VII and the
      Equal Pay Act.

245. _____. A WORKING WOMAN'S GUIDE TO HER JOB RIGHTS.
      Washington, D.C.: January 1983. 54 pp.

      A resource guide on employment rights of women and federal
      legislation that protect women workers. Includes topics on
      employment discrimination laws and regulations, sexual ha-
      rassment, pregnancy discrimination, and pay equity.

246. U.S. Department of Labor, Wage and Labor Standards Adminis-
      tration. Women's Bureau. HOW YOU CAN HELP REDUCE BARRIERS
      TO THE EMPLOYMENT OF MATURE WOMEN. Washington, D.C.:
      Government Printing Office, February 1969.

Analyzes the coverage, exceptions, enforcement provisions, and impact of the Age Discrimination Act on women workers who are over 40 years of age.

247. U.S. Equal Employment Opportunity Commission. TOWARD JOB EQUALITY FOR WOMEN. Washington, D.C.: Government Printing Office, 1969. 11 pp.

Summarizes employment rights of women, including the provisions of the Civil Rights of 1964.

248. _____. WOMEN: THE PATH TO EQUAL EMPLOYMENT. Washington, D.C.: Government Printing Office, 1977. 211 pp.

Reports on a ". . . study of female employment in the private sector between 1966 and 1975 [and] measures the progress of women toward fair-share goals in level of employment, job quality, and salary level." Includes discussions on salary gaps between women and men, female employment levels, labor market factors, availability of women in the labor market, and the progress made on closing the gap in the employment of women.

249. U.S. Department of Justice, Civil Rights Division. INTERIM REPORT TO THE PRESIDENT BY THE TASK FORCE ON SEX DISCRIMINATION. Washington, D.C.: Government Printing Office, 1978.

250. Walsh, Ethel Bent. "Sex Discrimination and the Impact of Title VII." LABOR LAW JOURNAL, 25 (March 1974), 150-154.

251. Wermiel, Stephen. "Sex Discrimination Suits May Force Big Changes in Retirement Benefits." WALL STREET JOURNAL, (January 10, 1983), 21.

Predicts that the Supreme Court decision in Norris v. Arizona will have a major impact on pension plans. The Supreme Court must decide whether expectancy or actuary tables used by insurance and pension industries are discriminatory. The tables show that women live longer than men as a class. Women, therefore, are required to pay more into pension plans than men are. Norris alleges the system violates Title VII.

252. Wolkinson, Benjamin W. and Dennis H. Liberson." The Arbitration of Sex Discrimination Grievances." THE ARBITRATION JOURNAL, 37 (June 1982), 35-44.

Analyzes a select group of arbitration decisions on sex discrimination which are reported in the Labor Arbitration

Reports between 1975 and 1980. Seeks to determine the similarity and dissimilarity in decisions between arbitrators,
courts and the Equal Employment Opportunity Commission
(EEOC). Concentrates on cases involving promotion, job
classification, sexual harassment, termination, preferential
treatment, and pregnancy. Concludes that arbitration decisions involving sex discrimination closely parallel decisions
issued by courts and the EEOC.

253. "Women's New Target: Job Bias in Offices." U.S. NEWS AND
     WORLD REPORT, 87 (July 30, 1979), 58-59.

254. Winslow, Mary. "Sex Discrimination In Employment: Current
     Federal Practice." DRAKE LAW REVIEW, 24 (Summer 1975),
     515-569.

     Provides a summary of employment practices that may violate
     Title VII on the basis of sex discrimination. Includes dis-
     cussions on seniority provisions that adversely affect women,
     the issue of pregnancy discrimination, and sex as a BFOQ.
     Explains various defenses to claims of sex discrimination and
     the burden of proving a claim of sex discrimination. Out-
     lines procedural provisions of Title VII, e.g., processing
     complaints, time limitations, litigation by the EEOC and
     private parties, and remedies available under Title VII.

255. Zarefsky, Paul. "How the Hishon Decision Will Affect Your
     Firm." AMERICAN BAR ASSOCIATION JOURNAL, 70 (September
     1984), 58-61.

PREGNANCY DISCRIMINATION

256. Bird, Roger A. "Title VII and the Pregnant Employee." NOTRE
     DAME LAWYER, 49 (February 1974), 568-578.

     Traces the development of sex discrimination before the
     passage of Title VII and evaluates the impact of Title VII on
     sex discrimination after its passage. Focuses specifically
     on the protection against sex discrimination due to pregnancy
     under Title VII, the EEOC's 1972 Guidelines on Pregnancy, and
     the Fourteenth Amendment.

257. Bureau of National Affairs, Inc. "Special Report: Pregnancy
     Disability Amendment to Title VII of the Civil Rights Act
     of 1964." FAIR EMPLOYMENT PRACTICES. Washington, D.C.,
     (No. 357). November 9, 1978.

     Gives a thorough review of the Amendment and its impact on
     pregnancy discrimination. Reviews major provisions of the
     Amendment, the Supreme Court decisions in General Electric

Co. v. Glbert and Nashville Gas Co. v. Satty, coverage for
abortions, pregnancy cost to employers, and responsibilities
of employers under the Amendment. Includes the full text of
the Amendment and the House and Senate Committee reports.

258. "Comment, Geduldig v. Aiello: Pregnancy Classifications and
      the Definition of Sex Discrimination." COLUMBIA LAW RE-
      VIEW, 75 (March 1975), 441-482.

259. Egger, Mary H. "Sexual Discrimination: Pregnancy Bene-
      fits As Interpreted by the EEOC and the Courts--Wetzel v.
      Liberty Mutual." UNIVERSITY OF DAYTON LAW REVIEW, 1 (May
      1976), 195-210.

260. Erickson, Nancy S. "Pregnancy Discrimination: An Analytical
      Approach." WOMEN'S RIGHTS LAW REPORTER, 7 (Fall 1981),
      11-26.

      A descriptive study and analysis of the constitutional,
      legislative, and judicial prohibition against sex discrimi-
      nation due to pregnancy. Includes discussions on maternity
      leave, sick leave plans, hiring and terminating pregnant
      workers, leave of absence, compensation, seniority, and
      insurance.

261. Furnish, Hannah Arterian. "Prenatal Exposure to Fetally
      Toxic Work Environments: The Dilemma of the 1978 Pregancy
      Amendment to Title VII of the Civil Rights Act of 1964."
      IOWA LAW REVIEW, 66 (October 1980), 63-129.

      Gives an in-depth study of the problem of protecting female
      employees and fetuses from toxic work environments without
      violating Title VII and the 1978 Pregnancy Amendment.

262. Greenlaw, Paul S. and Diana L. Foderaro. "Some Practical
      Implications of the Pregnancy Discrimination Act." PERSON-
      NEL JOURNAL, 58 (October 1979), 677.

      Briefly outlines court decisions which ultimately resulted
      in the passage of the Act, e.g., General Electric v. Gilbert.
      Analyzes major sections of the Act to determine whether the
      Act is a "miscarriage of justice."

263. Greenwald, Carol. "Maternity Leave Policy." GOOD GOVERN-
      MENT, (Spring 1974), 12-15.

      Analyzes the coverage and major provisions of the EEOC's
      guidelines on pregnancy discrimination that were issued in
      April of 1972. Reviews a study conducted by the Federal Re-
      serve Bank on the increase of labor cost to the bank if the

guidelines were implemented. Concludes that ". . . the cost
of implementing the new EEOC guidelines clearly indicate that
the cost would have a negligible impact on overall labor
cost."

* Institute of Industrial Relations, University of California,
  Los Angeles. 1980 REPORT - EQUAL EMPLOYMENT OPPORTUNITY
  AND AFFIRMATIVE ACTION - THE ROOTS GROW DEEPER. See Item
  929.

264. Kohn, Roger S. "Can Men Be Discriminated Against on the
     Basis of Pregnancy?: The Pregnancy Discrimination Act of
     1978 and Its Application in Newport. COLUMBIA HUMAN RIGHTS
     LAW REVIEW, 14 (Fall-Winter 1982-83), 383-432.

     Seeks to determine whether the Pregnancy Discrimination Act
     of 1978 is violated in situations where an employer's insur-
     ance program provides ". . . less comprehensive benefits
     for male employees' wives than for female employees' hus-
     bands." Analyzes the legislative history of the Act and
     court decisions, including Newport News Shipbuilding & Dry
     Dock Co. v. EEOC. Concludes that the above situation dis-
     criminates against males.

265. Lies, Mark A., II. "Current Trends in Pregnancy Benefits-
     1972 EEOC Guidelines Interpreted." DePAUL LAW REVIEW, 24
     (Fall 1974), 127-142.

     Explains the origin of the guidelines and discusses con-
     flicts between the Supreme Court's interpretation of preg-
     nancy discrimination and the EEOC's interpretation. Con-
     tends that the EEOC's action in issuing the guidelines
     was ". . . hastily enacted, poorly planned, and somewhat
     arbitrary . . ."

266. Lines, Patricia M. "Updated: New Rights for Pregnancy
     Employees." PERSONNEL JOURNAL, 58 (January 1979), 33-37.

     Discusses the implication of the 1978 Pregnancy Discrimi-
     nation Act. The Act requires ". . . employers to extend to
     pregnant women any disability and medical benefits extended
     to other employees for non-job related disabilities."

267. Mass, Michael A. "Sex Discrimination Based On Pregnancy:
     The Post-Gilbert Environment." EMPLOYEE RELATIONS LAW
     JOURNAL, 4 (Autumn 1978), 161-172.

268. "The Pregnancy Discrimination Act: Questions and Answers
     From the EEOC." EEO REVIEW, (October 1981), 6-7.

Answers commonly asked questions concerning pregnancy
disability, leave policy, and other benefits under the Act.

269.   Project on the Status and Education of Women of the Associa-
        tion of American Colleges. THE PREGNANCY DISCRIMINATION
        ACT OF 1978 AND ITS IMPACT ON EDUCATIONAL INSTITUTIONS.
        Washington, D.C., April 1979.

        Summarizes provisions of the Pregnancy Discrimination Act
        of 1978. States that the Act ". . . prohibits discrimination
        against women employees because of pregnancy, childbirth, or
        related medical conditions." Explains that the Act overides
        the Supreme Court's decision in General Electric v. Gilbert,
        which held that employers did not violate Title VII if they
        did not provide company benefits to pregnant employees. Out-
        lines procedures for educational institutions to follow in
        complying with the Act.

270.   Sape, George P. "1978 Pregnancy Disability Amendment to
        Title VII of the Civil Rights Act of 1964." EQUAL EMPLOY-
        MENT PRACTICE GUIDE. Edited by John R. Erickson and
        Katherine McGovern. Washington, D.C.: Bureau of National
        Affairs, 1979, pp. I-14 and I-25.

        Outlines the legislative history of the 1978 Pregnancy
        Disability Amendment. Finds that the Act does not require an
        employer to provide pregnancy benefits to pregnant employees.
        The Act does require that they be "treated even-handedly on
        the basis of their ability or inability to work." Explains
        that the Act requires pregnant employees to receive the same
        benefits as disabled workers.

271.   Sculnick, Michael W. "The Reach of the Pregnancy Discrimi-
        nation Act." EEO TODAY, 9 (Winter 1982-83), 305-308.

        Focuses ". . . on the question of whether [the Act] extends
        the reach of Title VII to dependent coverage provided under
        insurance programs offered by employers to their employees."
        Explains that presently, two federal courts of appeals [New-
        port News Shipbuilding and Drydock Co. v. EEOC and EEOC v.
        Lockheed Missiles and Space Co., Inc.] have reached different
        opinions on this issue. Predicts that the Supreme Court will
        ultimately have to decide the issue.

272.   Silton, Susan. "Maternity Benefits: Do's and Don'ts." EQUAL
        OPPORTUNITY FORUM, 7 (December 1979), 30-31.

        Outlines employers' obligations and responsibilities in
        complying with the Pregnancy Discrimination Act. Explains
        that the basic principle of the Act is that an employer can-
        not discharge, refuse to hire, promote or otherwise discrimi-
        nate against a female employee or female applicant because

she is pregnant. The Act is administered by the EEOC and is an amendment to the Civil Rights Act of 1964. Additionally, an insurance agent provides a list of insurance benefits that employees should consider when applying for an insurance plan.

273. Trotter, Richard; Susan R. Zacur; and Wallace Gatewood. "The Pregnancy Disability Amendment: What the Law Provides, Part II." PERSONNEL ADMINISTRATOR, 27 (March 1982), 55-58.

Discusses the Pregnancy Disability Amendment of 1978. Includes topics on coverage, job reassignment, benefit abuse, and the implication of the amendment on collective bargaining agreements. Feels that the amendment has had both legal and social implications on the status of working women.

274. U.S. Equal Employment Opportunity Commission. "Pregnancy Discrimination Act: Adoption of Interim Interpretative Guidelines, Questions, and Answers." FEDERAL REGISTER, 44 (March 9, 1979), 13278-13281.

Provides answers to commonly asked questions about the Act.

275. U.S. Office of Personnel Management, Intergovernmental Personnel Programs. "Establishing Policy for Absence for Maternity Purposes." EEO INFORMATION ON EQUAL EMPLOYMENT OPPORTUNITY FOR STATE AND LOCAL GOVERNMENTS. 2d rev. ed. Issue No. 13. Washington, D.C.: Government Printing Office, September 1979. 3 pp.

States that in 1978 Congress passed the Pregnancy Discrimination Act which prohibit discrimination based on pregnancy. Further, The EEOC modified their Guidelines on Sex Discrimination to comply with the Act. A provision of the EEOC's Guidelines established that pregnancy is a disability. Concludes that where employment policies or practices provide for benefits to an employee due to a disability, the same benefits must be provided to employees who have a pregnancy disability.

276. Wolfe, David L. "Complying with the New Pregnancy Discrimination Act." CHICAGO BAR RECORD, 60 (May-June 1979), 309-324.

Discusses the coverage, effective date, exceptions, liabilities, and the impact of the Act on personnel policy.

64   SEXUAL HARASSMENT

SEXUAL HARASSMENT IN EMPLOYMENT

277. Achiron, Marilyn. "Sexual Harassment on the Job." MADEMOI-
     SELLE, (October 1979), 116-118.

278. Alexander, Kathleen S. "Sexual Harassment at Marriott: A
     Practical Approach to the Problem." EEO TODAY, 8 (Spring
     1981), 63-68.

     Contends that employers in the hospitality industry may be
     more prone to receiving sexual harassment claims due to the
     nature of their business. States that "[e]mployees are
     encouraged to be outgoing and friendly; indeed, 'agressive
     hospitality' is the key phase." Finds that the Marriott
     Corporation, a hospitality company, has set up a system to
     prevent and correct sexual harassment claims.

279. Alliance Against Sexual Coercion. FIGHTING SEXUAL HARASS-
     MENT: AN ADVOCACY HANDBOOK. Cambridge, MA., 1979. 76 pp.

     Defines sexual harassment as ". . . any unwanted sexual
     attention a woman experiences on the job, ranging from leer-
     ing, pinching, patting, verbal comments, and subtle pressure
     for sexual activity, to attempted rape and rape." Discusses
     case studies, myths, and other facts relative to sexual
     harassment. Outlines procedures for developing outreach and
     education programs for women who are sexually harassed. In-
     cludes sample surveys on sexual harassment, an EEOC complaint
     form, a sample client intake sheet, and sample evaluation
     forms for vocational counselors, lawyers and therapists.
     Concludes that women who have been sexually harassed on the
     job may have a cause of action under Title VII, Worker Com-
     pensation, Occupational Safety and Health Act, Unemployment
     Insurance, various criminal statutes, civil lawsuits, union
     grievance procedures, and Title IX of the Civil Rights Act.

280. _____. UNIVERSITY GRIEVANCE PROCEDURES, TITLE IX,
     AND SEXUAL HARASSMENT ON CAMPUS, Cambridge, MA., 1980.
     29 pp.

     Designed to inform female students how to develop a griev-
     ance procedure for hearing and resolving sexual harassment
     complaints. Outlines provisions of Title IX of the Education
     Amendment of 1972, which prohibits sex discrimination in
     education. Explains the Department of Education Office for
     Civil Rights' responsibilities in enforcing Title IX.

281. American Federation of State, County and Municipal Employees.
     SEXUAL HARASSMENT, ON THE JOB SEXUAL HARASSMENT: WHAT THE
     UNION CAN DO. Washington, D.C., 1980. 40 pp.

Designed to inform local unions of AFSCME what their
responsibility entails in preventing and correcting sexual
harassment in the workforce. Contends that sexual harassment
is widespread in the workforce. Summarizes court decisions
and provides sample surveys, contract language, and policy
statements related to preventing sexual harassment in
employment.

282. The Assessment Task Group of the Sexual Harassment Committee.
      "Assessment of Sexual Harassment Within the University of
      Rhode Island." Mimeographed. Kingston, R.I.: University
      of Rhode Island, August 1980. 40 pp.

      Results of a survey conducted at the university to deter-
      mine the extent of sexual harassment on campus. Reports that
      of the 927 individuals who responded to the survey, 172 cited
      one or more situations where sexual assault occurred on cam-
      pus to someone other than themselves.

283. Axford, Naida B. "When Women Cry 'Wolf': Liability for
      False Charges of Sexual Harassment." EMPLOYMENT RELATIONS
      TODAY, 10 (Spring 1983), 73-81.

      Alerts employers that they may be liable for terminating an
      employee for alleged sexual harassment of another employee.
      Presents a case study to illustrate the various causes of
      action available to employees who are terminated. Suggests a
      procedure to minimize potential liability of employers when
      terminating an alleged sexual harasser.

284. Backhouse, Constance and Leah Cohen. SEXUAL HARASSMENT ON
      THE JOB: HOW TO AVOID THE WORKING WOMAN'S NIGHTMARE.
      Englewood Cliffs, N.J.: Prentice-Hall, Inc., 1981. 196
      pp.

      Presents case studies, court cases, legislation, and inter-
      views concerning sexual harassment in the workplace. Ex-
      plores the historical development of sexual harassment and
      answers commonly asked questions on the subject. Reveals
      that sexual harassment in the workplace is "rampant" and
      "affects all working women, regardless of their age, phy-
      sical appearance, social status, or job category."

285. _____. "The Other Side of the Coin: Women Who
      Exploit Their Sexuality for Gain." SEXUALITY IN ORGANIZA-
      TIONS: ROMANTIC AND COERCIVE BEHAVIORS AT WORK. Edited by
      Dail Ann Neugarten and Jay M. Shafritz. Oak Park, IL.:
      Moore Publishing Company, Inc., 1980, pp. 72-77.

      Indicates that there is another side of the coin to sexual
      harassment that involves women who use their sexuality to gain

employment favors. Explains why women use such tactics, the pitfalls they face, and the repercussions of such conduct.

286. Baxter, Ralph H., Jr. "How to Limit Employer Exposure to Sexual Harassment Claims." EEO TODAY, 8 (Spring 1981), 69-72.

Outlines various methods to prevent or limit sexual harassment claims. Recommends the following methods: Issue a statement of policy against sexual harassment; adopt a complaint procedure; educate supervisors; investigate complaints; and take appropriate corrective action.

287. Biles, George E. "A Program Guide for Preventing Sexual Harassment in the Workplace." PERSONNEL ADMINISTRATOR, 26 (June 1981), 49-56.

Outlines a program to prevent sexual harassment in the workplace. Four techniques of prevention include openly discussing the issue, establishing a reporting procedure for such conduct, corroborating allegations of harassment, and then taking the necessary corrective action.

288. Brothers, Joyce. "Sexual Harassment in the Secretary's Workplace." SECRETARY, 41 (October 1981), 13-15.

289. Bureau of National Affairs, Inc. SEXUAL HARASSMENT AND LABOR RELATIONS: A BNA SPECIAL REPORT. Washington, D.C., 1981. 100 pp.

A comprehensive study on sexual harassment in the workplace. Includes discussions on the EEOC's Guidelines, court cases, congressional hearings, state government developments, and the results of surveys on the issue of sexual harassment. The appendix include the full text of the guidelines, corporate policies on sexual harassment, bibliography, and a list of court cases.

290. Burns, M. Susan. "On the Job Sexual Harassment--Sexual Harassment as Sex Discrimination: Developments in Employer's Liability." HAMLINE LAW REVIEW, 4 (June 1981), 515-535.

Explains that an employer can be liable for sexual harassment acts of their supervisors and coworkers. Recommends that employers take steps to prevent and correct sexual harassment in the workplace, e.g., issuing a strong policy against sexual harassment and establishing a grievance procedure to hear sexual harassment complaints. Includes an in-depth analysis of the Minnesota Supreme Court's decision in Continental Can Co. v. Minnesota.

291. "Case Study: EEO and Sexual Harassment." EEO REVIEW, (May
     1982), 2-3.

     Presents a case study on a sexual harassment complaint.
     Provides comments and suggestions to managers and supervisors
     on how to effectively deal with EEO complaints in this area
     of the law.

292. "Case Study: Sexual Harassment and Unemployment Insurance
     Claims." EEO REVIEW, (July 1981), 4-6.

     Explains that some states allow women who claim they quit
     their job as a result of sexual harassment to receive unem-
     ployment insurance benefits. Advises employers to review
     such claims very closely to determine if the claim is valid.
     Presents a case study to illustrate that employers can win
     meritless claims of sexual harassment.

293. Chastain, Sherry. WINNING THE SALARY GAME: SALARY NEGOTIA-
     TION FOR WOMEN. New York: John Wiley & Sons, Inc., 1980.
     170 pp.

     Includes a chapter on the negative impact that sexual
     harassment can have on women who are attempting to negotiate
     a salary.

294. Collins, Eliza G.C. and Timothy B. Blodgett. "Sexual Harass-
     ment . . . Some See It . . . Some Won't." HARVARD BUSINESS
     REVIEW, 59 (March-April 1981), 76-95.

     Results of a survey on sexual harassment which was con-
     ducted by Redbook Magazine and Harvard Business Review. Con-
     cludes that "[m]ost people agree on what harassment is. But
     men and women disagree strongly on how frequently it occurs.
     The majority correlate the perceived seriousness of the be-
     havior with the power of the person making the advance. Top
     management appears isolated from situations involving harass-
     ment. Many women, in particular, despair of having tradi-
     tionally male-dominated management understand how much
     harassment humiliates and frustrates them, and they despair
     of having management's support in resisting it. Most people
     think that the EEOC guidelines-although reasonable in
     theory--will be difficult to implement because they are too
     vague."

295. "Comment, Employment Discrimination--Sexual Harassment and
     Title VII--Female Employees' Claim Alleging Verbal and
     Physical Advances by a Male Supervisor Dismissed as
     Nonactionable -- Corne v. Bausch and Lomb, Inc." NEW YORK
     UNIVERSITY LAW REVIEW, 51 (April 1976), 148-167.

296.   Commerce Clearing House, Inc. "Sexual Harassment: The Best
       Way to Handle a Delicate Matter." HUMAN RESOURCES MANAGE-
       MENT--IDEAS AND TRENDS IN PERSONNEL. Chicago, IL., (July
       9, 1982), 1.

       Suggests that employers issue a policy encouraging employ-
       ees to file complaints when they feel that they have been
       sexually harassed on the job. States that employers should
       in "good faith" investigate all sexual harassment complaints
       and take disciplinary action where warranted.

297.   Crull, Peggy. "The Impact of Sexual Harassment on the Job:
       A Profile of the Experiences of 92 Women." SEXUALITY IN
       ORGANIZATIONS: ROMANTIC AND COERCIVE BEHAVIORS AT WORK.
       Edited by Dail Ann Neugarten and Jay M. Shafritz. Oak
       Park, IL.: Moore Publishing Company, Inc., 1980,
       pp. 67-71.

       Analyzes questionnaires which were completed by women who
       had experienced sexual harassment on the job. The question-
       naire was designed to gather data on the age, salary, marital
       status, occupation, job performance, and attitude of persons
       were harassed. Concludes that sexual harassment is wide-
       spread in the workforce. Believes that sexual harassment has
       a negative affect on the productivity, health and economic
       status of women workers.

298.   D.C. Commission for Women. "Dealing with Sexual Harassment
       In the District of Columbia." Mimeographed. Washington,
       D.C.: Government of the District of Columbia, June 19,
       1979.

       Makes recommendations to the Mayor of Washington, D.C. on
       how to prevent and correct sexual harassment in the city's
       workforce and in the private sector. Includes recommenda-
       tions on training, employee counseling, proposed legisla-
       tion, and personnel guidelines.

299.   Desmarais, Mark B. and Katherine Desmarais. "Advances vs.
       Advancements: Employer Liability for Sexual Advances
       Under Equal Employment Opportunity Commission Guidelines."
       GONZAGA LAW REVIEW, 17 (No. 1 - 1981), 1-22.

       Analyzes Federal court decisions on sexual harassment and
       provisions of the EEOC's Guidelines On Sexual Harassment.
       Outlines specific procedures for employers to follow to avoid
       or reduce their liability in sexual harassment cases.

300.   Drey Fack, Madeleine. "Sexual Harassment: Can You Afford
       Not to Clamp Down?" SUPERVISION, 44 (April 1982), 8-10.

301. Driscoll, Jeanne Bosson. "Sexual Attraction and Harassment:
      Management's New Problems." PERSONNEL JOURNAL, 60 (January
      1981), 33.

      Explains the difference between "sexual attraction" and
      "sexual harassment." States that sexual attraction will
      exist within an organization and can be managed; however,
      sexual harassment does not have to exist in an organization
      and must be eliminated. Contends that organizations can no
      longer implement "non-fraternization policies" because women
      are entering the workforce in large numbers which will force
      women and men to learn to work together. Suggests that
      organizations review their policies on sexual attraction to
      be sure they are consistent and communicated to all employ-
      ees. Indicates that sexual harassment should be prohibited
      and corrected immediately where it is occurring. Outlines
      procedures to be followed by employees who have experienced
      sexual harassment on the job and for those who have been
      accused of sexual harassment.

302. _____ and Rosemary A. Bova. "The Sexual Side of
      Enterprise." MANAGEMENT REVIEW, 69 (July 1980), 51-54.

      Indicates that sexual harassment can have a negative impact
      on an organization and create a number of problems for man-
      agers and employees. Provides suggestions to managers and
      employees on how to effectively deal with sexual harassment
      in the workplace.

303. Eason, Yla. "When the Boss Wants Sex." ESSENCE, (March
      1981), 82.

      Outlines guidelines for women who are sexually harassed on
      the job. Discusses the psychological affect that sexual
      harassment can have on women. Explains that black women have
      been in the forefront fighting sexual harassment in employ-
      ment, because the major court cases dealing with sexual
      harassment were filed by black females. Believes that sexual
      harassment cases that were brought by black females had a
      major impact on the EEOC issuance of guidelines on sexual
      harassment.

304. Etzcorn, Pamela. "Dealing With Sexual Harassment." WOMEN'S
      WORK, V (September-October 1979), 11.

*   Executive Enterprises. SOLVING EEO PROBLEMS: A GUIDE TO
      EEO LAW AND PRACTICE. See Item 33.

305. Faley, Robert H. "Sexual Harassment: Critical Review of
      Legal Cases with General Principles and Preventive
      Measures." PERSONNEL PSYCHOLOGY, 35 (Autumn 1982), 583-
      600.

          Examines fifty-two court decisions ". . . to determine the
      standards set by the courts for establishing a claim of sex-
      ual harassment under Title VII of the Civil Rights Act of
      1964." Contends that the number of sexual harassment com-
      plaints will continue to be filed by women who are sexually
      harassed on the job. Suggests "preventive measures" employ-
      ers can take to curtail such conduct.

306. Farley, Lin. SEXUAL SHAKEDOWN: THE SEXUAL HARASSMENT OF
      WOMEN ON THE JOB. New York: McGraw-Hill, 1978. 228 pp.

          Defines sexual harassment as an . . . "unsolicited non-
      reciprocal male behavior that asserts a woman's sex role
      over her function as a worker." Presents case studies on
      sexual harassment and legal remedies. Discusses the role of
      employers and unions in preventing and correcting sexual
      harassment in the workplace. Suggests a plan of action for
      women on how to prevent and correct sexual harassment on the
      job.

307. Faucher, Mary D. and Kenneth J. McCulloch. "'Sexual Harass-
      ment in the Workplace--What Should the Employer Do?"
      SOLVING EEO PROBLEMS: A GUIDE TO EEO LAW AND PRACTICE.
      New York: Executive Enterprises Publications, Co., Inc.,
      1980, pp 193-201.

          Examines the various forms of sexual harassment, e.g.,
      verbal abuse and condition of employment. Outlines leading
      court decisions related to sexual harassment and provides
      suggestions to employers on how to prevent, correct and
      investigate charges of sexual harassment. Presents a flow
      chart for employers on procedures for processing a sexual
      harassment complaint.

308. Feinberg, Mortimer R. and Aaron Levenstein. "Sex and Romance
      in the Office and Plant." THE WALL STREET JOURNAL, (Novem-
      ber 29, 1982), 26.

          Highlights the results of a "mini-survey" on sexual harass-
      ment among executives. Concludes that there are four types
      of sexual involvements: Sexual harassment, courtship between
      single individuals who are interested in marriage, sexual
      relationships between single individuals who are not inter-
      ested in marriage, and sexual relationships between married
      and unmarried individuals. As to sexual harassment, believes
      that ". . . no self-respecting employer would approve of
      harassment in any form, but the line between harassment and
      voluntary involvement is not always easily discerned."

309. Field, Anne. "Harassment on Campus: Sex In A Tenured
      Position?" MS. (September 1981), 68.

310. Friedman, Karen. "AFSCME Targets Fight Against Sexual
      Harassment." PUBLIC EMPLOYEE, 45 (August 1980), 10.

311. Goodman, Jill Laurie. "Sexual Demands On the Job." CIVIL
      LIBERTIES REVIEW, 4 (March-April 1978), 55-58.

      Presents the problems of sexual harassment in the work-
      force. Reports that a number of Federal cases are finding
      that sexual harassment is a form of sex discrimination and
      violate Title VII. Indicates that an increasing number of
      women are bringing lawsuits to curtail sexual harassment,
      and various women's organizations are providing the public
      with methods on preventing and correcting sexual harassment
      in the workforce.

312. Greenbaum, Marcia L. and Bruce Fraser. "Sexual Harassment
      in the Workplace." THE ARBITRATION JOURNAL, 36 (December
      1981), 30-41.

      Presents the leading cases on sexual harassment in the
      workplace. Begins with Barnes v. Train, which was the first
      sexual harassment case litigated under Title VII. Explains
      employers' responsibilities in preventing and correcting
      sexual harassment. Discusses sexual harassment cases that
      have been arbitrated and the type of awards an arbitrator may
      award. Predicts that sexual harassment cases will continue
      to increase.

313. Greenlaw, Paul S. and John P. Kohl. "Sexual Harassment:
      Homosexuality, Bisexuality and Blackmail." PERSONNEL
      ADMINISTRATOR, 26 (June 1981), 59-62.

      Suggests that the EEOC guidelines on sexual harassment not
      only apply to males sexually harassing females, but also
      apply to "homosexual harassment," "women harassing men" and
      bi-sexual behavior.

314. Gutek, Barbara A. and Charles Y. Nakamura. SEXUALITY AND THE
      WORKPLACE. Los Angeles, CA.: University of California,
      1979.

315. "Harassment Survey: Results Announced." MANAGEMENT, (Summer
      1981), 18-20.

      Summarizes the U.S. Merit System Protection Board's finding
      that 42% of female and 15% of male federal employees reported
      that they had been sexually harassed on the job. Gives a

"manager's checklist" on dealing with sexual harassment and provides "tips for employees" on how to handle sexual harassment.

316. Harragan, Betty Lehan. GAMES MOTHER NEVER TAUGHT YOU. New York: Rawson Associates Publishers, 1977. 334 pp.

Focuses on peculiar problems that women workers face when entering the corporate workforce. Gives strategies and lesson plans to women workers on how to survive and progress. Includes a section on sexual harassment in the workforce which indicates such conduct is widespread in the workforce.

317. _____. "Sexual Harassment, A Power Game That Can Be Halted." THE ATLANTA JOURNAL AND CONSTITUTION, (April 26, 1981), 30.

Asserts that sexual harassment in the workforce is pervasive and cannot be eliminated unless women take the initiative to combat the problem. Explains that sexual harassment is a power move by men against women who are in vulnerable positions. Advises women to report occurrences of sexual harassment, but should do so with other women or/and contact the Working Women's Institute for information and support.

318. Hodle, Sharon F. "Sexual Harassment and the Management Response." SECRETARY, 39 (May 1979), 12-15.

319. Hopkins, Carter H. and David A. Johnson. "Sexual Harassment In The Workplace." JOURNAL OF COLLEGE PLACEMENT, 40 (Spring 1982), 30-36.

320. Horn, Patrice D. and Jack C. Horn. SEX IN THE OFFICE. Reading, MA.: Addison-Wesley Publishing Company, 1982. 168 pp.

Includes a chapter on the status of sexual harassment in employment. Indicates that sexual harassment is widespread in the workforce and can happen to both male and female workers, but mostly women. Discusses various surveys and studies conducted on sexual harassment, court decisions, and the EEOC's Guidelines on Sexual Harassment.

321. Hubbart, William S. "Sexual Harassment: Coping With the Controversy." ADMINISTRATIVE MANAGEMENT, 41 (August 1980), 34-35.

322. James, Jennifer. "Sexual Harassment." PUBLIC PERSONNEL MANAGEMENT JOURNAL, 10 (Winter 1981), 402-407.

Indicates that surveys on sexual harassment support that
sexual harassment is a major problem in the workplace and
causes employees to have stress and poor performance. States
that both men and women can be sexually harassed. Gives
specific examples of sexual harassment. Believes that defining sexual harassment for employees is an important step in
recognizing and preventing sexual harassment in the workplace. Cites other methods of preventing sexual harassment,
e.g., awareness programs and processing sexual harassment
claims through the grievance procedure.

323. Johnson, Theresa. "Sexual Harassment in the Workplace."
     CIVIL SERVICE REVIEW (Canada), 53 (December 1980), 8.

324. Karnes, C. Daniel. "Sexual Harassment: New Guidelines, New
     Cases, New Problems." SOLVING EEO PROGRAMS: A GUIDE TO
     EEO LAW AND PRACTICE. New York: Executive Enterprises
     Publications, Co., Inc., 1980, pp. 202-206.

     Alerts employers that five federal courts of appeals have
     held that sexual harassment violates Title VII and that
     federal agencies such as the Office of Federal Contract Com-
     pliance Programs and the EEOC are proposing guidelines on
     sexual harassment. Advises employers to establish a corpo-
     rate policy on sexual harassment and to implement an investi-
     gative procedure to handle sexual harassment complaints.

325. Kay, Herma H. and Carroll M. Brodsky. "Protecting Women
     From Sexual Harassment In the Workplace." TEXAS LAW
     REVIEW, 58 (March 1980), 671-694.

326. Kronenberger, George K. and David L. Bourke. "Effective
     Training and the Elimination of Sexual Harassment." PER-
     SONNEL JOURNAL, 60 (November 1981), 879-883.

     Contends that a comprehensive training program for employ-
     ees and management on sexual harassment will help prevent
     such conduct in the workforce. Outlines key components of
     what a sexual harassment training program should contain,
     e.g., corporate policy, court decisions, and inhouse cases.

327. Lawrence, Kenneth and Katharine A. Klos., eds. SEX DISCRIMI-
     NATION IN THE WORKPLACE. Germantown, MD.: Aspen Publica-
     tion, 1978. 532 pp.

     Presents a comprehensive study on laws and legislations,
     judicial decisions, personnel policies and practices, and
     affirmative action guidelines that prohibit sex discrimina-
     tion in employment.

328. Leap, Terry L. and Edmund R. Gray. "Corporate Responsibility
      In Cases of Sexual Harassment." BUSINESS HORIZONS, 23
      (October 1980), 58-65.

329. Ledgerwood, Donna E. and Sue Johnson-Dietz. "The EEOC's
      Foray into Sexual Harassment: Interpreting the New Guide-
      lines for Employer Liability." LABOR LAW JOURNAL, 31
      (December 1980), 741-744.

      A Review of the sex discrimination guidelines on sexual
      harassment and a review of the court's decisions in Miller v.
      Bank of America and Continental Can v. State of Minnesota.

330. _____. "Sexual Harassment: Implications for Employer
      Liability." Monthly Labor Review, 104 (April 1981), 45-47.

      Analyzes the EEOC's guidelines on sexual harassment and
      concludes that employers can be liable for the conduct of
      their supervisors who sexually harass employees under the
      doctrine of respondent superior.

331. LeVerone, Richard. "The Well-Intentioned Harasser." MANAGE-
      MENT, (Summer 1981), 21-22.

      Believes that sexual harassment may also occur when male
      supervisors actively sterotype female workers into roles as
      their daughter, wife, or lover. Explains that these stereo-
      typical attitudes from male supervisors may not be inten-
      tional; nevertheless, these attitudes are inconsistent with
      female workers' wishes to be treated equal.

332. Levin, Noel A. and Mark E. Brossman. "Sexual Harassment on
      the Job: Title VII & EEOC to the Rescue." NATIONAL LAW
      JOURNAL, 2 (June 2, 1980), 26.

333. Lindsey, Karen. "Sexual Harassment on the Job and How to
      Stop It." MS., 6 (November 1977), 47.

      Present a series of situations where women have received
      sexual demands, advances, and propositions on the job. Pro-
      vides a list of remedies available to women who find them-
      selves in these situations.

334. Linenberger, Patricia. "What Behavior Constitutes Sexual
      Harassment?" LABOR LAW JOURNAL, 34 (April 1983), 238-247.

      Attempts to further explain what behavior is considered
      sexual harassment and prohibited by Title VII, the EEOC
      guidelines, and by federal courts. Reviews court decisions
      that have held that sexual harassment violate Title VII and

decisions involving tort actions. Outlines ten factors to
consider when determining whether a certain behavior is sexual harassment.

335. _____ and Timothy J. Keaveny. "Sexual Harass-
     ment: The Employer's Legal Obligations." PERSONNEL, 58
     (November-December 1981), 60-68.

     Reviews various definitions of sexual harassment as set
     forth in Continental Can Co. v. Minnesota, hearings before
     the House Committee on Post Office and Civil Service, and by
     the Michigan Task Force on Sexual Harassment in the Work-
     place. Suggests that the Michigan Task Force definition is
     "less subjective and not as inclusive" as the other defini-
     tions. Discusses the EEOC's Interpretative Guidelines on
     Sexual Harassment, coverage of sexual harassment by the
     Civil Rights Act of 1964, and court cases that held employers
     liable for sexual harassment on the job. Recommends that
     efforts to control sexual harassment on the job by employers
     include the issuance of a strong policy statement condemning
     sexual harassment on the job and a system to process sexual
     harassment complaints through the grievance procedure.

336. Linnick, Stuart. "Investigation and Discovery in Sex
     Harassment, Wrongful Discharge and Age Discrimination
     Litigation." EMPLOYMENT LITIGATION AND ITS ALTERNATIVES.
     New York: Practicing Law Institute, 1984. 480 pp.

337. Lissy, William E. "EEOC's Guidelines On Sexual Harassment."
     SUPERVISION, 43 (April 1981), 19-21.

338. MacKinnon, Catherine A. SEXUAL HARASSMENT OF WORKING WOMEN:
     A CASE OF SEX DISCRIMINATION. New Haven, CT.: Yale Uni-
     versity Press, 1979. 312 pp.

339. Marmo, Michael. "Arbitrating Sex Harassment Cases." ARBI-
     TRATION JOURNAL, 35 (March 1980), 35-40.

     Examines 19 arbitration cases on sexual harassment that
     were heard between 1958 and 1978. Most cases in the study
     involved grievances filed by male employees who were disci-
     plined for sexually harassing a co-worker. Explains the
     difficulty in defining sexual harassment, the type of re-
     course available to women who are sexually harassed, manage-
     ment's response to such claims, and the dual role of the
     union in sexual harassment claims. Found in most cases that
     management responded quickly to claims of sexual harassment
     and discharged the employee who participated in the act; how-
     ever, in all of the cases examined in this study, the arbi-
     trator held that discharge as the disciplinary action was to
     severe.

340. Mayor's Task Force on Sexual Harassment. "Final Report."
      Mimeographed. Washington, D.C.: Government of the Dis-
      trict of Columbia, Office of the Corporation Counsel, May
      18, 1979. 6 pp.

      Makes recommendations to the Mayor of Washington, D.C. on
      what actions should be taken to prevent and correct sexual
      harassment within the city's workforce. Recommends that the
      Mayor develop a policy statement and a formal complaint pro-
      cedure; that sexual harassment be considered a form of sex
      discrimination; that a special unit be established to handle
      sexual harassment claims; and that department heads be held
      responsible for preventing and correcting sexual harassment
      in the workforce.

341. McIntyre, Douglas I. and James C. Renick. "Protecting Public
      Employees and Employers from Sexual Harassment." PUBLIC
      PERSONNEL MANAGEMENT, 11 (Fall 1982), 282-292.

      Focuses on the extent of sexual harassment in the public
      sector. Discusses various surveys which support that sexual
      harassment in the workforce is widespread. Explains the
      application of Title VII and the EEOC's guidelines in sexual
      harassment cases. Provides a list of suggestions for govern-
      mental employers on how to prevent and correct sexual harass-
      ment in the workplace.

342. Meier, Sara Beth. "Expanding Title VII to Prohibit a Sexu-
      ally Harassing Work Environment." GEORGETOWN LAW JOURNAL,
      70 (October 1981), 345-364.

      Analyzes the court's decision in Bundy v. Jackson, which
      held ". . . that the existence of a sexually harassing atmo-
      sphere alone is sufficient to constitute a discriminatory
      condition of employment."

343. Meyer, Coeli Mary; Inge M. Berchtold; Jeanne L. Oestreich;
      and Frederick J. Collins. SEXUAL HARASSMENT. Princeton,
      N.J.: Petrocelli Books, Inc., 1981. 200 pp.

      Defines sexual harassment and provides strategies for com-
      bating and dealing with the problem in the workforce. In-
      cludes the full text of the Equal Employment Opportunity
      Commission's Interpretive Guidelines on Sexual Harassment,
      sample policy statements, related court cases, a "self-help
      bibliography," and a survey conducted on the extent of sexual
      harassment in the workforce.

344. Middleton, Martha. EEOC Guidelines: What They Say. AMERICAN
      BAR ASSOCIATION JOURNAL, 66 (June 1980), 703.

Indicates that attitudes about the seriousness of sexual harassment on the job is changing, especially since the EEOC issued guidelines that prohibits sexual harassment on the job. Believes the guidelines will encourage women workers to "fight back" if they are sexually harassed on the job.

345. _____. "Sex Harassment on Job: New Rules Issued." AMERICAN BAR ASSOCIATION JOURNAL, 66 (June 1980), 703.

Briefly outlines the coverage and application of the EEOC's guidelines on sexual harassment in employment.

346. "Minimizing Company Liability for Sexual Harassment." SMALL BUSINESS REPORT, 7 (July 1980), 18-20.

Defines sexual harassment and explains what evidence is necessary to prove and defend a sexual harassment complaint. Encourages employers to establish a code of conduct prohibiting sexual harassment in the workplace. Suggests that employers establish an internal grievance procedure to hear and process sexual harassment complaints. Concludes that sexual harassment can be a costly expense to an employer, e.g., sick leave, medical care, turnover, and legal fees.

347. Montgomery, Alice. M. "Sexual Harassment in the Workplace: A Practitioner's Guide to Tort Actions." GOLDEN GATE UNIVERSITY LAW REVIEW, WOMEN'S LAW FORUM, 10 (Summer 1980), 879-928.

Explores basic principles of tort law and concludes that women who are sexually harassed on the job may bring a cause of action in tort, e.g., intentional infliction of emotional distress, assault and battery, fraud, and deceit. Envisions difficulties in processing a sexual harassment and worker's compensation claim simultaneously.

348. Morrow, Merle Helen. "EEOC Guidelines on Sexual Harassment." EQUAL EMPLOYMENT PRACTICE GUIDE. Vol. I. Edited by John R. Erickson, Katherine Savers McGovern and Richard T. Sampson. Washington, D.C.: Bureau of National Affairs, 1980, pp. III-167 - III-169.

Briefly discusses the Guidelines and court cases related to sexual harassment. Believes sexual harassment will not be eliminated in the workplace unless subsection (e) of the Guidelines are strictly adhered to by employers. Subsection (e) states in part that ". . . prevention is the best tool for the elimination of sexual harassment. . . ."

349. Neugarten, Dail Ann and Jay M. Shafritz, eds. SEXUALITY IN
      ORGANIZATIONS: ROMANTIC AND COERCIVE BEHAVIORS AT WORK.
      Oak Park, IL.: Moore Publishing Company, Inc., 1980.
      166 pp.

      A collection of articles on "sexual dynamics" in the work-
      place, the extent and scope of sexual harassment in employ-
      ment, employers' responses to sexual harassment, and the
      legal ramifications of sexual harassment under Title VII of
      the Civil Rights Act of 1964, as amended.

350. Niehouse, Oliver L. and Joanne R. Doades. "Sexual Harass-
      ment: An Old Issue--A New Problem." SUPERVISORY MANAGE-
      MENT, 25 (April 1980), 10-14.

351. Perry, Suzanne. "Sexual Harassment on the Campuses: Decid-
      ing Where to Draw the Line." CHRONICLE OF HIGHER EDUCA-
      TION, March 23, 1983, pp. 21-22.

      Reports on the extent of sexual harassment at colleges and
      universities. Contends that sexual harassment (professor-
      student relationship) on campuses ". . . is perpetrated by a
      small number of professors who harass multiple victims."
      Summarizes various studies on sexual harassment and reports
      on what some educational institutions are doing to correct
      the problem.

352. Peters, Cara and Erin Van Bronkhorst. HOW TO STOP SEXUAL
      HARASSMENT: STRATEGIES FOR WOMEN ON THE JOB. Seattle,
      WA.: Facts for Women, February 1982. 32 pp.

      Gives women workers practical advice on how to deal with
      sexual harassment on the job. Explains women's legal rights,
      where to seek assistance, how to deal with agencies and
      lawyers, and preventive strategies when faced with sexual
      harassment on the job.

353. Petersen, Donald J. and Douglas Massengill. "Sexual Harass-
      ment--A Growing Problem in the Workplace." PERSONNEL
      ADMINISTRATOR, 27 (October 1982), 79-89.

354. Picker, Jane M. "Sexual Harassment." PROCEEDINGS OF NEW
      YORK UNIVERSITY THIRTY-FOURTH ANNUAL NATIONAL CONFERENCE
      ON LABOR. Edited by Richard Adelman. New York: Matthew
      Bender, 1982, pp. 211-228.

      Presents the legal status of sexual harassment in the work-
      force. Discusses the Equal Opportunity Commission's guide-
      lines on sexual harassment, state legislation, Title VII
      prohibitions, common law principles, and leading decisions
      related to sexual harassment.

355. Pogrebin, Letty Cottin. "Sex Harassment." LADIES HOME
      JOURNAL, (June 1977), 24.

356. Project on the Status and Education of Women of the Associa-
      tion of American Colleges. SEXUAL HARASSMENT: A HIDDEN
      ISSUE. Washington, D.C., June 1978. 7 pp.

      Presents a list of "myths" about sexual harassment and
      provides the true "facts" on the subject. Defines sexual
      harassment and indicates that sexual harassment is widespread
      in the workplace and on college campuses. Briefly summarizes
      judical decisions that support that sexual harassment is a
      violation of Title VII and Title IX. Provides a list of
      suggestions on preventing sexual harassment, e.g., developing
      a grievance procedure, employee handbook, training materials,
      etc. Includes a bibliography and a list of women organi-
      zations.

357. "A Redbook Questionnaire: How Do You Handle . . . Sex on the
      Job?" REDBOOK MAGAZINE, 146 (January 1976), 74-75.

      A questionnaire designed to gather national statistics on
      the extent of sexual harassment in the workforce and to de-
      termine how women are handling sexual harassment on the job.

358. Rowe, Mary P. "Dealing With Sexual Harassment." HARVARD
      BUSINESS REVIEW, 28 (May-June 1981), 42-44.

      Provides "some practical approaches" to preventing and
      correcting sexual harassment in the workplace.

359. Safran, Claire. "Sexual Harassment: The View from the
      Top." REDBOOK MAGAZINE, 156 (March 1981), 45-51.

360. _____. "What Men Do To Women On The Job: A Shocking
      Look At Sexual Harassment." REDBOOK MAGAZINE, 148 (Novem-
      ber 1976), 149.

      Results of a national survey on the extent of sexual ha-
      rassment in the workplace. Reports that sexual harassment
      in the workplace ". . . is not epidemic; it is pandemic--an
      every day, every where occurrence." Suggests ways that
      women can handle passes on the job and how to send out and
      respond to "signals" on the job to potential harassers.

361. Sawyer, Sandra and Arthur Whatley. "Sexual Harassment: A
      Form of Sex Discrimination." PERSONNEL ADMINISTRATOR, 25
      (January 1980) 36.

Reviews recent court decisions on the issue of sexual harassment in the workplace. Determines that an employer may
be liable for his/her employees' conduct when the employer
has knowledge or reason to believe that employees are sexually harassing others on the job. Suggests that employers
develop a grievance procedure where employees may file internal complaints.

362. Schupp, Robert W.; Joyce Windham; and Scott Draughn. "Sexual
      Harassment Under Title VII: The Legal Status." LABOR LAW
      JOURNAL, 32 (April 1981), 238-252.

      Contends that sexual harassment is "widespread and the
      damages resulting therefrom are far-reaching." Focuses
      specifically on landmark decisions on sexual harassment and
      the EEOC's guidelines which prohibit such conduct in employ-
      ment practices. Sets forth the elements to present a prima
      facie case of sexual harassment and suggest ways employers
      can deal with such conduct.

363. "Sexual Harassment on Campus." JOURNAL OF THE NATIONAL
      ASSOCIATION FOR WOMEN DEANS, ADMINISTRATORS, AND COUNSEL-
      ORS, 46 (Winter 1983), 1-59.

      A collection of articles on the extent and complexity of
      sexual harassment on college campuses. Surveys how school
      administrators are preventing and correcting the situation
      on their campus. Explores the problem as it occurs between
      students and faculty, administrators and faculty, and between
      colleagues.

364. "Sexual Harassment Lands Companies in Court." BUSINESS WEEK,
      (October 1, 1979), 120-122.

365. Siniscalco, Gary R. "Sexual Harassment and Employer Lia-
      bility: The Flirtation That Could Cost A Fortune." EM-
      PLOYEE RELATIONS LAW JOURNAL, 6 (Autumn 1980), 227-293.

366. Skrocki, Merrill Rogers. "Sexual Pressure on the Job."
      MCCALLS, 105 (March 1978), 43.

      Cites the background and accomplishments of the Alliance
      Against Sexual Coercion, which is an organization whose pur-
      pose is to assist women who have been sexually harassed on
      the job. Advises women how to handle sexual harassment on
      the job.

367. Somers, Patricia A. and Judith Clementson-Mohr. "Sexual
      Extortion in the Workplace." PERSONNEL ADMINISTRATOR,
      24 (April 1979), 23-28.

Defines sexual harassment and presents studies to support that sexual harassment is widespread in the workplace. Outlines procedures women should follow when they are experiencing sexual harassment on the job. Believes that sexual harassment should not only be opposed on "moral and ethical grounds," but also because it can be costly to all parties involved, including the employer. Includes a list of organizations concerned with preventing and correcting sexual harassment in the workplace.

368. Stevens, George E. "Sexual Harassment of Female Employees and the Law of Slander." EEO TODAY, 9 (Summer 1982), 163-171.

Indicates that comments regarding a female's sexual preference or "good name" on the job may be a cause of action for sexual harassment under Title VII and an action for defamation. Analyzes the California case of Schomer v. Smidt, where an airline stewardess was awarded $36,000 in damages for being called a lesbian by a co-worker. Discusses legal standards for establishing a prima facie case of slander and various court decisions, including the Supreme Court decision in New York Times Co. v. Sullivan.

369. Stover, Patricia and Yvonne Gillies. "Conference Report, Stop Sexual Harassment in the Workplace." Mimeographed. Ann Arbor, MI.: Program on Women and Work, Institute of Labor and Industrial Relations, University of Michigan and Wayne State University, October 27, 1979. 69 pp.

A conference report which summarizes court decisions, workshop addresses, and case studies on sexual harassment in the workplace. Provides strategies on how to use the legal system, the union grievance procedure, the EEO complaint system, and the unemployment insurance claim when sexually harassed on the job.

370. "Symposium: Sexual Harassment." CAPITAL UNIVERSITY LAW REVIEW, 10 (Spring 1981), 445-708.

A collection of articles on sexual harassment in employment and education. Includes topics on the EEOC Guidelines, employer's liability, sexual harassment and Title VII, and procedures for filing a sexual harassment complaint. Concludes with a book review, film review, and a bibliography on sexual harassment.

371. Tillar, Darrel Long. "Sexual Harassment: New Rules to the Game." EQUAL OPPORTUNITY FORUM, 7 (July 1980), 17-19.

States that the EEOC's Guidelines on Sexual Harassment and the U.S. Court of Appeals' decision in Miller v. Bank of

America were major events that established the standards used
in determining whether sexual harassment exist in the workplace. Miller held that an employer may be liable for sexual
harassment on the job, even if the harasser is a co-worker.
Concludes that the guidelines support this decision. Recommends steps employers should take in preventing and correcting sexual harassment in the workplace.

372.   _____. "Sexual Harassment in Employment: The Double
            Bind." EQUAL OPPORTUNITY FORUM, 7 (December 1979), 7-9.

            States that no matter how women respond to sexual harass-
            ment on the job, they are faced with some form of adverse
            action or "negative consequences." Suggests preventive and
            corrective actions that employers may take, e.g., developing
            an internal complaint program to handle sexual harassment
            complaints. Discusses leading court decisions and monetary
            settlements involving sexual harassment.

373.   Thurston, Kathryn A. "Sexual Harassment: An Organizational
            Perspective." PERSONNEL ADMINISTRATOR, 25 (December 1980),
            59-64.

            States that sexual harassment in the workplace can be
            costly to the victim as well as the organization. Sexual
            harassment causes high levels of stress and anxiety, high
            employee turnover, legal cost, and possibly loss of federal
            contracts to the organization. Outlines procedures for
            employers to follow in protecting themselves from liability,
            e.g., issue a policy statement prohibiting such conduct and
            provide appropriate training for supervisors.

374.   "Unemployment Compensation Benefits for the Victim of Work-
            Related Sexual Harassment." HARVARD WOMEN'S LAW JOURNAL,
            3 (Spring 1980), 173-197.

375.   U.S. Commission on Civil Rights. SEXUAL HARASSMENT ON THE
            JOB: A GUIDE FOR EMPLOYERS. Washington, D.C.: Government
            Printing Office, September 1982. 22 pp.

            Answers basic questions on sexual harassment, e.g., "What
            is sexual harassment?", "Is it a problem?", "Who are the
            victims?" Explains that sexual harassment violate Title VII
            and the EEOC's guidelines. Briefly summarizes the leading
            court decisions and outlines procedures for employers to
            follow in preventing and correcting sexual harassment. In-
            cludes a model questionnaire and sample policy statement on
            sexual harassment.

376. U.S. Department of Labor, Women's Bureau. "Background Paper
      on Sexual Harassment on the Job." Prepared by the Commit-
      tee on the Status of Women, Atlanta Community Relations
      Commission. Mimeographed. Atlanta, GA., 1980.

      Presents a position paper on the issue of sexual harassment
      in the workforce. Indicates that sexual harassment is wide-
      spread in the workforce and is having a psychological and
      physical affect on the persons harassed. Contends that
      waitresses, clerical workers, and factory workers are the
      most likely to be harassed on the job because of their low
      economic status, i.e., they can't afford to quit or file a
      court action. Gives a brief summary of actual situations
      where women were forced to resign, discharged, suspended,
      and denied a promotion as a result of sexual harassment.

377. U.S. House of Representatives, Subcommittee on Investigations
      of the Committee on Post Office and Civil Service. SEXUAL
      HARASSMENT IN THE FEDERAL GOVERNMENT. Committee Print,
      96th Congress, 2nd Session. Washington, D.C.: Government
      Printing Office, 1979. 32 pp.

      As a result of a preliminary investigation, which indicated
      that sexual harassment was widespread in the federal govern-
      ment, the subcommittee held 3 days of hearings on the issue.
      Includes testimony and statements from officials of the
      federal government, women's organizations, and unions on the
      need for federal regulations prohibiting sexual harassment.

378. _____. SEXUAL HARASSMENT IN THE FEDERAL GOVERNMENT.
      Committee Print, 96th Congress, 1st Session. Washington,
      D.C.: Government Printing Office, 1980. 176 pp.

      Summarizes data collected by the subcommittee during hear-
      ings held in 1979 to determine the extent of sexual harass-
      ment in the workforce. Concludes that even though sexual
      harassment appears to be widespread in the workforce,
      federal agencies have not taken any corrective action. In-
      cludes policy statements from various federal agencies pro-
      hibiting sexual harassment that were written as a result of
      the hearing. Makes 21 recommendations to federal agencies
      and departments, the private sector, the White House, and
      state and local governments on methods of preventing and
      correcting sexual harassment. Includes a bibliography of
      materials available on the subject.

379. U.S. Merit Systems Protection Board, Office of Merit Systems
      Review and Studies. SEXUAL HARASSMENT IN THE FEDERAL
      WORKPLACE--IS IT A PROBLEM? Washington, D.C.: Government
      Printing Office, March 1981, 104 pp.

      Results of a comprehensive study conducted by the Merit
      Systems Protection Board on the extent of sexual harassment

in the federal workplace. Concludes that sexual harassment
is a widespread problem in the workplace and is costing the
Federal government million of dollars. Makes recommendations
on how to curtail the growth of sexual harassment in the
workforce.

380. U.S. Office of Personnel Management, Office of Affirmative
     Employment Programs, Mid-Atlantic Region. REFERENCE GUIDE
     ON SEXUAL HARASSMENT. Washington, D.C., 1981. 12 pp.

381. _____. WORKSHOP ON SEXUAL HARASSMENT: PARTICIPANTS
     MATERIAL. Washington, D.C.: Government Printing Office,
     1980. 23 pp.

     Designed as a training module for individuals receiving
     training on sexual harassment. Defines sexual harassment and
     explains what responsibilities employees and supervisors have
     in prohibiting sexual harassment in the work area. Includes
     procedures for processing an individual complaint of sexual
     harassment in the public sector.

382. _____. WORKSHOP ON SEXUAL HARASSMENT: TRAINER'S
     MANUAL. Washington, D.C.: Government Printing Office,
     1980. 77 pp.

     "A training module designed to . . . introduce partici-
     pants to the nature and seriousness of the problem of sexual
     harassment in the federal workforce." Includes lesson
     plans, handouts, policy statements, transparencies, and
     statements from various government officials prohibiting
     sexual harassment.

383. Vermuelen, Joan. "Comments on the Equal Employment Opportu-
     nity Commission's Proposed Amendment Adding Section
     1604.11, Sexual Harassment to Its Guidelines on Sexual
     Discrimination." WOMEN'S RIGHTS LAW REPORTER, 6 (Summer
     1980), 285-294.

     Expresses full support for the guidelines and analyzes each
     section. Acknowledges that sexual harassment in employment
     is widespread and identifies the type and affect such conduct
     has on women workers. Believes that the guidelines will be
     a major factor in eliminating sexual harassment from the
     workplace.

384. Vilkin, Richard. "Sexual Harassment Hits Home." THE NA-
     TIONAL LAW JOURNAL, 4 (September 6, 1982), 1.

     Reports that female lawyers can also be sexually harassed
     on the job and presents several cases where female lawyers
     were victims of sexual harassment.

385. Waks, Jay W. and Michael G. Starr. "Sexual harassment in the
     Workplace: The Scope of Employer's Liability." EMPLOYEE
     RELATIONS LAW JOURNAL, 7 (Winter 1981-72), 369-388.

     Concludes that sexual harassment is a form of sex discrimi-
     nation under Title VII of the Civil Rights Act of 1964. Dis-
     cusses the EEOC's guidelines on sexual harassment, an employ-
     er's liability for sexual harassment, court cases, harassment
     from supervisors and co-workers, and harassment from non-
     employees. Presents strategies to employers on how to pre-
     vent and avoid sexual harassment complaints.

386. Warren, Jerry K. "Sexual Harassment in the Employment Con-
     text: An Analysis of the New Title VII Cause of Action."
     BAYLOR LAW REVIEW, 32 (Fall 1980), 605-615.

     Reports that a number of federal courts have expanded Title
     VII to cover sexual harassment violations. Outlines specific
     procedures for employers to prevent and correct sexual
     harassment in the workforce.

387. Wehrwein, Austin C. "The Boss Must Pay for Office Wolf's
     Foray: Minnesota Court Rules in Harassment Case."
     NATIONAL LAW JOURNAL, 5 (June 23, 1980), 5.

388. White, Barbara M. "Job-Related Sexual Harassment and Union
     Women: What Are Their Rights? GOLDEN GATE UNIVERSITY LAW
     REVIEW, WOMEN'S LAW FORUM, 10 (Summer 1980), 929-962.

     Examines the issue of sexual harassment in the workplace
     and the union's responsibility to process sexual harassment
     claims in the grievance procedure. Finds that where the
     union breaches its duty to fairly represent women who file
     such claims, the union may be liable under Title VII for
     supporting such conduct of the employer.

389. Women Organized Against Sexual Harassment. SEXUAL HARASS-
     MENT: WHAT IT IS, WHAT TO DO ABOUT IT. Berkeley, CA.,
     1979. 8 pp.

     Defines sexual harassment and sets forth procedures that
     students should follow when sexually harassed on the campus
     of the University of California at Berkeley, Explains that
     men of all backgrounds can be harassers as can women from
     all backgrounds be harassed. Finds that 20% of Berkeley
     seniors who responded to a survey indicated that they had
     been sexually harassed by teachers.

390. Woodrum, Robert L. "Sexual Harassment: New Concern About
     an Old Problem." ADVANCED MANAGEMENT JOURNAL, 46 (Winter
     1981), 20-26.

391. Wymer, John F., III. "Compensatory and Punitive Damages
      for Sexual Harassment." PERSONNEL JOURNAL, 62 (March
      1983), 181-182.

      Reports that employers may not only be liable for sexual
      harassment under Title VII, but may also be liable under
      tort laws, e.g., assault, battery, and emotional distress.

392. Zemke, Ron. "Sexual Harassment: Is Training the Key to
      Prevention?" TRAINING, 18 (February 1981), 22.

      Provides a historical review of the sexual harassment issue
      and the legal implications. Gives "strategic advice" to
      women who are faced with sexual harassment on the job and
      explains the "true cost of the office romance." Suggests
      that a key to preventing sexual harassment in the workplace
      is to provide training to managers, supervisors, and line
      workers.

            THE EQUAL PAY ACT AND SEX WAGE DISCRIMINATION

393. Barnett, Edith. "Notes on Plaintiff's Litigation Under the
      Equal Pay Act." EQUAL EMPLOYMENT PRACTICE GUIDE. Vol I.
      Edited by John R. Erickson and Katherine Savers McGovern.
      Washington, D.C.: Bureau of National Affairs, 1979,
      pp. IV-1 - IV-14.

      States that the Act forbids wage discrimination between
      males and females when they are performing "substantially
      equal" work. Contends that the Act has proven to be success-
      ful in preventing discrimination and analyzes important case
      decisions involving the Act.

394. Bird, Caroline. EVERYTHING A WOMAN NEEDS TO KNOW TO GET
      PAID WHAT SHE'S WORTH. Edited by Helene Mandelbaum. New
      York: David McKay Company, 1973. 304 pp.

      Explains why women are underpaid and provides tactics that
      women can follow to get a career job and be paid what they
      are worth. Includes sections on avoiding job discrimination,
      men's jobs, affirmative action programs, and discrimination
      laws and regulations. Gives addresses of organizations that
      provide assistance to women in the area of employment.

395. Blau, Francine D. EQUAL PAY IN THE OFFICE. Lexington, MA.:
      Lexington Books, 1977. 158 pp.

396. _____. "Women's Place in the Labor Market." AMERICAN
      ECONOMIC REVIEW, 62 (1972), 161-166.

397. Blinder, Alan S. "Wage Discrimination: Reduced Form and
      Structural Estimates." JOURNAL OF HUMAN RESOURCES, 8 (Fall
      1973), 436-455.

398. Blumrosen, Ruth G. "Wage Discrimination, Job Segregation,
      and Title VII of the Civil Rights Act of 1964." UNIVER-
      SITY OF MICHIGAN JOURNAL OF LAW REFORM, 12 (Spring) 1979,
      399-502.

      A comprehensive analysis of job segregation and wage dis-
      crimination of minorities and women. Believes that women
      and minorities have been traditionally placed in low paying
      jobs, which result in "earning gaps" between them and white
      males. Contends ". . . that it is more probable than not
      that where jobs have been segregated, the valuation of the
      worth of those jobs has been influenced by the fact that
      they are jobs of a disfavored group" [minorities and women].
      Sees wage discrimination and job segregation as an inter-
      related problem that should not be viewed separate. Explains
      what is needed to establish a prima facie case of job segre-
      gation discrimination and explains various defenses that can
      be raised by the employer.

399. Buckley, John E. "Pay Differences Between Men and Women in
      the Same Job." MONTHLY LABOR REVIEW, 94 (November 1971),
      36-39.

400. Burns, John E. and Catherine G. Burns. "An Analysis of the
      Equal Pay Act." LABOR LAW JOURNAL, 24 (February 1973),
      92-99.

      Believes that the Equal Pay Act has benefited women in
      their struggle for equal pay. Gives a brief historical view
      of the Act. Provides statistical data on the success rate of
      complainants who have filed suit under the Act and concludes
      that the Act is applicable to a claim of discrimination when
      a female and male have "equal skill, effort, responsibility,
      and similar working conditions," but the female is paid less.

401. Elisburg, Donald. "Equal Pay in the United States: The
      Development and Implementation of the Equal Pay Act of
      1963." LABOR LAW JOURNAL, 29 (April 1978), 195-208.

      Discusses the historical development and implementation of
      the Equal Pay Act of 1963. Explains the coverage, exceptions
      and enforcement provisions of the Act. Cites leading court
      decisions involving the Act. Believes that the passage of
      the Act was a step in the right direction for ensuring equal
      pay between men and women.

402. Formby, John P. "The Extent of Wage and Salary Discrimi-
      nation Against Non-White Labor." SOUTHERN ECONOMIC JOUR-
      NAL, 35 (October 1968), 140-150.

403. Gitt, Cynthia E. and Marjorie Gelb. "Beyond the Equal Pay
      Act: Expanding Wage Differential Protections Under Title
      VII." LOYOLA UNIVERSITY OF CHICAGO LAW JOURNAL, 9 (Summer
      1977), 723-765.

      Contends that even with the passage of the Equal Pay Act of
      1963 and Title VII of the Civil Rights Act of 1964, women
      have not achieved "equal pay for equal work." Traces the
      legislative histories of both Acts and concludes that ". . .
      the Equal Pay Act was intended to cover narrow situations
      where men and women performed the same job, [but] no such
      limitations are part of the legislative history or objectives
      of Title VII. Therefore, Title VII can and should be used
      to remedy wage discrimination cases even where the positions
      involved are not substantially identical."

404. Greenlaw, Paul S. and John P. Kohl. "The EEOC's New Equal
      Pay Act Guidelines." PERSONNEL JOURNAL, 61 (July 1982),
      517-521.

      Analyzes the Equal Employment Opportunity Commission's
      (EEOC) guidelines on the Equal Pay Act (EPA). The enforce-
      ment responsibility of EPA was transferred on July 1, 1979
      from the Department of Labor (DOL) to EEOC. On September 1,
      1981, the EEOC issued proposed interpretative guidelines on
      the EPA. Discusses the meaning of "establishment," the prin-
      ciple of "red circle rates," the implication of EPA on em-
      ployee benefits and labor costs, and the implication of the
      guidelines on personnel management. Believes that the guide-
      lines are unclear, difficult to comply with, and create an
      additional burden on personnel managers to justify personnel
      practices and to document their pay system.

*   Hartman, Gerald S. "Management Personnel Practices: The Do's
      and Don'ts of EEO Compliance." See Item 43.

*   Landau, Eliot and Kermit L. Dunahoo. "Sex Discrimination In
      Employment: A Survey of State and Federal Remedies." See
      Item 215.

*   Larson, E. Richard. SUE YOUR BOSS--RIGHTS AND REMEDIES FOR
      EMPLOYMENT DISCRIMINATION. See Item 53.

405. Margolin, Bessie. "Equal Pay and Equal Employment Oppor-
      tunities for Women." PROCEEDINGS OF NEW YORK UNIVERSITY-
      NINETEENTH ANNUAL CONFERENCE ON LABOR. Edited by Thomas
      G.S. Christensen. New York: Matthew Bender, 1967, pp.
      297-315.

      Parallels the development and impact of Equal Pay Act of
      1963 with Title VII of the Civil Rights Act of 1964. Dis-
      cusses their significance, scope and coverage, background,
      impact, and accomplishments. Believes that the Equal Pay
      Act of 1963 was the "beginning step" to the larger goal of
      full equality of opportunity for women. Concludes that even
      without enforcement powers, Title VII has outstanding poten-
      tial for ensuring EEO for women.

406. Meek, Catherine M. "How to Assure Equal Pay for Equal Work."
      THE MANAGER'S GUIDE TO EQUAL EMPLOYMENT OPPORTUNITY.
      Edited by Robert Freiberg. New York: Executive Enter-
      prises Publication Co., Inc., 1977, pp. 62-70.

      Contends that even after the Equal Pay Act of 1963, the
      Civil Rights Act of 1964 and the Equal Employment Opportunity
      Act of 1972, women are still not provided equal pay for the
      same work that men are performing. Sees the earning gap
      between men and women further widening. Outlines procedures
      that employers can follow to ensure equal pay for equal work,
      e.g., analyzing positions and job descriptions, and conduct-
      ing salary surveys.

407. Murphy, Thomas E. "Female Wage Discrimination: A Study of
      the Equal Pay Act 1963-1970." UNIVERSITY OF CINCINNATI
      LAW REVIEW, 39 (Fall 1970), 615-649.

      Believes that sex discrimination in wages is analogous with
      race discrimination in America. Presents statistical data
      to support that there is a major earning gap between women
      and men workers. Explains the coverage and exceptions to
      the Act. Analyzes the Third Circuit's decision in Shultz v.
      Wheatson Glass, which interpreted the word "equal" as meaning
      "substantially equal." Reviews the application of the Wheat-
      son decision on industries and institutions that have had
      difficulties in implementing the Equal Pay Act.

408. Oaxaca, Ronald. "Sex Discrimination in Wages." DISCRIMINA-
      IN LABOR MARKETS. Edited by Orley Ashenfelter and Albert
      Rees. Princeton, N.J.: Princeton University Press, 1973,
      pp. 124-151.

      An empirical study on the extent of wage discrimination be-
      tween men and women. Provides a ". . . quantitative assess-
      ment of the causes of male-female wage differentials." Dis-
      cusses the concept of a "discrimination coefficient" and

develops a wage model that parallels the "post-schooling
investment model of human capital theory."

409. Pettman, Barrie O., ed. EQUAL PAY FOR WOMEN. Washington,
     D.C.: Hemisphere Publishing Corporation, 1977. 179 pp.

     A collection of studies on equal pay of women in seven
     industrialized countries, including America. Other countries
     include Great Britain, Australia, New Zealand, Germany,
     Canada, and Japan. Sees women as having made strides toward
     eliminating wage discrimination in America. Finds that women
     in several of the countries have made similar strides. Cites
     obstacles that women face in attempting to totally defeat all
     wage discrimination, e.g., education requirements, lack of
     guidance and training, and the unwillingness of trade unions
     to accept change.

410. Ratner, Ronnie Steinberg., ed. EQUAL EMPLOYMENT POLICY FOR
     WOMEN. Philadelphia, PA. Temple University Press, 1980.
     520 pp.

     A collection of essays and articles on equal pay and equal
     employment opportunities for women in the United States,
     Canada, and Western Europe.

411. Ross, Albert H. and Frank V. McDermott, Jr. "The Equal Pay
     Act of 1963: A Decade of Enforcement." BOSTON COLLEGE
     INDUSTRIAL AND COMMERCIAL LAW REVIEW, 16 (November 1974),
     1-73.

     A comprehensive discussion on the legislative history,
     major provisions, and affirmative defenses under the Act.
     Explains the relationship between the Act and Title VII.
     Analyzes the Supreme Court's decision in Brennan v. Corning
     Glass Works, and other court decisions related to the Act.
     Believes that the Act will be beneficial in eliminating sex
     discrimination in wages. Suggests ways that Congress can
     strenghten some weaknesses in the Act.

*   Sullivan, Charles A.; Michael J. Zimmer; and Richard F.
     Richards. FEDERAL STATUTORY LAW OF EMPLOYMENT DISCRIMI-
     NATION. See Item 105.

412. Tanenbaum, Susan G. and Michael M. Tarnow. "Recent Develop-
     ments Under the Equal Pay Act, 1979." NINTH ANNUAL INSTI-
     TUTE--EQUAL EMPLOYMENT OPPORTUNITY COMPLIANCE. New York:
     Practicing Law Institute, 1980, pp. 227-233.

     Cites the transfer of enforcement powers from the Depart-
     ment of Labor to the EEOC and the filing of a major equal

pay suit against Sears Roebuck Company by the EEOC as two
major developments under the Act.

413. U.S. Department of Labor, Employment Standards Administra-
      tion, Women's Bureau. THE EARNINGS GAP BETWEEN WOMEN AND
      MEN. Washington, D.C., October 1976. 12 pp.

      Provides statistical data to illustrate that there is a
      major earning gap between women and men workers. Concludes
      that once ". . . women are allowed easier access to more
      highly paid professional, technical, managerial, and craft
      occupations, only then will the earning differential narrow."

414. U.S. Department of Labor, Office of the Secretary, Women's
      Bureau. THE EARNINGS GAP BETWEEN WOMEN AND MEN. Govern-
      ment Printing Office, 1979. 22 pp.

      Presents statistical data that support that earning differ-
      entials still exist between men and women, and that women are
      concentrated in low-paying and dead end jobs. Gives several
      factors that cause this earning gap between men and female
      workers.

415. U.S. Equal Employment Opportunity Commission. EQUAL WORK-
      EQUAL PAY-MEN AND WOMEN. Washington, D.C.: Government
      Printing Office, December 1982. 4 pp.

      Briefly outlines the major provisions of the Equal Pay Act,
      including the coverage, exceptions, penalties for violation,
      and procedures for filing a complaint and lawsuit.

416. _____. HEARINGS . . . ON JOB SEGREGATION AND WAGE
      DISCRIMINATION. Washington, D.C.: Government Printing
      Office, 1980. 849 pp.

      Presents testimony on the extent of job segregation and
      wage discrimination of women and minorities in the workforce.
      Includes testimony from employer groups who argue that the
      EEOC's authority to correct job segregation should be limited
      to their enforcement powers under the Equal Pay Act of 1963.
      Also includes testimony from women groups who argue that the
      solution to job segregation and wage discrimination would be
      for the EEOC to issue guidelines on "equal pay for equal
      standards."

417. Vladeck, Judith. "The Equal Pay Act of 1963." PROCEEDING
      OF NEW YORK UNIVERSITY EIGHTEENTH ANNUAL CONFERENCE ON
      LABOR. Edited by Thomas G.S. Christensen. New York:
      BNA, Inc., 1966, pp. 381-399.

Explains the scope, coverage, exceptions, enforcement provisions, and the historical background of the Act. Concludes
that the Act will ensure equal pay between men and women,
but it will not be able to ensure equal employment opportunities for women in other areas, such as in hiring and
promotions.

418. Wegener, Elaine. "Does Competitive Pay Discriminate?"
      PERSONNEL ADMINISTRATOR, 25 (May 1980), 38-43.

COMPARABLE WORTH

419. Bennett, Michael J. "Labor Law--Sex Discrimination -- Equal
      Pay for Equal Work Standard Not Necessary for Title VII
      Sex-Based Wage Discrimination Claims. County of Washington
      v. Gunther, 101 S. Ct. 2242 (1981)." MARQUETTE LAW REVIEW,
      65 (Winter 1981), 269-281.

      Discusses the Supreme Court's decision in County of Wash-
      ington v. Gunther, which ". . . held that the Bennett Amend-
      ment to Title VII of the Civil Rights Act of 1964 did not
      require that Title VII sex-based wage discrimination claims
      meet the equal work standard of the Equal Pay Act." Believes
      the Gunther decision was a narrow decision but will open the
      door to more "sex based wage discrimination claims."

420. Brinks, James T. "The Comparable Worth Issue: A Salary
      Administration Bombshell." THE PERSONNEL ADMINISTRATOR,
      26 (November 1981), 37-40.

      Gives a brief summary of cases involving the comparable
      worth issue. Suggests ways to make job evaluation systems
      "defensible and explainable" when the comparable worth of a
      job is in question.

421. Bureau of National Affairs, Inc. "The Comparable Worth
      Issue: A BNA Special Report." FAIR EMPLOYMENT PRACTICE
      MANUAL. Washington, D.C. (Supplement 433, Part 2), Novem-
      ber 7, 1981. 144 pp.

      Examines several court decisions, surveys, hearings,
      studies, reports, and federal, state and local developments
      involving the comparable worth issue. The facts and impact
      of the County of Washington v. Gunther decision are high-
      lighted in this special report. Representatives from manage-
      ment, academia, labor, and women's organizations provide
      their opinions on comparable worth and predict what impact
      comparable worth will have on future court decisions. In-
      cludes a comparable worth bibliography and a table of cases.

422. Carter, Michael F. "Comparable Worth: An Idea Whose Time
      Has Come?" PERSONNEL JOURNAL, 60 (October 1981), 792-794.

      Begins with a brief update on the legal status of the
      comparable worth concept and discusses problem areas when
      implementing such a concept within a compensation system.
      Concludes that "[t]he practical solution is to allow employ-
      ers to price different jobs as they deem appropriate, while
      ensuring that women have equal access to all jobs . . ."
      States that ". . . recruiting women for traditional male jobs
      is a far more practical solution than pay equity legislation,
      regulation or litigation."

423. "Case Study: EEO and Comparable Worth." EEO REVIEW, (Janu-
      ary 1983), 2-3.

      Presents a case study on a comparable worth discrimination
      complaint. Provides comments and suggestions to managers and
      supervisors on how to effectively deal with EEO complaints in
      this area of the law.

424. Chandler, Melinda P. "Equal Pay for Comparable Work Value:
      The Failure of Title VII and the Equal Pay Act." NORTH-
      WESTERN UNIVERSITY LAW REVIEW, 75 (December 1980), 914-943.

      Argues that despite the passage of Title VII and the Equal
      Pay Act, women workers are paid less than men and are segre-
      gated in lower paying jobs. States that neither law speaks
      directly to the issue of comparable worth, nevertheless,
      believes that the courts can find sex-wage discrimination
      under Title VII. Discusses the legislative history of the
      Equal Pay Act, Title VII, and the Bennett Amendment. Out-
      lines a series of court cases on sex discrimination in wages
      and reviews the Supreme Court's decisions in Gunther v.
      County of Washington and General Electric Co. v. Gilbert.

425. "Comparable Worth - Catching on and Controversial." AMERICAN
      BAR ASSOCIATION JOURNAL, 70 (September 1984), 16.

426. Cody, Thomas G. "The Comparable Worth Slot Machine: Does
      Job Evaluation Give Every Player an Even Break?" EQUAL
      EMPLOYMENT PRACTICES GUIDE, VOL. I. Edited by John R.
      Erickson and Katherine Savers McGovern. Washington, D.C.:
      Bureau of National Affairs, 1979, pp. IV-15 - IV-32.

      Combines the principles of job evaluation with the compar-
      able worth issue. Concludes that job evaluation cannot solve
      nor was it designed to solve "macro issues" as equal pay,
      unless job evaluation techniques are improved.

427. Committee on Occupation Classification and Analysis, Assembly
     of Behavioral and Social Sciences National Research Coun-
     cil. Women, Work, and Wages: Equal Pay for Jobs of Equal
     Value. Edited by Donald J. Treiman and Heidi I. Hartmann.
     Washington, D.C.: National Academy Press, 1981. 136 pp.

     Commissioned by the Equal Employment Opportunity Commis-
     sion, the committee evaluated the process of "measuring the
     comparability of jobs." Seeks to determine whether tradi-
     tional methods of job evaluation to establish rates of com-
     pensation result in discrimination between women and men.
     Concentrates on the issue of comparable worth and discusses
     various empirical studies on pay differences between women
     and men. Concludes that "there is substantial discrimination
     in pay" between men and women, and suggest methods and ap-
     proaches in eliminating such differences.

428. Conference on Alternative State and Local Policies. MANUAL
     ON PAY EQUITY. Edited by Joy Ann Grune. Washington, D.C.:
     Conference on Alternative State and Local Policies, 1980.
     224 pp.

     Proceedings of the first national "Conference on Pay
     Equity" which was held on October 24, 1979. Includes
     speeches and summaries on job segregation and wage discrimi-
     nation. Focuses on the issue of comparable worth and equal
     pay. Provides "facts and figures" to support that wage
     discrimination against women workers exist. Sets forth the
     reasons why comparable worth should be supported.

429. Cook, Alice H. COMPARABLE WORTH: THE PROBLEM AND STATES'
     APPROACHES TO WAGE EQUITY. Honolulu, HI.: Industrial
     Relations Center, University of Hawaii at Manoa, 1983.
     84 pp.

     Defines comparable worth and explains the problem of wage
     inequity between men and women who perform comparable jobs.
     Summarizes the present status of comparable worth in a
     selected number of states, including discussions on state
     legislation, litigation, and case studies.

430. Doherty, Mary Helen and Ann Harriman. "Comparable Worth:
     The Equal Employment Issue of the 1980s." REVIEW OF
     PUBLIC PERSONNEL ADMINISTRATION, 1 (Summer 1981), 11-31.

     A review of court cases, legislation, case studies and "job
     evaluation methods" in the area of comparable worth.

431. Equal Employment Advisory Council. COMPARABLE WORTH: A
     SYMPOSIUM ON THE ISSUES AND ALTERNATIVES. Washington,
     D.C., November 21, 1980.

A collection of discussions from governmental officials,
representatives from private industry, and the academic field
on the reasons and solutions to the wage differential between
men and women workers. Seeks to determine ". . . whether
that earning gap is the result of illegal wage discrimination or job segregation, and whether the comparable worth
theory should be adopted as a practical means of ending that
differential."

432. "Equal Pay, Comparable Work, and Job Evaluation." YALE LAW
      JOURNAL, 90 (January 1981), 657-680.

      Contends that even after the passage of Title VII and the
      Equal Pay Act there is still disparity between the earnings
      of women and men. States that "[n]early half of all women
      workers hold traditionally female, substantially sex-segre-
      gated jobs." Argues that Title VII also covers equal pay
      between women and men when their jobs are of comparable worth
      to the employer. Outlines a job evaluation system to iden-
      tify jobs that are of comparable worth to employers.

433. Fulghum, Judy B. "The Employer's Liabilities Under Compar-
      able Worth." PERSONNEL JOURNAL, 62 (May 1983), 400-404.

434. Gasaway, Laura N. "Comparable Worth: A Post-Gunther Over-
      view." GEORGETOWN LAW JOURNAL, 69 (June 1981), 1123-1169.

      A comprehensive study on the issue of comparable worth.
      Begins with a discussion on the status of women in the work-
      force. Argues that women are still paid less than men and/or
      segregated in particular occupations. Discusses the legal
      basis of comparable worth, e.g., Title VII and the Equal Pay
      Act. Briefly outlines the facts and the court's decision in
      The County of Washington v. Gunther, and other related lower
      court decisions. Examines the positions of the Equal Employ-
      ment Opportunity Commission, the Office of Federal Contract
      Compliance Programs, and other state agencies on comparable
      worth. Provides information on how comparable worth is
      perceived abroad. Sees traditional job evaluation systems
      as an obstacle to implementing a successful comparable worth
      program.

435. Helmreich, Martha S. "Women, Wages, and Title VII: The
      Significance of County of Washington v. Gunther." UNIVER-
      SITY OF PITTSBURGH LAW REVIEW, 43 (Winter 1982), 467-499.

      Analyzes the impact of the Supreme Court's decision in the
      above referenced case on establishing a prima facie case of
      wage discrimination. States that the court held ". . . that
      it is possible to establish a prima facie case of intentional
      sex discrimination in the payment of wages without proof of
      substantially equal work." Interprets the implication of the

Bennett Amendment on the <u>Gunther</u> decision, and outlines
approaches for plaintiffs and defendants in presenting and
rebutting a claim of wage discrimination. Concludes that the
court in <u>Gunther</u> did not rule out the theory of "comparable
worth."

436.   "How to Prepare for Comparable Pay." EFFECTIVE MANAGER, 4
       (November 1980), 1-2.

437.   Kahn, Steven C. "Comparable Worth: Journey of a Thousand
       Miles." CORPORATION LAW REVIEW, 3 (Spring 1980), 136-142.

       Gives a brief discussion on the historical background of
       sex discrimination in wages, the comparable worth theory,
       and recent litigation on wage discrimination. Focuses on
       <u>Gunther v. County of Washington</u> and <u>Lemons v. City and County
       of Denver</u> decisions. Concludes that the EEOC and the courts
       will eventually be faced with the responsibility of deciding
       the legal status of comparable worth within the context of
       Title VII.

438.   Kaplan, Joel H. and Richard E. Lieberman. "Comparable Pay:
       A Management Perspective." SOLVING EEO PROGRAMS: A GUIDE
       TO EEO LAW AND PRACTICE. New York: Executive Enterprises
       Publications Co., Inc., 1980, pp. 177-190.

       Admits "[t]here has been an earnings gap between males and
       females in the workplace since biblical time . . .," but
       believes that the theory of comparable worth is not the
       solution to the problem. States that ". . . the comparable
       worth theory argues that through a combination of sex-biased
       market forces--historical female protective statutes, soci-
       etal influences, subjective male values, and intentional
       corporate discrimination--jobs held by women are underpaid
       compared to jobs held by men." Disagrees with advocates of
       comparable worth as to why there is a disparity between male
       and female workers. Believes that sex discrimination is not
       the major reason for disparity but" . . . factors such as
       female disinclination, intermittent female participation in
       the labor force, and lesser skills and education of female
       workers." Concludes that the comparable worth theory will
       further segregate women in certain jobs--with more money.

439.   Kramer, Susan D. "Comparable Worth." UNIVERSITY OF SAN
       FRANCISCO LAW REVIEW, 16 (Winter 1982), 357-375.

       Argues that the comparable worth theory should be used as a
       tool to eliminate wage discrimination. Presents the views of
       supporters and critics of the comparable worth issue. Iden-
       tifies applicable federal laws related to the comparable
       worth theory, e.g., Title VII, the the Equal Pay Act of 1963,
       and the Bennett Amendment. Reviews the Supreme Court's

decision in County of Washington v. Gunther, and concludes
that the decision is narrow and leaves unresolved some basic
questions on comparable worth.

440. Lauter, David. "Comparable Worth War: Pay Bias Enters a New
      Age." THE NATIONAL LAW JOURNAL, 6 (January 2, 1984), 1.

      Analyzes the District Courts decision in AFSCME v. State
      of Washington and its impact on the future of the comparable
      worth issue. In the Washington decision, the judge used the
      comparable worth theory to find sex discrimination against
      the state of Washington. Indicates that the decision may
      result in one billion dollars in damages against the state.

441. Legislative Research Commission, Program Review and Investi-
      gations Committee. SALARY DIFFERENTIALS BETWEEN MEN AND
      WOMEN IN KENTUCKY STATE GOVERNMENT. Frankfort, KY., March
      1983, 110 pp.

      Results of a state study on the extent of salary differen-
      tials between male and female state workers, and the topic of
      equal pay for equal work. Provides recommendations on how to
      prevent and correct salary differential between male and
      female employees in state government.

      Leap, Terry L.; William H. Holley, Jr.; and Hubert S. Feild.
      "Equal Employment Opportunity and its Implications for
      Personnel Practices in the 1980s." See Item 54.

442. Lindsay, Cotton M. EQUAL PAY FOR COMPARABLE WORK: AN ECO-
      NOMIC ANALYSIS OF A NEW ANTIDISCRIMINATION DOCTRINE. Coral
      Gables, FL.: Law and Economics Center, University of
      Miami, 1980. 36 pp.

443. Livernash, Robert E., ed. COMPARABLE WORTH: ISSUES AND
      ALTERNATIVES. Washington, D.C.: Equal Employment Advi-
      sory Council, 1980. 260 pp.

      A collection of articles which analyze the concept of
      comparable worth. Includes discussions on job evaluations,
      pay differentials between women and men, compensation sys-
      tems, statistical analysis on pay discrimination, how other
      countries are dealing with comparable worth, and the legal
      framework of the Equal Pay Act of 1963 and Title VII. Con-
      cludes that ". . . any attempted implementation of comparable
      worth would encounter substantial difficulties and would have
      disruptive and undesirable consequences. . . ." Sees the
      accelerated promotion of women in nontraditional and manage-
      rial positions as a "viable alternative" to the comparable
      worth concept.

444. Lorber, Lawrence Z. "Job Segregation and Wage Discrimination
      Under Title VII and The Equal Pay Act." PERSONNEL ADMINIS-
      TRATOR, 25 (May 1980), 31-34.

          Presents a position paper by the American Society of Per-
      sonnel Administration which opposes the EEOC's proposed
      guidelines on "equal pay for comparable worth." Sees the
      EEOC as having no authority to deviate from the "equality
      standard" as set forth by the Equal Pay Act and Title VII.
      Both laws support the theory that to prove a case of sex
      discrimination there must be a differential in pay between
      women and men on jobs that are equal in all respect. Be-
      lieves that there is no mention of a "comparability standard"
      in either law. Recommends that the EEOC submit the question
      of comparable worth to Congress, because it is a legislative
      issue.

445. McLennan, Barbara N. "Sex Discrimination In Employment and
      Possible Liabilities of Labor Unions: Implications of
      County of Washington v. Gunther. LABOR LAW JOURNAL, 33
      (January 1982), 26-35.

          Focuses on the liability of unions in sex discrimination
      cases filed under Title VII and under the National Labor
      Relations Act. Reviews the Supreme Court's decision in
      County of Washington v. Gunther to determine whether unions
      would also be liable in situations where women are paid less
      for jobs that are of equal value to those held by men.
      Advises unions that they can be liable under both Acts for
      violating the "equal pay for comparable worth theory" which
      was set forth in the Gunther decision.

446. Nellis, James Peter. "An Approach to Equal Pay Through
      Comparable Worth - Moving on From County of Washington v.
      Gunther." WOMEN LAWYER'S JOURNAL, 69 (No. 2 1983), 8-10.

          Compares Title VII's coverage, standard of proof, and com-
      plaint procedure with the Equal Pay Act. Believes that the
      Equal Pay Act is more technical and places a heavier burden
      on plaintiffs to prove their case. States that under the
      Equal Pay Act jobs must be substantially equal for the Act
      to be applicable. Advises plaintiffs in comparable worth
      cases to file under Title VII when the Equal Pay Act is not
      appropriate.

447. Newman, Winn and Jeanne M. Vonhof. "'Separate But Equal'--
      Job Segregation and Pay Equity in the Wake of Gunther."
      UNIVERSITY OF ILLINOIS LAW REVIEW, 1981 (No. 2), 269-331.

          Analyzes the Supreme Court's decision in Gunther, which
      held that sex-based wage discrimination under Title VII did
      not require the equal work standard as required in suits

filed under the Equal Pay Act. Provides an in-depth discussion on proving wage discrimination, the IUE v. Westinghouse case and other related cases, and remedies and defenses to wage discrimination suits.

448. Pekelis, Rosselle. "Equal Pay: Comparability vs. Identical Work." PROCEEDINGS OF NEW YORK UNIVERSITY - THIRTY-THIRD ANNUAL NATIONAL CONFERENCE ON LABOR. Edited by Richard Adelman. New York: Matthew Bender, 1981, pp. 367-382.

Discusses Gunter v. County of Washington and other court cases relative to the issue of "comparable worth." Believes that there is a "growing commitment to comparable worth principles and that employers should voluntarily begin to correct any disparity in wages between men and women."

449. Picus, Joy. "Equal Pay for Work of Comparable Value." GRADUATE WOMEN, 76 (July-August 1982), 36.

Gives a brief historical view on the status of women and the causes as to why women receive less pay than men for jobs of comparable worth. Feels that it will take an extended period of time before employers in the private and public sector can end this form of wage discrimination.

450. Rasnic, Carol D. "Robbing Peter to Pay Pauline: Proving and Defending Sex Based Wage Discrimination Claims." VIRGINIA BAR ASSOCIATION JOURNAL, (Winter 1983), 10.

Gives a brief review of the legislative history of the 1963 Equal Pay Act and Title VII, and discusses how to prove and defend a claim under each law. Recommends that comparable worth cases be filed under the Equal Pay Act, Title VII, and the Equal Protection Clause of the Constitution. Projects there will be a major increase in the number of comparable worth cases after the U.S. Supreme Court held in County of Washington v. Gunther that the four prong test used in the Equal Pay Act was not applicable in the Gunther case.

451. Remick, Helen. "Beyond Equal Pay for Equal Work: Comparable Worth in the State of Washington." EQUAL EMPLOYMENT POLICY FOR WOMEN. Edited by Lonnie Steinberg Ratner. Philadelphia, PA: Temple University Press, 1980, pp. 405-419.

States that an ". . . analysis of the workforce clearly shows that jobs held predominantly by women pay salaries substantially below those held predominantly by men; equal pay for equal work concepts are inadequate for understanding these differences." Recommends that the point factor evaluation system be used to correct pay inequities between men and women who are performing comparable jobs. Cites the Willis

Report as an example of how the point system can be implemented to eliminate and correct pay inequities between women
and men.

452.   Ruderfer, Faith D.   "Sex Based Wage Discrimination Under
       Title VII: Equal Pay for Equal Work or Equal Pay for
       Comparable Work?" WILLIAM AND MARY LAW REVIEW, 22 (Spring
       1981), 421-485.

       Attempts to clarify the coverage, procedural requirements,
       and the relationship between Title VII, the Equal Pay Act and
       the Bennett Amendment in wage discrimination cases. Analyzes
       the court's decisions in Gunther v. Washington and IUE v.
       Westinghouse. Concludes that the Westinghouse decision was
       "a narrower decision" than Gunther and more workable for the
       courts.

453.   Sager, Lawrence Gene.   "Gender-Based Wage Discrimination":
       County of Washington v Gunther. HARVARD LAW REVIEW, 95
       (November 1981), 300-310.

       Analyzes and attempts to rationalize the court's decision
       within the context of the Equal Pay Act and the Bennett
       Amendment.

454.   Schnebly, John R.   "Comparable Worth: A Legal Overview."
       PERSONNEL ADMINISTRATOR, 27 (April 1982), 43.

       Provides an overview of the legal standards for wage dis-
       crimination claims under the Equal Pay Act, Title VII, the
       Age Discrimination In Employment Act, Executive Order 11246
       and various state laws. Feels that the issue of comparable
       worth is still in the developmental stages; however, the
       court's decision in County of Washington v. Gunther has set
       the stage for future litigation on the issue of comparable
       worth. The Supreme Court held in Gunther that Title VII
       wage claims are not limited by the equal work standard of
       the Equal Pay Act. Discusses the implications of the Gunther
       decision and gives a synopsis of other cases related to com-
       parable worth.

455.   Thomas, Clarence.   "Pay Equity and Comparable Worth." LABOR
       LAW JOURNAL, 34 (January 1983), 3-12.

       Explains that women workers not only face the possibility
       of wage discrimination as prohibited by Title VII of the
       Civil Rights Act of 1964 and the Equal Pay Act, but also face
       wage discrimination on the theory of ". . . the now well-
       known but less clearly defined concept of comparable worth.
       . . ." Briefly outlines the history behind the comparable
       worth concept, the impact of the Bennett Amendment, recent

court decisions, comparable worth abroad and in the federal
sector, and the EEOC's progress in studying the issue.

456. Wasem, Mark R. "The Comparable Worth Theory: A Critical
      Analysis." BAYLOR LAW REVIEW, 32 (Fall 1980), 629-638.

      Contends that the Equal Pay Act and Title VII have not been
      completely successful in eradicating wage discrimination
      among the sexes. Explores the feasibility of the theory of
      comparable worth as a means of eliminating the disparity
      between men and women wages. Analyzes the Ninth Circuit's
      opinion in Gunther v. County of Washington, which supported
      the comparable worth theory.

457. Whaley, George L. "Controversy Swirls Over Comparable Worth
      Issue." PERSONNEL ADMINISTRATOR, 27 (April 1982), 51.

      Presents the pros and cons of the comparable worth issue.
      Includes tables on key comparable worth issues, women's
      relative earning by occupation between 1956-1975, and compar-
      able worth organization implications. Discusses the future
      implication of comparable worth, the Supreme Court's decision
      in the County of Washington v. Gunther, job evaluation, and
      the politics of adopting the comparable worth doctrine.

458. Williamson, Jane. "Equal Pay For Work Of Comparable Value."
      WORKING WOMAN, 6 (January 1981), 10.

THE VOCATIONAL REHABILITATION ACT OF 1973
AND HANDICAP DISCRIMINATION

459. Action, Norman. "Employment of Disabled Persons: Where Are
We Going?" INTERNATIONAL LABOR REVIEW, 120 (January-
February 1981), 1-14.

* "Affirmative Action for Disabled People." See Item 891.

460. Allbery, Charles, III and Michele Gressel. "Accessibility
for the Handicapped: The Impact of Section 504 on Architectural and Transportation Barriers." UNIVERSITY OF
DAYTON LAW REVIEW, 3 (Summer 1978), 431-447.

Discusses the coverage and compliance requirements, and
limitations of the Architectural Barriers Act, Section 504 of
the Rehabilitation Act of 1973, and the Urban Mass Transportation Assistance Act. States that each Act was designed to
remove physical barriers to handicapped employees in federally funded programs. Concludes that Section 504 ". . . is
the strongest federal anti-barriers legislation passed to
date."

461. Angel, Juvenal L. EMPLOYMENT OPPORTUNITIES FOR THE HANDI-
CAPPED. New York: World Trade Academy Press, Inc., 1969.
411 pp.

A comprehensive discussion on the employment problems and
particular needs of handicapped workers. Explains the employment potential of handicapped workers and provides a
listing of where to locate qualified handicapped workers.
Discusses the type of counseling and training handicapped
individuals need before and during placement. Gives suggestions to handicapped workers on preparing for job placement,
interviewing, and developing a resume. Gives a job analysis
of 350 occupations open to handicapped workers and a bibliography of resources available to handicapped workers.

462. Asher, Janet and Jules Asher. "How to Accommodate Workers
in Wheelchairs." JOB SAFETY AND HEALTH, (October 1976),
30-35.

Provides suggestions and ideas for modifying machines,
tools, and buildings to accommodate handicapped workers who
are confined to a wheelchair.

102

463. Battles, Michaele Snyder. "The Manager and Affirmative
     Action to Hire the Handicapped." THE MANAGER'S GUIDE TO
     EQUAL EMPLOYMENT OPPORTUNITY. Edited by Robert Freiberg.
     New York: Executive Enterprises Publications Co., Inc.,
     1977, pp. 105-114.

     Outlines federal contractors' responsibilities in hiring
     and promoting handicapped individuals as mandated by Section
     503 of the Rehabilitiation Act of 1973. Sees managers' roles
     in complying with the Act as "vital." Provides suggestions
     to managers on how to select, train, and accommodate handi-
     capped individuals.

464. Bennett, Keith W. "We Want to Hire the Handicapped,
     But . . .?" MANAGEMENT REVIEW, 61 (October 1972), 54-55.

465. Berwitz, Clement J. "Job Accommodation." AFFIRMATIVE ACTION
     FOR THE HANDICAPPED, by the U.S. Department of Labor, Em-
     ployment Standards Administration, Office of Federal Con-
     tract Compliance Programs. Washington, D.C.: Government
     Printing Office, April 1980, pp. 69-99.

     Explains the nature, types, and cost of accommodating
     handicapped applicants and employees. Provides specific
     examples of accommodating handicapped individuals who use
     wheelchairs or crutches; have limited ability to use reach,
     handle, finger, or feel; and who are blind or deaf.

466. Bogaards, Pieter. "The Rehabilitation Act of 1973: Who Is
     Handicapped Under Federal Law." UNIVERSITY OF SAN FRAN-
     CISCO LAW REVIEW, 16 (Spring 1982), 653-680.

467. Bowe, Frank. "Supreme Court to Rule on First '504' Case."
     EQUAL OPPORTUNITY FORUM, 6 (April 1979), 3.

     Reviews the facts in Davis v. Southeastern Community
     College. This case was the first case before the Supreme
     Court dealing with Section 504. The major issue before the
     Court was the applicability of Section 504 on educational
     institutions' admission policies that had an impact on the
     admission of handicapped students. Predicts that the Court's
     decision may have broad implications on admissions policies
     relative to handicapped individuals.

*   Brosnan, Ted. "There's More to Affirmative Action Than Just
     Just Hiring 'the Handicapped.'" See Item 904.

468. Bruck, Lilly. ACCESS: THE GUIDE TO A BETTER LIFE FOR DIS-
     ABLED AMERICANS. New York: Random House, Inc., 1978.
     251 pp.

A resource guide for handicapped or disabled Americans
regarding strategies for removing and overcoming barriers
that prohibit their full use of the market place, e.g.,
architectural, attitudinal, communication, and transportation. Includes chapters on employment discrimination, vocational rehabilitation, and affirmative action for handicapped
workers.

469. Burden, Charles A. "Hiring a Mental Rehabilitant." PER-
      SONNEL JOURNAL, 50 (December 1971), 920-923.

      Results of a study on twenty companies in the Atlanta,
      Georgia area who hired individuals that were previously
      emotionally handicapped individuals. Outlines the procedure
      followed in conducting physical examinations, presenting
      supervisory orientation, and getting co-workers and the union
      involved. Among the findings were that ". . . emotional
      rehabilitants were considered to be good employees. . . ."

470. Burgdorf, Marcia P. and Robert Burgdorf, Jr. "A History of
      Unequal Treatment: The Qualifications of Handicapped
      Persons as a 'Suspect Class' Under the Equal Protection
      Clause." SANTA CLARA LAWYER, 15 (1975), 855-910.

471. "Case Study: EEO and Handicapped Discrimination." EEO
      REVIEW, (October 1982), 2-3.

      Presents a case study on a handicap discrimination com-
      plaint. Provides comments and suggestions to managers and
      supervisors on how to effectively deal with EEO complaints
      in this area of the law.

472. Charlton, M. Melissa. "Enforcing the Rights of the Handi-
      capped: The Future of Section 504 in the Fifth Circuit."
      CUMBERLAND LAW REVIEW, 10 (1979), 423-439.

      Outlines the coverage, judicial limitation, and enforcement
      difficulities under the Act. Reports that the Court of
      Appeals for the Fifth Circuit has not had an opportunity to
      rule on Section 504; however, encourages the court ". . . to
      take the initiative and [to] follow Congress' stated intent
      of eliminating discrimination against the handicapped . . ."
      when the issue comes before the Court.

473. Clark, Blake S. "Are Disabled Trainees Handicapped by Our
      Designs?" TRAINING AND DEVELOPMENT JOURNAL, 36 (July
      1982), 56.

474. Conrad, Voris R. and Veronica M. Leona. "Hiring Your First
      Handicapped Person." JOURNAL OF COOPERATIVE EDUCATION, 18
      (Fall 1981), 50-57.

475. Cook, Timothy M. "Nondiscrimination in Employment Under the
      Rehabilitation Act of 1973." AMERICAN UNIVERSITY LAW
      REVIEW, 27 (1977), 31-75.

      Seeks to determine what impact the Rehabilitation Act,
      specifically Section 504, has on organizations who receive
      some form of federal assistance. Evaluates the Department
      of Health, Education, and Welfare's efforts to enforce the
      Act.

476. Craft, James A.; Thomas J. Benecki; and Yitzchak M. Shkop.
      "Who Hires the Seriously Handicapped?" INDUSTRIAL RELA-
      TIONS, 19 (Winter 1980), 94-99.

      "Investigates the types of employers with whom seriously
      handicapped persons are placed, the types and levels of jobs
      they obtain, and the factors contributing to these place-
      ments." Concludes ". . . that seriously handicapped workers
      are often placed in dead-end, low-paying jobs with secondary
      employers."

477. DeLury, Bernard E. "Equal Job Opportunity for the Handi-
      capped Means Positive Thinking and Positive Action."
      LABOR LAW JOURNAL, 26 (November 1975), 679-685.

      States that successful affirmative action programming for
      employing handicapped individuals require positive thinking
      and action. Briefly explains how affirmative action can be
      planned and implemented for the handicapped. Defines the
      meaning of "qualified handicap" and explains the coverage
      and enforcement section under Section 503 of the Rehabilita-
      tion Act of 1973.

478. "The Developing Law on Equal Employment Opportunity for
      Handicapped: An Overview and Analysis of the Major Is-
      sues." UNIVERSITY OF BALTIMORE LAW REVIEW, 7 (Spring
      1978), 183-278.

      Surveys state and federal laws and regulations that pro-
      hibit employment discrimination against handicapped workers.
      Analyzes the coverage, application, remedies, and defenses
      under handicap discrimination laws. Defines the meaning of
      "qualified handicap," reasonable accommodation, and "job-
      relatedness." "Concludes that the regulations promulgated
      by administrative agencies, pursuant to legislative mandate,
      impose onerous standards for compliance and may exceed the
      bound of statutory authority in some respects."

479. Donnell, Garry W. "Nondiscrimination Under Federal Grants--
     Striving Toward Equal Employment Opportunities for Handi-
     capped Individuals." UNIVERSITY OF DAYTON LAW REVIEW, 3
     (Summer 1978), 405-430.

480. Dystel, John Jay. "The Disabled in Court: A Lack of Judi-
     cial Understanding and Compassion." EQUAL OPPORTUNITY
     FORUM, 7 (November 1979), 12-13.

     Reviews the Court's decisions in Trageser v. Libbie Reha-
     bilitation Center, Inc.; Southeastern Community College v.
     Davis; and Hart v. County of Alameda. Concludes that judges
     do not accept handicapped citizens as humans even though they
     have the same rights as non-handicapped citizens.

481. Gordon, Sue. "Up Against the Accommodation Rule." UNIVER-
     SITY OF MISSOURI AT KANSAS CITY LAW REVIEW, 45 (1976),
     56-74.

482. Grazulis, Cheryl. "Understanding Section 503: What Does It
     Really Say?" PERSONNEL ADMINISTRATOR, 23 (January 1978),
     22-23.

     Briefly reviews the legal requirements for employers and
     contractors under Section 503 of the Rehabilitation Act of
     1973. Discusses the outreach assistance program, interview-
     ing techniques, job accommodation assistance, accessibility
     assistance, and human relations training provisions.

483. Grossman, Vigdor. EMPLOYING HANDICAPPED PERSONS: MEETING
     EEO OBLIGATIONS. Washington, D.C.: Bureau of National
     Affairs, 1980. 139 pp.

*   Hartman, Gerald S. "Management Personnel Practices: The
     Do's and Don'ts of EEO Compliance." See Item 43.

484. Hermann, Ann Marie and Lucinda Walker. HANDBOOK OF EMPLOY-
     MENT RIGHTS OF THE HANDICAPPED: SECTION 503 AND 504 OF
     THE REHABILITATION ACT OF 1973. Washington, D.C.: Re-
     gional Rehabilitation Research Institute On Attitudinal,
     Legal, and Leisure Barriers, 1978.

     Outlines employers' obligations under the Rehabilitation
     Act of 1973 to hire and promote qualified handicapped indi-
     viduals. Gives an overview of the Act's coverage, enforce-
     ment procedures, and reasonable accommodation provisions.
     Provides information on placement practices, training, wages,
     benefits, promotions, and layoffs of handicapped workers.

485. "Hiring the Handicapped. What the New Rules Say." EFFECTIVE
      MANAGER, 4 (February 1981), 6-7.

486. Hood, Michael A. "Federal Laws Barring Discrimination
      Against the Handicapped: An Overview." SOLVING EEO
      PROBLEMS: A GUIDE TO EEO LAW AND PRACTICE. New York:
      Executive Enterprises Publications Co., Inc., 1980,
      pp. 21-34.

      Discusses federal contractors' responsibilities to employ
      and promote qualified mentally and physically handicapped
      employees and prospective employees under the Rehabilitation
      Act of 1973. Defines who is a handicapped individual under
      the Act and explains which federal contractors are covered
      by the Act. Outlines affirmative action steps that federal
      contractors should follow to comply with the Act, e.g.,
      developing an affirmative action plan. Finds that Federal
      contractors who fail to comply with the Act can be debarred
      from receiving future government contracts.

487. "How Bias Strikes" Hidden Handicapped." U.S. NEWS AND WORLD
      REPORT, 90 (June 29, 1981), 73-74.

488. Hull, Kent. "Reasonable Accommodation Under Section 504 --
      Southeastern Community College v. Davis." AMICUS, (July-
      August 1979), 170-174.

      Examines the Circuit's and the Supreme Court's rulings in
      the Davis case. Points to ambiguities in the Supreme Court's
      decision and suggests that more litigation in this area is
      forthcoming from other handicapped individuals.

*   Institute of Industrial Relations, University of California,
      Los Angeles. 1980 REPORT-EQUAL EMPLOYMENT OPPORTUNITY
      AND AFFIRMATIVE ACTION - THE ROOTS GROW DEEPER. See Item
      929.

489. Jackson, Diane P. "Affirmative Action for the Handicapped
      and Veterans: Interpretative and Operational Guidelines."
      LABOR LAW JOURNAL, 26 (February 1978), 107-117.

      Reviews the coverage, recordkeeping, reporting, accommoda-
      tion and affirmative action programming provisions under
      Sections 503 of the Rehabilitation Act of 1973 and the
      Vietnam Era-Veteran's Readjustment Assistance Act of 1974.
      Interprets both Acts and outlines a plan of action to comply
      with both.

490. _____. "Update on Handicapped Discrimination." PER-
      SONNEL JOURNAL, 57 (September 1978), 488-491.

Reports that 90 out of 100 federal contractors investigated
by OFCCP concerning their personnel practices were found to
have violated the Rehabilitation Act of 1973. Believes that
non-compliance is basically due to federal contractors not
being aware of their responsibility to develop and implement
affirmative action for handicapped individuals. Explains the
coverage of the Act and provides a brief summary of what some
companies are doing to comply with the Act. Provides a list
of suggestions to other federal contractors on how to comply
with the Act and gives a summary of specific affirmative
action requirements for federal contractors.

491. Jacobs, Roger B. "Employment Discrimination and the Handi-
      capped: Some New Teeth For A 'Paper Tiger' -- The Reha-
      bilitation Act of 1973." HOWARD LAW JOURNAL, 23 (1980),
      481-519.

      Discusses the historical background, affirmative action
      requirements, amendments, coverage, administrative pro-
      cedures, enforcement provision, and remedies under the Act.
      Examines the Supreme Court's decisions in New York City
      Transit Authority v. Beazer and Southeastern CommunityCol-
      lege v. Davis. Contends that the administrative enforcement
      of the Act by the Office of Federal Contract Compliance Pro-
      gram is inadequate. Asserts that handicapped employees are
      still mostly underemployed or unemployed. Recommends that
      Title VII be amended to include handicap discrimination as
      a basis.

492. Kemp, John D. and Robert W. Young. "Handicapped Employment
      Discrimination Litigation: Meeting the Challenge." TRIAL,
      17 (February 1981), 36-38.

      Discusses barriers to litigating handicapped employment
      discrimination cases. Cites the slowness by government
      agencies in enforcing handicapped laws, the opposition to
      private handicapped suits, and the lack of understanding of
      the capabilities of handicapped workers as barriers to liti-
      gating handicap employment cases. Briefly discusses the
      decision in E. E. Black v. Marshall, which defined the mean-
      ing of "qualified handicapped individual" and supported DOL's
      position that a "perceived" handicap condition is a form of
      handicap discrimination. Indicates that private suits under
      Section 503 are still opposed by some courts because it is
      unclear whether private suits are permissible. Updates re-
      cent cases related to Section 504 under the Act and outlines
      "successful defenses" to handicap discrimination charges.

493. _____. SECTION 504 COMPLIANCE MANUAL FOR RECIPIENTS
      OF FEDERAL FINANCIAL ASSISTANCE. Mission, KS., 1973.

      A comprehensive compliance manual for designing and imple-
      menting programs for handicapped individuals. Outlines and

explains major provisions of Section 504 and the deadlines
for compliance. Focuses on employment practices that may
adversely affect handicapped workers. Includes a model
affirmative action plan for the employment of the handicapped, a bibilography of resources, and a guide to manufacturing "assistive devices" to accommodate handicapped
individuals.

494. Layton, James R. "Comments, Compensating the Handicapped:
      An Approach to Determining the Appropriateness of Damages
      for Violations of Section 504." BRIGHAM YOUNG LAW REVIEW,
      1981 (No. 1), 133-153.

      Traces the legislative history of Section 504 of the Reha-
      bilitation Act to determine whether compensatory damages are
      available to plaintiffs who successfully prove a 504 viola-
      tion. Advises courts to use the Supreme Court's decision
      in Davis v. Passman as a guide for determining the appropri-
      ateness of compensatory damages.

*   Leap, Terry L.; William H. Holley, Jr.; and Hubert S. Feild.
      "Equal Employment Opportunity and Its Implications for
      Personnel Practices in the 1980s." See Item 54.

495. Mason, Karol V. "Employment Discrimination Against Over-
      weight." UNIVERSITY OF MICHIGAN JOURNAL OF LAW REFORM,
      15 (Winter-1982), 337-362.

      Examines Title VII, the Rehabilitation Act of 1973, and
      state statutes to determine whether overweight individuals
      are protected from employment discrimination. Concludes that
      existing laws do not adequately protect overweight individ-
      uals from employment discrimination. ". . . argues for the
      passage of legislation designating weight as a classification
      protected from employment discrimination, and prohibiting the
      use of weight standards unrelated to job performance."

496. Massaro, Toni M. "Employment Rights of Handicapped Individ-
      uals: Statutory and Judicial Parameters." WILLIAM &
      MARY LAW REVIEW, 20 (Winter 1978), 291-327.

497. Matteson, Bob and Rick Stamm. "Make Room for the Able
      Disabled." MANAGEMENT WORLD, 9 (November 1980), 26-28.

      Reports that prior to 1980, the OFCCP had been slow about
      enforcing the Rehabilitation Act of 1973. Indicates that
      during the 1980s, the OFCCP is "cracking down" on federal
      contractors to develop affirmative action plans for hiring
      and promoting handicapped individuals. Outlines several
      specific requirements that federal contractors must meet to
      be in compliance with the Act.

498. McGraw, Cathy. "The Rehabilitation Act of 1973." LEGAL
      RIGHTS OF THE HANDICAPPED. Columbia, S.C.: South Carolina
      Bar Association, October 30, 1981.

      Outlines major sections of the Act and cites judicial
      decisions related to each section.

499. Milk, Leslie B. "But Can They Do The Job?" HUMAN RIGHTS, 9
      (Spring 1980), 16-17.

500. _____. "The Key to Job Accommodations." PERSONNEL
      ADMINISTRATOR, 24 (January 1979), 31.

      Explains who is handicapped and the meaning of "reasonable
      accommodations." Outlines the reasonable accommodation
      process which include: Getting top management to support
      affirmative action for handicapped individuals; reviewing job
      descriptions to determine the type of accommodation needed;
      and reviewing medical standards for jobs to ensure they are
      job related. Believes that "most accommodations require more
      imagination than expense." Cites examples of cost saving
      techniques in accommodating handicapped individuals.

501. _____. "Not Business as Usual: The Disabled in
      Employment." EQUAL OPPORTUNITY FORUM, 7 (November 1979),
      10-11.

      Explains why the Rehabilitation Act of 1973 was needed and
      the definition of "handicapped" under the Act.

502. _____. "What Is Reasonable Accommodation?" CIVIL
      SERVICE JOURNAL, 19 (October-December 1978), 34-36.

503. Miller, Lee. "Hiring the Handicapped: An Analysis of Laws
      Prohibiting Discrimination Against the Handicapped in
      Employment." GONZAGA LAW REVIEW, 16 (No. 1 1980), 23-55.

      Focuses specifically on major provisions of the Rehabilita-
      tion Act of 1973 and the Washington Law Against Discrimina-
      tion. Believes that these two statutes do not require pre-
      ferential treatment for handicapped individuals but require
      employers to give them an opportunity to succeed. Suggests
      a method for employers to follow when analyzing the employ-
      ability of handicapped individuals. Discusses major concerns
      that employers have when considering the employment of handi-
      capped employees, e.g., workmen's compensation, absenteeism,
      safety, etc.

504. Nathanson, Robert B. and Jeffrey Lambert. "Integrating
     Disabled Employees Into the Workplace." PERSONNEL JOURNAL,
     60 (February 1981), 109-113.

     Contends that negative attitudes and feelings projected
     from co-workers and management toward handicapped employees
     are a major obstacle to successfully integrating disabled
     employees in the workforce. Presents actual case studies to
     illustrate the type of negative feelings directed at disabled
     employees.

505. Nicolai, Don F. and William J. Ricci. "Access to Buildings
     and Equal Employment Opportunity for the Disabled: Survey
     of State Statutes." TEMPLE LAW QUARTERLY, 50 (No. 4,
     1977), 1067-1085.

     Surveys state anti-discrimination statutes that require
     equal access to buildings, facilities, and transportation for
     disabled individuals. Finds that state statutes are vague
     and are ineffective in ensuring that handicapped individuals
     have easy access to private and public facilities. Indicates
     that architectural barriers have a detrimental impact on
     employment opportunity for handicapped workers. Recommends
     that state architectural barrier statutes be modified to
     effectively achieve their goals and purposes.

*   Northrup, James P. OLD AGE, HANDICAPPED, AND VIETNAM - ERA
     ANTI-DISCRIMINATION. See Item 584.

506. "Notes, Rehabilitating the Rehabilitation Act of 1973.
     BOSTON UNIVERSITY LAW REVIEW, 58 (March 1978), 247-274.

507. "The 504 Notice: Moving Toward A Civil Rights Act?" AMICUS,
     (July 1976), 12-14.

     Traces the development of the Rehabilitation Act of 1973
     and the Amendments to the Act through Congressional Subcom-
     mittees, Court actions, and the administrative process.

508. Nouri, Clement J. "Equal Opportunity for the Handicapped."
     PERSONNEL ADMINISTRATOR, 17 (March-April 1972), 38-40.

509. Olenick, Donald Jay. "Accommodating the Handicapped: Reha-
     bilitating Section 504 After Southeastern." COLUMBIA LAW
     REVIEW, 80 (January 1980), 171-191.

510. Pati, Gopal C. "Countdown on Hiring the Handicapped."
     PERSONNEL JOURNAL, 57 (March 1978), 144-153.

Outlines procedures for employers to follow to comply with
the Vocational Rehabilitation Act of 1973. Presents a summary of major studies conducted on the employment of handicapped individuals.

511. _____ and John I. Adkins, Jr. "Hiring the Handi-
     capped -- Compliance Is Good Business." HARVARD BUSINESS
     REVIEW, 58 (January-February 1980), 14.

     Contends that the Vocational Rehabilitation Act of 1973 has
     not been actively enforced since its passage by the federal
     government. States that 91% of corporations who have federal
     contracts affirmative action programs are not in compliance
     with the Act. Alerts employees that OFCCP is ". . . stepping
     up their efforts to enforce affirmative action requirements."
     Advises employers what steps to take to bring their programs
     in compliance with the law.

512. _____ and Michael J. Mezey. "Designing an Affirmative
     Action Program for the Handicapped." TRAINING AND DEVELOP-
     MENT JOURNAL, 32 (June 1978), 14-22.

513. Petersen, Donald J. "Paving the Way for Hiring the Handi-
     capped." PERSONNEL, 58 (March-April 1981), 43-52.

     Outlines affirmative action requirements for federal con-
     tractors to hire and promote qualified handicapped individ-
     uals, as required under Section 503 of the 1973 Rehabilita-
     tion Act. Discusses recruitment, personnel practices, accom-
     modation, accessibility, and human relations training. Pre-
     sents the results of a survey which showed that employers saw
     advantages to hiring and utilizing handicapped workers, e.g.,
     "greater dependability and reliability, better attendance,
     lower turnover, greater loyalty to the organization. . . ."

514. President's Committee on Employment of the Handicapped. THE
     ABC's OF HIRING PEOPLE WITH DISABILITIES. Washington,
     D.C.: Government Printing Office, 1978. 8 pp.

     Outlines positive approaches for employers to take when
     seeking and hiring qualified physically or mentally handi-
     capped workers.

515. _____. ALL YOU'LL EVER NEED TO KNOW ABOUT HIRING
     PEOPLE WITH DISABILITIES. Washington, D.C.: Government
     Printing Office, 1977. 7 pp.

     A handicapped employer with 100 employees gives a personal
     view of his experiences with hiring handicapped workers.
     Discredits various myths about hiring handicapped workers and

encourages other employers to take affirmative action to
locate and hire qualified handicapped workers.

516. _____. AMERICAN PROFILE: WHAT STATES ARE DOING (AND
CAN DO) TO HIRE THE HANDICAPPED. Washington, D.C.: Government Printing Office, 1975. 69 pp.

Results of a questionnaire sent to cities and counties
regarding employment of handicapped individuals. Finds that
a large number of those governmental entities who responded
did not have formal affirmative action programs to hire
handicapped individuals, nevertheless, handicapped workers
were being placed.

517. _____. EQUALIZING THE HANDICAPPED. Washington, D.C.:
Government Printing Office, 1975. 10 pp.

Highlights affirmative action requirements for employing
handicapped individuals under Section 503 of the Rehabilitation Act of 1973. Explains the purpose of the Act and which
governmental contractors are covered by the Act. Defines who
is considered handicapped and the meaning of "reasonable
accommodation." Stresses that affirmative action programs
for handicapped workers should be considered positive programs and not punitive.

518. _____. GUIDE TO JOB PLACEMENT OF MENTALLY RESTORED
PEOPLE. Washington, D.C.: Government Printing Office,
1977. 47 pp.

Provides guidelines to employers on job placement for
individuals who have been mentally restored or rehabilitated.
Explains who the mentally restored individuals are and the
kinds of special considerations they need to be placed.
Briefly explains employers' legal responsibility to hire
mentally restored people under Section 503 of the Rehabilitation Act of 1973.

519. _____. SELECTED STATE AND FEDERAL LAWS AFFECTING
EMPLOYMENT AND CERTAIN RIGHTS OF PEOPLE WITH DISABILITIES.
Washington, D.C.: Government Printing Office, 1980.
172 pp.

Summarizes selected state and federal laws related to
". . . integrating handicapped people into the mainstream of
American life." Chapter II focuses specifically on EEO and
affirmative action programs for handicapped workers and
applicants, e.g., the Fair Labor Standards Act, the Rehabilitation Act of 1973, Executive Order 11914, the Civil Service
Reform Act of 1978, Title VII, and the 1978 Amendments to the
Rehabilitation Act. Believes that employment discrimination
against handicapped workers occurs because there is a lack of

understanding from people on the potential of handicapped
workers.

520.   Primentel, Lynn. "Hiring the Able Disabled." MANAGEMENT
       WORLD, 9 (March 1979), 4-7.

       Alerts Federal contractors that the Federal government is
       taking a more serious position in enforcing the Rehabilita-
       tion Act of 1973. Briefly outlines the coverage, compliance
       requirements, and how to develop an affirmative action plan
       for handicapped individuals. Advises employers that they can
       receive tax credits when hiring handicapped individuals, and
       at the same time obtain employees who have a history of lower
       absenteeism and a low turnover rate.

*   Rabby, Rami. LOCATING, RECRUITING AND HIRING THE DISABLED.
       See Item 866.

521.   Rappaport, Cyril M. "Hiring the Handicapped." PERSONNEL
       ADMINISTRATOR, 25 (November 1980), 81-88.

       Recommends that employers review their employment practices
       and policies to ensure that handicapped individuals are being
       placed within the organization. Advises employers to re-
       evaluate job descriptions that have physical requirements.
       Maintains that employers, especially those with federal con-
       tracts make every effort to accommodate handicapped individu-
       als. Other topics discussed include: developing an outreach
       program, defining who is a handicapped person, and legal
       requirements under the Rehabilitation Act.

522.   Ray, Nancy. "Legislation by Implication: The Exercise of
       Legislative Authority Under the 1978 Amendments to Section
       504 of the Rehabilitation Act of 1973." KENTUCKY LAW
       JOURNAL, 68 (1979-80), 141-182.

       Points to procedural and substantive sections of the Reha-
       bilitation Act of 1973 which are vague and need further
       clarification. States that the statute does not clearly
       indicate whether there is a private right of action and does
       not clearly define the term "otherwise qualified handicapped
       individual." Concludes that the 1978 Amendments to the Act
       did not resolve the problem and recommends that Congress
       takes further action to clarify these "preliminary issues."

523.   Rothstein, Laura F.   Rights of Physically Handicapped Per-
       sons. New York: McGraw-Hill Book Company, 1984.   487 pp.

524. Russell, Harold. "The Handicapped: 'Mutual Benefits' In
     Government Service." CIVIL SERVICE JOURNAL, 10 (October-
     December 1969), 10-11.

     A brief review of the federal government's program to hire
     handicapped employees. Suggests areas where improvements
     could be made.

*   Sahlein, Stephen. THE AFFIRMATIVE ACTION HANDBOOK. See
     Item 970.

525. Sale, Richard T. "Employment." WHITE HOUSE CONFERENCE ON
     HANDICAPPED INDIVIDUALS - VOLUME ONE: AWARENESS PAPERS.
     Washington, D.C.: Government Printing Office, 1977, pp.
     205-216.

     Insists that despite various laws, regulations and special
     programs, a large number of handicapped workers are still
     unemployed and underemployed. Sees a conflict in attitudes
     between employers and handicapped workers concerning employ-
     ment. Seeks to resolve the difference in perception between
     employers and handicapped workers concerning the kind and
     type of work handicapped workers can perform. Discusses
     educational training, placement, and the rehabilitation of
     handicapped individuals under Section 503 of the Rehabilita-
     tion Act of 1973.

526. Schoenfeld, Benjamin N. "Civil Rights for the Handicapped
     Under the Constitution and Section 504 of the Rehabilita-
     tion Act." UNIVERSITY OF CINCINNATI LAW REVIEW, 49
     (No. 3, 1980), 580-610.

     Discusses efforts made by congress to eliminate discrimi-
     natory practices that prohibit handicapped individuals from
     obtaining their full constitutional rights. Focuses specifi-
     cally on Section 504 of the Rehabilitation Act; the Rehabili-
     tation, Comprehensive Services, and Developmental Disabili-
     ties Amendment of 1978; and the judicial systems' interpreta-
     tion of those efforts. Concludes that Section 504 and the
     1978 Amendments have made some strides in eliminating some
     of the barriers that handicapped individuals face; however,
     the coverage of the Act needs to be expanded to include more
     affirmative action requirements.

527. Schweisheimer, W. "Jobs for Handicapped Workers." SUPER-
     VISION, 31 (February 1969), 5-6.

*   Schweitzer, Nancy J. and John Deely. "Interviewing the
     Disabled Job Applicant." See Item 848.

528.   "Section 504 and the New Rights Mandates." AMICUS, (September 1977), 1-48.

       A collection of articles on the legislative history of
       Section 504. Include discussions on the coverage, complaint
       procedure, and compliance deadlines.

529.   Stephen, D. Erf. "Potluck Protections for Handicapped
       Discriminatees: The Need to Amend Title VII to Prohibit
       Discrimination on the Basis of Disability." LOYOLA UNI-
       VERSITY OF CHICAGO LAW JOURNAL, 8 (Spring 1977), 814-845.

       Proposes that Title VII be amended to include handicap dis-
       crimination as a cause of action. States that only public
       employers and employers who are federal contractors are
       presently covered by federal requirements to hire and promote
       qualified handicapped individuals. Private employers are
       not under similar federal requirements. Suggests ways that
       workers' compensation statutes can be modified to remove
       any undue hardship on private employers, if Title VII is
       amended to require employers to hire and promote handicapped
       individuals.

530.   Strom, Linda J. and Gerald R. Ferris. "Issues in Hiring the
       Handicapped: A Positive Outlook." PERSONNEL ADMINISTRA-
       TOR, 27 (August 1982), 75-81.

       Contends that even with federal legislative action, handi-
       capped individuals still are "largely unemployed and iso-
       lated." Finds that recruiters and interviewers tend to focus
       on what handicapped applicants "can't do in order to see what
       they can do." Believes that the future may bring new federal
       legislation to include handicap discrimination as a part of
       the 1964 Civil Rights Act. Cites studies that support that
       handicapped employees are highly productive employees and the
       cost of accommodating them on the job can be inexpensive.

531.   "Symposium on Employment Rights of the Handicapped." DEPAUL
       LAW REVIEW, 27 (Summer 1978), 943-1169.

       A collection of articles on the plight of handicapped indi-
       viduals to achieve full employment without discrimination.
       Includes discussions on handicap as a BFOQ, litigating handi-
       cap cases, arbitrating handicap complaints, and handicap
       discrimination in the Federal sector.

532.   "A Symposium -- The Rights of the Handicapped: Federal Non-
       discrimination Requirements Under the Rehabilitation Act
       of 1973." UNIVERSITY OF DAYTON LAW REVIEW, 3 (Summer
       1978), 387-458.

A collection of articles on the coverage, prohibition, and application of Section 504 of the Rehabilitation Act of 1973.

533. Taking Down the Barriers. JOURNAL OF AMERICAN INSURANCE, 58 (Spring 1982), 11-17.

534. Tanenbaum, Susan G. and Michael M. Tarnow. "Discrimination Against the Handicapped." NINTH ANNUAL INSTITUTE -- EQUAL EMPLOYMENT OPPORTUNITY COMPLIANCE. New York: Practicing Law Institute, 1980, pp. 209-226.

States that there is no uniform definition of the term handicap between statutes and regulations. Believes, however, that agencies and courts will give the term handicap a liberal interpretation. Explains reasonable accommodation requirements as mandated by the Department of Labor. Draws an analogy between the Supreme Court's interpretation of reasonable accommodation in TWA v. Hardison and the Department of Labor's interpretation. Briefly discusses how handicap complaints are processed by OFCCP and HEW. Concludes with a summary of judicial developments since the adoption of the Rehabilitation Act.

535. Trammell, Brian H. "The Rehabilitation Act of 1973: Is There an Implied Right of Action Under Section 504?" TENNESSEE LAW REVIEW, 49 (Spring 1982), 577-593.

Seeks to determine whether there is an implied right of private action under Section 504 of the Rehabilitation Act. Concludes that the legislative intent was to provide a private cause of action under the Act. Discusses major court decisions that have reviewed this issue, e.g., Cort v. Ash and Southeastern Community College v. Davis.

536. Turney, Harriet. "Defining the Handicapped: Section 504 of the Rehabilitation Act." UNIVERSITY OF DAYTON LAW REVIEW, 3 (Summer 1978), 391-404.

Analyzes each section of the Act which defines who is a "handicapped individual." Concludes that the Act does not clearly answer the question as to who is specifically covered by the Act. Points to sections of the definition that appear to be ambiguous and will probably lead to controversy and litigation. Sees the term "substantially limits" as an example of a term that needs further clarification. Believes there will be controversy over the inclusion of alcoholics and addicts in the definition. Argues that "more detailed examples" should have been included in defining who is handicapped under the Act.

537.   U.S. Civil Service Commission, Bureau of Intergovernmental
       Personnel Programs. EMPLOYMENT OF THE HANDICAPPED IN
       STATE AND LOCAL GOVERNMENT. Washington, D.C., Government
       Printing Office, 1977. 21 pp.

       A pamphlet designed to explain the "do's and don'ts" when
       employing and utilizing handicapped workers. Suggests ways
       to overcome attitudinal and architectural barriers. Recom-
       mends that employers conduct a job analysis for each job to
       determine the skills and abilities needed to perform the
       tasks. Explains that the employment of handicapped workers
       may only require minor adjustments on the worksite and in
       the use of equipment. Concludes that after handicapped
       employees are recruited, selected and placed, they may need
       "post-employment considerations" such as follow-up placement
       and training.

538.   _____. HANDBOOK OF SELECTIVE PLACEMENT IN FEDERAL
       CIVIL SERVICE EMPLOYMENT OF THE PHYSICALLY HANDICAPPED,
       THE MENTALLY RESTORED, THE MENTALLY RETARDED, THE
       REHABILITATED OFFENDER. Washington, D.C.: Government
       Printing Office, 1969. 42 pp.

539.   _____. "Hiring the Handicapped." EEO FOR STATE AND
       LOCAL GOVERNMENTS. Washington, D.C.: Government Printing
       Office, (Issue No. 10). 6 pp.

       Defines who handicapped employees are, the purpose of the
       Rehabilitation Act of 1973, and provides affirmative action
       guidelines on how to hire and promote handicap workers.

540.   _____. Personnel Research and Development Center,
       Bureau of Policies and Standards. TESTING THE HANDICAPPED
       FOR EMPLOYMENT PURPOSES: ADAPTATIONS FOR PERSONS WITH
       MOTOR HANDICAPS. Washington, D.C.: Government Printing
       Office, 1978. 15 pp.

541.   U.S. Commission on Civil Rights. ACCOMMODATING THE SPECTRUM
       OF INDIVIDUAL ABILITIES. Washington, D.C.: Government
       Printing Office, September, 1983. 173 pp.

       Provides a historical view of how handicapped individuals
       have been discriminated against in all phases of life,
       including employment. Defines who handicapped individuals
       are, summarizes various Federal civil rights laws that pro-
       hibit handicap discrimination, and explains the meaning of
       "reasonable accommodation" and "qualified handicapped
       individual."

HANDICAP DISCRIMINATION   119

542. _____. CIVIL RIGHTS ISSUES OF HANDICAPPED AMERICANS:
     PUBLIC POLICY IMPLICATION. Washington, D.C.: Government
     Printing Office, 1981. 691 pp.

     A compilation of testimony presented at a consultation
     sponsored by the Commission during 1980 to ". . . identify
     and examine civil rights issues relating to disabled persons
     in our society and to address potential solutions." Includes
     testimony and comments from 30 experts, authorities, advocacy
     groups on the rights of handicapped individuals.

543. U.S. Department of Education. SUMMARY OF EXISTING LEGISLA-
     TION RELATING TO THE HANDICAPPED. Washington, D.C.: G
     overnment Printing Office, 1980. 156 pp.

544. U.S. Department of Labor, Employment Standards Adminis-
     tration, Office of Federal Contract Compliance Programs.
     AFFIRMATIVE ACTION FOR THE HANDICAPPED. Washington, D.C.:
     Government Printing Office, April 1980. 140 pp.

     A handbook designed for equal employment opportunity spe-
     cialists who monitor, review, and evaluate affirmative action
     compliance of federal contractors. Discusses accessibility,
     accommodation, outreach and recruitment programs, and medical
     limitations of handicapped workers.

545. _____. A STUDY OF ACCOMMODATIONS PROVIDED TO HANDI-
     CAPPED EMPLOYEES BY FEDERAL CONTRACTORS -- FINAL REPORT,
     VOL I: STUDY FINDING. Washington, D.C.: Government
     Printing Office, 1982.

     Results of a national survey on federal contractors' per-
     formance in accommodating handicapped workers. Major com-
     ponents of the study included: "a survey of 2000 federal
     contractors . . . telephone interviews with 85 firms . . . a
     survey of disabled workers . . . intensive case studies
     . . ." Defines accommodation and presents data on the pre-
     valence of handicapped workers, types and cost of accommo-
     dation, and the impact of accommodation on workers. One
     major conclusion reached by the study is that accommodation
     is very much needed to employ handicapped workers.

546. _____. A STUDY OF ACCOMMODATIONS PROVIDED TO HANDI-
     CAPPED EMPLOYEES BY FEDERAL CONTRACTORS -- FINAL REPORT --
     VOL II: TEN CASE STUDIES. Washington, D.C.: Government
     Printing Office, 1982.

     Results of ten case studies on accommodating handicapped
     workers. All ten case studies were completed on federal
     contractors, e.g., Dow Chemical, Dupont, IBM, Lockheed,
     Union Carbide, etc. Each case study provides background

information on the company, accommodation policy, hiring
practices, and conclusions reached from the study.

*   U.S. Equal Employment Opportunity Commission. LAWS ADMINIS-
        TERED BY EEOC. See Item 121.

*   U.S. Manpower Administration. INTERVIEWING GUIDES FOR SPE-
        CIFIC DISABILITIES, HEARING IMPAIRMENTS. See Item 851.

547.   U.S. National Institute of Mental Health and the President's
        Committee on Employment of the Handicapped. AFFIRMATIVE
        ACTION TO EMPLOY MENTALLY RESTORED PEOPLE. Washington,
        D.C.: Government Printing Office, 1981. 17 pp.

548.   U.S. Office of Personnel Management. HANDBOOK OF JOB ANALY-
        SIS FOR REASONABLE ACCOMMODATION. Washington, D.C.:
        Government Printing Office, April 1982. 17 pp.

        Presents in succinct, yet understandable terms how the
        process of job analysis is directly related to the process
        of accommodating handicapped workers. States that the major
        process of planning accommodation include: conducting a job
        analysis; determining the functional characteristics of the
        worker; evaluating the worker's physical or mental limitation
        and the job requirement; and developing remedies and alter-
        natives.

549.   _____. HANDBOOK OF SELECTIVE PLACEMENT OF PERSONS
        WITH PHYSICAL AND MENTAL HANDICAPS IN FEDERAL CIVIL-SERVICE
        EMPLOYMENT. Washington, D.C.: Government Printing
        Office, 1981. 72 pp.

        Summarizes federal laws, policies, and programs that are
        designed to ensure that handicapped individuals are employed
        and promoted in the federal workforce.

550.   _____. Office of Affirmative Employment Programs.
        HANDBOOK ON REASONABLE ACCOMMODATION. Washington, D.C.:
        Government Printing Office, March 1980. 12 pp.

        A pamphlet designed to assist federal agencies to reason-
        ably accommodate handicapped workers. Defines reasonable
        accommodation as ". . . a logical adjustment made to a job
        and/or the work environment that enables a qualified handi-
        capped person to perform the duties of that position." Ex-
        plains that an employer may be excused for not accommodating
        a handicapped employee or applicant if undue hardship occurs.
        Provides examples of how employees and applicants can be
        reasonably accommodated.

551. _____. REASONABLE ACCOMMODATION FOR DEAF EMPLOYEES
     IN WHITE COLLAR JOBS. Washington, D.C.: Government
     Printing Office, 1982. 40 pp.

     Identifies the major problems that deaf individuals face in
     the workplace and recommends methods and techniques to rea-
     sonably accommodate them.

552. U.S. Senate Committee on Labor and Human Resources. EQUAL
     EMPLOYMENT OPPORTUNITY ACT OF 1979: HEARINGS . . . ON
     S.446, TO AMEND TITLE VII OF THE CIVIL RIGHTS ACT TO
     PROHIBIT DISCRIMINATION AGAINST INDIVIDUALS BECAUSE THEY
     ARE HANDICAPPED. Washington, D.C.: Government Printing
     Office, 1979.

553. Waltz, Anne. "Integrating Disabled Workers Into Your Work-
     force." PUBLIC PERSONNEL MANAGEMENT, 10 (Winter 1981),
     412-417.

     Suggests techniques and methods for hiring and placing
     qualified handicapped workers in the workforce.

554. Williams, C. Arthur, Jr. "Is Hiring the Handicapped Good
     Business?" JOURNAL OF REHABILITATION, 38 (March-April
     1972), 30-34.

555. Wolkinson, Benjamin W. "Arbitration and the Employment
     Rights of the Physically Disadvantaged." ARBITRATION
     JOURNAL, 36 (March 1981), 23-30.

556. Wright, William A. "Equal Treatment of the Handicapped by
     Federal Contractors." EMORY LAW JOURNAL, 26 (Winter 1977),
     65-106.

     Outlines the coverage of the Rehabilitation Act of 1973 and
     explains federal contractors' responsibilities in hiring and
     promoting handicapped individuals under the Act. Defines
     "who is handicapped," the meaning of "qualified" handicap,
     and handicap discrimination under the Act. Believes that
     courts will have difficulty in determining who are qualified
     handicapped individuals under the Act. Makes recommenda-
     tions on how the Act can be more effective.

557. "Writing an Affirmative Action Program for the Handicap."
     EEO TODAY, 6 (Summer 1979), 151-159.

     Indicates that government contractors and subcontractors
     who employ 50 or more employees and receive contracts of
     $50,000 or more are required to develop and maintain an
     affirmative action program, including provisions for the

employment of handicapped individuals. Provides a sample
affirmative action plan for the employment of handicapped
individuals.

558. Zimmer, Arno B. EMPLOYING THE HANDICAPPED, A PRACTICAL
        COMPLIANCE MANUAL. New York: AMACOM, 1981. 374 pp.

        Designed to assist employers to understand their responsi-
        bilities in employing handicapped employees. Topics includes
        discussions on federal and state laws affecting employers,
        e.g., Rehabilitation Act of 1973. Outlines the functions and
        powers of the Office of Federal Contract Compliance Programs.
        Suggests ways to effectively accommodate handicapped employ-
        ees and procedures on developing an affirmative action plan.

559. _____. "Smoothing the Way for the Handicapped
        Worker." SUPERVISORY MANAGEMENT, 26 (April 1981), 2-8.

AGE DISCRIMINATION IN EMPLOYMENT

560. Agatstein, David Joseph. "The Age Discrimination In Employ-
      ment Act of 1967: A Critique." NEW YORK LAW FORUM, 19
      (Fall 1973), 309-323.

      Details the coverage, prohibitions, and remedies under the
      Act. Criticizes the upper and lower age limitations of the
      Act, and recommends that age limitations be removed and the
      coverage be extended to all workers.

561. "The Age Discrimination In Employment Act: Highlights from a
      Management Seminar." INDUSTRIAL GERONTOLOGY, 18 (1973), 1.

562. "Age Discrimination In Employment." NEW YORK UNIVERSITY LAW
      REVIEW, 50 (October 1975), 924-951.

      Analyzes the impact of the Equal Protection Clause of the
      Constitution and the Age Discrimination Act of 1967 on chal-
      lenges to mandatory retirement and age ceilings in employment
      hiring. Indicates that courts have not been favorable to
      constitutional challenges. Recommends that exceptions to the
      Act be interpreted narrowly to ensure that courts success-
      fully prohibit age discrimination in employment.

563. American Bar Association, Commission on Legal Problems of the
      Elderly. AGE DISCRIMINATION IN EMPLOYMENT ACT, A SYMPOSIUM
      HANDBOOK FOR LAWYERS AND PERSONNEL PRACTITIONERS. Washing-
      ton, D.C., 1983. 453 pp.

      A collection of articles and papers on recent developments
      under the Act, litigating an age discrimination case, avoid-
      ing age discrimination complaints, and the future implication
      of the Act on age discrimination in employment.

564. Baroni, Barry J. "Age Discrimination in Employment: Some
      Guidelines for Employers." PERSONNEL ADMINISTRATOR, 26
      (May 1981), 97-101.

      Updates changes in the Age Discrimination in Employment
      Act of 1967, which includes the 1978 amendment and recent
      court decisions, e.g., United States v. McMann and Hodgson
      v. Greyhound Lines, Inc.

565. Batten, Michael D. "Ending Age Discrimination." CIVIL
      RIGHTS DIGEST, 11 (Winter 1979), 26-35.

*   Berlin, Philip E. "Avoiding Charges of Age Discrimination."
      See Item 666.

566. Bureau of National Affairs, Inc. 1978 AGE DISCRIMINATION
      ACT AMENDMENTS. Washington, D.C., 1978. 184 pp.

      Summarizes the major features of the 1978 Amendments to the
      Age Discrimination Act. Includes the full text of the Act,
      as amended and the House and Senate Reports on the Act.

567. Clauss, Carin Ann. "The Age Discrimination In Employment
      Act." EQUAL EMPLOYMENT PRACTICE GUIDE. Vol. I. Edited by
      John R. Erickson and Katherine Savers McGovern. Washing-
      ton, D.C.: Bureau of National Affairs, 1979, pp. V-1 -
      V-56.

      Gives an in-depth study of the Age Discrimination in Em-
      ployment Act. Discusses the purpose of the Act, coverage,
      exceptions to the Act, prima facie cases of age discrimina-
      tion, recordkeeping requirements, the 1978 amendments, and
      remedies to age discrimination.

568. Cleveland, Michael G. "Problems in Age Discrimination."
      PROCEEDINGS OF NEW YORK UNIVERSITY-THIRTY-THIRD ANNUAL
      NATIONAL CONFERENCE ON LABOR. Edited by Richard Adelman.
      New York: Matthew Binder, 1981, pp. 351-365.

      Indicates that more age discrimination cases are a result
      of the 1978 amendments to the Federal Age Discrimination in
      Employment Act (ADEA), the EEOC being assigned enforcement
      responsibilities to process age discrimination complaints,
      and the large labor force of older Americans. Discusses ways
      to identify possible age discrimination complaints, statis-
      tics in ADEA cases, proving an age discrimination case, age
      as a BFOQ, and planning for the future to accommodate the
      older worker.

569. Commerce Clearing House, Inc. Labor Law Reports Employment
      Practices: NEW 1978 MANDATORY RETIREMENT AND AGE DISCRIMI-
      NATION RULES. Chicago, IL,, April 6, 1978. 79 pp.

      A comprehensive study of the Age Discrimination in Employ-
      ment Act and the 1978 amendments. Explains the coverage,
      enforcement procedures, and compliance procedures under the
      Act. Include a brief summary of state laws on age discrimi-
      nation, the full text of the Act, and the amendments.

570. Connolly, Walter B., Jr. "Age Discrimination In Employment
      Act Amendment of 1978." 1978 MANDATORY RETIREMENT-AGE LAW
      AMENDMENTS: PLANNING LEGAL AND PERSONNEL COMPLIANCE.
      Edited by Arthur H. Kroll. New York: Harcourt Brace
      Jovanovich, Publishers, 1978, pp. 27-48.

      Outlines provisions of the Age Discrimination in Employment
      Act Amendments of 1978 and explains the changes and modifi-
      cations that the Amendments had on the 1967 Act.

*   Cramer, Robert J. "State Deferral of Complaints Under the
      Age Discrimination in Employment Act." See Item 673.

571. Cuddy, Robert W. "Age Discrimination Amendments and Their
      Impact on Personnel." EMPLOYEE RELATIONS LAW JOURNAL, 4
      (Winter 1978-1979), 339-345.

572. Edelman, Charles D. and Ilene C. Siegler. FEDERAL AGE DIS-
      CRIMINATION IN EMPLOYMENT LAW: SLOWING DOWN THE GOLD WATCH.
      Charlottesville, VA.: The Michie Company, 1978. 353 pp.

      Provides backgound information on the science of gerontol-
      ogy. Explains the demographic profile, and the physical and
      attitudinal aspects of older workers. Gives an in-depth
      study of the Federal Age Discrimination in Employment Act of
      1967. Discusses the coverage, purpose, civil action, reme-
      dies, and recordkeeping. Includes a 1980 cumulative supple-
      ment which updates the bound volume.

573. Finger, Joel L. and Thomas C. Greble. "The Impact of Age
      Discrimination on Reductions-in-Force." NATIONAL LAW
      JOURNAL, 4 (August 30, 1982), 6.

      Advises employers to be conscious of the possibility of an
      age discrimination complaint when reducing the workforce.
      Indicates that there is a greater possibility of employers
      being charged with an age discrimination complaint because
      older workers are more knowledgeable about the law, have a
      more difficult time finding other employment, and because a
      large number of managers and executives are older. Summa-
      rizes exceptions and defenses to the Age Discrimination Act
      and analyzes recent court decisions related to layoffs and
      age discrimination.

*   Green, Ronald. "Trends in Age Discrimination Litigation."
      See Item 1042.

574. Greenberger, Robert S. "Fired Employees in 40s Filing more
      Bias Suits." WALL STREET JOURNAL, 198 (October 8, 1981),
      31.

575. Greenlaw, Paul S. and John P. Kohl. "Age Discrimination in
     Employment Guidelines." PERSONNEL JOURNAL, 61 (March
     1982), 224-228.

     Compares the similarities between the Department of Labor's
     (DOL) interpretations of the Age Discrimination in Employment
     Act of 1967 (ADEA) with the Equal Employment Opportunity
     Commission's (EEOC) guidelines on the ADEA. The enforcement
     responsibility of the ADEA was transferred from DOL to EEOC
     on July 1, 1979. The EEOC issued final guidelines on the Act
     on September 29, 1981. The new guidelines modified and
     extended DOL's interpretation of the Act. A major modifi-
     cation made by the EEOC's guidelines was to eliminate the
     wage-rate reductions prohibition. The guidelines also
     extended the protected age range.

*   Hartman, Gerald S. "Management Personnel Practices: The
     Do's and Don'ts of EEO Compliance." See Item 43.

576. International City Management Association. AGE DISCRIMINA-
     TION: WHAT YOU SHOULD KNOW. Washington, D.C., 1981.
     7 pp.

     Gives answers to commonly asked questions about the Age
     Discrimination Act. Provides a glossary of terms related to
     the Act and a list of regional offices of the EEOC.

577. Kovarsky, Irving and Joel Kovarsky. "Economic, Medical and
     Legal Aspects of the Age Discrimination Laws in Employ-
     ment." VANDERBILT LAW REVIEW, 27 (October 1974), 839-925.

578. Kroll, Arthur H. THE 1978 MANDATORY RETIREMENT-AGE LAW
     AMENDMENTS: PLANNING LEGAL AND PERSONNEL COMPLIANCE. New
     York: Harcourt Brace Jovanovich Publishers, 1978. 381 pp.

     A collection of articles on the coverage, procedural re-
     quirements, and modifications made by the Amendments on the
     1967 Age Discriminations Act. Discusses the impact the
     Amendments will have on retirement programs, judicial liti-
     gation, benefits, pension plans, and personnel policies.
     Includes various memorandums, conference reports, and spe-
     cial bulletins that have been issued from the private and
     public sector.

*   Larson, E. Richard. SUE YOUR BOSS -- RIGHTS AND REMEDIES
     FOR EMPLOYMENT DISCRIMINATION. See Item 53.

579. Lewis, Craig J. "The Age Discrimination in Employment Act
     of 1967: A Practical Application." BAYLOR LAW REVIEW, 24
     (Fall 1972), 601-609.

Highlights the coverage and exceptions to the Act and
focuses on the Fifth Circuit's decision in <u>Hodgson v. First
Federal Saving and Loan Association of Broward County,
Florida</u>, which involves the enforcement provisions of the
Act.

580.   Liddle, Jeffrey L.   "Disparate Treatment Claims Under ADEA:
       The Negative Impact of <u>McDonnell Douglas v. Green</u>." EM-
       PLOYEE RELATIONS LAW JOURNAL, 5 (Spring 1980), 549-559.

581.   Linenberger, Patricia and Timothy J. Keaveny, "Age Discrimi-
       nation In Employment: A Guide for Employers." THE PER-
       SONNEL ADMINISTRATOR, 24 (July 1979), 87-98.

       Explains the Age Discrimination In Employment Act of 1967
       (ADEA), the 1978 amendments, related court decisions, and the
       Department of Labor's interpretative statements. Indicates
       that the ADEA is a combination of Title VII and the Fair
       Labor Standards Act. The Act prohibits age discrimination
       in employment of employees between the ages of 40 and 70.
       Cites circumstances where the Act does not prohibit an em-
       ployer from discharging an employee between 40 and 70. Pro-
       vides suggestions to employers on how to prevent and reduce
       the number of age discrimination complaints. Concludes that
       where an employer is found to have discriminated on the basis
       of age, the penalty in dollars and cents can be costly.

*   Linnick, Stuart.   "Investigation and Discovery in Sex Harass-
       ment, Wrongful Discharge and Age Discrimination Litiga-
       tion." See Item 336.

582.   Macdonald, Robert M.   MANDATORY RETIREMENT AND THE LAW.
       Washington, D.C.: American Enterprise Institute for
       Public Policy Research, 1978. 29 pp.

       Discusses the major provisions of the Age Discrimination in
       Employment Act of 1967 and the 1978 amendments. Present the
       arguements for and against mandatory retirement. Explains
       how the Act ". . . will work to the advantage of some people,
       [and] to the disadvantage of others." Concludes that the
       Amendments will have a greater impact on the employment of
       individuals between the ages of 40 and 70 than was antici-
       pated.

583.   Marcus, Sumner and Jon Christoffersen.   "Discrimination and
       the Older Worker, Public Policy Not Yet Effective." BUSI-
       NESS HORIZON, 12 (October 1969), 83-89.

       Outlines various aspects of employment problems that older
       workers face. Evaluates the Age Discrimination Act of 1967
       and explains management's responsibilities under the Act.

584. Northrup, James P. OLD AGE, HANDICAPPED, AND VIETNAM - ERA
     ANTI-DISCRIMINATION. Rev. ed. Philadelphia, PA.: Univer-
     sity of Pennsylvania, Wharton School, Industrial Research
     Unit, 1980. 234 pp.

585. "Note, The Age Discrimination In Employment Act of 1967."
     HARVARD LAW REVIEW, 90 (December 1976), 380-411.

586. "Note, The Age Discrimination In Employment: The Problem of
     the Older Worker." NEW YORK UNIVERSITY LAW REVIEW, 41
     (1966), 383-424.

     Explains the social and economic impact that age discrimi-
     nation in employment has on older workers. Discusses the
     forms that age discrimination can come in, e.g., advertising,
     hiring, and promotion restrictions. Examines various state
     and federal laws that prohibit age discrimination in employ-
     ment, the exception under the Act, and the legal standards
     required to prove an age discrimination complaint. Maintains
     that the Federal government should take an active role in
     eliminating arbitrary age discrimination. Outlines various
     federal proposals to prohibit age discrimination.

587. "Protecting the Older Worker." UNIVERSITY OF MICHIGAN
     JOURNAL OF LAW REFORM, 6 (Fall 1972), 214-231.

588. Quinn, Joseph F. WAGE DETERMINATION AND DISCRIMINATION AMONG
     OLDER WORKERS. Madison, WI.: University of Wisconsin,
     1977.

589. Quirk, Daniel A. "Public Policy Note: Age Discrimination
     In Employment -- Some Recent Developments." INDUSTRIAL
     GERONTOLOGY, 1 (Summer 1974), 77-80.

*   Sahlein, Stephen. THE AFFIRMATIVE ACTION HANDBOOK. See
     Item 970.

590. Schuchat, Theodor. "The Age Discrimination In Employment
     Act." INDUSTRIAL GERONTOLOGY, No. 1 (Spring 1969), 31-33.

     Traces the events leading up to the passage of the Act.
     Explains the coverage, exceptions, enforcement powers,
     and the effective date of the Act. Projects that the Act
     will make progress in combating age discrimination in the
     workforce.

591. Schuster, Michael H. and Christopher S. Miller. "Performance
      Evaluations As Evidence In ADEA Cases." LABOR RELATIONS
      LAW JOURNAL, 6 (Spring 1981), 561-583.

592. Selden, Lauren. "The Supreme Court and Mandatory Retirement."
      EQUAL OPPORTUNITY FORUM, 6 (June 1979), 10.

      Analyzes Supreme Court decisions that have had an impact on
      the employment of older individuals. Concludes that "the
      Court has turned its back on the older citizen. . . ."

*   Sheblak, Vernon. "The Older Worker: Employment and Training."
      See Item 888.

593. Snyder, Robert A. and Billie Brandon. "Riding the Third
      Wave: Staying on Top of ADEA Complaints." PERSONNEL
      ADMINISTRATOR, 28 (February 1983), 41-47.

      Advises managers that the number of age discrimination
      complaints filed has increased substantially. Explains the
      reasons for the increase of age discrimination complaints and
      advises employers how to successfully defend such charges.

594. Steffeck, Cheri. "Age Discrimination? It's Illegal."
      DYNAMIC MATURITY, 9 (July 1974), 32-34.

*   Sullivan, Charles A.; Michael J. Zimmer; and Richard F.
      Richards. FEDERAL STATUTORY LAW OF EMPLOYMENT DISCRIMI-
      NATION. See Item 105.

595. U.S. Civil Service Commission. "Facts About Age Discrimi-
      nation." EEO FOR STATE AND LOCAL GOVERNMENTS. Issue
      No. 11. Washington, D.C.: Government Printing Office,
      1975. 6 pp.

      States that among the reasons the Age Discrimination Act
      was passed was that a large portion of unemployed workers
      were between the ages of 40-65 and employers arbitrarily set
      age limits on jobs without regard to performance. Finds that
      employers who have discriminated on the basis of age have
      found their actions costly. To prevent age discrimination,
      an employer should review recruitment practices, the employ-
      ment application, employment tests, and the selection pro-
      cedure to ensure compliance with the law.

596. U.S. Commission on Civil Rights. THE AGE DISCRIMINATION
      STUDY. Washington, D.C.: Government Printing Office,
      December 1977. 55 pp.

Studies ten federal programs to determine whether discrimination exist on the basis of age in the administration of the
programs. Finds that [d]iscrimination on the basis of age in
the delivery of federally-supported services and benefits
exist to some extent in each Federal program examined."
Examines the reasons age discrimination exist and recommends
various corrective actions, including amending the Age Discrimination Act of 1975 which prohibit discrimination in
federally assisted programs.

597. _____. THE AGE DISCRIMINATION STUDY-PART II. Washington, D.C.: Government Printing Office, January 1979.
298 pp.

Describes the methodology and data used in a report re-
leased by the Commission in 1978 which found that age discrimination existed in ten federally assisted programs.

598. U.S. Employment Standards Administration. AGE DISCRIMINA-
TION IN EMPLOYMENT ACT OF 1967, A REPORT COVERING ACTIVI-
TIES UNDER THE ACT DURING 1972. Washington, D.C.: Govern-
ment Printing Office, 1973.

*   U.S. Equal Employment Opportunity Commission. LAWS ADMINIS-
TERED BY EEOC. See Item 121.

599. _____. PERSONS 40-70: NOTE, AGE DISCRIMINATION IS
AGAINST THE LAW. Washington, D.C.: Government Printing
Office, December, 1982.

Briefly outlines the major provisions of the Age Discrimination Act, including the coverage, exceptions, filing private suits, and filing charges of discrimination.

600. U.S. Office of Personnel Management, Office of Planning and
Evaluation. AN INTERIM REPORT ON THE EFFECT OF AGE DIS-
CRIMINATION IN EMPLOYMENT ACT AMENDMENTS OF 1978 ON THE
FEDERAL WORKFORCE. Washington, D.C.: Government Printing
Office, 1981.

601. Walker, James W. and Harriet L. Lazer. THE END OF MANDATORY
RETIREMENT. New York: John Wiley & Sons, 1978. 223 pp.

Reviews the 1978 amendments to the Age Discrimination Act
and discusses the implications of the Act on mandatory retirement. Suggests that personnel selections, promotions
and the criteria for termination be absent of age bias. Provides a checklist for managers to follow in complying with
age discrimination laws. Summarizes court decisions related

to age discrimination and provides management with information on counseling employees for pre-retirement and career
development.

602. "What Happens When an Age Complaint is Filed." EEO REVIEW,
      (February 1977), 6-8.

      Briefly outlines the Department of Labor, Wage and Hour
      Division's procedures for processing age discrimination
      complaints.

603. Weaver, Peter. "Age Discrimination Is Against the Law."
      DYNAMIC YEAR, 16 (March-April 1981), 64-69.

THE CIVIL RIGHTS ACT OF 1972

604. Bureau of National Affairs, Inc. THE EQUAL EMPLOYMENT
OPPORTUNITY ACT OF 1972. Washington, D.C., 1974. 423 pp.

Gives a comprehensive analysis of the legislative history,
congressional reports, coverage, prohibitions, enforcement
powers, and exemptions under the Act. States that the Act
primarily expanded the coverage of Title VII of the Civil
Rights Act of 1964 and increased the enforcement powers of
the EEOC, e.g., the EEOC may now bring civil suits in federal district court to enforce the statute.

605. Dorman, J. Michael. - "Federal Employee Civil Actions Under
The Equal Employment Opportunity Act of 1972: The Right to
De Novo Review." HOUSTON LAW REVIEW, 12 (October 1974),
178-190.

Seeks to determine whether federal employees who file
discrimination suits in federal district court involves a
trial de novo (new record) or whether the court is merely
reviewing the EEOC's administrative record. Indicates that
neither the 1972 Act nor the legislative history is clear
on this issue. Recommends that administrative records be
admissible during a trial de novo.

606. Grossman, Harry. "The Equal Employment Opportunity Act of
1972, Its Implications for the State and Local Government
Manager." PUBLIC PERSONNEL MANAGEMENT, 2 (September-
October 1973), 370-379.

* Hunter, James M. and Milton C. Branch. "Equal Employment
Opportunities: Administrative Procedures and Judicial
Developments Under Title VII of the Civil Rights Act of
1964 and the Equal Employment Act of 1972." See Item 47.

* Margolin, Bessie. "Management-Union Confrontation 1972 New
Frontiers: Who Discriminates Against Women?" See Item
219.

607. McManis, Charles R. "Racial Discrimination in Government
Employment: A Problem of Remedies for Unclean Federal
Hands." GEORGETOWN LAW JOURNAL, 63 (July 1975), 1203-1244.

Explains that Congress' purpose in passing the Equal Employment Opportunity Act of 1972 was to provide EEO for
minorities in the public sector. Prior to passage of the
1972 amendment, various federal agencies had a track record
of discriminating against minorities. Finds that the 1972
amendment has not totally eliminated all the administrative
obstacles to Federal workers when filing an employment discrimination complaint.

*   National Association of Attorneys General, Committee on the
       Office of Attorney General. EQUAL EMPLOYMENT OPPORTUNITY:
       AN OVERVIEW OF LEGAL ISSUES. See Item 70.

608.   National Civil Service League. FEDERAL MANDATE FOR AFFIRMA-
       TIVE ACTION: A NATIONAL CIVIL SERVICE LEAGUE GUIDEBOOK
       FOR PUBLIC EMPLOYERS. Washington, D.C., 1974. 47 pp.

       Finds that with the passage of the Equal Employment Oppor-
       tunity Act of 1972, public employers are now prohibited from
       discriminating in employment decisions. Includes the full
       text of the 1972 Act, Title VII, the EEOC's Guidelines on
       Employee Selection Procedures, the EEOC's Guidelines on Dis-
       crimination Because of Sex, and Executive Order 11246.

609.   Rose, Winfield H. and Tiang Ping Chia. "The Impact of the
       Equal Employment Opportunity Act of 1972 on Black Employ-
       ment in the Federal Service: A Preliminary Analysis."
       PUBLIC ADMINISTRATION REVIEW, 38 (May/June 1978), 245-251.

       Sketches the historical development of black employment in
       the federal civil service from 1883 to the passage of the
       Equal Employment Opportunity Act of 1972. Analyzes the im-
       pact of the Act on the placement of blacks in selected pay
       schedules. Finds that blacks are generally placed in lower
       levels of all schedules and few in higher levels. Observes
       that some progress is being made to place blacks in higher
       schedules, however, sees no significant impact of the Act
       on the placement of blacks in higher level schedules.

610.   Sape, George P. and Thomas J. Hart. "Title VII Reconsidered:
       Equal Employment Opportunity of 1972." GEORGE WASHINGTON
       LAW REVIEW, 40 (July 1972), 824-889.

       Gives a comprehensive analysis of the legislative history,
       congressional proceedings, and major provisions of the 1972
       amendments to Title VII. Suggests that the amendments will
       strengthen the enforcement provisions of Title VII.

611.   U.S. Civil Service Commission, Bureau of Intergovernmental
       Programs. EQUAL EMPLOYMENT OPPORTUNITY IN STATE AND LOCAL
       GOVERNMENTS: A GUIDE FOR AFFIRMATIVE ACTION. Washington,
       D.C.: Government Printing Office, 1972.

       States that the Equal Employment Opportunity Act of 1972
       prohibit state and local governments from discriminating in
       employment as provided by the Civil Rights Act of 1964.
       Provides a step by step program for state and local govern-
       ment agencies to follow in developing an affirmative action
       program.

*   U.S. Equal Employment Opportunity Commission. JOB DISCRIMI-
       NATION - LAWS AND RULES YOU SHOULD KNOW. See Item 120.

THE UNIFORM SELECTION GUIDELINES AND ADVERSE IMPACT

612.   American Society for Personnel Administration.   "Adverse
       Impact Defense Invalid."   RESOURCE, (August 1982), 1.

       Interprets the Supreme Court's decision in Connecticut v.
       Teal as a rejection to the "bottom line" theory defense to
       adverse impact claims.   In Connecticut v. Teal, the court
       held that ". . . Title VII focuses on the individual rather
       than the minority group as a whole. Therefore, the 'correct'
       final selection of minorities does not eliminate the dis-
       crimination suffered by the applicants who were eliminated
       from the selection process because of the operation of a
       non-validated test." Advises employers to review all com-
       ponents of their selection process for discriminatory
       practices.

613.   Beatty, Richard W.; H. John Bernardin; and Walter Jensen, Jr.
       "The New Uniform Guidelines on Employee Selection Proce-
       dures In the Context of University Personnel Decisions."
       Personnel Psychology, 33 (Summer 1980), 301-316.

       Discusses the impact of the Guidelines on student evalua-
       tions as a valid criteria for faculty selection, retention,
       and as a basis for deciding other personnel related matters.
       Suggests that student evaluations are not in compliance with
       the Guidelines. Defines adverse impact, criterion related
       validity, and content validity.

614.   Bemis, Stephen E. "Systems for Measuring and Assessing Ad-
       verse Impact." PUBLIC PERSONNEL MANAGEMENT, 7 (November-
       December 1978) 354-357.

       Encourages employers to maintain an employment data system
       to monitor employment decisions as a means of determining
       whether adverse impact exist.

615.   Blumrosen, Alfred W. "The Bottom Line In Equal Employment
       Guidelines: Administering a Polycentric Problem."
       ADMINISTRATIVE LAW REVIEW, 33 (Summer 1981), 323-349.

616.   _____. "The 'Bottom Line' after Connecticut v. Teal."
       EMPLOYEE RELATIONS LAW JOURNAL, 8 (Spring 1983), 572-586.

Criticizes the Supreme Court's decision in Teal and concludes that the court erred in their decision and reasoning.
States that the Teal decision held that the "bottom line"
theory was not a complete defense to a claim of discrimination in a selection procedure, even were the selection procedure had no adverse impact on the employment of minorities.
Believes that the decision may have a negative impact on
affirmative action, and advises the EEOC to amend the Uniform Guidelines On Employee Selection to further protect
employers who have taken affirmative action to hire and promote minorities.

617.   Boisseau, Richard R. and James L. Mackay. "Job-Related
       Selection Procedures Under the Uniform Guidelines." EEO
       TODAY, 7 (Winter 1980-81), 301-312.

       States that the Uniform Guidelines on Employee Selection
       Procedures, 29 C.F.R. Part 1609, were adopted by the Equal
       Employment Opportunity Commission, the Justice and Labor
       Departments, and the Civil Service Commission. Under the
       Guidelines, adverse impact exists when the ". . . selection
       rate for minority applicants is less than 80 percent of the
       selection rate for majority applicants." If adverse impact
       exist, the "test or other selection criterion" must be vali-
       dated to prove that it is job-related. Concludes that the
       Guidelines recognize three acceptable methods of validating a
       "test or other selection criterion": criterion-related vali-
       dation, content validation, and construct validation.

618.   Cahoon, Susan A. "Employee Selection Procedures--Uniform
       Guidelines at Last." SOLVING EEO PROBLEMS: A GUIDE TO
       EEO LAW AND PRACTICE. New York: Executive Enterprises
       Publication, Co., Inc., 1980, pp. 137-145.

       Traces the origin and events that led to the issuance of
       the Proposed Uniform Guidelines on Employee Selection Pro-
       cedures by the EEOC and other federal agencies. Summarizes
       the basic features of the Guidelines and predicts the future
       impact of the Guidelines on employers' efforts to prevent
       employment discrimination.

619.   Cronbach, Lee J.; Elanna Yalow; and Gary Schaeffer. "A
       Mathematical Structure for Analyzing Fairness in Selec-
       tion." PERSONNEL PSYCHOLOGY, 33 (Winter 1980), 693-704.

*   Curry, Theodore H. "A Common-sense Management Approach to
       Employee Selection and EEO Compliance for the Smaller
       Employer." See Item 24.

*   Executive Enterprises Publication Co. SOLVING EEO PROBLEMS:
       A GUIDE TO EEO LAW AND PRACTICE. See Item 33.

*   Greenlaw, Paul S. and John P. Kohl. "Selection Interviewing
        and the New Uniform Federal Guidelines." See Item 835.

620.   Hills, Frederick S. "Job Relatedness v. Adverse Impact in
        Personnel Decision-Making." PERSONNEL JOURNAL, 59 (March
        1980), 211.

*   Horstman, Dee Ann S. "New Judicial Standards for Adverse
        Impact: Their Meaning for Personnel Practices." See Item
        1046.

621.   Klinefelter, John and James Thompkins. "Adverse Impact in
        Employment Selection." PUBLIC PERSONNEL MANAGEMENT, 5
        (May-June 1976), 199-204.

        Defines adverse impact as ". . . the total employment pro-
        cess which results in a significantly higher percentage of a
        protected group in the candidate population being rejected
        for employment, placement, or promotion." The four basic
        approaches to proving adverse impact include "disparate
        rejection rates, restricted policy, population comparisons,
        [and the] McDonnell Douglas test." Concludes that the
        "disparate rejection rates" are used more often than the
        other approaches.

622.   Koral, Alan M. "Practical Applications of the Uniform Guide-
        lines: What to Do 'Til the Agency Comes." EMPLOYEE RELA-
        TIONS LAW JOURNAL, 5 (Spring 1980), 473-492.

        Provides an overview of "crucial provisions" of the Uniform
        Selection Guidelines. Explains adverse impact, the bottom
        line concept, and validation of selection procedures. Ad-
        vises employers to use external availability numbers rather
        than applicant flow data when the bottom line assessment is
        made; to examine each component of personnel procedures when
        adverse impact is shown, especially test; and to analyze the
        benefits, cost and alternative selection procedure before
        validating the procedure.

623.   Marr, Richard and Joseph Schneider. "Self-assessment test
        for the 1978 Uniform Guidelines on Employee Selection
        Procedures." THE PERSONNEL ADMINISTRATOR, 26 (May 1981),
        103-108.

        Presents twenty-five questions on the Uniform Guidelines on
        Employee Selection Procedures test the reader's knowledge
        and understanding of the guidelines.

*   McCullough, Kenneth J. SELECTING EMPLOYEES SAFELY UNDER THE
        LAW. See Item 62.

624. Miner, Mary Green and John B. Miner. UNIFORM GUIDELINES ON
      EMPLOYEE SELECTION PROCEDURES. Washington, D.C.: The
      Bureau of National Affairs, 1980. 80 pp.

      Briefly analyzes major provisions of the Uniform Guide-
      lines. Provides a summary on what steps an employer should
      follow to comply with the guidelines, the "bottom-line" con-
      cept, "suitable alternative procedures" and "documentation
      requirements." Includes the full text of the Guidelines,
      the EEOC's Questions and Answers on the Guidelines, and a
      bibliography on testing.

625. Mobley, William H. "Meeting Government Guidelines on Testing
      and Selection." THE PERSONNEL ADMINISTRATOR, 19 (November-
      December 1974), 42-48.

      Examines five major issues involving employment testing:
      "the legality and utility of testing, the 'adverse effect'
      criterion, evidence of validity, the differential prediction
      hypothesis, and where to go from here." States that some
      employers have abandoned testing because of the high cost of
      validation and to avoid compliance reviews. Employers who
      use testing as a selection device should conduct a statisti-
      cal analysis to determine whether minority applicants are
      being disqualified at a significantly higher rate than non-
      minorities. Evidence of test validation may be necessary
      where adverse impact exist. Believes that tests can be used
      in a non-discriminatory manner where they are developed "by
      sound reasoning and good research."

626. Quaintance, Marilyn K. "The Impact of the Uniform Selection
      Guidelines on Public Merit Systems." PUBLIC PERSONNEL
      MANAGEMENT, 9 (No. 3, 1980), 125-133.

      Highlights the implications of the guidelines on personnel
      selections in the public sector and outlines a "plan-of-
      action" for employers to comply with the regulations.

627. Robertson, Clendenin P. "Uniform Selection Guidelines in a
      Nutshell." EQUAL EMPLOYMENT PRACTICE GUIDE. Edited by
      John R. Erickson and Katherine Savers McGovern. Washing-
      ton, D.C.: Bureau of National Affairs, 1979, pp. II-1 -
      II-15.

      Believes that the guidelines are easy to understand and
      that the government acted responsibly in issuing the guide-
      lines. Concludes that employers have flexibility in comply-
      ing with the guidelines.

628. Robertson, Peter C. "EEO Issues and Employment: The Search
      for Alternatives - The Need For Research Under The Uniform

Guidelines on Employee Selection Procedures." LABOR LAW
JOURNAL, 30 (August 1979), 483-489.

Focuses on the Guidelines' requirement that an employer
search for alternative selection procedures when the procedures do not predict "probable job performance" or/and have
an adverse impact on protected class individuals. Recommends
that futher research be conducted to find ". . . alternative
employment systems and alternative methods of employee selection . . . which will eliminate the adverse impact that
existing systems have on minorities and women. . . ."

629. Rubenfeld, Stephen A. and Michael D. Crino. "The Uniform
     Guidelines: A Personnel Decision-Making Perspective."
     EMPLOYEE RELATIONS LAW JOURNAL, 7 (Summer 1981), 105-121.

     Gives an analytical overview of the Uniform Guidelines on
     Employee Selection Procedures. States that the guidelines
     apply ". . . not only to tests but to virtually all aspects
     of the processes used in selection, promotion, demotion, and
     the determination of eligibility for training or transfer."
     In most cases where no adverse impact has been found in the
     selection process, the guidelines are not applicable. If
     adverse impact is found in the selection process the employer
     has violated the guidelines. Where "bottom line" numbers of
     minorities and women selected indicate that no adverse impact
     exist, the guidelines do not apply. Nevertheless, there are
     exceptions to the "bottom line" principles that will permit
     an employer's selection process to be reviewed by govern-
     mental enforcement agencies. Suggests the following options
     to employers to comply with the guidelines where adverse
     impact exist: review the recruitment procedures to adjust
     applicant flow data; provide personnel and EEO training to
     persons who make personnel selections to ensure they under-
     stand personnel policy; and make adjustments in the selection
     process to comply with the guidelines. In making adjust-
     ments, the abandonment of an entire selection device, e.g.,
     testing, interviewing, may create more problems than it
     solves, especially in cost. Concludes that where the selec-
     tion process or device has an adverse impact, the process or
     device may be justified due to a business necessity.

630. Rubin, Ronald B. "The Uniform Guidelines on Employee Selec-
     tion Procedures: Compromises and Controversies." CATHOLIC
     UNIVERSITY LAW REVIEW, 28 (Spring 1979), 605-634.

     Compares the Uniform Selection Guidelines with prior fed-
     eral regulations on employment testing. Discusses test
     validation, judicial interpretation of the guidelines, and
     adverse impact. Indicates that the guidelines "undoubtedly
     will advance fair employment laws" and will ensure that
     selection procedures are more standardized. Concludes that
     even with the many positive benefits derived from the guide-
     lines, there still exist the conflict between "test validity"

and "test fairness." Believes that the guidelines fail to
resolve this issue.

631. Schanie, Charles F. and William L. Holley. "An Interpreta-
      tive Review of the Federal Uniform Guidelines on Employee
      Selection Procedures." PERSONNEL ADMINISTRATOR, 25 (June
      1980), 44-48.

      Discusses selection procedures, validation and record-keep-
      ing requirements under the guidelines. Concludes that em-
      ployers should validate their selection procedures, regard-
      less of what the selection rates indicate. Believes that
      validating selection procedures will ". . . ensure the
      selection of the best candidates available."

*   Schwartz, Donald J. and Patricia E. Shahen. "Avoiding Dis-
      crimination Suits." See Item 1069.

632. Sharf, James C. "Uniform Guidelines: Competence or Num-
      bers?" EQUAL EMPLOYMENT PRACTICE GUIDE. Edited by John
      R. Erickson and Katherine Savers McGovern. Washington,
      D.C.: Bureau of National Affairs, 1979, pp. II-70 - II-84.

      Argues that if the guidelines are literally applied, it is
      a "numbers game." Believes that the guidelines force employ-
      ers to hire employees based on race and sex to avoid adverse
      impact. Concludes that the guidelines go beyond the intent
      of Congress and Supreme Court decisions.

*   Siegel, Jerome. PERSONNEL TESTING UNDER EOO. See Item 660.

633. Simon, William A., Jr. "A Practical Approach to the Uniform
      Selection Guidelines." THE PERSONNEL ADMINISTRATOR, 24
      (November 1979), 75-80.

      Discusses adverse impact, the bottom line provision, vali-
      dation techniques, documentation and affirmative action pro-
      visions under the guidelines. Concludes that there are
      "ambiguities inherent" in the guidelines which will lead to
      future litigation. Concludes that personnel administrators
      must fully understand the guidelines and comply with them to
      avoid costly litigation.

634. Sloan, Allen. "An Analysis of Uniform Guidelines on Employee
      Selection Procedures." EMPLOYEE RELATIONS LAW JOURNAL, 4
      (Winter 1978-1979), 346-356.

635. Sparks, Paul C. "How to Identify Systemic Discrimination."
      MANAGER'S GUIDE TO EQUAL EMPLOYMENT OPPORTUNITY. Edited

by Robert Freiberg. New York: Executive Enterprise Publication Co., Inc., 1977, pp. 21-27.

Defines systemic discrimination as "seemingly neutral
policies or practices [which] result in adverse impact."
Advises employers to maximize their recruitment efforts to
attract minorities and women as a means of preventing systemic discrimination. Explains the importance of job analysis in preventing discrimination. Advises employers to
determine whether minority and female employees are concentrated only in low paying or the most undesirable jobs; if
so, employers should seek to determine why the situation
exist and to take corrective action. Briefly mentions the
issue of equal pay for women and "reasonable accommodation"
in religious discrimination cases.

636. Thompson, Duane E. and Patricia S. Christiansen. "Court
      Acceptance of Uniform Guidelines Provisions: The Bottom
      Line and the Search for Alternatives." EMPLOYEE RELATIONS
      LAW JOURNAL, (Spring 1983), 587-602.

Seeks to determine the extent of acceptance of the Uniform
Guidelines by the Supreme Court. Analyzes leading Supreme
Court decisions related to personnel selection, test validation, and the Uniform Guidelines. Finds that the Court's
decisions have been in agreement with the guidelines on the
definition of discrimination. However, sees some differences
between the Court and the guidelines in ". . . the definition
of adverse impact in terms of the bottom line and with the
requirement that a validation study must include a search for
alternatives if there is adverse impact." Recommends that
the provisions on the bottom line theory and alternative
selection procedures be revised to comply with the court's
interpretation of adverse impact.

637. "Uniform Selection Guidelines." EEO TODAY, 5 (Winter 1978-
      1979), 271-288.

Asserts that the complexity of employee selection within
EEO guidelines has been a difficult task for employers since
the effective date of Title VII and Executive Order 11246.
A major element of the complexity in employee selection has
been pre-employment tests. Two federal agencies, the EEOC
and OFCCP have had the responsibility of developing guidelines for employers to follow in using pre-employment tests
in employee selection. The EEOC issued "Employee Selection
Guidelines" in 1970. These guidelines expanded EEOC's in-
volvement in employee selection pass the issue of pre-employment test. The guidelines affect almost every facet of
employment selection. The 1970 guidelines were affirmed in
the Supreme Court's decision in Griggs v. Duke Power. The
Supreme Court in 1975, further held in Albermarle Paper Co.
v. Moody, that even if an employer proves that the selection
criteria was job related, other evidence can be presented to

challenge the selection criteria to show pretext for discrimination. In 1978, the EEOC and other federal agencies
jointly issued the Uniform Guidelines which set forth validation requirements and adopted the 80 percent selection rule.

TESTING

*   Arvey, Richard D. FAIRNESS IN SELECTING EMPLOYEES. See Item
    4.

638. Byham, William C. and Morton Edward Spitzer. THE LAW AND
      PERSONNEL TESTING. New York: American Management Associa-
      tion, 1971. 238 pp.

      Focuses on the use of tests in personnel selections. Be-
      gins with a brief discussion of Title VII's implications on
      personnel testing and enforcement agencies, e.g., EEOC and
      the Office of Federal Contract Compliance. Discusses pecu-
      liar problems in recruiting minorities and suggests strate-
      gies on how to increase the number of minority applicants.
      Believes that once minority applicants are recruited, the
      next step in the selection process is to give a fair and
      accurate test. Discusses the various types of tests, test
      administration, limitations on testing, and test content.
      Cites "language bias" on tests as a factor that should be
      considered in developing test content. Gives a "Ghetto
      Language Test" to illustrate the problem of "language bias."
      Suggests affirmative action steps be taken to ensure that
      personnel testing is fair and accurate.

639. Campbell, Joel J. "Tests Are Valid For Minority Groups Too."
      PUBLIC PERSONNEL MANAGEMENT, 2 (January-February 1973),
      70-73.

      Results from a study on tests and job performance which was
      conducted by the United States Civil Service Commission and
      the Educational Testing Service. Concludes that ". . . apti-
      tude tests do predict as well for minority groups as for
      majority groups, and where there is a discrepancy, the test
      is more apt to overpredict than to underpredict job per-
      formance for minorities." Feels that this study challenges
      the popular belief that tests poorly predict how well minori-
      ties will perform a job.

640. "Case Study: EEO and Testing." EEO REVIEW, (July 1980),
      2-4.

      Presents a case study on a testing discrimination com-
      plaint. Provides comments and suggestions to managers and
      supervisors on how to effectively deal with EEO complaints
      in this area of the law.

*   Cooper, George and Richard B. Sobol. "Seniority and Testing
      Under Fair Employment Laws: A General Approach to Objec-
      tive Criteria of Hiring and Promotion." See Item 703.

641. DeVaney, Michael Jay. "Civil Rights -- Employee Testing."
      WAKE FOREST LAW REVIEW, 7 (June 1971), 425-439.

      Examines ". . . some of the points of conflict created by
      the commencement of a testing program, what the requirements
      of objectivity are, the motive of Congress in passing Title
      VII of the Civil Rights Act of 1964, the guidelines set forth
      by the Equal Employment Opportunity Commission Agency created
      to enforce the provisions of the Civil Rights Act of 1964,
      and judicial construction of the many facets of fair employ-
      ment." Advises employers who use employment tests to deter-
      mine whether the test is job related, and in compliance with
      EEOC guidelines and the Supreme Court's decision in Griggs v.
      Duke Power Co.

642. "Employment Testing: The Aftermath of Griggs v. Duke Power
      Co." COLUMBIA LAW REVIEW, 72 (May 1972), 900-925.

      Reviews the Supreme Court's decision in Griggs and its
      impact on employment testing. States that the decision re-
      quires employment testing be job related, and that discrimi-
      natory intent is not a prerequisite to proving a Title VII
      case. Believes that the decision did not answer all the
      questions related to employment testing, e.g., what is a
      prima facie case, the meaning of test validation, and testing
      for professional jobs. Provides solutions and alternatives
      to the remaining problems of employment testing.

643. Fay, Julie D. "Challenges to Preemployment Tests After
      Washington v. Davis." HOFSTRA LAW REVIEW, 5 (Summer 1977),
      893-910.

      Seeks to determine what proof is sufficient to establish a
      prima facie case of employment discrimination. Analyzes the
      Washington v. Davis decision and concludes that there is a
      different standard of proof in a Title VII claim of discrimi-
      nation. Contends that Title VII considers the impact of the
      employers' action on the complainant; whereas, discriminatory
      intent must be proved under a constitutional claim of dis-
      crimination.

644. Finzen, Bruce A. "Civil Rights Law -- Fair Employment Test-
      ing and Title VII of the Civil Rights Act of 1964."
      UNIVERSITY OF KANSAS LAW REVIEW, 20 (Winter 1972), 334-344.

      Analyzes the facts and decision in the Griggs v. Duke Power
      case, and related court cases on employment testing. States

that the Griggs' decision held ". . . that Title VII prohibits an employment practice that requires an applicant to pass
a standardized intelligence test as a condition of employment
when the test is shown not to be significantly related to job
performance and has the effect of disqualifying Negroes at a
higher rate than Whites."

645. Guion, Robert M. "Employment Tests and Discriminatory Hiring." INDUSTRIAL RELATIONS, 5 (February 1966), 20-37.

646. Haney, Craig. "Employment Tests and Employment Discrimination: A Dissenting Psychological Opinion." INDUSTRIAL
RELATIONS LAW JOURNAL, 5 (No. 1, 1982), 1-86.

Gives an in-depth analysis of the use of employment tests
and their impact on employment discrimination. Recommends
that the testing industry be more rigorously regulated to
ensure that tests are job-related. Gives recommendations on
how to ensure that employment tests are nondiscriminatory.

*   Johnson, James G. "Albermarle Paper Company v. Moody: The
Aftermath of Griggs and the Death of Employee Testing."
See Item 1048.

647. Katzell, Raymond A. "EEO In Relation to Personnel Testing
and Selection." PROCEEDINGS OF NEW YORK UNIVERSITY THIR-
TIETH ANNUAL NATIONAL CONFERENCE ON LABOR. Edited by
Richard Adelman. New York: Matthew Bender, 1977, pp.
101-107.

Gives a historical view of the development of equal employment laws and guidelines as they relate to employment testing. Focuses on the EEOC's selection guidelines that were
issued in 1970 and the Federal Executive Agency's guidelines
on testing. Advises employers that the elimination of employment testing within their organization does not totally
relieve them of liability where "adverse impact" is still
occuring in the selection procedure.

648. Kirkpatrick, James J.; Robert B. Ewen; Richard S. Barrett;
and Raymond A. Katzell. TESTING AND FAIR EMPLOYMENT:
FAIRNESS AND VALIDITY OF PERSONNEL TEST FOR DIFFERENT
EITHNIC GROUPS. New York: New York University Press,
1968. 145 pp.

An empirical study of five work situations where employment
tests were administered to whites, blacks, and Spanish speaking workers. Concludes that ". . . tests proposed for personnel selection be studied separately in the specific ethnic
group and job settings for which they are to be used."

649. Kirkwood, John H. "Selection Techniques: To Test or Not to
      Test?" PERSONNEL, 44 (November-December 1967), 18-26.

650. Kulhavy, Raymond W. "Personnel Testing: Validating Selec-
      tion Instruments." PERSONNEL, 48 (September-October 1971),
      20-24.

651. Lawer, Neil. "Developing New Employment Tests for Minori-
      ties." PUBLIC ADMINISTRATION REVIEW, 31 (July-August
      1971), 459-461.

652. Noffke, Richard. "The Validity of Employment Testing."
      UNIVERSITY OF ILLINOIS LAW FORUM, (1972), 388-407.

      Seeks to determine the impact of the Supreme Court's deci-
      sion in Griggs v. Duke Power Co. and the EEOC's Guidelines on
      Employment Selection Procedures on employment testing.

653. Northcross, Wilson. "The Limits On Employment Testing."
      JOURNAL OF URBAN LAW, 50 (February 1973), 349-370.

654. "Notes, Legal Implications of the Use of Standardized Ability
      Tests In Employment and Education." COLUMBIA LAW REVIEW,
      68 (April 1968), 691-744.

      Defines "racially discriminatory test as one on which
      Negroes score lower than less qualified or equally qualified
      whites." Explains test theory and practice as it relates to
      employment discrimination. Discusses the Civil Rights Act of
      1964, judicial interpretation of the Act, Executive Order
      11246, and state fair employment laws. Believes that testing
      has eliminated some "subjective" procedures in employment
      selection, but testing may also include racial bias.

655. Nugent, P. Michael, Jr. "Employment Testing and the Federal
      Executive Agency Guidelines on Employee Selection Proce-
      dures: One Step Forward and Two Steps Backward for Equal
      Employment Opportunity." CATHOLIC UNIVERSITY LAW REVIEW,
      26 (Summer 1977), 852-874.

      Discusses the impact the guidelines will have on employment
      testing and EEO laws. Believes that the guidelines eased the
      requirements on test validation and fail ". . . to require
      separate validation studies for each racial or cultural group
      of test takers. . . ."

*   Petersen, Donald J. "The Impact of Duke Power on Testing."
      See Item 1083.

*   Reiter, Michael. "Compensating for Race or National Origin
        in Employment Testing. See Item 186.

656.   Romero, Carlos J. "The PACE Exam and Federal Employment."
        EQUAL OPPORTUNITY FORUM, 7 (October 1979), 21.

        Provides test statistics which indicate that non-minority
        applicants pass the PACE exam at a higher rate than minority
        applicants. Concludes that the PACE exam adversely affects
        the selection of minorities and women for federal employment.
        Makes recommendations to Congress and the Office of Personnel
        Management on how to implement affirmative action to ensure
        that minorities and women are equally represented in the
        federal workforce.

657.   Roth, David C. and Philip C. Stahl. "Application of the EEOC
        Guidelines to Employment Test Validation: A Uniform Stan-
        dard for Both Public and Private Employers." GEORGE
        WASHINGTON LAW REVIEW, 41 (March 1973), 505-537.

        Advises courts to adopt the EEOC Guidelines on Employee
        Selection Procedures that were promulgated in 1972 to elimi-
        nate discrimination in selection practices, especially test-
        ing procedures. Believes there would be a uniform standard
        of review of discrimination cases by courts if the guidelines
        were adopted. Discusses the Griggs' decision on establishing
        a prima facie case, and test validation.

*   Rowe, Benjamen T. and S. Dagnal Rowe. "Employment Testing
        and Title VII of the Civil Rights Act of 1964: After
        Albermarle Paper Co. v. Moody." See Item 1066.

658.   Sandman, Bonnie and Faith Urban. "Employment Testing and
        the Law." LABOR LAW JOURNAL, 27 (January 1976), 38-54.

        Reviews and summarizes leading cases related to unvalidated
        selection procedures and promotional tests. Defines the
        various types of test validations and analyzes court deci-
        sions on the adequacy of validity studies.

659.   Seelman, Frederick G., Jr. "Employment Testing Law: The
        Federal Agencies Go Public with the Problems." URBAN
        LAWYER, 10 (winter 1978), 1-73.

*   Schick, Richard and Barry S. Bader. "Supreme Court Mandates
        Job Related Examinations: The Griggs Decision." JUDICIAL
        MANDATES FOR AFFIRMATIVE ACTION. See Item 1086.

660. Siegel, Jerome. PERSONNEL TESTING UNDER EEO. New York:
      American Management Association, 1980. 92 pp.

      Summarizes governmental requirements for using employment
      tests as a selection device. Explains that employers are
      faced with the dilemma of whether to "test or not to test."
      Interviews various private and public sector managers, per-
      sonnel executives, professionals, and consultants for their
      suggestions and recommendations on complying with EEO regula-
      tions when testing. Recommendations include monitoring the
      workforce for adverse impact, validating tests, and con-
      ducting job analysis. Discusses the elements of a test,
      test validation, job analysis, the Uniform Guidelines On
      Selection, affirmative action, and preparing for an EEO
      investigation.

661. U.S. Commission on Civil Rights. EMPLOYMENT TESTING: GUIDE
      SIGNS, NOT STOP SIGNS. Washington, D.C.; Government
      Printing Office, 1968. 30 pp.

      Expresses concern that the exclusive use of employment
      tests may inadvertently discriminate and exclude qualified
      blacks from hiring and promotion opportunities. Provides
      comments from personnel and management experts who also feel
      that certain employment practices, including testing are
      discriminatory. Identifies the "perils and pitfalls of test-
      ing," and outlines how some companies are modifying their
      testing and selection practices to avoid employment discrimi-
      nation against blacks.

662. U.S. Equal Employment Opportunity Commission. GUIDELINES ON
      EMPLOYMENT TESTING PROCEDURES. Washington, D.C.: Govern-
      ment Printing Office, August, 1966. 8 pp.

663. _____. PERSONNEL TESTING AND EQUAL EMPLOYMENT OPPOR-
      TUNITY. Washington, D.C.: Government Printing Office,
      December 1970. 48 pp.

      Contains a collection of papers on employment testing.
      Concentrates on how the use of tests can lead to discrimina-
      tion and can prevent the employment of qualified minorities.

664. Weitzul, James. "Employment Tests: Fair or Unfair Discrimi-
      nation?" MANAGEMENT REVIEW, 69 (August 1980), 50-52.

665. Wigdor, Alexandra K. and Wendell R. Garner. "Employment
      Testing and Equal Opportunity." NEW ENGLAND JOURNAL OF
      HUMAN SERVICES, 3 (Spring 1983), 27-36.

Reports on a study conducted by the National Academy of
Sciences on the use of testing in employment practices.
Focuses on the use of testing in the military, the Federal
Civil Service, state and local government, and in the private
sector. Analyzes the rationale for using tests, test validity, the quality of testing, and alternatives to testing.
Summarizes the study's conclusions on the state of employment
testing and the committee's recommendations to governmental
authorities and employers on improving the use of employment
testing.

*   Berg, Richard K. "Equal Employment Opportunity Under the
       Civil Rights Act of 1964." See Item 10.

666.   Berlin, Philip E. "Avoiding Charges of Age Discrimination."
       THE MANAGER'S GUIDE TO EQUAL EMPLOYMENT OPPORTUNITY.
       Edited by Robert Freiberg. New York: Executive Enter-
       prises Publication Co., Inc., 1977, pp. 115-130.

       Outlines guidelines for corporate managers to adhere to
       when making and implementing personnel policies to avoid age
       discrimination complaints. States that ". . . management
       should make sure that: (1) applicants and employees are
       evaluated on their individual merits, not on suspected
       incapacities due to age; (2) all policies are consistently
       applied and enforced; and (3) all job requirements are re-
       lated to the performance of a given job." Discusses how the
       Age Discrimination in Employment Act of 1967 prohibit dis-
       crimination in selections, terms, conditions, and privileges
       of employment, and when terminating employees.

667.   Brownstein, Paul. "Initial Contact: Charge and Investiga-
       tion." EQUAL EMPLOYMENT OPPORTUNITIES COMPLIANCE. Edited
       by John Ross. New York: Practicing Law Institute, 1972.

       Provides guidance to employers on how to be prepared for
       an EEO investigation that is conducted by a civil rights
       organization.

668.   "Case Study: EEO and Retaliation." EEO REVIEW, (September
       1982), 2-3.

       Presents a case study on a retaliation discrimination com-
       plaint. Provides comments and suggestions to managers and
       supervisors on how to effectively deal with EEO complaints
       in this area of the law.

669.   "Case Study: Responding to EEOC Investigators' Questions."
       EEO REVIEW, (December 1979), 2-3.

       Presents a case study on how managers and supervisors
       should respond to questions from an EEOC investigator during
       the investigation of a discrimination complaint. Proposes

commonly asked questions during an investigation and recommends the appropriate answers.

670. Clark, Charles E. "Definition of Discrimination: Employers'
      Hiring." MERCER LAW REVIEW, 19 (Winter 1968), 334-365.

      Surveys more than 200 discrimination findings against em-
      ployers by the Equal Employment Opportunity Commission (EEOC)
      concerning hiring practices. Summarizes the EEOC's rationale
      for finding discrimination and outlines the EEOC's complaint
      processing system.

671. Cole, Craig W. "Some In-House EEO Grievance Procedures
      Actually Work." SOLVING EEO PROBLEMS: A GUIDE TO EEO LAW
      AND PRACTICE. New York: Executive Enterprises Publica-
      tions, Co., Inc., 1980, pp. 79-88.

      Cites four reasons why an employer should have an internal
      EEO grievance procedure: "to bring EEO complaints to the
      surface; to allow for examination of complaints; to diffuse
      hostility; and to resolve complaints without outside inter-
      vention." Provides suggestions on structuring and imple-
      menting an EEO grievance procedure. Concludes that unless
      employees have a system to air grievances it will have a
      negative impact on productivity and morale of the employees.

672. Cousens, Frances Reissman. PUBLIC CIVIL RIGHTS AGENCIES AND
      FAIR EMPLOYMENT. New York: Frederick A. Praeger, 1969.
      162 pp.

      Evaluates employment patterns and employment practices that
      adversely affect "Negroes" in selected industries, e.g.,
      financial institutions, utilities, retail stores, manufac-
      turing, etc. Analyzes the operation and effectiveness of
      government civil rights agencies in combating employment
      discrimination.

673. Cramer, Robert J. "State Deferral of Complaints Under the
      Age Discrimination in Employment Act." NOTRE DAME LAW
      REVIEW, 51 (February 1976), 492-504.

674. Dominick, Peter H. "Let's Be Fair About Equal Employment."
      NATION'S BUSINESS, 59 (October 1971), 40-42.

      Proposes that discrimination laws be enforced by Federal
      courts rather than the Equal Employment Opportunity Commis-
      sion (EEOC). Believes the EEOC should only investigate,
      process, and conciliate complaints.

675. Drake, E. Thayer. "Discrimination Grievances: What to Do
      and How to Do It." THE MANAGER'S GUIDE TO EQUAL EMPLOYMENT
      OPPORTUNITY. Edited by Robert Freiberg. New York: Execu-
      tive Enterprises Publication Co., Inc., 1977, pp. 85-96.

      Defines a "discrimination grievance" as ". . . a grievance
      by an 'employee' alleging discrimination by an 'employer' in
      connection with the employee-employer relationship. . ."
      Outlines procedures that employers should follow when dealing
      with federal and state agencies who investigate "discrimina-
      tion grievances." Lists the type of data an employer should
      present to EEO enforcement agencies and how to explain their
      position. Explains the Equal Employment Opportunity Commis-
      sion's proceedings and advises employers how to resolve and
      avoid "discrimination grievances."

*   Executive Enterprises Publication, Co., Inc. CONDUCTING THE
      LAWFUL EMPLOYMENT INTERVIEW: HOW TO AVOID CHARGES OF DIS-
      CRIMINATION WHEN INTERVIEWING JOB CANDIDATES. See Item
      831.

676. "Facing a Bias Charge." EEO COMPLIANCE MANUAL VOL. I.
      Englewood Cliffs, N.J.: Prentice-Hall, Inc., 1979.

      Explains who can file a charge of discrimination under
      Title VII and provides suggestions to employers on how to
      handle such claims.

677. Gordon, Leonard J. HOW TO HANDLE DISCRIMINATION COMPLAINTS,
      THE DO'S AND DON'TS MANAGERS AND SUPERVISORS MUST UTILIZE
      TO AVOID COSTLY AA/EEO VIOLATIONS. Urbana, Il.: L.J.
      Gordon Associates, 1981. 16 pp.

678. "How Communication Can Prevent-or Provoke - Discrimination
      Charges." EEO REVIEW, (May 1980), 6-7.

      States that "[a] large number of complaints filed with
      state human rights agencies and with the EEOC are the result
      of a manager's and supervisor's failure to communicate,
      rather than the result of discrimination." Recommends tech-
      niques for supervisors and managers on how to effectively
      communicate information and policy to employees as a means
      of preventing the filing of discrimination complaints.

*   Jackson, Tom. INTERVIEWING WOMEN: AVOIDING CHARGES OF
      DISCRIMINATION. See Item 839.

679. Jauvtis, Robert L. "The Corporate EEO Officer and Limits of
      Lawful Protest." PERSONNEL ADMINISTRATOR, 28 (February
      1983), 31.

Defines the duties of an EEO officer, and identifies the
"tolerable limits" of how far an EEO officer can go in pro-
testing an unlawful employment practice of their employer,
before they ". . . overstep the bounds of the job." Discusses court decisions involving EEO officers who filed EEO
charges against their employer on the basis of retaliation.
Concludes that EEO officers are quasi-managers and ". . . are
obligated to perform defined duties which may restrict the
manner of opposition to practices they believe to be unfair
or unlawful."

680. "Job Discrimination Is Still Very, Very Serious." U.S. NEWS
      AND WORLD REPORT, INC., 94 (March 14, 1983), 67-68.

      An interview with Clarence Thomas, Chairman of the EEOC,
      reveals that employment discrimination still exists in Amer-
      ica. Gives opinions on affirmative action, quotas, and
      complaint processing by the EEOC.

681. Kahn, Dona S. and Judith E. Harris. "Dealing With Compliance
      Agencies." THE MANAGER'S GUIDE TO EQUAL EMPLOYMENT OPPOR-
      TUNITY. Edited by Robert Freiberg. New York: Executive
      Enterprises Publication Co., Inc., 1977, pp. 131-135.

      A brief summary of what an employer should do to prevent
      litigation when a charge of discrimination is filed against
      the company. Advises employers to try to settle complaints
      and to have complainants withdraw their charges. Where this
      is not feasible, recommends that employers conduct a thorough
      internal investigation and provide all important data to the
      Equal Employment Opportunity Commission.

*   Leap, Terry L.; William H. Holley, Jr.; and Hubert S. Feild.
      "Equal Employment Opportunity and its Implications for
      Personnel Practices in the 1980s." See Item 54.

682. Norton, Eleanor Holmes. "EEOC Today." EQUAL OPPORTUNITY
      FORUM, 6 (April 1979), 10-11.

      Contends that internal reform at the EEOC has caused the
      backlog of complaints to be reduced. Believes that the rapid
      charge processing system provide many benefits to the com-
      plainant and respondent. Believes businesses will also bene-
      fit from the reorganization of equal employment functions
      within the federal system, e.g., will reduce the duplication
      of compliance reviews. Briefly discusses the Bakke and Weber
      decisions and the impact of the EEOC's Affirmative Action
      Guidelines on these decisions.

683. Peres, Richard. DEALING WITH EMPLOYMENT DISCRIMINATION.
      New York: McGraw-Hill Book Company, 1977. 330 pp.

A comprehensive text on how to prevent and correct discrimination in the workplace. Discusses the legal terminology of
discrimination and the basis of discrimination. Provides an
outline on how to prevent discrimination complaints in the
areas of hiring, discharge, and discriminatory working environment. Gives advice on the best way to handle EEO investigations and how to resolve complaints.

684. _____. PREVENTING DISCRIMINATION COMPLAINTS: A
      GUIDE FOR SUPERVISORS. New York: McGraw Hill, 1979.
      88 pp.

      Written specifically for supervisors on the "do's and
      dont's" of EEO Compliance. Focuses on hiring, discharge,
      discipline and job performance of employees. Stresses that
      the prevention of EEO complaints rest in the hands of the
      supervisor.

685. Pingpank, Jeffrey C. "Preventing and Defending EEO Charges."
      PERSONNEL ADMINISTRATOR, 28 (February 1983), 35.

      Provides suggestions and strategies to personnel managers
      on how to develop sound personnel policies that may prevent,
      or at least assist them in defending EEO charges.

686. Sheahan, Robert H. "Responding to Employment Discrimination
      Charges." PERSONNEL JOURNAL, 60 (March 1981), 217-220.

      Discusses how to respond to a complaint of discrimination.
      Contends that how an employer responds to an EEOC complaint
      may influence any subsequent litigation on the complaint.
      Focuses on the EEOC's administrative procedures, the charge
      of discrimination, the fact-finding conferences, and the com-
      pany's investigation, settlement procedures, and the EEOC's
      investigation, determination and conciliation.

687. Shemetulskis, Richard. "How to Hire and Fire Safely."
      MANAGEMENT WORLD, 10 (December 1981), 25-27.

      Advises employers that EEO complaints can be avoided if
      they are consistent and fair in their hiring and termination
      practices. Provides tips on how to conduct an employment
      interview without projecting a prejudice disposition and how
      to terminate employees without making discriminatory state-
      ments.

688. Smith, Thomas Royall and Christopher J. Kelleher. "Dealing
      With the EEO Officer Who Files a Discrimination Complaint."
      EMPLOYEE RELATIONS LAW JOURNAL, 8 (Summer 1982), 92-109.

Contends that Section 704(a) of Title VII of the Civil Rights Act (retaliation provision) does not totally immunize EEO officers from receiving a disciplinary action, including termination when they oppose their employer's EEO/Affirmative Action programs. Discusses three leading court cases involving EEO officers who received some form of discipline and later brought suit under Section 704(a). Provides strategies for employers to follow when they receive a discrimination complaint from their EEO officer.

689. "Supervising the Employee who has Filed a Discrimination Charge." EEO REVIEW, (June 1977), 6-8.

Provides suggestions to supervisors and managers on how to effectively supervise employees who have filed EEO complaints and at the same time avoid retaliation charges.

690. Thomas, William C. "When the Charge is Discrimination." SUPERVISORY MANAGEMENT, 15 (February 1970), 7-10.

*   U.S. Commission on Civil Rights. EQUAL EMPLOYMENT OPPORTU- NITY UNDER FEDERAL LAW. See Item 110.

691. U.S. Civil Service Commission. EQUAL EMPLOYMENT OPPORTUNITY COUNSELING. Washington, D.C.: Government Printing Office, 1974.

Designed as a training manual for EEO counselors. Includes discussions on counseling techniques, conducting interviews, gathering information, and resolving complaints.

692. _____. EQUAL EMPLOYMENT OPPORTUNITY COUNSELING, A GUIDEBOOK. Washington, D.C.: Government Printing Office, October 1977. 28 pp.

Provides guidelines to managers on selecting, training, and assigning EEO counselors within the federal government. Outlines the duties of an EEO counselor and provides instructions on performing such duties, e.g., scheduling, counseling complainants, and principles of interviewing.

693. _____. INVESTIGATING COMPLAINTS OF DISCRIMINATION IN FEDERAL EMPLOYMENT. Washington, D.C.: Government Printing Office, 1975. 35 pp.

Provides a step by step guide to investigating complaints of discrimination. Includes topics on preparing for the investigation, interviewing witnesses, conducting the investigation, and collecting evidence.

694. U.S. Equal Employment Opportunity Commission. FILING A
      CHARGE, ABOUT FILING A CHARGE . . . JOB DISCRIMINATION.
      Washington, D.C.: Government Printing Office, January
      1983. 12 pp.

      Outlines steps for filing a charge of discrimination with
      the EEOC. Briefly explains what is discussed at the initial
      interview, the fact-finding conference, the meaning of a no
      cause determination, and litigation procedures. Provides the
      addresses of EEOC District and Area Offices.

695. U.S. Office of Personnel Management. "Equal Employment
      Opportunity Counseling." EEO INFORMATION ON EQUAL EMPLOY-
      MENT OPPORTUNITY FOR STATE AND LOCAL GOVERNMENTS. Issue
      No. 18. Washington, D.C., January 1979. 6 pp.

      Suggests that informal counseling programs may prevent
      formal EEO complaints which are expensive and time consuming.
      Believes that "[t]he careful selection of persons to serve as
      EEO counselors is critical." Concludes that counselors
      should receive training and be readily assessible to employ-
      ees.

696. U.S. Postal Service. EEO COUNSELING MODEL. Washington,
      D.C.: Government Printing Office, 1980. 47 pp.

      Describes the job duties and responsibilities of an EEO
      counselor. Presents a four phase model on EEO counseling,
      which includes the initial interview, interviews with manage-
      ment, an analysis and decision, and the final interview.

*   Vernon, Richard G. and Peter S. Gray. "Affirmative Action as
      an Affirmative Defense to EEO Charges." See Item 999.

697. Walker, Wayne. "Title VII: Complaint and Enforcement Pro-
      cedures and Relief and Remedies." BOSTON COLLEGE INDUS-
      TRIAL COMMERCIAL LAW REVIEW, 7 (Spring 1966), 495-524.

      Outlines problems with enforcement procedures and remedies
      under Title VII. Indicates that it is unclear whether a com-
      plaint must first be filed with the EEOC before a court
      action can be commenced. Includes discussions on the timeli-
      ness of filing a complaint, attorney's fees, jury trials,
      class actions, joinder of defendants, and equitable and law
      remedies under Title VII.

698. Wrong, Elaine Gale. "Selecting an Arbitrator for a Discrimi-
      nation Grievance." PERSONNEL ADMINISTRATOR, 28 (January
      1983), 58.

      Believes that the ". . . careful selection of an arbitrator
      for hearing a work-related grievance can help deter future

action by a dissatisfied party." Outlines the problems that
management and the union will have in selecting an arbitrator. For example, there are varying opinions among arbitrators as to who prevails when there is a conflict between the
labor contract and public laws. Recommends that employers
review arbitrators' past record of awards in discrimination
grievances to determine their general disposition on an
issue.

LAYOFFS AND SENIORITY SYSTEMS

699. Adams, Avril V.; Joseph Krislov; and David R. Lairson.
"Plant-wide Seniority, Black Employment, and Employer
Affirmative Action." INDUSTRIAL AND LABOR RELATIONS
REVIEW, 26 (October 1972), 686-690.

* American Bar Association, Section of Labor Relations Law.
PROCEEDINGS OF THE THIRD ABA NATIONAL INSTITUTE ON EQUAL
EMPLOYMENT LAW. See Item 1.

700. Bagby, Thomas R. "The Supreme Court Reaffirms Broad Immunity
for Seniority Systems." LABOR LAW JOURNAL, 33 (July 1982),
409-416.

Analyzes the Supreme Court's decisions in <u>American Tobacco
Company v. Patterson</u> and <u>Pullman-Standard v. Swint</u>. Indicates that in both cases the Court reaffirmed its position
that Section 703(h) of Title VII provides immunity for bona
fide seniority systems, even if the systems adversely affects
minorities.

* Blumrosen, Alfred W. BLACK EMPLOYMENT AND THE LAW. See
Item 133.

701. Bureau of National Affairs, Inc. LAYOFFS, RIFs, AND EEO IN
THE PUBLIC SECTOR, A BNA SPECIAL REPORT. Washington, D.C.:
February 5, 1982. 70 pp.

States that major federal budget cuts have had an adverse
impact on women and minorities. Large numbers of women and
minorities who were hired as a result of affirmative action
are being laid-off under the practice of last hired, first
fired. Discusses the issue of EEO and layoffs in the federal
sector, and provides data on how some states have implemented
regulations and policies to lessen the impact of layoffs on
affirmative action programs.

* Cebulski, Bonnie G. "Affirmative Action versus Seniority -
Is Conflict Inevitable?" See Item 909.

702. "Comments, _Teamsters_, _Evans_, and Title VII: Will Women be
      the Ultimate Losers?" NORTHWESTERN UNIVERSITY LAW REVIEW,
      72 (November-December 1977), 761-788.

      Finds that the Supreme Court in International Brotherhood
      of Teamsters v. United States and United Airlines v. Evans
      refused to strike down a "neutral" departmental seniority
      system which perpetuated past discrimination. The Court held
      that the seniority system did not violate Title VII. Exam-
      ines whether Section 1981 of 42 U.S.C. would prohibit senior-
      ity systems that perpetuate past discrimination. Section
      1981 "prohibits discrimination in the making and enforcement
      of contracts." Concludes that Section 1981 is broader in
      scope than Title VII and would be applicable.

703. Cooper, George and Richard B. Sobol. "Seniority and Testing
      Under Fair Employment Laws: A General Approach to Objec-
      tive Criteria of Hiring and Promotion." HARVARD LAW
      REVIEW, 82 (1969), 1598-1679.

704. Depuy, Warner, K. "Last-Hired, First-Fired: Discriminatory
      or Sacrosanct?" DICKINSON LAW REVIEW, 80 (Summer 1976),
      747-767.

      Reviews the legislative intent of Title VII of the Civil
      Rights Act of 1964 and judicial decisions to determine
      whether present day seniority systems violate the Act. Con-
      cludes that "[t]he last-hired, first-fired doctrine governing
      workforce reductions is not discriminatory and not prohibited
      by law." Suggests ways to decrease the "adverse affects"
      that seniority systems have on minorities and women during
      lay-offs, e.g., work sharing.

705. Doeringer, Peter B. "Discriminatory Promotion Systems"
      MONTHLY LABOR REVIEW, 90 (March 1967), 27-28.

706. Feil, Clyde Hurt. "The Problem of Last-Hired, First-Fired:
      Retroactive Seniority as a Remedy Under Title VII."
      GEORGIA LAW REVIEW, 9 (Spring 1975), 611-657.

      Traces the legislative history of Title VII and evaluates
      the affects of Title VII on discriminatory seniority systems
      that perpetuate past discrimination. Analyzes a series of
      court cases where seniority systems were challenged under
      Title VII.

*   Finger, Joel L. and Thomas C. Greble. "The Impact of Age
      Discrimination on Reductions-in-Force." See Item 573.

707. Gould, William B. "Employment Security, Seniority and Race:
      The Rule of Title VII of the Civil Rights Act of 1964."
      HOWARD LAW JOURNAL, 13 (Winter 1967), 1-50.

      Discusses the problems of racial discrimination in "com-
      petitive status seniority." Advises the EEOC, inter alia,
      to issue guidelines prohibiting racial discrimination in
      seniority systems. Alerts unions and employers that they
      may have to negotiate or amend their agreement to comply
      with the guidelines. Written prior to the EEOC having en-
      forcement powers.

708. Gregory, Alan G. "Frank V. Bowan Transportation Co.:
      Expanding the Remedy for Employment Discrimination."
      DETROIT COLLEGE OF LAW REVIEW, 1976 (No. 3), 609-624.

*   Hunter, James M. and Milton C. Branch. "Equal Employment
      Opportunities: Administrative Procedures and Judicial
      Developments Under Title VII of the Civil Rights Act of
      1964 and the Equal Employment Act of 1972." See Item 47.

*   Jackson, Gary W. "Executive Order 11246 as an Alternative to
      Title VII: The Elimination of Discrimination in Bona Fide
      Seniority Systems." See Item 1008.

*   Johnson, Ronald D. "Voluntary Affirmative Action in the
      Post-Weber Era: Issues and Answers." See Item 930.

709. Jones, James E., Jr. "Title VII, Seniority and the Supreme
      Court: Clarification or Retreat." UNIVERSITY OF KANSAS
      LAW REVIEW, 26 (Fall 1977), 1-60.

      Provides an analysis of judicial decisions relative to the
      issue of Title VII and seniority systems. Discusses deci-
      sions preceding and after the Supreme Court's decision in
      Franks v. Bowman Transportation Company. Concludes that the
      issue of seniority and Title VII is still unclear and will
      require further interpretation from the court.

710. Joseph, Ellen R. "Last-Hired, First-Fired Seniority, Lay-
      offs, and Title VII: Questions of Liability and Remedy."
      COLUMBIA JOURNAL OF LAW AND SOCIAL PROBLEMS, 11 (Spring
      1975), 343-402.

      Explores the issue of whether a bona fide "date-of-hire
      seniority system" which adversely affects minorities and
      women in a lay-off violate Title VII. Concludes that such a
      system may violate Title VII ". . . where it perpetuates the
      effects of past hiring discrimination. . . ." Analyzes the
      leading cases in the area of EEO and seniority systems:

Waters v. Wisconsin Steel Works, Watkins v. Steelworkers Local 2369 and Franks v. Bowman Transportation Co.

711. Kelley, Maryellen R. "Discrimination in Seniority Systems: A Case Study." INDUSTRIAL AND LABOR RELATIONS REVIEW, 36 (October 1982), 40-55.

Presents an empirical study on the Supreme Court's decision in Teamsters v. U.S. and the decision's impact on seniority systems that perpetrate discriminatory treatment against women and minority employees.

712. Klotchman, Janissee and Linda L. Neider. "EEO Alert: Watch Out for Discrimination in Discharge Decisions." PERSONNEL, 60 (January-February 1983), 60-66.

Advises employment managers to be impartial and consistent when administering personnel policy that involves termination and layoffs. Contends that employment managers who follow this practice and document employment actions may avoid discriminatory practices. Summarizes Federal laws, executive orders, and court cases that are related to terminations and layoffs.

713. "'Last-Hired, First-Fired', Takes it on the Chin." BUSINESS WEEK, (March 9, 1974), 166.

714. Levine, Marvin J. "The Conflict Between Negotiated Seniority Provisions and Title VII of the Civil Rights Act of 1964: Recent Developments." LABOR LAW JOURNAL, 29 (June 1978), 352-363.

States that maintaining an affirmative action program during a time of layoffs may cause a conflict with "conventional seniority provisions and equal employment opportunity laws." Seniority systems which were not designed to intentionally discriminate are valid under Title VII. Explains that "reverse discrimination" may also exist where less qualified minorities or women obtain jobs over white males. Discusses the landmark decision in Teamsters v. U.S. and its impact on seniority systems.

715. McCully, Carol L. "The Continuing Validity of Seniority Systems Under Title VII: Sharing the Burden of Discrimination." LOYOLA UNIVERSITY OF CHICAGO LAW JOURNAL, 8 (Summer 1977), 882-912.

Analyzes the impact of Title VII and seniority systems on the employment of minorities. Focuses specifically on two Supreme Court decisions: Franks v. Bowman Transportation Co. and Griggs v. Duke Power Co. Includes a brief analysis of lower court decisions related to the practice of "last-hired, first-fired."

716. Poplin, Caroline. "Fair Employment in a Depressed Economy: The Layoff Problem." UCLA LAW REVIEW, 23 (December 1975), 177-234.

A comprehensive article on the implication of Title VII on layoffs during a recessionary period. Typically, in a layoff situation, the last-hired will be the first-fired. Because blacks are usually the last-hired, they normally will be the first to be laid off. Focuses on two court cases that involve the issue of layoffs and Title VII: Watkins v. United Steele Workers of America, Local 2369 and Waters v. Wisconsin Steelworkers.

717. Powell, John H., Jr. "Reconciling Equal Employment Opportunity with Seniority: The Case for Sensitive Application of Traditional Equitable Principles." DICKINSON LAW REVIEW, 80 (Summer 1976), 653-665.

Supports the Supreme Court's decision in Franks v. Bowman Transportation Company, which held that retroactive seniority was an acceptable remedy where an applicant had previously been denied employment due to their race. Argues that this remedy is an appropriate remedy under Title VII for correcting discrimination in employment.

718. Roberts, Robert N. "'Last-Hired, First-Fired and Public Employee Layoffs: The Equal Employment Opportunity Dilemma." REVIEW OF PUBLIC PERSONNEL ADMINISTRATION, 2 (Fall 1981), 29-48.

Contends that gains made by minorities and women in employment during the last two decades are being hampered by layoffs that are based on seniority systems. Finds that minorities and women who were recently hired pursuant to affirmative action plans are the first to be terminated during a layoff. Discusses the impact of Title VII and the Civil Rights Acts of 1866 and 1871 on seniority systems. Analyzes the Supreme Court's decisions in Franks v. Bowman Transportation Co. and International Brotherhood of Teamsters v. United States. Concludes that even though the Court has provided clarification as to what a bona fide seniority system entails under Title VII, the conflict still remains between the principle of "last-hired, first-fired" and equal employment opportunity programs.

719. Sculnick, Michael W. "New Ruling on Seniority Systems." EEO TODAY, 8 (Winter 1981-82), 289-296.

Finds that the position of the EEOC and the Department of
Labor that seniority systems which perpetuate past discrimination violate Executive Order 11246 was struck down by the
United States Court of Appeals for the District of Columbia
in United States v. Trucking Management, Inc. The Court held
that "[a] bona fide seniority system found lawful under section 703(h) of Title VII may not be found unlawful under
Executive Order 11246." Analyzes the court's decisions in
Trucking Management, Inc. and Southbridge Plastics v. Local
759, Rubber Workers. Interprets the Southbridge Plastic case
to mean that an employer that joins with the EEOC in a conciliation agreement that modifies a seniority system may be
held liable if a court subsequently finds that the seniority
system was a bona fide plan.

720. "Seniority Squeezes Out Minorities in Layoffs." BUSINESS
      WEEK, (May 5, 1975), 66.

721. Simon, Ruth. "Seniority v. Affirmative Action." THE
      NATIONAL LAW JOURNAL, 5 (September 20, 1982), 1.

      Illustrates the problems that Federal Courts are faced
      with in trying to preserve affirmative action programs in
      the midst of a recession. Discusses court cases which were
      brought by white employees who had more seniority than black
      employees but were reduced in force due to the preservation
      of affirmative action.

*   Sovern, Michael I. RACIAL DISCRIMINATION IN EMPLOYMENT.
      See Item 148.

722. Spurlock, Delbert L., Jr. EMPLOYMENT AND LAYOFFS. Cali-
      fornia: League of California Cities - Employee Relations
      Service. (no date). 10 pp.

      As a result of Proposition 13 many state and local agencies
      in California are faced with major budget cuts which could
      possibly result in a reduction in force of government employ-
      ees. Provides information to agencies on how to minimize the
      destruction of their affirmative action program during a
      reduction in force. Recommends specific guidelines to follow
      if protected class individuals are adversely affected by the
      reduction in force. Briefly discusses affirmative action
      requirements under Executive Order 11246 and quotas under
      Title VII.

723. Stanley, D.T. "Trying to Avoid Layoffs." PUBLIC ADMINISTRA-
      TION REVIEW, 37 (September-October), 515-517.

724. Stickler, K. Bruce and Mark D. Nelson. "Implementing Layoffs
      and Reductions in Force: A Practical Guide." EMPLOYMENT
      RELATIONS TODAY, 10 (Spring 1983), 65-72.

      Advises employers that their reduction in force practices
      and policies may potentially lead to EEO charges and liabil-
      ity. Provides guidelines on preparing and implementing a
      layoff system that will reduce the possibility of a finding
      of discrimination if an EEO charge is filed and litigated.

725. "The Supreme Court on Seniority." EEO TODAY, 4 (Autumn
      1977), 159-166.

      The Supreme Court's decision in Teamsters v. United States
      basically ended the issue of whether a "bona fide" seniority
      plan can violate Title VII. To prove that a seniority plan
      is discriminatory, the claimant must prove that the seniority
      plan was intentionally designed to discriminate. In United
      Airlines v. Evans, the Supreme Court held that even if a
      "bona fide" seniority plan perpetuates past discrimination,
      the plan itself is not discriminatory. The Supreme Court
      further held in Franks v. Bowman Transportation, that retro-
      active seniority would still be an appropriate remedy for
      other types of Title VII violations, i.e., hiring discrimi-
      nation, but not for a "bona fide" seniority system.

726. Thorp, Cary D., Jr. "Racial Discrimination and Seniority."
      LABOR LAW JOURNAL, 23 (July 1972), 398-413.

      Points out the applicable sections of Title VII that are
      pertinent to claims of discrimination in seniority systems.
      Discusses seniority systems, bona fide seniority systems, and
      types of preferential treatment. Analyzes court cases in-
      volving seniority systems that were held to be discrimina-
      tory.

727. "Title VII, Seniority Discrimination, and the Incumbent
      Negro." HARVARD LAW REVIEW, 80 (1966-1967), 1260-1283.

      Focuses on the problems of protecting "seniority rights of
      white workers" and complying with Title VII's requirement of
      eliminating race discrimination in seniority systems. Sug-
      gests that the "rightful place" approach be used to correct
      past discrimination practices in seniority systems. "The
      'right place' approach would allow an incumbent Negro to bid
      for openings in 'white' jobs comparable to those held by
      whites of equal tenure on the basis of his full length of
      service with the employer."

728. U.S. Civil Service Commission. "Reducing the Effects of Lay-
      offs on Your Affirmative Action Program." EEO FOR STATE
      AND LOCAL GOVERNMENTS. Washington, D.C.: Government
      Printing Office, Issue No. 15. 9 pp.

729. U.S. Commission on Civil Rights. LAST-HIRED, FIRST-FIRED:
      LAYOFFS AND CIVIL RIGHTS. Washington, D.C.: Government
      Printing Office, February 1977. 89 pp.

      Analyzes the impact of layoffs during a recession (1974-75)
      on affirmative action programs and the employment of minori-
      ties in the workforce. Concludes that strict adherence to
      seniority procedures during a layoff may have a disparate
      impact on minorities and women. Provides some alternatives
      to lessen the conflict between seniority systems and equal
      employment opportunity.

730. _____. LAST-HIRED, FIRST-FIRED. Washington, D.C.:
      Government Printing Office, October 12, 1976. 105 pp.

      Reviews proceedings before the Commission on the impact of
      seniority-based layoffs on minorities and women. Contends
      that affirmative action gains that have been made in the
      employment of women and minorities are in the process of being
      eroded due to seniority-based layoffs.

731. U.S. Department of Labor, Employment and Training Administra-
      tion. LAYOFF TIME TRAINING: A KEY TO UPGRADING WORKFORCE
      UTILIZATION AND EEOC AFFIRMATIVE ACTION. Washington, D.C.:
      Government Printing Office, 1978. 117 pp.

      Results of a study on an experimental and demonstration
      project which was funded by the Department of Labor to pro-
      vide training and stipends for laid-off, low-skilled workers
      in the California canning industry. The purpose of the pro-
      ject was to train workers when they were laid off so they
      might return to work sooner or to a better paying job. After
      the first year of the program, it was found that the employ-
      ment status of women was improved and the project accelerated
      the affirmative action process.

732. Weiner, Paul I. "Seniority Systems in the Post-Teamsters
      Era -- An Update." EMPLOYMENT DISCRIMINATION LITIGATION.
      Edited by Paul I. Weiner. New York: Practicing Law
      Institute, 1979, pp. 345-372.

      Concentrates on the definition of "bona fide" seniority
      system and the implication of such definition on both parties
      in a discrimination suit. Reviews the Supreme Court's land-
      mark decision in Teamsters v. U.S. The Court held ". . .
      that 'bona fide' seniority systems which tend to perpetuate
      the effects of pre-act discrimination were protected."

166   LAYOFFS AND SENIORITY SYSTEMS

733. _____. "Seniority Systems Under Teamsters and
     Bryant." EMPLOYEE RELATIONS LAW JOURNAL, 6 (Winter 1980-
     81), 437-458.

734. Westerfield, Rebecca A. "Title VII and Seniority Systems:
     Back to the Foot of the Line?" KENTUCKY LAW JOURNAL, 64
     (No. 1, 1975-76), 114-145.

     Describes the conflict between the operation of seniority
     systems and the principles of equal employment opportunity.
     Reviews efforts made by Federal District and Circuit Courts
     in their decisions to reconcile the conflict. Discusses
     remedies available under Title VII for unlawful seniority
     systems and other alternative remedies. Recommends pos-
     sible methods of resolving the conflict through affirmative
     action planning and modifications in collective bargaining
     agreements.

735. "Who Gets the Pink Slip? Conflict Between Ban on Hiring
     Discrimination and Layoffs." TIME, 105 (February 3,
     1975), 58.

     Briefly highlights the conflict with traditional seniority
     systems and affirmative action. Concludes that it will take
     further legislation or some direction from the U.S. Supreme
     Court before the conflict is resolved.

736. Wise, Nancy J. "EEOC: Seniority Rights During Layoffs in
     Light of Title VII -- Jersey Central Power and Light Co.
     v. Local 327, IBEW," 508 F.2d 687 (3rd Cir. 1975). UNIVER-
     OF DAYTON LAW REVIEW, 1 (January 1976), 71-77.

     Analyzes the court's decision in the above case, which ill-
     ustrates the conflict between contractual seniority systems
     and Title VII. States that the court held that contractual
     seniority systems did not violate Title VII; therefore, the
     employer was permitted to layoff according to another system
     that would have maintained a certain percentage of minority
     employees. Concludes that the court's decision ". . . indi-
     cates a decided unwillingness on the part of the courts to
     implement congressional policies during a recession."

737. Youngdahl, James E. "How Can Seniority, Anti-Discrimination
     and Affirmative Action Be Reconciled In A Layoff Economy:
     The Union View Point." PROCEEDINGS OF NEW YORK UNIVERSITY
     TWENTY-EIGHTH ANNUAL CONFERENCE ON LABOR. Edited by
     Richard Adelman. New York: Matthew Bender, 1976,
     pp. 297-316.

     Seeks to reconcile the conflict between plant seniority and
     the implementation of affirmative action programs. Discusses

alternatives to seniority systems, solutions to possible conflict, and employers' liability to laid-off employees who
have been victims of discrimination.

738. Zimmer, Michael J. "Teamsters: Redefinition and Retrench-
      ment of Concepts of Discrimination." PROCEEDINGS OF NEW
      YORK UNIVERSITY THIRTIETH ANNUAL NATIONAL CONFERENCE ON
      LABOR. Edited by Richard Adelman. New York: Matthew
      Bender, 1977, pp. 51-86.

      Analyzes the Supreme Court's decision in International
      Brotherhood of Teamsters v. United States. Concludes that
      the decision ". . . rearranges and restructures the law of
      employment discrimination."

REVERSE DISCRIMINATION - PREFERENTIAL TREATMENT - QUOTAS

*   Abraham, Henry J. "Some Post-<u>Bakke</u> and <u>Weber</u> Reflections on
    'Reverse Discrimination.'" See Item 1089.

739. Brown, William H., III. "Problems In 'Reverse Discrimina-
    tion': A Management View." PROCEEDINGS OF NEW YORK UNI-
    VERSITY THIRTY-SECOND ANNUAL NATIONAL CONFERENCE ON LABOR.
    New York: Matthew Bender, 1980, pp. 239-247.

740. "Case Study: EEO and Reverse Discrimination." EEO REVIEW,
    (December 1982), 2-3.

    Presents a case study on a reverse discrimination com-
    plaint. Provides comments and suggestions to managers and
    supervisors on how to effectively deal with EEO complaints
    in this area of the law.

741. Chen, Edward. "Comments, The Case for Minority Participation
    in Reverse Discrimination Litigation." CALIFORNIA LAW
    REVIEW, 67 (January 1979), 191-229.

    Argues that minority groups should intervene as a party to
    reverse discrimination litigation because they are the bene-
    ficiary of the race-conscious affirmative action program that
    is at issue. Cites the <u>Bakke</u> and <u>Weber</u> cases as examples of
    where a race-conscious affirmative action program was at
    issue and both plaintiff and defendant were white.

742. "Civil Rights - Employment Discrimination - Preferential
    Minority Treatment as an Appropriate Remedy Under Section
    703(j) of Title VII." TENNESSEE LAW REVIEW, 42 (Winter
    1975), 397-405.

    Examines federal court decisions which have prescribed some
    form of preferential remedial action to correct continuing
    effects of past discrimination on present employment oppor-
    tunities for minorities. Reviews the court's rationale in
    reconciling their decision with section 703(j) of Title VII
    which prohibits preferential treatment.

*   Cohen, David M. "An End to Affirmative Action?" See Item
    911.

743. Cohen, Carl. "Why Racial Preference Is Illegal and Immoral."
      COMMENTARY, 67 (June 1979), 40-52.

744. Coleman, Jules L. "Justice and Preferential Hiring." JOUR-
      NAL OF CRITICAL ANALYSIS, 5 (July-October 1973), 27-30.

745. "Court Turning Against Reverse Discrimination." U.S. NEWS
      AND WORLD REPORT, 81 (July 12, 1976), 63-64.

      Indicates that there is a conflict among lower courts'
      decisions as to whether preferential treatment for blacks and
      women in employment situations is legal. States that whites
      and males are winning some major reverse discrimination cases
      and so are blacks and women. Suggests that there is a need
      for the Supreme Court to give further clarification on this
      issue.

746. Davidson, Kenneth M. "Preferential Treatment and Equal
      Opportunity." OREGON LAW REVIEW, 55 (No. 1, 1976),
      53-83.

      Argues that ". . . preferential treatment is necessary to
      overcome long standing patterns of discrimination." Dis-
      cusses the legality of preferential treatment under the Con-
      stitution and Title VII. Explains the need for preferential
      treatment and provides guidelines on how preferential reme-
      dies can be implemented and at the same time minimize the
      displacement of white individuals.

747. D'Zurilla, William T. "Labor Law -- Employment Discrimina-
      tion - Voluntary Affirmative Action Plan With Racial Quota
      Does Not Violate Title VII of the Civil Rights Act of
      1964." TULANE LAW REVIEW, 54 (December 1979), 244-262.

      Outlines the facts in the Weber decision and related court
      decisions on racial quotas and preferential hiring of minori-
      ties. States that the Supreme Court's decision in Weber
      approved the use of quota-type affirmative action plans in
      situations where minorities have been excluded due to race
      discrimination. Recommends that courts approve Executive
      Order 11246's requirement that preferential hiring be used
      to correct past discrimination.

748. Edwards, Harry T. "Affirmative Action or Reverse Discrimina-
      tion: The Head and Tail of Weber." CREIGHTON LAW REVIEW,
      13 (1980), 713-767.

      Begins with an overview of the status of "race discrimi-
      nation" in America, specifically in employment. Provides
      statistical data to support that blacks have not made sig-
      nificant employment gains since the passage of Title VII.

Analyzes the Supreme Court's decisions in the __Bakke__ and __Weber__ cases, with special emphasis on the impact of the __Weber__ decision on affirmative action.

749. _____ and Barry L. Zaretsky. "Preferential Remedies for Employment Discrimination." MICHIGAN LAW REVIEWS, 74 (November 1975), 1-47.

750. Elliot, Robert M. "Reverse Discrimination: The Balancing of Human Rights." INDUSTRIAL RELATIONS LAW DIGEST, 9 (Spring 1977), 57-78.

Focuses on the growing concern and litigation over preferential treatment of protected class individuals in hirings and promotions. Attempts to balance the potential conflict between the employment rights of white male employees and protected class individuals. Provides a list of factors to be considered when balancing the interest between groups.

751. Ely, John Hart. "The Constitutionality of Reverse Racial Discrimination," UNIVERSITY OF CHICAGO LAW REVIEW, 41 (Summer 1974), 723-741.

752. Fried, Marlene Gerber. "In Defense of Preferential Hiring." PHILOSOPHICAL FORUM, 5 (Fall-Winter 1973-1974), 309-319.

753. Fullinwider, Robert K. "Preferential Hiring and Compensation." SOCIAL THEORY AND PRACTICE, 3 (Spring 1975), 307-320.

754. _____. THE REVERSE DISCRIMINATION CONTROVERSY: A MORAL AND LEGAL ANALYSIS. Totowa, N.J.: Rowman and Littlefield, 1980. 300 pp.

Provides a philosophical approach to reviewing the issue of reverse discrimination. Presents both sides of the argument on preferential hiring. Concludes that neither the Constitution nor principles of equality absolutely bar the use of racial preference in employment.

755. Goldman, Alan H. JUSTICE AND REVERSE DISCRIMINATION. Princeton, N.J.: Princeton University Press, 1979. 251 pp.

Defines reverse discrimination and preferential treatment. Considers the pros and cons of the issue and explains when and under what circumstances preferential treatment is permissible and when it is not.

756. Goodman, Carl F. "Equal Employment Opportunity: Preferential Quotas and Unrepresented Third Parties." PUBLIC PERSONNEL MANAGEMENT, 6 (November-December 1977), 371-397.

Examines the issue of ". . . whether the courts may properly order preferential employment plans where the beneficiaries have not shown particularized injury from discrimination and where individuals disadvantaged by the plans are not represented in court." Does an in-depth analysis of Carter v. Gallagher. In Gallagher, the Eight Circuit approved a preferential plan to hire minorities in a fire department that was initially all-white. Disagrees with the court's imposed remedy of eliminating past discrimination in employment practices. Believes that qualified white applicants would be denied employment due to their race and the legislative history of Title VII does not support racial quotas.

757. Greenawalt, Kent. "The Unresolved Problems of Reverse Discrimination." CALIFORNIA LAW REVIEW, 67 (January 1979), 87-130.

Analyzes the Supreme Court's decision in Regents of the University of California v. Bakke. Seeks to determine "what is clear and what is not clear" in the decision. Indicates that the decision did not clearly resolve the issue of "reverse discrimination."

758. Greenberg, Deborah. "Reverse Discrimination in Employment." PROCEEDINGS OF NEW YORK UNIVERSITY THIRTIETH ANNUAL NATIONAL CONFERENCE ON LABOR. New York: Matthew Bender, 1977, pp. 87-99.

Discusses the legal standards for establishing a claim of reverse discrimination in employment within the framework of the Thirteenth and Fourteenth Amendments to the Constitution, Section 1981 and 1983 of Title 42 of the U.S. Code, Title VII, and under other state laws. Explains what is permissible affirmative action and what action employers should take to protect themselves from claims of "reverse discrimination."

759. Gross, Barry R. DISCRIMINATION IN REVERSE: IS TURNABOUT FAIR PLAY? New York: New York University Press, 1978. 168 pp.

Gives a philosophical view of the problems of reverse discrimination. Seeks to determine how "invidious discriminatory practices" can be eliminated without infringing on the rights of others. Approaches the issue from a moral perspective and not from a legal perspective. Presents arguments for and against reverse discrimination. Concludes that reverse discrimination is morally wrong and goes against the American system of equal justice.

760. _____, ed. REVERSE DISCRIMINATION. Buffalo, New York: Prometheus Books, 1977. 401 pp.

A collection of articles by sociologists, political scientists, economists, lawyers, judges and philosophers which examine the present status of minorities, the pros and cons of affirmative action, and the controversial issue of reverse discrimination.

761. "Job 'Quotas' to Fight Bias -- Furor Goes On." U.S. NEWS AND WORLD REPORT, 89 (July 7, 1980), 45-47.

Indicates that the battle over affirmative action and job quotas continues. Briefly discusses court ordered hiring of minorities in Louisville, Kentucky; Los Angeles County; Cleveland; and in Atlanta. Believes that affirmative action programming will continue in the future but courts may give affirmative action programming a new direction.

*   Johnson, Ronald D. "Voluntary Affirmative Action in the Post-Weber Era: Issues and Answers." See Item 930.

762. Jones, James E., Jr. "'Reverse Discrimination' in Employment: Judicial Treatment of Affirmative Action Programs in the United States." HOWARD LAW JOURNAL, 25 (No. 2, 1982), 217-245.

763. Karnes, Daniel C. "The Legality of Preferential Treatment After Weber." OFCCP AND FEDERAL CONTRACT COMPLIANCE. Edited by David A. Corpus and Linda Rosenzweig. New York: Practicing Law Institute, 1981, pp. 169-196.

Presents five employment situations where preferential treatment may occur. Believes that goals and timetables developed by federal contractors to correct the underutilization of minorities and women is a form of preferential treatment. Questions whether the OFCCP requirement to establish race and sex-conscious preferential treatment is valid under Title VII or the Constitution. Analyzes the court's decisions in Weber, Bakke and other Circuit Court cases, and concludes that the OFCCP requirements" are "constitutionally suspect."

*   Kilberg, William J. and Stephen E. Tallent. "From Bakke to Fullilove: The Use of Racial and Ethnic Preferences in Employment." See Item 1102.

*   Larson, E. Richard. "Race Consciousness in Employment After Bakke." See Item 1103.

764. MacGuigan, Mark R.   "Reverse Discrimination Reversed."
      PHILOSOPHICAL LAW.   Edited by Richard Bronaugh.   Westport,
      CT.: Greenwood Press, 1978, pp. 84-92.

*   Marino, Kenneth E. "Conducting an Internal Compliance Review
      of Affirmative Action." See Item 943.

765. McGuiness, Kenneth C., ed.   PRFERENTIAL TREATMENT IN EMPLOY-
      MENT -- AFFIRMATIVE ACTION OR REVERSE DISCRIMINATION?
      Washington, D.C.: Equal Employment Advisory Council,
      1977. 143 pp.

      Gives an in-depth analysis of preferential treatment in the
      employment of protected class individuals. Includes topics
      on the OFCCP affirmative action requirements, preferential
      treatment within the realms of the Constitution, Title VII,
      and Supreme Court decisions. Explains the dilemma that
      employers face in giving preferential treatment to women and
      minorities and at the same time ensuring that white males are
      treated fairly.

766. Newton, Lisa H. "Reverse Discrimination as Unjustified."
      ETHICS, 83 (July 1973), 308-312.

*   Notes, "Employment Discrimination: Statistics and Prefer-
      ences Under Title VII." See Item 817.

767. Nyren, Karl. "Affirmative Action and Charges of 'Reverse
      Bias.'" LIBRARY JOURNAL, 101 (April 15, 1976), 985-987.

      A series of comments from library administrators on how
      they are ensuring affirmative action within their organiza-
      tion and at the same time avoiding charges of reverse dis-
      crimination. Reveals that there is a major disagreement
      among library administrators on whether reverse discrimina-
      tion is a problem.

768. Oster, Patrick. "'Reverse Discrimination,' Has it Gone Too
      Far?" U.S. NEWS AND WORLD REPORT, 80 (March 29, 1976),
      26-29.

      Attempts to determine whether courts and governmental
      agencies have gone too far in preventing and correcting dis-
      crimination. Presents both the critics' views on affirmative
      action and the supporters' views. Concludes that the Supreme
      Court has the final responsibility to decide ". . . where the
      anti-discrimination rights of minorities and women end and
      where those of whites and males begin?"

769. Reed, Janet L. "The Employer's Dilemma: Quotas, Reverse
      Discrimination, and Voluntary Compliance." LOYOLA UNI-
      VERSITY OF CHICAGO LAW JOURNAL, 8 (Winter 1977), 369-389.

      Examines the dilemma that employers are faced with when
      attempting to comply with quota provisions in a consent
      decree, defending claims of reverse discrimination, and when
      implementing a voluntary affirmative action program. Recom-
      mends that Congress, the courts, and the EEOC provide some
      direction to employers on which affirmative action remedies
      are legal under Title VII.

770. "'Reverse' Discrimination Still a Problem-Government Policy
      Changes on Remedial Quotas." EMPLOYMENT RELATIONS TODAY,
      10 (Spring 1983), 23-27.

      Finds that the Justice Department-Civil Rights Division,
      during the Reagan administration is against the use of hiring
      quotas and preferential treatment of minorities, as a means
      of correcting past discrimination. Briefly summarizes lead-
      ing employment discrimination cases where the Justice Depart-
      ment sided with white plaintiffs in contesting affirmative
      action programs that included hiring quotas for minorities.

771. Richards, John E. "Equal Protection and Racial Quotas:
      Where Does Fullilove v. Klutznick Leave Us?" BAYLOR LAW
      REVIEW, 33 (Winter 1981), 601-617.

      Analyzes the Supreme Court's decisions in University of
      California v. Bakke, United Steelworkers of America v. Weber,
      and Fullilove v. Klutznick. Concludes that the issue of
      racial quotas and preferential treatment for minorities is
      not settled. Maintains that the Supreme Court failed to give
      clear direction on which equal protection test to use when
      racial quotas are at issue. Summarizes the three decisions
      in this manner: (1) "Congress has the power to establish
      preferential quotas; (2) a state may or may not have such
      power, but may consider race as a factor in granting bene-
      fits; and (3) a private group may use quotas so long as they
      relate to traditionally segregated job categories and do not
      violate Title VII."

772. Roberts, Michael A. "Affirmative Action Without Reverse
      Discrimination." EEO TODAY, 4 (Autumn 1977), 193-199.

      Focuses specifically on governmental contractors who are
      required to develop an affirmative program as a requirement
      to do business with the federal government. In developing
      programs, an employer must determine whether women and minor-
      ities are under-utilized in the contractor's workforce. To
      prevent reverse discrimination, ". . . an employer "should
      not hire, train, or promote a woman or minority who is less
      qualified than identifiable white male candidates for the

same job, training opportunity, or promotion, unless there
is a court order or conciliation agreement directing that
this be done."

773. Robertson, David E. and Ronald D. Johnson. "Reverse Dis-
    crimination: Did Weber Decide the Issue?" LABOR LAW
    JOURNAL, 31 (November 1980), 693-699.

    Argues that the Weber decision did not completely settle
    the issue of whether "reverse discrimination" occurs when
    minorities receive preferential treatment under a voluntary
    affirmative plan. States the Supreme Court interpreted Sec-
    tion 703 of Title VII to mean that Congress did not intend
    to prohibit all race-conscious affirmative action programs.
    This position taken by the Supreme Court did not completely
    make the issue of "reverse discrimination" clear.

774. Rose, Stephen. "Reverse Discrimination Developments Under
    Title VII." HOUSTON LAW REVIEW, 15 (October 1977), 136-
    156.

    Presents a series of cases contesting the use of affirma-
    tive action programs, quotas, and preferential hiring of
    minorities. Analyzes the court decisions, corrective ac-
    tions, and consent decrees in discrimination suits. Indi-
    cates that the use of quotas and preferential treatment in
    hiring procedures are becoming disfavored by non-minorities.
    Suggests that the use of quotas be de-emphasized, and that
    non-discriminatory policies and criteria in hiring procedures
    be implemented by employers.

775. Rossum, Ralph A. REVERSE DISCRIMINATION: THE CONSTITUTIONAL
    DEBATE. New York: Marcel Dekker, Inc., 1980. 224 pp.

    Sees reverse discrimination as both a social and constitu-
    tional issue. Examines the argument for and against reverse
    discrimination, and reviews the Appellate and Supreme Court
    decisions in Regents of the University of California v. Bakke
    and DeFunis v. Odegaard.

*   Sahlein, Stephen. THE AFFIRMATIVE ACTION HANDBOOK. See
    Item 970.

776. Sher, George. "Justifying Reverse Discrimination in Employ-
    ment." PHILOSOPHY AND PUBLIC AFFAIRS, 4 (1975), 1159-1170.

    Examines the justifications for preferential hiring of
    minorities and women over ". . . the best qualified applicant
    for a given job." Indicates that not every black or woman
    has been disadvantaged by past discrimination, therefore,
    preferential treatment may not be justified as a whole but on

an individual basis. Suggests that poor whites have been
victims of past discrimination and deserve preferential
hiring just like blacks.

777. Slate, Martin. "Preferential Relief In Employment Cases."
      LOYOLA UNIVERSITY OF CHICAGO LAW JOURNAL, 5 (Summer 1974),
      315-348.

      Examines various approaches used by courts in ordering
      preferential relief to victims in cases brought under the
      Civil Rights Acts of 1866 and 1870, and Title VII, as
      amended. Outlines the legal and social theories that courts
      have used to support the use of preferential relief. Con-
      cludes that courts are taking a "middle of the road" approach
      in using this relief to avoid possible conflict.

778. Stewart, Shirley E. "The Myth of Reverse Racial Discrimina-
      tion: An Historical Perspective." CLEVELAND STATE LAW
      REVIEW, 23 (Spring 1974), 319-336.

      Gives a historical view of past discrimination of blacks
      and its affect on present day discrimination. Analyzes the
      impact of affirmative action and preferential treatment on
      employment and education discrimination. Recommends that
      America take immediate action to ensure equality among all
      races. Concludes that "[w]hite Americans can no longer name
      the game, stack the deck, and then demand, under the guise
      of equal protection, to walk away with all of the prizes."

779. Taylor, Paul W. "Reverse Discrimination and Compensatory
      Justice." ANALYSIS, 33 (June 1973), 177-182.

      Advocates that groups of individuals who have been discrim-
      inated against due to a "morally irrelevant characteristic
      [such as being a woman, being black, being a Jew, etc.],"
      should receive "compensatory justice." Describes "compensa-
      tory justice" as involving reverse discrimination. Believes
      it is necessary to correct a past injustice.

780. Vaughn, Dennis H. "Employment Quotas - Discrimination or
      Affirmative Action?" EMPLOYEE RELATIONS LAW JOURNAL, 7
      (Spring 1982), 552-566.

781. Venick, Shelley J. and Ronald A. Lane. "Doubling the Price
      of Past Discrimination: The Employer's Burden After
      McDonald v. Santa Fe Trail Transportation Co." LOYOLA
      UNIVERSITY OF CHICAGO LAW JOURNAL, 8 (Summer 1977), 789-812.

      Gives a historical view of reverse discrimination in em-
      ployment and analyzes the court's decision in McDonald.
      Explains the dilemma employers are in when implementing

affirmative action and ensuring equal opportunities for all
employees, including white employees.

782. Wilson, James B. "Some Practical Problems in Defending a
     Reverse Discrimination Case." HOWARD LAW JOURNAL, 21
     (No. 2, 1977), 579-584.

     Gives a brief account of practical problems that defense
     attorneys will have in defending a case, involving a reverse
     discrimination claim. Points to the main issue of whether
     race can be used as a factor for selection into an educa-
     tional program or in employment without violating the
     Constitution.

*   Zashin, Elliot M. "Affirmative Action, Preferential Selec-
     tion, and Federal Employment." See Item 1002.

AVAILABILITY AND THE LABOR MARKET

*   American Bar Association, Section of Labor Relations Law.
        PROCEEDINGS OF THE THIRD ABA NATIONAL INSTITUTE ON EQUAL
        EMPLOYMENT LAW. See Item 1.

783.   Ashenfelter, Orley C. "Racial Discrimination and Labor
        Markets." Ph.D. dissertation, Princeton University, 1970.

        Presents an empirical and theoretical study on the economic
        implication of race discrimination in the labor market.
        Major topics include: "Racial Discrimination and Trade
        Unionism," "The Inter-Industry Structure of the Relative
        Wages of Negro Workers," and "Changes in Labor Market Dis-
        crimination Over Time."

784.   _____ and Albert Rees, eds. DISCRIMINATION IN LABOR
        MARKETS. Princeton, N.J.: Princeton University Press,
        1973. 181 pp.

        A collection of papers presented during a conference on
        "Discrimination in the Labor Markets," held at Princeton Uni-
        versity on October 7 and 8, 1971. A majority of the articles
        are written by economists who give a theoretical and quanti-
        tative analysis of discrimination in the labor market.

*   Becker, Gary S. THE ECONOMICS OF DISCRIMINATION. See Item
        6.

785.   Bloch, Howard R. and Robert L. Pennington. "Measuring
        Discrimination: What is a Relevant Labor Market?"
        PERSONNEL, 57 (July-August 1980), 21-29.

        Explains how to determine the relevant labor market when
        determining whether an employer is engaged in discriminatory
        hiring practices. Analyzes the court decision in U.S. v.
        County of Fairfax, which supported the county's claim ". . .
        that the government's designation of its relevant labor
        market didn't match its applicant flow, and for good non-
        discriminatory reasons." Concludes that factors such as the
        expense of commuting to a geographical area and the salary
        status of a position in a particular geographical region may
        cause the relevant labor market to be smaller for the purpose
        of establishing EEO goals and determining whether hiring
        practices are discriminatory.

786. _____. "Labor Market Analysis As A Test of Discrimi-
     nation." PERSONNEL JOURNAL, 59 (August 1980), 649-652.

787. Chiswick, Barry R. "Racial Discrimination in the Labor
     Market: A Test of Alternative Hypotheses." JOURNAL OF
     POLITICAL ECONOMY, 81 (November-December 1973), 1330-1349.

788. Equal Employment Advisory Council. PERSPECTIVES ON AVAIL-
     ABILITY: A SYMPOSIUM ON DETERMINING PROTECTED GROUP REPRE-
     SENTATION IN INTERNAL AND EXTERNAL LABOR MARKETS. Washing-
     ton, D.C., 1977. 243 pp.

     A collection of articles on the problems of determining the
     availability of women and minorities in the labor market when
     establishing goals and timetables for affirmative action.

789. Gastwirth, Joseph L. and Sheldon E. Haber. "Defining The
     Labor Market for Equal Employment Standards." MONTHLY
     LABOR REVIEW, 99 (March 1976), 32-36.

     Presents a model for determining and estimating the rele-
     vant labor market of blacks. The major operating component
     of the model is the utilization of data on applicants' resi-
     dential location and the proximity of the job. Sees inade-
     quacies in the use of SMSA data when measuring or determining
     employment discrimination in hiring. Sees their model as
     providing more reliable data for establishing fair employment
     standards.

790. Knauer, Leslie Zeoli. "The 1970 Census and Other Data
     Sources Relevant to Equal Employment Opportunity." EQUAL
     EMPLOYMENT PRACTICE GUIDE. Vol. I. Edited by John R.
     Erickson and Katherine Savers McGovern. Washington, D.C.:
     Bureau of National Affairs, 1979, pp. VI-1 - VI-22.

     Explains how the 1970 Census data is collected and tabu-
     lated. States that census data is a "key source" of data
     used in preparing affirmative action programs and in Title
     VII cases. Believes that the 1980 Census will provide even
     more statistical information on minorities.

*   Koral, Alan M. "Practical Application of the Uniform Guide-
     lines: What to do 'Til the Agency Comes.'" See Item 622.

*   Marshall, Ray. "Equal Employment Opportunities: Problems
     and Prospects." See Item 60.

180   AVAILABILITY AND THE LABOR MARKET

791.   Potter, Stewart G.   "The Black Labor Market -- What?--
       Where?--When?" PERSONNEL ADMINISTRATOR, 16 (January-
       February 1971), 17-20.

792.   Schneider, Stephen A.   The AVAILABILITY OF MINORITIES AND
       WOMEN FOR PROFESSIONAL AND MANAGERIAL POSITIONS - 1970-
       1985. Philadelphia, PA.:   University of Pennsylvania,
       1977. 280 pp.

       States that affirmative action planning requires that goals
       and timetables be developed to project the hiring of minori-
       ties and women. To develop meaningful affirmative action
       plans, the employer must have data on the availability of
       qualified minority and female workers. Examines various
       sources of data on minorities and women in the field of engi-
       neering, law, accounting, business chemistry, physics, medi-
       cine, and dentistry. Concludes that by 1985, minority and
       female participation will have substantially improved in the
       professions he has studied.

793.   Snider, Patricia J.   "Measurement of Availability: A Con-
       ceptual Issue." EQUAL EMPLOYMENT PRACTICE GUIDE. Edited
       by John R. Erickson and Katherine Savers McGovern. Wash-
       ington, D.C.:   Bureau of National Affairs, 1979, pp.
       VI-23 - VI-34.

       Defines and explains the concept of "measuring availabil-
       ity" of women and minorities in the labor market for assess-
       ing under utilization and establishing affirmative action
       goals. Concludes that employers and enforcement agencies are
       at conflict in determining whether availability should be
       used as a "benchmark or mechanism" in causing social change.

794.   U.S. Equal Employment Opportunity Commission. JOB PATTERNS
       FOR MINORITIES AND WOMEN IN PRIVATE INDUSTRY. Washington,
       D.C.:   Government Printing Office, 1970.

       Presents statistical data on the occupational distribution
       of minorities and women in the workforce. Provides nation-
       wide and state totals by occupation, sex, and by selected
       industries.

795.   _____.   MINORITIES AND WOMEN IN APPRENTICESHIP PRO-
       GRAMS AND REFERRAL UNIONS. Washington, D.C.:   Government
       Printing Office, February 1980.

       Provides a statistical report on the makeup of minorities
       and women in apprenticeship programs as of 1978. Includes
       the number of graduates, dropouts, and applicants by indus-
       try, craft, union, and geographical location.

796. _____ . Office of Planning, Research and Systems.
     BLACK EXPERIENCES VERSUS EXPECTATION, A CASE FOR FAIR-
     SHARE EMPLOYMENT. Prepared by Melvin Humphrey, Ph.D.
     Washington, D.C.: Government Printing Office, 1977,
     pp. 94.

     Analyzes the status of black employment within private
     industry between 1969 and 1974. Statistical data for the
     analysis is derived from employers who are required to submit
     an EEO-1 Employer Information Report to the Equal Employment
     Opportunity Commission. One major finding of the report con-
     clude that black workers as a class are still adversely
     affected by employment discrimination.

797. _____ . Office of Program Planning and Evaluation.
     JOB PATTERNS FOR MINORITIES AND WOMEN IN PRIVATE INDUSTRY,
     1980, Vol. I AND II. Washington, D.C.: Government Print-
     ing Office, 1982.

     A statistical report on the makeup of minorities and women
     employed by private industry as of 1980. Summarizes data
     collected on EEO-1 surveys. The EEO-1 survey is conducted
     annually by the Commission and reports employment data by job
     classification and salary.

798. _____ . Office of Program Planning and Evaluation.
     JOB PATTERNS FOR MINORITIES AND WOMEN IN STATE AND LOCAL
     GOVERNMENT, 1980. Washington, D.C.: Government Printing
     Office, 1982.

     A statistical report on the makeup of minorities and women
     employed by state and local government as of 1980. Summa-
     rizes data collected from the State and Local Government
     Information Report-EEO-4. Reports employment data by job
     classification and salaries.

799. U.S. General Accounting Office. ACHIEVING REPRESENTATION OF
     MINORITIES AND WOMEN IN THE FEDERAL WORKFORCE. REPORT TO
     THE CONGRESS BY THE COMPTORLLER GENERAL OF THE UNITED
     STATES. Washington, D.C.: Government Printing Office,
     1980.

800. U.S. Office of Personnel Management. A GUIDE FOR ASSESSING
     THE DISTRIBUTION OF MINORITIES AND WOMEN IN RELEVANT LABOR
     MARKETS. Washington, D.C.: Government Printing Office,
     1979. 79 pp.

801. U.S. Women's Bureau. UNDER-UTILIZATION OF WOMEN WORKERS.
     Rev. ed. Washington, D.C.: Government Printing Office,
     1971. 25 pp.

A statistical study on the inequities in pay for women in professional and technical occupations, recent college graduates, and in the education field.

802. Wallace, Phyllis A. "Employment Discrimination: Some Policy Considerations." DISCRIMINATION IN THE LABOR MARKETS. Edited by Orley Ashenfelter and Albert Rees. Princeton, N.J.: Princeton University Press, 1973, pp. 155-175.

Outlines the federal system of enforcing equal employment laws, regulations, and executive orders. Includes a discussion of the Civil Rights Act of 1964 as amended, and Executive Order 11246. Briefly discusses the enforcement and internal procedures of the Equal Employment Opportunity Commission, the Office of Federal Contract Compliance, and the U.S. Civil Service Commission. Contends that the federal system of enforcing equal employment is ". . . cumbersome, ad hoc, and not so comprehensive as it could be." Sets forth alternative strategies for improving the system.

803. Wolfe, Barbara L. "How the Disabled Fare In The Labor Market." MONTHLY LABOR REVIEW, 103 (September 1980), 48-52.

STATISTICS

804. Aigner, Dennis J. and Glen C. Cain. "Statistical Theories
of Discrimination in Labor Market." INDUSTRIAL AND LABOR
RELATIONS REVIEW, 30 (January 1977), 175-187.

805. Cohn, Richard M. "On the Use of Statistics In Employment
Discrimination Cases." INDIANA LAW JOURNAL, 55 (1980),
493-513.

Indicates that the use of quantitative data to prove or
disprove employment discrimination cases is becoming very
common. Explains and illustrates how statistics can be used
and misused in such cases. Advises civil rights litigants to
become aware of at least ". . . the basic logic of statistical inference, the proper measures to indicate discrimination
and the analytic procedures which can be used to demonstrate
discrimination."

806. Connolly, Walter B., Jr. and David W. Peterson. THE USE OF
STATISTICS IN EQUAL EMPLOYMENT OPPORTUNITY LITIGATION.
New York: Law Journal Seminars-Press, Inc., 1980. 374 pp.

Discusses the use of statistics in proving and defending
civil right cases. Explains the various statistical methods
of determining the extent of employment discrimination in
personnel practices. Focuses on discriminatory practices
in ". . . recruiting, hiring, discipline, discharge, job
assignment, transfers, promotions, testing, selection procedures, and matters pertaining to pay."

807. "EEO: What the Numbers Mean-and How They Work." EEO REVIEW,
(May 1977), 6-8.

Advises managers and supervisors on the importance of EEO
statistical data. States that some courts will find discrimination if there is a statistical imbalance of minorities
and women in the employer's workforce. Explains how to
determine the percentage of minorities and women in the workforce and their availability in the labor market. Advises
managers and supervisors to maintain applicant flow data and
to discover any under-representation of minorities and women
in the workforce.

808. Grady, John S. "Statistics in Employment Discrimination."
      LABOR LAW JOURNAL, 30 (December 1979), 748-753.

      States that statistics may be used as evidence to prove or
      disprove a case of discrimination and explains how to use
      statistics in promotion and discharge cases.

809. Haertel, Robert J. "The Statistical Procedure for Calculat-
      ing Adverse Impact." PERSONNEL ADMINISTRATOR, 29, (January
      1984), 55-58.

      Explains how to determine whether adverse impact exist as
      defined by the Uniform Guidelines on Employee Selection, the
      procedure for computing the 80 percent rule, Chi-square, and
      standard deviation tests.

810. Hallock, Marcy M. "The Numbers Game-The Use and Misuse of
      Statistics in Civil Rights Litigation." VILLANOVA LAW
      REVIEW, 23 (November 1977), 5-34.

      A comprehensive study on the use of statistics during the
      litigation of an employment discrimination case. Focuses on
      the judicial application and acceptance of statistics by
      courts in rendering a decision.

811. Hay, Howard C. "The Use of Statistics to Disprove Employment
      Discrimination." LABOR LAW JOURNAL, 29 (July 1978), 430-
      440.

      Indicates that statistics may be used to prove or disprove
      discrimination cases involving disparate treatment and dis-
      parate impact. "Pass/fail comparison and population/work-
      force comparison" are the typical statistical data presented.
      Concludes that employers can defend against a complaint by
      maintaining an applicant flow system and to "recruit in a
      nondiscriminatory manner."

812. Holley, William H. and Hubert S. Feild. "Using Statistics
      in Employment Discrimination Cases." EMPLOYEE RELATIONS
      LAW JOURNAL, 4 (Summer 1978), 24-33.

813. Joseph, Michael E. "Evidence: Statistical Proof in Employ-
      ment Discrimination Cases." OKLAHOMA LAW REVIEW, 28
      (1975), 885-894.

      Illustrates the use of statistical evidence in discrimina-
      tion cases under Title VII and explains the weight accorded
      to statistical evidence by courts. Concludes that statisti-
      cal data ". . . can prove objective criteria by which a judge
      or jury can view the consequences of particular employment

practices." Warns that statistical data can also be used
inappropriately in employment discrimination cases.

814.   Kolesar, Peter J. "Statistical Concepts in EEO Litigation."
       EMPLOYMENT DISCRIMINATION 1979.   Edited by Paul I. Weiner.
       New York: Practicing Law Institute, 1979, pp. 231-265.

       Explains how plaintiffs in discrimination complaints can
       use statistics in establishing a prima facie case and how
       the respondent (employer) can rebut such statistical data.
       Discusses basic statistical concepts, e.g., random samples,
       probability, expected values, variance, standard deviation,
       and binomial probability law. Concludes that statistics can
       be used to scientifically determine whether there is a cor-
       relation between "age and layoff, sex and seniority and
       performance rating, and pay, etc."

815.   McGuire, J.P. "The Use of Statistics in Title VII Cases."
       LABOR LAW JOURNAL, 30 (June 1979), 361-370.

       Analyzes the use of statistical evidence in employment de-
       cisions rendered under Title VII, the "Reconstruction" Civil
       Rights Acts, the Fourteenth Amendment, and under the state of
       Ohio employment discrimination laws.

816.   Montlack, Kenneth. "Using Statistical Evidence to Enforce
       the Laws Against Discrimination." CLEVELAND STATE LAW
       REVIEW, 22 (Spring 1973), 259-280.

817.   "Notes, Employment Discrimination: Statistics and Prefer-
       ences Under Title VII." VIRGINIA LAW REVIEW, 59 (March
       1973), 463-491.

       Explains the use of statistics in proving a Title VII case
       and the statistical method used, e.g., "comparative and demo-
       graphic." In proving a practice of discrimination, the sta-
       tistical data must show that minorities were substantially
       impacted. Discusses the remedies used by the court when dis-
       crimination has been found, e.g., quotas, affirmative action,
       and preferential treatment. Indicates that the remedies used
       by the court may raise statutory and constitutional issues.

818.   Phelps, Edmunds. "The Statistical Theory of Racism and
       Sexism." AMERICAN ECONOMIC REVIEW, 62 (September 1972),
       659-669.

819.   Smith, Arthur B., Jr. and Thomas G. Abram. "Quantitative
       Analysis and Proof of Employment Discrimination." UNIVER-
       SITY OF ILLINOIS LAW REVIEW, 1981 (No. 1), 33-74.

820. U.S. Civil Service Commission. "Statistical Tools for Affir-
      mative Action Planning." EEO FOR STATE AND LOCAL GOVERN-
      MENTS. Issue No. 12. Washington, D.C.: Government Print-
      ing Office, 1975. 9 pp.

      Provides step by step guidelines on how to use statistics
      in doing a workforce analysis. Explains that after statis-
      tics have been compiled and analyzed, the employer can deter-
      mine where minorities and women are under-utilized within the
      organization. Provides a list of publications on the avail-
      ability of minorities and women in various occupations.

821. U.S. Office of Personnel Management, Office of Intergovern-
      mental Personnel Programs. APPLICANT EEO DATA SYSTEMS IN
      STATE AND LOCAL GOVERNMENTS, PRACTICAL APPLICATION AND
      CURRENT DEVELOPMENTS. Washington, D.C.: Government Print-
      ing Office, 1981.

822. _____. "Collecting Race, Sex, and Ethnic Group Sta-
      tistics on Job Applicants." EEO INFORMATION ON EQUAL EM-
      PLOYMENT OPPORTUNITY FOR STATE AND LOCAL GOVERNMENT. Issue
      No. 19. Washington, D.C.: Government Printing Office, May
      1979. 14 pp.

      Finds that State governments are collecting EEO data on
      job applicants ". . . for the purpose of evaluating personnel
      selection procedures for adverse impact against certain
      groups." Indicates that various methods of collecting EEO
      data on applicants are used. Maintains that where self-
      identification is used, some applicants intentionally give
      the wrong information or no information at all. Legal re-
      quirements for the collection of EEO data are derived from
      various civil right laws and regulations, including the
      Supreme Court's decision in Griggs v. Duke Power Company and
      the Uniform Guidelines on Employee Selection Procedures.

823. _____. EEO STATISTICAL REPORT ON EMPLOYMENT IN STATE
      AND LOCAL GOVERNMENT, EMPLOYMENT SECURITY, HEALTH, AND
      WELFARE PROGRAMS, COMPARISON OF 1970, 1974, 1976. Washing-
      ton, D.C.: Government Printing Office, 1979. 7 pp.

      Examines trends and changes in the employment of women and
      minorities in state and local employment security, health and
      welfare programs. Finds that women and minorities are em-
      ployed at a higher rate in the security, health and welfare
      functions of state and local government than other functions
      which were reported to the Equal Employment Opportunity Com-
      mission. Concludes that a greater effort should be made in
      employing women and minorities in the officials/administra-
      tors, professionals and technician categories.

824. Westcott, Diane Nilsen. "Blacks in the 1970's: Did They
      Scale The Job Ladder?" MONTHLY LABOR REVIEW, 105 (June
      1982), 29-38.

      Reviews statistical data on the 1970 Decennial Census popu-
      lation counts. Concludes that more blacks have been hired
      into white-collar jobs; however, very few blacks have moved
      up the ladder to highly professional or managerial positions.
      The mobility of blacks slowed down in the 1970's due to a
      sluggish economy, inflation, and three recessions. States
      that blacks achieved more advancements during the 1960's be-
      cause of the passage of the Civil Rights Act of 1964, the
      establishment of the Equal Employment Opportunity Commission,
      and because of "favorable economic conditions."

INTERVIEWING AND EMPLOYMENT APPLICATIONS

*   Arvey, Richard D. FAIRNESS IN SELECTING EMPLOYEES. See
       Item 4.

825. Austin, David. "Is the Interview an Analog?" PERSONNEL
      ADMINISTRATOR, (January-February 1972), 13-15.

      Reviews the Supreme Court's decision in Griggs v. Duke
      Power. Concludes that the behavior an applicant displays in
      an interview is not comparable to the behavior required or
      needed to perform most job assignments; therefore, the data
      collected during interviews may not sufficiently predict an
      applicant's success on the job.

826. Bernstein, Leonard S. "How to 'Discriminate' in Hiring."
      DUN'S, 100 (October 1972), 105.

827. Burrington, Debra D. "A Review of State Government Employ-
      ment Application Forms for Suspect Inquires." PUBLIC PER-
      SONNEL MANAGEMENT, 11 (Spring 1982), 55-60.

      Finds that employment applications presently being used by
      state governmental agencies have pre-employment inquiries
      that would be considered "suspicious" and may violate various
      civil rights laws. Gives examples of inquiries that are in-
      appropriate and provides revisions that would be more appro-
      priate to ask of applicants.

828. Citti, Richard M. "When You Say 'No' to Job Applicants:
      How to Avoid Charges of Bias." SUPERVISORY MANAGEMENT, 18
      (January 1973), 2-6.

829. Cook, Suzanne H. "The EEO Interview: Turning a Gamble Into
      a Good Bet." MANAGEMENT WORLD, 7 (November 1978), 18-21.

      Outlines specific employment interviewing procedures that
      are designed to minimize EEO complaints from job applicants.
      Provides a list of pre-employment questions that are con-
      sidered non-discriminatory.

830. Dipboye, Robert L.; Richard D. Arvey; and David E. Terpstra.
      "Equal Employment and the Interview." PERSONNEL JOURNAL,
      55 (October 1976), 520.

831. Executive Enterprises Publication Co., Inc. CONDUCTING THE
      LAWFUL EMPLOYMENT INTERVIEW: HOW TO AVOID CHARGES OF
      DISCRIMINATION WHEN INTERVIEWING JOB CANDIDATES. 2nd rev.
      ed. New York, 1979. 32 pp.

      A pamphlet designed to assist employment interviewers on
      how to obtain employment data from applicants in a non-
      discriminatory manner. Gives a concise description of fed-
      eral EEO laws and regulations, e.g., Title VII, the Equal Pay
      Act, the Age Discrimination Act, etc. Provides answers to
      commonly asked questions from interviewers concerning the
      application of federal EEO laws and regulations.

832. Fear, Richard A. and James F. Ross. JOBS, DOLLARS, AND EEO-
      HOW TO HIRE MORE PRODUCTIVE ENTRY-LEVEL WORKERS. New York:
      McGraw-Hill Book Company, 1983. 226 pp.

      Outlines procedures on selecting the "best-qualified" indi-
      viduals for employment within EEO requirements. Focuses spe-
      cifically on understanding EEO laws and regulations, selec-
      tion procedures, and how to conduct employment interviews.

833. Friedman, Mark Joel. "Differences In Assessment Center Per-
      formance as a Function of the Race and Sex of Ratees and
      the Race of Assessors." Ph.D. dissertation, University of
      Tennessee, 1980.

      Seeks to determine whether the race or sex of the ratees
      and assessors in an assessment center selection program were
      factors in the ratings given to the ratees. The study in-
      volved 256 employees at a large southeastern utility company
      who were considered for a management development and training
      program. Finds that the assessment center ". . . appear[ed]
      to be free of biases related to sex or race discrimination
      [and] that it may be used to promote equal employment oppor-
      tunities." Includes discussions on the operation, validity,
      and reliability of assessment centers as a selection device.

834. Gatewood, Robert D. and James Ledvinka. "Selection Inter-
      viewing and EEO: Mandate for Objectivity." THE PERSONNEL
      ADMINISTRATOR, 24 (December 1979), 51-54.

      Contends that interviews "must be job related just as tests
      must be." Believes that interviews must comply with EEOC
      guidelines and conform to court decisions that suggest that
      interview systems be standardized and supported by documen-
      tation.

835. Greenlaw, Paul S. and John P. Kohl. "Selection Interviewing
      and the New Uniform Federal Guidelines." PERSONNEL ADMIN-
      ISTRATOR, 25 (August 1980), 74-80.

      States that the guidelines are applicable to employment
      interviewing. Discusses the applicability of adverse impact
      and selection validation to interviewing. Believes that
      adverse impact will be minimized and validation unnecessary
      if interviewers are properly trained, and if interviewees are
      counseled on how to prepare for an interview.

836. "How to Check Out a Job Applicant - Legally." EEO REVIEW,
      (April 1980), 6-7.

      Provides suggestions and helpful hints to managers and
      supervisors on how to collect data on job applicants and at
      the same time avoid discrimination complaints.

837. "Interviewing Women: Evaluating the Applicants." EEO
      REVIEW, (September 1977), 6-8.

      Designed to assist managers and supervisors to fairly
      evaluate women applicants to avoid employment discrimination
      complaints. Includes an "evaluation checklist" for recording
      a summary of applicants' evaluation ratings.

838. Jablin, Fredric M. "Use of Discriminatory Questions in
      Screening Interviews." PERSONNEL ADMINISTRATOR, 27 (March
      1982), 41-94.

      Reports on a survey of college placement directors' views
      on the types and frequency of discriminatory questions asked
      of applicants during the interviewing process. Concludes
      that ". . . illegal questions related to the sex of inter-
      viewees occur more often than inquiries into other poten-
      tially discriminating areas. Moreover, women appear to be
      the focus of this sexual discrimination, often being asked
      questions about their marital and family plans or the manage-
      ment of these activities." An applicant's age was the second
      most common area of discriminatory questions asked.

839. Jackson, Tom. INTERVIEWING WOMEN: AVOIDING CHARGES OF DIS-
      CRIMINATION. New York: Executive Enterprises Publications
      Co., 1976. 46 pp.

      Indicates that sex stereotypes and biased attitudes from
      employment interviewers may prevent qualified females from
      being hired, especially for non-traditional or male oriented
      positions. Outlines guidelines and procedures for conducting
      an effective, yet a lawful interview with female applicants.

Believes the ". . . result will be better interviewing, better selection, and more women in meaningful jobs."

840. Koen, Clifford M., Jr. "The Pre-Employment Inquiry Guide." PERSONNEL JOURNAL, 59 (October 1980), 825-829.

Maintains that EEO and affirmative action regulations and court decisions have made various pre-employment inquiries unlawful. Provides a step by step guide to what can and cannot be legally asked of an applicant during an employment interview.

841. Lowell, Richard S. and Jay A. DeLoach. "Equal Employment Opportunity: Are You Overlooking the Application Form?" PERSONNEL, 59 (July-August 1982), 49-58.

Examines job application forms of 50 major U.S. companies. Finds that 48 of the applications reviewed violated EEOC regulations. The most prevalent violations were questions involving the applicant's ". . . military background, education, arrest records, physical handicaps, age and name." Believes that the violations existed ". . . as a result of either the employer's ignorance of Title VII regulations or sheer deception."

*   Macleod, Jennifer S. "Making the System Work For Instead of Against Affirmative Action Job Candidates." See Item 941.

*   McCullough, Kenneth J. SELECTING EMPLOYEES SAFELY UNDER THE LAW. See Item 62.

842. Miller, Ernest C. "An EEO Examination of Employment Applications." THE PERSONNEL ADMINISTRATOR, 25 (March 1980), 63.

Analyzes the results of a research study on a sample of Fortune 500 organizations' employment applications. Provides a list of inappropriate questions on employment applications and suggests substitute questions.

843. Paylo, Joan. "Avoiding Pitfalls in Interviewing Women." MANAGER'S GUIDE TO EQUAL EMPLOYMENT OPPORTUNITY. Edited by Robert Freiberg. New York: Executive Enterprises Publication Co., Inc., 1977, pp. 51-61.

Warns that interviewers who are unfamiliar or lack a clear understanding of EEO laws and regulations may ask the "wrong questions" of women applicants. Believes there may be cultural stereotypes and assumptions from both the applicant

and interviewer. For these reasons, suggest that the interviewer be aware of the social and legal implications of interviewing women applicants. Outlines various EEO laws and
regulations. Briefly explains traditional stereotypes of
women in the workforce and suggests ways on how to conduct a
lawful interview.

844. Peterson, Mark A. "How to Conduct the Lawful Employment
      Interview." MANAGER'S GUIDE TO EQUAL EMPLOYMENT OPPOR-
      TUNITY. Edited by Robert Freiberg. New York: Executive
      Enterprises Publication Co., Inc., 1977, pp. 39-50.

      Provides questions, answers and case studies related to
      employment interviewing, testing, and application forms.

845. Pickens, William, III. "The Interview--The Black Viewpoint."
      BUSINESS HORIZONS, 13 (October 1970), 13-22.

      Provides suggestions to managers on how to conduct a fair
      and sensitive interview with black applicants.

846. Pursell, Elliott D.; Michael A. Campion; and Sarah R. Gay-
      lord. "Structured Interviewing: Avoiding Selection Prob-
      lems." PERSONNEL ADMINISTRATOR, 59 (November 1980), 907-
      912.

      Recommends that traditional interviewing techniques be
      discontinued by employers and that they establish a more
      structured interviewing format. Includes discussions on job
      analysis, developing sample questions for interviews, and
      developing performance appraisals.

847. Rogers, Jean L. and Walter L. Fortson. FAIR EMPLOYMENT
      INTERVIEWING. Reading, MA.: Addison-Wesley Publishing
      Company, 1976. 155 pp.

848. Schweitzer, Nancy J. and John Deely. "Interviewing the
      Disabled Job Applicant." PERSONNEL JOURNAL, 61 (March
      1982), 205-209.

      Provides interviewing tips to personnel managers and other
      interviewers on how to comply with Section 503 of the Voca-
      tional Rehabilitation Amendments of 1978 when interviewing
      handicapped applicants and at the same time eliminate any
      feeling of uneasiness. Suggests four areas that interviewers
      should be skilled in: ". . . being aware of attitudinal
      barriers; acquiring information about specific disabilities;
      understanding the reasonable accommodation process; and uti-
      lizing referral sources."

849. Taylor, Vernon R. "You Just Can't Get Through to Whitey:
     Interviewing Minority Group Members." PUBLIC PERSONNEL
     REVIEW, 30 (October 1969), 199-204.

     Provides suggestions on how to fairly interview minorities
     and disadvantaged applicants.

850. Terpstra, David E. "The Effects of Applicant Race and
     Qualification and type of Job on Hiring Decisions." Ph.D.
     dissertation, University of Tennessee, 1978.

     Seeks to determine whether black job applicants ". . .
     receive less favorable hirability and starting salary assign-
     ment . . ." on jobs traditionally held by whites and whether
     the same results occur to white applicants who apply for jobs
     traditionally held by blacks. Finds that ". . . blacks re-
     ceived significantly higher hirability and salary assignment
     rating than whites for the black type jobs, while whites were
     rated more favorably than blacks for white type jobs.

851. U.S. Manpower Administration. INTERVIEWING GUIDES FOR
     SPECIFIC DISABILITIES, HEARING IMPAIRMENTS. Washington,
     D.C.: Government Printing Office, 1971.

852. U.S. Office of Personnel Management, Office of Intergovern-
     mental Personnel Programs. APPLICANT EEO DATA SYSTEMS IN
     STATE AND LOCAL GOVERNMENT. Washington, D.C.: Government
     Printing Office, January 1981. 38 pp.

     Details procedures and methods for state and local govern-
     ments on how to collect and maintain EEO data on applicants.
     States that such data is needed to determine whether an
     employer's selection procedure has an adverse impact on
     minorities and women.

*   U. S. Office of Personnel, Intergovernmental Personnel Pro-
     grams. "Collecting Race, Sex, and Ethnic Group Statistics
     on Job Applicants." EEO INFORMATION ON EQUAL EMPLOYMENT
     OPPORTUNITY FOR STATE AND LOCAL GOVERNMENT. See Item 822.

853. Young, Richard A. "Interviewing Minority Job Applicants,
     Don't Go By the Book." SUPERVISORY MANAGEMENT, 14 (Decem-
     ber 1969), 2-6.

     Sees conventional approaches to interviewing minorities
     as insufficient and suggests nine techniques to successfully
     interview minorities.

854. Blumrosen, Alfred W. "The Duty of Fair Recruitment Under
     the Civil Rights Act of 1964." RUTGERS UNIVERSITY LAW
     REVIEW, 22 (1967-68), 465-536.

     Contends that the high rate of unemployment among "Negroes"
     is directly related to discriminatory hiring and recruitment
     practices. Provides examples of discriminatory recruitment
     and hiring practices. Discusses the implication of Section
     703(a)(1) and (2) of Title VII on discriminatory hiring prac-
     tices. Briefly discusses affirmative action files as a tool
     for remedying discrimination in recruitment and hiring prac-
     tices. Defines the affirmative action filing process as the
     practice of placing qualified minority applicants in a sepa-
     rate file from white applicants. When a job becomes avail-
     able, minority applicant files are reviewed and a minority
     is referred or hired. Believes that the affirmative action
     file may cause "discrimination in the reverse" towards white
     applicants. Nevertheless, the affirmative action file is an
     appropriate remedy to correct discriminatory recruitment and
     hiring practices. Other areas discussed, include fair quali-
     fication standards, e.g., testing, education and experience
     requirements.

855. Bowe, Frank. "Outreach and Recruitment: Strategies Employ-
     ers Find Effective." AFFIRMATIVE ACTION FOR THE HANDI-
     CAPPED, by the U.S. Department of Labor, Employment Stand-
     ards Administration, Office of Federal Contract Compliance
     Programs. Washington, D.C: Government Printing Office,
     April 1980, pp. 101-134.

     Describes the frustrations that employers have in recruit-
     ing and hiring qualified handicapped workers. Explains that
     the handicapped worker is mutually frustrated when seeking
     employment. Provides strategies to employers on developing
     and implementing an outreach program for recruiting handi-
     capped workers.

856. Calvert, Robert, Jr. EQUAL EMPLOYMENT OPPORTUNITY FOR
     MINORITY GROUP COLLEGE GRADUATES: LOCATING, RECRUITING,
     EMPLOYING. Garrett Park, MD.: Garrett Park Press 1972.
     247 pp.

     Designed to assist employers to recruit qualified minority
     groups, including Hispanics and American Indians. Provides
     statistical data on the size of minority groups in the United

194

States, selected cities, colleges, and various career fields.
Suggests techniques that employers should develop in preparing to recruit minorities. Includes the names and addresses
of minority newspapers, periodicals, radio stations, sorori-
ties, fraternities, colleges and universities, consulting and
accounting firms, and banks.

857. Doss, Martha Merrill, ed. DIRECTORY OF SPECIAL OPPORTUNITIES
      FOR WOMEN. Garrett Park, MD.: Garrett Park Press, 1981.
      293 pp.

      Includes a listing of national and state organizations,
      associations, women's programs, agencies, colleges and uni-
      versities that provide career information and counseling to
      women.

858. Edwards, John L. "What is a 'Qualified Minority'?" NATIONAL
      LAW JOURNAL, 5 (August 8, 1983), 13.

      Argues that white law firms have not made a sincere effort
      to recruit black lawyers and are only "paying lip service" to
      the principle of equal employment opportunity. Believes that
      white law firms use the term "qualified minority" as a bar-
      rier to deny blacks employment. Sees the standards used to
      determine "qualified minority" as "arbitrary hiring prac-
      tices." Suggests objective standards for hiring minority
      lawyers for firms who are sincere in their efforts to hire
      minorities.

*   Farley, Jennie. AFFIRMATIVE ACTION AND THE WOMAN WORKER:
      GUIDELINES FOR PERSONNEL MANAGEMENT. See Item 917.

859. Foxley, Cecelia. LOCATING, RECRUITING, AND EMPLOYING WOMEN:
      AN EQUAL OPPORTUNITY APPROACH. Garrett Park, MD.: Garrett
      Park Press, 1976. 357 pp.

      A source book on women in the workforce. Provides statis-
      tical data on their earnings, placement, occupational status,
      labor force participation, and unemployment rates. Cites
      and discredits various myths about women workers. Explains
      laws and regulations that affect women workers and outlines
      major elements of an affirmative action program for women
      workers. Includes a list of women organizations and train-
      ing programs.

860. Johnson, Fred R. "Recruitment, Retaining, and Advancing
      Minority Employees." TRAINING AND DEVELOPMENT JOURNAL,
      26 (January 1972), 28-31.

861. Johnson, Willis L., ed. DIRECTORY OF SPECIAL PROGRAMS FOR
      MINORITY GROUP MEMBERS: CAREER INFORMATION SERVICES,
      EMPLOYMENT SKILLS BANK, FINANCIAL AID SOURCES. Garrett
      Park, MD.: Garrett Park Press, 1980. 612 pp.

862. Levine, Marvin J. "Hiring, Recruiting and EEO." EEO TODAY,
      4 (Autumn 1977), 185-191.

      "A non-discriminatory employment procedure for recruiting
      and selecting employees is one that does not intentionally or
      inadvertently work to screen out minority group members and
      females." Recommends that employers review their recruitment
      procedures to ensure that minorities and women are not dis-
      criminated against. Discusses methods and procedures to
      achieve non-discrimination in hiring and recruiting, e.g.,
      collecting applicant flow data and developing an affirmative
      action file.

*   McCullough, Kenneth J. SELECTING EMPLOYEES SAFELY UNDER THE
      LAW. See Item 62.

863. Orlov, Darlene. "Networking: The New Way to Find Female and
      Minority Managers." SOLVING EEO PROBLEMS: A GUIDE TO EEO
      LAW AND PRACTICE. New York: Executive Enterprises Publi-
      cation Co., Inc., 1980, pp. 146-152.

      Concludes that traditional methods of recruitment, e.g.,
      advertisement, employment agencies and search firms, fail to
      provide employers with a large pool of minority and female
      applicants. Suggests the concept of "networking" as a system
      to find qualified minority and female applicants. Networking
      involves contacting successful females and minorities within
      the organization to refer other qualified females and minori-
      ties for employment.

864. Peterson, Robin. "Action Recruiting." PERSONNEL ADMINIS-
      TRATION, 34 (January-February 1971), 44-47.

865. Project on the Status and Education of Women of the Associa-
      tion of American Colleges. RECRUITING WOMEN FOR TRADITION-
      ALLY "MALE" CAREERS: PROGRAMS AND RESOURCES FOR GETTING
      WOMEN INTO THE MEN'S WORLD. Washington, D.C.: October
      1977. 9 pp.

      A resource guide for recruiting women in traditionally male
      occupations. Provides a list of programs and publications
      that are available to assist employers in recruiting women to
      enter the fields of medicine, law, engineering, and science.

866. Rabby, Rami. LOCATING, RECRUITING AND HIRING THE DISABLED.
      New York: Pilot Publishing Co., 1981.

867. "The Recruitment of Job Applicants Under Title VII of the
      Civil Rights Act of 1964." COLUMBIA JOURNAL OF LAW AND
      SOCIAL PROBLEMS, 9 (1973), 131-165.

868. Renetzky, Alvin; Daniel J. Jacobson; and Hyndra Rudd, eds.
      DIRECTORY OF CAREER RESOURCES FOR WOMEN. Santa Monica,
      CA.: Ready Reference Press, 1979. 287 pp.

      A comprehensive listing of organizations that provide
      information on employment opportunities and educational
      training for women. Includes information on career coun-
      seling, talent banks, fellowships, job placements, and skill
      assessment.

869. _____ and Others. DIRECTORY OF CAREER RESOURCES FOR
      MINORITIES: A GUIDE TO CAREER RESOURCES AND OPPORTUNITIES
      FOR MINORITIES. Santa Monica, CA.: Ready Reference
      Press, 1980. 335 pp.

      A comprehensive listing of organizations that provide
      information on employment opportunities and educational
      training for women. Includes information on career coun-
      seling, talent banks, fellowships, job placements, and skill
      assessment.

870. Stanton, Erwin S. SUCCESSFUL PERSONNEL RECRUITMENT AND
      SELECTION: WITHIN EEO/AFFIRMATIVE ACTION GUIDELINES.
      New York: American Management Associations, 1977. 214 pp.

      "Introduces the Sequential Selection System; a step by step
      system designed to optimize the time of the personnel spe-
      cialist or manager so that he or she can more quickly and
      effectively select qualified applicants without spending a
      lot of unnecessary time in fruitless, non-productive activ-
      ity." Summarizes various EEO laws and briefly outlines the
      personnel selection requirements under each. The Appendix
      includes: "Tested Questions for the Structured Selection
      Interview, Sample Psychological Evaluation, Selected Sources
      for Recruiting Minority Group and Women Applicants."

871. U.S. Civil Service Commission, Bureau of Intergovernmental
      Personnel Programs. "Tips on Recruitment of Hispanic
      Americans," EEO INFORMATION ON EQUAL EMPLOYMENT OPPORTUNITY
      FOR STATE AND LOCAL GOVERNMENT. Rev. ed. Issue No. 9.
      Washington, D.C.: Government Printing Office, 1977. 4 pp.

      Indicates that "Hispanics are the fastest growing segment
      of the U.S. population" and special recruitment programs

may be necessary to eliminate barriers that hinder their
employment. Outlines a program for recruiting Hispanics in
public employment and provides tips on making the program
successful.

872.   U.S. Commission on Civil Rights. CIVIL RIGHTS DIRECTORY,
       1981. Washington, D.C.: Government Printing Office,
       1981. 549 pp.

       A comprehensive directory of private and public organiza-
       tions that provide services related to civil rights.

873.   U.S. Department of Health and Human Services. HISTORICALLY
       BLACK COLLEGES AND UNIVERSITIES: FACT BOOK, Vols. I, II,
       and III, January 1983.

       Provides an alphabetical listings and fact sheets on his-
       torically black public colleges and graduate schools, com-
       munity colleges, private colleges, and graduate schools.

874.   U.S. Equal Employment Opportunity Commission, Educational
       Programs Division, Office of Voluntary Programs. A DIREC-
       TORY OF RESOURCES FOR AFFIRMATIVE RECRUITMENT. Washington,
       D.C.: Government Printing Office, March 1975. 91 pp.

       A directory of minority and female recruitment sources.
       Includes the names and addresses of organizations that have
       referral sources and assist in the employment of minorities
       and women.

*   U.S. Equal Employment Opportunity Commission. ELIMINATING
       DISCRIMINATION IN EMPLOYMENT: A COMPELLING NATIONAL
       PRIORITY. See Item 993.

875.   U.S. Office of Personnel Management, Hispanic Employment
       Program. HISPANIC EMPLOYMENT: A RECRUITMENT SOURCES
       BOOKLET. Washington, D.C.: Government Printing Office,
       September, 1980. 136 pp.

       Includes population statistics on Hispanics as of 1976 in
       selected areas; a listing of national, state and local His-
       panic organizations; and radio and TV stations servicing the
       Hispanic community. Outlines procedures for developing a
       recruitment program for Hispanics.

876.   _____. Intergovernmental Personnel Programs. "Out-
       reach Recruitment of Minorities and Women for Professional
       and Technical Positions." EEO INFORMATION ON EQUAL EMPLOY-
       MENT OPPORTUNITY FOR STATE AND LOCAL GOVERNMENTS. Issue

No. 21. Washington, D.C.: Government Printing Office,
December, 1979. 7 pp.

Gives strategies on how to recruit minorities and women
for professional and technical positions in state and local
governments.

877. Women's Action Alliance. WOMEN HELPING WOMEN: A STATE-BY-
STATE DIRECTORY OF SERVICES. New York: Neal-Schuman
Publishers, Inc., 1981. 179 pp.

A state directory of social, political, and management services available to women, e.g., career counseling services
and skilled trades training centers.

878. Young, Richard A. RECRUITING AND HIRING MINORITY EMPLOYEES.
New York; American Management Association, 1969.

Cites traditional approaches to recruiting and hiring
minorities as creating barriers to the full employment of
minority individuals. Suggests various techniques that companies should use to overcome "stumbling blocks" and "pitfalls" when recruiting and hiring minorities. Discusses
communication problems between minority applicants and the
interviewer, the employment application, employment testing,
reference checks, medical examinations, and orientation.

EEO AND TRAINING

879. "Case Study: EEO and Training." EEO REVIEW, (December
    1980), 2-4.

    Presents a case study on a complaint filed by women who
    alleged that the trainer provided different training and
    testing to the male employees. Provides comments and sugges-
    tions to managers and supervisors on how to effectively pre-
    vent discrimination in training programs.

880. Delaney, Martin E. and Chris Johnson. "Four Myths About
    EEO - and What Trainers Can Do About Them." TRAINING,
    17 (April 1980), 42.

    Addresses four negative myths concerning EEO programs and
    their origin. Explains how EEO trainers can use the wrong
    training approach which can further complicate the problem.
    Outlines a training program for employers to implement which
    can effectively overcome and dispel the myths without ". . .
    exploiting their employees' fears, without putting them on
    the defensive and without putting them to sleep."

881. DeSanto, John F. "A Training Seminar for Supervisors of
    Minority Group Employees." PUBLIC PERSONNEL REVIEW, 32
    (April 1977), 71-76.

882. Fisher, Barbara. "The Role of Women in Training and Develop-
    ment." TRAINING AND DEVELOPMENT JOURNAL, 25 (June 1971),
    32-34.

    Presents ". . . a case study of the author's experiences as
    a woman trainer." Indicates that women trainers are not
    identified as professionals like their peers and within the
    organization. Compares the stereotypical attitudes directed
    at blacks with those directed at women trainers. Concludes
    that prejudice exists within the training field toward women.

883. Geiger, Adrianne H. "Managing Effectively While Implementing
    EEO." TRAINING AND DEVELOPMENT JOURNAL, 35 (May 1981), 87.

    Indicates that managers and supervisors are frustrated and
    aggravated when implementing EEO policies and procedures.
    Provides suggestions to managers and supervisors on how to
    implement EEO programs successfully and logically. Believes

200

that EEO training for managers and supervisors is one method
of preventing discriminatory practices.

884. Gordon, Steven R. "The Impact of Fair Employment Laws on
     Training." TRAINING AND DEVELOPMENT JOURNAL, (November
     1978), 29-45.

     Finds that EEOC decisions and court cases have had a "con-
     siderable impact" on training programs and on the process of
     selecting trainees for entry level jobs. Contends that
     courts have eliminated or modified various tests, age and
     education requirements that have had a discriminatory impact
     on the selection of protected class individuals into training
     programs. Sees unvalidated tests as the most common source
     of discrimination in selecting trainees. Includes a review
     of Griggs v. Duke Power Co., Albemarle Paper Co. v. Moody,
     U.S. v. Bethlehem Steel Corporation, and Washington v. Davis.

885. Hall, Francine S. and Maryann H. Albrecht. "Training for
     EEO: What Kinds and for Whom?" PERSONNEL ADMINISTRATOR,
     22 (October 1977), 25-28.

     Reports on a study to assess the need for EEO training
     within an organization. The study was conducted by the Per-
     sonnel and Industrial Relations Association of Wisconsin.
     Reveals that personnel administrators need more training in
     the area of EEO and affirmative action; especially in the
     area of developing and implementing affirmative action pro-
     grams. Suggests that university curriculums and in-house
     training programs be designed to train managers on how to
     solve EEO problems.

886. "Helpful Advice to Make EEO Programs Run More Smoothly."
     TRAINING, 17 (November 1980), 20.

*   Johnson, Fred R. "Recruitment, Retaining, and Advancing
     Minority Employees." See Item 860.

*   Kronenberger, George K. and David L. Bourke. "Effective
     Training and the Elimination of Sexual Harassment." See
     Item 326.

887. Patten, Thomas H., Jr. and Lester E. Dorey. "An Equal
     Employment Opportunity Sensitivity Workshop." TRAINING
     AND DEVELOPMENT JOURNAL, 26 (January 1972), 42.

     Outlines procedures followed in developing a sensitivity
     training seminar on equal employment within the U.S. Army
     Tank-Automotive Command.

888. Russell, James S. "A Review of Fair Employment Cases in the
      Field of Training." PERSONNEL PSYCHOLOGY, 37 (Summer
      1984), 261-276.

889. St. John, Robert L. "A New Approach to Affirmative Action."
      PERSONNEL, 56 (May-June 1979), 25-30.

      Reports on a special training program for women to enter
      nontraditional jobs at New York Telephone Company. Concludes
      that properly designed affirmative action programs, specifi-
      cally training, can be extremely useful for placing women in
      positions traditionally held by men.

*   U.S. Department of Labor, Employment and Training Administra-
      tion. LAYOFF TIME TRAINING: A KEY TO UPGRADING WORKFORCE
      UTILIZATION AND EEOC AFFIRMATIVE ACTION. See Item 731.

*   U.S. Office of Personnel Management. WORKSHOP ON SEXUAL
      HARASSMENT: TRAINER'S MANUAL. See Item 382.

890. Wells, Theodora. "Equalizing Advancement Between Women and
      Men." TRAINING AND DEVELOPMENT JOURNAL, 27 (August 1973),
      20-24.

      Identifies the primary ways that women and men within an
      organization can acquire training and development for ad-
      vancement. Analyzes how women receive unfair treatment in
      the distribution of training and suggests ways in which
      organizations can equalize advancement opportunities between
      women and men.

*   Zemke, Ron. "Sexual Harassment: Is Training the Key to Pre-
      vention?" See Item 392.

2. AFFIRMATIVE ACTION

AFFIRMATIVE ACTION PROGRAMS

*   Affirmative Action Coordinating Center. "Some Facts
       About Weber v. Kaiser Aluminum and United Steelworkers
       Union." See Item 1115.

891.   "Affirmative Action for Disabled People." EQUAL OPPORTUNITY
       FORUM, 7 (November 1979), 14-15.

       Outlines a guide for developing an affirmative action plan
       for employing and accommodating handicapped individuals.
       Includes topics on pre-employment exams and complaints from
       handicapped individuals. Lists organizations that can assist
       in developing a plan and recruiting handicapped individuals.

892.   Baker, Rob. "Turnabout: Blue-Collar Support for Affirmative
       Action Grows." EQUAL OPPORTUNITY FORUM, 6 (April 1979),
       8-9.

       Unlike the Bakke case, trade unions have submitted "a
       blizzard of amicus curiae briefs" against Weber. Contends
       that unions recognize that if the Supreme Court finds in
       favor of Weber, they will be faced with expensive court bat-
       tles across the country where affirmative action clauses have
       been incorporated into collective bargaining agreement.

893.   Baldwin, Carol A. "The Thirteenth Amendment as an Effective
       Source of Constitutional Authority for Affirmative Action
       Legislation." COLUMBIA JOURNAL OF LAW AND SOCIAL PROBLEMS,
       18 (No. 1, 1983), 77-114.

       Argues that employment discrimination still exist even
       after the Civil Rights Act of 1964 was enacted approximately
       20 years ago. Believes that the EEOC has failed in its mis-
       sion to effectively combat employment discrimination. Pro-
       poses that the U.S. Congress enact affirmative action legis-
       lation to eliminate employment discrimination. Outlines
       major provisions needed in affirmative action legislation.
       Contends that Congress has the power to enact affirmative
       action legislation under the thirteenth amendment to the
       Constitution.

*   Battles, Michaele Snyder. "The Manager and Affirmative
       Action to Hire the Handicapped." See Item 463.

894. Beazley, Paul. "Comments on OFCCP final Regulations." Mim-
      eographed. Columbia, SC.: South Carolina Human Affairs
      Commission, 1983.

      Examines the OFCCP's proposed final regulations on affir-
      mative action for Federal contractors. Argues that "[t]he
      final regulations constitute a significant weakening of
      affirmative action requirements. . . ." Reviews major pro-
      visions of the regulations and recommends other means of
      modifying the regulations without jeopardizing the effective-
      ness of affirmative action.

895. Bellone, Carl J. and Douglas H. Darling. "Implementing
      Affirmative Action Programs: Problems and Strategies."
      PUBLIC PERSONNEL MANAGEMENT, 9 (1980), 184-191.

      Identifies problems in planning and implementing an affir-
      mative action plan and provides strategies and solutions to
      those problems. States that one major obstacle employers
      face is making the workforce knowledgeable of the program.
      Suggests that employers survey their current employees to
      determine their understanding of affirmative action. There-
      after, the employer should design a training program to en-
      lighten the workforce of the objective, purpose, and mechan-
      ics of the program. Reports on the results of Alameda
      County's (California) survey and concludes that the survey
      had a positive impact on their affirmative action program.

896. Belohlav, James A. and Eugene Ayton. "Equal Opportunity Law:
      Some Common Problems." PERSONNEL JOURNAL, 61 (April 1982),
      282-285.

      Briefly discusses the behavioral reactions to affirmative
      action and equal employment opportunity (AA/EEO) on the job.
      Explains that there has been some abuse of AA/EEO laws from
      both protected class individuals and employers. Cites prob-
      lems in the recruitment of minorities and women and believes
      that "tokenism" is still a common practice in some organiza-
      tions. States that unless managers are held accountable for
      AA/EEO there is little incentive for them to change their
      behavior. Sees the most "insidious problems" facing AA/EEO
      are situations where individuals profess to understand AA/EEO
      principles but fail to change their own behaviors to comply
      with those principles.

897. Benokraitis, Nijole V. and Joe R. Feagin. AFFIRMATIVE ACTION
      AND EQUAL OPPORTUNITY: ACTION, INACTION, REACTION. Boul-
      der, CO.: Westview Press, 1978. 255 pp.

      Traces the history of equal employment opportunities and
      affirmative action (AA/EEO) laws and guidelines. Contends
      that despite various AA/EEO laws and guidelines, minorities
      and women are still being discriminated against. Suggests

that federal enforcement agencies are ineffective when enforcing their AA/EEO compliance powers. Examines public
reaction to affirmative action programs, e.g., setting goals
and timetables, and quotas. Explains why affirmative action
is needed; why it is failing; and predicts the future of
affirmative action programs.

898. Berry, Margaret C., ed. "Affirmative "Action?" JOURNAL OF
      THE NATIONAL ASSOCIATION FOR WOMEN DEANS, ADMINISTRATORS,
      AND COUNSELORS, 39 (Winter 1976), 1-60.

      A collection of articles related to sex discrimination in
      the field of education. Written on the premise that affirma-
      tive action has not worked in the field of education, even
      though there are a large number of highly qualified women.
      Concludes that discrimination in hiring and promotion prac-
      tices still exist for women in the field of education.

899. Berwitz, Clement J. THE JOB ANALYSIS APPROACH TO AFFIRMATIVE
      ACTION. New York: John Wiley & Sons, 1975. 327 pp.

      Analyzes the Wagner College Affirmative Action Plan that
      was designed to comply with governmental requirements (Re-
      vised Order No. 4). Provides ". . . conceptual guidelines
      and methods for developing an affirmative action program in
      compliance with governmental regulations." Focuses primarily
      on job analysis techniques.

900. Blumrosen, Alfred W. "The Bottom Line Concept in Equal
      Employment Opportunity Law." NORTH CAROLINA CENTRAL LAW
      JOURNAL, 12 (Fall 1980), 1-20.

      Defines the "bottom line" theory as the process of hiring
      "an acceptable number of minorities and women in various job
      categories." Believes that employers who apply the "bottom
      line" theory will be protected against claims of discrimina-
      tion from minorities, women, and white males. Maintains that
      the Weber decision and the EEOC guidelines further support
      the "bottom line" theory.

901. Boyle, M. Barbara. "Equal Opportunity for Women is Smart
      Business." HARVARD BUSINESS REVIEW, 51 (May-June 1973),
      85-95.

      Presents ten steps for employers to follow when developing
      an affirmative action program for employing women in the cor-
      porate sector. Advises employers that the implementation of
      an affirmative action program is not costly but the absence
      of one could be.

*   Brady, Robert L. LAW FOR PERSONNEL MANAGERS: HOW TO HIRE
       THE PEOPLE YOU NEED WITHOUT DISCRIMINATING. See Item 12.

902.   Brookmire, David A. and Amy A. Burton. "A Format for Pack-
       aging Your Affirmative Action Program" PERSONNEL JOURNAL,
       57 (June 1978), 294-304.

       Presents a model affirmative action manual that is designed
       to comply with all AA/EEO laws and regulations. The manual
       was reviewed and approved by several federal agencies. In-
       cludes charts on calculating workforce analysis, applicant
       flow, and establishing goals and timetables.

903.   _____. "Designing and Implementing Your Company's
       Affirmative Action Program" PERSONNEL JOURNAL, 58 (April
       1979), 232-237.

       Outlines procedures for designing and implementing an
       affirmative action program as required of federal contractors
       under Executive Orders 11246 and 11375. Provides suggestions
       on determining the availability and underutilization of mi-
       norities and women. Explains how to successfully implement a
       program with little or no resistance from management. Feels
       that affirmative action goals can be achieved by implementing
       or modifying personnel practices, e.g., devising a recruit-
       ment plan to increase the applicant flow of minorities and
       women. Concludes that affirmative action programs can be
       successful by developing well planned strategies and by
       gaining top management support.

904.   Brosnan, Ted. "There's More to Affirmative Action Than Just
       Hiring 'The Handicapped'." PERSONNEL ADMINISTRATOR, 23
       (January 1978), 18-21.

       Outlines a seven phase project to hire handicapped employ-
       ees at C&P Telephone Company. Phase seven of the project
       include: "Handicap awareness program, outreach and place-
       ment, reasonable job accommodations, job inventory, archi-
       tectural accessibility, information program, and follow-up
       and counseling."

905.   Brownstein, Paul. "Affirmative Action Programs." Edited by
       John J. Ross. EQUAL EMPLOYMENT OPPORTUNITY --RESPONSIBLE
       MANAGEMENT. New York: Practicing Law Institute, 1974.

       Outlines federal requirements for federal contractors on
       how to develop and implement an affirmative action plan. In-
       cludes a compliance checklist for contractors and a model
       affirmative action program.

906. Bulwik, Helen C. and Suzanne R. Elicks. AFFIRMATIVE ACTION
     FOR WOMEN: MYTH AND REALITY. Berkeley, CA.: Institute
     of Business and Economic Research, University of Cali-
     fornia, 1972.

907. Cadei, Raymond M. "Hiring Goals, California State Government
     and Title VII: Is This Numbers Game Legal?" PACIFIC LAW
     JOURNAL, 8 (January 1977), 49-71.

908. Calvert, Robert, Jr. AFFIRMATIVE ACTION: A COMPREHENSIVE
     RECRUITMENT MANUAL. Garnett, MD.: Garrett Park Press,
     1979. 380 pp.

909. Cebulski, Bonnie G. AFFIRMATIVE ACTION VERSUS SENIORITY -
     IS CONFLICT INEVITABLE? Edited by B.V. H. Schneider.
     Berkeley, CA: Institute of Industrial Relations, Univer-
     sity of California, 1977. 52 pp.

     Explores the controversial issue of ". . . can traditional
     seniority systems and effective affirmative action plans
     co-exist?" Believes that finding an alternative to layoffs
     may avoid the potential conflict between affirmative action
     and seniority. Alternatives to layoff include ". . . payless
     vacations and holidays, payless workdays, waiver of employer
     contribution to fringe benefits, early retirement, elimina-
     tion of overtime, [and] temporary leave without pay for em-
     ployees to pursue travel. . . ." Discusses case law on
     seniority systems and the EEOC's position on seniority and
     layoffs. Analyzes a case study on seniority, layoffs and
     affirmative action.

910. Cohen, David M. "An End to Affirmative Action?" LABOR LAW
     JOURNAL, 28 (April 1977), 218-229.

     Reviews a series of lower court decisions that challenged
     affirmative action plans and quotas. Four of these cases
     were brought by white males. In each case, the court was
     not supportive of affirmative action and quotas. Believes
     that the Supreme Court will be forced to decide the issue
     of affirmative action and reverse discrimination. Written
     prior to the Supreme Court's decision in Bakke.

911. Coil, James H. III. "Action Needed on Affirmative Action."
     EMPLOYMENT RELATIONS TODAY, 4 (Winter 1983-1984), 351-357.

912. Cole, Craig W. "Affirmative Action: Change it or Lose it."
     EEO TODAY, 8 (Autumn 1981), 262-271.

Addresses the issue of why affirmative action has failed
in many organizations and the need for proponents of affirmative action ". . . to strive for affirmative action programs
that are more fair, more workable, and less cumbersome to
employers. . . ." Believes that unless these changes come
about, conservative lobbying groups will continue to strive
to weaken affirmative action programs.

913. _____. "Decentralizing EEO Management: How to Share
the Responsibility." PERSONNEL ADMINISTRATOR, 24 (August
1979), 17.

Proposes that EEO and affirmative action programs be decentralized. "Maintains that "[l]ike any other management program, EEO and affirmative action must involve a coordinated
effort by all supervisory personnel." Believes management
will take EEO and affirmative action more seriously when
they share in the responsibility of implementation. Concludes that managers should be encouraged to take the responsibility and receive training to be knowledgeable of EEO
and affirmative action laws and regulations.

914. Cruz, Nester. "An Antitrust Approach to Equal Employment
Opportunity Laws." LABOR LAW JOURNAL, 32 (February 1981),
67-70.

Present an empirical study on how discrimination creates
the same kind of problems as in a monopoly situation. Begins
with the basic elements of a monopoly and the "free competition" system. Presents evidence that discrimination ". . .
costs the economy substantial amounts yearly because of
inefficient allocation of labor resources." Contends that
Federal laws and regulations on EEO support the "free competition theory" by allowing all qualified applicants to be
equally qualified.

915. _____. "Real Politik" and "Affirmative Action."
PUBLIC PERSONNEL MANAGEMENT, 9 (1980), 192-195.

*   D'Zurilla, William T. "Labor Law -- Employment Discrimina-
tion-Voluntary Affirmative Action Plan With Racial Quota
Does Not Violate Title VII of the Civil Rights Act of
1964." See Item 747.

916. "EEOC's Affirmative Action Guidelines." EEO TODAY, 6 (Spring
1979), 17-21.

Contends that the EEOC will routinely dismiss reverse discrimination complaints against an employer who has implemented a "bona fide" affirmative action program. States that
the EEOC issued the Affirmative Action Guidelines after the

Fifth Circuit held in <u>Weber v. Kaiser</u> that a white male had
been discriminated against due to the employer's affirmative
action program.

* Edwards, Harry T. "Affirmative Action or Reverse Discrimination: The Head and Tail of <u>Weber</u>." See Item 748.

917. Farley, Jennie. AFFIRMATIVE ACTION AND THE WOMAN WORKER:
     GUIDELINES FOR PERSONNEL MANAGEMENT. New York: American
     Management Associations, 1979. 225 pp.

     Concentrates on affirmative action programs for women in
     recruitment, selection and training.

918. Galloway, Russell W., Jr. "Administrative and Judicial
     Nullification of Federal Affirmative Action Law." SANTA
     CLARA LAW REVIEW, 17 (Summer 1977), 559-593.

     Criticizes the OFCCP and the judicial system for their
     efforts to fully enforce Executive Order 11246. Believes
     that the OFCCP is failing to require federal contractors to
     comply with the Order. Argues that private individuals
     should be allowed to seek damages under the Order, since the
     OFCCP is not vigorously enforcing the Order.

919. Gaymon, Donald. "Underutilization in Affirmative Action
     Programs: What Is It and What Can We Do About It?"
     PERSONNEL JOURNAL, 58 (July 1979), 457-459.

     Explains that "utilization rates" and "underutilization"
     involves the issue of whether ". . . protected classes are
     being utilized at all levels and in all kinds of positions
     proportionally to their availability in the workforce."
     Contends that employers have a difficult time determining
     what the underutilization rate should be for setting goals
     and timetables. Believes that since the government has
     the responsibility to monitor an employer's affirmative
     action progress, the government should provide sufficient
     and updated statistics to employers on how to determine
     underutilization.

920. Ginger, Ann Fagan. "A Personal Analysis: Who Needs Affirma-
     tive Action?" HARVARD CIVIL RIGHTS-CIVIL LIBERTIES LAW
     REVIEW, BAKKE SYMPOSIUM: CIVIL RIGHTS PERSPECTIVES, 14
     (Spring 1979), 265-313.

     Argues that affirmative action programs are still needed
     for minorities and women. Contends that such programs have
     also benefited non-minorities. Believes that affirmative
     action programs have worked and at the same time have not
     prevented qualified persons from finding work. Discusses

the Bakke decision, focusing specifically on the "inadequate record" which the court's decision was based on.

921. Goeke, Joseph R. and Caroline S. Weymar. "Barriers to Hiring the Blacks." HARVARD BUSINESS REVIEW, 47 (September-October 1969), 144-146.

922. Haber, Sheldon E. "The Mobility of Professional Workers and Fair Hiring." INDUSTRIAL & LABOR RELATIONS REVIEW, 34 (January 1981), 257-264.

923. Hall, Francine S. and Maryann H. Albrecht. THE MANAGEMENT OF AFFIRMATIVE ACTION. Santa Monica, CA.: Goodyear Publishing Co., 1979. 398 pp.

Provides techniques on how management can integrate EEO and affirmative action laws and regulations into the daily operation of personnel functions. Concentrates on how to administer EEO and affirmative action programs and gives sample forms and reports to use when implementing such programs.

924. Hall, Samuel M., Jr. "Affirmative Action: Some Observations." EQUAL OPPORTUNITY FORUM, 6 (April 1979), 31.

Gives his personal observation of affirmative action. States that affirmative action has not given ethnic minorities "an edge in the hiring process." Finds that monetary gaps between whites and ethnic minorities still exist. Concludes that the search for ethnic minorities for employment has shifted to the search for women.

925. Hammer, Tove H. "Affirmative Action Programs: Have we Forgotten the First-Line Supervisor?" PERSONNEL JOURNAL, 58 (June 1979), 384-389.

Contends that the effectiveness of an affirmative action program on the "shop floor" depends heavily on front-line supervisors' understanding of the program; yet the first-line supervisors are the last persons to be explained what their roles are for implementation. Suggests that affirmative action planning include not only staff and line management personnel but also the front-line supervisors.

*   Harris, Rich and Jack Hartog. "The Catch-22 Case: Is Kaiser v. Weber Rigged Against Affirmative Action?" See Item 1119.

*   Hartman, Gerald S. "Management Personnel Practices: The Do's and Don'ts of EEO Compliance." See Item 43.

926. Hatch, Orrin G. "Senator Hatch Wrestles with Affirmative
      Action." PERSONNEL ADMINISTRATOR, 25 (October 1980), 78.

      Argues that affirmative action "is illegal, immoral and
      won't work." Contends that enforcement of affirmative action
      regulations cost the American economy billions of dollars.
      Believes that the Weber decision was not decisive and employ-
      ers may find themselves in trouble if they make employment
      decisions based on Weber.

927. Higgins, Chester A., Sr. "Interview with Clarence Thomas,
      Chairman, EEOC . . . (conclusion) 'I Am Opposed to Affirma-
      tive Action!'" CRISIS, 90 (March 1983), 34-38.

      The Chairman of the EEOC during the Reagan Administration
      shares his views on affirmative action and addresses criti-
      cism directed at him from the press and the minority com-
      munity. Describes the future direction, policies, and goals
      of the EEOC in prohibiting employment discrimination. Indi-
      cates that the EEOC will concentrate on patterns and prac-
      tices of discrimination in lieu of individual complaints.

928. Humanic Designs Division of Information Science Incorporated.
      HOW TO ELIMINATE DISCRIMINATORY PRACTICES: A GUIDE TO EEO
      COMPLIANCE. New York: AMACOM, 1975. 80 pp.

      Defines systemic discrimination as ". . . policies, pro-
      cedures, and employment systems which, however, inadvertently
      or neutrally applied, affect some people [protected class
      individuals] differently from others." Outlines a self-audit
      procedure to determine whether an employment system is sys-
      temically discriminatory. Elements of the self-audit in-
      cludes analyzing the workforce, recruitment and hiring prac-
      tices, promotions, transfers, and terminations. If an em-
      ployment system is found to be systemically discriminatory,
      the employer should develop an affirmative action plan which
      includes goals and timetables to eliminate the discriminatory
      practice. Includes a discussion on Revised Order No. 4, a
      vocabulary of EEO terms, and a selected reading list.

*   Hunter, James M. and Milton C. Branch. "Equal Employment
      Opportunities: Administrative Procedures and Judicial
      Developments Under Title VII of the Civil Rights Act of
      1964 and the Equal Employment Act of 1972." See Item 47.

929. Institute of Industrial Relations, University of California,
      Los Angeles. 1980 REPORT - EQUAL EMPLOYMENT OPPORTUNITY
      AND AFFIRMATIVE ACTION - THE ROOTS GROW DEEPER. Los
      Angeles, CA.: Institute of Industrial Relations Publica-
      tions, 1980. 349 pp.

Discusses new developments in affirmative action and EEO.
Explains the meaning of the <u>Weber</u> decision, voluntary affirmative action in the public sector, and the EEOC position on
affirmative action programs. Reviews the substantive and
procedural changes made to the Age Discrimination in Employment Act. Suggests that discrimination due to religion is
growing in momentum. Explains the <u>Hardison</u> decision and the
EEOC new guidelines on discrimination due to religion. Provides an update on new developments in sex discrimination,
e.g., pregnancy disability, sexual harassment, and comparable
worth. Gives an overview of the Uniform Guidelines on Employee Selection and the Rehabilitation Act of 1973.

*   Jackson, Diane P. "Affirmative Action for the Handicapped
         and Veterans: Interpretative and Operational Guidelines."
         See Item 489.

930.   Johnson, Ronald D. "Voluntary Affirmative Action In the
         Post-<u>Weber</u> Era: Issues and Answers. LABOR LAW JOURNAL,
         32 (September 1981), 609-620.

         Points to affirmative action and possible reverse discrimi-
         nation issues in the <u>Weber</u> decision. Defines the meaning of
         voluntary affirmative action. Explains that the <u>Weber</u> deci-
         sion supports the use of quotas; however, quotas should be
         reasonable and should not absolutely bar white employees'
         rights to advancement. Affirmative action goals should be
         reasonable and reflect the availability of minorities in the
         labor market. Briefly discusses the affects of <u>Weber</u> on
         seniority systems. Concludes that the Supreme Court's inten-
         tions were to have the <u>Weber</u> decision applied narrowly; how-
         ever, the decision has not been applied narrowly and has in
         fact set standards for lower courts to follow. Believes that
         the possibilities of winning a reverse discrimination case
         are "slim and none."

931.   Jones, James E., Jr. "The Development of Modern Equal
         Employment Opportunity and Affirmative Action Law: A Brief
         Chronological Overview." HOWARD LAW JOURNAL, 20 (No. 1,
         1977), 74-99.

         Sketches a chronological order of major events and court
         decisions involving EEO and affirmative action. Concludes
         that EEO law "is still in the infancy" stage of development.

*   _____. "'Reverse Discrimination' in Employment:
         Judicial Treatment of Affirmative Action Programs in the
         United States." See Item 762.

932. Jongeward, Dorothy and Dru Scott. AFFIRMATIVE ACTION FOR
      WOMEN: A PRACTICAL GUIDE FOR WOMEN AND MANAGEMENT.
      Reading, MA.: Addison-Wesley Publishing Company, 1977.
      334 pp.

      A collection of articles related to establishing and imple-
      menting affirmative action programs for women. Provides
      information on federal legislation and regulation affecting
      women and employers. Reviews the effectiveness of affirma-
      tive action programs for women in the federal government.
      Analyzes the impact of religion on the advancement of women
      and discusses the special needs and problems of the work-
      ing black woman. Identifies obstacles to women in manage-
      ment and gives strategies to women workers on how to reach
      their career goals. Other areas discussed include women in
      psychotherapy and how to eliminate sexist language in written
      materials.

933. Jordan, Isaac, L., Sr. and E. Cassandra McBryde Jordan.
      "Affirmative Action and the Black Manager." PERSONNEL
      JOURNAL, 62 (February 1983), 155-157.

      Outlines the "serious dilemma" that black managers in cor-
      porations are faced with when implementing affirmative action
      programs. Explains that black affirmative action managers
      often find themselves isolated and have no one within the
      organization to share ideas on affirmative action implementa-
      tion. Suggests that black affirmative action managers are
      expected to do a good job but if they begin making serious
      "efforts of good faith" they may receive "negative reactions"
      from their supervisor. Provides suggestions to black man-
      agers on how they can project a successful image to their
      supervisors and provides guidelines on self improvement.

934. Jreisat, J.E. and F.W. Swierczek. "Affirmative Action In
      Public Administration in the South: A Human Resources
      Approach." SOUTHERN REVIEW OF PUBLIC ADMINISTRATION, 5
      (Summer 1981), 148-161.

935. Kelso, William. "From Bakke to Fullilove: Has the Supreme
      Court Finally Settled the Affirmative Action Controversy?"
      REVIEW OF PUBLIC PERSONNEL ADMINISTRATION, 1 (Fall 1980),
      57-76.

936. "Labor Department Says It Will Ease Affirmative Action Rules."
      THE CHRONICLE OF HIGHER EDUCATION, (April 13, 1983), 9-10.

      Summarizes the Labor Department's proposed new rules to
      revise existing affirmative action requirements for federal
      contractors.

*   Ledvinka, James. FEDERAL REGULATION OF PERSONNEL AND HUMAN
      RESOURCE MANAGEMENT. See Item 55.

937. Liebers, Donald E. "Making Equal Employment Opportunities
      a Reality In a Major Corporation." PROCEEDING OF NEW YORK
      UNIVERSITY TWENTY-SIXTH ANNUAL CONFERENCE ON LABOR.
      Edited by Emanuel Stein and S. Theodore Reiner. New York:
      Matthew Bender, 1974, pp. 157-167.

      Identifies three problems associated with complying with
      EEO laws: commitment from managers, providing support for
      new programs, and confronting the issue of reverse discrimi-
      nation. Recommends techniques for developing a successful
      EEO program, e.g., implementation of new and radical EEO and
      affirmative action programs, and at the same time maintaining
      management prerogatives.

938. Loggins, Philip R. "Calculating Staff Affirmative Action
      Goals and Timetables." JOURNAL OF COLLEGE AND UNIVERSITY
      PERSONNEL ASSOCIATION, 24 (September 1973), 64-77.

939. Lovell, Catherine. "Three Key Issues in Affirmative Action."
      PUBLIC ADMINISTRATION REVIEW, 34 (May-June 1974), 235-237.

      Proposes three key issues that must be resolved before any
      attempt is made to implement an affirmative action program.
      Those issues include: the difference between affirmative
      action and nondiscrimination policy; the need for prefer-
      ential hiring and promotion; and the need for a reexamina-
      tion of what the term "qualified" means when considering
      applicants.

940. Lyle, Jerolyn R. AFFIRMATIVE ACTION PROGRAMS FOR WOMEN: A
      SURVEY OF INNOVATIVE PROGRAMS. Washington, D.C.: Govern-
      ment Printing Office, 1973. 150 pp.

      Analyzes the status of women in the American economy from
      working in the household to working outside the household.
      Examines pay differentials between men and women and explains
      the mechanics of the system that establishes pay inequities.
      Reports on a study conducted on the effectiveness of affir-
      mative action in a selected group of companies and makes
      recommendations to the Equal Employment Opportunity Commis-
      sion on how to combat sex discrimination in employment.

941. Macleod, Jennifer S. "Making the System Work FOR Instead
      of AGAINST Affirmative Action Job Candidates." EEO TODAY,
      5 (Winter 1978-79), 325-328.

      Believes there is a tendency for managers to select one of
      the first three candidates interviewed to fill a job vacancy.

The first three candidates are typically white males since
there is an abundance of qualified white males. Recommends
that employment managers make an attempt to have minority and
female candidates interviewed first and have white male
candidates interviewed after the first two or three minority
or female candidates have been interviewed.

942. _____. "Personnel Policies: Keys to Successful
      Affirmative Action." EEO TODAY, 6 (Summer 1979), 139-142.

      Finds that personnel policies within an organization have
      a direct and indirect impact on affirmative action; there-
      fore, personnel policies should be reviewed on a continuous
      basis to ensure that disparate impact does not exist in the
      selection of "protected" class individuals.

943. Marino, Kenneth E. "Conducting an Internal Compliance Re-
      view of Affirmative Action." PERSONNEL, 57 (March-April
      1980), 24-34.

      Interviews fifty federal compliance officers to determine
      whether employers should use the "good faith-effort strategy"
      or the "quota strategy" when designing and implementing an
      affirmative action program. Recommends that employers use
      the good faith approach because employment quotas have not
      been clearly explained by the courts nor the federal govern-
      ment. Summarizes the overall objectives of an affirmative
      action program and suggest possible tactics in meeting those
      objectives.

944. Mazaroff, Stanley, "A Tightrope for Employers - Affirmative
      Action-Post-Bakke." EEO TODAY, 5 (Autumn 1978), 244-252.

      Analyzes the U.S. Supreme Court's decision in Bakke and the
      implication of the Court's decision on affirmative action,
      Title VII, and on other Supreme Court decisions relative to
      employment discrimination.

945. Miller, Lee E. "EEO Audits: An Ounce of Prevention." EEO
      TODAY, 9 (Spring 1982), 63-85.

      Outlines guidelines for preparing and conducting an EEO
      audit. Defines an EEO audit as a review of personnel func-
      tions to determine whether they are in compliance with EEO
      laws and regulations. Contends that a thorough EEO audit
      will alert employers to possible violations of the law which
      can be corrected to prevent costly court cases. Substantive
      areas to be reviewed by the employer include recruitment,
      hiring, assignments, promotions, transfers, training, compen-
      sation, benefits, layoffs, and disciplinary practices. Pro-
      vides a check-list to follow when conducting an EEO audit.

946. Morgan, John S. and Richard L. VanDyke. WHITE-COLLAR BLACKS:
      A BREAKTHROUGH? New York: American Management Associa-
      tion, Inc. 1970. 214 pp.

      Analyzes the status of blacks in white-collar positions.
      Examines ". . . promotion practices, identification of poten-
      tial, attitudes of white co-workers, salary differential be-
      tween whites and blacks, recruitment and treatment on the
      job." Advises employers what action to take to ensure that
      the work environment is free of discrimination.

947. National Civil Service League. JUDICIAL MANDATES FOR AFFIR-
      MATIVE ACTION, NCSL's NATIONAL PROGRAM CENTER, GUIDEBOOK
      FOR PUBLIC EMPLOYERS. Washington, D.C., 1973. 36 pp.

948. _____. MODELS FOR AFFIRMATIVE ACTION. Washington,
      D.C., 1973. 63 pp.

      Defines what an affirmative action plan entails and out-
      lines the major components of a plan. Includes a collection
      of affirmative action plans and policies from state and local
      governments, e.g. San Diego, Sacramento, Flint, and San
      Bernadino County.

949. National Education Association. WHAT IS AFFIRMATIVE ACTION?
      COMBATING DISCRIMINATION IN EMPLOYMENT. Washington, D.C.,
      1973. 17 pp.

      Focuses on how to prevent and correct employment discrimi-
      nation through affirmative action plans. Outlines how to
      develop and implement affirmative action plans that will
      comply with federal requirements.

950. National Urban League, Office of the Vice President for
      Washington Operations. AFFIRMATIVE ACTION 1981: DEBATE,
      LITIGATE, ELIMINATE? Washington, D.C., 1981. 64 pp.

951. Neisser, Eric. "Affirmative Action In Hiring Court Staff:
      The Ninth Circuit's Experience." HOWARD LAW JOURNAL, 26
      (No. 1, 1983), 53-89.

      Outlines affirmative action steps taken by the United
      States Court of Appeal for the Ninth Circuit to recruit and
      place qualified minorities on the legal staff.

952. Nigro, Lloyd G. ed. "A Mini-Symposium: Affirmative Action
      in Public Employment." PUBLIC ADMINISTRATION REVIEW, 34
      (May-June 1974), 234-246.

A collection of articles that focus specifically on peculiar problems administrators face when developing and implementing an affirmative action program in the public sector.

*   "Note, Executive Order 11246 and Reverse Discrimination
        Challenges: Presidential Authority to Require Affirmative
        Action." See Item 1015.

*   Norton, Eleanor Holmes. "The Bakke's Decision and the
        Future of Affirmative Action." See Item 1107.

*   Nyren, Karl. "Affirmative Action and Charges of 'Reverse
        Bias'." See Item 767.

953.   Ornati, Oscar A. and Anthony Pisano. "Affirmative Action:
        Why It Isn't Working." PERSONNEL ADMINISTRATOR, September/
        October 1972), 50-52.

954.   Panken, Peter M. and Denise M. Davin. "Model Affirmative
        Action Program." RESOURCE MATERIALS: LABOR AND EMPLOYMENT
        LAW. Edited by Peter M. Panken. 2d.ed. Philadelphia,
        PA.: American Law Institute -- American Bar Association
        Committee on Continuing Professional Education, 1984,
        pp. 389-442.

        A model affirmative action program for federal contractors.
        Designed to assist contractors in developing a program that
        complies with the Office of Federal Contract Compliance Pro-
        gram's audit requirements.

955.   Paoli, Heidi. "How to Write Your Affirmative Action Plan."
        EEO COMPLIANCE MANUAL, VOL. 1. Englewood Cliffs, NJ.:
        Prentice-Hall, Inc., 1979.

        Provides a step by step outline for developing a plan.
        Explains federal requirements, how to conduct a utilization
        analysis, and how to set goals and timetables. Identifies
        problem areas that arise when developing a plan and suggest
        remedies.

956.   Pati, Gopal C. and Michael J. Mezey. "Designing an Affirma-
        tive Action Program for the Handicapped." TRAINING AND
        DEVELOPMENT JOURNAL, 32 (June 1978), 14-22.

        Outlines steps for developing and implementing an affirma-
        tive action program for handicapped individuals as required
        by the Vocational Rehabilitation Act of 1973 and the Vietnam
        Era Vietnam's Readjustment Act of 1974.

957. Pearson, David W. "Federal Guidelines Force Affirmative
      Action Programs." PERSONNEL ADMINISTRATOR, 16 (September-
      October 1971), 26-28.

958. Perlmutter, Cathy. "Congressional Attacks on Affirmative
      Action." 7 EQUAL OPPORTUNITY FORUM, (November 1979), 4-5.

      Discusses various anti-affirmative action amendments that
      have been passed in the House of Representatives and con-
      sidered by the Senate. The amendments would prohibit quotas,
      goals, and timetables as a means of employing women and
      minorities. Feels that such action on the part of legisla-
      tors is a result of a growing national mood of conservatism.

959. Peskin, Dean B. THE BUILDING BLOCKS OF EEO: HOW TO MAKE
      EQUAL EMPLOYMENT OPPORTUNITY LAWS WORK FOR YOU. New York:
      World Publishing Company, 1971. 234 pp.

      Explains the fundamentals of EEO law and its applicability
      to operating a business. Believes that EEO programs can be
      implemented in a positive manner and outlines a step by step
      guide for employers to follow in complying with the law.

960. Plevin, Mark D. "The Constitutionality of Affirmative Action
      in Public Employment: Judicial Deference to Certain
      Politically Responsible Bodies." VIRGINIA LAW REVIEW, 67
      (September 1981), 1235-1249.

      Examines the Supreme Court's decisions in Weber, Bakke, and
      Fullilove v. Klutznick to determine whether public employers'
      affirmative action programs are constitutional. Focuses
      specifically on Justice Powell's opinion that ". . . race-
      conscious affirmative action programs are remedial, and
      therefore constitutional, only if a 'competent' body makes
      sufficient 'findings' of past discrimination justifying the
      affirmative action program." Powell held that the Board of
      Regents in the Bakke case was not a competent body. Seeks
      to reconcile Justice Powell's opinion with Justice Brennan's
      opinion ". . . that the [Board of Regents'] affirmative
      action program was constitutionally permissible because it
      was directed at remedying prior discrimination. . . ."
      Brennan maintained that the Board of Regents' general alle-
      gation of past discrimination was sufficient.

*   Posner, Richard A. "The Bakke Case and the Future of Affir-
      mative Action." See Item 1109.

*   Powers, Thompson, ed. EQUAL EMPLOYMENT OPPORTUNITY: COM-
      PLIANCE AND AFFIRMATIVE ACTION. See Item 82.

961. President's Committee on Employment of the Handicapped.
      AFFIRMATIVE ACTION TO EMPLOY DISABLED VETERANS AND VETER-
      ANS OF THE VIETNAM ERA. Washington, D.C., 1977.

      Outlines the legal obligation of employers to hire and
      promote veterans through affirmative action.

962. Project on the Status and Education of Women of the Associa-
      tion of American Colleges. AFFIRMATIVE ACTION AND PREFER-
      ENCE. Washington, D.C., September, 1976.

      States that ". . . 'affirmative action' refers to the con-
      cept that discrimination can be eliminated when employers
      take positive steps to identify and change policies, prac-
      tices and any other institutional barriers that cause or
      perpetuate inequity." An employer is involved in affirmative
      action when it voluntarily develops an affirmative action
      plan, voluntarily accepts a federal contract, signs a con-
      ciliation agreement or when a court directs the employer to
      develop a plan. Explains the difference between goals and
      quotas. Stresses that goals do not require preferential
      treatment.

963. Rambo, Lewis M. "So You've Hired a Black American."
      PERSONNEL ADMINISTRATION, 33 (May-June 1970), 4.

      Contends that corporations are in search of "Super Black"
      employees to hire. Believes that the "manhunt" for black
      employees is a result of pressures from the EEOC and OFCCP.
      Recruiters are requiring prospective black employees to have
      "unreasonable academic credentials" for jobs that have
      "limited potential." Prospective black employees are "inter-
      viewed, screened and re-interviewed" by a chain of corporate
      personnel . . . where white applicants rarely require such
      extensive consensual validation." Explains that when a black
      employee is finally hired, he/she is expected to adapt imme-
      diately ". . . to obscure and unwritten corporate mores,
      prescriptions, and proscriptions." States that ". . . any
      black who fails or succeeds on a job is automatically a
      template for other Negroes to follow. If he fails -- 'We
      tried one in that department and he just didn't work out.'
      If he succeeds -- 'Find some more like him for our X, Z, and
      M Divisions.'" Concludes that corporations who are in search
      of "Super Blacks" should begin to ask themselves why, spe-
      cifically, whether they understand the purpose and need of
      equal employment opportunity.

964. Reed, Leonard. "What's Wrong with Affirmative Action."
      WASHINGTON MONTHLY, 12 (January 1981), 24-26.

965. Reid, Herbert O., Sr. "Assault on Affirmative Action: The
     Delusion of a Color-Blind America." HOWARD LAW JOURNAL,
     23 (No. 3, 1980), 381-428.

     Traces the legal status of Blacks from the Dred Scott case
     in 1857 to Supreme Court decisions on affirmative action
     during the 1970s and 80s. Concludes that affirmative action
     programs are valid and are needed ". . . if blacks are to
     escape from a permanent state of second class citizenship."

966. Reynolds, William Bradford. "Justice Department Policies on
     Equal Employment and Affirmative Action." PROCEEDING OF
     NEW YORK UNIVERSITY THIRTY-FIFTH ANNUAL NATIONAL CONFERENCE
     ON LABOR. Edited by Richard Adelman. New York: Matthew
     Bender, 1983, pp. 443-453.

*   Roberts, Michael A. "Affirmative Action Without Reverse
     Discrimination." See Item 772.

967. Rodriquez, Armando M. "A Look at Equal Employment.Opportu-
     nity." LABOR LAW JOURNAL, 33 (May 1982), 259-264.

     A commissioner on the Equal Employment Opportunity Com-
     mission briefly discusses the past history of equal employ-
     ment opportunity and affirmative action programs. Vigorously
     supports voluntary affirmative action and believes that em-
     ployers and employees should work together to find a model
     affirmative action plan that is workable.

968. Rosenbloom, David H. "Evaluating Affirmative Action In the
     Federal Service: A Comparison of Blacks and Women." Mime-
     ographed. Syracuse, N.Y.: Syracuse University, 1980.

     Reviews employment statistical data on females and minori-
     ties in the federal workforce between 1967 and 1978. Finds
     that female employment in the Federal workforce increased
     at a higher rate than minority employment. Indicates that
     women have benefited more from affirmative action and equal
     employment opportunity laws than minorities.

969. Ross, John J. AFFIRMATIVE ACTION WORKSHOP. New York:
     Practicing Law Institute, 1973. 225 pp.

     Details federal affirmative action requirements for federal
     contractors. Includes a comprehensive guide for developing a
     plan, e.g., utilization analysis, establishing goals and
     timetables, dissemination of the plan, and monitoring.

*   Ruzicho, Andrew J. "The Weber Case -- Its Impact on Affirma-
     tive Action." See Item 1125.

970. Sahlein, Stephen. THE AFFIRMATIVE ACTION HANDBOOK. Edited
      by Jeff Baron. New York: Executive Enterprises Publica-
      tions Co., 1978. 112 pp.

      A handbook for supervisors on the application of EEO laws
      and regulations. Written in "simple terms" with case studies
      on hiring, evaluation, promotion, and discipline practices.
      Discusses the basis of discrimination, e.g., sex, race,
      national origin, religion, age, handicap, and reverse dis-
      crimination. Outlines various federal laws against discrimi-
      nation and explains EEO guidelines for part-time and tempo-
      rary employees. Includes a glossary of EEO terms.

*   Silbergeld, Arthur F. "New Affirmative Action Regulations
      for Government Contractors." See Item 1023.

*   Simon, Ruth. "Seniority v. Affirmative Action." See Item
      721.

*   Singer, James W. "Weber: A Boost to Affirmative Action."
      See Item 1129.

971. Siniscalo, Gary. "Affirmative Action Plan for the XYZ
      Company." EEO TODAY, 8 (Spring 1981), 73-80.

      Provides a model affirmative action plan and a narrative
      for each section of the plan.

972. Sloan, Allan. "Affirmative Action After Bakke." EMPLOYEE
      RELATIONS LAW JOURNAL, 4 (Autumn 1978), 153-160.

*   Smith, Arthur B., Jr.; Charles B. Craver; and Leroy D. Clark,
      EMPLOYMENT DISCRIMINATION LAW. See Item 102.

973. Sowell, Thomas. "A Dissenting Opinion About Affirmative
      Action." ACROSS THE BOARD, 18 (January 1981), 64-72.

974. "Special Issue on Affirmative Action." PUBLIC PERSONNEL
      MANAGEMENT, 7 (November-December 1978), 347-398.

      Presents a series of papers that review the judicial
      standard and measurement of adverse impact.

975. Squires, Gregory D. AFFIRMATIVE ACTION, A GUIDE FOR THE
      PERPLEXED. East Lansing, MI.: Institute for Community
      Development, Continuing Education Service, Michigan State
      University, May 1977. 204 pp.

Gives a concise summary of federal civil rights laws and
regulations. Outlines federal requirements for developing
and implementing an affirmative action program. Includes a
directory of civil rights agencies, listings of reading
materials available on civil rights and affirmative action,
and a collection of articles written on affirmative action.

976. Sturdevant, Annette K. and Robert B. Patterson, Jr. A HAND-
     BOOK FOR AFFIRMATIVE ACTION PROGRAM PLANNING: UTILIZING
     THE STRUCTURED PERSONNEL MANAGEMENT PROCESS. Athens, OH.:
     Organization Development, Inc., 1980. 289 pp.

977. Swanson, Stephen C. "Affirmative Action Goals: Acknow-
     ledging the Employer's Interest." PERSONNEL JOURNAL, 62
     (March 1983), 216-220.

     Contends that officials in the Justice Department during
     the Reagan Administration advocate that the Weber decision
     was " wrongly decided"; therefore, numerical affirmative
     action goals may not be legitimate. Explains what the court
     said in Weber and advises employers on how goals should be
     properly used.

978. Terry, Robert W. "Obstacles to Affirmative Action." AFFIR-
     MATIVE ACTION: A GUIDE FOR THE PERPLEXED. Edited by
     Gregory D. Squires. East Lansing, MI.: Institute for
     Community Development Continuing Education Service,
     Michigan State University, May 1977.

979. Thayer, Robert. "Affirmative Action: What's Really Fair?"
     HOSPITALS, 53 (April 16, 1979), 88.

980. U.S. Civil Service Commission, Bureau of Intergovernmental
     Personnel Program. "EEO - A Time for Affirmative Action."
     EEO FOR STATE AND LOCAL GOVERNMENTS. Washington, D.C.:
     Government Printing Office, Issue No. 3. 3 pp.

     Discusses why affirmative action is needed and how to
     develop and implement an affirmative action program.

981. _____. GOALS AND TIMETABLES FOR EFFECTIVE AFFIRMA-
     TIVE ACTION -- A GUIDE FOR STATE AND LOCAL GOVERNMENT.
     Washington, D.C.: Government Printing Office, 1976.

     Designed to assist state and local governments ". . . in
     establishing goals and timetables to achieve equal employment
     opportunity. . . ." Maintains that prior to establishing
     numerical goals, a self assessment of the workforce should be
     made to determine the number of minorities and women in each
     job category. The numerical data should then be compared to

the availability of qualified minorities and women in the
labor force. Thereafter, goals and timetables are developed
to correct the underutilization of minorities and women in
the workforce. The "recruitment area," "applicant flow
data," and the progress of affirmative action programs should
be reviewed and evaluated on a continuous basis to ensure
that obstacles to equal employment have been removed.

982. _____. GUIDELINES FOR THE DEVELOPMENT OF AN AFFIRMA-
      TIVE ACTION PLAN. Washington, D.C.: Government Printing
      Office, 1975. 78 pp.

      A step by step outline for developing an affirmative action
      plan. Includes topics on recruitment, selection, training,
      upward mobility, labor market analysis, and evaluating an EEO
      program.

983. _____. "Guidelines for Internal Evaluation of Equal
      Employment Opportunity Programs." EEO FOR STATE AND LOCAL
      GOVERNMENTS. Washington, D.C.: Government Printing
      Office, (Issue No. 4). 3 pp.

      Provides an outline of procedures to follow in conducting a
      "periodic self-assessment" of an equal employment and affir-
      mative action program.

*   U.S. Civil Service Commission, Bureau of Intergovernmental
      Personnel Programs. "Reducing the Effects of Layoffs on
      your Affirmative Action Program." See Item 728.

*   U.S. Civil Service Commission, Bureau of Intergovernmental
      Personnel Programs. "Statistical Tools for Affirmative
      Action Planning." See Item 820.

984. _____. "Upward Mobility," EEO FOR STATE AND LOCAL
      GOVERNMENTS. Washington, D.C.: Government Printing
      Office, Issue No. 6. 4 pp.

      Indicates that an essential component of an affirmative
      action plan is the upward mobility program. States that
      components of an upward mobility program include "career
      systems," which determines whether opportunities exist for
      employees with lower-level jobs to be advanced to higher-
      level jobs. States that career counseling, guidance, and
      training, are also a part of an upward mobility program.
      Recommends that career development plans be developed for
      employees and communicated, monitored and evaluated contin-
      uously.

985. U.S. Commission on Civil Rights. AFFIRMATIVE ACTION IN
      EMPLOYMENT IN HIGHER EDUCATION. Washington, D.C.: Govern-
      ment Printing Office, 1977. 239 pp.

      Reports on proceedings of a consultation conference held by
      the Commission during the Fall of 1975. Includes panel dis-
      cussions and presentations. Focuses specifically on ". . .
      policy and practice relating to student recruitment, admis-
      sions, and scholarship grant; and faculty recruitment, pro-
      motion, and tenure policy and practice."

986. _____. Affirmative Action in the 1980's: DISMANTLING
      THE PROCESS OF DISCRIMINATION -- A STATEMENT. Washington,
      D.C.: Government Printing Office, 1981. 55 pp.

      "Views discrimination against minorities and women as pro-
      cesses that will continue unless systematically dismantled."
      Argues that affirmative action programs provide a systematic
      approach of dismantling employment discrimination. Includes
      discussions on developing an affirmative action program,
      goals and quotas, preferential treatment, and civil rights
      laws and regulations.

987. _____. PROMISES AND PERCEPTIONS: FEDERAL EFFORTS TO
      ELIMINATE EMPLOYMENT DISCRIMINATION THROUGH AFFIRMATIVE
      ACTION. Washington, D.C.: Government Printing Office,
      October 1981. 44 pp.

      Results of a study conducted by thirteen State Advisory
      Committees to the U.S. Commission on Civil Rights concerning
      the enforcement of affirmative action and equal employment
      opportunity. The study was conducted through fact finding
      meetings in 10 cities around the country. The purpose of
      the study was to examine ". . . the laws and regulations
      under which the major Federal enforcement agencies discharge
      their responsibilities in the area of equal employment
      opportunity." One of the Committee's general observation
      was that employment discrimination still widely exists.

988. _____. STATE GOVERNMENT: AFFIRMATIVE ACTION IN
      MID-AMERICA. Washington, D.C.: Government Printing
      Office, June 1978. 107 pp.

      A report from the Advisory Committees in Iowa, Kansas,
      Missouri, and Nebraska on the status of affirmative action in
      state government. Finds that minorities and women are under-
      utilized in employment by state agencies and that state
      government is not taking the lead in ensuring equal employ-
      ment opportunity and affirmative action. Recommends that
      recruitment efforts be improved to increase the number of
      minorities and women in state government.

989. _____. STATE GOVERNMENT AFFIRMATIVE ACTION IN
MID-AMERICA: AN UPDATE. Washington, D.C.: Government
Printing Office, March 1982. 299 pp.

Reports on the progress made by state government in the
states of Iowa, Missouri, Nebraska, and Kansas on affirmative
action since their study on affirmative action in 1978. Reviews state agency affirmative action plans and evaluates the
effectiveness of each plan to hire and promote minorities and
women. Summarizes the Advisory Committee's findings and
recommends steps to be taken by each state to ensure that
minorities and women are recruited and selected for meaningful positions.

990. _____. STATEMENT ON AFFIRMATIVE ACTION FOR EQUAL
EMPLOYMENT OPPORTUNITIES. Washington, D.C.: Government
Printing Office, 1973. 24 pp.

Presents the Commission's policy on affirmative action and
equal employment opportunity. Cites the aims of affirmative
action and provides common examples of barriers to equal
opportunity. Briefly discusses the Civil Rights Act of 1964
and Executive Order 11246. Distinguishes goals and timetables from quotas and denies that the purpose of affirmative
action is to give preferential treatment to minorities and
women.

991. U.S. Equal Employment Opportunity Commission. AFFIRMATIVE
ACTION AND EQUAL EMPLOYMENT: A GUIDEBOOK FOR EMPLOYERS,
VOL. 1. Washington, D.C.: Government Printing Office,
1974. 70 pp.

A comprehensive step by step guide to developing an affirmative action plan, including a summary of various EEO and
affirmative action laws and regulations.

992. _____. AFFIRMATIVE ACTION AND EQUAL EMPLOYMENT: A
GUIDE FOR EMPLOYERS, VOL. 2, APPENDICES. Washington, D.C.:
Government Printing Office, 1974. 32 pp.

A resource guide to sample documents and forms for developing an affirmative action program. Includes data sources
for determining underutilization, recruitment resources, EEO
guidelines and regulations, and a selected list of EEOC
publications.

993. _____. ELIMINATING DISCRIMINATION IN EMPLOYMENT: A
COMPELLING NATIONAL PRIORITY. Washington, D.C.: Government Printing Office, 1979.

A handbook for state, county and municipal governments on
how to comply with employment discrimination laws. The handbook provides information on all employment discrimination
laws, regulations, including laws prohibiting discrimination
in federally funded programs. Makes recommendations on how
to comply with EEO/AA laws and provides resources for developing an affirmative action program. Resources include
information on affirmative action recruitment, data sources
for utilization analysis, and a list of publications available on affirmative action.

994. _____. Office of Interagency Coordination. FEDERAL
AGENCY EQUAL EMPLOYMENT OPPORTUNITY PUBLIC INFORMATION
MATERIALS: AN ANNOTATED BIBLIOGRAPHY. Washington, D.C.:
Government Printing Office, June 1981.

Contains an annotated bibliography of materials published
by various Federal agencies concerning equal employment
opportunity and affirmative action.

995. U.S. General Accounting Office. HOW TO MAKE SPECIAL EMPHASIS
PROGRAMS AN EFFECTIVE PART OF AGENCIES' EEO ACTIVITIES.
REPORT TO THE CONGRESS BY THE CONTROLLER GENERAL OF THE
UNITED STATES. Washington, D.C.: Government Printing
Office, 1980.

*   U.S. National Institute of Mental Health and the President's
Committee on Employment of the Handicapped. AFFIRMATIVE
ACTION TO EMPLOY MENTALLY RESTORED PEOPLE. See Item 547.

996. U.S. Office of Personnel Management. EEO AFFIRMATIVE ACTION
PLAN, TRANSITION YEAR 1980. Washington, D.C.: Government
Printing Office, 1980.

997. _____. Intergovernmental Personnel Programs. "Build-
ing a Merit Promotion Program that Meets Federal EEO
Requirements for Selection." EEO INFORMATION ON EQUAL
EMPLOYMENT OPPORTUNITY FOR STATE AND LOCAL GOVERNMENTS.
Issue No. 20. Washington, D.C.: Government Printing
Office, June 1979.

Outlines promotion procedures that are based on merit and
at the same time allows minorities and women to receive
advancement within the organization.

998. VanderWaerdt, Lois. AFFIRMATIVE ACTION IN HIGHER EDUCATION,
A SOURCEBOOK. New York: Garland Publishing, Inc., 1982.
259 pp.

Explores the affects that affirmative action has had on college and university campuses in the hiring and placement of minority and female employees. Indicates that even after the passage of the Civil Rights Act of 1964, minorities and women are still under-represented. Outlines a procedure for designing and implementing an affirmative action program for hiring and promoting minorities and women. Discusses grievances, charges of discrimination, and compliance reviews. Includes a glossary of affirmative action terms, a list of key cases, and a bibliography.

999.   Vernon, Richard G. and Peter S. Gray. "Affirmative Action as an Affirmative Defense to EEO Charges." EEO TODAY, 6 (Autumn 1979), 209-213.

Affirmative action plans that have been adopted by employers to increase the number of minorities and women do not guarantee that the employer will not receive a charge of discrimination. Contends that "[p]lans or practices in place when allegations of disparate treatment are made provide evidence of the employer's state of mind, or motive, and may help to defeat a claim of intentional discrimination." Concludes that the U.S. Supreme Court decision in United Steelworkers v. Weber may also provide some protection to employers who implement affirmative action programs.

1000. West, Wayne K. "A Self-Audit for Affirmative Action Programs. PERSONNEL JOURNAL, 57 (December 1978), 688.

1001. Wright, James R. "Affirmative Action: A Plan for America." FREEDOMWAYS, 17 (First Quarter 1977), 30-34.

Believes that affirmative action is still needed to eliminate and combat employment discrimination. Contends that the "old buddy" system for hiring is still practiced. Discredits the notion that minorities "have now made it in the job market."

*   "Writing an Affirmative Action Program for the Handicap." See Item 557.

1002. Zashin, Elliot M. "Affirmative Action, Preferential Selection, and Federal Employment." PUBLIC PERSONNEL MANAGEMENT, 7 (November-December 1978), 378-393.

Briefly outlines the historical roots of affirmative action in the federal system and explains the differences between goals and quotas. Analyzes opponents' criticism of affirmative action and proponents' defenses to affirmative action.

EXECUTIVE ORDER 11246 AND FEDERAL CONTRACT COMPLIANCE

1003.   Ashe, R. Lawrence, Jr. and Donald R. Stacy. "Executive
        Order 11246: An Overview." OFCCP AND FEDERAL CONTRACT
        COMPLIANCE. Edited by David A. Copus and Linda Rosenz-
        weig. New York: Practicing Law Institute, 1981, pp. 1-37.

        Examines the origin, components, and sanctions under Execu-
        tive Order 11246.

*   Brownstein, Paul. "Affirmative Action Programs." Edited by
        John J. Ross. EQUAL EMPLOYMENT OPPORTUNITY -- RESPONSIBLE
        MANAGEMENT. See Item 905.

1004.   Callahan, Michael T. "Defending Enforcement of Executive
        Order 11246 Against Federal Construction Contractors: A
        Quagmire of Uncertainty." ADMINISTRATIVE LAW REVIEW, 30
        (Fall 1978), 519-533.

1005.   Corpus, David A. and Linda E. Rosenzweig, eds. OFCCP AND
        FEDERAL CONTRACT COMPLIANCE. New York: Practicing Law
        Institute, 1981. 233 pp.

        Views the Office of Federal Contract Compliance Program
        (OFCCP) as the most active federal agency enforcing equal
        employment and affirmative action (EEO/AA). Presents arti-
        cles on the enforcement powers of OFCCP under Executive Order
        11246 and the responsibility of federal contractors to ensure
        EEO/AA.

1006.   Executive Order 11246: Anti-discrimination Obligation in
        Government Contracts. NEW YORK UNIVERSITY LAW REVIEW,
        44 (May 1969), 590-611.

*   Hartman, Gerald S. "Management Personnel Practices: The
        Do's and Don'ts of EEO Compliance." See Item 43.

1007.   Humphrey, Kathy. CONTRACT COMPLIANCE: A LOCAL GOVERNMENT
        APPROACH. Berkeley, CA.: Institute for Local Self
        Government, 1978. 133 pp.

        As recipients of Federal funds, local governments have a
        responsibility to ensure that equal employment opportunity

228

guidelines are met on federally supported construction projects. This responsibility is mandated by Executive Order
11246. This manual outlines compliance programs for local
governments to meet EEO and affirmative action regulations.
Includes topics on the functions of a contract compliance
officer, the components of a compliance program, and how to
develop a minority business enterprise program.

1008. Jackson, Gary W. "Executive Order 11246 as an Alternative
      to Title VII: The Elimination of Discrimination in Bona
      Fide Seniority Systems." DUKE LAW JOURNAL, 1978 (December
      No. 5), 1268-1293.

1009. Jones, James E., Jr. "Federal Contract Compliance in Phase
      II: The Dawning of the Age of Enforcement of Equal Employ-
      ment Obligations. GEORGIA LAW REVIEW, 4 (1970), 756-778.

1010. McLanahan, Bruce. "The Equal Opportunity Obligations to
      Supply and Service Contractors." OFCCP AND FEDERAL CON-
      TRACT COMPLIANCE. Edited by David A. Corpus and Linda
      Rosenzweig. New York: Practicing Law Institute, 1981,
      pp. 39-93.

      Explains equal employment and affirmative action obliga-
      tions of supply and service contractors under Executive Order
      11246. Outlines the components of an affirmative action pro-
      gram for contractors, e.g., goal setting, workforce analysis,
      eight factor analysis, applicant flow data, and adverse
      impact.

1011. Moeller, James L. "Executive Order 11246: Presidential
      Power to Regulate Employment Discrimination." MISSOURI
      LAW REVIEW, 43 (Summer 1978), 451-502.

1012. Moroze, M. Brian. "Backpay Awards: A Remedy Under Execu-
      tive Order 11246." BUFFALO LAW REVIEW, 22 (Winter 1973),
      439-455.

      Argues that a backpay award is an appropriate remedy in
      discrimination suits against federal contractors who have
      violated Executive Order 11246.

1013. Nelson, Bruce A. and Mary Lu Christie. "Affirmative Action
      Requirements for the Construction Industry Under Execu-
      tive Order 11246." OFCCP AND FEDERAL CONTRACT COMPLIANCE.
      Edited by David A. Corpus and Linda Rosenzweig. New York:
      Practicing Law Institute, 1981, pp. 95-127.

      Outlines affirmative action requirements for federal con-
      struction contractors. Under Executive Order 11246, the

Rehabilitation Act of 1973, and the Vietnam Era Veterans'
Readjustment Assistance Act of 1974, contractors and subcontractors of any federal agency or employed by an organization
receiving federal assistance are required to have an affirmative plan. Briefly outlines the Philadelphia Plan which was
developed by the Department of Labor to obtain minority participation on federal construction contracts. Other topics
discussed include reverse discrimination, compliance problems
under Executive Order 11246, and the utilization of goals for
hiring minorities and women.

1014.   "Note, Executive Order 11246: Anti-Discrimination Obliga-
        tions in Government Contracts." NEW YORK UNIVERSITY LAW
        REVIEW, 44 (May 1969), 590-611.

        Details the coverage, sanctions, affirmative action re-
        quirements, and the judicial and administrative enforcement
        provisions of the Order. Includes the text of Burlington
        Industries' Affirmative Action Program to illustrate how one
        federal contractor is making an effort to comply with the
        Order.

1015.   "Note, Executive Order 11246 and Reverse Discrimination
        Challenges: Presidential Authority to Require Affirma-
        tive Action." NEW YORK UNIVERSITY LAW SCHOOL, 54 (May
        1979), 376-412.

1016.   THE OFFICE OF FEDERAL CONTRACT COMPLIANCE PROGRAM SPEAKS:
        REVISED AFFIRMATIVE ACTION REQUIREMENTS AND COMPLIANCE
        REVIEW PROCESS FOR FEDERAL CONTRACTORS. New York: Har-
        court Brace Jovanovich, Publishers, 1980.

        A collection of directives and guidelines from the OFCCP
        that explain affirmative action requirements for governmen-
        tal contractors. Includes the full text of Executive Order
        11246, as amended and a model affirmative action plan.

1017.   Panken, Peter M. "The Obligation of Federal Contractors
        to Take Affirmative Action." ALI-ABA COURSE MATERIALS
        JOURNAL, 3 (April 1979), 81-107.

        Designed as a training course on affirmative action re-
        quirements for federal contractors. Gives a step-by-step
        review of Executive Order 11246, affirmative action compli-
        ance programs, OFCCP affirmative action requirements, the
        Rehabilitation Act of 1973, and the Vietnam Era Veterans
        Readjustment Act.

1018. _____. "Use of Federal Purchasing Power to Require
      Affirmative Action." RESOURCE MATERIALS: LABOR AND
      EMPLOYMENT LAW. Edited by Peter M. Panken. 2d.ed.
      Philadelphia, PA.: American Law Institute -- American Bar
      Association Committee on Continuing Professional Education,
      1984, pp. 327-387.

      Outlines federal contractor's affirmative action obliga-
      tions under Executive Order 11246. Briefly compares the
      enforcement efforts of the Order under the Carter and Reagan
      administrations. Sees a softening of affirmative action
      requirements and enforcement efforts during the Reagan
      administration.

1019. Pratt, L. Steven. "Federal Contract Compliance: Use of
      Special Contract Provisions to Encourage Minority Employ-
      ment." LOYOLA UNIVERSITY OF CHICAGO LAW JOURNAL, 8 (Summer
      1977), 913-933.

      Gives an overview of various anti-discrimination programs
      in the construction industry, e.g., Executive Order 11246,
      Hometown Plans, Office of Minority Business Enterprise, and
      state programs. Indicates that the major obstacle to such
      programs is that they discriminate against white contrac-
      tors; however, believes that the programs will survive a
      constitutional challenge.

1020. Price, W.S. "The Affirmative Action Concept of Equal Employ-
      ment Opportunity." LABOR LAW JOURNAL, 16 (October 1965),
      603-619.

      Evaluates the implementation of Executive Order 10925,
      which established the President's Committee on Equal Employ-
      ment Opportunity and Executive Order 11246. Explains that
      Executive Order 11246 require governmental contractors to
      take affirmative action to employ minorities.

1021. Robinette, Mark B. "Fullilove v. Klutznick: An Initial
      Victory for Congressional Affirmative Action." OHIO
      NORTHERN UNIVERSITY LAW REVIEW, VII (No. 2, 1981), 377-387.

      Analyzes the Supreme Court's decision in Fullilove v.
      Klutznick in which the Court held that Congress was within
      its constitutional powers to establish an affirmative action
      program to ensure that minority businesses participated in
      federally funded public works projects. Sees the decision
      as a "victory" for congressional affirmative action programs.
      Concludes that the Court failed to set forth what limits were
      placed on Congress to use race as a classification. The
      Court also failed to establish the standard of review under
      the Equal Protection Clause of the Fourteenth Amendment for
      congressional affirmative action projects.

1022. Schmid, Carol. "Backpay Relief Under Executive Order 11,246:
       Justice or Just a Duplicative Government Regulation."
       UCLA-ALASKA LAW REVIEW, 10 (Fall 1980), 63-84.

1023. Silbergeld, Arthur F. "New Affirmative Action Regulations
       for Government Contractors." LABOR LAW JOURNAL, 33
       (April 1982), 230-237.

1024. U.S. Department of Health, Education, and Welfare, Office of
       Civil Rights. EXECUTIVE ORDER 11246: NONDISCRIMINATION
       UNDER FEDERAL CONTRACTS. Washington, D.C.: Government
       Printing Office, 1975. 19 pp.

       Provides the full text of the Order as signed by President
       Johnson and amendments 11375 and 11478. Provides the ad-
       dresses of the national and regional offices of H.E.W.

1025. _____. HIGHER EDUCATION GUIDELINES, EXECUTIVE ORDER
       11246. Washington, D.C.: Government Printing Office,
       1975.

       Outlines EEO and affirmative action requirements for col-
       leges and universities who receive federal contracts. Dis-
       cusses the major provisions of Executive Order 11246 and
       Revised Order No. 4. Advises employers that personnel poli-
       cies and practices must be "valid predictors of performance"
       and nondiscriminatory. Briefly discusses personnel policies
       and practices within the academic setting that may be sus-
       ceptible to discrimination. Concludes by giving a step-by-
       step formula for developing an "effective affirmative action
       program."

1026. U.S. Department of Labor, Employment Standards Administra-
       tion, Office of Federal Contract Complaince Programs.
       OFCCP: MAKING EEO AND AFFIRMATIVE ACTION WORK. Washing-
       ton, D.C.: Government Printing Office, 1979. 15 pp.

       Explains the functions of the Office of Federal Contract
       Compliance Programs for enforcing equal employment opportu-
       nity and affirmative action.

1027. U.S. Department of Labor, Wage and Labor Standards Adminis-
       tration, Office of Federal Contract Compliance. PHILA-
       DELPHIA PLAN, QUESTIONS AND ANSWERS. Washington, D.C.:
       Government Printing Office, 1969.

       Discusses federal requirements for federal construction
       projects to submit affirmative action plans to the Office of
       Federal Contract Compliance Programs.

1028.   U.S. Senate, Committee on Labor and Human Resources.
        COMMITTEE ANALYSIS OF EXECUTIVE ORDER 11246 (AFFIRMATIVE
        ACTION PROGRAM). Committee Print, 97th Congress, 2nd
        Session. Washington, D.C.: Government Printing Office,
        April 1982. 96 pp.

        Summarizes the findings of a study by the Committee on the
        effectiveness of Executive Order 11246 in eliminating dis-
        crimination and increasing the employment opportunities of
        protected class individuals. Provides comments from both
        supporters and critics of the Order. Concludes with four-
        teen recommendations to improve the effectiveness in the
        administration and enforcement of the Order.

3. LITIGATION AND RELATED ARTICLES

1029. Agid, Susan R. FAIR EMPLOYMENT LITIGATION, PROVING AND
DEFENDING A TITLE VII CASE. New York: Practicing Law
Institute, 1979. 961 pp.

Provides guidance to attorneys on litigating Title VII
cases. Focuses on procedural requirements under Title VII.
Explains the process of litigating a VII case from the initial filing of the complaint to award and settlement provisions under VII. Other topics include: motions to dismiss,
class actions, discovery, negotiating settlements, burdens
of proof, test validation, and counsel fees.

1030. Bell, Derrick A., Jr., ed. CIVIL RIGHTS: LEADING CASES.
Boston, MA.: Little, Brown and Company, 1980. 476 pp.

Analyzes opinions of the Supreme Court in selected civil
rights cases. Examines cases from the Dred Scott decision,
which was rendered in 1857 to the 1979 Weber decision. In
addition to the Weber decision, other major employment discrimination cases reported include Griggs, Bakke, and
Washington v. Davis.

1031. "Bias Charges in Hiring: AT&T Fights Back." U.S. NEWS AND
WORLD REPORT, 73 (August 14, 1972), 66-68.

Discusses the landmark employment discrimination case
against the American Telephone and Telegraph Company (AT&T).
Outlines AT&T's strategies for defending their EEO policy.

1032. Brown, William H. III. "Preparing for Trial from Defendant's
Point of View." EQUAL EMPLOYMENT OPPORTUNITY COMPLIANCE.
New York: Practicing Law Institute, 1976, pp. 81-94.

Outlines techniques for defending a claim of discrimination
under Title VII and the Civil Rights Act of 1866. Focuses
specifically on the issues of jurisdiction, multiple forums,
trial de novo, discovery, and defenses.

1033. Bureau of National Affairs, Inc. FAIR EMPLOYMENT PRACTICE
CASES. Washington, D.C., 1982.

Contains opinions of state and federal courts, and EEOC
decisions relative to race, color, religion, sex, sexual

orientation, national orgin, age, and disability discrimination. Includes a loose-leaf update on the most recent decisions and bound volumes of earlier decisions.

1034. Cathcart, David A. and Michael L. Bender. "A Guide to Em-
       ployment Discrimination Litigation." RESOURCE MATERIALS:
       LABOR AND EMPLOYMENT LAW. Philadelphia, PA.: American
       Law Institute - American Bar Association Committee on
       Continuing Professional Education, 1981, pp. 79-149.

       A comprehensive outline on litigating an employment dis-
       crimination case. Begins with pre-trial issues through
       post-trial remedies under Title VII. Includes discussions
       on class actions, discovery, age discrimination, equal
       pay cases, settlements, burdens of proof, and statistical
       evidence.

1035. Clothier, Janice Shaw. "Civil Rights: Defendant's Burden
       of Proof in Title VII Disparate Treatment Cases."
       WASHBURN LAW JOURNAL, 21 (Fall 1981), 143-150.

       Analyzes the Supreme Court's decisions in Texas Department
       of Community Affairs v. Burdine and McDonnell Douglas Corp.
       v. Green to determine the defendant's burden in proving a
       Title VII disparate treatment case. Concludes that the
       Burdine decision reaffirmed the Court's decision in McDonnell
       Douglas, which held that after the plaintiff establishes a
       prima facie case of discrimination, the burden of proof
       shifts to the defendant to "articulate some legitimate, non-
       discriminatory reason for the employee's rejection." States
       that the Court in Burdine went further to explain that the
       burden of persuasion to prove discrimination remains with
       the plaintiff throughout the case.

1036. Cohen, Leonard E. and Monte Fried. "'Multiple Jeopardy' in
       Employment Discrimination Cases." MARYLAND LAW REVIEW,
       31 (1971), 101-133.

1037. Commerce Clearing House, Inc. EEOC DECISIONS. Chicago,
       IL., 1983.

       Reports on administrative decisions issued by the EEOC
       between January 20, 1973 through April 21, 1983.

1038. _____. EMPLOYMENT PRACTICES DECISIONS. Chicago,
       IL., 1982.

       A full text reporter on state and federal court decisions
       related to race, color, sex, religion, national origin, and
       age discrimination. Includes a loose-leaf update on the most
       recent decisions and bound volumes of earlier decisions.

*   Connolly, Walter B., Jr. and David W. Peterson. The Use
        of Statistics in Equal Employment Opportunity Litigation.
        See Item 806.

1039.   Cooper, George and Harriet Rabb. EQUAL EMPLOYMENT LAW AND
        LITIGATION: MATERIALS FOR A CLINICAL LAW COURSE. New
        York: Employment Rights Project, Columbia Law School,
        1973. 500 pp.

        Written as a casebook for students in an employment dis-
        crimination clinical program at Columbia Law School. Dis-
        cusses civil rights laws and regulations, remedies, pro-
        cedures for litigating a discrimination case, theories of
        discrimination, brief writing, and injunctions.

1040.   Fields, Cheryl. "High Court Rules that Job-Bias Plaintiffs
        Need Not Prove Direct Discrimination." THE CHRONICLE OF
        HIGHER EDUCATION, (April 13, 1983), 9-10.

        Reports on the Supreme Court's decision in U.S. Postal
        Service Board of Governors v. Aiken, which held that plain-
        tiff in a Title VII suit need not prove discriminatory
        intent on the part of the defendant to prove a prima facie
        case. The Court reaffirmed the procedure to establish a
        prima facie case as outlined in McDonnell Douglas v. Green.

1041.   Freeman, Alan David. "Legitimizing Racial Discrimination
        Through Anti-discrimination Law: A Critical Review of
        Supreme Court Doctrine." MINNESOTA LAW REVIEW, 62 (July
        1978), 1049-1119.

1042.   Goldman, Alan. "Employment Discrimination, Washington v.
        Davis: Splitting the Causes of Action Against Racial
        Discrimination in Employment." LOYOLA UNIVERSITY OF
        CHICAGO LAW JOURNAL, 8 (Fall 1976), 225-249.

        Examines the impact of the Washington decision on employ-
        ment discrimination litigation. States that the decision
        held that the standard for proving discrimination established
        under Griggs does not apply to discrimination cases which
        are brought under the Constitution. The Court also estab-
        lished a new "job relatedness" standard. The Court held that
        since Washington was brought under 42 U.S.C., section 1981
        and the Fifth Amendment, "intentional discriminatory purpose"
        had to be proven and the Court's new standard for "job
        relatedness" was applicable. Concludes that the decision
        established three distinct causes of action for race dis-
        crimination suits.

1043. Green, Ronald. "Trends in Age Discrimination Litigation."
       PROCEEDING OF NEW YORK UNIVERSITY THIRTY FIFTH ANNUAL
       NATIONAL CONFERENCE OF LABOR. Edited by Richard Adelman.
       New York: Matthew Bender, 1983, pp. 353-377.

1044. Holmes, Grace W. and Quenda B. Story, eds. HANDLING THE
       EMPLOYMENT DISCRIMINATION CASE. Ann Arbor, MI.: The
       Institute of Continuing Legal Education, 1975. 285 pp.

       Includes articles from plaintiff and defense attorneys on
       litigating employment discrimination cases. Recommends ways
       to select the best forum for litigating employment discrimi-
       nation cases. Discusses financing the litigation, discovery,
       relief, and peculiar problems in litigating employment dis-
       crimination cases.

1045. Holt, Thaddeus. "Personnel Selection and the Supreme
       Court." CONTEMPORARY PROBLEMS IN PERSONNEL. Edited by
       W. Clay Hammer and Frank L. Schmidt. rev. ed. Chicago,
       IL.: St. Clair Press, 1979, pp. 147-159.

       Examines six Supreme Court decisions that were rendered
       between 1971-76 in the area of EEO and personnel selection.
       The Supreme Court decision in Griggs v. Duke Power Company,
       established that it was unnecessary for the plaintiff to
       prove that the employer intended to discriminate. It is
       sufficient to prove that an employment practice is not job
       related and has an adverse impact on protected class indi-
       viduals. Two years after the Griggs decision, the Supreme
       Court outlined in McDonnell Douglas Corp. v. Green, what is
       needed to establish a prima facie case. In Albemarle Paper
       Co. v. Moody, the Supreme Court held that an employer must
       show by a preponderance of evidence that the selection de-
       vice is job related. In Washington v. Davis, the court held
       that "an adverse effect on a minority group, standing alone,
       is not enough to make out a prima facie case of discrimina-
       tion under the Equal Protection Clause: Under the constitu-
       tional provision, there must also be some proof of an intent
       to discriminate." In Johnson v. Railway Express Agency, the
       Court held that the Civil Rights Act of 1866 prohibited dis-
       crimination in the making of contracts and was not affected
       by Title VII. At the same time that the Supreme Court handed
       down the Johnson case, the Court held in McDonald v. Santa Fe
       Trail Transportation Co., that Title VII and the Civil Rights
       Act of 1866 applies to whites just like it applies to Blacks.
       Maintains that these cases represent the most significant
       Supreme Court decisions on EEO during this time period.

1046. Horstman, Dee Ann S. "New Judicial Standards for Adverse
       Impact: Their Meaning for Personnel Practices." PUBLIC
       PERSONNEL MANAGEMENT, 7 (November-December 1978), 347-353.

Summarizes leading court decisions on statistical methods
of establishing adverse impact.

*   Hunter, James M. and Milton C. Branch. "Equal Employment
        Opportunities: Administrative Procedures and Judicial
        Developments Under Title VII of the Civil Rights Act of
        1964 and the Equal Employment Act of 1972." See Item 47.

1047.   Jacobs, Roger B. "Ricks v. Delaware State College: An
        End to Continuing Violations?" EMPLOYEE RELATIONS LAW
        JOURNAL, 7 (Summer 1981), 85-104.

        Analyzes the Supreme Court's decision in Ricks and explains
        the impact that the decision will have on the continuing vio-
        lation theory in Title VII litigation cases.

1048.   Johnson, James G. "Albemarle Paper Company v. Moody: The
        Aftermath of Griggs and the Death of Employee Testing."
        HASTINGS LAW JOURNAL, 27 (July 1976), 1239-1262.

        Analyzes the Supreme Court's decision in Albemarle Paper
        Company, which held that testing practices used by the com-
        pany violated Title VII. The court based the decision in
        part on the Griggs' decision and the EEOC's Guidelines on
        Employee Selection Procedures. Believes that the guidelines
        are "unrealistic and unworkable." Concludes that if courts
        strictly enforce the guidelines, employers will be forced
        to abandon testing as a selection device.

1049.   Kilberg, William J. "How to Settle A Discrimination Case."
        PROCEEDINGS OF NEW YORK UNIVERSITY TWENTY-EIGHTH ANNUAL
        CONFERENCE ON LABOR. Edited by Richard Adelman. New
        York: Matthew Bender, 1976, pp. 101-110.

        Outlines procedures for attorneys to follow in settling em-
        ployment discrimination cases. Focuses primarily on settle-
        ments with multi-employers, e.g., American Telephone and
        Telegraph.

*   Kolesar, Peter J. "Statistical Concepts in EEO Litigation."
        See Item 814.

*   Ledvinka, James. FEDERAL REGULATION OF PERSONNEL AND
        HUMAN RESOURCE MANAGEMENT. See Item 55.

1050.   Martin-Howard, Jane. "A Critical Analysis of Judicial
        Opinions in Professional Employment Discrimination Cases."
        HOWARD LAW JOURNAL, 26 (No. 2, 1983), 721-757.

Asserts that the "bulk" of employment discrimination cases since the passage of Title VII has involved employers who employed blue collar employees, with an increasingly number of employers who employ white collar employees. Explains why the number of employment discrimination cases involving professional positions has "lagged" behind other job classifications. Reviews discrimination cases involving professional positions and analyzes the Court's rationale in reaching the decision.

1051. McClory, Robert. "Sears Suit: Substance or Pre-Emptive Strike?" EQUAL OPPORTUNITY FORUM, 6 (April 1979), 4-5.

Presents both sides of the Sears suit. Sears insist that conflicting federal regulations prohibit them from hiring minorities and women; therefore, EEOC enforcement powers should be curtailed. Opponents of the suit argue that the suit has no substance and was a scheme to circumvent civil rights regulations, guidelines, handicap and age discrimination regulations, and affirmative action. Believes that if Sears prevails it will mean an end to the enforcement of Griggs v. Duke Power and will disallow the use of statistical disparity in showing discrimination.

1052. Mendez, Miguel Angel. "Presumptions of discriminatory Motive in Title VII Disparate Treatment Cases." STANFORD LAW REVIEW, 32 (July 1980), 1129-1162.

1053. Miller, Paul O., III. "Class Actions and Employment Discrimination Under Title VII of the Civil Rights Act of 1964." MISSISSIPPI LAW JOURNAL, 43 (1972), 275-286.

Examines the use of class action suits as a device to enforce Title VII's prohibitions against employment discrimination. Discusses a series of court decisions where class actions were brought and explains procedures for filing a class action suit under Title VII.

1054. Modjeska, Lee. "Decisions of the Supreme Court, 1979-1980 - Labor Relations and Employment Discrimination Law." INDUSTRIAL RELATIONS LAW JOURNAL, 4 (No. 1, 1980), 1-28.

Summarizes and analyzes Supreme Court decisions issued in the area of employment discrimination during 1979 and 1980. Includes decisions on seniority, class actions, attorney's fees, and filing limitations.

1055. _____. HANDLING EMPLOYMENT DISCRIMINATION CASES. Rochester, N.Y.: The Lawyers Co-Operative Publishing Co., 1980. 559 pp.

Attempts to explain EEO laws, executive orders, regulations, and cases in a "basic and understandable form." Begins with a discussion of Title VII's coverage, prohibitions,
and exceptions. Other chapters focus on the EEOC's administrative and enforcement powers, the Equal Pay Act, the Age
Discrimination in Employment Act, and the Rehabilitation Act
of 1973. The appendix includes the full text of various
Civil Rights statutes and the EEOC's regulations on employment discrimination. Includes an annual supplement which
reports on new developments.

1056.   National Employment Law Project. LEGAL SERVICES MANUAL FOR
        TITLE VII LITIGATION. New York, October 1973. 104 pp.

        Outlines the coverage and procedures for litigating a Title
        VII case. Explains the procedural prerequisites to filing a
        case and federal court procedures. Updates substantive de_
        velopment in employment discrimination law, e.g., testing,
        seniority and promotions, discrimination in labor unions, and
        sex discrimination.

1057.   Nelson, Bruce. "Title VII Litigation." ALI-ABA COURSE
        MATERIAL JOURNAL, 2 (April 1978), 47-64.

        Designed as training course material for litigating employ-
        ment discrimination cases under Title VII of the Civil Rights
        Act of 1964. Gives a step by step review of Title VII,
        jurisdictional prerequisites, burden of proof requirements,
        class actions, intervention by the EEOC, settlement formulas,
        jury trials, remedial relief, and litigating reverse dis-
        crimination claims.

1058.   Northrup, Herbert R. and John A. Larson. THE IMPACT OF THE
        AT&T - EEO CONSENT DECREE. Philadelphia, PA.: University
        of Pennsylvania, Industrial Research Unit, The Wharton
        School, 1979. 239 pp.

        Summarizes the events leading up to the consent decree, its
        terms, and impact on the employment of minorities and women
        over a five-year span.

1059.   Patten, Thomas, Jr., "Pay Discrimination Lawsuits: The
        Problems of Expert Witnesses and the Effects on the Dis-
        covery Process." PERSONNEL, 55 (November-December 1978),
        27-35.

1060.   Pemberton, John de J., Jr., ed. EQUAL EMPLOYMENT OPPORTU-
        NITY -- RESPONSIBILITIES, RIGHTS, REMEDIES. New York:
        Practicing Law Institute, 1975. 517 pp.

A collection of articles on EEO cases, civil rights laws
and regulations, affirmative action, handling EEO charges,
litigating EEO cases, defining discrimination and remedies
available under Title VII. Explores every aspect of discrimination, e.g., race, sex, age, and national origin.
Analyzes every major EEO decision that was rendered prior
to 1975, including Griggs and McDonnell Douglas.

1061. Peterson, William B. and Michael C. Lynch. "Limiting
       Employer Backpay Liability in Employment Discrimination
       Cases: Ford Motor Co. v. EEOC." EMPLOYEE RELATIONS LAW
       JOURNAL, 9 (Autumn 1983), 276-291.

1062. Player, Mack A. EMPLOYMENT DISCRIMINATION LAW: CASES AND
       MATERIALS. St. Paul, MN.: West Publishing Co., 1980.
       876 pp.

1063. Polhemus, Craig E. "Good Faith Discrimination and Backpay."
       MONTHLY LABOR REVIEW, 98 (October 1975) 57-60.

       Provides an overview of the Court's decision in Albemarle
       Paper Co. The court held that a good faith attempt on the
       part of the employer to prevent discrimination is not suffi-
       cient to prevent an award of backpay to an employee who has
       been discriminated against. The court also held that the
       employer's validation study was not in compliance with EEOC
       guidelines.

1064. Ray, Paula M. "Civil Rights." CREIGHTON LAW REVIEW, 13
       (1980), 1189-1212.

       Gives an analysis of significant civil rights decisions in
       the Eighth Circuit between January 1, 1979 to December 31,
       1979.

1065. Rodwig, Susan Talley. "Employment Discrimination -- Plain-
       tiff's Prima Facie Case and Defendant's Rebuttal in a
       Disparate Impact Case." TULANE LAW REVIEW, 54 (June 1979),
       1187-1197.

1066. Rowe, Benjamen T. and S. Dagnal Rowe. "Employment Testing
       and Title VII of the Civil Rights Act of 1964: After
       Albemarle Paper Co. v. Moody." ALABAMA LAWYER, 38 (July
       1977), 357-375.

       Traces the issue of discrimination in employment testing
       after Griggs v. Duke Power to Albemarle Paper Co. v. Moody.
       The Supreme Court endorsed the EEOC guidelines on selection
       in Albemarle and held that the test used by Albemarle was
       not job related nor sufficiently validated. Concludes that

the EEOC guidelines on selection favor quotas and discourage
employment testing.

1067.   Ruzicho, Andrew J. CIVIL RIGHTS LITIGATION: AN INVESTIGA-
        TION, PREPARATION & TRIAL MANUAL. Cincinnati, OH.: Ander-
        son Publishing Co., 1976. 372 pp.

        Presents tactics and strategies for EEO investigators,
        negotiators, and trial attorneys involved in litigating
        employment discrimination cases.

1068.   _____. "Comments on the Sears Suit." EQUAL OPPOR-
        TUNITY FORUM, 6 (April 1979), 16-17.

        Summarizes the complaint and facts in Sears v. Attorney
        General. States that the complaint "is a work of art and a
        masterpiece of a document." Believes that Sears has spent
        time and money in attempting to comply with EEO laws, but
        their efforts are not sufficient according to the EEOC.
        Concludes that whether Sears prevails or not, the suit has
        required federal EEO enforcement agencies to consider more
        than workforce statistics when determining whether discrimi-
        nation exist.

1069.   Schwartz, Donald J. and Patricia E. Shahen. "Avoiding Dis-
        crimination Suits." THE NATIONAL LAW JOURNAL, 4 (August 2,
        1982), 14.

        Defines adverse impact and the "bottom line" principle.
        Explains that during an EEO investigation on a discrimina-
        tion complaint or in a court of law, the burden is on the
        complainant to prove that adverse impact exist due to the
        employment practice in question. If the employer is guilty
        of adverse impact he/she is given an opportunity to show that
        the employment practice is job related. Briefly discusses
        the Supreme Court's decision in Teal v. Connecticut, which
        held that in some cases the "bottom line" principle may not
        prevent the finding of adverse impact. Believes that dis-
        crimination complaints may be avoided by closely analyzing
        personnel selection procedures and by establishing a system
        to monitor employment practices for adverse impact.

1070.   Schwemm, Robert G. "From Washington to Arlington Heights
        and Beyond: Discriminatory Purpose in Equal Protection
        Litigation." UNIVERSITY OF ILLINOIS LAW FORUM, (No. 4,
        1977), 961-1052.

        Analyzes the Court's decision in Washington v. Davis, which
        held that discriminatory purpose or intent must be shown by
        the plaintiff to establish a claim of race discrimination
        under the Equal Protection Clause of the Constitution.

States that the <u>Davis</u> decision was reaffirmed in the <u>Arlington</u> decision.

1071.   Shanor, Gloria J. and Charles A. Shanor. "Employment Discrimination." MERCER LAW REVIEW, 33 (Summer 1982), 1119-1146.

Surveys employment discrimination cases that were heard in the Fifth Circuit during 1981. Indicates that the Fifth Circuit's decision in <u>Patsy v. Florida International University</u> had national ramifications. The Fifth Circuit held that ". . . 'adequate and appropriate' state administrative remedies must be exhausted before a Section 1983 action may proceed in federal court."

1072.   Thomas, Clarence. "Current Litigation Trends and Goals at the EEOC." LABOR LAW JOURNAL, 34 (April 1983), 208-214.

Outlines six major court cases won by the EEOC during 1982. States that three of the cases were age discrimination cases and the other three were sex discrimination cases. Indicates that due to the number of women entering the workforce and the recession, there will be more cases involving sex discrimination and reductions in force in the future. Discusses the future of affirmative action and the present misunderstanding of its purpose and goal.

1073.   U.S. Office of Personnel Management. EQUAL EMPLOYMENT OPPORTUNITY COURT CASES. Washington, D.C.: Government Printing Office, 1979. 146 pp.

Summarizes major Title VII decisions of the U.S. Appellate Courts and the U.S. Supreme Court.

1074.   _____. EQUAL EMPLOYMENT OPPORTUNITY COURT CASES, 1980 SUPPLEMENT. Washington, D.C.: Government Printing Office, 1980. 238 pp.

Summarizes major Title VII decisions of the U.S. Appellate Courts and the U.S. Supreme Court between 1979 and 1980.

1075.   Wallace, Phyllis A., ed. EQUAL OPPORTUNITY AND THE AT&T CASE. Cambridge, Mass: The MIT Press, 1976. 355 pp.

THE GRIGGS DECISION

1076. Aronson, Albert H. "Duke Power Company Case: An Interpre-
       tative Commentary on the U.S. Supreme Court Decision,
       with Particular Reference to Its Implications for Govern-
       ment Personnel Selection Practices." PUBLIC EMPLOYMENT
       PRACTICES BULLETIN. No. 1. (1971), 1-5.

       Sees the Griggs' decision as establishing standards for
       promotion opportunities which are based on merit and effi-
       ciency.

1077. Barnabas, Bentley. "What Did the Supreme Court Really Say?"
       PERSONNEL ADMINISTRATOR, 16 (July-August 1971), 22-25.

1078. Blumrosen, Alfred W. "Strangers In Paradise: Griggs v.
       Duke Power Co. and The Concept of Employment Discrimi-
       nation." MICHIGAN LAW REVIEW, 71 (November 1972), 59-110.

1079. Cleveland, Christopher C. American Tobacco Co. v. Patterson:
       A Pre-Griggs Approach to Seniority Systems Under Title
       VII." WISCONSIN LAW REVIEW, 1984 (No. 3), 831-857.

       Analyzes the Supreme Court's decision in American Tobacco
       Co., which held that the disparate impact theory outlined in
       the Griggs' decision is not applicable when challenging a
       "bona fide seniority systems" under Title VII. Concludes
       that "[t]he message of Americans Tobacco is that employers
       and unions are free to devise seniority systems which per-
       petuate past intentional discrimination, so long as the
       seniority system itself is facially neutral and was itself
       not adopted with a discriminatory purpose."

*   "Employment Testing: The Aftermath of Griggs v. Duke
       Power Co." See Item 642.

1080. Fiss, Owen M. "A Theory of Fair Employment." UNIVERSITY OF
       CHICAGO LAW REVIEW, 38 (Winter 1971), 235-314.

*   Holt, Thaddeus. "Personnel Selection and the Supreme
       Court." CONTEMPORARY PROBLEMS IN PERSONNEL. See Item
       1045.

*   Johnson, James G. "Albemarle Paper Company v. Moody: The
       Aftermath of Griggs and the Death of Employee Testing."
       See Item 1048.

1081. McBrearty, James C. "Legality of Employment Tests: The
       Impact of Duke Power Co." LABOR LAW JOURNAL, 22 (July
       1971), 387-393.

       Analyzes the Griggs' decision and its impact on selection
       and promotion tests.

1082. McCarthy, J. James. "The Meaning of the Griggs Case in the
       Federal Service." GOOD GOVERNMENT, 88 (Winter 1971), 8-9.

       Highlights the U.S. Civil Service Commission's views on
       the impact of the Griggs' decision on federal employment
       practices. Asserts that the decision ". . . is identical
       to that which civil service statutes have long prescribed
       for public employment. . . ."

1083. Petersen, Donald J. "The Impact of Duke Power on Testing."
       PERSONNEL, 51 (March-April 1974), 30-37.

       Results of a questionnaire mailed to 185 companies to de-
       termine whether they will discontinue the use of employment
       tests, what efforts they will make to validate employment
       tests, and who will be doing the validation. Indicates that
       smaller companies will tend to discontinue the use of tests
       altogether; whereas, larger companies will tend to validate
       employment tests and will continue their use.

1084. Price, Robert N. "Griggs v. Duke Power Company: The First
       Landmark Under Title VII of the Civil Rights Act of
       1964." SOUTHWESTERN LAW JOURNAL, 25 (1971), 484-493.

1085. Rush, Floyd L. "The Impact on Employment Procedures of the
       Supreme Court Decision in the Duke Power Case." PERSONNEL
       JOURNAL, 50 (October 1971), 777-783.

1086. Schick, Richard and Barry S. Bader. "Supreme Court Mandates
       Job Related Examinations: The Griggs Decision." JUDICIAL
       MANDATES FOR AFFIRMATIVE ACTION. Washington, D.C.: NCSL's
       National Program Center Guidebook for Public Employers,
       1973, pp. 6-7.

       States that the Supreme Court's decision in Griggs v. Duke
       Power Co. held that "unvalidated basic intelligence and apti-
       tude tests" may violate Title VII of the Civil Rights Act
       of 1964. Indicates that not all employment tests or employ-
       ment practices are required to be validated. Concludes that
       where the test or selection device does not disproportion-
       ately screen out minority applicants, validation may not be
       necessary.

1087.   University of Richmond Law Review Association. "Civil
        Rights Act and Professionally Developed Ability Tests--
        Griggs v. Duke Power Co." UNIVERSITY OF RICHMOND LAW
        REVIEW, 5 (Fall 1970), 157-166.

        Advocates that the Fourth Circuit decision in Griggs v.
        Duke Power Co. was incorrect and was a misinterpretation of
        Title VII of the Civil Rights Act of 1964. The Fourth Cir-
        cuit held that tests being used by Duke Power were valid,
        served a "genuine business purpose," and were not designed
        to discriminate against "Negro" employees. Supports the
        Equal Employment Opportunity Commission position that em-
        ployment tests must be job-related.

*   Veil, Fred W. "Title VII of the Civil Rights Act of 1964-
        Educational and Testing Requirement Invalid Unless Job-
        related." See Item 130.

1088.   Wilson, Hugh S. "A Second Look at Griggs v. Duke Power
        Company: Ruminations on Job Testing, Discrimination, and
        the Role of the Federal Courts." VIRGINIA LAW REVIEW, 58
        (May 1972), 844-874.

        Focuses on the Supreme Court's decision in Griggs and the
        implication of the decision on job testing. Reviews the
        Court's interpretation of Title VII's legislative history,
        test validation, and the application of the Griggs decision
        on federal courts.

                         THE BAKKE DECISION

1089.   Abraham, Henry J. "Some Post-Bakke-and-Weber Reflections
        on 'Reverse Discrimination.'" UNIVERSITY OF RICHMOND LAW
        REVIEW, 14 (Winter 1980), 373-388.

1090.   Alleyne, Reginald. "Regents v. Bakke: Implementing Pre-
        Bakke Admissions Policies with Post-Bakke Admissions
        Procedures." BLACK LAW JOURNAL, 7 (No. 2, 1982), 290-295.

        Analyzes the Supreme Court's decision in Regents of the
        University of California v. Bakke. Indicates that there are
        differences of opinions as to who actually won the decision-
        plaintiff or defendant. Believes that the decision supports
        affirmative action, although the decision does not clearly
        state so.

1091.   Baker, Rob. "Turnabout: Blue-Collar Support for Affirma-
        tive Action Grows." EQUAL OPPORTUNITY FORUM, 6 (April
        1979), 8-9.

Asserts that unlike the Bakke case, trade unions have submitted "a blizzard of amicus curiae briefs" against Weber.
Contends that unions recognize that if the Supreme Court
finds in favor of Weber, they will be faced with expensive
court battles across the country where affirmative action
clauses have been incorporated into collective bargaining
agreements.

1092.   Bennett, William J. and Terry Eastland. "Why Bakke Won't
        End Reverse Discrimination." COMMENTARY, 66 (September
        1978), 29-35.

1093.   Blasi, Vincent. "Bakke as Precedent: Does Mr. Justice
        Powell Have a Theory?" CALIFORNIA LAW REVIEW, 67 (January
        1979), 21-68.

        Gives a critical analysis of the Supreme Court's decision
        in Regents of the University of California v. Bakke. Gives
        special attention to Justice Powell's opinion which indicates
        that race may be a factor in selecting an applicant for
        admission to school.

1094.   Buchanan, Richard G. "Affirmative Action After Bakke."
        EEO TODAY, 5 (Autumn 1978), 225-227.

        Believes that the Bakke decision supports the use of volun-
        tary affirmative action programs that establish flexible
        goals for the employment of minorities. The establishment
        of rigid quotas for the employment of minorities is prohibi-
        ted. Indicates that the U.S. Supreme Court's decision in
        Bakke cited Harvard University admission plan as a favorable
        affirmative action plan.

1095.   Carty-Bernia, Denise. "Bakke: Some Views - Extraordinary
        Split." CIVIL RIGHTS DIGEST, 10 (Summer 1978), 10-11.

        Briefly analyzes the Supreme Court Justices' opinions in
        the Bakke decision. Indicates that the decision was a ". . .
        4-1-4 split among the Justices in their perceptions, reason-
        ing, and conclusions about almost every issue raised." Con-
        centrates on Justice Powell's opinion, which held that racial
        classification could be considered, however, "strict judicial
        review" would be applicable.

1096.   College Entrance Examination Board. THE BAKKE DECISION:
        RETROSPECT AND PROSPECT. New York, 1978. 85 pp.

        Summarizes discussions presented during six meetings of
        college admissions officers and educators on the implication

of the <u>Bakke</u> decision on admission programs at colleges and
universities.

1097. Dixon, Robert G., Jr. "<u>Bakke</u>: A Constitutional Analysis."
       CALIFORNIA LAW REVIEW, 67 (January 1979), 69-86.

       Analyzes the Supreme Court's decision in <u>Regents of the
       University of California v. Bakke</u> and the decision's impact
       on constitutional principles. Focuses particularly on Jus-
       tice Powell's opinion which states in part ". . . that race
       may be a factor but not the factor in the admissions criteria
       of state universities. . . ."

1098. Dreyfuss, Joel and Charles Lawrence III. THE BAKKE CASE:
       THE POLITICS OF INEQUALITY. New York: Harcourt Brace
       Jovanovich, Inc., 1979. 278 pp.

       Traces the development of the <u>Bakke</u> cases through its
       inception to Bakke's first day as a medical student at the
       University of California at Davis.

1099. Farrell, Charles S. "Five Years Later, Allan Bakke Is A
       Doctor, but Effects of His Suit are Still Debated."
       CHRONICLE OF HIGHER EDUCATION, XXVI (June 22, 1983), 11.

       Finds that minority student enrollment is declining in
       medical and law schools, but indicates that the <u>Bakke</u> deci-
       sion was not the primary cause for such decline.

1100. Gold, Bertran. "<u>Bakke</u>: Some Views-Both Sides Won." CIVIL
       RIGHTS DIGEST, 10 (Summer 1978), 12-13.

       Contends that the Supreme Court took a middle of the road
       position on the issue of racial quotas. Believes that the
       decision will allow the American Jewish Committee, an oppo-
       nent of racial quotas, to again renew their coalition with
       other civil rights groups.

1101. "Impact of <u>Bakke</u> Decision." U.S. NEWS AND WORLD REPORT,
       85 (July 10, 1978), 14-18.

       Gives an assessment of the decision's impact on affirma-
       tive action programs in both private and public employment.
       States that the Supreme Court held that race could be a fac-
       tor in affirmative action programs but "strict numerical
       quotas" could not. Outlines other landmarks in the civil
       rights movement for minorities since 1954. Includes statis-
       tical data on minorities in graduate and professional schools
       during 1970-71 and 1977-78, and summarizes each Supreme Court
       Justices' opinion in the <u>Bakke</u> decision.

1102.   Kilberg, William J. and Stephen E. Tallent. "From Bakke to
        Fullilove: The Use of Racial and Ethnic Preferences in
        Employment." EMPLOYEE RELATIONS LAW JOURNAL, 6 (Winter
        1980-81), 364-379.

1103.   Larson, E. Richard. "Race Consciousness in Employment After
        Bakke." HARVARD CIVIL RIGHTS - CIVIL LIBERTIES LAW REVIEW,
        BAKKE SYMPOSIUM: CIVIL RIGHTS PERSPECTIVES, 14 (Spring
        1979), 215-267.

        Reviews the Bakke decision and speculates as to whether
        race-conscious employment programs are permissible after the
        Bakke decision. Concludes that Justice Powell's opinion
        supports a "wide range of race-conscious employment programs"
        by the government and by private employers.

1104.   Maltz, Earl M. "Bakke Primer." OKLAHOMA LAW REVIEW, 32
        (Winter 1979), 119-137.

        Examines the Supreme Court justices' opinions in the Bakke
        decision and predicts what impact the decision will have on
        affirmative action. Concludes that both sides of the Bakke
        issue won a partial victory. Indicates that the court ap-
        proved some usage of race as a classification, however, the
        court did not make it clear when and to what extent.

1105.   Margolis, Emanuel. "The Aching Bakke: Is There A Cure?"
        CONNECTICUT BAR JOURNAL, 51 (December 1977), 417-434.

        Outlines the facts, issues, arguments, and trial proceed-
        ings in the Bakke case.

*   Mazaroff, Stanley. "A Tightrope for Employers -- Affirmative
        Action Post-Bakke." See Item 944.

1106.   Morse, Thomas Rainbow and Anthony Joseph Rusciano. "Bakke v.
        The Regents of the University of California: Preferential
        Racial Admissions, An Unconstitutional Approach Paved with
        Good Intentions?" NEW ENGLAND LAW REVIEW, 12 (Winter
        1977), 719-761.

        Argues that the Supreme Court could have upheld the minor-
        ity admission program in the Bakke decision as being consti-
        tutional. Sets forth four major premises to support their
        claim that the Equal Protection Clause of the Constitution
        allows preferential treatment in special situations.

1107.   Norton, Eleanor Holmes. "The Bakke's Decision and the
        Future of Affirmative Action." EQUAL OPPORTUNITY FORUM,
        5 (August 1978), 18-19.

A former chairperson of the EEOC analyzes the Bakke decision and predicts the future of affirmative action. Concludes that the court approved race-conscious remedies for
correcting past discrimination. States that the EEOC will
also continue using numerical remedies. Believes that affirmative action must be taken to save affirmative action.
Cites the guidelines on affirmative action as a good tool to
"head off reverse discrimination suits."

1108. _____. "Comment on the Bakke Decision." PERSONNEL
ADMINISTRATOR, 23 (August 1978), 26-28.

Believes that affirmative action programs are still oper-
able under the law even after the Bakke decision. Encourages
employers to continue to take affirmative action to eliminate
discrimination in employment. Discusses the EEOC's guidelines on affirmative action. States that the guidelines provide direction on how to design a legally acceptable affirmative action program. Believes that employers will be in a
better position to fight a reverse discrimination claim if
they have complied with the guidelines.

*   Plevin, Mark D. "The Constitutionality of Affirmative Ac-
         tion in Public Employment: Judicial Deference to Certain
         Politically Responsible Bodies." See Item 960.

1109.   Posner, Richard A. "The Bakke Case and the Future of Affir-
        mative Action." California Law Review, 67 (January 1979),
        171-189.

        Analyzes the Supreme Court's decision in Bakke v. Regents
        of the University of California. Focuses on Justice Powell's
        opinion in the decision. Explains that Powell's opinion was
        the deciding vote in the Bakke decision and that his opinion
        is crucial to predicting the future of affirmative action and
        the status of reverse discrimination. Concludes that imposed
        affirmative action by the government may be illegal if Jus-
        tice Powell's constitutional standards analysis in Bakke is
        applicable to Title VII employment discrimination cases.

*   Richards, John E. "Equal Protection and Racial Quotas:
         Where Does Fullilove v. Klutznick Leave Us?" See Item 771.

1110.   Roberts, Steven V. "The Bakke Case Moves to the Factory."
        NEW YORK TIMES MAGAZINE, (February 25, 1979), 36.

1111.   Segal, Phyllis N. "Bakke-Some Views - A Feminist Perspec-
        tive." Civil Rights Digest, 10 (Summer 1978), 14-15.

Asserts that the decision is applicable to sex discrimination as well as race discrimination in employment practices.

*   Sloan, Allan. "Affirmative Action After Bakke." See Item
        972.

1112.   Tallent, Stephen E. "A Legal Perspective on the Bakke
        Decision." PERSONNEL JOURNAL, 58 (May 1979), 296.

        Analyzes the Supreme Court's decision in Bakke and the
        impact of the decision on personnel practices and affirma-
        tive action.

1113.   U.S. Commission on Civil Rights. TOWARD AN UNDERSTANDING
        OF BAKKE. Washington, D.C.: Government Printing Office,
        May 1979. pp. 189.

        Gives a brief comparison of the U.S. Supreme Court's de-
        cisions in Regents of the University of California v. Bakke,
        and Brown v. Board of Education, and provides a summary of
        the Justices' opinions in the Bakke decision.

1114.   Vieira, Norman. "Permissible Classification by Race and
        the Bakke Case." IDAHO LAW REVIEW, 14 (Fall 1977), 1-19.

        Provides a historical view of court cases involving the
        permissible use of classification by race. Discusses the
        race classification issue in the Japanese relocation cases,
        voting right cases, school desegregation cases, and the
        Supreme Court's decision in Bakke.

                          THE WEBER DECISION

*   Abraham, Henry J. "Some Post-Bakke and Weber Reflections on
        'Reverse Discrimination.'" See Item 1089.

1115.   Affirmative Action Coordinating Center. "Some Facts about
        Weber v. Kaiser Aluminum and United Steelworkers Union."
        EQUAL OPPORTUNITY FORUM, 6 (April 1979), 15.

        Briefly explains Kaiser's affirmative action plan, lower
        courts' decisions on affirmative action, the EEOC Guidelines
        on Affirmative Action, and the impact of the Supreme Court
        decision on affirmative action.

1116.   Boyd, William E. "Affirmative Action in Employment - The
        Weber Decision. IOWA, 66 (October 1980), 1-61.

Gives an in-depth analysis of the <u>Weber</u> decision and its impact on the future of affirmative action.

*   Edwards, Harry T. "Affirmative Action or Reverse Discrimination: The Head and Tail of Weber." See Item 748.

1117. Gallagher, John J. "The <u>Weber</u> Decision: Summary and Analysis." EEO TODAY, 6 (Autumn 1979), 231-241.

A study of the <u>Weber</u> decision and its impact on affirmative action. Believes that "<u>Weber</u> answers many legal questions and provides some protection for employers against reverse discrimination lawsuits." Nevertheless, it left unanswered a number of questions, e.g., "When is affirmative action permissible?"

1118. Goins, Patricia A. "The <u>Weber</u> Decision: Positive But Narrow." EQUAL OPPORTUNITY FORUM, 7 (December 1979), 26-27.

Concludes that <u>Weber</u> reinforced affirmative action principles and approved quotas in employment as a means of correcting past acts of discrimination. However, the court stressed that their decision was narrow and limited. Believes that the Supreme Court fail to promote or encourage affirmative action in the <u>Bakke</u> and <u>Weber</u> decisions.

1119. Harris, Rich and Jack Hartog. "The Catch-22 Case: Is <u>Kaiser v. Weber</u> Rigged Against Affirmative Action?" CIVIL SERVICE DIGEST, 11 (Winter 1979), 3-11.

1120. Herndon, Randolph K. "The Presence of State Action in <u>United Steelworkers v. Weber</u>." DUKE LAW JOURNAL, (November 1980), 1172-1200.

Seeks to determine whether Kaiser's affirmative action plan could have survived a Fifth Amendment challenge under the Constitution. Distinguishes the <u>Weber</u> suit which was brought under Title VII and from the <u>Fullilove v. Klutznich</u> suit which was brought under the Fifth Amendment. The <u>Fullilove</u> case involved a contract set aside program which was enacted by Congress. Concludes that a state action existed in the <u>Weber</u> set of facts and projects that courts in the future will be faced with whether similar affirmative action programs are constitutional.

*   Institute of Industrial Relations, University of California, Los Angeles. 1980 REPORT-EQUAL EMPLOYMENT OPPORTUNITY AND AFFIRMATIVE ACTION-THE ROOTS GROW DEEPER. See Item 929.

1121. Johnson, Barbara J. "One of Weber's Unanswered Questions:
       How much Prior Discrimination Justifies Voluntary
       Preferential Affirmative Action." DICKINSON LAW REVIEW,
       83 (Summer 1979), 835-851.

       Analyzes the Weber decision and concludes that the court
       approved voluntary affirmative action programs as a remedial
       tool to correct employment discrimination. Believes the
       court failed to clarify how far a voluntary affirmative
       action program can go to correct past discrimination before
       a claim of reverse discrimination becomes valid.

*   Johnson, Ronald D. "Voluntary Affirmative Action in the
       Post-Weber Era: Issues and Answers. See Item 930.

1122. Kandel, William L. "The Aftermath of Weber: State Court
       Decisions." EMPLOYEE RELATIONS LAW JOURNAL, 6 (Summer
       1980), 137-144.

*   Karnes, Daniel C. "The Legality of Preferential Treatment
       After Weber." OFCCP AND FEDERAL CONTRACT COMPLIANCE. See
       Item 763.

1123. Meltzer, Bernard D. "The Weber Case: The Judicial Abroga-
       tion of Antidiscrimination Standard in Employment." UNI-
       VERSITY OF CHICAGO LAW REVIEW, 47 (Spring 1980), 423-466.

       Analyzes the Supreme Court's decision in United Steel-
       workers v. Weber. Indicates that the decision conflicts with
       the legislative intent of Title VII. Points out deficiencies
       in the Court's analysis in the majority's opinion. Supports
       Justice Rehnquist's dissenting opinion that implies that the
       majority decision may cause further "racial polarization in
       our society."

*   Plevin, Mark D. "The Constitutionality of Affirmative Ac-
       tion in Public Employment: Judicial Deference to Certain
       Politically Responsible Bodies." See Item 960.

1124. Rabin, Robert J. "Affirmative Action Programs Before and
       After Weber?" PROCEEDING OF NEW YORK UNIVERSITY THIRTY-
       SECOND ANNUAL NATIONAL CONFERENCE OF LABOR. Edited by
       Richard Adelman. New York: Matthew Bender, 1980. pp.
       205-237.

*   Robertson, David E. and Ronald D. Johnson. "Reverse Dis-
       crimination: Did Weber Decide the Issue?" See Item 773.

1125. Ruzicho, Andrew J. "The Weber Case--Its Impact on Affirma-
       tive Action." PERSONNEL ADMINISTRATOR, 25 (June 1980),
       69-72.

       Answers several questions raised by the Supreme Court's
       decision in Kaiser Aluminum v. Weber. Concludes that Weber
       is an important decision because it ". . . did not outlaw
       preferential treatment, did not extend Bakke to private
       employers and did not mandate a quota affirmative action plan
       be adopted."

1126. Schlosser, Charles, W., Jr. "United Steelworkers of America
       v. Weber: Title VII Revised." DENVER LAW JOURNAL, 57
       (1980), 649-660.

       Analyzes the Supreme Court's decision in Weber and attempts
       to rationalize the Court's decision with Title VII and the
       Constitution. Commends the Supreme Court on the decision and
       believes the decision was less confusing than the Bakke deci-
       sion. However, concludes that the Weber decision has some
       inconsistencies with prior court decisions, with Title VII,
       and the Constitution.

1127. "Significant Post-Weber Litigation: Maehren v. City of
       Seattle." EEO TODAY, 6 (Winter 1979-80), 283-287.

       Compares the Maehren case with Weber and finds that a pub-
       lic employer must show that a compelling governmental inter-
       est exist when developing an affirmative action plan that
       provides for preferential selection based on race. Concludes
       that the question of equal protection is at issue in the
       Maehren case, whereas, Weber was decided purely on Title VII,
       since the employer was private and not a governmental agency.

1128. Sindelar, Karen Ann. "Employment Discrimination - Weber v.
       Kaiser Aluminum and Chemical Corp.: Does Title VII Limit
       Executive Order 11246?" NORTH CAROLINA LAW REVIEW, 57
       (May 1979), 695-725.

       Attempts to reconcile the Fifth Circuit's decision in
       Weber, which held that the affirmative action plan used by
       Kaiser violated Title VII and Executive Order 11246. Traces
       the legislative history of Title VII and Executive Order
       11246 and concludes that Title VII and Executive Order 11246
       are "complementary and not contradictory."

1129. Singer, James W. "Weber: A Boost to Affirmative Action."
       NATIONAL JOURNAL, 11 (August 4, 1979), 1297.

1130. Spataro, John F. "The Impact of <u>United Steelworkers of</u>
       <u>America v. Weber</u> On Affirmative Action Planning." OHIO
       NORTHERN UNIVERSITY LAW REVIEW, VII (No. 4, 1980), 987-
       1004.

       Analyzes the Supreme Court's decision in <u>Weber</u> and focuses
       specifically on the features and provisions of Kaiser's
       affirmative action plan. Reviews related court decisions on
       affirmative action and concludes that the Supreme Court
       approved voluntary affirmative action plans, but failed to
       provide guidelines on what was and was not a permissible
       plan.

1131. Temko, William D. <u>"Weber v. Kaiser Aluminum and Chemical</u>
       <u>Corp.</u>: The Challenge To Voluntary Compliance Under Title
       VII." COLUMBIA JOURNAL OF LAW AND SOCIAL PROBLEMS, 14
       (No. 2, 1978), 123-187.

       Presents the Fifth Circuit's majority and dissenting opin-
       ions in <u>Weber</u>, and reviews the Court's standard for estab-
       lishing a voluntary affirmative action plan.

1132. "<u>Weber</u> Reaches the Supreme Court." EEO TODAY, 6 (Spring
       1979), 25-29.

       Explores the judicial process in <u>Weber v. Kaiser Aluminum</u>
       from the decisions of the District Court and Fifth Circuit
       to the Supreme Court's decision. Finds that both lower
       courts held that Kaiser's training program was unlawful.
       The Fifth Circuit ". . . also held that Executive Order
       11246 and Order 4 were not in conflict with Title VII's ban
       on preferences in the absence of discrimination."

*   Vernon, Richard G. and Peter S. Gray. "Affirmative Action
       As An Affirmative Defense to EEO Charges." See Item 999.

1133. "What the <u>Weber</u> Ruling Does." TIME, 114 (July 9, 1979),
       48-49.

4. RESOURCE INFORMATION

RECRUITMENT SOURCES FOR MINORITIES*

Affirmative Action
Coordinating Center
126 W. 119th Street
New York, N.Y. 10026
(212) 864-4000

Alpha Kappa Alpha Fraternity
5211 South Greenwood Avenue
Chicago, IL. 60615
(312) 684-1283

Alpha Phi Alpha Fraternity, Inc.
4432 South Dr. Martin Luther
King, Jr. Drive
Chicago, IL. 60653
(312) 373-1879

American Association of Blacks
in Energy
915 15th Street, NW., Suite 600
Washington, D.C. 20005
(202) 737-1359

American Economic Association
Committee on the Status of Minority in the Economics Profession
1313 21st Avenue
Nashville, TN. 37212

Americans for Indian Opportunity
1010 Massachusetts Avenue
Washington, D.C. 20001
(202) 371-1280

American Political Science
Association
1527 New Hampshire Avenue, NW.
Washington, D.C. 20036
(202) 483-2512

American Society for Public
Administration
Conference of Minority Public
Administrators
1120 G. Street, N.W.
Washington, D.C. 20005
(202) 484-2390

Aspira of America, Inc.
114 E. 28th, Suite 300
New York, N.Y. 10016
(212) 889-6101

Association for the Study of
Afro-American Life and History
P.O. Box 6024
Washington, D.C. 2005
(202) 667-2822

Association of American Indian
Affairs
432 Park Avenue, South
New York, N.Y. 10016
(212) 689-8720

Association of Black Psychologists
1118 19th Street, N.W.
Washington, D.C. 20013
(202) 289-3663

Association of Black Sociologists
Dept. of Sociology/Anthropology
Virginia Commonwealth University
Richmond, VA 23284
(804) 257-1028

Black Caucus of American Library
Association
499 Wilson Library
University of Minneapolis
Minneapolis, MN 55455
(612) 376-9396

*Addresses change periodically.

Black Music Association
1500 Locust Street
Philadelphia, PA. 19102
(215) 545-8600

Black Psychiatrists of America
Connecticut Mental Health Center
34 Park Street
New Haven, CT. 06519
(203) 789-7419

Chinese for Affirmative Action
121 Waverly Place
San Francisco, CA. 94108
(415) 398-8212

Coalition of Black Trade
  Unionists
P.O. Box 13055
Washington, D.C. 20009
(202) 452-4837

Congressional Black Caucus
H2-344 House Annex #2
Washington, D.C. 20515
(202) 226-2322

Delta Sigma Theta Sorority, Inc.
1707 New Hampshire Avenue, NW.
Washington, D.C. 20009
(202) 483-5460

Indian Rights Association
1505 Race Street
Philadelphia, PA 19102
(215) 563-8349

International City Management
  Association
Attn: Minority Placement Service
1120 G. Street, NW., Suite 300
Washington, D.C. 20005
(202) 626-4600

Interracial Council for Business
  Opportunity
800 Second Avenue, Room 307
New York, N.Y. 10017
(212) 599-0677

League of United Latin American
  Citizens
400 First Street, N.W., Suite 716
Washington, D.C. 200017
(202) 628-0717

Links, Inc.
1522 K. Street, N.W.
Washington, D.C. 20005
(202) 783-3883

Mexican American Women's National
  Association
1201 16th Street, N.W.
Washington, D.C. 20024
(202) 223-3440

National Alliance of Black
  Educators
1118 9th Street, N.W.
Washington, D.C. 20005
(202) 289-5384

National Alliance of Business
1015 1th Street, N.W.
Washington, D.C. 20005
(202) 457-0040

National Association for Equal
  Opportunity in Higher Education
2243 Wisconsin Avenue, N.W.
Washington, D.C. 20007
(202) 333-3855

National Association for the
  Advancement of Colored People
186 Remsen Street
Brooklyn, N.Y. 11201
(212) 858-0800

National Association of Black
  Accountants, Inc.
1642 R Street, N.W.
Washington, D.C. 20009
(202) 387-7066

National Association of Black
  Professors
c/o Sarah Miles Woods
Roosevelt University
430 S. Michigan Avenue
Chicago, IL 60605

National Association of Black
  Social Workers
1969 Madison Avenue
New York, N.Y. 10035´
(212) 749-0470

National Association of Blacks
  Within Government
1836 9th Street, N.W.
Washington, D.C. 20006

National Association of Black
  Women Attorneys
1625 I. Street, NW., Suite 626
Washington, D.C. 20006
(202) 822-9124

National Association of College
  and University Attorneys
c/o Affirmative Action and Non-
  Discrimination Section
One Dupont Circle, Suite 650
Washington, D.C. 20036
(202) 296-0207

National Association of Colored
  Women's Clubs
5806 16th Street, NW.
Washington, D.C. 20011
(202) 726-2044

National Association of
  Minority CPA Firms
1424 K. Street, N.W.
Washington, D.C. 20006
(202) 842-4830

National Association of Spanish
  Broadcasters
1120 Connectivut Avenue, N.W.
Washington, D.C. 20007

National Bankers Association
400 South Capitol Street, SW.,
  Suite 520
Washington, D.C. 20003
(202) 488-5550

National Bar Association
1773 T Street, NW.
Washington, D.C. 20009
(202) 797-9002

National Black Child Development
  Institute
1463 Rhode Island Avenue, N.W.
Washington, D.C. 20005
(202) 387-1281

National Black Media Coalition
516 U Street, N.W.
Washington, D.C. 20001
(202) 387-8155

National Black Nurses'
  Association, Inc.
P.O. Box 18358
Boston, MA 02118
(617) 266-9703

National Black Police
  Association, Inc.
P.O. Box 138
Jamaica, N.Y. 11412
(516) 286-3361

National Business League
4324 Georgia Avenue, N.W.
Washington, D.C. 20011
(202) 829-5000

National Conference of Black
  Lawyers
126 W. 119th Street
New York, N.Y. 10026
(212) 864-4000

National Conference of Black
Mayors, Inc.
1430 West Peachtree Street, N.W.
  Suite 318
Atlanta, GA 30309
(404) 892-0127

National Conference of Puerto
  Rican Women
P.O. Box 1281
Boston, MA 02104
(617) 742-4898

National Congress of American
Indians
2025 I Street, N.W.
Washington, D.C. 20002
(202) 546-1168

National Consortium for Black
Professional Development
1359 S. Third Street
Louisville, KY   40208
(502) 451-8199

National Council of Negro
Women
701 N. Fairfax Street
Suite 330
Alexandria, VA   22314
(703) 684-5733

National Dental Association
5506 Connecticut Avenue, NW.
Suites 24 and 25
Washington, D.C.   20015
(202) 244-7555

National Hook-up of Black
Women, Inc.
1100 Sixth Street, NW., Room 5
Washington, D.C.   20001
(202) 662-6993

National Insurance Association
2400 South Michigan Avenue
Chicago, IL   60616
(312) 842-5125

National Medical Association
1301 Pennsylvania Avenue, NW.
Suite 310
Washington, D.C.   20004
(202) 347-1895

National Network of Minority
Women in Science
Office of Opportunities in
Science
1776 Massachusetts Avenue, NW.
Washington, D.C.   20036
(202) 467-5431

National Pharmaceutical
Association, Inc.
Howard University
P.O. Box 934
Washington, D.C.   20059
(202) 636-7963, - 6530

National Puerto Rican Forum, Inc.
450 Park Avenue, South
New York, NY   10016
(121) 683-2311

National Society of Black
Engineers
Purdue University
Electrical Engineering Building
West Lafayette, IN   47907
(317) 494-3362

National Urban League, Inc.
500 East 62nd Street
New York, NY   10021
(212) 310-9000

The National Technical
Assocation
1425 H Street, N.W., Suite 701
Washington, D.C.   20005
(202) 638-6370

Omega Psi Phi Fraternity, Inc.
2714 Georgia Avenue, N.W.
Washington, D.C.   20001
(202) 667-7158

Opportunities Industrialization
Centers of America
100 West Coulter Street
Philadelphia, PA   19144
(215) 849-3010

People United to Save Humanity
(PUSH)
930 East 50th Street
Chicago, IL   60615
(312) 373-3366

Scientific Manpower Commission
1500 Massachusetts Avenue, N.W.
Washington, D.C.   20036

Society of Black Physicists   Zeta Phi Beta
Department of Physics   1734 New Hampshire Avenue, N.W.
Morehouse College   Washington, D.C. 20009
Atlanta, GA. 30314   (202) 387-3103

Southern Christian Leadership
  Conference (SCLC)
334 Auburn Avenue, NE.
Atlanta, GA. 30303
(404) 522-1420

RECRUITMENT SOURCES FOR WOMEN*

Alliance of Women in
  Architecture
P.O. Box 5136, F.D.R. Station
New York, N.Y. 10022
(212) 267-7853

American AGRI-Women Resource
  Center
Route 2, Box 175
Bango, MI 49013
(616) 621-3062

American Alliance for Health,
  Physical Education and
  Recreation
Placement Program
1900 Association Drive
Reston, VA 22091
(703) 476-3400

American Anthropological Association Committee on the Status
  of Women in Anthropology
1703 New Hampshire Avenue, N.W.
Washington, D.C. 20009
(202) 232-8800

American Association for the
  Advancement of Science
Women's Section-Office of Opportunities in Science
1515 Massachusetts Avenue, N.W.
Washington, D.C. 20005
(202) 467-4400

American Association of School
  Administrator Project Award
1801 North Moore Street
Arlington, VA 22209
(703) 528-0700

American Association of
  University Professors
Committee on the Status of Women
  in the Academic
One Dupont Circle
Washington, D.C. 20036
(202) 466-8050

American Association of University Women
2401 Virginia Avenue, N.W.
Washington, D.C. 20037
(202) 785-7700

American Association of Women
Community and Junior Colleges
1519 Clearlake Road
Cocoa, FL 32922
(305) 632-1111

American Dental Association
211 E. Chicago Avenue
Chicago, IL 60611
(312) 440-2500

American Education Research
  Association
1230 17th Street, N.W.
Washington, D.C. 20036
(202) 223-9485

American Economic Association
Committee on the Status of
  Women in Economic
1313 21st Avenue
Nashville, TN 37212
(615) 322-2959

*Addresses change periodically.

261

American Federation of Teachers
11 Dupont Circle, N.W.
Washington, D.C. 20036
(202) 797-4400

American Geological Institute
5205 Leesburg Pike
Falls Church, VA 22041
(703) 379-2480

American Historical Association
400 A Street, S.E.
Washington, D.C. 20003
(202) 544-2422

American Institute of Chemists
7315 Wisconsin Avenue
Washington, D.C. 20014
(301) 652-8634

American Institute of Planners
1313 E. 60th Street
Chicago, IL 60637
(312) 947-2560

American Library Association
50 E. Huron Street
Chicago, IL 60611
(312) 944-6780

American Medical Women's
   Association
456 Grand Street
New York, N.Y. 10002
(212) 533-5104

American News Women Club
1607 22nd Street, N.W.
Washington, D.C. 20008
(202) 332-6770

American Nurses Association
2420 Pershing Road
Kansas City, MO 64108
(816) 474-5720

American Personnel and Guidance
   Association
Two Skyline Place, Suite 400
5203 Leesburg Pike
Fall Church, VA 22041
(703) 820-4700

American Physical Society
Committee on the Status of Women
   in Physics
335 45th Street
New York, N.Y. 10017
(212) 683-7341

American Psychiatric Association
1400 K Street, N.W.
Washington, D.C. 20009
(202) 682-6000

American Psychological Association Committee on Women in
   Psychology
1200 17th Street, N.W.
Washington, D.C. 20036
(202) 833-7600

American Public Health
   Association, Inc.
1015 18th Street, N.W.
Washington, D.C. 20005
(202) 789-5600

American Society for Cell Biology
9650 Rockville Pike
Bethesda, MD 20814
(413) 256-0409

American Society for Micro-
   biology
1913 I Street, N.W.
Washington, D.C. 20006
(202) 833-9680

American Society for Public
   Administration
Committee on Women in Public
   Administration
1120 G Street, N.W.
Washington, D.C. 20005
(202) 393-7878

American Society for Training
   and Development
600 Maryland Ave., SW, Suite 305
Washington, D.C. 20025
(202) 484-2390

American Society of Biological
  Chemists
9650 Rockville Pike
Bethesda, MD. 20014
(301) 530-7145

American Society of Planning
  Officials
1313 East 60th Street
Chicago, IL 60637
(312) 955-9100

American Society of Women
  Accountants
35 E. Wacker Drive
Chicago, IL 60601
(312) 341-9078

American Sociological Association
1722 N Street, NW.
Washington, D.C. 20036
(202) 833-3410

American Speech and Hearing
  Association
108 01 Rockville Pike
Rockville, MD 20852
(301) 897-5700

American Statistical Association
806 15th Street, N.W.
Washington, D.C. 20005
(202) 393-3253

American Studies Association
  Women's Committee
4025 Chestnut Street
University of Pennsylvania
Philadelphia, PA. 19104
(215) 243-5808

American Women in Radio and
ʹ Television, Inc.
1321 Connecticut Avenue, NW.
Washington, D.C. 20036
(202) 296-0009

American Women's Society of
  Certified Public Accountants
500 N. Michigan Avenue
Suite 1400
Chicago, IL 60611

Association for Women in
  Psychology
c/o Ethel Tobach
CUNY Graduate Center
33 W. 42nd Street
New York, NY 10036

Association for Women in Science
1346 Connecticut Avenue, N.W.
  Suite 1122
Washington, D.C. 20036
(202) 833-1998

Association of American Colleges
  Project on the Status and
  Education of Women
1818 R Street, N.W.
Washington, D.C. 20009
(202) 387-3760

Association of American Women
  Dentists
211 Chicago Avenue, Suite 948
Chicago, IL 60611
(312) 337-1563

Business and Professional Women's
  Foundation
2012 Massachusetts Avenue, N.W.
Washington, D.C. 20036
(202) 293-1200

Catalyst
14 E. 60th Street
New York, NY 10023
(212) 759-9700

Coalition for Women's Appointment in Government
1411 K Street, N.W.
Washington, D.C. 20005

Coalition of Labor Union Women
15 Union Square
New York, N.Y. 10003
(212) 777-3600

Committee on the Status of
   Women in Linguistics
3520 Prospect Street, NW.
Washington, D.C. 20007
(202) 298-7120

Delta Sigma Theta Sorority,
   Inc.
1707 New Hampshire Avenue, N.W.
Washington, D.C. 20009
(202) 483-5460

Federal Employed Women
1010 Vermont Avenue, NW.,
   Suite 821
Washington, D.C. 20005
(202) 638-4404

Federal Women's Program
c/o Office of Personnel
   Management
1900 E Street, NW., Room 7540
Washington, D.C. 20415
(202) 632-6870

Federal Organization for
   Professional Women
2000 P Street, NW., Suite 403
Washington, D.C. 20036
(202) 466-3544

International Association for
   Personnel Women
211 E. 43rd Street, Suite 1601
New York, N.Y. 10017
(212) 867-4194

International Federation of
   Women Lawyers
150 Nassau
New York, N.Y. 10038
(212) 227-8339

Links, Inc.
1522 K Street, N.W.
Washington, D.C. 20005
(202) 783-3888

Mexican American Women's
   National Association
1201 16th Street, N.W.
Washington, D.C. 20024
(202) 628-5663

Ohio Black Women's Leadership
   Caucus
422 W. Princeton Avenue
Youngstown, Ohio 44511

National Assocation for Women
   Deans, Administrators and
   Counselors
1625 I Street, N.W., 624A
Washington, D.C. 20006
(202) 659-9330

National Association of Commissions for Women
1 Dupon Circle, N.W.
Washington, D.C.
(202) 833-4692

National Association of Bank
   Women
500 N. Michigan Avenue
Chicago, IL 60601
(312) 661-1700

National Association of Executive
   Secretaries (NAES)
9301 Lee Highway, Suite 210
Fairfax, VA 22031
(703) 273-2988

National Association of Hispanic
   Nurses
12044 Seventh Avenue, N.W.
Seattle, Washington 98177
(206) 543-9455

National Association of Insurance Women
1847 East 15th Street
P.O. Box 4694
Tulsa, Oklahoma 74104
(918) 932-5195

National Conference of Puerto
Rican Women, Inc.
P.O. Box 1281
Boston, MA 02104
(617) 742-4898

National Association of Media
Women
1185 Niskey Lake Road, SW.
Atlanta, GA. 30331
(404) 344-5862

National Council of Career Women
1629 K Street, N.W.
Washington, D.C. 20006
(202) 775-8199

National Association of Negro
Business & Professional
Women's Clubs
1806 New Hampshire Ave., N.W.
Washington, D.C. 20009
(202) 483-4206

National Education Association
1201 16th Street, N.W.
Washington, D.C. 20036
(202) 833-4000

National Association of
Social Workers
1425 H Street, NW.
Washington, D.C. 20005
(202) 347-9893

National Federation of Business
and Professional Women's Club,
Inc.
2012 Massachusetts Avenue, N.W.
Washington, D.C. 20036
(202) 293-1100

National Association of Women
Federal Contractors
1511 K Street, NW., Suite 839
Washington, D.C. 20005
(202) 638-3336

National Federation of Press
Women
Box 99
Blue Springs, MO 64015
(816) 229-1666

National Association of Women
Lawyers
American Bar Center
1155 E. 60 Street
Chicago, IL. 60637
(312) 947-4000

National Forum for Executive
Women
1101 Fifteenth Street, N.W.
Washington, D.C. 20005
(202) 331-0270

National Black Nurses'
Association, Inc.
P.O. Box 18358
Boston, MA. 02118

National League for Nursing
10 Columbus Circle
New York, N.Y. 10019
(212) 582-1022

National Commission on Working
Women
2000 P Street, NW.
Washington, D.C. 20036
(202) 872-1782

National Organization for Women
425 Thirteenth Street, N.W.,
Suite 1048
Washington, D.C. 20004
(202) 347-2279

National Recreation and Park
  Association
Office of Women and Minority
  Programs
1601 N. Kent Street
Arlington, VA. 22209
(703) 525-0606

National Women's Political
  Caucus
1411 K Street, NW., Suite 1110
Washington, D.C. 20005
(202) 347-4456

National Women's Education Fund
1410 Q Street, NW.
Washington, D.C. 20009
(202) 462-8606

Organization of Chinese American Women
3214 Quesada Street, NW.
Washington, D.C. 20015
(703) 527-8704

Organization of Pan Asian
  Women, Inc.
2025 I Street, NW., Suite 926
Washington, D.C. 20006
(202) 293-7087

Professional Secretaries
  International
2440 Pershing Road, Suite G-10
Kansas City, MO. 64108
(816) 474-5755

Society of Women Engineers
United Engineering Center
345 East 47th Street
New York, N.Y. 10017
(212) 705-7855

Women's Bureau
U.S. Department of Labor
Washington, D.C. 20210
(202) 523-6653

Women's Equity Action League
805 15th Street, N.W., Suite 822
Washington, D.C. 20005
(202) 638-1961

Wider Opportunities for Women,
  Inc.
1325 G Street, N.W.
Washington, D.C. 20005
(202) 638-3143

Women Office Workers
680 Lexington Avenue
New York, NY 10022
(212) 688-4160

Working Woman Institute
593 Park Avenue
New York, NY 10021
(212) 838-4420

Zeta Phi Beta Sorority, Inc.
1734 New Hampshire Ave., N.W.
Washington, D.C. 20009
(202) 387-3103

LIST OF PREDOMINANTLY BLACK COLLEGES AND UNIVERSITIES*

Alabama A&M University
P.O. Box 271
Normal, Alabama 35762

Alabama State University
915 South Jackson Street
Montgomery, Alabama 36195

Albany State College
504 College Drive
Albany, Georgia 31705

Alcorn State University
P.O. Box 114
Lorman, Mississippi 39096

Allen University
1530 Harden Street
Columbia, South Carolina 29204

Arkansas Baptist College
1600 High Street
Little Rock, Arkansas 72202

University of Arkansas at Pine
   Bluff
North Cedar Street
Pine Bluff, Arkansas 71601

Atlanta University
223 Chestnut Street, SW
Atlanta, Georgia 30314

Barber-Scotia College
145 Cabarrus Avenue
Concord, North Carolina 28025

Benedict College
Harden & Blanding Streets
Columbia, South Carolina 29203

Bennett College
900 Washington Street
Greensboro, North Carolina 27420

Bethune-Cookman College
640 Second Avenue
Daytona Beach, Florida 32015

Bishop College
3837 Simpson-Stuart Road
Dallas, Texas 75241

Bowie State College
Bowie, Maryland 20715

Central State University
Wilberforce, Ohio 45384

Cheyney State College
Cheyney, Pennsylvania 193..9

Claflin College
College Avenue
East Orangeburg, S. C. 29115

Clark College
240 Chestnut Street, S.W.
Atlanta, Georgia 30314

Coppin State College
2500 West North Avenue
Baltimore, Maryland 21216

Delaware State College
North DuPont Highway
Dover, Delaware 19901

*Addresses change periodically.

267

Dillard University
2601 Gentilly Boulevard
New Orleans, Louisiana 70122

University of the District of
  Columbia
4200 Connecticut Ave., NW
Washington, D.C. 20008

Edward Waters College
1658 Kings Road
Jacksonville, Florida 32209

Elizabeth City State University
1001 Parkview Drive
Elizabeth City, N. Carolina
  27909

Fayetteville State University
Fayetteville, N. Carolina 28301

Fisk University
17th Avenue, North
Nashville, TN 37203

Florida Agricultural and
  Mechanical University
Tallahasee, Florida 32307

Florida Memorial College
15800 N.W. 42nd Avenue
Miami, Florida 33054

The Fort Valley State College
805 State College Drive
Fort Valley, Georgia 31030

Grambling State University
P.O. Drawer 605
Grambling, Louisiana 71245

Hampton Institute
Hampton, Virginia 23668

Howard University
2400 6th Street, N.W.
Washington, D.C. 20059

Huston-Tillotson College
1820 East 8th Street
Austin, Texas 78702

Inter-Denominational Theological
  Center
671 Beckwith Street, S.W.
Atlanta, Georgia 30314

Jackson State University
1440 Lynch Street
Jackson, Mississippi 37917

Jarvis Christian College
P.O. Box G
Hawkins, Texas 75765

Johnson C. Smith University
100-300 Beatties Ford Road
Charlotte, N. Carolina 28216

Kentucky State University
East Main Street
Frankfort, Kentucky 40601

Knoxville College
901 College Street
Knoxville, Tennessee 37921

Lane College
545 Lane Avenue
Jackson, Tennessee 38301

Langston University
P.O. Box 907
Langston, Oklahoma 73050

LeMoyne-Owen College
807 Walker Avenue
Memphis, Tennessee 38126

Lincoln University
820 Chestnut Street
Jefferson City, Missouri 65101

Lincoln University
Lincoln University, Pennsylvania
  19352

Livingston College
701 West Monroe Street
Salisbury, N. Carolina   28144

University of Maryland
(Eastern Shore Campus)
Princess Anne, Maryland   21853

Medgar Evers College of the
  City University of New York
1150 Carroll Street
Brooklyn, New York   11225

Meharry Medical College
1005 18th Avenue, North
Nashville, Tennessee   37208

Miles College
P.O. Box 3800
Birmingham, Alabama   35208

Mississippi Industrial College
Memphis Street
Holly Springs, Mississippi
  38635

Mississippi Valley State
  University
Itta Bena, Mississippi   38941

Morehouse College
830 Westview Drive, S.W.
Atlanta, Georgia   30314

Morgan State University
Cold Spring Lane & Hillen Road
Baltimore, Maryland

Morris Brown College
643 Martin Luther Drive, N.W.
Atlanta, Georgia   30314

Morris College
North Main Street
Sumter, South Carolina   29150

Norfolk State University
2401 Corprew Avenue
Norfolk, Virginia   23504

North Carolina Agricultural and
  Technical State University
I601 East Market Street
Greensboro, N. Carolina   27411

North Carolina Central University
1801 Fayetteville Street
Durham, North Carolina   27707

Oakwood College
Oakwood Road
Huntsville, Alabama   35806

Paine College
1235 Fifteenth Street
Augusta, Georgia   30901

Paul-Quinn College
1020 Elm Street
Waco, Texas   76704

Philander Smith College
812 West 13th Street
Little Rock, Arkansas   72202

Prairie View Agricultural and
  Mechanical University
P.O. Box 2746
Prairie View, Texas   77445

Rio Grande College
218 N. College Avenue
Rio Grande, Ohio   45674

Rust College
One Rust Avenue
Holly Springs, Mississippi
  38635

Saint Augustine's College
1315 Oakwood Avenue
Raleigh, North Carolina   27610

Saint Paul's College
Highway 46 North
Lawrenceville, Virginia   23868

Savannah State College
State College Branch
Savannah, Georgia   31404

Shaw College at Detroit
7351 Woodward Avenue
Detroit, Michigan 48202

Shaw University
118 East South Street
Raleigh, N. C. 27602

Simmons University
1811 Dumesnill Street
Louisville, Kentucky 40210

Sojourner-Douglass College
500 North Caroline Street
Baltimore, Maryland 21205

South Carolina State College
P.O. Box 1885
Orangebury, S. Carolina 29117

Southern University & Agricul-
   tural & Mechanical College
Southern Branch
P.O. 9562
Baton Rouge, Louisiana 70813

Southern University in New
   Orleans
Division of Southern University
   & Agricultural & Mechanical
6400 Press Drive
New Orleans, Louisiana 70126

Spelman College
350 Spelman Lane, S.W.
Atlanta, Georgia 30314

Stillman College
P.O. box 1430-F
Tuscaloosa, Alabama 35403

Talladega College
627 West Battle Street
Talladega, Alabama 35160

Tennessee State University
3500 John Merritt Boulevard
Nashville, Tennessee 37203

Texas College
2404 North Grand Avenue
Tyler, Texas 75702

Texas Southern University
3200 Cleburne Street
Houston, Texas 77004

Tougaloo College
Tougaloo, Mississippi 39174

Tuskegee Institute
Tuskegee Institute, Alabama
   36088

Virginia Seminary
2057 Garfield Avenue
Lynchburg, Virginia 24501

Virginia State University
P.O. Box 1
Petersburg, Virginia 23803

Virginia Union University
1500 North Lombardy Street
Richmond, Virginia 23220

Voorhees College
Denmark, South Carolina 29042

Wilberforce University
Wilberforce, Ohio 45384

Wiley College
711 Rosborough Spring Road
Marshall, Texas 75670

Winston-Salem State University
Winston-Salem, N. Carolina 27102

Xaiver University of Louisiana
7325 Palmetto Street
New Orleans, Louisiana 70125

STATE AND LOCAL FAIR EMPLOYMENT PRACTICE AGENCIES*

Alaska State Commission for
Human Rights
431 W. 7th Avenue, Suite 105
Anchorage, Alaska 99501

Alexandria Human Rights
Commission
110 North Royal, Suite 501
Alexandria, Virginia 22313

Arizona Attorney General's
Office
1275 W. Washington Street
Phoenix, Arizona 85007

Austin Human Relations
Commission
P.O. Box 1088
Austin, Texas 78767

Baltimore Community Relations
Commission
100 North Eutaw Street
Baltimore, Maryland 21201

Broward County (FL) Human
Relations Division
Governor's Club #602
236 S.E. 1st Avenue
Fort Lauderdale, Florida 33301

Clearwater (FL) Community
Relations Department
P.O. Box 4748
Clearwater, FL 33518

Colorado Civil Rights Division
1525 Sherman Street, Rm. 600C
Denver, Colorado 80203

Connecticut Commission on Human
Rights and Opportunities
90 Washington Street
Hartford, Connecticut 06115

Corpus Christi Human Relations
Commission
P.O. Box 9277
101 N. Shoreline
Corpus Christi, Texas 78408

Date County Fair Housing and
Employment Appeals Board
1515 N.W. 7th Street, Room 205
Miami, Florida 33125

D.C. Office of Human Rights
Lansburgh Building, 2nd Floor
421 Eighth Street, N.W.
Washington, D.C. 20004

Delaware Department of Labor
Anti-Discrimination Section
820 North French St., 6th Floor
State Office Building
Wilmington, Delaware 19801

The Department of Fair
Employment and Housing
1201 I Street, 2nd Fl., Suite 211
Sacramento, CA 95814

Department of Tourism and
Commerce
Division of Human Rights
State Capitol Building
500 E Capitol
Pierre, S.D. 57501

East Chicago Human Rights
Commission
City Hall, Room 9
4525 Indianapolis Boulevard
East Chicago, Indiana 46312

*Addresses change periodically

271

Fairfax County Human Rights
  Commission
10530 Page Avenue
Fairfax, Virginia 22030

Indiana Civil Rights Commission
311 West Washington Street
Fair Bldg., 3rd Floor, Suite 319
Indianpolis, Indiana 46204

Florida Commission on Human
  Relations
2562 Executive Center Circle
  East, Suite 1000
Tallahassee, FL 32301

Iowa Civil Rights Commission
Colony Building
507 Tenth Street, 8th Floor
Des Moines, Iowa 50319

Fort Worth Human Relations
  Commission
1000 Throckmorton Street
Fort Worth, Texas 76102

Jacksonville Equal Employment
  Opportunity Commission
220 East Bay Street, Room 701
Jacksonville, FL 32202

Fort Wayne Metropolitan Human
  Relations Commission
City-County Building, Room 680
One Main Street
Fort Wayne, Indiana 46802

Kansas City (MO) Human
  Relations Department
4th Floor, City Hall
Kansas City, MO 64106

Gary Human Relations Commission
475 Broadway, Rm. 108-109-110
Gary, Indiana 46402

Kansas Commission on Civil Rights
535 Kansas Avenue, 5th Floor
Topeka, Kansas 66603

Georgia Office of Fair Employ-
  ment Practices
State Labor Building
254 Washington St., S.W.,
  Suite 685
Atlanta, Georgia 30334

Lexington-Fayette Human Rights
  Commission
207 North Upper Street
Lexington, Kentucky 40507

Hawaii Department of Labor
  and Industrial Relations-
  Enforcement Division
888 Mililani Street, Room 401
Honolulu, Hawaii 96813

Maine Human Rights Commission
Statehouse
Augusta, Maine 04333

Idaho Human Rights Commission
Statehouse
Boise, Idaho 83720

Maryland Commission on Human
  Relations
20 E. Franklin Street
Baltimore, Maryland 21202

Illinois Department of Human
  Rights
32 W. Randolph Street
Room 890
Chicago, Illinois 60601

Massachusetts Commission Against
  Discrimination
One Asburton Place, Room 601
Boston, Massachusetts 02108

Michigan Department of Civil
  Rights
Michigan Plaza Building
1200 Sixth Avenue
Detroit, Michigan 48226

Minneapolis Department of
  Civil Rights
2649 Park Avenue, South
Minneapolis, Minnesota 55407

Minnesota Department of Human
  Rights
5th Fl. Bremer Tower
7th Place and Minnesota Street
St. Paul, Minnesota 55101

Missouri Commission on Human
  Rights
P.O. box 1129
Jefferson City, MO 65102

Montana Human Rights Division
23 South Last Chance Gulch
Helena, Montana 59620

Montgomery County Human
  Relations Commission
6400 Democracy Boulevard
Bethesda, Maryland 20817

Nebraska Equal Opportunity
  Commission
301 Centennial Mall South,
  5th Floor
Lincoln, Nebraska 68509

Nevada Equal Rights Commission
1515 E. Tropicana Avenue,
  Suite 590
Las Vegas, Nevada 89158

New Hampshire State Commission
  for Human Rights
61 South Spring Street
Concord, New Hampshire 03301

New Hanover Human Relations
  Commission
320 Chestnut, Room 409
Wilmington, N. Carolina 28401

New Jersey Division on Civil
  Rights
1100 Raymond Boulevard
Newark, New Jersey 07112

New Mexico Human Rights
  Commission
303 Bataan Memorial Building
Santa Fe, New Mexico 87503

New York City Commission on
  Human Rights
32 Duane Street
New York, New York 10007

New York State Division of
  Human Rights
2 World Trade Center
New York, New York 10047

North Dakota Department of Labor
State Capitol Building
Bismarck, North Dakota 58501

Ohio Civil Rights Commission
220 Parsons Avenue
Columbus, Ohio 43215

Oklahoma Human Rights Commission
P.O. Box 52945
Oklahoma City, Oklahoma 73152

Omaha Human Relations Department
1819 Farnam Street, Suite 502
Omaha, Nebraska 68183

Oregon Bureau of Labor and
  Industries, Civil Rights
  Division
1400 Southwest 5th
Portland, Oregon 97201

Orlando Human Relations Dept.
400 South Orange Avenue,
  Suite 103
Orlando, Florida 32801

Pennsylvania Human Relations
  Commission
101 South Second St., Suite 300
P.O. Box 3145
Harrisburgh, Pennsylvania
  17105-3145

Philadelphia Commission on
  Human Relations
601 City Hall Annex
Philadelphia, Pennsylvania 19107

Pittsburgh Commission on
  Human Relations
908 City County Building
Pittsburgh, Pennsylvania 15219

Puerto Rico Dept. of Labor
  and Human Resources
Anti-Discrimination Unit
Commonwealth of Puerto Rico
505 Munoz Rivera Ave., Guyama St.
Hata Rey, Puerto Rico 00918

Rhode Island Commission for
  Human Rights
334 Westminister Mall
Providence, Rhode Island 02903

Seattle Human Rights Department
104 14th Avenue, Suite C
Seattle, Washington 98122

South Carolina Human Affairs
  Commission
P.O. Box 11300
Columbia, South Carolina 29211

South Bend Human Rights
  Commission
1200 County-City Building
227 W. Jefferson Boulevard
South Bend, Indiana 46601

St. Louis Civil Rights
  Enforcement Agency
3rd Floor, Civil Courts Building
St. Louis, Missouri 63101

St. Petersburg (FL) Office of
  Human Relations
P.O. Box 2841
St. Petersburg, FL 33731

Tacoma Human Relations Commission
740 St. Helens Avenue, Room 1420
Tacoma, Washington 98402

Tennessee Commission for Human
  Development
208 Tennessee Building
Nashville, Tennessee 37219

Utah Industrial Commission
Anti-Discrimination Division
560 South 300 East
Salt Lake City, Utah 84111

Vermont Attorney General's
  Office Civil Rights Division
109 State Street
Montpelier, Vermont 05602

Virgin Islands Department of
  Labor
P.O. Box 148, Charlotte Amalie
St. Thomas, Virgin Islands 00801

Washington State Human Rights
  Commission
402 Evergreen Plaza Bldg. (FJ-41)
Olympia, WA 98504

West Virginia Human Rights
  Commission
215 Professional Building
1036 Quarrier Street
Charleston, WV 25301

Wisconsin Equal Rights Division
  Department of Industry, Labor
  and Human Relations
201 E. Washington Avenue
Madison, Wisconsin 53702

Wyoming Fair Employment Practices
  Commission
Hathaway Building
Cheyenne, Wyoming 82002

York City Human Relations
  Commission
225 East Princess Street
York, Pennsylvania 17403

DISTRICT OFFICES AND THE NATIONAL OFFICE OF THE EQUAL
EMPLOYMENT OPPORTUNITY COMMISSION*

Albuquerque Area Office
Western Bank Building,
  Suite 1515
505 Marquette N.W.
Albuquerque, New Mexico 87101

Detroit District Office
Equal Employment Opportunity
  Commission
First National Bldg., Suite 600
660 Woodward Avenue
Detroit, Michigan 48226

Atlanta District Office
Citizens Trust Bldg., 10th Fl.
75 Piedmont Avenue, N.E.
Atlanta, Georgia 30335

Houston District Office
405 Main Street, 6th Floor
Houston, Texas 77002

Baltimore District Office
Rotunda Building, Suite 210
711 W. 40th Street
Baltimore, Maryland 21211

Indianapolis District Office
Federal Building, U.S. Courthouse
46 East Ohio Street, Room 456
Indianapolis, Indiana 46204

Boston Area Office
150 Causeway St., Suite 1000
Boston, Massachusetts 02114

Los Angeles District Office
3255 Wilshire Boulevard, 9th Fl.
Los Angeles, California 90010

Charlotte District Office
1201 E. Morehead Street
Charlotte, N. Carolina 28204

Mimphis District Office
1407 Union Avenue, Suite 502
Memphis, Tennessee 38104

Chicago District Office
Federal Building, Rm. 234
536 South Clark Street
Chicago, Illinois 60605

Miami District Office
DuPont Plaza Center, Suite 414
300 Biscayne Blvd. Way
Miami, Florida 33131

Cleveland District Office
Engineers' Building, Rm. 602
1365 Ontario Street
Cleveland, Ohio 44114

Milwaukee District Office
342 North Water Street, Rm. 612
Milwaukee, Wisconsin 53202

Dallas District Office
1900 Pacific Ave., Building
Dallas, Texas 75201

New York District Office
90 Church St., Rm. 1301
New York, N.Y. 10007

Denver District Office
1531 Scout Street, 6th Fl.
Denver, Colorado 80202

Philadelphia District
127 N. 4th Street, Suite 200
Philadelphia, Pennsylvania 19106

*Addresses change periodically.

Phoenix District Office
135 N. Second Ave., 4th Fl.
Phoenix, AZ 85003

Pittsburgh Area Office
Federal Building, Room 2038A
100 Liberty Avenue
Pittsburgh, Pennsylvania 15222

St. Louis District Office
625 N. Euclid Street
St. Louis, Missouri 63108

San Antonio Area Office
727 E. Durango, Suite B-601
San Antonio, TX 78206

San Francisco District Office
10 UN Plaza, 4th Floor
San Francisco, CA 94102

Seattle District Office
Dexter Horton Building
710 Second Avenue
Seattle, Washington 98104

Washington Area Office
1717 H. Street, N.W., Suite 402
Washington, D.C. 20096

National Office:
2401 E. Street, N.W.
Washington, D.C. 30506

SELECTED CASE CITATIONS*

TITLE VII - PROCEDURAL ISSUES

Albemarle Paper Co. v. Moody, 422 U.S. 405 (1975).
Issue: Back-pay, attorney fees, and prima facie case

Alexander v. Gardner - Denver Co., 415 U.S. 36 (1974).
Issue: Prior arbitration proceeding and Title VII

Baldwin County Welcome Center v. Brown - U.S. Ct. - (1984), 33 EPD
34,287.
Issue: Right-to-sue limitation

Board of Trustees v. Sweeney, 439 U.S. 24 (1978).
Issue: Prima facie case

Brown v. GSA, 425 U.S. 820 (1976).
Issue: Federal employees

Christiansburg Garment Co. v. EEOC, 434 U.S. 412 (1978).
Issue: Attorney fees for prevailing defendants

Connecticut v. Teal 102 S. Ct. 2525 (1982).
Issue: Burden of proof and the bottom line concept

Delaware State College v. Ricks, 449 U.S. 250 (1980).
Issue: Tolling of the statute of limitation

Dothard v. Rawlinson, 433 U.S. 321 (1977).
Issue: Disparate impact

EEOC v. Anchor Hocking Corp., 666 F.2d 1037 (6th Cir. 1981).
Issue: Preliminary injunctions

EEOC v. Shell Oil Co., 676 F.2d 322 (8th Cir. 1982), Cert.
granted, 103 S. Ct. 1181 (1983).
Issue: EEOC Commissioner's charges

Ford Motor Co. v. EEOC, 102 S. Ct. 3057 (1983).
Issue: Accrual of backpay liability

Furnco Construction Corporation v. Waters, 438 U.S. 567 (1978).
Issue: Employer's rebuttal to a prima facie case

General Telephone Company v. EEOC, 446 U.S. 318 (1980).
Issue: Certification of Class Action

*Lower court decisions should be updated before citing.

General Telephone Company of the Southwest v. Falcon, 102 Sup.
  Ct. 2364 (1982).
Issue: Certification of class action

Griggs v. Duke Power Co., 401 U.S. 424 (1971).
Issue: Disparate impact

Hensley v. Eckerhart, 103 S. Ct. 1933 (1983).
Issue: Attorney's fees on unsuccessful claims

Johnson v. Railway Express Agency, 421 U.S. 454 (1975).
Issue: Timely filings and remedies under Title VII

King v. New Hampshire Department of Resources and Economic Development, 567 F.2d 80 (1st Cir. 1977).
Issue: Prima facie case

Kremer v. Chemical Construction Corp., 102 S. Ct. 1883 (1982).
Issue: Res judicata

Love v. Pullman Co., 404 U.S. 522 (1972).
Issue: Filing limitations

McDonald v. Santa Fe Trail Transportation Co., 427 U.S. 273 (1976).
Issue: Whites also covered by Title VII

McDonnell Douglas Corporation v. Green, 411 U.S. 792 (1973).
Issue: Prima facie case and disparate treatment

Monell v. Department of Social Services 436 U.S. 658 (1978).
Issue: Back-pay and municipal immunity

New York Gas Light Club v. Carney, 447 U.S. 54 (1980).
Issue: Attorney fees for administrative proceeding

Pantchenko v. C.B. Dolge Co., 581 F.2d 1052 (5th Cir. 1978).
Issue: Retaliation

Roadway Express, Inc. v. Piper, 447 U.S. 752 (1980).
Issue: Attorney fees

Sias v. City Demonstration Agency, 588 F.2d 692 (9th Cir. (1978).
Issue: Retaliation

Teamsters v. United States, 431 U.S. 324 (1977).
Issue: Disparate treatment theory

Texas Department of Community Affairs v. Burdine, 450 U.S. 248
  (1981).
Issue: Burden of proof

RACE DISCRIMINATION*

Albemarle Paper Co. v. Moody, 422 U.S. 405 (1975).
Issue: Pre-employment test

DeGrace v. Rumsfeld, 614 F. 2d 796 (1st Cir. 1980).
Issue: Racial harassment

General Building Contractors Association v. Pennsylvania, 458 U.S.
  375 (1982).
Issue: Hiring hall

Green v. Missouri Pacific Railroad Company, 523 F. 2d 1290 (8th Cir.
  1975).
Issue: Conviction record

Griggs v. Duke Power, 401 U.S. 424 (1971).
Issue: Testing

Knight v. Nassau County Civil Service Commission, 649 F. 2d 157
  (2d Cir.), Cert. denied, 454 U.S. 818 (1981).
Issue: BFOQ

Lindsey v. Mississippi Research and Development Center, 652 F. 2d
  488 (5th Cir. 1981).

Johnson v. Georgia Highway Express Inc., 488 F.2d 714 (5th Cir.
  1974).
Issue: Employment practices

Washington v. Davis, 426 U.S. 229 (1976).
Issue: Testing

RELIGIOUS DISCRIMINATION

Anderson v. General Dynamics, 648 F.2d 1247 (9th Cir. 1981).
Issue: Reasonable accommodation

Burns v. Southern Pacific Transportation Co., 589 F. 2d 403 (9th
  Cir. 1978).
Issue: Reasonable accommodation

Cooper v. General Dynamics, 533 F.2d 163 (5th Cir. 1976), cert.
  denied, 433 U.S. 908 (1977).
Issue: Union membership

Cummins v. Parker Seal Co., 516 F. 2d 544 (6th Cir. 1975), aff'd
  mem., 429 U.S. 65 (1976), vacated and remanded, 433 U.S. 903
  (1977).
Issue: Reasonable accommodation

*Also see reverse discrimination section.

Dewey v. Reynolds Metal, 429 F. 2d 324 (6th Cir. 1970), aff'd mem.
  402 U.S. 689 (1971).
Issue: Duty to accommodate

EEOC v. Pacific Press Publishing Assn., 676 F.2d 1272 (Cir. 1982).
Issue: Free exercise clause of the First Amendment

Huston v. Auto Workers Local 93, 559 F.2d 477 (8th Cir. 1977).
Issue: Reasonable accommodation

Jordan v. N.C. National Bank, 565 F.2d 72 (4th Cir. 1977).
Issue: Reasonable accommodation

McGinnis v. U.S. Postal Service 512 F. Supp. 517 (N.D. Cal. 1980).
Issue: Bona fide religious belief

Nottelson v. Smith Steelworkers, 643 F.2d 445 (7th Cir. 1981).
Issue: Reasonable accommodation

Redmond v. GAF Corporation, 574 F.2d 897 (7th Cir. 1978).
Issue: Definition

Trans World Airlines, Inc. v. Hardison, 432 U.S. 63 (1977).
Issue: Accommodation

NATIONAL ORIGIN DISCRIMINATION

Ambach v. Norwick, 60 L.Ed. 2d 49 (1979).
Issue: Citizenship

Espinoza v. Farah Manufacturing Co., Inc., 414 U.S. 86 (1973).
Issue: Citizenship

Foley v. Connelie, 435 U.S. 291 (1978).
Issue: Citizenship

Garcia v. Gloor, 618 F.2d 264 (1980), cert. denied, 449 U.S. 113
  (1981).
Issue: Speak only English rule

General Telephone Co. v. Falcon, 102 S. Ct. 2364 (1982).
Issue: Mexican-American class action

Hampton v. Mow Sun Wong, 426 U.S. 88 (1976).
Issue: Aliens

Manzanares v. Safeway Stores, 593 F.2d 968 (10th Cir. 1979).
Issue: Speak only English rule

Sumitomo Shoji America Inc. v. Avagliano, 102 S. St. 2374 (1982).
Issue: Japanese Companies

SEX DISCRIMINATION

Abraham v. Graphic Arts International Union, 660 F.2d 811 (D.C. Cir. 1981).
Issue: Lack of pregnancy leave policy

Arizona Governing Committee for Tax Deferred Annuity and Deferred Compensation Plans v. Norris, 103 S. Ct. 3492 (1983).
Issue: Retirement benefits

Cleveland Board of Education v. LaFleur, 414 U.S. 632 (1974).
Issue: Pregnancy leave

Costa v. Markey, 706 F.2d 1 (1st Cir. 1983).
Issue: Height requirement for females

Dothard v. Rawlinson, 433 U.S. 321 (1977).
Issue: Height and weight requirement

EEOC v. Lockheed Missiles and Space Co., Inc., 680 F.2d 1243 (9th Cir. 1982).
Issue: Pregnancy benefits

Fountain v. Safeway Stores, 555 F.2d 753 (9th Cir. 1977).
Issue: Grooming code

Frontiero v. Richardson, 411 U.S. 677 (1973).
Issue: Classification

Geduldig v. Aiello, 417 U.S. 484 (1974).
Issue: Disability insurance

General Electric Co. v. Gilbert, 429 U.S. 125 (1976).
Issue: Pregnancy benefits

Holloway v. Arthur Anderson & Company, 566 F.2d 659 (9th Cir. 1977).
Issue: Transexual employees

Kouba v. Allstate Insurance Co., 691 F.2d 873 (9th Cir. 1982).
Issue: Salaries

Loper v. American Airlines, 582 F.2d 956 (5th Cir. 1978).
Issue: Marriage restriction

Los Angeles Department of Water and Power v. Manhart, 435 U.S. 702 (1978).
Issue: Pension funds

Nashville Gas Co. v. Satty, 434 U.S. 136 (1977).
Issue: Seniority rights after pregnancy leave

Newport News Shipbuilding & Dry Dock Co. v. EEOC, 103 S. Ct. 2622 (1983).
Issue: Benefit for spouses of male employees

Personnel Administrator v. Feeney, 442 U.S. 256 (1979).
Issue: Veteran's preference

Weeks v. Southern Bell Telephone & Telegraph Co., 408 F.2d 228 (5th
  Cir. 1969).
Issue: BFOQ

Willingham v. Macon Telegraph Publishing Company, 507 F.2d 1084 (5th
  Cir. 1975).
Issue: Dress Code

Wright v. Olin Corp., 697 F.2d 1172 (4th Cir. 1982).
Issue: Fetal rights

SEXUAL HARASSMENT

Barnes v. Costle, 561 F.2d 983 (D.C. Cir. 1977).
Issue: Employer's liability

Brown v. City of Gutherie, 22 FEP 1627 W.D. Okla. 1980).
Issue: EEOC Interim Guidelines

Bundy v. Jackson, 641 F.2d 934 (D.C. Cir. 1981).
Issue: Employer's liability

Clark v. World Airways, Inc., 24 FEP 305 (D.D.C. 1980).
Issue: EEOC Interim Guidelines

Continental Can Co. v. State of Minn., 297 N.W.2d 241 (1981).
Issue: Employer's liability and definition of sexual harassment

Corne v. Bausch and Lomb, Inc., 562 F.2d 55 (9th Cir. 1977).
Issue: Employer's liability for supervisor's conduct

EEOC v. Sage Realty Corp., 507 F. Supp. 599 (S.D.N.Y. 1981).
Issue: Sexually revealing costumes

Fisher v. Flynn, 598 F.2d 663 (1st Cir. 1979).
Issue: Term or condition of employment

Garber v. Saxon Business Products, Inc., 552 F.2d 1032 (4th Cir.
  1977).
Issue: Employer's liability

Heelan v. Johns-Manville Corp., 451 F. Supp. 1382 (D. Colo. 1978).
Issue: Term or condition of employment

Henson v. City of Dundee, 682 F.2d 897 (11th Cir. 1982).
Issue: Employer's liability and work environment

Huebschen v. Department of Health and Social Services, 547 F. Supp.
  1168 (W.D. Wisc. 1982), rev'd and remanded, 716 F.2d 1167 (7th
  Cir. 1983).
Issue: Civil liability

Katz v. Dole, 709 F.2d 251 (4th Cir. 1983).
Issue: Employer's liability

Kyriazi v. Western Electric Co., 476 F. Supp. 335 (D.N.J. 1979).
Issue: Tort action

Ludington v. Sambo's Restaurants, Inc., 474 F. Supp. 480 (E.D. Wis.
1979).
Issue: Employer's liability

Miller v. Bank of America, 600 F.2d 211 (9th Cir 1979).
Issue: Supervisor's liability

Neidhardt v. D.H. Holmes Co., 21 FEP 452 (E.D. La 1979).
Issue: Employer's liability

Phillips v. Smalley Maintenance Services, 711 F.2d 1524 (11th Cir.
1983).
Issue: Employer's liability

Smith v. Rust Engineering Co., 18 EPD 8698 (N.D. Ala. 1978).
Issue: Term or condition of employment

Tompkins v. Public Service Electric and Gas Co., 568 F.2d 1044 (3rd
Cir. 1977).
Issue: Employer's liability

Wright v. Methodist Youth Services, Inc., 511 F. Supp 307 (N.D. Ill.
1981).
Issue: Homosexual advances

EQUAL PAY ACT

Bartelt v. Berlitz School, 698 F.2d 1003 (9th Cir. 1983).
Issue: Comparing wages

Brennan v. Corning Glassworks, 94 S. Ct. 2223 (1974).
Issue: Affirmative defenses and legislative history

Brennan v. South Davis Community Hospital, 538 F.2d 859 (10th Cir.
1976).
Issue: Job must be substantially equal

EEOC v. Central Kan. Medical Center, 705 F.2d 1270 (10th Cir. 1983).
Issue: Comparing job description

Hodgson v. American Bank of Commerce, 447 F.2d 416 (5th Cir. 1971).
Issue: Job must be substantially equal

Hodgson v. Brook Haven General Hospital, 436, F.2d 719 (5th Cir.
1970).
Issue: Interpretation of terms

Hodgson v. City Stores, Inc., 332 F. Supp. 942 (M.D. Ala. 1971),
  aff'd 479 F.2d 235 (5th Cir. 1973).
Issue: Interpretation of terms

Kouba v. Allstate Insurance Co., 691 F.2d 873 (9th Cir. 1982).
Issue: Setting salary

Laffey v. Northwest Airlines, 567 F.2d 429 (D.C. Cir. 1976), cert.
  denied, 434 U.S. 1086 (1978).
Issue: Job must be substantially equal

Murphy v. Miller Brewing, 457 F.2d 221 (7th Cir. 1972).
Issue: Job must be substantially equal

Pearce v. Wichita County, 590 F.2d 128 (5th Cir. 1979).
Issue: Equal pay judgment

Shultz v. Wheatson, 421 F.2d 259 (3rd Cir.), cert. denied, 398 U.S.
  905 (1970).
Issue: Job must be substantially equal

Usery v. Columbia University, 568 F.2d 953 (2d Cir. 1977).
Issue: Job must be substantially equal

Wetzel v. Liberty Mutual Ins. Co., 17 FEP 232 (W.D. Pa. 1978).
Issue: Jobs must be substantially equal

COMPARABLE WORTH

AFSCME v. State of Washington, 242 Daily Lab. Rep. (Dec 15, 1983).
Issue: Prima facie case

Briggs v. City of Madison, 536 F. Supp 435 (W.D. Wis 1982).
Issue: Marketplace impact on wages

Christensen v. State of Iowa, 563 F.2d 353 (8th Cir. 1977).
Issue: Prima facie case

County of Washington v. Gunther, 452 U.S. 161 (1981).
Issue: Title VII coverage

Electrical Workers, IUE v. Westinghouse Electric Corp., 631 F.2d
  1094 (3rd Cir. 1980), cert. denied 449 U.S. 1009 (1980).
Issue: Wage structure

Lemon v. City and County of Denver, 620 F.2d 228 (10th Cir. 1980),
  cert. denied, 449 U.S. 888 (1981).
Issue: Comparable value of jobs and Title VII coverage

Oaks v. City of Fairhope, 515 F. Supp. 1004 (S.D. Ala. 1981).
Issue: Comparison of different job classification

Plemer v. Parsons-Bilbane, 713 F.2d 1127 (5th Cir. 1983).
Issue: Comparison of different job classification

Power v. Barry County, 29 FEP 559 (W.D. Mich. 1982).
Issue: Limitation of Title VII

HANDICAP DISCRIMINATION

Carmi v. Metropolitan St. Louis Sewer District, 620 F.2d 672 (8th
    Cir. 1980), cert. denied, 101 S. Ct. 249 (1980).
Issue: Employment

Consolidated Rail Corporation v. Darrone, ___U.S. Sup. Ct. ___ No.
    82-862, Feb. 28, 1984
Issue: Section 504

Cort v. Ash, 422 U.S. 66 (1975).
Issue: Private action of Section 503

E. E. Black, Ltd. v. Marshall, 497 F. Supp. 1088 (D. Hawaii 1980).
Issue: Perceived handicapped condition

Gurmankin v. Costanzo, 556 F.2d 184 (3rd Cir. 1977), cert. denied,
    450 U.S. 923 (1981).
Issue: Due process issue

Holland v. Boeing Co., 583 P.2d 621 (1978).
Issue: Accommodation

Lewis v. Remmele Engineering, Inc., 314 N.W. 2d 1 (Minn. Sup. Ct.
    1981).
Issue: Safety

Lloyd V. Regional Transportation Authority, 548 F.2d 1277 (7th Cir.
    1977).
Issue: Private court action

New York City Transit Authority v. Beazer, 440 U.S. 568 (1979).
Issue: Due process clause

Prewitt v. U.S. Postal Service, 662 F.2d 292 (5th Cir. 1981).
Issue: Accommodation

Rogers v. Frito-Lay, Inc., 611 F.2d 1074 (5th Cir.), cert. denied,
    449 U.S. 889 (1980).
Issue: Section 503 of the Rehabilitation Act of 1973

Simon v. St. Louis County, 656 F.2d 316 (8th Cir 1981, cert. denied,
    455 U.S. 976 (1982).
Issue: Reasonable accommodation

Southeastern Community College v. Davis, 442 U.S. 397 (1979).
Issue: Reasonable accommodation

Trageser v. Libbie Rehabilitation Center, Inc., 590 F.2d 87 (4th
    Cir. 1978), cert. denied, 442 U.S. 947 (1979).
Issue: Section 504 coverage

AGE DISCRIMINATION

Ackerman v. Diamond Shamrock Corp., 670 F.2d 66 (6th Cir. 1982).
Issue: Voluntary retirement

Allison v. Western Union Telegraph Co., 29 FEP 393 (11th Cir. 1982).
Issue: Reduction-in-Force

Arritt v. Gisell, 567 F.2d 1267 (4th Cir. 1977).
Issue: City employees

Brennan v. Paragon Employment Agency, Inc., 356 F. Supp. 286 (S.D.
  N.Y.), aff'd 489 F.2d 752 (2d Cir. 1974).
Issue: Advertisement

Cancellier v. Federated Department Stores, 672 F.2d 1312 (9th Cir.
  1982), cert. denied, 103 S. Ct. 131 (1982).
Issue: Burden of proof and lay-offs

DePriest v. Safeway Food Town, Inc., 29 FEP 647 (E.D. Mich. 1982).
Issue: Filing limitations

EEOC v. Liggett & Meyers, Inc., 29 FEP 1611 (E.D. N.C. 1982).
Issue: Reduction-in-Force

EEOC v. Missouri Highway Patrol, 30 FEP 1096 (W.D. Mo. 1982).
Issue: BFOQ

EEOC v. Wyoming, 103 S. Ct. 1054 (1983).
Issue: State and local government

Ford v. General Motors Corp., 656 F.2d 117 (5th Cir. 1981).
Issue: Burden of proof

Hodgson v. Approved Personnel Service, Inc., 529 F.2d 760 (4th Cir.
  1975).
Issue: Advertisement

Hodgson v. First Federal Saving and Loan Association of Broward
  County, Florida, 455 F.2d 818 (5th Cir. 1972).
Issue: Inference of discrimination

Hodgson v. Greyhound Lines, Inc., 499 F.2d 859 (7th Cir. 1974),
  cert. denied, 419 U.S. 1122 (1975).
Issue: BFOQ

Kanzanzas v. Walt Disney World Co., 704 F.2d 1527 (11th Cir. 1983).
Issue: Failure to display a poster prohibiting age discrimination

Kelly v. American Standard, Inc., 640 F.2d 974 (9th Cir. 1981).
Issue: Prima facie case

Leftwich v. Harris-Stowe State College, 31 FEP 376 (8th Cir. 1983).
Issue: Statistical proof

Lehman v. Nakshian, 453 U.S. 156 (1981).
Issue: Jury trials

Loeb v. Textron Inc., 600 F.2d 1003 (1st Cir. 1979).
Issue: Burden of Proof

Lorillard v. Pons, 434 U.S. 575 (1978).
Issue: Jury trial

Marshall v. Goodyear Tire & Rubber Co., 554 F.2d 730 (1977).
Issue: Prima facie case

Massachusetts Board of Retirement v. Murgia, 427 U.S. 307 (1976).
Issue: Rational basis test

Moses v. Falstaff Brewing Corp., 550 F.2d 1113 (8th Cir. 1977).
Issue: Burden of proof in discharge cases

Naton v. Bank of California, 694 F.2d 691 (9th Cir. 1981).
Issue: Class actions

Oscar Mayer & Company v. Evans, 441 U.S. 750 (1979).
Issue: Prerequisites to filing an age discrimination suit

Pirone v. Home Insurance Co., 507 F. Supp. 1281 (S.D. N.Y. 1981).
Issue: Factors other than age

Sahadi v. Reynolds Chemical, 636 F.2d 1116 (6th Cir. 1980).
Issue: Burden of Proof

Slate v. Noll, 62 L.Ed. 2d 637 (1979).
Issue: Mandatory retirement

Stacey v. Allied Stores Corp., 34 FEP 616 (1984).
Issue: Legitimate business reasons for discharges

Stanojev v. Ebasco Services, Inc., 643 F.2d 914 (2d Cir. 1981).
Issue: Direct evidence

Sutton v. Atlantic Richfield Co., 646 F.2d 407 (9th Cir. 1981).
Issue: Allocation of proof

Tribble v. Westinghouse Elec. Corp., 669 F.2d 1193 (8th Cir. 1982),
   cert. denied, 103 S. Ct. 1767 (1983).
Issue: Voluntary retirement

Usery v. Tamiami Trail Tours, Inc., 531 F.2d 224 (5th Cir. 1976).
Issue: BFOQ

Vance v. Bradley, 440 U.S. 93 (1979).
Issue: Mandatory retirement

Williams v. General Motors Corp., 656 F.2d 120 (5th Cir. 1981),
   cert. denied, 455 U.S. 943 (1982).
Issue: Prima facie case

STATISTICS

Albemarle Paper Co. v. Moody, 422 U.S. 405 (1975).
Issue: Prima facie case

Castenada v. Partida, 430 U.S. 482 (1977).
Issue: Adverse impact

Chance v. Board of Examiners, 458 F.2d 1167 (2d Cir. 1972).
Issue: Adverse impact

Detroit Police Officers Association v. Young, 608 F.2d 671 (6th Cir.
   1979), cert. denied, 452 U.S. 938 (1981).
Issue: Adverse impact

Dothard v. Rawlinson, 433 U.S. 321 (1977).
Issue: Workforce analysis and applicant flow data

Gay v. Waiters Union, Local 30, 30 FEP 605 (9th Cir. 1982).
Issue: Sufficient standard deviations

Griggs v. Duke Power Co., 401 U.S. 424 (1971).
Issue: Adverse impact

Harper v. TransWorld Airlines, Inc., 525 F.2d 409 (8th Cir. 1975).
Issue: Statistical sample

Hazelwood School District v. United States, 433 U.S. 299 (1977).
Issue: Appropriate labor market

Hudson v. IBM, 620 F.2d 351 (2d Cir.), cert. denied, 101 S. Ct. 794
   (1980).
Issue: Prima facie case

Markey v. Tenneco Oil Co., 635 F.2d 497 (5th Cir. 1981).
Issue: Labor market analysis

McDonnell Douglas Corp. v. Green, 411 U.S. 792 (1971).
Issue: Prima facie case

New York City Transit Authority v. Beazer, 440 U.S. 568 (1979).
Issue: Applicant flow data and burden of proof

Pouncy v. Prudential Ins. Co., 668 F.2d 795 (5th Cir. 1982).
Issue: Adverse impact

Robinson v. Dallas, 514 F.2d 1271 (5th Cir. 1975).
Issue: Prima facie case

Teamsters v. United States, 431 U.S. 324 (1977).
Issue: Applicant flow data

United States v. Fairfax County, 629 F.2d 932 (4th Cir. 1980),
   cert. denied, 449 U.S. 1078 (1981).
Issue: SMSA

SENIORITY

American Tobacco Co. v. Patterson, 456 U.S. 63 (1982).
Issue: Bona fide seniority systems

Boston Chapter, NAACP v. Beecher, 504 F.2d 1017 (1st Cir. 1974),
  cert. denied, 421 U.S. 910 (1975).
Issue: Promotions and selections

Boston Chapter, NAACP v. Beecher, 679 F.2d 965 (1st Cir. 1982),
  cert. granted, 103 S. Ct. 293 (1982).
Issue: Modification of consent decree requiring hiring goals

California Brewers Association v. Bryant, 444 U.S. 598 (1980).
Issue: Defines bona fide seniority systems

Franks v. Bowman, 424 U.S. 747 (1976).
Issue: Retroactive seniority status

Freeman v. Motors Convey, Inc., 700 F.2d 1339 (11th Cir. 1983).
Issue: Bona fide seniority system

James v. Stockham Valves and Fittings Co., 559 F.2d 310 (5th Cir.
  1977), cert. denied, 434 U.S. 1034 (1978).
Issue: Bona fide seniority systems

Papermakers, Local 189 v. United States, 416 F.2d 980 (5th Cir.
  1969), cert. denied, 379 U.S. 919 (1970).
Issue: Past discrimination in seniority systems

Pettway v. American Cast Iron Pipe Co., 576 F.2d 1157 (5th Cir.
  1978), cert. denied, 439 U.S. 1115 (1979).
Issue: Seniority rights

Pullman-Standard v. Swint, 456 U.S. 273 (1982).
Issue: Bona fide seniority systems

Quarles v. Philip Morris, Inc., 279 F. Supp. 505 (E.D. Va. 1968).
Issue: Past discrimination in seniority systems

Robinson v. Polaroid Corp., 567 F. Supp. 192 (D. Mass. 1983).
Issue: Adverse impact on minorities and reduction-in-force pro-
          cedures

Sears v. Atchison, Topeka & Santa Fe Railway, 645 F.2d 1365 (10th
  Cir. 1981), cert. denied, 456 U.S. 964 (1982)
Issue: Bona fide seniority system

Sledge v. J. P. Stevens & Co., Inc., 585 F.2d 625 (4th Cir. 1978),
  cert. denied, 440 U.S. 981 (1979).
Issue: Court ordered quotas

Southbridge Plastics v. Local 759, Rubber Workers, 565 F.2d 913 (5th
  Cir. 1978).
Issue: Bona fide seniority systems vs. conciliation agreements

Stotts v. Memphis Fire Department, 679 F.2d 541 (6th Cir. 1982),
  cert. granted 103 S. Ct. 2451 (1983)
Issue: Affirmative action consent decrees vs. provisions of collec-
        tive bargaining agreement

Teamsters v. United States, 431 U.S. 324 (1977).
Issue: Past discrimination in seniority systems

United Air Lines, Inc. v. Evans, 431 U.S. 553 (1977).
Issue: Timely charges

United States v. Bethlehem Steel Corp., 446 F.2d 652 (2d Cir. 1971).
Issue: Departmental assignments

United States v. Navajo Freight Lines, Inc., 525 F.2d 1318 (9th Cir.
  1975).
Issue: Remedies to discriminatory seniority systems

Watkins v. United Steelworkers, Local 2369, 516 F.2d 41 (5th Cir.
  1975).
Issue: Lay-off procedures

Williams v. New Orleans Steamship Ass'n, 673 F.2d 742 (5th Cir.
  1982), cert. denied, 103 S. Ct. 1428 (1983).
Issue: Custom and practice

Woods v. Southwestern Bell Telephone Co., 637 F.2d 1188 (8th Cir.
  1980), cert. denied, 102 S. Ct. 142 (1981).
Issue: Departmental seniority

W. R. Grace & Co. v. Local 759, 103 S. Ct. 2177 (1983).
Issue: Collective bargaining agreement vs. EEOC conciliation
        agreement

                        REVERSE DISCRIMINATION

Boston Chapter, NAACP, Inc. v. Beecher, 504 F.2d 1017 (1st Cir.
  1974), cert. denied, 421 U.S. 910 (1975).
Issue: Promotion quotas

Boston Firefighters Union Local, 718 v. Boston Chapter, NAACP, Inc.
  461 U.S. ___, (1983).
Issue: Reverse seniority layoffs

Bratton v. City of Detroit, 704 F.2d 878 (6th Cir. 1983), vacated
  and remanded on reconsideration, 712 F.2d 222 (6th Cir. 1983).
Issue: Affirmative action program

Bridgeport Guardians, Inc. v. Bridgeport Civil Service Commission,
  482 F.2d 1333 (2d Cir. 1973), cert. denied, 421 U.S. 991 (1975).
Issue: Promotion quotas

Buccinna v. City of New York, 82 Civ. 8460 ____ (S.D. N.Y. 1982).
Issue: Promotional exams

Contractors Association of Eastern Pennsylvania v. Secretary of
Labor, 442 F.2d 159 (3rd Cir. 1970), cert. denied, 404 U.S. 854
(1971).
Issue: Philadelphia Plan (affirmative action plan)

Detroit Police Officers Assoc. v. Young, 608 F.2d 671 (6th Cir.
1979), cert. denied, 452 U.S. 938 (1981).
Issue: Affirmative action goals

EEOC v. American Telephone & Telegraph Co., 556 F.2d 167 (3rd Cir.
1977), cert. denied, 438 U.S. 915 (1978).
Issue: Quotas

Electrical Workers, IBEW, Local 35 v. City of Hartford, 625 F.2d 416
(2d Cir. 1980), cert. denied, 453 U.S. 913 (1981)
Issue: Affirmative action

Fullilove v. Klutznick, 448 U.S. 448 (1980).
Issue: Minority businesses

Kirkland v. New York State Department of Correctional Services, 520
F.2d 420 (2nd Cir. 1975), cert. denied, 429 U.S. 823 (1976)
Issue: Court ordered quotas

Lehman v. Yellow Freight System, Inc., 651 F.2d 520 (7th Cir. 1981).
Issue: Informal affirmative action plans

McDonald v. Santa Fe Trail Transportation Co., 427 U.S. 273 (1976).
Issue: Title VII coverage of white employees

Morrow v. Dillard, 580 F.2d 1284 (5th Cir. 1978).
Issue: Court ordered quotas

Parker v. Baltimore & Ohio Railroad, 652 F.2d 1012 (D.C. Cir. 1981).
Issue: Affirmative action program

Setser v. Novack Investment Co., 638 F.2d 1137 (8th Cir. 1980), cert.
denied, 454 U.S. 1064 (1981).
Issue: Affirmative action plans

United States v. Commonwealth of Virginia Department of Highways and
Transportation. No. 82-09338 E.D. Vir. 1983.
Issue: Quotas

United States v. Navajo Freight Lines, Inc., 525 F.2d 1318 (9th Cir.
1975).
Issue: Remedies

United Steelworkers of America v. Weber, 443 U.S. 193 (1979).
Issue: Affirmative action programs

University of California Regents v. Bakke, 438 U.S. 265 (1978).
Issue: Affirmative action programs

Valentine v. Smith, 654 F.2d 503 (8th Cir. 1981).
Issue: Accelerating hiring of minorities

Williams v. City of New Orleans, 673 F.2d 742 (5th Cir. 1982),
  cert. denied, 460 U.S. 1038 (1983).
Issue: Promotional quotas

CIVIL RIGHTS ACT OF 1964 AS AMENDED

AN ACT To enforce the constitutional right to vote, to confer jurisdiction upon the district courts of the United States to provide injunctive relief against discrimination in public accommodations, to authorize the Attorney General to institute suits to protect constitutional rights in public facilities and public education, to extend the Commission on Civil Rights, to prevent discrimination in federally assisted programs, to establish a Commission on Equal Employment Opportunity, and for other purposes.

Be it enacted by the Senate and House of Representatives of the United States of America in Congress assembled, That this Act may be cited as the "Civil Rights Act of 1964".

* * * * * * *

TITLE VII—EQUAL EMPLOYMENT OPPORTUNITY [1]

DEFINITIONS

Sec. 701. For the purposes of this title—

(a) The term "person" includes one or more individuals, *governments, governmental agencies, political subdivisions,* labor unions, partnerships, associations, corporations, legal representatives, mutual companies, joint-stock companies, trusts, unincorporated organizations, trustees, trustees in bankruptcy, or receivers.

(b) The term "employer" means a person engaged in an industry affecting commerce who has *fifteen* or more employees for each working day in each of twenty or more calendar weeks in the current or preceding calendar year, and any agent of such a person, but such term does not include (1) the United States, a corporation wholly owned by the Government of the United States, an Indian tribe, or *any department or agency of the District of Columbia subject by statute to procedures of the competitive service (as defined in section 2102 of title 5 of the United States Code*), or (2) a bona fide private membership club (other than a labor organization) which is exempt from taxation under section 501(c) of the Internal Revenue Code of 1954, *except that during the first year after the date of enactment of the Equal Employment Opportunity Act of 1972,* persons having fewer than *twenty-five* employees (and their agents) shall not be considered *employers.*

(c) The term "employment agency" means any person regularly undertaking with or without compensation to procure employees for an employer or to procure for employees opportunities to work for an employer and includes an agent of such a person.

(d) The term "labor organization" means a labor organization engaged in an industry affecting commerce, and any agent of such an organization, and includes any organization of any kind, any agency, or employee representation committee, group, association, or plan so engaged in which employees participate and which exists for the

---

[1] Includes 1972 amendments made by P.L. 92–261 printed in italic.

purpose, in whole or in part, of dealing with employers concerning grievances, labor disputes, wages, rates of pay, hours, or other terms or conditions of employment, and any conference, general committee, joint or system board, or joint council so engaged which is subordinate to a national or international labor organization.

(e) A labor organization shall be deemed to be engaged in an industry affecting commerce if (1) it maintains or operates a hiring hall or hiring office which procures employees for an employer or procures for employees opportunities to work for an employer, or (2) the number of its members (or, where it is a labor organization composed of other labor organizations or their representatives, if the aggregate number of the members of such other labor organization) is (A) *twenty-five* or more during the first year after the *date of enactment of the Equal Employment Opportunity Act of 1972*, or (B) *fifteen* or more thereafter, and such labor organization—

(1) is the certified representative of employees under the provisions of the National Labor Relations Act, as amended, or the Railway Labor Act, as amended;

(2) although not certified, is a national or international labor organization or a local labor organization recognized or acting as the representative of employees of an employer or employers engaged in an industry affecting commerce; or

(3) has chartered a local labor organization or subsidiary body which is representing or actively seeking to represent employees of employers within the meaning of paragraph (1) or (2); or

(4) has been chartered by a labor organization representing or actively seeking to represent employees within the meaning of paragraph (1) or (2) as the local or subordinate body through which such employees may enjoy membership or become affiliated with such labor organization; or

(5) is a conference, general committee, joint or system board, or joint council subordinate to a national or international labor organization, which includes a labor organization engaged in an industry affecting commerce within the meaning of any of the preceding paragraphs of this subsection.

(f) The term "employee" means an individual employed by an employer, *except that the term 'employee' shall not include any person elected to public office in any State or political subdivision of any State by the qualified voters thereof, or any person chosen by such officer to be on such officer's personal staff, or an appointee on the policymaking level or an immediate adviser with respect to the excercise of the constitutional or legal powers of the office. The exemption set forth in the preceding sentence shall not include employees subject to the civil service laws of a State government, governmental agency or political subdivision.*

(g) The term "commerce" means trade, traffic, commerce, transportation, transmission, or communication among the several States; or between a State and any place outside thereof; or within the District of Columbia, or a possession of the United States; or between points in the same State but through a point outside thereof.

(h) The term "industry affecting commerce" means any activity, business, or industry in commerce or in which a labor dispute would hinder or obstruct commerce or the free flow of commerce and includes any activity or industry "affecting commerce" within the meaning of the Labor-Management Reporting and Disclosure Act of 1959, *and further includes any governmental industry, business, or activity.*

(i) The term "State" includes a State of the United States, the District of Columbia, Puerto Rico, the Virgin Islands, American Samoa, Guam, Wake Island, the Canal Zone, and Outer Continental Shelf lands defined in the Outer Continental Shelf Lands Act.

(j) *The term "religion" includes all aspects of religious observance and practice, as well as belief, unless an employer demonstrates that he is unable to reasonably accommodate to an employee's or prospective employee's, religious observance or practice without undue hardship on the conduct of the employer's business.*

EXEMPTION

Sec. 702. This title shall not apply to an employer with respect to the employment of aliens outside any State, or to a religious corporation, association, *educational institution,* or society with respect to the employment of individuals of a particular religion to perform work connected with the carrying on by such corporation, association, *educational institution,* or society of its *activities.*

DISCRIMINATION BECAUSE OF RACE, COLOR, RELIGION, SEX, OR NATIONAL ORIGIN

Sec. 703. (a) It shall be an unlawful employment practice for an employer—

(1) to fail or refuse to hire or to discharge any individual, or otherwise to discriminate against any individual with respect to his compensation, terms, conditions, or privileges of employment, because of such individual's race, color, religion, sex, or national origin; or

(2) to limit, segregate, or classify his employees *or applicants for employment* in any way which would deprive or tend to deprive any individual of employment opportunities or otherwise adversely affect his status as an employee, because of such individual's race, color, religion, sex, or national origin.

(b) It shall be an unlawful employment practice for an employment agency to fail or refuse to refer for employment, or otherwise to discriminate against, any individual because of his race, color, religion, sex, or national origin, or to classify or refer for employment any individual on the basis of his race, color, religion, sex, or national origin.

(c) It shall be an unlawful employment practice for a labor organization—

(1) to exclude or to expel from its membership, or otherwise to discriminate against, any individual because of his race, color, religion, sex, or national origin;

(2) to limit, segregate, or classify its membership, *or applicants for membership* or to classify or fail or refuse to refer for employment any individual, in any way which would deprive or tend to deprive any individual of employment opportunities, or would limit such employment opportunities or otherwise adversely affect his status as an employee or as an applicant for employment, because of such individual's race, color, religion, sex, or national origin; or

(3) to cause or attempt to cause an employer to discriminate against an individual in violation of this section.

(d) It shall be an unlawful employment practice for any employer, labor organization, or joint labor-management committee controlling apprenticeship or other training or retraining, including on-the-job training programs to discriminate against any individual because of his race, color, religion, sex, or national origin in admission to, or employment in, any program established to provide apprenticeship or other training.

(e) Notwithstanding any other provision of this title, (1) it shall not be an unlawful employment practice for an employer to hire and employ employees, for an employment agency to classify, or refer for employment any individual, for a labor organization to classify its membership or to classify or refer for employment any individual, or for an employer, labor organization, or joint labor-management committee controlling apprenticeship or other training or retraining programs to admit or employ any individual in any such program, on the basis of his religion, sex, or national origin in those certain instances where religion, sex, or national origin is a bona fide occupational qualification reasonably necessary to the normal operation of that particular business or enterprise, and (2) it shall not be an unlawful employment practice for a school, college, university, or other educational institution or institution of learning to hire and employ employees of a particular religion if such school, college, university, or other educational institution or institution of learning is, in whole or in substantial part, owned, supported, controlled, or managed by a particular religion or by a particular religious corporation, association, or society, or if the curriculum of such school, college, university, or other educational institution or institution of learning is directed toward the propagation of a particular religion.

(f) As used in this title, the phrase "unlawful employment practice" shall not be deemed to include any action or measure taken by an employer, labor organization, joint labor-management committee, or employment agency with respect to an individual who is a member of the Communist Party of the United States or of any other organization required to register as a Communist-action or Communist-front organization by final order of the Subversive Activities Control Board pursuant to the Subversive Activities Control Act of 1950.

(g) Notwithstanding any other provision of this title, it shall not be an unlawful employment practice for an employer to fail or refuse to hire and employ any individual for any position, for an employer to discharge any individual from any position, or for an employment agency to fail or refuse to refer any individual for employment in any position, or for a labor organization to fail or refuse to refer any individual for employment in any position, if—

(1) the occupancy of such position, or access to the premises in or upon which any part of the duties of such position is performed or is to be performed, is subject to any requirement imposed in the interest of the national security of the United States under any security program in effect pursuant to or administered under any statute of the United States or any Executive order of the President; and

(2) such individual has not fulfilled or has ceased to fulfill that requirement.

(h) Notwithstanding any other provision of this title, it shall not be an unlawful employment practice for an employer to apply different standards of compensation, or different terms, conditions, or privileges of employment pursuant to a bona fide seniority or merit system, or a system which measures earnings by quantity or quality of production or to employees who work in different locations, provided that such differences are not the result of an intention to discriminate because of race, color, religion, sex, or national origin, nor shall it be an unlawful employment practice for an employer to give and to act upon the results of any professionally developed ability test provided that such test, its administration or action upon the results is not designed, intended or used to discriminate because of race, color, religion, sex or national origin. It shall not be an unlawful employment practice under this title for any employer to differentiate upon the basis of sex in determining the amount of the wages or compensation paid or to be paid to employees of such employer if such differentiation is authorized by the provisions of section 6(d) of the Fair Labor Standards Act of 1938, as amended (29 U.S.C. 206(d)).

(i) Nothing contained in this title shall apply to any business or enterprise on or near an Indian reservation with respect to any publicly announced employment practice of such business or enterprise under which a preferential treatment is given to any individual because he is an Indian living on or near a reservation.

(j) Nothing contained in this title shall be interpreted to require any employer, employment agency, labor organization, or joint labor-management committee subject to this title to grant preferential treatment to any individual or to any group because of the race, color, religion, sex, or national origin of such individual or group on account of an imbalance which may exist with respect to the total number or percentage of persons of any race, color, religion, sex, or national origin employed by any employer, referred or classified for employment by any employment agency or labor organization, admitted to membership or classified by any labor organization, or admitted to, or employed in, any apprenticeship or other training program, in comparison with the total number or percentage of persons of such race, color, religion, sex, or national origin in any community, State, section, or other area, or in the available work force in any community, State, section, or other area.

OTHER UNLAWFUL EMPLOYMENT PRACTICES

SEC. 704. (a) It shall be an unlawful employment practice for an employer to discriminate against any of his employees or applicants for employment, for an employment agency, *or joint labor-management committee controlling apprenticeship or other training or retraining, including on-the-job training programs,* to discriminate against any individual, or for a labor organization to discriminate against any member thereof or applicant for membership, because he has opposed any practice made an unlawful employment practice by this title, or because he has made a charge, testified, assisted, or participated in any manner in an investigation, proceeding, or hearing under this title.

(b) It shall be an unlawful employment practice for an employer, labor organization, employment *agency, or joint labor-management committee controlling apprenticeship or other training or retraining, in-*

cluding on-the-job training programs, to print or publish or cause to be printed or published any notice or advertisement relating to employment by such an employer or membership in or any classification or referral for employment by such a labor organization, or relating to any classification or referral for employment by such an employment *agency, or relating to admission to, or employment in, any program established to provide apprenticeship or other training by such a joint labor-management committee* indicating any preference, limitation, specification, or discrimination, based on race, color, religion, sex, or national origin, except that such a notice or advertisement may indicate a preference, limitation, specification, or discrimination based on religion, sex, or national origin when religion, sex, or national origin is a bona fide occupational qualification for employment.

EQUAL EMPLOYMENT OPPORTUNITY COMMISSION

SEC. 705. (a) There is hereby created a Commission to be known as the Equal Employment Opportunity Commission, which shall be composed of five members, not more than three of whom shall be members of the same political party. *Members of the Commission shall be appointed by the President by and with the advice and consent of the Senate for a term of five years. Any individual chosen to fill a vacancy shall be appointed only for the unexpired term of the member whom he shall succeed, and all members of the Commission shall continue to serve until their successors are appointed and qualified, except that no such member of the Commission shall continue to serve (1) for more than sixty days when the Congress is in session unless a nomination to fill such vacancy shall have been submitted to the Senate, or (2) after the adjournment sine die of the session of the Senate in which such nomination was submitted.* The President shall designate one member to serve as Chairman of the Commission, and one member to serve as Vice Chairman. The Chairman shall be responsible on behalf of the Commission for the administrative operations of the Commission, and *except as provided in subsection (b),* shall appoint, in accordance with the *provisions of title 5, United States Code, governing appointments in the competitive service, such officers, agents, attorneys, hearing examiners, and employees as he deems necessary to assist it in the performance of its functions and to fix their compensation in accordance with the provisions of chapter 51 and subchapter III of chapter 53 of title 5, United States Code, relating to classification and General Schedule pay rates: Provided, That assignment, removal, and compensation of hearing examiners shall be in accordance with sections 3105, 3344, 5362, and 7521 of title 5, United States Code.*

(b)(1) There shall be a General Counsel of the Commission appointed by the President, by and with the advice and consent of the Senate, for a term of four years. The General Counsel shall have responsibility for the conduct of litigation as provided in sections 706 and 707 of this title. The General Counsel shall have such other duties as the Commission may prescribe or as may be provided by law and shall concur with the Chairman of the Commission on the appointment and supervision of regional attorneys. The General Counsel of the Commission on the effective date of this Act shall continue in such position and perform the functions specified in this subsection until a successor is appointed and qualified.

(*2*) *Attorneys appointed under this section may, at the direction of the Commission, appear for and represent the Commission in any case in court, provided that the Attorney General shall conduct all litigation to which the Commission is a party in the Supreme Court pursuant to this title.*

(*c*) A vacancy in the Commission shall not impair the right of the remaining members to exercise all the powers of the Commission and three members thereof shall constitute a quorum.

(*d*) The Commission shall have an official seal which shall be judicially noticed.

(*e*) The Commission shall at the close of each fiscal year report to the Congress and to the President concerning the action it has taken; the names, salaries, and duties of all individuals in its employ and the moneys it has disbursed; and shall make such further reports on the cause of and means of eliminating discrimination and such recommendations for further legislation as may appear desirable.

(*f*) The principal office of the Commission shall be in or near the District of Columbia, but it may meet or exercise any or all its powers at any other place. The Commission may establish such regional or State offices as it deems necessary to accomplish the purpose of this title.

(*g*) The Commission shall have power—

(1) to cooperate with and, with their consent, utilize regional, State, local, and other agencies, both public and private, and individuals;

(2) to pay to witnesses whose depositions are taken or who are summoned before the Commission or any of its agents the same witness and mileage fees as are paid to witnesses in the courts of the United States;

(3) to furnish to persons subject to this title such technical assistance as they may request to further their compliance with this title or an order issued thereunder;

(4) upon the request of (i) any employer, whose employees or some of them, or (ii) any labor organization, whose members or some of them, refuse or threaten to refuse to cooperate in effectuating the provisions of this title, to assist in such effectuation by conciliation or such other remedial action as is provided by this title;

(5) to make such technical studies as are appropriate to effectuate the purposes and policies of this title and to make the results of such studies available to the public;

(6) to *intervene* in a civil action brought *under section 706* by an aggrieved party *against a respondent other than a government, governmental agency, or political subdivision.*

(*h*) The Commission shall, in any of its educational or promotional activities, cooperate with other departments and agencies in the performance of such educational and promotional activities.

(*i*) All officers, agents, attorneys, and employees of the Commission shall be subject to the provisions of section 9 of the Act of August 2, 1939, as amended (the Hatch Act), notwithstanding any exemption contained in such section.

PREVENTION OF UNLAWFUL EMPLOYMENT PRACTICES

SEC. 706. (a) *The Commission is empowered, as hereinafter provided, to prevent any person from engaging in any unlawful employment practice as set forth in section 703 or 704 of this title.*

(b) Whenever a *charge is filed by or on behalf of a* person claiming to be aggrieved, or by a member of the Commission, *alleging* that an employer, employment agency, labor *organization, or joint labor-management committee controlling apprenticeship or other training or retraining, including on-the-job training programs,* has engaged in an unlawful employment practice, the Commission shall *serve a notice of the charge (including the date, place and circumstances of the alleged unlawful employment practice)* on such employer, employment agency, labor *organization, or joint labor-management committee* (hereinafter referred to as the "respondent") *within ten days, and shall make an investigation thereof. Charges shall be in writing under oath or affirmation and shall contain such information and be in such form as the Commission requires. Charges* shall not be made public by the Commission. If the Commission *determines* after such investigation that there is *not* reasonable cause to believe that the charge is true, *it shall dismiss the charge and promptly notify the person claiming to be aggrieved and the respondent of its action. In determining whether reasonable cause exists, the Commission shall accord substantial weight to final findings and orders made by State or local authorities in proceedings commenced under State or local law pursuant to the requirements of subsections (c) and (d). If the Commission determines after such investigation that there is reasonable cause to believe that the charge is true,* the Commission shall endeavor to eliminate any such alleged unlawful employment practice by informal methods of conference, conciliation, and persuasion. Nothing said or done during and as a part of such *informal* endeavors may be made public by the *Commission, its officers or employees, or used as evidence in a subsequent proceeding* without the written consent of the *persons concerned.* Any *person* who *makes* public information in violation of this subsection shall be fined not more than $1,000 or imprisoned *for* not more than one *year, or both. The Commission shall make its determination on reasonable cause as promptly as possible and, so far as practicable, not later than one hundred and twenty days from the filing of the charge or, where applicable under subsection (c) or (d) from the date upon which the Commission is authorized to take action with respect to the charge.*

(c) In the case of an alleged unlawful employment practice occurring in a State, or political subdivision of a State, which has a State or local law prohibiting the unlawful employment practice alleged and establishing or authorizing a State or local authority to grant or seek relief from such practice or to institute criminal proceedings with respect thereto upon receiving notice thereof, no charge may be filed under subsection (a) by the person aggrieved before the expiration of sixty days after proceedings have been commenced under the State or local law, unless such proceedings have been earlier terminated, provided that such sixty-day period shall be extended to one hundred and twenty days during the first year after the effective date of such State or local law. If any requirement for the commencement of such proceedings is imposed by a State or local authority other than a requirement of the filing of a written and signed statement of the facts upon which the proceeding is based, the proceeding shall be deemed to have been commenced for the purposes of this subsection at the time such statement is sent by registered mail to the appropriate State or local authority.

(d) In the case of any charge filed by a member of the Commission alleging an unlawful employment practice occurring in a State or political subdivision of a State which has a State or local law prohibiting the practice alleged and establishing or authorizing a State or local authority to grant or seek relief from such practice or to institute criminal proceedings with respect thereto upon receiving notice thereof, the Commission shall, before taking any action with respect to such charge, notify the appropriate State or local officials and, upon request, afford them a reasonable time, but not less than sixty days (provided that such sixty-day period shall be extended to one hundred and twenty days during the first year after the effective *date* of such State or local law), unless a shorter period is requested, to act under such State or local law to remedy the practice alleged.

(e) A charge under *this section* shall be filed within *one hundred and eighty* days after the alleged unlawful employment practice *occurred and notice of the charge (including the date, place and circumstances of the alleged unlawful employment practice) shall be served upon the person against whom such charge is made within ten days thereafter,* except that in *a* case of an unlawful employment practice with respect to which the person aggrieved has *initially instituted proceedings with a State or local agency with authority to grant or seek relief from such practice or to institute criminal proceedings with respect thereto upon receiving notice thereof,* such charge shall be filed by *or on behalf of* the person aggrieved within *three hundred* days after the alleged unlawful employment practice occurred, or within thirty days after receiving notice that the State or local agency has terminated the proceedings under the State or local law, whichever is earlier, and a copy of such charge shall be filed by the Commission with the State or local agency.

(f)(1) If within thirty days after a charge is filed with the Commission or within thirty days after expiration of any period of reference under subsection (c) *or (d)*, the Commission has been unable to *secure from the respondent a conciliation agreement acceptable to the Commission,* the Commission *may bring a civil action against any respondent not a government, governmental agency, or political subdivision named in the charge. In the case of a respondent which is a government, governmental agency, or political subdivision, if the Commission has been unable to secure from the respondent a conciliation agreement acceptable to the Commission, the Commission shall take no further action and shall refer the case to the Attorney General who may bring a civil action against such respondent in the appropriate United States district court. The person or persons aggrieved shall have the right to intervene in a civil action brought by the Commission or the Attorney General in a case involving a government, governmental agency, or political subdivision. If a charge filed with the Commission pursuant to subsection (b) is dismissed by the Commission, or if within one hundred and eighty days from the filing of such charge or the expiration of any period of reference under subsection (c) or (d), whichever is later, the Commission has not filed a civil action under this section or the Attorney General has notified a civil action in a case involving a government, governmental agency, or political subdivision, or the Commission has not entered into a conciliation agreement to which the person aggrieved is a party, the Commission, or the Attorney General in a case involving a government, governmental agency, or political subdivision, shall so notify the person aggrieved and within ninety days after the giving of such notice a civil action may* be brought against the respondent named in the charge (A) by the person claiming to be aggrieved, or (B) if such charge was filed by a member of the Commission, by any person whom the charge alleges was aggrieved by the alleged unlawful employment practice. Upon application by the complainant and in such circumstances as the court may deem just, the court may appoint an attorney for such complainant and may authorize the commencement of the action without the payment of fees, costs, or security. Upon timely application, the court may, in its discretion, permit the *Commission,* or the Attorney General in a case involving a government, governmental agency, or political subdivision, to intervene in such civil action *upon certification* that the case is of general public importance. Upon request, the court may, in its discretion, stay further proceedings for not more than sixty days pending the termination of State or local proceedings described in subsections (c) or (d) *of this section or further* efforts of the Commission to obtain voluntary compliance.

(2) Whenever a charge is filed with the Commission and the Commission concludes on the basis of a preliminary investigation that prompt judicial action is necessary to carry out the purposes of this Act, the Commission, or the Attorney General in a case involving a government, governmental agency, or political subdivision, may bring an action for appropriate temporary or preliminary relief pending final disposition of such charge. Any temporary restraining order or other order granting preliminary or temporary relief shall be issued in accordance with rule 65 of the Federal Rules of Civil Procedure. It shall be the duty of a court having jurisdiction over proceedings under this section to assign cases for hearing at the earliest practicable date and to cause such cases to be in every way expedited.

(3) Each United States district court and each United States court of a place subject to the jurisdiction of the United States shall have jurisdiction of actions brought under this title. Such an action may be brought in any judicial district in the State in which the unlawful employment practice is alleged to have been committed, in the judicial district in which the employment records relevant to such practice are maintained and administered, or in the judicial district in which the aggrieved person would have worked but for the alleged unlawful employment practice, but if the respondent is not found within any such district, such an action may be brought within the judicial district in which the respondent has his principal office. For purposes of sections 1404 and 1406 of title 28 of the United States Code, the judicial district in which the respondent has his principal office shall in all cases be considered a district in which the action might have been brought.

(4) It shall be the duty of the chief judge of the district (or in his absence, the acting chief judge) in which the case is pending immediately to designate a judge in such district to hear and determine the case. In the event that no judge in the district is available to hear and determine the case, the chief judge of the district, or the acting chief judge, as the

case may be, shall certify this fact to the chief judge of the circuit (or in his absence, the acting chief judge) who shall then designate a district or circuit judge of the circuit to hear and determine the case.

(5) It shall be the duty of the judge designated pursuant to this subsection to assign the case for hearing at the earliest practicable date and to cause the case to be in every way expedited. If such judge has not scheduled the case for trial within one hundred and twenty days after issue has been joined, that judge may appoint a master pursuant to rule 53 of the Federal Rules of Civil Procedure.

(g) If the court finds that the respondent has intentionally engaged in or is intentionally engaging in an unlawful employment practice charged in the complaint, the court may enjoin the respondent from engaging in such unlawful employment practice, and order such affirmative action as may be appropriate, which may include, but is not limited to, reinstatement or hiring of employees, with or without back pay (payable by the employer, employment agency, or labor organization, as the case may be, responsible for the unlawful employment practice), or any other equitable relief as the court deems appropriate. Back pay liability shall not accrue from a date more than two years prior to the filing of a charge with the Commission. Interim earnings or amounts earnable with reasonable diligence by the person or persons discriminated against shall operate to reduce the back · pay otherwise allowable. No order of the court shall require the admission or reinstatement of an individual as a member of a union, or the hiring, reinstatement, or promotion of an individual as an employee, or the payment to him of any back pay, if such individual was refused admission, suspended, or expelled, or was refused employment or advancement or was suspended or discharged for any reason other than discrimination on account of race, color, religion, sex, or national origin or in violation of section 704(a).

(h) The provisions of the Act entitled "An Act to amend the Judicial Code and to define and limit the jurisdiction of courts sitting in equity, and for other purposes," approved March 23, 1932 (29 U.S.C. 101–115), shall not apply with respect to civil actions brought under this section.

(i) In any case in which an employer, employment agency, or labor organization fails to comply with an order of a court issued in a civil action brought under *this section*, the Commission may commence proceedings to compel compliance with such order.

(j) Any civil action brought under *this section* and any proceedings brought under subsection (i) shall be subject to appeal as provided in sections 1291 and 1292, title 28, United States Code.

(k) In any action or proceeding under this title the court, in its discretion, may allow the prevailing party, other than the Commission or the United States, a reasonable attorney's fee as part of the costs, and the Commission and the United States shall be liable for costs the same as a private person.

SEC. 707. (a) Whenever the Attorney General has reasonable cause to believe that any person or group of persons is engaged in a pattern or practice of resistance to the full enjoyment of any of the rights secured by this title, and that the pattern or practice is of such a nature and is intended to deny the full exercise of the rights herein described, the Attorney General may bring a civil action in the appropriate district court of the United States by filing with it a complaint (1) signed by him (or in his absence the Acting Attorney General), (2) setting forth facts pertaining to such pattern or practice, and (3) requesting such relief, including an application for a permanent or temporary injunction, restraining order or other order against the person or persons responsible for such pattern or practice, as he deems necessary to insure the full enjoyment of the rights herein described.

(b) The district courts of the United States shall have and shall exercise jurisdiction of proceedings instituted pursuant to this section, and in any such proceeding the Attorney General may file with the clerk of such court a request that a court of three judges be convened to hear and determine the case. Such request by the Attorney General shall be accompanied by a certificate that, in his opinion, the case is of general public importance. A copy of the certificate and request for a three-judge court shall be immediately furnished by such clerk to the chief judge of the circuit (or in his absence, the presiding circuit judge of the circuit) in which the case is pending. Upon receipt of such request it shall be the duty of the chief judge of the circuit or the presiding circuit judge, as the case may be, to designate immediately three judges in such circuit, of whom at least one shall be a circuit judge and another of whom shall be a district judge of the court in which the proceeding was instituted, to hear and determine such case, and it shall be the duty of the judges so designated to assign the case for hearing at the earliest practicable date, to participate in the hearing and determination thereof, and to cause the case to be in every way expedited. An appeal from the final judgment of such court will lie to the Supreme Court.

In the event the Attorney General fails to file such a request in any such proceeding, it shall be the duty of the chief judge of the district (or in his absence, the acting chief judge) in which the case is pending immediately to designate a judge in such district to hear and determine the case. In the event that no judge in the district is available to hear and determine the case, the chief judge of the district, or the acting chief judge, as the case may be, shall certify this fact to the chief judge of the circuit (or in his absence, the acting chief judge) who shall then designate a district or circuit judge of the circuit to hear and determine the case.

It shall be the duty of the judge designated pursuant to this section to assign the case for hearing at the earliest practicable date and to cause the case to be in every way expedited.

(c) *Effective two years after the date of enactment of the Equal Employment Opportunity Act of 1972, the functions of the Attorney General under this section shall be transferred to the Commission, together with such personnel, property, records, and unexpended balances of appropriations, allocations, and other funds employed, used, held, available, or to be made available in connection with such functions unless the President submits, and neither House of Congress vetoes, a reorganization plan pursuant to chapter 9, of title 5, United States Code, inconsistent with the provisions of this subsection. The Commission shall carry out such functions in accordance with subsections (d) and (e) of this section.*

(d) *Upon the transfer of functions provided for in subsection (c) of this section, in all suits commenced pursuant to this section prior to the date of such transfer, proceedings shall continue without abatement, all court orders and decrees shall remain in effect, and the Commission shall be substituted as a party for the United States of America, the Attorney General, or the Acting Attorney General, as appropriate.*

(e) *Subsequent to the date of enactment of the Equal Employment Opportunity Act of 1972, the Commission shall have authority to investigate and act on a charge of a pattern or practice of discrimination, whether filed by or on behalf of a person claiming to be aggrieved or by a member of the Commission. All such actions shall be conducted in accordance with the procedures set forth in section 706 of this Act.*

EFFECT ON STATE LAWS

SEC. 708. Nothing in this title shall be deemed to exempt or relieve any person from any liability, duty, penalty, or punishment provided by any present or future law of any State or political subdivision of a State, other than any such law which purports to require or permit the doing of any act which would be an unlawful employment practice under this title.

INVESTIGATIONS, INSPECTIONS, RECORDS, STATE AGENCIES

SEC. 709. (a) In connection with any investigation of a charge filed under section 706, the Commission or its designated representative shall at all reasonable times have access to, for the purposes of examination, and the right to copy any evidence of any person being investigated or proceeded against that relates to unlawful employment practices covered by this title and is relevant to the charge under investigation.

(b) The Commission may cooperate with State and local agencies charged with the administration of State fair employment practices laws and, with the consent of such agencies, may, for the purpose of carrying out its functions and duties under this title and within the limitation of funds appropriated specifically for such purpose, *engage in and contribute to the cost of research and other projects of mutual interest undertaken by such agencies, and* utilize the services of such agencies and their employees, and, notwithstanding any other provision of law, *pay by advance or reimbursement* such agencies and their employees for services rendered to assist the Commission in carrying out this title. In furtherance of such cooperative efforts, the Commission may enter into written agreements with such State or local agencies and such agreements may include provisions under which the Commission shall refrain from processing a charge in any cases or class of cases specified in such agreements or under which the Commission shall relieve any person or class of persons in such State or locality from requirements imposed under this section. The Commission shall rescind any such agreement whenever it determines that the agreement no longer serves the interest of effective enforcement of this title.

(c) *Every* employer, employment agency, and labor organization subject to this title shall (1) make and keep such records relevant to the determinations of whether unlawful employment practices have been or are being committed, (2) preserve such records for such periods, and (3) make such reports therefrom, as the Commission shall prescribe by regulation or order, after public hearing, as reasonable, necessary, or appropriate for the enforcement of this title or the regulations or orders thereunder. The Commission shall, by regulation, require each employer, labor organization, and joint labor-management committee subject to this title which controls an apprenticeship or other training program to maintain such records as are reasonably necessary to carry out the purpose of this title, including, but not limited to, a list of applicants who wish to participate in such program, including the chronological order in which applications were received, and *to* furnish to the Commission upon request, a detailed description of the manner in which persons are selected to participate in the apprenticeship or other training program. Any employer, employment agency, labor organization, or joint labor-management committee which believes that the application to it of any regulation or order issued under this section would result in undue hardship may apply to the Commission for an exemption from the application of such regulation or order, *and, if such application for an exemption is denied,* bring a civil action in the United States district court for the district where such records are kept. If the Commission or the court, as the case may be, finds that the application of the regulation or order to the employer, employment agency, or labor organization in question would impose an undue hardship, the Commission or the court, as the case may be, may grant appropriate relief. *If any person required to comply with the provisions of this subsection fails or refuses to do so, the United States district court for the district in which such person is found, resides, or transacts business, shall, upon application of the Commission, or the Attorney General in a case involving a government, governmental agency or political subdivision, have jurisdiction to issue to such person an order requiring him to comply.*

(d) In prescribing requirements pursuant to subsection (c) of this section, the Commission shall consult with other interested State and Federal agencies and shall endeavor to coordinate its requirements with those adopted by such agencies. The Commission shall furnish upon request and without cost to any State or local agency charged with the administration of a fair employment practice law information obtained pursuant to subsection (c) of this section from any employer, employment agency, labor organization, or joint labor-management committee subject to the jurisdiction of such agency. Such information shall be furnished on condition that it not be made public by the recipient agency prior to the institution of a proceeding under State or local law involving such information. If this condition is violated by a recipient agency, the Commission may decline to honor subsequent requests pursuant to this subsection.

(e) It shall be unlawful for any officer or employee of the Commission to make public in any manner whatever any information obtained by the Commission pursuant to its authority under this section prior to the institution of any proceeding under this title involving such information. Any officer or employee of the Commission who shall make public in any manner whatever any information in violation of this subsection shall be guilty of a misdemeanor and upon conviction thereof, shall be fined not more than $1,000, or imprisoned not more than one year.

INVESTIGATORY POWERS

Sec. 710. For the purpose of all hearings and investigations conducted by the Commission or its duly authorized agents or agencies, section 11 of the National Labor Relations Act (49 Stat. 455; 29 U.S.C. 161) shall apply.

NOTICES TO BE POSTED

SEC. 711. (a) Every employer, employment agency, and labor organization, as the case may be, shall post and keep posted in conspicuous places upon its premises where notices to employees, applicants for employment, and members are customarily posted a notice to be prepared or approved by the Commission setting forth excerpts from, or summaries of, the pertinent provisions of this title and information pertinent to the filing of a complaint.

(b) A willful violation of this section shall be punishable by a fine of not more than $100 for each separate offense.

VETERANS' PREFERENCE

SEC. 712. Nothing contained in this title shall be construed to repeal or modify any Federal, State, territorial, or local law creating special rights or preference for veterans.

RULES AND REGULATIONS

SEC. 713. (a) The Commission shall have authority from time to time to issue, amend, or rescind suitable procedural regulations to carry out the provisions of this title. Regulations issued under the section shall be in conformity with the standards and limitations of the Administrative Procedure Act.

(b) In any action or proceeding based on any alleged unlawful employment practice, no person shall be subject to any liability or punishment for or on account of (1) the commission by such person of an unlawful employment practice if he pleads and proves that the act or omission complained of was in good faith, in conformity with, and in reliance on any written interpretation or opinion of the Commission, or (2) the failure of such person to publish and file any information required by any provision of this title if he pleads and proves that he failed to publish and file such information in good faith, in conformity with the instructions of the Commission issued under this title regarding the filing of such information. Such a defense, if established, shall be a bar to the action or proceeding, notwithstanding that (A) after such act or omission, such interpretation or opinion is modified or rescinded or is determined by judicial authority to be invalid or of no legal effect, or (B) after publishing or filing the description and annual reports, such publication or filing is determined by judicial authority not to be in conformity with the requirements of this title.

FORCIBLY RESISTING THE COMMISSION OR ITS REPRESENTATIVES

SEC. 714. The provisions of *sections 111 and 1114* title 18, United States Code, shall apply to officers, agents, and employees of the Commission in the performance of their official duties. *Notwithstanding the provisions of sections 111 and 1114 of title 18, United States Code, whoever in violation of the provisions of section 1114 of such title kills a person while engaged in or on account of the performance of his official*

310

functions under this Act shall be punished by imprisonment for any term of years or for life.

EQUAL EMPLOYMENT OPPORTUNITY COORDINATING COUNCIL

Sec. 715. There shall be established an Equal Employment Opportunity Coordinating Council (hereinafter referred to in this section as the Council) composed of the Secretary of Labor, the Chairman of the Equal Employment Opportunity Commission, the Attorney General, the Chairman of the United States Civil Service Commission, and the Chairman of the United States Civil Rights Commission, or their respective delegates. The Council shall have the responsibility for developing and implementing agreements, policies and practices designed to maximize effort, promote efficiency, and eliminate conflict, competition, duplication and inconsistency among the operations, functions and jurisdictions of the various departments, agencies and branches of the Federal government responsible for the implementation and enforcement of equal employment opportunity legislation, orders, and policies. On or before July 1 of each year, the Council shall transmit to the President and to the Congress a report of its activities, together with such recommendations for legislative or administrative changes as it concludes are desirable to further promote the purposes of this section.

EFFECTIVE DATE

Sec. 716. (a) This title shall become effective one year after the date of its enactment.

(b) Notwithstanding subsection (a), sections of this title other than sections 703, 704, 706, and 707 shall become effective immediately.

(c) The President shall, as soon as feasible after the enactment of this title, convene one or more conferences for the purpose of enabling the leaders of groups whose members will be affected by this title to become familiar with the rights afforded and obligations imposed by its provisions, and for the purpose of making plans which will result in the fair and effective administration of this title when all of its provisions become effective. The President shall invite the participation in such conference or conferences of (1) the members of the President's Committee on Equal Employment Opportunity, (2) the members of the Commission on Civil Rights, (3) representatives of State and local agencies engaged in furthering equal employment opportunity, (4) representatives of private agencies engaged in furthering equal employment opportunity, and (5) representatives of employers, labor organizations, and employment agencies who will be subject to this title.

NONDISCRIMINATION IN FEDERAL GOVERNMENT EMPLOYMENT

Sec. 717. (a) All personnel actions affecting employees or applicants for employment (except with regard to aliens employed outside the limits of the United States) in military departments as defined in section 102 of title 5, United States Code, in executive agencies (other than the General Accounting Office) as defined in section 105 of title 5, United States Code (including employees and applicants for employment who are paid from nonappropriated funds), in the United States Postal Service and the Postal Rate Commission, in those units of the Government of the District of Columbia having positions in the competitive service, and in those units of the legislative and judicial branches of the Federal Government having positions in the competitive service, and in the Library of Congress shall be made free from any discrimination based on race, color, religion, sex, or national origin.

(b) Except as otherwise provided in this subsection, the Civil Service Commission shall have authority to enforce the provisions of subsection (a) through appropriate remedies, including reinstatement or hiring of employees with or without back pay, as will effectuate the policies of this section, and shall issue such rules, regulations, orders, and instructions as it deems necessary and appropriate to carry out its responsibilities under this section. The Civil Service Commission shall—

(1) be responsible for the annual review and approval of a national and regional equal employment opportunity plan which each department and agency and each appropriate unit referred to in subsection (a) of this section shall submit in order to maintain an affirmative program of equal employment opportunity for all such employees and applicants for employment;

(2) be responsible for the review and evaluation of the operation of all agency equal employment opportunity programs, periodically obtaining and publishing (on at least a semiannual basis) progress reports from each such department, agency, or unit; and

(3) consult with and solicit the recommendations of interested individuals, groups, and organizations relating to equal employment opportunity.

The head of each such department, agency, or unit shall comply with such rules, regulations, orders, and instructions which shall include a provision that an employee or applicant for employment shall be notified of any final action taken on any complaint of discrimination filed by him thereunder. The plan submitted by each department, agency, and unit shall include, but not be limited to—

(1) provision for the establishment of training and education programs designed to provide a maximum opportunity for employees to advance so as to perform at their highest potential; and

(2) a description of the qualifications in terms of training and experience relating to equal employment opportunity for the principal and operating officials of each such department, agency, or unit responsible for carrying out the equal employment opportunity program and of the allocation of personnel and resources proposed by such department, agency, or unit to carry out its equal employment opportunity program.

With respect to employment in the Library of Congress, authorities granted in this subsection to the Civil Service Commission shall be exercised by the Librarian of Congress.

(c) Within thirty days of receipt of notice of final action taken by a department, agency, or unit referred to in subsection 717(a), or by the Civil Service Commission upon an appeal from a decision or order of such department, agency, or unit on a complaint of discrimination based on race, color, religion, sex, or national origin, brought pursuant to subsection (a) of this section, Executive Order 11478 or any succeeding Executive orders, or after one hundred and eighty days from the filing of the initial charge with the department, agency, or unit or with the Civil Service Commission on appeal from a decision or order of such department, agency, or unit until such time as final action may be taken by a department, agency, or unit, an employee or applicant for employment, if aggrieved by the final disposition of his complaint, or by the failure to take final action on his complaint, may file a civil action as provided in section 706, in which civil action the head of the department, agency, or unit, as appropriate, shall be the defendant.

(d) The provisions of section 706(f) through (k), as applicable, shall govern civil actions brought hereunder.

(e) Nothing contained in this Act shall relieve any Government agency or official of its or his primary responsibility to assure nondiscrimination in employment as required by the Constitution and statutes or of its or his responsibilities under Executive Order 11478 relating to equal employment opportunity in the Federal Government.

SPECIAL PROVISIONS WITH RESPECT TO DENIAL, TERMINATION, AND SUSPENSION OF GOVERNMENT CONTRACTS

SEC. 718. No Government contract, or portion thereof, with any employer, shall be denied, withheld, terminated, or suspended, by any agency or officer of the United States under any equal employment opportunity law or order, where such employer has an affirmative action plan which has previously been accepted by the Government for the same facility within the past twelve months without first according such employer full hearing and adjudication under the provisions of title 5, United States Code, section 554, and the following pertinent sections: Provided, That if such employer has deviated substantially from such previously agreed to affirmative action plan, this section shall not apply: Provided further, That for the purposes of this section an affirmative action plan shall be deemed to have been accepted by the Government at the time the appropriate compliance agency has accepted such plan unless within forty-five days thereafter the Office of Federal Contract Compliance has disapproved such plan.

PROVISIONS OF EQUAL EMPLOYMENT OPPORTUNITY ACT OF 1972 WHICH RELATE TO BUT DO NOT AMEND THE CIVIL RIGHTS ACT OF 1964

SEC. 9. (a) Section 5314 of title 5 of the United States Code is amended by adding at the end thereof the following new clause:

"(58) Chairman, Equal Employment Opportunity Commission."

(b) Clause (72) of section 5315 of such title is amended to read as follows:

"(72) Members, Equal Employment Opportunity Commission (4)."

(c) Clause (111) of section 5316 of such title is repealed.

(d) Section 5316 of such title is amended by adding at the end thereof the following new clause:

"(131) General Counsel of the Equal Employment Opportunity Commission."

SEC. 12. Section 5108(c) of title 5, United States Code, is amended by—

(1) striking out the word "and" at the end of paragraph (9);

(2) striking out the period at the end of paragraph (10) and inserting in lieu thereof a semicolon and the word "and"; and

(3) by adding immediately after paragraph (10) the last time it appears therin in the following new paragraph:

"(11) the Chairman of the Equal Employment Opportunity Commission, subject to the standards and procedures prescribed by this chapter, may place an additional ten positions in the Equal Employment Opportunity Commission in GS–16, GS–17, and GS–18 for the purposes of carrying out title VII of the Civil Rights Act of 1964."

SEC. 14. The amendments made by this Act to section 706 of the Civil Rights Act of 1964 shall be applicable with respect to charges pending with the Commission on the date of enactment of this Act and all charges filed thereafter.

○

FRIDAY, AUGUST 25, 1978
PART IV

EQUAL EMPLOYMENT
OPPORTUNITY
COMMISSION

CIVIL SERVICE
COMMISSION

DEPARTMENT OF LABOR

DEPARTMENT OF
JUSTICE

■

ADOPTION BY FOUR AGENCIES
OF UNIFORM GUIDELINES ON
EMPLOYEE SELECTION
PROCEDURES (1978)

315

[6570-06]

Title 29—Labor

CHAPTER XIV—EQUAL EMPLOYMENT OPPORTUNITY COMMISSION

PART 1607—UNIFORM GUIDELINES ON EMPLOYEE SELECTION PROCEDURES (1978)

Title 5—Administrative Personnel

CHAPTER I—CIVIL SERVICE COMMISSION

PART 300—EMPLOYMENT (GENERAL)

Title 28—Judicial Administration

CHAPTER I—DEPARTMENT OF JUSTICE

PART 50—STATEMENTS OF POLICY

Title 41—Public Contracts and Property Management

CHAPTER 60—OFFICE OF FEDERAL CONTRACT COMPLIANCE PROGRAMS, DEPARTMENT OF LABOR

PART 60-3—UNIFORM GUIDELINES ON EMPLOYEE SELECTION PROCEDURES (1978)

Adoption of Employee Selection Procedures

AGENCIES: Equal Employment Opportunity Commission, Civil Service Commission, Department of Justice and Department of Labor.

ACTION: Adoption of uniform guidelines on employee selection procedures as final rules by four agencies.

SUMMARY: This document sets forth the uniform guidelines on employee selection procedures adopted by the Equal Employment Opportunity Commission, Civil Service Commission, Department of Justice, and the Department of Labor. At present two different sets of guidelines exist. The guidelines are intended to establish a uniform Federal position in the area of prohibiting discrimination in employment practices on grounds of race, color, religion, sex, or national origin. Cross reference documents are published at 5 CFR 300.103(c) (Civil Service Commission), 28 CFR 50.14 (Department of Justice), 29 CFR Part 1607 (Equal Employment Opportunity Commission), and 41 CFR Part 60-3 (Department of Labor) elsewhere in this issue.

EFFECTIVE DATE: September 25, 1978.

FOR FURTHER INFORMATION CONTACT:

Doris Wooten, Associate Director, Donald J. Schwartz, Staff Psychologist, Office of Federal Contract Compliance Programs, Room C-3324, Department of Labor, 200 Constitution Avenue NW., Washington, D.C. 20210, 202-523-9426.

Peter C. Robertson, Director, Office of Policy Implementation, Equal Employment Opportunity Commission, 2401 E Street NW., Washington, D.C. 20506, 202-634-7060.

David L. Rose, Chief, Employment Section, Civil Rights Division, Department of Justice, 10th Street and Pennsylvania Avenue NW., Washington, D.C. 20530, 202-739-3831.

A. Diane Graham, Director, Federal Equal Employment Opportunity, Civil Service Commission, 1900 E Street NW., Washington, D.C. 20415, 202-632-4420.

H. Patrick Swygert, General Counsel, Civil Service Commission, 1900 E Street NW., Washington, D.C. 20415, 202-632-4632.

SUPPLEMENTARY INFORMATION:

AN OVERVIEW OF THE 1978 UNIFORM GUIDELINES ON EMPLOYEE SELECTION PROCEDURES

I. BACKGROUND

One problem that confronted the Congress - which adopted the Civil Rights Act of 1964 involved the effect of written preemployment tests on equal employment opportunity. The use of these test scores frequently denied employment to minorities in many cases without evidence that the tests were related to success on the job. Yet employers wished to continue to use such tests as practical tools to assist in the selection of qualified employees. Congress sought to strike a balance which would proscribe discrimination, but otherwise permit the use of tests in the selection of employees. Thus, in title VII, Congress authorized the use of "any professionally developed ability test provided that such test, its administration or action upon the results is not designed, intended or used to discriminate * * *".[1]

At first, some employers contended that, under this section, they could use any test which had been developed by a professional so long as they did not intend to exclude minorities, even if such exclusion was the consequence of the use of the test. In 1966, the Equal Employment Opportunity Commission (EEOC) adopted guidelines to advise employers and other users what the law and good industrial psycholo-

gy practice required.[2] The Department of Labor adopted the same approach in 1968 with respect to tests used by Federal contractors under Executive Order 11246 in a more detailed regulation. The Government's view was that the employer's intent was irrelevant. If tests or other practices had an adverse impact on protected groups, they were unlawful unless they could be justified. To justify a test which screened out a higher proportion of minorities, the employer would have to show that it fairly measured or predicted performance on the job. Otherwise, it would not be considered to be "professionally developed."

In succeeding years, the EEOC and the Department of Labor provided more extensive guidance which elaborated upon these principles and expanded the guidelines to emphasize all selection procedures. In 1971 in *Griggs v. Duke Power Co.*,[3] the Supreme Court announced the principle that employer practices which had an adverse impact on minorities and were not justified by business necessity constituted illegal discrimination under title VII. Congress confirmed this interpretation in the 1972 amendments to title VII. The elaboration of these principles by courts and agencies continued into the mid-1970's,[4] but differences between the EEOC and the other agencies (Justice, Labor, and Civil Service Commission) produced two different sets of guidelines by the end of 1976.

With the advent of the Carter administration in 1977, efforts were intensified to produce a unified government position. The following document represents the result of that effort. This introduction is intended to assist those not familiar with these matters to understand the basic approach of the uniform guidelines. While the guidelines are complex and technical, they are based upon the principles which have been consistently upheld by the courts, the Congress, and the agencies.

The following discussion will cite the sections of the Guidelines which embody these principles.

II. ADVERSE IMPACT

The fundamental principle underlying the guidelines is that employer policies or practices which have an adverse impact on employment opportunities of any race, sex, or ethnic group are illegal under title VII and the Executive order unless justified by business necessity.[3] A selection procedure

---

[1] Section 703(h), 42 U.S.C. 2000e(2)(h).

[1] See 35 U.S.L.W. 2137 (1966).

[2] 401 U.S. 424 (1971).

[4] See, e.g., *Albemarle Paper Co.* v. *Moody*, 422 U.S. 405 (1975).

[3] *Griggs,* note 3, supra; uniform guidelines on employee selection procedures (1978), section 3A. (hereinafter cited by section number only).

which has no adverse impact generally does not violate title VII or the Executive order.[5] This means that an employer may usually avoid the application of the guidelines by use of procedures which have no adverse impact.[7] If adverse impact exists, it must be justified on grounds of business necessity. Normally, this means by validation which demonstrates the relation between the selection procedure and performance on the job.

The guidelines adopt a "rule of thumb" as a practical means of determining adverse impact for use in enforcement proceedings. This rule is known as the "⅘ths" or "80 percent" rule.[8] It is not a legal definition of discrimination, rather it is a practical device to keep the attention of enforcement agencies on serious discrepancies in hire or promotion rates or other employment decisions. To determine whether a selection procedure violates the "⅘ths rule", an employer compares its hiring rates for different groups.[9] But this rule of thumb cannot be applied automatically. An employer who has conducted an extensive recruiting campaign may have a larger than normal pool of applicants, and the "⅘ths rule" might unfairly expose it to enforcement proceedings.[10] On the other hand, an employer's reputation may have discouraged or "chilled" applicants of particular groups from applying because they believed application would be futile. The application of the "⅘ths" rule in that situation would allow an employer to evade scrutiny because of its own discrimination.[11]

III. IS ADVERSE IMPACT TO BE MEASURED BY THE OVERALL PROCESS?

In recent years some employers have eliminated the overall adverse impact of a selection procedure and employed sufficient numbers of minorities or women to meet this "⅘th's rule of thumb". However, they might continue use of a component which does have an adverse impact. For example, an employer might insist on a minimum passing score on a written test which is not job related and which has an adverse impact on minorities.[12] However, the employer might compensate for this adverse impact by hiring a sufficient proportion of minorities who do meet its standards, so that its overall hiring is on a par with or higher than the applicant flow. Employers have argued that as long as their "bottom line" shows no overall

adverse impact, there is no violation at all, regardless of the operation of a particular component of the process.

Employee representatives have argued that rights under equal employment opportunity laws are individual, and the fact that an employer has hired some minorities does not justify discrimination against other minorities. Therefore, they argue that adverse impact is to be determined by examination of each component of the selection procedure, regardless of the "bottom line." This question has not been answered definitively by the courts. There are decisions pointing in both directions.

These guidelines do not address the underlying question of law. They discuss only the exercise of prosecutorial discretion by the Government agencies themselves.[13] The agencies have decided that, generally, their resources to combat discrimination should be used against those respondents whose practices have restricted or excluded the opportunities of minorities and women. If an employer is appropriately including all groups in the workforce, it is not sensible to spend Government time and effort on such a case, when there are so many employers whose practices do have adverse effects which should be challenged. For this reason, the guidelines provide that, in considering whether to take enforcement action, the Government will take into account the general posture of the employer concerning equal employment opportunity, including its affirmative action plan and results achieved under the plan.[14] There are some circumstances where the government may intervene even though the "bottom line" has been satisfied. They include the case where a component of a selection procedure restricts promotional opportunities of minorities or women who were discriminatorily assigned to jobs, and where a component, such as a height requirement, has been declared unlawful in other situations.[15]

What of the individual who is denied the job because of a particular component in a procedure which otherwise meets the "bottom line" standard? The individual retains the right to proceed through the appropriate agencies, and into Federal court.[16]

IV. WHERE ADVERSE IMPACT EXISTS: THE BASIC OPTIONS

Once an employer has established that there is adverse impact, what

steps are required by the guidelines? As previously noted, the employer can modify or eliminate the procedure which produces the adverse impact, thus taking the selection procedure from the coverage of these guidelines. If the employer does not do that, then it must justify the use of the procedure on grounds of "business necessity."[17] This normally means that it must show a clear relation between performance on the selection procedure and performance on the job. In the language of industrial psychology, the employer must validate the selection procedure. Thus the bulk of the guidelines consist of the Government's interpretation of standards for validation.

V. VALIDATION: CONSIDERATION OF ALTERNATIVES

The concept of validation as used in personnel psychology involves the establishment of the relationship between a test instrument or other selection procedure and performance on the job. Federal equal employment opportunity law has added a requirement to the process of validation. In conducting a validation study, the employer should consider available alternatives which will achieve its legitimate business purpose with lesser adverse impact.[18] The employer cannot concentrate solely on establishing the validity of the instrument or procedure which it has been using in the past.

This same principle of using the alternative with lesser adverse impact is applicable to the manner in which an employer uses a valid selection procedure.[19] The guidelines assume that there are at least three ways in which an employer can use scores on a selection procedure: (1) To screen out of consideration those who are not likely to be able to perform the job successfully; (2) to group applicants in accordance with the likelihood of their successful performance on the job, and (3) to rank applicants, selecting those with the highest scores for employment.[20]

The setting of a "cutoff score" to determine who will be screened out may have an adverse impact. If so, an employer is required to justify the initial cutoff score by reference to its need for a trustworthy and efficient work force.[21] Similarly, use of results for

---

[5] *Furnco v. Waters*, 98 S.Ct. 2943 (1978).
[6] Section 6.
[7] Section 4D.
[8] Section 16R (definition of selection rate).
[10] *Ibid* (user's actions have discouraged applicants).
[11] *Ibid* (special recruiting programs).
[12] See, e.g., *Griggs v. Duke Power Co.*, 401 U.S. 424 (1971).

[13] Section 4C.
[14] Section 4E.
[15] Section 4C.
[16] The processing of individual cases is excluded from the operation of the bottom line concept by the definition of "enforcement action," section 16I. Under section 4C, where adverse impact has existed, the employer must keep records of the effect of each component for 2 years after the adverse effect has dissipated.

[17] A few practices may be used without validation even if they have adverse impact. See, e.g., *McDonnell Douglas v. Green*, 411 U.S. 792 (1973) and section 6B.
[18] *Albermarle Paper Co. v. Moody*, 422 U.S. 405 (1975); *Robinson v. Lorillard Corp.*, 444 F. 2d 791 (4th Cir. 1971).
[19] Sections 3B; 5G.
[20] *Ibid.*
[21] See sections 3B; 5H. See also sections 14B(6) (criterion-related validity); 14C(9) (content validity); 14D(1) (construct validity).

grouping or for rank ordering is likely to have a greater adverse effect than use of scores solely to screen out unqualified candidates. If the employer chooses to use a rank order method, the evidence of validity must be sufficient to justify that method of use.[22]

VI. TESTING FOR HIGHER LEVEL JOBS

Normally, employers test for the job for which people are hired. However, there are situations where the first job is temporary or transient, and the workers who remain are promoted to work which involves more complex activities. The guidelines restrict testing for higher level jobs to users who promote a majority of the employees who remain with them to the higher level job within a reasonable period of time.[23]

VII. HOW IS VALIDATION TO BE CONDUCTED

Validation has become highly technical and complex, and yet is constantly changing as a set of concepts in industrial psychology. What follows here is a simple introduction to a highly complex field. There are three concepts which can be used to validate a selection procedure. These concepts reflect different approaches to investigating the job relatedness of selection procedures and may be interrelated in practice. They are (1) criterion-related validity,[24] (2) content validity,[25] and (3) construct validity.[26] In criterion-related validity, a selection procedure is justified by a statistical relationship between scores on the test or other selection procedure and measures of job performance. In content validity, a selection procedure is justified by showing that it representatively samples significant parts of the job, such as a typing test for a typist. Construct validity involves identifying the psychological trait (the construct) which underlies successful performance on the job and then devising a selection procedure to measure the presence and degree of the construct. An example would be a test of "leadership ability."

The guidelines contain technical standards and documentation requirements for the application of each of the three approaches.[27] One of the problems which the guidelines attempt to meet is the "borderline" be-

tween "content validity" and "construct validity." The extreme cases are easy to understand. A secretary, for example, may have to type. Many jobs require the separation of important matters which must be handled immediately from those which can be handled routinely. For the typing function, a typing test is appropriate. It is justifiable on the basis of content validity because it is a sample of an important or critical part of the job. The second function can be viewed as involving a capability to exercise selective judgment in light of the surrounding circumstances, a mental process which is difficult to sample.

In addressing this situation, the guidelines attempt to make it practical to validate the typing test by a content strategy,[28] but do not allow the validation of a test measuring a construct such as "judgment" by a content validity strategy.

The bulk of the guidelines deals with questions such as those discussed in the above paragraphs. Not all such questions can be answered simply, nor can all problems be addressed in the single document. Once the guidelines are issued, they will have to be interpreted in light of changing factual, legal, and professional circumstances.

VIII. SIMPLIFICATION OF REPORTING AND RECORDKEEPING REQUIREMENTS

The reporting and recordkeeping provisions which appeared in the December 30 draft which was published for comment have been carefully reviewed in light of comments received and President Carter's direction to limit paperwork burdens on those regulated by Government to the minimum necessary for effective regulation. As a result of this review, two major changes have been made in the documentation requirements of the guidelines:

(1) A new section 15A(1) provides a simplified recordkeeping option for employers with fewer than 100 employees;

(2) Determinations of the adverse impact of selection procedures need not be made for groups which constitute less than 2 percent of the relevant labor force.

Also, the draft has been changed to make clear that users can assess adverse impact on an annual basis rather than on a continuing basis.

Analysis of comments. The uniform guidelines published today are based upon the proposition that the Federal Government should speak to the public and to those whom it regulates with one voice on this important subject; and that the Federal Government ought to impose upon itself obligations for equal employment opportunity which are at least as demanding as

those it seeks to impose on others. These guidelines state a uniform Federal position on this subject, and are intended to protect the rights created by title VII of the Civil Rights Act of 1964, as amended, Executive Order 11246, as amended, and other provisions of Federal law. The uniform guidelines are also intended to represent "professionally acceptable methods" of the psychological profession for demonstrating whether a selection procedure validly predicts or measures performance for a particular job. *Albemarle Paper Co.* v. *Moody,* 442 U.S. 405, 425. They are also intended to be consistent with the decisions of the Supreme Court and authoritative decisions of other appellate courts.

Although the development of these guidelines preceded the issuance by President Jimmy Carter of Executive Order 12044 designed to improve the regulatory process, the spirit of his Executive order was followed in their development. Initial agreement among the Federal agencies was reached early in the fall of 1977, and the months from October 1977 until today have been spent in extensive consultation with civil rights groups whose clientele are protected by these guidelines; employers, labor unions, and State and local governments whose employment practices are affected by these guidelines; State and local government antidiscrimination agencies who share with the Federal Government enforcement responsibility for discriminatory practices; and appropriate members of the general public. For example, an earlier draft of these guidelines was circulated informally for comment on October 28, 1977, pursuant to OMB Circular A-85. Many comments were received from representatives of State and local governments, psychologists, private employers, labor organizations, civil rights groups, the American Psychological Association and components thereof, and many individual employers, psychologists, and personnel specialists. On March 3, 1978, notice was given of a public hearing and meeting to be held on April 10, 1978, 43 FR 9131. After preliminary review of the comments, the agencies identified four issues of particular interest, and invited testimony particularly on those issues, 43 FR 11812 (March 21, 1978). In the same notice the agencies published questions and answers on four

---

[22] Sections 5G, 14B(6); 14C(9); 14D(1).

[23] Section 5I.

[24] Sections 5B, (General Standards); 14B (Technical Standards); 15B (Documentation); 16F (Definition).

[25] Sections 5B (General Standards); 14C (Technical Standards); 15C (Documentation); 16D (Definition).

[26] Sections 5B (General Standards); 14D (Technical Standards); 15D (Documentation); 16E (Definition).

[27] Technical standards are in section 14; documentation requirements are in section 15.

[28] Section 14C.

issues of concern to the commenters. The questions and answers were designed to clarify the intent of the December 30, 1977, draft, so as to provide a sharper focus for the testimony at the hearing.

At a full day of testimony on April 10, 1978, representatives of private industry, State and local governments, labor organizations, and civil rights groups, as well as psychologists, personnel specialists, and others testified at the public hearing and meeting. The written comments, testimony, and views expressed in subsequent informal consultations have been carefully considered by the four agencies. We set forth below a summary of the comments, and the major issues raised in the comments and testimony, and attempt to explain how we have resolved those issues.

The statement submitted by the American Psychological Association (A.P.A.) stated that "these guidelines represent a major step forward and with careful interpretation can provide a sound basis for concerned professional work." Most of the A.P.A. comments were directed to clarification and interpretation of the present language of the proposal. However, the A.P.A. recommended substantive change in the construct validity section and in the definition of work behavior.

Similarly, the Division of Industrial and Organizational Psychology (division 14) of the A.P.A. described the technical standards of the guidelines as "superior" in terms of congruence with professional standards to "most previous orders and guidelines but numerous troublesome aspects remain." Division 14 had substantial concerns with a number of the provisions of the general principles of the draft.

Civil rights groups generally found the uniform guidelines far superior to the FEA guidelines, and many urged their adoption, with modifications concerning ranking and documentation. Others raised concerns about the "bottom line" concept and other provisions of the guidelines.

The Ad Hoc Group on Employee Selection Procedures representing many employers in private industry supported the concept of uniform guidelines, but had a number of problems with particular provisions, some of which are described below. The American Society for Personnel Administration (ASPA) and the International Personnel Management Association, which represents State and local governments, generally took the same position as the ad hoc group. Major industrial unions found that the draft guidelines were superior to the FEA guidelines, but they perceived them to be inferior to the EEOC guidelines. They challenged particularly the

bottom line concept and the construct validity section.

The building trade unions urged an exclusion of apprenticeship programs from coverage of the guidelines. The American Council on Education found them inappropriate for employment decisions concerning faculty at institutions of higher education. Other particular concerns were articulated by organizations representing the handicapped, licensing and certifying agencies, and college placement offices.

General Principles

1. *Relationship between validation and elimination of adverse impact, and affirmative action.* Federal equal employment opportunity law generally does not require evidence of validity for a selection procedure if there is no adverse impact; e.g., *Griggs v. Duke Power Co.,* 401 U.S. 424. Therefore, a user has the choice of complying either by providing evidence of validity (or otherwise justifying use in accord with Federal law), or by eliminating the adverse impact. These options have always been present under Federal law, 29 CFR 1607.3; 41 CFR 60-3.3(a); and the Federal Executive Agency Guidelines, 41 FR 51734 (November 23, 1976). The December 30 draft guidelines, however, clarified the nature of the two options open to users.

Psychologists expressed concern that the December 30 draft of section 6A encouraged the use of invalid procedures as long as there is no adverse impact. Employers added the concern that the section might encourage the use of illegal procedures not having an adverse impact against the groups who have historically suffered discrimination (minorities, women), even if they have an adverse impact on a different group (whites, males).

Section 6A was not so intended, and we have revised it to clarify the fact that illegal acts purporting to be affirmative action are not the goal of the agencies or of the guidelines; and that any employee selection procedure must be lawful and should be as job related as possible. The delineation of examples of alternative procedures was eliminated to avoid the implication that particular procedures are either prescribed or are necessarily appropriate. The basic thrust of section 6A, that elimination of adverse impact is an alternative to validation, is retained.

The inclusion of excerpts from the 1976 Equal Employment Opportunity Coordinating Council Policy Statement on Affirmative Action in section 13B of the December 30 draft was criticized as not belonging in a set of guidelines for the validation of selection procedures. Section 13 has been revised. The general statement of

policy in support of voluntary affirmative action, and the reaffirmation of the policy statement have been retained, but this statement is now found in the appendix to the guidelines.

2. *The "bottom line" (section 4C).* The guidelines provide that when the overall selection process does not have an adverse impact the Government will usually not examine the individual components of that process for adverse impact or evidence of validity. The concept is based upon the view that the Federal Government should not generally concern itself with individual components of a selection process, if the overall effect of that process is nonexclusionary. Many commenters criticized the ambiguity caused by the word "generally" in the December 30 draft of section 4C which provided, "the Federal enforcement agencies * * * generally will not take enforcement action based upon adverse impact of any component" of a process that does not have an overall adverse impact. Employer groups stated the position that the "bottom line" should be a rule prohibiting enforcement action by Federal agencies with respect to all or any part of a selection process where the bottom line does not show adverse impact. Civil rights and some labor union representatives expressed the opposing concerns that the concept may be too restrictive, that it may be interpreted as a matter of law, and that it might allow certain discriminatory conditions to go unremedied.

The guidelines have been revised to clarify the intent that the bottom line concept is based upon administrative and prosecutorial discretion. The Federal agencies cannot accept the recommendation that they never inquire into or take enforcement action with respect to any component procedure unless the whole process of which it is a part has an adverse impact. The Federal enforcement agencies believe that enforcement action may be warranted in unusual circumstances, such as those involving other discriminatory practices, or particular selection procedures which have no validity and have a clear adverse impact on a national basis. Other unusual circumstances may warrant a high level agency decision to proceed with enforcement actions although the "bottom line" has been satisfied. At the same time the agencies adhere to the bottom line concept of allocating resources primarily to those users whose overall selection processes have an adverse impact. See overview, above, part III.

3. *Investigation of alternative selection procedures and alternative methods of use (section 3B).* The December 30 draft included an obligation on the user, when conducting a validity

study, to investigate alternative procedures and uses, in order to determine whether there are other procedures which are substantially equally valid, but which have less adverse impact. The American Psychological Association stated:

"We would concur with the drafters of the guidelines that it is appropriate in the determination of a selection strategy to consider carefully a variety of possible procedures and to think carefully about the question of adverse impact with respect to each of these procedures. Nevertheless, we feel it appropriate to note that a rigid enforcement of these sections, particularly for smaller employers, would impose a substantial and expensive burden on these employers."

Since a reasonable consideration of alternatives is consistent with the underlying principle of minimizing adverse impact consistent with business needs, the provision is retained.

Private employer representatives challenged earlier drafts of these guidelines as being inconsistent with the decision of the Supreme Court in *Albemarle Paper Co.* v. *Moody*, 422 U.S. 405. No such inconsistency was intended. Accordingly, the first sentence of section 3B was revised to paraphrase the opinion in the *Albemarle* decision, so as to make it clear that section 3B is in accord with the principles of the *Albemarle* decision.

Section 3B was further revised to clarify the intent of the guidelines that the obligation to investigate alternative procedures is a part of conducting a validity study, so that alternative procedures should be evaluated in light of validity studies meeting professional standards, and that section 3B does not impose an obligation to search for alternatives if the user is not required to conduct a validity study.

Just as, under section 3B of the guidelines, a user should investigate alternative selection procedures as a part of choosing and validating a procedure, so should the user investigate alternative uses of the selection device chosen to find the use most appropriate to his needs. The validity study should address the question of what method of use (screening, grouping, or rank ordering) is appropriate for a procedure based on the kind and strength of the validity evidence shown, and the degree of adverse impact of the different uses.

4. *Establishment of cutoff scores and rank ordering.* Some commenters from civil rights groups believed that the December 30 draft guidelines did not provide sufficient guidance as to when it was permissible to use a selection procedure on a ranking basis rather than on a pass-fail basis. They also objected to section 5G in terms of setting cutoff scores. Other comments noted a lack of clarity as to how the determi-

nation of a cutoff score or the use of a procedure for ranking candidates relates to adverse impact.

As we have noted, users are not required to validate procedures which do not have an adverse impact. However, if one way of using a procedure (e.g., for ranking) results in greater adverse impact than another way (e.g., pass/ fail), the procedure must be validated for that use. Similarly, cutoff scores which result in adverse impact should be justified. If the use of a validated procedure for ranking results in greater adverse impact than its use as a screening device, the evidence of validity and utility must be sufficient to warrant use of the procedures as a ranking device.

A new section 5G has been added to clarify these concepts. Section 5H (formerly section 5G) addresses the choice of a cutoff score when a procedure is to be used for ranking.

5. *Scope: Requests for exemptions for certain classes of users.* Some employer groups and labor organizations (e.g., academic institutions, large public employers, apprenticeship councils) argued that they should be exempted from all or some of the provisions of these guidelines because of their special needs. The intent of Congress as expressed in Federal equal employment opportunity law is to apply the same standards to all users, public and private.

These guidelines apply the same principles and standards to all employers. On the other hand, the nature of the procedures which will actually meet those principles and standards may be different for different employers, and the guidelines recognize that fact. Accordingly, the guidelines are applicable to all employers and other users who are covered by Federal equal employment opportunity law.

Organizations of handicapped persons objected to excluding from the scope of these guidelines the enforcement of laws prohibiting discrimination on the basis of handicap, in particular the Rehabilitation Act of 1973, sections 501, 503, and 504. While this issue has not been addressed in the guidelines, nothing precludes the adoption of the principles set forth in these guidelines for other appropriate situations.

Licensing and certification boards raised the question of the applicability of the guidelines to their licensing and certification functions. The guidelines make it clear that licensing and certification are covered "to the extent" that licensing and certification may be covered by Federal equal employment opportunity law.

Voluntary certification boards, where certification is not required by law, are not users as defined in section 16 with respect to their certifying

functions and therefore are not subject to these guidelines. If an employer relies upon such certification in making employment decisions, the employer is the user and must be prepared to justify, under Federal law, that reliance as it would any other selection procedure.

6. *The "Four-Fifths Rule of Thumb"* *(section 4D).* Some representatives of employers and some professionals suggest that the basic test for adverse impact should be a test of statistical significance, rather than the four-fifths rule. Some civil rights groups, on the other hand, still regard the four-fifths rule as permitting some unlawful discrimination.

The Federal agencies believe that neither of these positions is correct. The great majority of employers do not hire, promote, or assign enough employees for most jobs to warrant primary reliance upon statistical significance. Many decisions in day-to-day life are made on the basis of information which does not have the justification of a test of statistical significance. Courts have found adverse impact without a showing of statistical significance. *Griggs* v. *Duke Power Co.*, supra; *Vulcan Society of New York* v. *CSC of N.Y.*, 490 F. 2d 387, 393 (2d Cir. 1973); *Kirkland* v. *New York St. Dept. of Corr. Serv.*, 520 F. 2d 420, 425 (2d Cir. 1975).

Accordingly, the undersigned believe that while the four-fifths rule does not define discrimination and does not apply in all cases, it is appropriate as a rule of thumb in identifying adverse impact.

Technical Standards

7. *Criterion-related validity (section 14B).* This section of the guidelines found general support among the commenters from the psychological profession and, except for the provisions concerning test fairness (sometimes mistakenly equated with differential prediction or differential validity), generated relatively little comment.

The provisions of the guidelines concerning criterion-related validity studies call for studies of fairness of selection procedures where technically feasible.

Section 14B(8). Some psychologists and employer groups objected that the concept of test fairness or unfairness has been discredited by professionals and pointed out that the term is commonly misused. We recognize that there is serious debate on the question of test fairness; however, it is accepted professionally that fairness should be examined where feasible. The A.P.A. standards for educational and psychological tests, for example, direct users to explore the question of fairness on finding a difference in group performances (section E9, pp. 43-44). Similarly the concept of test fairness is one which is closely related to the basic thrust of Federal equal employment opportunity law; and that concept was endorsed by the Supreme Court in *Albemarle Paper Co. v. Moody*, 422 U.S. 405.

Accordingly, we have retained in the guidelines the obligation upon users to investigate test fairness where it is technically feasible to do so.

8. *Content validity.* The Division of Industrial and Organizational Psychology of A.P.A. correctly perceived that the provisions of the draft guidelines concerning content validity, with their emphasis on observable work behaviors or work products, were "greatly concerned with minimizing the inferential leap between test and performance." That division expressed the view that the draft guidelines neglected situations where a knowledge, skill or ability is necessary to an outcome but where the work behavior cannot be replicated in a test. They recommended that the section be revised.

We believe that the emphasis on observable work behaviors or observable work products is appropriate; and that in order to show content validity, the gap between the test and performance on the job should be a small one. We recognize, however, that content validity may be appropriate to support a test which measures a knowledge, skill, or ability which is a necessary prerequisite to the performance of the job, even though the test might not be close enough to the work behavior to be considered a work sample, and the guidelines have been revised appropriately. On the other hand, tests of mental processes which are not directly observable and which may be difficult to determine on the basis of observable work behaviors or work products should not be supported by content validity.

Thus, the Principles for the Validation and Use of Personnel Selection Procedures (Division of Industrial and Organizational Psychology, American Psychological Association, 1975, p. 10), discuss the use of content validity to support tests of "specific items of knowledge, or specific job skills," but call attention to the inappropriateness of attempting to justify tests for traits or constructs on a content validity basis.

9. *Construct validity (section 14D).* Business groups and professionals expressed concern that the construct validity requirements in the December 30 draft were confusing and technically inaccurate. As section 14D indicates, construct validity is a relatively new procedure in the field of personnel selection and there is not yet substantial guidance in the professional literature as to its use in the area of employment practices. The provisions on construct

validity have been revised to meet the concerns expressed by the A.P.A. The construct validity section as revised clarifies what is required by the Federal enforcement agencies at this stage in the development of construct validity. The guidelines leave open the possibility that different evidence of construct validity may be accepted in the future, as new methodologies develop and become incorporated in professional standards and other professional literature.

10. *Documentation (section 15).* Commenters stated that the documentation section did not conform to the technical requirements of the guidelines or was otherwise inadequate. Section 15 has been clarified and two significant changes have been made to minimize the recordkeeping burden. (See overview, part VIII.)

11. *Definitions (section 16).* The definition of work behavior in the December 30, 1977 draft was criticized by the A.P.A. and others as being too vague to provide adequate guidance to those using the guidelines who must identify work behavior as a part of any validation technique. Other comments criticized the absence or inadequacies of other definitions, expecially "adverse impact." Substantial revisions of and additions to this section were therefore made.

UNIFORM GUIDELINES ON EMPLOYEE SELECTION PROCEDURES (1978)

NOTE.—These guidelines are issued jointly by four agencies. Separate official adoptions follow the guidelines in this part IV as follows: Civil Service Commission, Department of Justice, Equal Employment Opportunity Commission, Department of Labor.

For official citation see section 18 of these guidelines.

TABLE OF CONTENTS

GENERAL PRINCIPLES

SECTION 1. *Statement of purpose.*—A. *Need for uniformity—Issuing agencies.* The Federal government's need for a uniform set of principles on the question of the use of tests and other selection procedures has long been recognized. The Equal Employment Opportunity Commission, the Civil Service Commission, the Department of Labor, and the Department of Justice jointly have adopted these uniform guidelines to meet that need, and to apply the same principles to the Federal Government as are applied to other employers.

B. *Purpose of guidelines.* These guidelines incorporate a single set of principles which are designed to assist employers, labor organizations, employment agencies, and licensing and certification boards to comply with requirements of Federal law prohibiting employment practices which discriminate on grounds of race, color, religion, sex, and national origin. They are designed to provide a framework for determining the proper use of tests and other selection procedures. These guidelines do not require a user to conduct validity studies of selection procedures where no adverse impact results. However, all users are encouraged to use selection procedures which are valid, especially users operating under merit principles.

C. *Relation to prior guidelines.* These guidelines are based upon and supersede previously issued guidelines on employee selection procedures. These guidelines have been built upon court decisions, the previously issued guidelines of the agencies, and the practical experience of the agencies, as well as the standards of the psychological profession. These guidelines are intended to be consistent with existing law.

SEC. 2. *Scope.*—A. *Application of guidelines.* These guidelines will be applied by the Equal Employment Opportunity Commission in the enforcement of title VII of the Civil Rights Act of 1964, as amended by the Equal Employment Opportunity Act of 1972 (hereinafter "Title VII"); by the Department of Labor, and the contract compliance agencies until the transfer of authority contemplated by the President's Reorganization Plan No. 1 of 1978, in the administration and enforcement of Executive Order 11246, as amended by Executive Order 11375 (hereinafter "Executive Order 11246"); by the Civil Service Commission and other Federal agencies subject to section 717 of Title VII; by the Civil Service Commission in exercising its responsibilities toward State and local governments under section 208(b)(1) of the Intergovernmental-Personnel Act; by the Department of Justice in exercising its responsibilities under Federal law; by the Office of Revenue Sharing of the Department of the Treasury under the State and Local Fiscal Assistance Act of 1972, as amended; and by any other Federal agency which adopts them.

B. *Employment decisions.* These guidelines apply to tests and other selection procedures which are used as a basis for any employment decision. Employment decisions include but are not limited to hiring, promotion, demotion, membership (for example, in a labor organization), referral, retention, and licensing and certification, to the extent that licensing and certification may be covered by Federal equal employment opportunity law. Other selection decisions, such as selection for training or transfer, may also be considered employment decisions if they lead to any of the decisions listed above.

C. *Selection procedures.* These guidelines apply only to selection procedures which are used as a basis for making employment decisions. For example, the use of recruiting procedures designed to attract members of a particular race, sex, or ethnic group, which were previously denied employment opportunities or which are currently underutilized, may be necessary to bring an employer into compliance with Federal law, and is frequently an essential element of any effective affirmative action program; but recruitment practices are not considered by these guidelines to be selection procedures. Similarly, these guidelines do not pertain to the question of the lawfulness of a seniority system within the meaning of section 703(h), Executive Order 11246 or other provisions of Federal law or regulation, except to the extent that such systems utilize selection procedures to determine qualifications or abilities to perform the job. Nothing in these guidelines is intended or should be interpreted as discouraging the use of a selection procedure for the purpose of determining qualifications or for the purpose of selection on the basis of relative qualifications, if the selection procedure had been validated in accord with these guidelines for each such purpose for which it is to be used.

D. *Limitations.* These guidelines apply only to persons subject to Title VII, Executive Order 11246, or other equal employment opportunity requirements of Federal law. These guidelines do not apply to responsibilities under the Age Discrimination in Employment Act of 1967, as amended, not to discriminate on the basis of age, or under sections 501, 503, and 504 of the Rehabilitation Act of 1973, not to discriminate on the basis of handicap.

E. *Indian preference not affected.* These guidelines do not restrict any obligation imposed or right granted by Federal law to users to extend a preference in employment to Indians living on or near an Indian reservation in connection with employment opportunities on or near an Indian reservation.

SEC. 3. *Discrimination defined: Relationship between use of selection procedures and discrimination.—A. Procedure having adverse impact constitutes discrimination unless justified.* The use of any selection procedure which has an adverse impact on the hiring, promotion, or other employment or membership opportunities of members of any race, sex, or ethnic group will be considered to be discriminatory and inconsistent with these guidelines, unless the procedure has been validated in accordance with these guidelines, or the provisions of section 6 below are satisfied.

B. *Consideration of suitable alternative selection procedures.* Where two or more selection procedures are available which serve the user's legitimate interest in efficient and trustworthy workmanship, and which are substantially equally valid for a given purpose, the user should use the procedure which has been demonstrated to have the lesser adverse impact. Accordingly, whenever a validity study is called for by these guidelines, the user should include, as a part of the validity study, an investigation of suitable

alternative selection procedures and suitable alternative methods of using the selection procedure which have as little adverse impact as possible, to determine the appropriateness of using or validating them in accord with these guidelines. If a user has made a reasonable effort to become aware of such alternative procedures and validity has been demonstrated in accord with these guidelines, the use of the test or other selection procedure may continue until such time as it should reasonably be reviewed for currency. Whenever the user is shown an alternative selection procedure with evidence of less adverse impact and substantial evidence of validity for the same job in similar circumstances, the user should investigate it to determine the appropriateness of using or validating it in accord with these guidelines. This subsection is not intended to preclude the combination of procedures into a significantly more valid procedure, if the use of such a combination has been shown to be in compliance with the guidelines.

SEC. 4. *Information on impact.—A. Records concerning impact.* Each user should maintain and have available for inspection records or other information which will disclose the impact which its tests and other selection procedures have upon employment opportunities of persons by identifiable race, sex, or ethnic group as set forth in subparagraph B below in order to determine compliance with these guidelines. Where there are large numbers of applicants and procedures are administered frequently, such information may be retained on a sample basis, provided that the sample is appropriate in terms of the applicant population and adequate in size.

B. *Applicable race, sex, and ethnic groups for recordkeeping.* The records called for by this section are to be maintained by sex, and the following races and ethnic groups: Blacks (Negroes), American Indians (including Alaskan Natives), Asians (including Pacific Islanders), Hispanic (including persons of Mexican, Puerto Rican, Cuban, Central or South American, or other Spanish origin or culture regardless of race), whites (Caucasians) other than Hispanic, and totals. The race, sex, and ethnic classifications called for by this section are consistent with the Equal Employment Opportunity Standard Form 100, Employer Information Report EEO-1 series of reports. The user should adopt safeguards to insure that the records required by this paragraph are used for appropriate purposes such as determining adverse impact, or (where required) for developing and monitoring affirmative action programs, and that such records are not used improperly. See sections 4E and 17(4), below.

C. *Evaluation of selection rates. The "bottom line."* If the information called for by sections 4A and B above shows that the total selection process for a job has an adverse impact, the individual components of the selection process should be evaluated for adverse impact. If this information shows that the total selection process does not have an adverse impact, the Federal enforcement agencies, in the exercise of their administrative and prosecutorial discretion, in usual circumstances, will not expect a user to evaluate the individual components for adverse impact, or to validate such individual components, and will not take enforcement action based upon adverse impact of any component of that process, including the separate parts of a multipart selection procedure or any separate procedure that is used as an alternative method of selection. However, in the following circumstances the Federal enforcement agencies will expect a user to evaluate the individual components for adverse impact and may, where appropriate, take enforcement action with respect to the individual components: (1) where the selection procedure is a significant factor in the continuation of patterns of assignments of incumbent employees caused by prior discriminatory employment practices, (2) where the weight of court decisions or administrative interpretations hold that a specific procedure (such as height or weight requirements or no-arrest records) is not job related in the same or similar circumstances. In unusual circumstances, other than those listed in (1) and (2) above, the Federal enforcement agencies may request a user to evaluate the individual components for adverse impact and may, where appropriate, take enforcement action with respect to the individual component.

D. *Adverse impact and the "four-fifths rule."* A selection rate for any race, sex, or ethnic group which is less than four-fifths (⅘) (or eighty percent) of the rate for the group with the highest rate will generally be regarded by the Federal enforcement agencies as evidence of adverse impact, while a greater than four-fifths rate will generally not be regarded by Federal enforcement agencies as evidence of adverse impact. Smaller differences in selection rate may nevertheless constitute adverse impact, where they are significant in both statistical and practical terms or where a user's actions have discouraged applicants disproportionately on grounds of race, sex, or ethnic group. Greater differences in selection rate may not constitute adverse impact where the differences are based on small numbers and are not statistically significant, or where special recruiting or other programs cause the pool of minority or female candidates to be atypical of the normal pool of applicants from that group. Where the user's evidence concerning the impact of a selection procedure indicates adverse impact but is based upon numbers which are too small to be reliable, evidence concerning the impact of the procedure over a longer period of time and/or evidence concerning the impact which the selection procedure had when used in the same manner in similar circumstances elsewhere may be considered in determining adverse impact. Where the user has not maintained data on adverse impact as required by the documentation section of applicable guidelines, the Federal enforcement agencies may draw an inference of adverse impact of the selection process from the failure of the user to maintain such data, if the user has an underutilization of a group in the job category, as compared to the group's representation in the relevant labor market or, in the case of jobs filled from within, the applicable work force.

E. *Consideration of user's equal employment opportunity posture.* In carrying out their obligations, the Federal enforcement agencies will consider the general posture of the user with respect to equal employment opportunity for the job or group of jobs in question. Where a user has adopted an affirmative action program, the Federal enforcement agencies will consider the provisions of that program, including the goals and timetables which the user has adopted and the progress which the user has made in carrying out that program and in meeting the goals and timetables. While such affirmative action programs may in design and execution be race, color, sex, or ethnic conscious, selection procedures under such programs should be based upon the ability or relative ability to do the work.

SEC. 5. *General standards for validity studies.—A. Acceptable types of validity studies.* For the purposes of satisfying these guidelines, users may rely upon criterion-related validity studies, content validity studies or construct validity studies, in accordance with the standards set forth in the technical standards of these guidelines, section 14 below. New strategies for showing the validity of selection procedures will be evaluated as they become accepted by the psychological profession.

B. *Criterion-related, content, and construct validity.* Evidence of the validity of a test or other selection procedure by a criterion-related validity study should consist of empirical data demonstrating that the selection procedure is predictive of or significantly correlated with important elements of job performance. See section 14B

below. Evidence of the validity of a test or other selection procedure by a content validity study should consist of data showing that the content of the selection procedure is representative of important aspects of performance on the job for which the candidates are to be evaluated. See section 14C below. Evidence of the validity of a test or other selection procedure through a construct validity study should consist of data showing that the procedure measures the degree to which candidates have identifiable characteristics which have been determined to be important in successful performance in the job for which the candidates are to be evaluated. See section 14D below.

C. *Guidelines are consistent with professional standards.* The provisions of these guidelines relating to validation of selection procedures are intended to be consistent with generally accepted professional standards for evaluating standardized tests and other selection procedures, such as those described in the Standards for Educational and Psychological Tests prepared by a joint committee of the American Psychological Association, the American Educational Research Association, and the National Council on Measurement in Education (American Psychological Association, Washington, D.C., 1974) (hereinafter "A.P.A. Standards") and standard textbooks and journals in the field of personnel selection.

D. *Need for documentation of validity.* For any selection procedure which is part of a selection process which has an adverse impact and which selection procedure has an adverse impact, each user should maintain and have available such documentation as is described in section 15 below.

E. *Accuracy and standardization.* Validity studies should be carried out under conditions which assure insofar as possible the adequacy and accuracy of the research and the report. Selection procedures should be administered and scored under standardized conditions.

F. *Caution against selection on basis of knowledges, skills, or ability learned in brief orientation period.* In general, users should avoid making employment decisions on the basis of measures of knowledges, skills, or abilities which are normally learned in a brief orientation period, and which have an adverse impact.

G. *Method of use of selection procedures.* The evidence of both the validity and utility of a selection procedure should support the method the user chooses for operational use of the procedure, if that method of use has a greater adverse impact than another method of use. Evidence which may be sufficient to support the use of a selec-

tion procedure on a pass/fail (screening) basis may be insufficient to support the use of the same procedure on a ranking basis under these guidelines. Thus, if a user decides to use a selection procedure on a ranking basis, and that method of use has a greater adverse impact than use on an appropriate pass/fail basis (see section 5H below), the user should have sufficient evidence of validity and utility to support the use on a ranking basis. See sections 3B, 14B (5) and (6), and 14C (5) and (9).

H. *Cutoff scores.* Where cutoff scores are used, they should normally be set so as to be reasonable and consistent with normal expectations of acceptable proficiency within the work force. Where applicants are ranked on the basis of properly validated selection procedures and those applicants scoring below a higher cutoff score than appropriate in light of such expectations have little or no chance of being selected for employment, the higher cutoff score may be appropriate, but the degree of adverse impact should be considered.

I. *Use of selection procedures for higher level jobs.* If job progression structures are so established that employees will probably, within a reasonable period of time and in a majority of cases, progress to a higher level, it may be considered that the applicants are being evaluated for a job or jobs at the higher level. However, where job progression is not so nearly automatic, or the time span is such that higher level jobs or employees' potential may be expected to change in significant ways, it should be considered that applicants are being evaluated for a job at or near the entry level. A "reasonable period of time" will vary for different jobs and employment situations but will seldom be more than 5 years. Use of selection procedures to evaluate applicants for a higher level job would not be appropriate:

(1) If the majority of those remaining employed do not progress to the higher level job;

(2) If there is a reason to doubt that the higher level job will continue to require essentially similar skills during the progression period; or

(3) If the selection procedures measure knowledges, skills, or abilities required for advancement which would be expected to develop principally from the training or experience on the job.

J. *Interim use of selection procedures.* Users may continue the use of a selection procedure which is not at the moment fully supported by the required evidence of validity, provided: (1) The user has available substantial evidence of validity, and (2) the user has in progress, when technically feasible, a study which is designed to produce the additional evidence required by these guidelines within a reasonable time. If such a study is not technically feasible, see section 6B. If the study does not demonstrate validity, this provision of these guidelines for interim use shall not constitute a defense in any action, nor shall it relieve the user of any obligations arising under Federal law.

K. *Review of validity studies for currency.* Whenever validity has been shown in accord with these guidelines for the use of a particular selection procedure for a job or group of jobs, additional studies need not be performed until such time as the validity study is subject to review as provided in section 3B above. There are no absolutes in the area of determining the currency of a validity study. All circumstances concerning the study, including the validation strategy used, and changes in the relevant labor market and the job should be considered in the determination of when a validity study is outdated.

SEC. 6. *Use of selection procedures which have not been validated.—A. Use of alternate selection procedures to eliminate adverse impact.* A user may choose to utilize alternative selection procedures in order to eliminate adverse impact, or as part of an affirmative action program. See section 13 below. Such alternative procedures should eliminate the adverse impact in the total selection process, should be lawful and should be as job related as possible.

B. *Where validity studies cannot or need not be performed.* There are circumstances in which a user cannot or need not utilize the validation techniques contemplated by these guidelines. In such circumstances, the user should utilize selection procedures which are as job related as possible and which will minimize or eliminate adverse impact, as set forth below.

(1) *Where informal or unscored procedures are used.* When an informal or unscored selection procedure which has an adverse impact is utilized, the user should eliminate the adverse impact, or modify the procedure to one which is a formal, scored or quantified measure or combination of measures and then validate the procedure in accord with these guidelines, or otherwise justify continued use of the procedure in accord with Federal law.

(2) *Where formal and scored procedures are used.* When a formal and scored selection procedure is used which has an adverse impact, the validation techniques contemplated by these guidelines usually should be followed if technically feasible. Where the user cannot or need not follow the validation techniques anticipated by these guidelines, the user should

either modify the procedure to eliminate adverse impact or otherwise justify continued use of the procedure in accord with Federal law.

SEC. 7. *Use of other validity studies.—A. Validity studies not conducted by the user.* Users may, under certain circumstances, support the use of selection procedures by validity studies conducted by other users or conducted by test publishers or distributors and described in test manuals. While publishers of selection procedures have a professional obligation to provide evidence of validity which meets generally accepted professional standards (see section 5C above), users are cautioned that they are responsible for compliance with these guidelines. Accordingly, users seeking to obtain selection procedures from publishers and distributors should be careful to determine that, in the event the user becomes subject to the validity requirements of these guidelines, the necessary information to support validity has been determined and will be made available to the user.

B. *Use of criterion-related validity evidence from other sources.* Criterion-related validity studies conducted by one test user, or described in test manuals and the professional literature, will be considered acceptable for use by another user when the following requirements are met:

(1) *Validity evidence.* Evidence from the available studies meeting the standards of section 14B below clearly demonstrates that the selection procedure is valid;

(2) *Job similarity.* The incumbents in the user's job and the incumbents in the job or group of jobs on which the validity study was conducted perform substantially the same major work behaviors, as shown by appropriate job analyses both on the job or group of jobs on which the validity study was performed and on the job for which the selection procedure is to be used; and

(3) *Fairness evidence.* The studies include a study of test fairness for each race, sex, and ethnic group which constitutes a significant factor in the borrowing user's relevant labor market for the job or jobs in question. If the studies under consideration satisfy (1) and (2) above but do not contain an investigation of test fairness, and it is not technically feasible for the borrowing user to conduct an internal study of test fairness, the borrowing user may utilize the study until studies conducted elsewhere meeting the requirements of these guidelines show test unfairness, or until such time as it becomes technically feasible to conduct an internal study of test fairness and the results of that study can be acted upon, Users obtaining selection procedures from publishers should

consider, as one factor in the decision to purchase a particular selection procedure, the availability of evidence concerning test fairness.

C. *Validity evidence from multiunit study,* if validity evidence from a study covering more than one unit within an organization satisfies the requirements of section 14B below, evidence of validity specific to each unit will not be required unless there are variables which are likely to affect validity significantly.

D. *Other significant variables.* If there are variables in the other studies which are likely to affect validity significantly, the user may not rely upon such studies, but will be expected either to conduct an internal validity study or to comply with section 6 above.

SEC. 8. *Cooperative studies.—A. Encouragement of cooperative studies.* The agencies issuing these guidelines encourage employers, labor organizations, and employment agencies to cooperate in research, development, search for lawful alternatives, and validity studies in order to achieve procedures which are consistent with these guidelines.

B. *Standards for use of cooperative studies.* If validity evidence from a cooperative study satisfies the requirements of section 14 below, evidence of validity specific to each user will not be required unless there are variables in the user's situation which are likely to affect validity significantly.

SEC. 9. *No assumption of validity.—* A. *Unacceptable substitutes for evidence of validity.* Under no circumstances will the general reputation of a test or other selection procedures, its author or its publisher, or casual reports of it's validity be accepted in lieu of evidence of validity. Specifically ruled out are: assumptions of validity based on a procedure's name or descriptive labels; all forms of promotional literature; data bearing on the frequency of a procedure's usage; testimonial statements and credentials of sellers, users, or consultants; and other nonempirical or anecdotal accounts of selection practices or selection outcomes.

B. *Encouragement of professional supervision.* Professional supervision of selection activities is encouraged but is not a substitute for documented evidence of validity. The enforcement agencies will take into account the fact that a thorough job analysis was conducted and that careful development and use of a selection procedure in accordance with professional standards enhance the probability that the selection procedure is valid for the job.

SEC. 10. *Employment agencies and employment services.—A. Where selection procedures are devised by agency.* An employment agency, including pri-

326

vate employment agencies and State employment agencies, which agrees to a request by an employer or labor organization to devise and utilize a selection procedure should follow the standards in these guidelines for determining adverse impact. If adverse impact exists the agency should comply with these guidelines. An employment agency is not relieved of its obligation herein because the user did not request such validation or has requested the use of some lesser standard of validation than is provided in these guidelines. The use of an employment agency does not relieve an employer or labor organization or other user of its responsibilities under Federal law to provide equal employment opportunity or its obligations as a user under these guidelines.

B. *Where selection procedures are devised elsewhere.* Where an employment agency or service is requested to administer a selection procedure which has been devised elsewhere and to make referrals pursuant to the results, the employment agency or service should maintain and have available evidence of the impact of the selection and referral procedures which it administers. If adverse impact results the agency or service should comply with these guidelines. If the agency or service seeks to comply with these guidelines by reliance upon validity studies or other data in the possession of the employer, it should obtain and have available such information.

SEC. 11. *Disparate treatment.* The principles of disparate or unequal treatment must be distinguished from the concepts of validation. A selection procedure—even though validated against job performance in accordance with these guidelines—cannot be imposed upon members of a race, sex, or ethnic group where other employees, applicants, or members have not been subjected to that standard. Disparate treatment occurs where members of a race, sex, or ethnic group have been denied the same employment, promotion, membership, or other employment opportunities as have been available to other employees or applicants. Those employees or applicants who have been denied equal treatment, because of prior discriminatory practices or policies, must at least be afforded the same opportunities as had existed for other employees or applicants during the period of discrimination. Thus, the persons who were in the class of persons discriminated against during the period the user followed the discriminatory practices should be allowed the opportunity to qualify under less stringent selection procedures previously followed, unless the user demonstrates that the increased standards are required by business necessity. This section does not prohibit

a user who has not previously followed merit standards from adopting merit standards which are in compliance with these guidelines; nor does it preclude a user who has previously used procedures from developing and using procedures which are in accord with these guidelines.

SEC. 12. *Retesting of applicants.* Users should provide a reasonable opportunity for retesting and reconsideration. Where examinations are administered periodically with public notice, such reasonable opportunity exists, unless persons who have previously been tested are precluded from retesting. The user may however take reasonable steps to preserve the security of its procedures.

SEC. 13. *Affirmative action.*—A. *Affirmative action obligations.* The use of selection procedures which have been validated pursuant to these guidelines does not relieve users of any obligations they may have to undertake affirmative action to assure equal employment opportunity. Nothing in these guidelines is intended to preclude the use of lawful selection procedures which assist in remedying the effects of prior discriminatory practices, or the achievement of affirmative action objectives.

B. *Encouragement of voluntary affirmative action programs.* These guidelines are also intended to encourage the adoption and implementation of voluntary affirmative action programs by users who have no obligation under Federal law to adopt them; but are not intended to impose any new obligations in that regard. The agencies issuing and endorsing these guidelines endorse for all private employers and reaffirm for all governmental employers the Equal Employment Opportunity Coordinating Council's "Policy Statement on Affirmative Action Programs for State and Local Government Agencies" (41 FR 38814, September 13, 1976). That policy statement is attached hereto as appendix, section 17.

TECHNICAL STANDARDS

SEC. 14. *Technical standards for validity studies.* The following minimum standards, as applicable, should be met in conducting a validity study. Nothing in these guidelines is intended to preclude the development and use of other professionally acceptable techniques with respect to validation of selection procedures. Where it is not technically feasible for a user to conduct a validity study, the user has the obligation otherwise to comply with these guidelines. See sections 6 and 7 above.

A. *Validity studies should be based on review of information about the job.* Any validity study should be

based upon a review of information about the job for which the selection procedure is to be used. The review should include a job analysis except as provided in section 14B(3) below with respect to criterion-related validity. Any method of job analysis may be used if it provides the information required for the specific validation strategy used.

B. *Technical standards for criterion-related validity studies.*—(1) *Technical feasibility.* Users choosing to validate a selection procedure by a criterion-related validity strategy should determine whether it is technically feasible (as defined in section 16) to conduct such a study in the particular employment context. The determination of the number of persons necessary to permit the conduct of a meaningful criterion-related study should be made by the user on the basis of all relevant information concerning the selection procedure, the potential sample and the employment situation. Where appropriate, jobs with substantially the same major work behaviors may be grouped together for validity studies, in order to obtain an adequate sample. These guidelines do not require a user to hire or promote persons for the purpose of making it possible to conduct a criterion-related study.

(2) *Analysis of the job.* There should be a review of job information to determine measures of work behavior(s) or performance that are relevant to the job or group of jobs in question. These measures or criteria are relevant to the extent that they represent critical or important job duties, work behaviors or work outcomes as developed from the review of job information. The possibility of bias should be considered both in selection of the criterion measures and their application. In view of the possibility of bias in subjective evaluations, supervisory rating techniques and instructions to raters should be carefully developed. All criterion measures and the methods for gathering data need to be examined for freedom from factors which would unfairly alter scores of members of any group. The relevance of criteria and their freedom from bias are of particular concern when there are significant differences in measures of job performance for different groups.

(3) *Criterion measures.* Proper safeguards should be taken to insure that scores on selection procedures do not enter into any judgments of employee adequacy that are to be used as criterion measures. Whatever criteria are used should represent important or critical work behavior(s) or work outcomes. Certain criteria may be used without a full job analysis if the user can show the importance of the criteria to the particular employment con-

text. These criteria include but are not limited to production rate, error rate, tardiness, absenteeism, and length of service. A standardized rating of overall work performance may be used where a study of the job shows that it is an appropriate criterion. Where performance in training is used as a criterion, success in training should be properly measured and the relevance of the training should be shown either through a comparsion of the content of the training program with the critical or important work behavior(s) of the job(s), or through a demonstration of the relationship between measures of performance in training and measures of job performance. Measures of relative success in training include but are not limited to instructor evaluations, performance samples, or tests. Criterion measures consisting of paper and pencil tests will be closely reviewed for job relevance.

(4) *Representativeness of the sample.* Whether the study is predictive or concurrent, the sample subjects should insofar as feasible be representative of the candidates normally available in the relevant labor market for the job or group of jobs in question, and should insofar as feasible include the races, sexes, and ethnic groups normally available in the relevant job market. In determining the representativeness of the sample in a concurrent validity study, the user should take into account the extent to which the specific knowledges or skills which are the primary focus of the test are those which employees learn on the job.

Where samples are combined or compared, attention should be given to see that such samples are comparable in terms of the actual job they perform, the length of time on the job where time on the job is likely to affect performance, and other relevant factors likely to affect validity differences; or that these factors are included in the design of the study and their effects identified.

(5) *Statistical relationships.* The degree of relationship between selection procedure scores and criterion measures should be examined and computed, using professionally acceptable statistical procedures. Generally, a selection procedure is considered related to the criterion, for the purposes of these guidelines, when the relationship between performance on the procedure and performance on the criterion is statistically significant at the 0.05 level of significance, which means that it is sufficiently high as to have a probability of no more than one (1) in twenty (20) to have occurred by chance. Absence of a statistically significant relationship between a selection procedure and job performance should not necessarily discourage

other investigations of the validity of that selection procedure.

(6) *Operational use of selection procedures.* Users should evaluate each selection procedure to assure that it is appropriate for operational use, including establishment of cutoff scores or rank ordering. Generally, if other factors reman the same, the greater the magnitude of the relationship (e.g., coorelation. coefficent) between performance on a selection procedure and one or more criteria of performance on the job, and the greater the importance and number of aspects of job performance covered by the criteria, the more likely it is that the procedure will be appropriate for use. Reliance upon a selection procedure which is significantly related to a criterion measure, but which is based upon a study involving a large number of subjects and has a low correlation coefficient will be subject to close review if it has a large adverse impact. Sole reliance upon a single selection instrument which is related to only one of many job duties or aspects of job performance will also be subject to close review. The appropriateness of a selection procedure is best evaluated in each particular situation and there are no minimum correlation coefficients applicable to all employment situations. In determining whether a selection procedure is appropriate for operational use the following considerations should also be taken into account: The degree of adverse impact of the procedure, the availability of other selection procedures of greater or substantially equal validity.

(7) *Overstatement of validity findings.* Users should avoid reliance upon techniques which tend to overestimate validity findings as a result of capitalization on chance unless an appropriate safeguard is taken. Reliance upon a few selection procedures or criteria of successful job performance when many selection procedures or criteria of performance have been studied, or the use of optimal statistical weights for selection procedures computed in one sample, are techniques which tend to inflate validity estimates as a result of chance. Use of a large sample is one safeguard: cross-validation is another.

(8) *Fairness.* This section generally calls for studies of unfairness where technically feasible. The concept of fairness or unfairness of selection procedures is a developing concept. In addition, fairness studies generally require substantial numbers of employees in the job or group of jobs being studied. For these reasons, the Federal enforcement agencies recognize that the obligation to conduct studies of fairness imposed by the guidelines generally will be upon users or groups of users with a large number of persons in a a job class, or test developers;

and that small users utilizing their own selection procedures will generally not be obligated to conduct such studies because it will be technically infeasible for them to do so.

(a) *Unfairness defined.* When members of one race, sex, or ethnic group characteristically obtain lower scores on a selection procedure than members of another group, and the differences in scores are not reflected in differences in a measure of job performance, use of the selection procedure may unfairly deny opportunities to members of the group that obtains the lower scores.

(b) *Investigation of fairness.* Where a selection procedure results in an adverse impact on a race, sex, or ethnic group identified in accordance with the classifications set forth in section 4 above and that group is a significant factor in the relevant labor market, the user generally should investigate the possible existence of unfairness for that group if it is technically feasible to do so. The greater the severity of the adverse impact on a group, the greater the need to investigate the possible existence of unfairness. Where the weight of evidence from other studies shows that the selection procedure predicts fairly for the group in question and for the same or similar jobs, such evidence may be relied on in connection with the selection procedure at issue.

(c) *General considerations in fairness investigations.* Users conducting a study of fairness should review the A.P.A. Standards regarding investigation of possible bias in testing. An investigation of fairness of a selection procedure depends on both evidence of validity and the manner in which the selection procedure is to be used in a particular employment context. Fairness of a selection procedure cannot necessarily be specified in advance without investigating these factors. Investigation of fairness of a selection procedure in samples where the range of scores on selection procedures or criterion measures is severely restricted for any subgroup sample (as compared to other subgroup samples) may produce misleading evidence of unfairness. That factor should accordingly be taken into account in conducting such studies and before reliance is placed on the results.

(d) *When unfairness is shown.* If unfairness is demonstrated through a showing that members of a particular group perform better or poorer on the job than their scores on the selection procedure would indicate through comparison with how members of other groups perform, the user may either revise or replace the selection instrument in accordance with these guidelines, or may continue to use the selection instrument operationally with appropriate revisions in its use to assure compatibility between the probability of successful job performance and the probability of being selected.

(e) *Technical feasibility of fairness studies.* In addition to the general conditions needed for technical feasibilities for the conduct of a criterion-related study (see section 16, below) an investigation of fairness requires the following:

(i) An adequate sample of persons in each group available for the study to achieve findings of statistical significance. Guidelines do not require a user to hire or promote persons on the basis of group classifications for the purpose of making it possible to conduct a study of fairness; but the user has the obligation otherwise to comply with these guidelines.

(ii) The samples for each group should be comparable in terms of the actual job they perform, length of time on the job where time on the job is likely to affect performance, and other relevant factors likely to affect validity differences; or such factors should be included in the design of the study and their effects identified.

(f) *Continued use of selection procedures when fairness studies not feasible.* If a study of fairness should otherwise be performed, but is not technically feasible, a selection procedure may be used which has otherwise met the validity standards of these guidelines, unless the technical infeasibility resulted from discriminatory employment practices which are demonstrated by facts other than past failure to conform with requirements for validation of selection procedures. However, when it becomes technically feasible for the user to perform a study of fairness and such a study is otherwise called for, the user should conduct the study of fairness.

C. *Technical standards for content validity studies.*—(1) *Appropriateness of content validity studies.* Users choosing to validate a selection procedure by a content validity strategy should determine whether it is appropriate to conduct such a study in the particular employment context. A selection procedure can be supported by a content validity strategy to the extent that it is a representative sample of the content of the job. Selection procedures which purport to measure knowledges, skills, or abilities may in certain circumstances be justified by content validity, although they may not be representative samples, if the knowledge, skill, or ability measured by the selection procedure can be operationally defined as provided in section 14C(4) below, and if that knowledge, skill, or ability is a necessary prerequisite to successful job performance.

A selection procedure based upon inferences about mental processes cannot be supported solely or primarily on the basis of content validity. Thus, a content strategy is not appropriate for demonstrating the validity of selection procedures which purport to measure traits or constructs, such as intelligence, aptitude, personality, commonsense, judgment, leadership, and spatial ability. Content validity is also not an appropriate strategy when the selection procedure involves knowledges, skills, or abilities which an employee will be expected to learn on the job.

(2) *Job analysis for content validity.* There should be a job analysis which includes an analysis of the important work behavior(s) required for successful performance and their relative importance and, if the behavior results in work product(s), an analysis of the work product(s). Any job analysis should focus on the work behavior(s) and the tasks associated with them. If work behavior(s) are not observable, the job analysis should identify and analyze those aspects of the behavior(s) that can be observed and the observed work products. The work behavior(s) selected for measurement should be critical work behavior(s) and/or important work behavior(s) constituting most of the job.

(3) *Development of selection procedures.* A selection procedure designed to measure the work behavior may be developed specifically from the job and job analysis in question, or may have been previously developed by the user, or by other users or by a test publisher.

(4) *Standards for demonstrating content validity.* To demonstrate the content validity of a selection procedure, a user should show that the behavior(s) demonstrated in the selection procedure are a representative sample of the behavior(s) of the job in question or that the selection procedure provides a representative sample of the work product of the job. In the case of a selection procedure measuring a knowledge, skill, or ability, the knowledge, skill, or ability being measured should be operationally defined. In the case of a selection procedure measuring a knowledge, the knowledge being measured should be operationally defined as that body of learned information which is used in and is a necessary prerequisite for observable aspects of work behavior of the job. In the case of skills or abilities, the skill or ability being measured should be operationally defined in terms of observable aspects of work behavior of the job. For any selection procedure measuring a knowledge, skill, or ability the user should show that (a) the selection procedure measures and is a representative sample of that knowl-

edge, skill, or ability; and (b) that knowledge, skill, or ability is used in and is a necessary prerequisite to performance of critical or important work behavior(s). In addition, to be content valid, a selection procedure measuring a skill or ability should either closely approximate an observable work behavior, or its product should closely approximate an observable work product. If a test purports to sample a work behavior or to provide a sample of a work product, the manner and setting of the selection procedure and its level and complexity should closely approximate the work situation. The closer the content and the context of the selection procedure are to work samples or work behaviors, the stronger is the basis for showing content validity. As the content of the selection procedure less resembles a work behavior, or the setting and manner of the administration of the selection procedure less resemble the work situation, or the result less resembles a work product, the less likely the selection procedure is to be content valid, and the greater the need for other evidence of validity.

(5) *Reliability.* The reliability of selection procedures justified on the basis of content validity should be a matter of concern to the user. Whenever it is feasible, appropriate statistical estimates should be made of the reliability of the selection procedure.

(6) *Prior training or experience.* A requirement for or evaluation of specific prior training or experience based on content validity, including a specification of level or amount of training or experience, should be justified on the basis of the relationship between the content of the training or experience and the content of the job for which the training or experience is to be required or evaluated. The critical consideration is the resemblance between the specific behaviors, products, knowledges, skills, or abilities in the experience or training and the specific behaviors, products, knowledges, skills, or abilities required on the job, whether or not there is close resemblance between the experience or training as a whole and the job as a whole.

(7) *Content validity of training success.* Where a measure of success in a training program is used as a selection procedure and the content of a training program is justified on the basis of content validity, the use should be justified on the relationship between the content of the training program and the content of the job.

(8) *Operational use.* A selection procedure which is supported on the basis of content validity may be used for a job if it represents a critical work behavior (i.e., a behavior which is necessary for performance of the job) or

work behaviors which constitute most of the important parts of the job.

(9) *Ranking based on content validity studies.* If a user can show, by a job analysis or otherwise, that a higher score on a content valid selection procedure is likely to result in better job performance, the results may be used to rank persons who score above minimum levels. Where a selection procedure supported solely or primarily by content validity is used to rank job candidates, the selection procedure should measure those aspects of performance which differentiate among levels of job performance.

D. *Technical standards for construct validity studies.* — (1) *Appropriateness of construct validity studies.* Construct validity is a more complex strategy than either criterion-related or content validity. Construct validation is a relatively new and developing procedure in the employment field, and there is at present a lack of substantial literature extending the concept to employment practices. The user should be aware that the effort to obtain sufficient empirical support for construct validity is both an extensive and arduous effort involving a series of research studies, which include criterion related validity studies and which may include content validity studies. Users choosing to justify use of a selection procedure by this strategy should therefore take particular care to assure that the validity study meets the standards set forth below.

(2) *Job analysis for construct validity studies.* There should be a job analysis. This job analysis should show the work behavior(s) required for successful performance of the job, or the groups of jobs being studied, the critical or important work behavior(s) in the job or group of jobs being studied, and an identification of the construct(s) believed to underlie successful performance of these critical or important work behaviors in the job or jobs in question. Each construct should be named and defined, so as to distinguish it from other constructs. If a group of jobs is being studied the jobs should have in common one or more critical or important work behaviors at a comparable level of complexity.

(3) *Relationship to the job.* A selection procedure should then be identified or developed which measures the construct identified in accord with subparagraph (2) above. The user should show by empirical evidence that the selection procedure is validly related to the construct and that the construct is validly related to the performance of critical or important work behavior(s). The relationship between the construct as measured by the selection procedure and the related work behavior(s) should be supported by empirical evidence from one or more criterion-related studies involving the job or jobs in question which satisfy the provisions of section 14B above.

(4) *Use of construct validity study without new criterion-related evidence.* — (a) *Standards for use.* Until such time as professional literature provides more guidance on the use of construct validity in employment situations, the Federal agencies will accept a claim of construct validity without a criterion-related study which satisfies section 14B above only when the selection procedure has been used elsewhere in a situation in which a criterion-related study has been conducted and the use of a criterion-related validity study in this context meets the standards for transportability of criterion-related validity studies as set forth above in section 7. However, if a study pertains to a number of jobs having common critical or important work behaviors at a comparable level of complexity, and the evidence satisfies subparagraphs 14B (2) and (3) above for those jobs with criterion-related validity evidence for those jobs, the selection procedure may be used for all the jobs to which the study pertains. If construct validity is to be generalized to other jobs or groups of jobs not in the group studied, the Federal enforcement agencies will expect at a minimum additional empirical research evidence meeting the standards of subparagraphs section 14B (2) and (3) above for the additional jobs or groups of jobs.

(b) *Determination of common work behaviors.* In determining whether two or more jobs have one or more work behavior(s) in common, the user should compare the observed work behavior(s) in each of the jobs and should compare the observed work product(s) in each of the jobs. If neither the observed work behavior(s) in each of the jobs nor the observed work product(s) in each of the jobs are the same, the Federal enforcement agencies will presume that the work behavior(s) in each job are different. If the work behaviors are not observable, then evidence of similarity of work products and any other relevant research evidence will be considered in determining whether the work behavior(s) in the two jobs are the same.

DOCUMENTATION OF IMPACT AND VALIDITY EVIDENCE

SEC. 15. *Documentation of impact and validity evidence.* — A. *Required information.* Users of selection procedures other than those users complying with section 15A(1) below should maintain and have available for each job information on adverse impact of the selection process for that job and, where it is determined a selection process has an adverse impact, evidence of validity as set forth below.

(1) *Simplified recordkeeping for users with less than 100 employees.* In order to minimize recordkeeping burdens on employers who employ one hundred (100) or fewer employees, and other users not required to file EEO-1, et seq., reports, such users may satisfy the requirements of this section 15 if they maintain and have available records showing, for each year:

(a) The number of persons hired, promoted, and terminated for each job, by sex, and where appropriate by race and national origin;

(b) The number of applicants for hire and promotion by sex and where appropriate by race and national origin; and

(c) The selection procedures utilized (either standardized or not standardized).

These records should be maintained for each race or national origin group (see section 4 above) constituting more than two percent (2%) of the labor force in the relevant labor area. However, it is not necessary to maintain records by race and/or national origin (see § 4 above) if one race or national origin group in the relevant labor area constitutes more than ninety-eight percent (98%) of the labor force in the area. If the user has reason to believe that a selection procedure has an adverse impact, the user should maintain any available evidence of validity for that procedure (see sections 7A and 8).

(2) *Information on impact.* — (a) *Collection of information on impact.* Users of selection procedures other than those complying with section 15A(1) above should maintain and have available for each job records or other information showing whether the total selection process for that job has an adverse impact on any of the groups for which records are called for by sections 4B above. Adverse impact determinations should be made at least annually for each such group which constitutes at least 2 percent of the labor force in the relevant labor area or 2 percent of the applicable workforce. Where a total selection process for a job has an adverse impact, the user should maintain and have available records or other information showing which components have an adverse impact. Where the total selection process for a job does not have an adverse impact, information need not be maintained for individual components except in circumstances set forth in subsection 15A(2)(b) below. If the determination of adverse impact is made using a procedure other than the "four-fifths rule," as defined in the first sentence of section 4D above, a justification, consistent with section 4D above, for

the procedure used to determine adverse impact should be available.

(b) *When adverse impact has been eliminated in the total selection process.* Whenever the total selection process for a particular job has had an adverse impact, as defined in section 4 above, in any year, but no longer has an adverse impact, the user should maintain and have available the information on individual components of the selection process required in the preceding paragraph for the period in which there was adverse impact. In addition, the user should continue to collect such information for at least two (2) years after the adverse impact has been eliminated.

(c) *When data insufficient to determine impact.* Where there has been an insufficient number of selections to determine whether there is an adverse impact of the total selection process for a particular job, the user should continue to collect, maintain and have available the information on individual components of the selection process required in section 15(A)(2)(a) above until the information is sufficient to determine that the overall selection process does not have an adverse impact as defined in section 4 above, or until the job has changed substantially.

(3) *Documentation of validity evidence.*—(a) *Types of evidence.* Where a total selection process has an adverse impact (see section 4 above) the user should maintain and have available for each component of that process which has an adverse impact, one or more of the following types of documentation evidence:

(i) Documentation evidence showing criterion-related validity of the selection procedure (see section 15B, below).

(ii) Documentation evidence showing content validity of the selection procedure (see section 15C, below).

(iii) Documentation evidence showing construct validity of the selection procedure (see section 15D, below).

(iv) Documentation evidence from other studies showing validity of the selection procedure in the user's facility (see section 15E, below).

(v) Documentation evidence showing why a validity study cannot or need not be performed and why continued use of the procedure is consistent with Federal law.

(b) *Form of report.* This evidence should be compiled in a reasonably complete and organized manner to permit direct evaluation of the validity of the selection procedure. Previously written employer or consultant reports of validity, or reports describing validity studies completed before the issuance of these guidelines are acceptable if they are complete in regard to the documentation requirements

contained in this section, or if they satisfied requirements of guidelines which were in effect when the validity study was completed. If they are not complete, the required additional documentation should be appended. If necessary information is not available the report of the validity study may still be used as documentation, but its adequacy will be evaluated in terms of compliance with the requirements of these guidelines.

(c) *Completeness.* In the event that evidence of validity is reviewed by an enforcement agency, the validation reports completed after the effective date of these guidelines are expected to contain the information set forth below. Evidence denoted by use of the word "(Essential)" is considered critical. If information denoted essential is not included, the report will be considered incomplete unless the user affirmatively demonstrates either its unavailability due to circumstances beyond the user's control or special circumstances of the user's study which make the information irrelevant. Evidence not so denoted is desirable but its absence will not be a basis for considering a report incomplete. The user should maintain and have available the information called for under the heading "Source Data" in sections 15B(11) and 15D(11). While it is a necessary part of the study, it need not be submitted with the report. All statistical results should be organized and presented in tabular or graphic form to the extent feasible.

B. *Criterion-related validity studies.* Reports of criterion-related validity for a selection procedure should include the following information:

(1) *User(s), location(s), and date(s) of study.* Dates and location(s) of the job analysis or review of job information, the date(s) and location(s) of the administration of the selection procedures and collection of criterion data, and the time between collection of data on selection procedures and criterion measures should be provided (Essential). If the study was conducted at several locations, the address of each location, including city and State, should be shown.

(2) *Problem and setting.* An explicit definition of the purpose(s) of the study and the circumstances in which the study was conducted should be provided. A description of existing selection procedures and cutoff scores, if any, should be provided.

(3) *Job anlysis or review of job information.* A description of the procedure used to analyze the job or group of jobs, or to review the job information should be provided (Essential). Where a review of job information results in criteria which may be used without a full job analysis (see section 14B(3)), the basis for the selection of

these criteria should be reported (Essential). Where a job analysis is required a complete description of the work behavior(s) or work outcome(s), and measures of their criticality or importance should be provided (Essential). The report should describe the basis on which the behavior(s) or outcome(s) were determined to be critical or important, such as the proportion of time spent on the respective behaviors, their level of difficulty, their frequency of performance, the consequences of error, or other appropriate factors (Essential). Where two or more jobs are grouped for a validity study, the information called for in this subsection should be provided for each of the jobs, and the justification for the grouping (see section 14B(1)) should be provided (Essential).

(4) *Job titles and codes.* It is desirable to provide the user's job title(s) for the job(s) in question and the corresponding job title(s) and code(s) from U.S. Employment Service's Dictionary of Occupational Titles.

(5) *Criterion measures.* The bases for the selection of the criterion measures should be provided, together with references to the evidence considered in making the selection of criterion measures (essential). A full description of all criteria on which data were collected and means by which they were observed, recorded, evaluated, and quantified, should be provided (essential). If rating techniques are used as criterion measures, the appraisal form(s) and instructions to the rater(s) should be included as part of the validation evidence, or should be explicitly described and available (essential). All steps taken to insure that criterion measures are free from factors which would unfairly alter the scores of members of any group should be described (essential).

(6) *Sample description.* A description of how the research sample was identified and selected should be included (essential). The race, sex, and ethnic composition of the sample, including those groups set forth in section 4A above, should be described (essential). This description should include the size of each subgroup (essential). A description of how the research sample compares with the relevant labor market or work force, the method by which the relevant labor market or work force was defined, and a discussion of the likely effects on validity of differences between the sample and the relevant labor market or work force, are also desirable. Descriptions of educational levels, length of service, and age are also desirable.

(7) *Description of selection procedures.* Any measure, combination of measures, or procedure studied should be completely and explicitly described or attached (essential). If commercial-

ly available selection procedures are studied, they should be described by title, form, and publisher (essential). Reports of reliability estimates and how they were established are desirable.

(8) *Techniques and results.* Methods used in analyzing data should be described (essential). Measures of central tendency (e.g., means) and measures of dispersion (e.g., standard deviations and ranges) for all selection procedures and all criteria should be reported for each race, sex, and ethnic group which constitutes a significant factor in the relevant labor market (essential). The magnitude and direction of all relationships between selection procedures and criterion measures investigated should be reported for each relevant race, sex, and ethnic group and for the total group (essential). Where groups are too small to obtain reliable evidence of the magnitude of the relationship, need not be reported separately. Statements regarding the statistical significance of results should be made (essential). Any statistical adjustments, such as for less then perfect reliability or for restriction of score range in the selection procedure or criterion should be described and explained; and uncorrected correlation coefficients should also be shown (essential). Where the statistical technique categorizes continuous data, such as biserial correlation and the phi coefficient, the categories and the bases on which they were determined should be described and explained (essential). Studies of test fairness should be included where called for by the requirements of section 14B(8) (essential). These studies should include the rationale by which a selection procedure was determined to be fair to the group(s) in question. Where test fairness or unfairness has been demonstrated on the basis of other studies, a bibliography of the relevant studies should be included (essential). If the bibliography includes unpublished studies, copies of these studies, or adequate abstracts or summaries, should be attached (essential). Where revisions have been made in a selection procedure to assure compatability between successful job performance and the probability of being selected, the studies underlying such revisions should be included (essential). All statistical results should be organized and presented by relevant race, sex, and ethnic group (essential).

(9) *Alternative procedures investigated.* The selection procedures investigated and available evidence of their impact should be identified (essential). The scope, method, and findings of the investigation, and the conclusions reached in light of the findings, should be fully described (essential).

(10) *Uses and applications.* The methods considered for use of the selection procedure (e.g., as a screening device with a cutoff score, for grouping or ranking, or combined with other procedures in a battery) and available evidence of their impact should be described (essential). This description should include the rationale for choosing the method for operational use, and the evidence of the validity and utility of the procedure as it is to be used (essential). The purpose for which the procedure is to be used (e.g., hiring, transfer, promotion) should be described (essential). If weights are assigned to different parts of the selection procedure, these weights and the validity of the weighted composite should be reported (essential). If the selection procedure is used with a cutoff score, the user should describe the way in which normal expectations of proficiency within the work force were determined and the way in which the cutoff score was determined (essential).

(11) *Source data.* Each user should maintain records showing all pertinent information about individual sample members and raters where they are used, in studies involving the validation of selection procedures. These records should be made available upon request of a compliance agency. In the case of individual sample members these data should include scores on the selection procedure(s), scores on criterion measures, age, sex, race, or ethnic group status, and experience on the specific job on which the validation study was conducted, and may also include such things as education, training, and prior job experience, but should not include names and social security numbers. Records should be maintained which show the ratings given to each sample member by each rater.

(12) *Contact person.* The name, mailing address, and telephone number of the person who may be contacted for further information about the validity study should be provided (essential).

(13) *Accuracy and completeness.* The report should describe the steps taken to assure the accuracy and completeness of the collection, analysis, and report of data and results.

C. *Content validity studies.* Reports of content validity for a selection procedure should include the following information:

(1) *User(s), location(s) and date(s) of study.* Dates and location(s) of the job analysis should be shown (essential).

(2) *Problem and setting.* An explicit definition of the purpose(s) of the study and the circumstances in which the study was conducted should be provided. A description of existing selection procedures and cutoff scores, if any, should be provided.

(3) *Job analysis—Content of the job.* A description of the method used to analyze the job should be provided (essential). The work behavior(s), the associated tasks, and, if the behavior results in a work product, the work products should be completely described (essential). Measures of criticality and/or importance of the work behavior(s) and the method of determining these measures should be provided (essential). Where the job analysis also identified the knowledges, skills, and abilities used in work behavior(s), an operational definition for each knowledge in terms of a body of learned information and for each skill and ability in terms of observable behaviors and outcomes, and the relationship between each knowledge, skill, or ability and each work behavior, as well as the method used to determine this relationship, should be provided (essential). The work situation should be described, including the setting in which work behavior(s) are performed, and where appropriate, the manner in which knowledges, skills, or abilities are used, and the complexity and difficulty of the knowledge, skill, or ability as used in the work behavior(s).

(4) *Selection procedure and its content.* Selection procedures, including those constructed by or for the user, specific training requirements, composites of selection procedures, and any other procedure supported by content validity, should be completely and explicitly described or attached (essential). If commercially available selection procedures are used, they should be described by title, form, and publisher (essential). The behaviors measured or sampled by the selection procedure should be explicitly described (essential). Where the selection procedure purports to measure a knowledge, skill, or ability, evidence that the selection procedure measures and is a representative sample of the knowledge, skill, or ability should be provided (essential).

(5) *Relationship between the selection procedure and the job.* The evidence demonstrating that the selection procedure is a representative work sample, a representative sample of the work behavior(s), or a representative sample of a knowledge, skill, or ability as used as a part of a work behavior and necessary for that behavior should be provided (essential). The user should identify the work behavior(s) which each item or part of the selection procedure is intended to sample or measure (essential). Where the selection procedure purports to sample a work behavior or to provide a sample of a work product, a comparison should be provided of the manner, setting, and the level of complexity of the selection procedure with those of

the work situation (essential). If any steps were taken to reduce adverse impact on a race, sex, or ethnic group in the content of the procedure or in its administration, these steps should be described. Establishment of time limits, if any, and how these limits are related to the speed with which duties must be performed on the job, should be explained. Measures of central tend- ency (e.g., means) and measures of dispersion (e.g., standard deviations) and estimates of reaIibiIity should be reported for all selection procedures if available. Such reports should be made for relevant race, sex, and ethnic subgroups, at least on a statistically reliable sample basis.

(6) *Alternative procedures investigated.* The alternative selection procedures investigated and available evidence of their impact should be identified (essential). The scope, method, and findings of the investigation, and the conclusions reached in light of the findings, should be fully described (essential).

(7) *Uses and applications.* The methods considered for use of the selection procedure (e.g., as a screening device with a cutoff score, for grouping or ranking, or combined with other procedures in a battery) and available evidence of their impact should be described (essential). This description should include the rationale for choosing the method for operational use, and the evidence of the validity and utility of the procedure as it is to be used (essential). The purpose for which the procedure is to be used (e.g., hiring, transfer, promotion) should be described (essential). If the selection procedure is used with a cutoff score, the user should describe the way in which normal expectations of proficiency within the work force were determined and the way in which the cutoff score was determined (essential). In addition, if the selection procedure is to be used for ranking, the user should specify the evidence showing that a higher score on the selection procedure is likely to result in better job performance.

(8) *Contact person.* The name, mailing address, and telephone number of the person who may be contacted for further information about the validity study should be provided (essential).

(9) *Accuracy and completeness.* The report should describe the steps taken to assure the accuracy and completeness of the collection, analysis, and report of data and results.

D. *Construct validity studies.* Reports of construct validity for a selection procedure should include the following information:

(1) *User(s), location(s), and date(s) of study.* Date(s) and location(s) of the job analysis and the gathering of other evidence called for by these guidelines should be provided (essential).

(2) *Problem and setting.* An explicit definition of the purpose(s) of the study and the circumstances in which the study was conducted should be provided. A description of existing selection procedures and cutoff scores, if any, should be provided.

(3) *Construct definition.* A clear definition of the construct(s) which are believed to underlie successful performance of the critical or important work behavior(s) should be provided (essential). This definition should include the levels of construct performance relevant to the job(s) for which the selection procedure is to be used (essential). There should be a summary of the position of the construct in the psychological literature, or in the absence of such a position, a description of the way in which the definition and measurement of the construct was developed and the psychological theory underlying it (essential). Any quantitative data which identify or define the job constructs, such as factor analyses, should be provided (essential).

(4) *Job analysis.* A description of the method used to analyze the job should be provided (essential). A complete description of the work behavior(s) and, to the extent appropriate, work outcomes and measures of their criticality and/or importance should be provided (essential). The report should also describe the basis on which the behavior(s) or outcomes were determined to be important, such as their level of difficulty, their frequency of performance, the consequences of error or other appropriate factors (essential). Where jobs are grouped or compared for the purposes of generalizing validity evidence, the work behavior(s) and work product(s) for each of the jobs should be described, and conclusions concerning the similarity of the jobs in terms of observable work behaviors or work products should be made (essential).

(5) *Job titles and codes.* It is desirable to provide the selection procedure user's job title(s) for the job(s) in question and the corresponding job title(s) and code(s) from the United States Employment Service's dictionary of occupational titles.

(6) *Selection procedure.* The selection procedure used as a measure of the construct should be completely and explicitly described or attached (essential). If commercially available selection procedures are used, they should be identified by title, form and publisher (essential). The research evidence of the relationship between the selection procedure and the construct, such as factor structure, should be included (essential). Measures of central tendency, variability and reliability of the selection procedure should be provided (essential). Whenever feasible, these measures, should be provided separately for each relevant race, sex and ethnic group.

(7) *Relationship to job performance.* The criterion-related study(ies) and other empirical evidence of the relationship between the construct measured by the selection procedure and the related work behavior(s) for the job or jobs in question should be provided (essential). Documentation of the criterion-related study(ies) should satisfy the provisions of section 15B above or section 15E(1) below, except for studies conducted prior to the effective date of these guidelines (essential). Where a study pertains to a group of jobs, and, on the basis of the study, validity is asserted for a job in the group, the observed work behaviors and the observed work products for each of the jobs should be described (essential). Any other evidence used in determining whether the work behavior(s) in each of the jobs is the same should be fully described (essential).

(8) *Alternative procedures investigated.* The alternative selection procedures investigated and available evidence of their impact should be identified (essential). The scope, method, and findings of the investigation, and the conclusions reached in light of the findings should be fully described (essential).

(9) *Uses and applications.* The methods considered for use of the selection procedure (e.g., as a screening device with a cutoff score, for grouping or ranking, or combined with other procedures in a battery) and available evidence of their impact should be described (essential). This description should include the rationale for choosing the method for operational use, and the evidence of the validity and utility of the procedure as it is to be used (essential). The purpose for which the procedure is to be used (e.g., hiring, transfer, promotion) should be described (essential). If weights are assigned to different parts of the selection procedure, these weights and the validity of the weighted composite should be reported (essential). If the selection procedure is used with a cutoff score, the user should describe the way in which normal expectations of proficiency within the work force were determined and the way in which the cutoff score was determined (essential).

(10) *Accuracy and completeness.* The report should describe the steps taken to assure the accuracy and completeness of the collection, analysis, and report of data and results.

(11) *Source data.* Each user should maintain records showing all pertinent

information relating to its study of construct validity.

(12) *Contact person.* The name, mailing address, and telephone number of the individual who may be contacted for further information about the validity study should be provided (essential).

E. *Evidence of validity from other studies.* When validity of a selection procedure is supported by evidence not done by the user, the evidence from the original study or studies should be compiled in a manner similar to that required in the appropriate section of this section 15 above. In addition, the following evidence should be supplied:

(1) *Evidence from criterion-related validity studies.—a. Job information.* A description of the important job behavior(s) of the user's job and the basis on which the behaviors were determined to be important should be provided (essential). A full description of the basis for determining that these important work behaviors are the same as those of the job in the original study (or studies) should be provided (essential).

b. *Relevance of criteria.* A full description of the basis on which the criteria used in the original studies are determined to be relevant for the user should be provided (essential).

c. *Other variables.* The similarity of important applicant pool or sample characteristics reported in the original studies to those of the user should be described (essential). A description of the comparison between the race, sex and ethnic composition of the user's relevant labor market and the sample in the original validity studies should be provided (essential).

d. *Use of the selection procedure.* A full description should be provided showing that the use to be made of the selection procedure is consistent with the findings of the original validity studies (essential).

e. *Bibliography.* A bibliography of reports of validity of the selection procedure for the job or jobs in question should be provided (essential). Where any of the studies included an investigation of test fairness, the results of this investigation should be provided (essential). Copies of reports published in journals that are not commonly available should be described in detail or attached (essential). Where a user is relying upon unpublished studies, a reasonable effort should be made to obtain these studies. If these unpublished studies are the sole source of validity evidence they should be described in detail or attached (essential). If these studies are not available, the name and address of the source, an adequate abstract or summary of the validity study and data, and a contact person in the source organization should be provided (essential).

(2) *Evidence from content validity studies.* See section 14C(3) and section 15C above.

(3) *Evidence from construct validity studies.* See sections 14D(2) and 15D above.

F. *Evidence of validity from cooperative studies.* Where a selection procedure has been validated through a co-operative study, evidence that the study satisfies the requirements of sections 7, 8 and 15E should be provided (essential).

G. *Selection for higher level job.* If a selection procedure is used to evaluate candidates for jobs at a higher level than those for which they will initially be employed, the validity evidence should satisfy the documentation provisions of this section 15 for the higher level job or jobs, and in addition, the user should provide: (1) a description of the job progression structure, formal or informal; (2) the data showing how many employees progress to the higher level job and the length of time needed to make this progression; and (3) an identification of any anticipated changes in the higher level job. In addition, if the test measures a knowledge, skill or ability, the user should provide evidence that the knowledge, skill or ability is required for the higher level job and the basis for the conclusion that the knowledge, skill or ability is not expected to develop from the training or experience on the job.

H. *Interim use of selection procedures.* If a selection procedure is being used on an interim basis because the procedure is not fully supported by the required evidence of validity, the user should maintain and have available (1) substantial evidence of validity for the procedure, and (2) a report showing the date on which the study to gather the additional evidence commenced, the estimated completion date of the study, and a description of the data to be collected (essential).

DEFINITIONS

SEC. 16. *Definitions.* The following definitions shall apply throughout these guidelines:

A. *Ability.* A present competence to perform an observable behavior or a behavior which results in an observable product.

B. *Adverse impact.* A substantially different rate of selection in hiring, promotion, or other employment decision which works to the disadvantage of members of a race, sex, or ethnic group. See section 4 of these guidelines.

C. *Compliance with these guidelines.* Use of a selection procedure is in compliance with these guidelines if such use has been validated in accord with these guidelines (as defined below), or if such use does not result in adverse

impact on any race, sex, or ethnic group (see section 4, above), or, in unusual circumstances, if use of the procedure is otherwise justified in accord with Federal law. See section 6B, above.

D. *Content validity.* Demonstrated by data showing that the content of a selection procedure is representative of important aspects of performance on the job. See section 5B and section 14C.

E. *Construct validity.* Demonstrated by data showing that the selection procedure measures the degree to which candidates have identifiable characteristics which have been determined to be important for successful job performance. See section 5B and section 14D.

F. *Criterion-related validity.* Demonstrated by empirical data showing that the selection procedure is predictive of or significantly correlated with important elements of work behavior. See sections 5B and 14B.

G. *Employer.* Any employer subject to the provisions of the Civil Rights Act of 1964, as amended, including State or local governments and any Federal agency subject to the provisions of section 717 of the Civil Rights Act of 1964, as amended, and any Federal contractor or subcontractor or federally assisted construction contractor or subcontractor covered by Executive Order 11246, as amended.

H. *Employment agency.* Any employment agency subject to the provisions of the Civil Rights Act of 1964, as amended.

I. *Enforcement action.* For the purposes of section 4 a proceeding by a Federal enforcement agency such as a lawsuit or an administrative proceeding leading to debarment from or withholding, suspension, or termination of Federal Government contracts or the suspension or withholding of Federal Government funds; but not a finding of reasonable cause or a conciliation process or the issuance of right to sue letters under title VII or under Executive Order 11246 where such finding, conciliation, or issuance of notice of right to sue is based upon an individual complaint.

J. *Enforcement agency.* Any agency of the executive branch of the Federal Government which adopts these guidelines for purposes of the enforcement of the equal employment opportunity laws or which has responsibility for securing compliance with them.

K. *Job analysis.* A detailed statement of work behaviors and other information relevant to the job.

L. *Job description.* A general statement of job duties and responsibilities.

M. *Knowledge.* A body of information applied directly to the performance of a function.

N. *Labor organization.* Any labor organization subject to the provisions of the Civil Rights Act of 1964, as amended, and any committee subject thereto controlling apprenticeship or other training.

O. *Observable.* Able to be seen, heard, or otherwise perceived by a person other than the person performing the action.

P. *Race, sex, or ethnic group.* Any group of persons identifiable on the grounds of race, color, religion, sex, or national origin.

Q. *Selection procedure.* Any measure, combination of measures, or procedure used as a basis for any employment decision. Selection procedures include the full range of assessment techniques from traditional paper and pencil tests, performance tests, training programs, or probationary periods and physical, educational, and work experience requirements through informal or casual interviews and unscored application forms.

R. *Selection rate.* The proportion of applicants or candidates who are hired, promoted, or otherwise selected.

S. *Should.* The term "should" as used in these guidelines is intended to connote action which is necessary to achieve compliance with the guidelines, while recognizing that there are circumstances where alternative courses of action are open to users.

T. *Skill.* A present, observable competence to perform a learned psychomoter act.

U. *Technical feasibility.* The existence of conditions permitting the conduct of meaningful criterion-related validity studies. These conditions include: (1) An adequate sample of persons available for the study to achieve findings of statistical significance; (2) having or being able to obtain a sufficient range of scores on the selection procedure and job performance measures to produce validity results which can be expected to be representative of the results if the ranges normally expected were utilized; and (3) having or being able to devise unbiased, reliable and relevant measures of job performance or other criteria of employee adequacy. See section 14B(2). With respect to investigation of possible unfairness, the same considerations are applicable to each group for which the study is made. See section 14B(8).

V. *Unfairness of selection procedure.* A condition in which members of one race, sex, or ethnic group characteristically obtain lower scores on a selection procedure than members of another group, and the differences are not reflected in differences in measures of job performance. See section 14B(7).

W. *User.* Any employer, labor organization, employment agency, or licensing or certification board, to the

extent it may be covered by Federal equal employment opportunity law, which uses a selection procedure as a basis for any employment decision. Whenever an employer, labor organization, or employment agency is required by law to restrict recruitment for any occupation to those applicants who have met licensing or certification requirements, the licensing or certifying authority to the extent it may be covered by Federal equal employment opportunity law will be considered the user with respect to those licensing or certification requirements. Whenever a State employment agency or service does no more than administer or monitor a procedure as permitted by Department of Labor regulations, and does so without making referrals or taking any other action on the basis of the results, the State employment agency will not be deemed to be a user.

X. *Validated in accord with these guidelines or properly validated.* A demonstration that one or more validity study or studies meeting the standards of these guidelines has been conducted, including investigation and, where appropriate, use of suitable alternative selection procedures as contemplated by section 3B, and has produced evidence of validity sufficient to warrant use of the procedure for the intended purpose under the standards of these guidelines.

Y. *Work behavior.* An activity performed to achieve the objectives of the job. Work behaviors involve observable (physical) components and unobservable (mental) components. A work behavior consists of the performance of one or more tasks. Knowledges, skills, and abilities are not behaviors, although they may be applied in work behaviors.

APPENDIX

17. *Policy statement on affirmative action* (see section 13B). The Equal Employment Opportunity Coordinating Council was established by act of Congress in 1972, and charged with responsibility for developing and implementing agreements and policies designed, among other things, to eliminate conflict and inconsistency among the agencies of the Federal Government responsible for administering Federal law prohibiting discrimination on grounds of race, color, sex, religion, and national origin. This statement is issued as an initial response to the requests of a number of State and local officials for clarification of the Government's policies concerning the role of affirmative action in the overall equal employment opportunity program. While the Coordinating Council's adoption of this statement expresses only the views of the signatory agencies concerning this important subject, the principles set forth below

should serve as policy guidance for other Federal agencies as well.

(1) Equal employment opportunity is the law of the land. In the public sector of our society this means that all persons, regardless of race, color, religion, sex, or national origin shall have equal access to positions in the public service limited only by their ability to do the job. There is ample evidence in all sectors of our society that such equal access frequently has been denied to members of certain groups because of their sex, racial, or ethnic characteristics. The remedy for such past and present discrimination is twofold.

On the one hand, vigorous enforcement of the laws against discrimination is essential. But equally, and perhaps even more important are affirmative, voluntary efforts on the part of public employers to assure that positions in the public service are genuinely and equally accessible to qualified persons, without regard to their sex, racial, or ethnic characteristics. Without such efforts equal employment opportunity is no more than a wish. The importance of voluntary affirmative action on the part of employers is underscored by title VII of the Civil Rights Act of 1964, Executive Order 11246, and related laws and regulations—all of which emphasize voluntary action to achieve equal employment opportunity.

As with most management objectives, a systematic plan based on sound organizational analysis and problem identification is crucial to the accomplishment of affirmative action objectives. For this reason, the Council urges all State and local governments to develop and implement results oriented affirmative action plans which deal with the problems so identified.

The following paragraphs are intended to assist State and local governments by illustrating the kinds of analyses and activities which may be appropriate for a public employer's voluntary affirmative action plan. This statement does not address remedies imposed after a finding of unlawful discrimination.

(2) Voluntary affirmative action to assure equal employment opportunity is appropriate at any stage of the employment process. The first step in the construction of any affirmative action plan should be an analysis of the employer's work force to determine whether percentages of sex, race, or ethnic groups in individual job classifications are substantially similar to the percentages of those groups available in the relevant job market who possess the basic job-related qualifications.

When substantial disparities are found through such analyses, each element of the overall selection process should be examined to determine which elements operate to exclude persons on the basis of sex, race, or ethnic group. Such elements include, but are not limited to, recruitment, testing, ranking certification, interview, recommendations for selection, hiring, promotion, etc. The examination of each element of the selection process should at a minimum include a determination of its validity in predicting job performance.

(3) When an employer has reason to believe that its selection procedures have the exclusionary effect described in paragraph 2 above, it should initiate affirmative steps to remedy the situation. Such steps, which in design and execution may be race, color, sex, or ethnic "conscious," include, but are not limited to, the following:

(a) The establishment of a long-term goal, and short-range, interim goals and timetables for the specific job classifications, all of which should take into account the availability of basically qualified persons in the relevant job market;

(b) A recruitment program designed to attract qualified members of the group in question;

(c) A systematic effort to organize work and redesign jobs in ways that provide opportunities for persons lacking "journeyman" level knowledge or skills to enter and, with appropriate training, to progress in a career field;

(d) Revamping selection instruments or procedures which have not yet been validated in order to reduce or eliminate exclusionary effects on particular groups in particular job classifications;

(e) The initiation of measures designed to assure that members of the affected group who are qualified to perform the job are included within the pool of persons from which the selecting official makes the selection;

(f) A systematic effort to provide career advancement training, both classroom and on-the-job, to employees locked into dead end jobs; and

(g) The establishment of a system for regularly monitoring the effectiveness of the particular affirmative action program, and procedures for making timely adjustments in this program where effectiveness is not demonstrated.

(4) The goal of any affirmative action plan should be achievement of genuine equal employment opportunity for all qualified persons. Selection under such plans should be based

upon the ability of the applicant(s) to do the work. Such plans should not require the selection of the unqualified, or the unneeded, nor should they require the selection of persons on the basis of race, color, sex, religion, or national origin. Moreover, while the Council believes that this statement should serve to assist State and local employers, as well as Federal agencies, it recognizes that affirmative action cannot be viewed as a standardized program which must be accomplished in the same way at all times in all places.

Accordingly, the Council has not attempted to set forth here either the minimum or maximum voluntary steps that employers may take to deal with their respective situations. Rather, the Council recognizes that under applicable authorities, State and local employers have flexibility to formulate affirmative action plans that are best suited to their particular situations. In this manner, the Council believes that affirmative action programs will best serve the goal of equal employment opportunity.

Respectfully submitted,

HAROLD R. TYLER, Jr.,
Deputy Attorney General and Chairman of the Equal Employment Coordinating Council.

MICHAEL H. MOSKOW,
Under Secretary of Labor.

ETHEL BENT WALSH,
Acting Chairman, Equal Employment Opportunity Commission.

ROBERT E. HAMPTON,
Chairman, Civil Service Commission.

ARTHUR E. FLEMMING,
Chairman, Commission on Civil Rights.

Because of its equal employment opportunity responsibilities under the State and Local Government Fiscal Assistance Act of 1972 (the revenue sharing act), the Department of Treasury was invited to participate in the formulation of this policy statement; and it concurs and joins in the adoption of this policy statement.

Done this 26th day of August 1976.

RICHARD ALBRECHT,
General Counsel,
Department of the Treasury.

Section 18. Citations. The official title of these guidelines is "Uniform

Guidelines on Employee Selection Procedures (1978)". The Uniform Guidelines on Employee Selection Procedures (1978) are intended to establish a uniform Federal position in the area of prohibiting discrimination in employment practices on grounds of race, color, religion, sex, or national origin. These guidelines have been adopted by the Equal Employment Opportunity Commission, the Department of Labor, the Department of Justice, and the Civil Service Commission.

The official citation is:

"Section ——, Uniform Guidelines on Employee Selection Procedure (1978); 43 FR —— (August 25, 1978)."

The short form citation is:

"Section ——, U.G.E.S.P. (1978); 43 FR —— (August 25, 1978)."

When the guidelines are cited in connection with the activities of one of the issuing agencies, a specific citation to the regulations of that agency can be added at the end of the above citation. The specific additional citations are as follows:

Equal Employment Opportunity Commission
29 CFR Part 1607,

Department of Labor
Office of Federal Contract Compliance Programs
41 CFR Part 60-3

Department of Justice
28 CFR 50.14

Civil Service Commission
5 CFR 300.103(c)

Normally when citing these guidelines, the section number immediately preceding the title of the guidelines will be from these guidelines series 1-18. If a section number from the codification for an individual agency is needed it can also be added at the end of the agency citation. For example, section 6A of these guidelines could be cited for EEOC as follows: "Section 6A, Uniform Guidelines on Employee Selection Procedures (1978); 43 FR ——, (August 25, 1978); 29 CFR Part 1607, section 6A."

ELEANOR HOLMES NORTON,
Chair, Equal Employment Opportunity Commission.

ALAN K. CAMPBELL,
Chairman,
Civil Service Commission.

RAY MARSHALL,
Secretary of Labor.

GRIFFIN B. BELL,
Attorney General.

[6570-06]

CIVIL SERVICE COMMISSION

Title 5—Administrative Personnel

CHAPTER 1—CIVIL SERVICE COMMISSION

PART 300—EMPLOYMENT (GENERAL)

Uniform Guidelines on Employee Selection Procedures (1978)

The Uniform Guidelines on Employee Selection Procedures (1978) which are printed at the beginning of this part IV in today's FEDERAL REGISTER are adopted by the Civil Service Commission, in conjunction with the Equal Employment Opportunity Commission, Department of Justice, and the Department of Labor to establish uniformity in prohibiting discrimination in employment practices on grounds of race, color, religion, sex, or national origin. Cross reference documents are published at 29 CFR parts 1607 (Equal Employment Opportunity Commission), 28 CFR 50.14 (Department of Justice), and 41 CFR 60-3 (Department of Labor) elsewhere in this issue of the FEDERAL REGISTER.

By virtue of the authority vested in it by sections 3301, 3302, 7151, 7154, and 7301 of title 5 and section 4763(b) of title 42, United States Code, and Executive Order 10577, 3 CFR 1954-58 comp. page 218 and Executive Order 11478, 3 CFR 1959 comp. 133, and section 717 of the Civil Rights Act of 1964, as amended (42 U.S.C. 2000e-16), the Civil Service Commission amends title 5, part 300, subpart A, § 300.103(c) of the Code of Federal Regulations to read as follows:

§ 300.103 Basic requirements.

"(c) Equal employment opportunity. An employment practice shall not discriminate on the basis of race, color, religion, sex, age, national origin, partisan political affiliation, or other non-merit factor. Employee selection procedures shall meet the standards established by the "Uniform Guidelines on Employee Selection Procedures (1978), 43 FR—— (August 25, 1978)."

The Civil Service Commission rescinds the Guidelines on Employee Selection Procedures, 41 FR 51752, Federal Personnel Manual part 900, subpart F and adopts the Uniform Guidelines on Employee Selection Procedures (1978), to be issued as identical supplement appendices to supplements 271-1, Development of Qualification Standards; 271-2, Tests and Other Applicant Appraisal Procedures; 335-1, Evaluation of Employees for Promotion and Internal Placement; and 990-1 (Book III), part 900, subpart F, Administration of Standards for a Merit System of Personnel Administration of the Federal Personnel Manual in order to insure the examining, testing standards, and employment practices are not affected by discrimination on the basis of race, color, religion, sex or national origin.

Effective date: September 25, 1978.

ALAN K. CAMPBELL,
*Chairman,
Civil Service Commission.*

[6570-06]

DEPARTMENT OF JUSTICE

Title 28—Judicial Administration

CHAPTER 1—DEPARTMENT OF JUSTICE

PART 50—STATEMENTS OF POLICY

Uniform Guidelines on Employee Selection Procedures (1978)

The Uniform Guidelines on Employee Selection Procedures which are provided at the beginning of this part IV in today's FEDERAL REGISTER are adopted by the Department of Justice, in conjunction with the Civil Service Commission, Equal Employment Opportunity Commission, and the Department of Labor to establish a uniform Federal position in the area of prohibiting discrimination in employment practices on grounds of race, color, religion, sex, or national origin. Cross reference documents are published at 5 CFR 300.103(c), (Civil Service Commission) 29 CFR 1607 (Equal Employment Opportunity Commission), and 41 CFR 60-3 (Department of Labor), elsewhere in this issue of the FEDERAL REGISTER.

By virtue of the authority vested in me by 28 U.S.C. 509 and 5 U.S.C. 301, Sec. 50.14 of part 50 of chapter 1 of title 28 of the Code of Federal Regulations is amended by substituting the Uniform Guidelines on Employee Selection Procedures (1978) for part I through part IV.

Effective date: September 25, 1978.

GRIFFIN B. BELL,
Attorney General.

[6570-06]

EQUAL EMPLOYMENT OPPORTUNITY COMMISSION

Title 29—Labor

CHAPTER XIV—EQUAL EMPLOYMENT OPPORTUNITY COMMISSION

PART 1607—UNIFORM GUIDELINES ON EMPLOYEE SELECTION PROCEDURES (1978)

The Uniform Guidelines on Employee Selection Procedures which are printed at the beginning of this part IV in today's FEDERAL REGISTER' are adopted by the Equal Employment Opportunity Commission, in conjunction with the Civil Service Commission, Department of Justice, and the Department of Labor to establish a uniform Federal position in the area of prohibiting discrimination in employment practices on grounds of race, color, religion, sex, or national origin. Cross reference documents are published at 5 CFR 300.103(c) (Civil Service Commission), 28 CFR 50.14 (Department of Justice) and 41 CFR 60-3 Department of Labor), elsewhere in this issue.

By virtue of the authority vested in it by sections 713 and 709 of title VII of the Civil Rights Act of 1964 (78 Stat. 265), as amended by the Equal Employment Opportunity Act of 1972 (Pub. L. 92-261), (42 U.S.C. 2000e-12 and 2000e-8), the Equal Employment Opportunity Commission hereby revises part 1607 of chapter XIV of title 29 of the Code of Federal Regulations by rescinding the Guidelines on Employee Selection Procedures (see 35 FR 12333, August 1, 1970; and 41 FR 51984, November 24, 1976) and adopting the Uniform Guidelines on Employee Selection Procedures (1978) as a new part 1607.

Effective date: September 25, 1978.

ELEANOR HOLMES NORTON,
Chair.

339

[6570–06]

DEPARTMENT OF LABOR

Title 41—Public Contracts and Property Management

CHAPTER 60—OFFICE OF FEDERAL CONTRACT COMPLIANCE PROGRAMS, DEPARTMENT OF LABOR

PART 60–3—UNIFORM GUIDELINES ON EMPLOYEE SELECTION PROCEDURES (1978)

The Uniform Guidelines on Employee Selection Procedures which are printed at the beginning of this part IV of today's FEDERAL REGISTER are adopted by the Department of Labor, in conjunction with the Civil Service Commission, Department of Justice, and the Equal Employment Opportunity Commission to establish a uniform Federal position in the area of prohibiting discrimination in employment practices on grounds of race, color, religion, sex, or national origin. Cross reference documents are published at 5 CFR 300.103(c) (Civil Service Commission), 28 CFR 50.14 (Department of Justice) and 29 CFR 1607 (Equal Employment Opportunity Commission), elsewhere in this issue of the FEDERAL REGISTER.

By virtue of the authority of sections 201, 202, 203, 203(a), 205, 206(a), 301, 303(b), and 403(b) of Executive Order 11246, as amended, 30 FR 12319; 32 FR 14303; section 60–1.2 of part 60–1 of 41 CFR chapter 60, and section 715 of the Civil Rights Act of 1964, as amended (42 U.S.C. 2000e–14), part 60–3 of chapter 60 of title 41 of the Code of Federal Regulations is revised by rescinding the Guidelines on Employee Selection Procedures (see 41 FR 51744, November 23, 1976) and adopting the Uniform Guidelines on Employee Selection Procedures (1978) as a new part 60–3.

Effective date: September 25, 1978.

RAY MARSHALL,
Secretary of Labor.

[FR Doc. 76-23997 Filed 8-22-78; 4:48 pm]

FRIDAY, MARCH 2, 1979
PART IV

EQUAL EMPLOYMENT
OPPORTUNITY
COMMISSION

OFFICE OF PERSONNEL
MANAGEMENT

DEPARTMENT OF JUSTICE

DEPARTMENT OF LABOR

DEPARTMENT OF THE
TREASURY

■

ADOPTION OF QUESTIONS AND
ANSWERS TO CLARIFY AND
PROVIDE A COMMON
INTERPRETATION OF THE
UNIFORM GUIDELINES ON
EMPLOYEE SELECTION
PROCEDURES

federal register

344

[6570-06-M]

Title 29—Labor

CHAPTER XIV—EQUAL EMPLOYMENT OPPORTUNITY COMMISSION

PART 1607—UNIFORM GUIDELINES ON EMPLOYEE SELECTION PROCEDURES (1978)

Title 5—Administrative Personnel

OFFICE OF PERSONNEL MANAGEMENT

PART 300—EMPLOYMENT (GENERAL)

Title 28—Judicial Administration

CHAPTER I—DEPARTMENT OF JUSTICE

PART 50—STATEMENTS OF POLICY

Title 31—Money and Finance: Treasury

CHAPTER I—MONETARY OFFICES: DEPARTMENT OF THE TREASURY

PART 51—FISCAL ASSISTANCE TO STATE AND LOCAL GOVERNMENTS

Title 41—Public Contracts and Property Management

CHAPTER 60—OFFICE OF FEDERAL CONTRACT COMPLIANCE PROGRAMS, DEPARTMENT OF LABOR

PART 60-3—UNIFORM GUIDELINES ON EMPLOYEE SELECTION PROCEDURES (1978)

Adoption of Questions and Answers To Clarify and Provide a Common Interpretation of the Uniform Guidelines on Employee Selection Procedures

AGENCIES: Equal Employment Opportunity Commission, Office of Personnel Management, Department of Justice, Department of Labor and Department of Treasury.

ACTION: Adoption of questions and answers designed to clarify and provide a common interpretation of the Uniform Guidelines on Employee Selection Procedures.

SUMMARY: The Uniform Guidelines on Employee Selection Procedures were issued by the five Federal agen-

cies having primary responsibility for the enforcement of Federal equal employment opportunity laws, to establish a uniform Federal government position. See 43 FR 38290, et seq. (Aug. 25, 1978) and 43 FR 40223 (Sept. 11, 1978). They became effective on September 25, 1978. The issuing agencies recognize the need for a common interpretation of the Uniform Guidelines, as well as the desirability of providing additional guidance to employers and other users, psychologists, and investigators, compliance officers and other Federal enforcement personnel. These Questions and Answers are intended to address that need and to provide such guidance.

EFFECTIVE DATE: March 2, 1979.

FOR FURTHER INFORMATION CONTACT:

A. Diane Graham, Assistant Director, Affirmative Employment Programs, Office of Personnel Management, 1900 E Street, NW., Washington, D.C. 20415, 202/632-4420.

James Hellings, Special Assistant to the Assistant Director, Intergovernmental Personnel Programs, Office of Personnel Management, 1900 E Street, NW., Washington, D.C. 20415, 202/632-6248.

Kenneth A. Millard, Chief, State and Local Section, Personnel Research and Development Center, Office of Personnel Management, 1900 E St., NW., Washington, D.C. 20415, 202-632-8238.

Peter C. Robertson, Director, Office of Policy Implementation, Equal Employment Opportunity Commission, 2401 E Street, NW., Washington, D.C. 20506, 202/634-7060.

David L. Rose, Chief, Employment Section, Civil Rights Division, Department of Justice, 10th Street and Pennsylvania Avenue, NW., Washington, D.C. 20530, 202/633-3831.

Donald J. Schwartz, Psychologist, Office of Federal Contract Compliance Programs, Room C-3324, Department of Labor, 200 Constitution Avenue, NW., Washington, D.C. 20210, 202/523-9426.

Herman Schwartz, Chief Counsel, Office of Revenue Sharing, Department of the Treasury, 2401 E Street, NW., Washington, D.C. 20220, 202/634-5182.

James O. Taylor, Jr., Research Psychologist, Office of Systemic Programs, Equal Employment Opportunity Commission, 2401 E St., NW., Washington, D.C. 20506, 202/254-3036.

INTRODUCTION

The problems addressed by the Uniform Guidelines on Employee Selection Procedures (43 FR 38290 et seq., August 25, 1978) are numerous and im-

portant, and some of them are complex. The history of the development of those Guidelines is set forth in the introduction to them (43 FR 38290-95). The experience of the agencies has been that a series of answers to commonly asked questions is helpful in providing guidance not only to employers and other users, but also to psychologists and others who are called upon to conduct validity studies, and to investigators, compliance officers and other Federal personnel who have enforcement responsibilities.

The Federal agencies which issued the Uniform Guidelines—the Departments of Justice and Labor, the Equal Employment Opportunity Commission, the Civil Service Commission (which has been succeeded in relevant part by the Office of Personnel Management), and the Office of Revenue Sharing, Treasury Department—recognize that the goal of a uniform position on these issues can best be achieved through a common interpretation of the same guidelines. The following Questions and Answers are part of such a common interpretation. The material included is intended to interpret and clarify, but not to modify, the provisions of the Uniform Guidelines. The questions selected are commonly asked questions in the field and those suggested by the Uniform Guidelines themselves and by the extensive comments received on the various sets of proposed guidelines prior to their adoption. Terms are used in the questions and answers as they are defined in the Uniform Guidelines.

The agencies recognize that additional questions may be appropriate for similar treatment at a later date, and contemplate working together to provide additional guidance in interpreting the Uniform Guidelines. Users and other interested persons are invited to submit additional questions.

ELEANOR HOLMES NORTON,
Chair, Equal Employment Opportunity Commission.

ALAN K. CAMPBELL,
Director, Office of Personnel Management.

DREW S. DAYS III,
Assistant Attorney General, Civil Rights Division, Department of Justice.

WELDEN ROUGEAU,
Director, Office of Federal Contract Compliance, Department of Labor.

KENT A. PETERSON,
Acting Deputy Director, Office of Revenue Sharing.

I. PURPOSE AND SCOPE

1. Q. What is the purpose of the Guidelines?
A. The guidelines are designed to aid in the achievement of our nation's

goal of equal employment opportunity without discrimination on the grounds of race, color, sex, religion or national origin. The Federal agencies have adopted the Guidelines to provide a uniform set of principles governing use of employee selection procedures which is consistent with applicable legal standards and validation standards generally accepted by the psychological profession and which the Government will apply in the discharge of its responsibilities.

2. Q. What is the basic principle of the Guidelines?

A. A selection process which has an adverse impact on the employment opportunities of members of a race, color, religion, sex, or national origin group (referred to as "race, sex, and ethnic group," as defined in Section 16P) and thus disproportionately screens them out is unlawful unless the process or its component procedures have been validated in accord with the Guidelines, or the user otherwise justifies them in accord with Federal law. See Sections 3 and 6.[1] This principle was adopted by the Supreme Court unanimously in Griggs v. Duke Power Co., 401 U.S. 424, and was ratified and endorsed by the Congress when it passed the Equal Employment Opportunity Act of 1972, which amended Title VII of the Civil Rights Act of 1964.

3. Q. Who is covered by the Guidelines?

A. The Guidelines apply to private and public employers, labor organizations, employment agencies, apprenticeship committees, licensing and certification boards (see Question 7), and contractors or subcontractors, who are covered by one or more of the following provisions of Federal equal employment opportunity law: Title VII of the Civil Rights Act of 1964, as amended by the Equal Employment Opportunity Act of 1972 (hereinafter Title VII); Executive Order 11246, as amended by Executive Orders 11375 and 12086 (hereinafter Executive Order 11246); the State and Local Fiscal Assistance Act of 1972, as amended; Omnibus Crime Control and Safe Streets Act of 1968, as amended; and the Intergovernmental Personnel Act of 1970, as amended. Thus, under Title VII, the Guidelines apply to the Federal Government with regard to

Federal employment. Through Title VII they apply to most private employers who have 15 or more employees for 20 weeks or more a calendar year, and to most employment agencies, labor organizations and apprenticeship committees. They apply to state and local governments which employ 15 or more employees, or which receive revenue sharing funds, or which receive funds from the Law Enforcement Assistance Administration to impose and strengthen law enforcement and criminal justice, or which receive grants or other federal assistance under a program which requires maintenance of personnel standards on a merit basis. They apply through Executive Order 11246 to contractors and subcontractors of the Federal Government and to contractors and subcontractors under federally-assisted construction contracts.

4. Q. Are college placement officers and similar organizations considered to be users subject to the Guidelines?

A. Placement offices may or may not be subject to the Guidelines depending on what services they offer. If a placement office uses a selection procedure as a basis for any employment decision, it is covered under the definition of "user". Section 16. For example, if a placement office selects some students for referral to an employer but rejects others, it is covered. However, if the placement office refers all interested students to an employer, it is not covered, even though it may offer office space and provision for informing the students of job openings. The Guidelines are intended to cover all users of employee selection procedures, including employment agencies, who are subject to Federal equal employment opportunity law.

5. Q. Do the Guidelines apply only to written tests?

A. No. They apply to all selection procedures used to make employment decisions, including interviews, review of experience or education from application forms, work samples, physical requirements, and evaluations of performance. Sections 2B and 16Q, and see Question 6.

6. Q. What practices are covered by the Guidelines?

A. The Guidelines apply to employee selection procedures which are used in making employment decisions, such as hiring, retention, promotion, transfer, demotion, dismissal or referral. Section 2B. Employee selection procedures include job requirements (physical, education, experience), and evaluation of applicants or candidates on the basis of application forms, interviews, performance tests, paper and pencil tests, performance in training programs or probationary periods, and any other procedures used to make an employment decision whether admin-

istered by the employer or by an employment agency. See Section 2B.

7. Q. Do the Guidelines apply to the licensing and certification functions of state and local governments?

A. The Guidelines apply to such functions to the extent that they are covered by Federal law. Section 2B. The courts are divided on the issue of such coverage. The Government has taken the position that at least some kinds of licensing and certification which deny persons access to employment opportunity may be enjoined in an action brought pursuant to Section 707 of the Civil Rights Act of 1964, as amended.

8. Q. What is the relationship between Federal equal employment opportunity law, and State and Local government merit system laws or regulations requiring rank ordering of candidates and selection from a limited number of the top candidates?

A. The Guidelines permit ranking where the evidence of validity is sufficient to support that method of use. State or local laws which compel rank ordering generally do so on the assumption that the selection procedure is valid. Thus, if there is adverse impact and the validity evidence does not adequately support that method of use, proper interpretation of such a state law would require validation prior to ranking. Accordingly, there is no necessary or inherent conflict between Federal law and State or local laws of the kind described.

Under the Supremacy Clause of the Constitution (Art. VI, Cl. 2), however, Federal law or valid regulation overrides any contrary provision of state or local law. Thus, if there is any conflict, Federal equal opportunity law prevails. For example, in Rosenfeld v. So. Pacific Co., 444 F. 2d 1219 (9th Cir., 1971), the court held invalid state protective laws which prohibited the employment of women in jobs entailing long hours or heavy labor, because the state laws were in conflict with Title VII. Where a State or local official believes that there is a possible conflict, the official may wish to consult with the State Attorney General, County or City attorney, or other legal official to determine how to comply with the law.

II. ADVERSE IMPACT, THE BOTTOM LINE AND AFFIRMATIVE ACTION

9. Q. Do the Guidelines require that only validated selection procedures be used?

A. No. Although validation of selection procedures is desirable in personnel management, the Uniform Guidelines require users to produce evidence of validity only when the selection procedure adversely affects the opportunities of a race, sex, or ethnic group

---

[1] Section references throughout these questions and answers are to the sections of the Uniform Guidelines on Employee Selection Procedures (herein referred to as "Guidelines") that were published by the Equal Employment Opportunity Commission, the Civil Service Commission, the Department of Labor, and the Department of Justice on Aug. 25, 1978; 43 FR 38290. The Uniform Guidelines were adopted by the Office of Revenue Sharing of the Department of Treasury on September 11, 1978. 43 FR 40223.

for hire, transfer, promotion, retention or other employment decision. If there is no adverse impact, there is no validation requirement under the Guidelines. Sections 1B and 3A. See also, Section 8A.

10. Q. What is adverse impact?

A. Under the Guidelines adverse impact is a substantially different rate of selection in hiring, promotion or other employment decision which works to the disadvantage of members of a race, sex or ethnic group. Sections 4D and 16B. See Questions 11 and 12.

11. Q. What is a substantially different rate of selection?

A. The agencies have adopted a rule of thumb under which they will generally consider a selection rate for any race, sex, or ethnic group which is less than four-fifths (4/5ths) or eighty percent (80%) of the selection rate for the group with the highest selection rate as a substantially different rate of selection. See Section 4D. This "4/5ths" or "80%" rule of thumb is not intended as a legal definition, but is a practical means of keeping the attention of the enforcement agencies on serious discrepancies in rates of hiring, promotion and other selection decisions.

For example, if the hiring rate for whites other than Hispanics is 60%, for American Indians 45%, for Hispanics 48%, and for Blacks 51%, and each of these groups constitutes more than 2% of the labor force in the relevant labor area (see Question 16), a comparison should be made of the selection rate for each group with that of the highest group (whites). These comparisons show the following impact ratios: American Indians 45/60 or 75%; Hispanics 48/60 or 80%; and Blacks 51/60 or 85%. Applying the 4/5ths or 80% rule of thumb, on the basis of the above information alone, adverse impact is indicated for American Indians but not for Hispanics or Blacks.

12. Q. How is adverse impact determined?

A. Adverse impact is determined by a four step process.

(1) calculate the rate of selection for each group (divide the number of persons selected from a group by the number of applicants from that group).

(2) observe which group has the highest selection rate.

(3) calculate the impact ratios, by comparing the selection rate for each group with that of the highest group (divide the selection rate for a group by the selection rate for the highest group).

(4) observe whether the selection rate for any group is substantially less (i.e., usually less than 4/5ths or 80%) than the selection rate for the highest group. If it is, adverse impact is indicated in most circumstances. See Section 4D.

For example:

Applicants	Hires	Selection rate Percent hired
80 White	48	48/80 or 60%
40 Black	12	12/40 or 30%

A comparison of the black selection rate (30%) with the white selection rate (60%) shows that the black rate is 30/60, or one-half (or 50%) of the white rate. Since the one-half (50%) is less than 4/5ths (80%) adverse impact is usually indicated.

The determination of adverse impact is not purely arithmetic however; and other factors may be relevant. See, Section 4D.

13. Q. Is adverse impact determined on the basis of the overall selection process or for the components in that process?

A. Adverse impact is determined first for the overall selection process for each job. If the overall selection process has an adverse impact, the adverse impact of the individual selection procedure should be analyzed. For any selection procedures in the process having an adverse impact which the user continues to use in the same manner, the user is expected to have evidence of validity satisfying the Guidelines. Sections 4C and 5D. If there is no adverse impact for the overall selection process, in most circumstances there is no obligation under the Guidelines to investigate adverse impact for the components, or to validate the selection procedures used for that job. Section 4C. But see Question 25.

14. Q. The Guidelines designate the "total selection process" as the initial basis for determining the impact of selection procedures. What is meant by the "total selection process"?

A. The "total selection process" refers to the combined effect of all selection procedures leading to the final employment decision such as hiring or promoting. For example, appraisal of candidates for administrative assistant positions in an organization might include initial screening based upon an application blank and interview, a written test, a medical examination, a background check, and a supervisor's interview. These in combination are the total selection process. Additionally, where there is more than one route to the particular kind of employment decision, the total selection process encompasses the combined results of all routes. For example, an employer may select some applicants for a particular kind of job through appropriate written and performance tests. Others may be selected through an internal upward mobility program, on the basis

of successful performance in a directly related trainee type of position. In such a case, the impact of the total selection process would be the combined effect of both avenues of entry.

15. Q. What is meant by the terms "applicant" and "candidate" as they are used in the Uniform Guidelines?

A. The precise definition of the term "applicant" depends upon the user's recruitment and selection procedures. The concept of an applicant is that of a person who has indicated an interest in being considered for hiring, promotion, or other employment opportunities. This interest might be expressed by completing an application form, or might be expressed orally, depending upon the employer's practice.

The term "candidate" has been included to cover those situations where the initial step by the user involves consideration of current employees for promotion, or training, or other employment opportunities, without inviting applications. The procedure by which persons are identified as candidates is itself a selection procedure under the Guidelines.

A person who voluntarily withdraws formally or informally at any stage of the selection process is no longer an applicant or candidate for purposes of computing adverse impact. Employment standards imposed by the user which discourage disproportionately applicants of a race, sex or ethnic group may, however, require justification. Records should be kept for persons who were applicants or candidates at any stage of the process.

16. Q. Should adverse impact determinations be made for all groups regardless of their size?

A. No. Section 15A(2) calls for annual adverse impact determinations to be made for each group which constitutes either 2% or more of the total labor force in the relevant labor area, or 2% or more of the applicable workforce. Thus, impact determinations should be made for any employment decision for each group which constitutes 2% or more of the labor force in the relevant labor area. For hiring, such determination should also be made for groups which constitute more than 2% of the applicants; and for promotions, determinations should also be made for those groups which constitute at least 2% of the user's workforce. There are record keeping obligations for all groups, even those which are less than 2%. See Question 86.

17. Q. In determining adverse impact, do you compare the selection rates for males and females, and blacks and whites, or do you compare selection rates for white males, white females, black males and black females?

A. The selection rates for males and females are compared, and the selection rates for the race and ethnic groups are compared with the selection rate of the race or ethnic group with the highest selection rate. Neutral and objective selection procedures free of adverse impact against any race, sex or ethnic group are unlikely to have an impact against a subgroup. Thus there is no obligation to make comparisons for subgroups (e.g., white male, white female, black male, black female). However, there are obligations to keep records (see Question 87), and any apparent exclusion of a subgroup may suggest the presence of discrimination.

18. Q. Is it usually necessary to calculate the statistical significance of differences in selection rates when investigating the existence of adverse impact?

A. No. Adverse impact is normally indicated when one selection rate is less than 80% of the other. The federal enforcement agencies normally will use only the 80% (4/5ths) rule of thumb, except where large numbers of selections are made. See Questions 20 and 22.

19. Q. Does the 4/5ths rule of thumb mean that the Guidelines will tolerate up to 20% discrimination?

A. No. The 4/5ths rule of thumb speaks only to the question of adverse impact, and is not intended to resolve the ultimate question of unlawful discrimination. Regardless of the amount of difference in selection rates, unlawful discrimination may be present, and may be demonstrated through appropriate evidence. The 4/5ths rule merely establishes a numerical basis for drawing an initial inference and for requiring additional information.

With respect to adverse impact, the Guidelines expressly state (section 4D) that differences in selection rates of less than 20% may still amount to adverse impact where the differences are significant in both statistical and practical terms. See Question 20. In the absence of differences which are large enough to meet the 4/5ths rule of thumb or a test of statistical significance, there is no reason to assume that the differences are reliable, or that they are based upon anything other than chance.

20. Q. Why is the 4/5ths rule called a rule of thumb?

A. Because it is not intended to be controlling in all circumstances. If, for the sake of illustration, we assume that nationwide statistics show that use of an arrest record would disqualify 10% of all Hispanic persons but only 4% of all whites other than Hispanic (hereafter non-Hispanic), the selection rate for that selection procedure is 90% for Hispanics and 96% for non-Hispanics. Therefore, the 4/5 rule of thumb would not indicate the presence of adverse impact (90% is approximately 94% of 96%). But in this example, the information is based upon nationwide statistics, and the sample is large enough to yield statistically significant results, and the difference (Hispanics are 2½ times as likely to be disqualified as non-Hispanics) is large enough to be practically significant. Thus, in this example the enforcement agencies would consider a disqualification based on an arrest record alone as having an adverse impact. Likewise, in *Gregory* v. *Litton Industries*, 472 F. 2d 631 (9th Cir., 1972), the court held that the employer violated Title VII by disqualifying persons from employment solely on the basis of an arrest record, where that disqualification had an adverse impact on blacks and was not shown to be justified by business necessity.

On the other hand, a difference of more than 20% in rates of selection may not provide a basis for finding adverse impact if the number of persons selected is very small. For example, if the employer selected three males and one female from an applicant pool of 20 males and 10 females, the 4/5ths rule would indicate adverse impact (selection rate for women is 10%; for men 15%; 10/15 or 66⅔% is less than 80%), yet the number of selections is too small to warrant a determination of adverse impact. In these circumstances, the enforcement agency would not require validity evidence in the absence of additional information (such as selection rates for a longer period of time) indicating adverse impact. For recordkeeping requirements, see Section 15A(2)(c) and Questions 84 and 85.

21. Q. Is evidence of adverse impact sufficient to warrant a validity study or an enforcement action where the numbers involved are so small that it is more likely than not that the difference could have occurred by chance? For example:

Applicants	Not hired	Hired	Selection rate percent hired
80 White	64	16	20
20 Black	17	3	15

White Selection Rate 20
Black Selection Rate 15
15 divided by 20 = 75% (which is less than 80%).

A. No. If the numbers of persons and the difference in selection rates are so small that it is likely that the difference could have occurred by chance, the Federal agencies will not assume the existence of adverse impact, in the absence of other evidence. In this example, the difference in selection rates is too small, given the small number of black applicants, to constitute adverse impact in the absence of other information (see Section 4D). If only one more black had been hired instead of a white the selection rate for blacks (20%) would be higher than that for whites (18.7%). Generally, it is inappropriate to require validity evidence or to take enforcement action where the number of persons and the difference in selection rates are so small that the selection of one different person for one job would shift the result from adverse impact against one group to a situation in which that group has a higher selection rate than the other group.

On the other hand, if a lower selection rate continued over a period of time, so as to constitute a pattern, then the lower selection rate would constitute adverse impact, warranting the need for validity evidence.

22. Q. Is it ever necessary to calculate the statistical significance of differences in selection rates to determine whether adverse impact exists?

A. Yes. Where large numbers of selections are made, relatively small differences in selection rates may nevertheless constitute adverse impact if they are both statistically and practically significant. See Section 4D and Question 20. For that reason, if there is a small difference in selection rates (one rate is more than 80% of the other), but large numbers of selections are involved, it would be appropriate to calculate the statistical significance of the difference in selection rates.

23. Q. When the 4/5th rule of thumb shows adverse impact, is there adverse impact under the Guidelines?

A. There usually is adverse impact, except where the number of persons selected and the difference in selection rates are very small. See Section 4D and Questions 20 and 21.

24. Q. Why do the Guidelines rely primarily upon the 4/5ths rule of thumb, rather than tests of statistical significance?

A. Where the sample of persons selected is not large, even a large real difference between groups is likely not to be confirmed by a test of statistical significance (at the usual .05 level of significance). For this reason, the Guidelines do not rely primarily upon a test of statistical significance, but use the 4/5ths rule of thumb as a practical and easy-to-administer measure of whether differences in selection rates are substantial. Many decisions in day-to-day life are made without reliance upon a test of statistical significance.

25. Q. Are there any circumstances in which the employer should evaluate components of a selection process, even though the overall selection process results in no adverse impact?

A. Yes, there are such circumstances: (1) Where the selection procedure is a significant factor in the continuation of patterns of assignments of incumbent employees caused by prior discriminatory employment practices. Assume, for example, an employer who traditionally hired blacks as employees for the "laborer" department in a manufacturing plant, and traditionally hired only whites as skilled craftsmen. Assume further that the employer in 1962 began to use a written examination not supported by a validity study to screen incumbent employees who sought to enter the apprenticeship program for skilled craft jobs. The employer stopped making racial assignments in 1972. Assume further that for the last four years, there have been special recruitment efforts aimed at recent black high school graduates and that the selection process, which includes the written examination, has resulted in the selection of black applicants for apprenticeship in approximately the same rates as white applicants.

In those circumstances, if the written examination had an adverse impact, its use would tend to keep incumbent black employees in the laborer department, and deny them entry to apprenticeship programs. For that reason, the enforcement agencies would expect the user to evaluate the impact of the written examination, and to have validity evidence for the use of the written examination if it has an adverse impact.

(2) Where the weight of court decisions or administrative interpretations holds that a specific selection procedure is not job related in similar circumstances.

For example, courts have held that because an arrest is not a determination of guilt, an applicant's arrest record by itself does not indicate inability to perform a job consistent with the trustworthy and efficient operation of a business. Yet a no arrest record requirement has a nationwide adverse impact on some minority groups. Thus, an employer who refuses to hire applicants solely on the basis of an arrest record is on notice that this policy may be found to be discriminatory. *Gregory v. Litton Industries*, 472 F. 2d 631 (9th Cir., 1972) (excluding persons from employment solely on the basis of arrests, which has an adverse impact, held to violate Title VII). Similarly, a minimum height requirement disproportionately disqualifies women and some national origin groups, and has been held not to be job related in a number of cases. For example, in *Dothard v. Rawlinson*, 433 U.S. 321 (1977), the Court held that height and weight requirements not shown to be job related were violative of Title VII. Thus an employer using a minimum height requirement should have evidence of its validity.

(3) In addition, there may be other circumstances in which an enforcement agency may decide to request an employer to evaluate components of a selection process, but such circumstances would clearly be unusual. Any such decision will be made only at a high level in the agency. Investigators and compliance officers are not authorized to make this decision.

26. Q. Does the bottom line concept of Section 4C apply to the administrative processing of charges of discrimination filed with an issuing agency, alleging that a specific selection procedure is discriminatory?

A. No. The bottom line concept applies only to enforcement actions as defined in Section 16 of the Guidelines. Enforcement actions include only court enforcement actions and other similar proceedings as defined in Section 16I. The EEOC administrative processsing of charges of discrimination (investigation, finding of reasonable cause/no cause, and conciliation) required by Section 706(b) of Title VII are specifically exempted from the bottom line concept by the definition of an enforcement action. The bottom line concept is a result of a decision by the various enforcement agencies that, as a matter of prosecutorial discretion, they will devote their limited enforcement resources to the most serious offenders of equal employment opportunity laws. Since the concept is not a rule of law, it does not affect the discharge by the EEOC of its statutory responsibilities to investigate charges of discrimination, render an administrative finding on its investigation, and engage in voluntary conciliation efforts. Similarly, with respect to the other issuing agencies, the bottom line concept applies not to the processing of individual charges, but to the initiation of enforcement action.

27. Q. An employer uses one test or other selection procedure to select persons for a number of different jobs. Applicants are given the test, and the successful applicants are then referred to different departments and positions on the basis of openings available and their interests. The Guidelines appear to require assessment of adverse impact on a job-by-job basis (Section 15A(2)(a)). Is there some way to show that the test as a whole does not have adverse impact even though the proportions of members of each race, sex or ethnic group assigned to different jobs may vary?

A. Yes, in some circumstances. The Guidelines require evidence of validity only for those selection procedures which have an adverse impact, and which are part of a selection process which has an adverse impact. If the test is administered and used in the same fashion for a variety of jobs, the impact of that test can be assessed in

the aggregate. The records showing the results of the test, and the total number of persons selected, generally would be sufficient to show the impact of the test. If the test has no adverse impact, it need not be validated.

But the absence of adverse impact of the test in the aggregate does not end the inquiry. For there may be discrimination or adverse impact in the assignment of individuals to, or in the selection of persons for, particular jobs. The Guidelines call for records to be kept and determinations of adverse impact to be made of the overall selection process on a job by job basis. Thus, if there is adverse impact in the assignment or selection procedures for a job even though there is no adverse impact from the test, the user should eliminate the adverse impact from the assignment procedure or justify the assignment procedure.

28. Q. The Uniform Guidelines apply to the requirements of Federal law prohibiting employment practices which discriminate on the grounds of race, color, religion, sex or national origin. However, records are required to be kept only by sex and by specified race and ethnic groups. How can adverse impact be determined for religious groups and for national origin groups other than those specified in Section 4B of the Guidelines?

A. The groups for which records are required to be maintained are the groups for which there is extensive evidence of continuing discriminatory practices. This limitation is designed in part to minimize the burden on employers for recordkeeping which may not be needed.

For groups for which records are not required, the person(s) complaining may obtain information from the employer or others (voluntarily or through legal process) to show that adverse impact has taken place. When that has been done, the various provisions of the Uniform Guidelines are fully applicable.

Whether or not there is adverse impact, Federal equal employment opportunity law prohibits any deliberate discrimination or disparate treatment on grounds of religion or national origin, as well as on grounds of sex, color, or race.

Whenever "ethnic" is used in the Guidelines or in these Questions and Answers, it is intended to include national origin and religion, as set forth in the statutes, executive orders, and regulations prohibiting discrimination. See Section 16P.

29. Q. What is the relationship between affirmative action and the requirements of the Uniform Guidelines?

A. The two subjects are different, although related. Compliance with the Guidelines does not relieve users of their affirmative action obligations, including those of Federal contractors and subcontractors under Executive Order 11246. Section 13.

The Guidelines encourage the development and effective implementation of affirmative action plans or programs in two ways. First, in determining whether to institute action against a user on the basis of a selection procedure which has adverse impact and which has not been validated, the enforcement agency will take into account the general equal employment opportunity posture of the user with respect to the job classifications for which the procedure is used and the progress which has been made in carrying out any affirmative action program. Section 4E. If the user has demonstrated over a substantial period of time that it is in fact appropriately utilizing in the job or group of jobs in question the available race, sex or ethnic groups in the relevant labor force, the enforcement agency will generally exercise its discretion by not initiating enforcement proceedings based on adverse impact in relation to the applicant flow. Second, nothing in the Guidelines is intended to preclude the use of selection procedures, consistent with Federal law, which assist in the achievement of affirmative action objectives. Section 13A. See also, Questions 30 and 31.

30. Q. When may a user be race, sex or ethnic-conscious?

A. The Guidelines recognize that affirmative action programs may be race, sex or ethnic conscious in appropriate circumstances, (See Sections 4E and 13; See also Section 17, Appendix). In addition to obligatory affirmative action programs (See Question 29), the Guidelines encourage the adoption of voluntary affirmative action programs. Users choosing to engage in voluntary affirmative action are referred to EEOC's Guidelines on Affirmative Action (44 F.R. 4422, January 19, 1979). A user may justifiably be race, sex or ethnic-conscious in circumstances where it has reason to believe that qualified persons of specified race, sex or ethnicity have been or may be subject to the exclusionary effects of its selection procedures or other employment practices in its work force or particular jobs therein. In establishing long and short range goals, the employer may use the race, sex, or ethnic classification as the basis for such goals (Section 17(3) (a)).

In establishing a recruiting program, the employer may direct its recruiting activities to locations or institutions which have a high proportion of the race, sex, or ethnic group which has been excluded or underutilized (section 17(3) (b)). In establishing the pool of qualified persons from which final

selections are to be made, the employer may take reasonable steps to assure that members of the excluded or underutilized race, sex, or ethnic group are included in the pool (Section 17(3) (e)).

Similarly, the employer may be race, sex or ethnic-conscious in determining what changes should be implemented if the objectives of the programs are not being met (Section 17(3) (g)).

Even apart from affirmative action programs a user may be race, sex or ethnic-conscious in taking appropriate and lawful measures to eliminate adverse impact from selection procedures (Section 6A).

31. Q. Section 6A authorizes the use of alternative selection procedures to eliminate adverse impact, but does not appear to address the issue of validity. Thus, the use of alternative selection procedures without adverse impact seems to be presented as an option in lieu of validation. Is that its intent?

A. Yes. Under Federal equal employment opportunity law the use of any selection procedure which has an adverse impact on any race, sex or ethnic group is discriminatory unless the procedure has been properly validated, or the use of the procedure is otherwise justified under Federal law. *Griggs* v. *Duke Power Co.*, 401 U.S. 424 (1971); Section 3A. If a selection procedure has an adverse impact, therefore, Federal equal employment opportunity law authorizes the user to choose lawful alternative procedures which eliminate the adverse impact rather than demonstrating the validity of the original selection procedure.

Many users, while wishing to validate all of their selection procedures, are not able to conduct the validity studies immediately. Such users have the option of choosing alternative techniques which eliminate adverse impact, with a view to providing a basis for determining subsequently which selection procedures are valid and have as little adverse impact as possible.

Apart from Federal equal employment opportunity law, employers have economic incentives to use properly validated selection procedures. Nothing in Section 6A should be interpreted as discouraging the use of properly validated selection procedures; but Federal equal employment opportunity law does not require validity studies to be conducted unless there is adverse impact. See Section 2C.

III. GENERAL QUESTIONS CONCERNING VALIDITY AND THE USE OF SELECTION PROCEDURES

32. Q. What is "validation" according to the Uniform Guidelines?

A. Validation is the demonstration of the job relatedness of a selection procedure. The Uniform Guidelines

recognize the same three validity strategies recognized by the American Psychological Association:

(1) Criterion-related validity—a statistical demonstration of a relationship between scores on a selection procedure and job performance of a sample of workers.

(2) Content validity—a demonstration that the content of a selection procedure is representative of important aspects of performance on the job.

(3) Construct validity—a demonstration that (a) a selection procedure measures a construct (something believed to be an underlying human trait or characteristic, such as honesty) and (b) the construct is important for successful job performance.

33. Q. What is the typical process by which validity studies are reviewed by an enforcement agency?

A. The validity study is normally requested by an enforcement officer during the course of a review. The officer will first determine whether the selection process has an adverse impact, and if so, which component selection procedures have an adverse impact. See Section 15A(3). The officer will then ask for the evidence of validity for each procedure which has an adverse impact. See Sections 15B, C, and D. This validity evidence will be referred to appropriate personnel for review. Agency findings will then be communicated to the user.

34. Q. Can a user send its validity evidence to an enforcement agency before a review, so as to assure its validity?

A. No. Enforcement agencies will not review validity reports except in the context of investigations or reviews. Even in those circumstances, validity evidence will not be reviewed without evidence of how the selection procedure is used and what impact its use has on various race, sex, and ethnic groups.

35. Q. May reports of validity prepared by publishers of commercial tests and printed in test manuals or other literature be helpful in meeting the Guidelines?

A. They may be. However, it is the user's responsibility to determine that the validity evidence is adequate to meet the Guidelines. See Section 7, and Questions 43 and 66. Users should not use selection procedures which are likely to have an adverse impact without reviewing the evidence of validity to make sure that the standards of the Guidelines are met.

The following questions and answers (36-81) assume that a selection procedure has an adverse impact and is part of a selection process that has an adverse impact.

36. Q. How can users justify continued use of a procedure on a basis other than validity?

A. Normally, the method of justifying selection procedures with an adverse impact and the method to which the Guidelines are primarily addressed, is validation. The method of justification of a procedure by means other than validity is one to which the Guidelines are not addressed. See Section 6B. In *Griggs* v. *Duke Power Co.*, 401 U.S. 424, the Supreme Court indicated that the burden on the user was a heavy one, but that the selection procedure could be used if there was a "business necessity" for its continued use; therefore, the Federal agencies will consider evidence that a selection procedure is necessary for the safe and efficient operation of a business to justify continued use of a selection procedure.

37. Q. Is the demonstration of a rational relationship (as that term is used in constitutional law) between a selection procedure and the job sufficient to meet the validation requirements of the Guidelines?

A. No. The Supreme Court in *Washington* v. *Davis*, 426 U.S. 229 (1976) stated that different standards would be applied to employment discrimination allegations arising under the Constitution than would be applied to employment discrimination allegations arising under Title VII. The *Davis* case arose under the Constitution, and no Title VII violation was alleged. The Court applied a traditional constitutional law standard of "rational relationship" and said that it would defer to the "seemingly reasonable acts of administrators and executives." However, it went on to point out that under Title VII, the appropriate standard would still be an affirmative demonstration of the relationship between the selection procedure and measures of job performance by means of accepted procedures of validation and it would be an "insufficient response to demonstrate some rational basis" for a selection procedure having an adverse impact. Thus, the mere demonstration of a rational relationship between a selection procedure and the job does not meet the requirement of Title VII of the Civil Rights Act of 1964, or of Executive Order 11246, or the State and Local Fiscal Assistance Act of 1972, as amended (the revenue sharing act) or the Omnibus Crime Control and Safe Streets Act of 1968, as amended, and will not meet the requirements of these Guidelines for a validity study. The three validity strategies called for by these Guidelines all require evidence that the selection procedure is related to successful performance on the job. That evidence may be obtained through local validation or through validity studies done elsewhere.

38. Q. Can a user rely upon written or oral assertions of validity instead of evidence of validity?

A. No. If a user's selection procedures have an adverse impact, the user is expected to produce evidence of the validity of the procedures as they are used. Thus, the unsupported assertion by anyone, including representatives of the Federal government or State Employment Services, that a test battery or other selection procedure has been validated is not sufficient to satisfy the Guidelines.

39. Q. Are there any formal requirements imposed by these Guidelines as to who is allowed to perform a validity study?

A. No. A validity study is judged on its own merits, and may be performed by any person competent to apply the principles of validity research, including a member of the user's staff or a consultant. However, it is the user's responsibility to see that the study meets validity provisions of the Guidelines, which are based upon professionally accepted standards. See Question 42.

40. Q. What is the relationship between the validation provisions of the Guidelines and other statements of psychological principles, such as the *Standards for Educational and Psychological Tests*, published by the American Psychological Association ("Wash., D.C., 1974") (hereinafter "American Psychological Association *Standards*")?

A. The validation provisions of the Guidelines are designed to be consistent with the generally accepted standards of the psychological profession. These Guidelines also interpret Federal equal employment opportunity law, and embody some policy determinations of an administrative nature. To the extent that there may be differences between particular provisions of the Guidelines and expressions of validation principles found elsewhere, the Guidelines will be given precedence by the enforcement agencies.

41. Q. When should a validity study be carried out?

A. When a selection procedure has adverse impact on any race, sex or ethnic group, the Guidelines generally call for a validity study or the elimination of adverse impact. See Sections 3A and 6, and Questions 9, 31, and 36. If a selection procedure has adverse impact, its use in making employment decisions without adequate evidence of validity would be inconsistent with the Guidelines. Users who choose to continue the use of a selection procedure with an adverse impact until the procedure is challenged increase the risk that they will be found to be engaged in discriminatory practices and will be liable for back pay awards, plaintiffs' attorneys' fees, loss of Federal contracts, subcontracts or grants, and the like. Validation studies begun on the eve of litigation have seldom been found to be adequate. Users who choose to validate selection procedures should consider the potential benefit from having a validation study completed or well underway before the procedures are administered for use in employment decisions.

42. Q. Where can a user obtain professional advice concerning validation of selection procedures?

A. Many industrial and personnel psychologists validate selection procedures, review published evidence of validity and make recommendations with respect to the use of selection procedures. Many of these individuals are members or fellows of Division 14 (Industrial and Organizational Psychology) or Division 5 (Evaluation and Measurement) of the American Psychological Association. They can be identified in the membership directory of that organization. A high level of qualification is represented by a diploma in Industrial Psychology awarded by the American Board of Professional Psychology.

Individuals with the necessary competence may come from a variety of backgrounds. The primary qualification is pertinent training and experience in the conduct of validation research.

Industrial psychologists and other persons competent in the field may be found as faculty members in colleges and universities (normally in the departments of psychology or business administration) or working as individual consultants or as members of a consulting organization.

Not all psychologists have the necessary expertise. States have boards which license and certify psychologists, but not generally in a specialty such as industrial psychology. However, State psychological associations may be a source of information as to individuals qualified to conduct validation studies. Addresses of State psychological associations or other sources of information may be obtained from the American Psychological Association, 1200 Seventeenth Street, NW., Washington, D.C. 20036.

43. Q. Can a selection procedure be a valid predictor of performance on a job in a certain location and be invalid for predicting success on a different job or the same job in a different location?

A. Yes. Because of differences in work behaviors, criterion measures, study samples or other factors, a selection procedure found to have validity in one situation does not necessarily have validity in different circumstances. Conversely, a selection procedure not found to have validity in one situation may have validity in different circumstances. For these reasons, the Guidelines requires that certain standards be satisfied before a user may rely upon findings of validity in another situation. Section 7 and Section 14D. See also, Question 66. Cooperative and multi-unit studies are however encouraged, and, when those standards of the Guidelines are satisfied, validity evidence specific to each location is not required. See Section 7C and Section 8.

44. Q. Is the user of a selection procedure required to develop the procedure?

A. No. A selection procedure developed elsewhere may be used. However, the user has the obligation to show that its use for the particular job is consistent with the Guidelines. See Section 7.

45. Q. Do the Guidelines permit users to engage in cooperative efforts to meet the Guidelines?

A. Yes. The Guidelines not only permit but encourage such efforts. Where users have participated in a cooperative study which meets the validation standards of these Guidelines and proper account has been taken of variables which might affect the applicability of the study to specific users, validity evidence specific to each user will not be required. Section 8.

46. Q. Must the same method for validation be used for all parts of a selection process?

A. No. For example, where a selection process includes both a physical performance test and an interview, the physical test might be supported on the basis of content validity, and the interview on the basis of a criterion-related study.

47. Q. Is a showing of validity sufficient to assure the lawfulness of the use of a selection procedure?

A. No. The use of the selection procedure must be consistent with the validity evidence. For example, if a research study shows only that, at a given passing score the test satisfactorily screens out probable failures, the study would not justify the use of substantially different passing scores, or of ranked lists of those who passed. See Section 5G. Similarly, if the research shows that a battery is valid when a particular set of weights is used, the weights actually used must conform to those that were established by the research.

48. Q. Do the Guidelines call for a user to consider and investigate alternative selection procedures when conducting a validity study?

A. Yes. The Guidelines call for a user, when conducting a validity study, to make a reasonable effort to become aware of suitable alternative selection procedures and methods of

use which have as little adverse impact as possible, and to investigate those which are suitable. Section 3B.

An alternative procedure may not previously have been used by the user for the job in question and may not have been extensively used elsewhere. Accordingly, the preliminary determination of the suitability of the alternative selection procedure for the user and job in question may have to be made on the basis of incomplete information. If on the basis of the evidence available, the user determines that the alternative selection procedure is likely to meet its legitimate needs, and is likely to have less adverse impact than the existing selection procedure, the alternative should be investigated further as a part of the validity study. The extent of the investigation should be reasonable. Thus, the investigation should continue until the user has reasonably concluded that the alternative is not useful or not suitable, or until a study of its validity has been completed. Once the full validity study has been completed, including the evidence concerning the alternative procedure, the user should evaluate the results of the study to determine which procedure should be used. See Section 3B and Question 50.

49. Q. Do the Guidelines call for a user continually to investigate "suitable alternative selection procedures and suitable alternative methods of using the selection procedure which have as little adverse impact as possible"?

A. No. There is no requirement for continual investigation. A reasonable investigation of alternatives is called for by the Guidelines as a part of any validity study. Once the study is complete and validity has been found, however, there is generally no obligation to conduct further investigations, until such time as a new study is called for. See, Sections 3B and 5K. If a government agency, complainant, civil rights organization or other person having a legitimate interest shows such a user an alternative procedure with less adverse impact and with substantial evidence of validity for the same job in similar circumstances, the user is obliged to investigate only the particular procedure which has been presented. Section 3B.

50. Q. In what circumstances do the Guidelines call for the use of an alternative selection procedure or an alternative method of using the procedure?

A. The alternative selection procedure (or method of use) should be used when it has less adverse impact and when the evidence shows that its validity is substantially the same or greater for the same job in similar circumstances. Thus, if under the original selection procedure the selection rate for black applicants was only one

half (50 percent) that of the selection rate for white applicants, whereas under the alternative selection procedure the selection rate for blacks is two-thirds (67 percent) that of white applicants, the new alternative selection procedure should be used when the evidence shows substantially the same or greater validity for the alternative than for the original procedure. The same principles apply to a new user who is deciding what selection procedure to institute.

51. Q. What are the factors to be considered in determining whether the validity for one procedure is substantially the same as or greater than that of another procedure?

A. In the case of a criterion-related validity study, the factors include the importance of the criteria for which significant relationships are found, the magnitude of the relationship between selection procedure scores and criterion measures, and the size and composition of the samples used. For content validity, the strength of validity evidence would depend upon the proportion of critical and/or important job behaviors measured, and the extent to which the selection procedure resembles actual work samples or work behaviors. Where selection procedures have been validated by different strategies, or by construct validity, the determination should be made on a case by case basis.

52. Q. The Guidelines require consideration of alternative procedures and alternative methods of use, in light of the evidence of validity and utility and the degree of adverse impact of the procedure. How can a user know that any selection procedure with an adverse impact is lawful?

A. The Uniform Guidelines (Section 5G) expressly permit the use of a procedure in a manner supported by the evidence of validity and utility, even if another method of use has a lesser adverse impact. With respect to consideration of alternative selection procedures, if the user made a reasonable effort to become aware of alternative procedures, has considered them and investigated those which appear suitable as a part of the validity study, and has shown validity for a procedure, the user has complied with the Uniform Guidelines. The burden is then on the person challenging the procedure to show that there is another procedure with better or substantially equal validity which will accomplish the same legitimate business purposes with less adverse impact. Section 3B. See also, *Albemarle Paper Co. v. Moody*, 422 U.S. 405.

53. Q. Are the Guidelines consistent with the decision of the Supreme Court in *Furnco Construction Corp. v. Waters*, ―― *U.S.* ――, 98 S. Ct. 2943 (1978) where the Court stated: "Title

VII * * * does not impose a duty to adopt a hiring procedure that maximizes hiring of minority employees."

A. Yes. The quoted statement in *Furnco* v. *Waters* was made on a record where there was no adverse impact in the hiring process, no different treatment, no intentional discrimination, and no contractual obligations under E.O. 11246. Section 3B of the Guidelines is predicated upon a finding of adverse impact. Section 3B indicates that, when two or more selection procedures are available which serve a legitimate business purpose with substantially equal validity, the user should use the one which has been demonstrated to have the lesser adverse impact. Part V of the Overview of the Uniform Guidelines, in elaborating on this principle, states: "Federal equal employment opportunity law has added a requirement to the process of validation. In conducting a validation study, the employer should consider available alternatives which will achieve its legitimate purpose with lesser adverse impact."

Section 3B of the Guidelines is based on the principle enunciated in the Supreme Court decision in *Albermarle Paper Co.* v. *Moody*, 422 U.S. 405 (1975) that, even where job relatedness has been proven, the availability of other tests or selection devices which would also serve the employer's legitimate interest in "efficient and trustworthy workmanship" without a similarly undesirable racial effect would be evidence that the employer was using its tests merely as a pretext for discrimination.

Where adverse impact still exists, even though the selection procedure has been validated, there continues to be an obligation to consider alternative procedures which reduce or remove that adverse impact if an opportunity presents itself to do so without sacrificing validity. Where there is no adverse impact, the *Furnco* principle rather than the *Albermarle* principle is applicable.

IV. TECHNICAL STANDARDS

54. Q. How does a user choose which validation strategy to use?

A. A user should select a validation strategy or strategies which are (1) appropriate for the type of selection procedure, the job, and the employment situation, and (2) technically and administratively feasible. Whatever method of validation is used, the basic logic is one of prediction; that is, the presumption that level of performance on the selection procedure will, on the average, be indicative of level of performance on the job after selection. Thus, a criterion-related study, particularly a predictive one, is often regarded as the closest to such an ideal.

See American Psychological Association *Standards*, pp. 26-27.

Key conditions for a criterion-related study are a substantial number of individuals for inclusion in the study, and a considerable range of performance on the selection and criterion measures. In addition, reliable and valid measures of job performance should be available, or capable of being developed. Section 14B(1). Where such circumstances exist, a user should consider use of the criterion-related strategy.

Content validity is appropriate where it is technically and administratively feasible to develop work samples or measures of operationally defined skills, knowledges, or abilities which are a necessary prerequisite to observable work behaviors. Content validity is not appropriate for demonstrating the validity of tests of mental processes or aptitudes or characteristics; and is not appropriate for knowledges, skills or abilities which an employee will be expected to learn on the job. Section 14C(1)

The application of a construct validity strategy to support employee selection procedures is newer and less developed than criterion-related or content validity strategies. Continuing research may result in construct validity becoming more widely used. Because construct validity represents a generalization of findings, one situation in which construct validity might hold particular promise is that where it is desirable to use the same selection procedures for a variety of jobs. An overriding consideration in whether or not to consider construct validation is the availability of an individual with a high level of expertise in this field.

In some situations only one kind of validation study is likely to be appropriate. More than one strategy may be possible in other circumstances, in which case administrative considerations such as time and expense may be decisive. A combination of approaches may be feasible and desirable.

55. Q. Why do the Guidelines recognize only content, construct and criterion-related validity?

A. These three validation strategies are recognized in the Guidelines since they represent the current professional consensus. If the professional community recognizes new strategies or substantial modifications of existing strategies, they will be considered and, if necessary, changes will be made in the Guidelines. Section 5A.

56. Q. Why don't the Uniform Guidelines state a preference for criterion-related validity over content or construct validity?

A. Generally accepted principles of the psychological profession support the use of criterion-related, content or

construct validity strategies as appropriate. American Psychological Association *Standards*, E, pp. 25-26. This use was recognized by the supreme Court in *Washington* v. *Davis*, 426 U.S. 229, 247, fn. 13. Because the Guidelines describe the conditions under which each validity strategy is inappropriate, there is no reason to state a general preference for any one validity strategy.

57. .Q. Are the Guidelines intended to restrict the development of new testing strategies, psychological theories, methods of job analysis or statistical techniques?

A. No. The Guidelines are concerned with the validity and fairness of selection procedures used in making employment decisions, and are not intended to limit research and new developments. See Question 55.

58. Q. Is a full job analysis necessary for all validity studies?

A. It is required for all content and construct studies, but not for all criterion-related studies. See Sections 14A and 14B(2). Measures of the results or outcomes of work behaviors such as production rate or error rate may be used without a full job analysis where a review of information about the job shows that these criteria are important to the employment situation of the user. Similarly, measures such as absenteeism, tardiness or turnover may be used without a full job analysis if these behaviors are shown by a review of information about the job to be important in the specific situation. A rating of overall job performance may be used without a full job analysis only if the user can demonstrate its appropriateness for the specific job and employment situation through a study of the job. The Supreme Court held in *Albermarle Paper Co.* v. *Moody*, 422 U.S. 405 (1975), that measures of overall job performance should be carefully developed and their use should be standardized and controlled.

59. Q. Section 5J on interim use requires the user to have available substantial evidence of validity. What does this mean?

A. For purposes of compliance with 5J, "substantial evidence" means evidence which may not meet all the validation requirements of the Guidelines but which raises a strong inference that validity pursuant to these standards will soon be shown. Section 5J is based on the proposition that it would not be an appropriate allocation of Federal resources to bring enforcement proceedings against a user who would soon be able to satisfy fully the standards of the Guidelines. For example, a criterion-related study may have produced evidence which meets almost all of the requirements of the Guidelines with the exception that the gathering of the data of test fairness is still in progress and the fairness study has not yet produced results. If the correlation coefficient for the group as a whole permits the strong inference that the selection procedure is valid, then the selection procedure may be used on an interim basis pending the completion of the fairness study.

60. Q. What are the potential consequences to a user when a selection procedure is used on an interim basis?

A. The fact that the Guidelines permit interim use of a selection procedure under some conditions does not immunize the user from liability for back pay, attorney fees and the like, should use of the selection procedure later be found to be in violation of the Guidelines. Section 5J. For this reason, users should take steps to come into full compliance with the Guidelines as soon as possible. It is also appropriate for users to consider ways of minimizing adverse impact during the period of interim use.

61. Q. Must provisions for retesting be allowed for job-knowledge tests, where knowledge of the test content would assist in scoring well on it the second time?

A. The primary intent of the provision for retesting is that an applicant who was not selected should be given another chance. Particularly in the case of job-knowledge tests, security precautions may preclude retesting with the same test after a short time. However, the opportunity for retesting should be provided for the same job at a later time, when the applicant may have acquired more of the relevant job knowledges.

62 Q. Under what circumstances may a selection procedure be used for ranking?

A. Criterion-related and construct validity strategies are essentially empirical, statistical processes showing a relationship between performance on the selection procedure and performance on the job. To justify ranking under such validity strategies, therefore, the user need show mathematical support for the proposition that persons who receive higher scores on the procedure are likely to perform better on the job.

Content validity, on the other hand, is primarily a judgmental process concerned with the adequacy of the selection procedure as a sample of the work behaviors. Use of a selection procedure on a ranking basis may be supported by content validity if there is evidence from job analysis or other empirical data that what is measured by the selection procedure is associated with differences in levels of job performance. Section 14C(9); see also Section 5G.

Any conclusion that a content validated procedure is appropriate for

ranking must rest on an inference that higher scores on the procedure are related to better job performance. The more closely and completely the selection procedure approximates the important work behaviors, the easier it is to make such an inference. Evidence that better performance on the procedure is related to greater productivity or to performance of behaviors of greater difficulty may also support such an inference.

Where the content and context of the selection procedure are unlike those of the job, as, for example, in many paper-and-pencil job knowledge tests, it is difficult to infer an association between levels of performance on the procedure and on the job. To support a test of job knowledge on a content validity basis, there must be evidence of a specific tie-in between each item of knowledge tested and one or more work behaviors. See Question 79. To justify use of such a test for ranking, it would also have to be demonstrated from empirical evidence either that mastery of more difficult work behaviors, or that mastery of a greater scope of knowledge corresponds to a greater scope of important work behaviors.

For example, for a particular warehouse worker job, the job analysis may show that lifting a 50-pound object is essential, but the job analysis does not show that lifting heavier objects is essential or would result in significantly better job performance. In this case a test of ability to lift 50 pounds could be justified on a content validity basis for a pass/fail determination. However, ranking of candidates based on relative amount of weight that can be lifted would be inappropriate.

In another instance, a job analysis may reflect that, for the job of machine operator, reading of simple instructions is not a major part of the job but is essential. Thus, reading would be a critical behavior under the Guidelines. See Section 14C(8), since the job analysis in this example did not also show that the ability to read such instructions more quickly or to understand more complex materials would be likely to result in better job performance, a reading test supported by content validity alone should be used on a pass/fail rather than a ranking basis. In such circumstances, use of the test for ranking would have to be supported by evidence from a criterion-related (or construct) validity study.

On the other hand, in the case of a person to be hired for a typing pool, the job analysis may show that the job consists almost entirely of typing from manuscript, and that productivity can be measured directly in terms of finished typed copy. For such a job,

typing constitutes not only a critical behavior, but it constitutes most of the job. A higher score on a test which measured words per minute typed, with adjustments for errors, would therefore be likely to predict better job performance than a significantly lower score. Ranking or grouping based on such a typing test would therefore be appropriate under the Guidelines.

63. Q. If selection procedures are administered by an employment agency or a consultant for an employer, is the employer relieved of responsibilities under the Guidelines?

A. No. The employer remains responsible. It is therefore expected that the employer will have sufficient information available to show: (a) What selection procedures are being used on its behalf; (b) the total number of applicants for referral by race, sex and ethnic group; (c) the number of persons, by race, sex and ethnic group, referred to the employer; and (d) the impact of the selection procedures and evidence of the validity of any such procedure having an adverse impact as determined above.

A. CRITERION-RELATED VALIDITY

64. Q. Under what circumstances may success in training be used as a criterion in criterion-related validity studies?

A. Success in training is an appropriate criterion when it is (1) necessary for successful job performance or has been shown to be related to degree of proficiency on the job and (2) properly measured. Section 14B(3). The measure of success in training should be carefully developed to ensure that factors which are not job related do not influence the measure of training success. Section 14B(3).

65. Q. When may concurrent validity be used?

A. A concurrent validity strategy assumes that the findings from a criterion-related validity study of current employees can be applied to applicants for the same job. Therefore, if concurrent validity is to be used, differences between the applicant and employee groups which might affect validity should be taken into account. The user should be particularly concerned with those differences between the applicant group and current employees used in the research sample which are caused by work experience or other work related events or by prior selection of employees and selection of the sample. See Section 14B(4).

66. Q. Under what circumstances can a selection procedure be supported (on other than an interim basis) by a criterion-related validity study done elsewhere?

A. A validity study done elsewhere may provide sufficient evidence if four conditions are met (Sec. 7B):

1. The evidence from the other studies clearly demonstrates that the procedure was valid in its use elsewhere.

2. The job(s) for which the selection procedure will be used closely matches the job(s) in the original study as shown by a comparison of major work behaviors as shown by the job analyses in both contexts.

3. Evidence of fairness from the other studies is considered for those groups constituting a significant factor in the user's labor market. Section 7B(3). Where the evidence is not available the user should conduct an internal study of test fairness, if technically feasible. Section 7B(3).

4. Proper account is taken of variables which might affect the applicability of the study in the new setting, such as performance standards, work methods, representativeness of the sample in terms of experience or other relevant factors, and the currency of the study.

67. Q. What does "unfairness of a selection procedure" mean?

A. When a specific score on a selection procedure has a different meaning in terms of expected job performance for members of one race, sex or ethnic group than the same score does for members of another group, the use of that selection procedure may be unfair for members of one of the groups. See section 16V. For example, if members of one group have an average score of 40 on the selection procedure, but perform on the job as well as another group which has an average score of 50, then some uses of the selection procedure would be unfair to the members of the lower scoring group. See Question 70.

68. Q. When should the user investigate the question of fairness?

A. Fairness should be investigated generally at the same time that a criterion-related validity study is conducted, or as soon thereafter as feasible. Section 14B(8).

69. Q. Why do the Guidelines require that users look for evidence of unfairness?

A. The consequences of using unfair selection procedures are severe in terms of discriminating against applicants on the basis of race, sex or ethnic group membership. Accordingly, these studies should be performed routinely where technically feasible and appropriate, whether or not the probability of finding unfairness is small. Thus, the Supreme Court indicated in Albemarle Paper Co. v. Moody, 422 U.S. 405, that a validation study was "materially deficient" because, among other reasons, it failed to investigate fairness where it was not shown to be unfeasible to do so. Moreover,

the American Psychological Association Standards published in 1974 call for the investigation of test fairness in criterion-related studies wherever feasible (pp. 43–44).

70. Q. What should be done if a selection procedure is unfair for one or more groups in the relevant labor market?

A. The Guidelines discuss three options. See Section 14B(8)(d). First, the selection instrument may be replaced by another validated instrument which is fair to all groups. Second, the selection instrument may be revised to eliminate the sources of unfairness. For example, certain items may be found to be the only ones which cause the unfairness to a particular group, and these items may be deleted or replaced by others. Finally, revisions may be made in the method of use of the selection procedure to ensure that the probability of being selected is compatible with the probability of successful job performance.

The Federal enforcement agencies recognize that there is serious debate in the psychological profession on the question of test fairness, and that information on that concept is developing. Accordingly, the enforcement agencies will consider developments in this field in evaluating actions occasioned by a finding of test unfairness.

71. Q. How is test unfairness related to differential validity and to differential prediction?

A. Test unfairness refers to use of selection procedures based on scores when members of one group characteristically obtain lower scores than members of another group, and the differences are not reflected in measures of job performance. See Sections 16V and 14B(8)(a), and Question 67.

Differential validity and test unfairness are conceptually distinct. Differential validity is defined as a situation in which a given instrument has significantly different validity coefficients for different race, sex or ethnic groups. Use of a test may be unfair to some groups even when differential validity is not found.

Differential prediction is a central concept for one definition of test unfairness. Differential prediction occurs when the use of the same set of scores systematically overpredicts or underpredicts job performance for members of one group as compared to members of another group.

Other definitions of test unfairness which do not relate to differential prediction may, however, also be appropriately applied to employment decisions. Thus these Guidelines are not intended to choose between fairness models as long as the model selected is appropriate to the manner in which the selection procedure is used.

72. Q. What options does a user have if a criterion-related study is appropriate but is not feasible because there are not enough persons in the job?

A. There are a number of options the user should consider, depending upon the particular facts and circumstances, such as:

1. Change the procedure so as to eliminate adverse impact (see Section 6A);

2. Validate a procedure through a content validity strategy, if appropriate (see Section 14C and Questions 54 and 74);

3. Use a selection procedure validated elsewhere in conformity with the Guidelines (see Sections 7-8 and Question 66);

4. Engage in a cooperative study with other facilities or users (in cooperation with such users either bilaterally or through industry or trade associations or governmental groups), or participate in research studies conducted by the state employment security system. Where different locations are combined, care is needed to insure that the jobs studied are in fact the same and that the study is adequate and in conformity with the Guidelines (see Sections 8 and 14 and Question 45).

5. Combine essentially similar jobs into a single study sample. See Section 14B(1).

B. CONTENT VALIDITY

73. Q. Must a selection procedure supported by content validity be an actual "on the job" sample of work behaviors?

A. No. The Guidelines emphasize the importance of a close approximation between the content of the selection procedure and the observable behaviors or products of the job, so as to minimize the inferential leap between performance on the selection procedure and job performance. However, the Guidelines also permit justification on the basis of content validity of selection procedures measuring knowledges, skills, or abilities which are not necessarily samples of work behaviors if: (1) the knowledge, skill, or ability being measured is operationally defined in accord with Section 14C(4); and (2) that knowledge, skill, or ability is a prerequisite for critical or important work behaviors. In addition users may justify a requirement for training, or for experience obtained from prior employment or volunteer work, on the basis of content validity, even though the prior training or experience does not duplicate the job. See Section 14B(6).

74. Q. Is the use of a content validity strategy appropriate for a procedure measuring skills or knowledges which are taught in training after initial employment?

A. Usually not. The Guidelines state (Section 14C(1)) that content validity is not appropriate where the selection procedure involves knowledges, skills, or abilities which the employee will be expected to learn "on the job". The phrase "on the job" is intended to apply to training which occurs after hiring, promotion or transfer. However, if an ability, such as speaking and understanding a language, takes a sub- stantial length of time to learn, is required for successful job performance, and is not taught to those initial hires who possess it in advance, a test for that ability may be supported on a content validity basis.

75. Q. Can a measure of a trait or construct be validated on the basis of content validity?

A. No. Traits or constructs are by definition underlying characteristics which are intangible and are not directly observable. They are therefore not appropriate for the sampling approach of content validity. Some selection procedures, while labeled as construct measures, may actually be samples of observable work behaviors. Whatever the label, if the operational definitions are in fact based upon observable work behaviors, a selection procedure measuring those behaviors may be appropriately supported by a content validity strategy. For example, while a measure of the construct "dependability" should not be supported on the basis of content validity, promptness and regularity of attendance in a prior work record are frequently inquired into as a part of a selection procedure, and such measures may be supported on the basis of content validity.

76. Q. May a test which measures what the employee has learned in a training program be justified for use in employment decisions on the basis of content validity?

A. Yes. While the Guidelines (Section 14C(1)) note that content validity is not an appropriate strategy for knowledges, skills or abilities which an employee "will be expected to learn on the job", nothing in the Guidelines suggests that a test supported by content validity is not appropriate for determining what the employee has learned on the job, or in a training program. If the content of the test is relevant to the job, it may be used for employment decisions such as retention or assignment. See Section 14C(7).

77. Q. Is a task analysis necessary to support a selection procedure based on content validity?

A. A description of all tasks is not required by the Guidelines. However, the job analysis should describe all important work behaviors and their relative importance and their level of difficulty. Sections 14C(2) and 15C(3). The job analysis should focus on observable work behaviors and, to the extent appropriate, observable work products, and the tasks associated with the important observable work behaviors and/or work products. The job analysis should identify how the critical or important work behaviors are used in the job, and should support the content of the selection procedure.

78. Q. What is required to show the content validity of a paper-and-pencil test that is intended to approximate work behaviors?

A. Where a test is intended to repli- cate a work behavior, content validity is established by a demonstration of the similarities between the test and the job with respect to behaviors, products, and the surrounding environmental conditions. Section 14B(4).

Paper-and-pencil tests which are intended to replicate a work behavior are most likely to be appropriate where work behaviors are performed in paper and pencil form (e.g., editing and bookkeeping). Paper-and-pencil tests of effectiveness in interpersonal relations (e.g., sales or supervision), or of physical activities (e.g., automobile repair) or ability to function properly under danger (e.g., firefighters) generally are not close enough approximations of work behaviors to show content validity.

The appropriateness of tests of job knowledge, whether or not in pencil and paper form, is addressed in Question 79.

79. Q. What is required to show the content validity of a test of a job knowledge?

A. There must be a defined, well recognized body of information, and knowledge of the information must be prerequisite to performance of the required work behaviors. The work behavior(s) to which each knowledge is related should be identified on an item by item basis. The test should fairly sample the information that is actually used by the employee on the job, so that the level of difficulty of the test items should correspond to the level of difficulty of the knowledge as used in the work behavior. See Section 14C(1) and (4).

80. Q. Under content validity, may a selection procedure for entry into a job be justified on the grounds that the knowledges, skills or abilities measured by the selection procedure are prerequisites to successful performance in a training program?

A. Yes, but only if the training material and the training program closely approximate the content and level of difficulty of the job and if the knowledges, skills or abilities are not those taught in the training program. For example, if training materials are at a level of reading difficulty substantially in excess of the reading difficulty of materials used on the job, the Guidelines would not permit justification on a content validity basis of a reading test based on those training materials for entry into the job.

Under the Guidelines a training program itself is a selection procedure if passing it is a prerequisite to retention or advancement. See Section 2C and 14C(17). As such, the content of the training program may only be justified by the relationship between the program and critical or important behaviors of the job itself, or through a demonstration of the relationship between measures of performance in training and measures of job performance.

Under the example given above, therefore, where the requirements in the training materials exceed those on the job, the training program itself could not be validated on a content validity basis if passing it is a basis for retention or promotion.

C. CONSTRUCT VALIDITY

81. Q. In Section 5, "General Standards for Validity Studies," construct validity is identified as no less acceptable than criterion-related and content validity. However, the specific requirements for construct validity, in Section 14D, seem to limit the generalizability of construct validity to the rules governing criterion-related validity. Can this apparent inconsistency be reconciled?

A. Yes. In view of the developing nature of construct validation for employment selection procedures, the approach taken concerning the generalizability of construct validity (section 14D) is intended to be a cautious one. However, construct validity may be generalized in circumstances where transportability of tests supported on the basis of criterion-related validity would not be appropriate. In establishing transportability of criterion-related validity, the jobs should have substantially the same major work behaviors. Section 7B(2). Construct validity, on the other hand, allows for situations where only some of the important work behaviors are the same. Thus, well-established measures of the construct which underlie particular work behaviors and which have been shown to be valid for some jobs may be generalized to other jobs which have some of the same work behaviors but which are different with respect to other work behaviors. Section 14D(4).

As further research and professional guidance on construct validity in employment situations emerge, additional extensions of construct validity for employee selection may become generally accepted in the profession. The agencies encourage further research and professional guidance with respect to the appropriate use of construct validity.

V. Records and Documentation

82. Q. Do the Guidelines have simplified recordkeeping for small users (employers who employ one hundred or fewer employees and other users not required to file EEO-1, et seq. reports)?

A. Yes. Although small users are fully covered by Federal equal employment opportunity law, the Guidelines have reduced their record-keeping burden. See option in Section 15A(1). Thus, small users need not make adverse impact determinations nor are they required to keep applicant data on a job-by-job basis. The agencies also recognize that a small user may find that some or all validation strategies are not feasible. See Question 54. If a small user has reason to believe that its selection procedures have adverse impact and validation is not feasible, it should consider other options. See Sections 7A and 8 and Questions 31, 36, 45, 66, and 72.

83. Q. Is the requirement in the Guidelines that users maintain records of the race, national origin, and sex of employees and applicants constitutional?

A. Yes. For example, the United States Court of Appeals for the First Circuit rejected a challenge on constitutional and other grounds to the Equal Employment Opportunity Commission regulations requiring State and local governmental units to furnish information as to race, national origin and sex of employees. *United States* v. *New Hampshire*, 539 F. 2d 277 (1st Cir. 1976), *cert. denied*, sub nom. *New Hampshire* v. *United States*, 429 U.S. 1023. The Court held that the recordkeeping and reporting requirements promulgated under Title VII of the Civil Rights Act of 1964, as amended, were reasonably necessary for the Federal agency to determine whether the state was in compliance with Title VII and thus were authorized and constitutional. The same legal principles apply to recordkeeping with respect to applicants.

Under the Supremacy Clause of the Constitution, the Federal law requiring maintenance of records identifying race, sex and national origin overrides any contrary provision of State law. See Question 8.

The agencies recognize, however, that such laws have been enacted to prevent misuse of this information. Thus, employers should take appropriate steps to ensure proper use of all data. See Question #88.

84. Q. Is the user obliged to keep records which show whether its selection processes have an adverse impact on race, sex, or ethnic groups?

A. Yes. Under the Guidelines users are obliged to maintain evidence indicating the impact which their selection processes have on identifiable race, sex or ethnic groups. Sections 4 A and B. If the selection process for a job does have an adverse impact on one or more such groups, the user is expected to maintain records showing the impact for the individual procedures. Section 15A(2).

85. Q. What are the recordkeeping obligations of a user who cannot determine whether a selection process for a job has adverse impact because it makes an insufficient number of selections for that job in a year?

A. In such circumstances the user should collect, maintain, and have available information on the impact of the selection process and the component procedures until it can determine that adverse impact does not exist for the overall process or until the job has changed substantially. Section 15A(2)(c).

86. Q. Should applicant and selection information be maintained for race or ethnic groups constituting less than 2% of the labor force and the applicants?

A. Small employers and other small users are not obliged to keep such records. Section 15A(1). Employers with more than 100 employees and other users required to file EEO-1 et seq. reports should maintain records and other information upon which impact determinations could be made, because section 15A2 requires the maintenance of such information for "any of the groups for which records are called for by section 4B above." See also, Section 4A.

No user, regardless of size, is required to make adverse impact determinations for race or ethnic groups constituting less than 2% of the labor force and the applicants. See Question 16.

87. Q. Should information be maintained which identifies applicants and persons selected both by sex and by race or ethnic group?

A. Yes. Although the Federal agencies have decided not to require computations of adverse impact by subgroups (white males, black males, white females, black females—see Question 17), the Guidelines call for record keeping which allows identification of persons by sex, combined with race or ethnic group, so as to permit the identification of discriminatory practices on any such basis. Section 4A and 4B.

88. Q. How should a user collect data on race, sex or ethnic classifications for purposes of determining the impact of selection procedures?

A. The Guidelines have not specified any particular procedure, and the enforcement agencies will accept different procedures that capture the necessary information. Where applications are made in person, a user may maintain a log or applicant flow chart based upon visual observation, identifying the number of persons expressing an interest, by sex and by race or national origin; may in some circumstances rely upon personal knowledge of the user; or may rely upon self-identification. Where applications are not made in person and the applicants are not personally known to the employer, self-identification may be appropriate. Wherever a self-identification form is used, the employer should advise the applicant that identification by race, sex and national origin is sought, not for employment decisions, but for record-keeping in compliance with Federal law. Such self-identification forms should be kept separately from the application, and should not be a basis for employment decisions; and the applicants should be so advised. See Section 4B.

89. Q. What information should be included in documenting a validity study for purposes of these Guidelines?

A. Generally, reports of validity studies should contain all the information necessary to permit an enforcement agency to conclude whether a selection procedure has been validated. Information that is critical to this determination is denoted in Section 15 of the Guidelines by the word "(essential)".

Any reports completed after September 25, 1978, (the effective date of the Guidelines) which do not contain this information will be considered incomplete by the agencies unless there is good reason for not including the information. Users should therefore prepare validation reports according to the format of Section 15 of the Guidelines, and should carefully document the reasons if any of the information labeled "(essential)" is missing.

The major elements for all types of validation studies include the following:

When and where the study was conducted.

A description of the selection procedure, how it is used, and the results by race, sex, and ethnic group.

How the job was analyzed or reviewed and what information was obtained from this job analysis or review.

The evidence demonstrating that the selection procedure is related to the job. The nature of this evidence varies, depending upon the strategy used.

What alternative selection procedures and alternative methods of using the selection procedure were studied and the results of this study.

The name, address and telephone number of a contact person who can provide further information about the study.

The documentation requirements for each validation strategy are set forth in detail in Section 15 B, C, D, E, F, and G. Among the requirements for each validity strategy are the following:

1. *Criterion-Related Validity*

A description of the criterion measures of job performance, how and why they were selected, and how they were used to evaluate employees.

A description of the sample used in the study, how it was selected, and the size of each race, sex, or ethnic group in it.

A description of the statistical methods used to determine whether scores on the selection procedure are related to scores on the criterion measures of job performance, and the results of these statistical calculations.

2. *Content Validity*

The content of the job, as identified from the job analysis.

The content of the selection procedure.

The evidence demonstrating that the content of the selection procedure is a representative sample of the content of the job.

3. *Construct Validity*

A definition of the construct and how it relates to other constructs in the psychological literature.

The evidence that the selection procedure measures the construct.

The evidence showing that the measure of the construct is related to work behaviors which involve the construct.

90. Q. Although the records called for under "Source Data", Section 15B(11) and section 15D(11), are not listed as "Essential", the Guidelines state that each user should maintain such records, and have them available upon request of a compliance agency. Are these records necessary? Does the absence of complete records preclude the further use of research data compiled prior to the issuance of the Guidelines?

A. The Guidelines require the maintenance of these records in some form "as a necessary part of the study." Section 15A(3)(c). However, such records need not be compiled or maintained in any specific format. The term "Essential" as used in the Guidelines refers to information considered essential to the validity report. Section 15A(3)(b). The Source Data records need not be included with reports of validation or other formal reports until and unless they are specifically requested by a compliance agency. The absence of complete records does not preclude use of research data based on those records that are available. Validation studies submitted to comply with the requirements of the Guidelines may be considered inadequate to the extent that important data are missing or there is evidence that the collected data are inaccurate.

[FR Doc. 79-6323 Filed 3-1-79; 8:45 am]

Friday
April 20, 1979

Part VIII

Equal Employment Opportunity Commission

Guidelines on Sex Discrimination

Adoption of Final Interpretive Guidelines

Questions and Answers

EQUAL EMPLOYMENT OPPORTUNITY COMMISSION

29 CFR Part 1604

Guidelines on Sex Discrimination; Adoption of Final Interpretive Guidelines; Question and Answers

AGENCY: Equal Employment Opportunity Commission.

ACTION: Final Amendments to Guidelines on Discrimination Because of Sex, and Addition of Questions and Answers concerning the Pregnancy Discrimination Act, Public Law 95–555, 92 Stat. 2076 (1978).

SUMMARY: On October 31, 1978, President Carter signed into law the Pregnancy Discrimination Act, Pub. L. 95–555, 92 Stat. 2076, as an amendment to Title VII of the Civil Rights Act of 1964, as amended. The act makes clear that discrimination on the basis of pregnancy, childbirth or related medical conditions constitutes unlawful sex discrimination under Title VII. The amendments to the Equal Employment Opportunity Commission's Guidelines on Discrimination Because of Sex bring the Guidelines into conformity with Pub. L. 95–555. The accompanying questions and answers respond to concerns raised by the public about compliance with the Pregnancy Discrimination Act.

EFFECTIVE DATE: April 20, 1979.

FOR FURTHER INFORMATION CONTACT: Peter C. Robertson, Director, Office of Policy Implementation, Room 4002A, Equal Employment Opportunity Commission, 2401 E Street, N.W., Washington, D.C. 20506, (202) 634–7060.

SUPPLEMENTARY INFORMATION: The Pregnancy Discrimination Act makes clear that Title VII of the Civil Rights Act of 1964, as amended, forbids discrimination on the basis of pregnancy, childbirth and related medical conditions. As reflected in the Committee Reports (Senate Report 95–331, 95th Cong., 1st Session (1977) and House of Representatives Report 95–948, 95th Cong. 2d Session (1978)), Congress believed that the Equal Employment Opportunity Commission (EEOC or the Commission), in its Guidelines on Discrimination Because of Sex (29 CFR Part 1604, published at 39 FR 6836, April 5, 1972) had "rightly implemented the Title VII prohibition of sex discrimination in the 1964 act." H.R. 95–948 at p. 2.

Contrary to the EEOC's Guidelines and rulings by eighteen District Courts and all seven Courts of Appeal which faced the issue, in *General Electric Co.*

v. *Gilbert*, 429 U.S. 125 (1976), the Supreme Court ruled that General Electric's exclusion of pregnancy related disabilities from its comprehensive disability plan did not violate Title VII. The Supreme Court further indicated that it believed that the EEOC Guidelines located at 29 CFR 1604.10(b) incorrectly interpreted the Congressional intent in the statute.

The Pregnancy Discrimination Act reaffirms EEOC's Guidelines with but minor modifications. For that reason, the Commission believed that only slight modifications of its Guidelines were necessary and issued them on an interim basis on March 9, 1979 at 44 FR 13278. Along with these amended Sex Discrimination Guidelines, the Commission published a list of questions and answers concerning the Pregnancy Discrimination Act. These responded to urgent concerns raised by employees, employers, unions and insurers who sought the Commission's guidance in understanding their rights and obligations under the Pregnancy Discrimination Act.

Fringe benefit programs subject to Title VII which existed on October 31, 1978, must be modified in accordance with the Pregnancy Discrimination Act no later than April 29, 1979. It is the Commission's desire, therefore, that all interested parties be made aware of EEOC's view of their rights and obligations in advance of April 29, 1979, so that they may be in compliance by that date. For that reason, the Commission has determined that the amendment to 29 CFR 1604.10 and the questions and answers, which will be appended to 29 CFR Part 1604, are not subject to the requirements of Executive Order 12044. See section 6(b)(6) of Executive Order 12044.

The Commission, however, invited and received comments from the public and affected Federal agencies. The Commission has considered the comments and determined that its Sex Discrimination Guidelines at 29 CFR 1604.10 should be issued in final form as they were published in 44 FR 13278 (March 9, 1979), except that the word "opportunities" has been inserted in Subsection (a) of Section 1604.10 to emphasize that this subsection applies to all employment-related policies or practices, since there was apparent confusion on this point. Also as a result of the comments, the Commission has added several questions and answers which will be of further assistance to those seeking Commission guidance with respect to their rights and obligations under the Pregnancy Discrimination Act, and has amended

two of the originally published questions and answers.

Question 21 was amended by changing the second paragraph of the answer to read "non-spouse dependents" instead of "other dependents", to clarify the intent of the answers. Question 30 [now question 34] has been amended to include women who are contemplating an abortion within the prohibition against discrimination on the basis of abortion.

Questions 29 and 30 were added to address many of the concerns which had been raised with respect to "extended benefits" provisions.

Question 18(A) was added in response to questions and comments which pertain to child care leave.

A majority of the comments questioned the appropriateness of the Commission's answer to Question 21 of the questions and answers at 44 FR 13278. Question 21 asked whether an employer has to make available health insurance coverage for the medical expenses of pregnancy-related conditions of the spouses of male employees and of the non-spouse dependents of all employees.

The Commission concluded that health insurance benefits for the pregnancy-related conditions of the male employee's spouse must be available to the same extent as health insurance benefits are available to the female employee's spouse. The pregnancy-related conditions of non-spouse dependents, however, would not have to be covered under the health insurance program so long as that practice applied to the non-spouse dependents of male and female employees equally.

The Pregnancy Discrimination Act amends Title VII of the Civil Rights Act of 1964, as amended. To the extent that a specific question is not directly answered by a reading of the Pregnancy Discrimination Act, existing principles of Title VII must be applied to resolve that question. The legislative history of the Pregnancy Discrimination Act states explicitly that existing principles of Title VII law would have to be applied to resolve the question of benefits for dependents. (S. Rep. No. 95–331 at 6.)

The Commission, being responsible for interpreting and implementing Title VII, utilized Title VII principles to arrive at the position reached on the dependent question.

The underlying principle of Title VII is that applicants for employment or employees be treated equally without regard to their race, sex, color, religion, or national origin. This equality of treatment encompasses the receiving of fringe benefits made available in connection with employment. Title VII does not require employers to provide the same coverage for the pregnancy-related medical conditions of spouses of male employees as it provides for the pregnancy-related costs of its female employees. However, if an employer makes available to female employees insurance which covers the costs of all of the medical conditions of their spouses, but provides male employees with insurance coverage for only *some* of the medical conditions (i.e., all but pregnancy-related expenses) of their spouses, male employees are receiving a less favorable fringe benefit package. This view was explicitly supported in the Senate by Senators Bayh and Cranston, 123 Cong. Rec. S15037, S15058 (daily ed. Sept. 16, 1977), and not specifically opposed.

Absent a state statute to the contrary, it would not be a violation of Title VII if an employer's health insurance policy denied pregnancy benefits for the other dependents of employees (e.g. daughters) so long as the exclusion applied equally to non-spouse dependents of male employees and non-spouse dependents of female employees. Since male and female employees have an equal chance of having pregnant dependent daughters, male and female employees would be equally affected by such an exclusion.

Although costs may increase as a result of providing pregnancy benefits for the spouses of male employees where benefits are made available for the spouses of female employees, the Pregnancy Discrimination Act provides that where costs were apportioned on the date of enactment between employers and employees, any payments or contributions required to comply with the Act may be made by employers and employees in the same proportion, if that apportionment was non-discriminatory.

As a result of the many comments and questions raised on the dependent question, questions 22 and 23 were added to provide additional guidance to interested parties.

With the exception of the addition of questions 18(A), 22, 23, 29, and 30, and the amendments to questions 21 and 30 (now 34); the questions and answers are issued in final form as they were published in 44 FR 13278 (March 9, 1979).

By virtue of the authority vested in it by Section 713 of Title VII of the Civil Rights Act, as amended, 42 U.S.C. 2000-12, 78 Stat. 265, the Equal Employment Opportunity Commission hereby approves as final § 1604.10 and adopts questions and answers concerning the Pregnancy Discrimination Act, Pub. L. 95–555, 92 Stat. 2076 (1978), as an appendix to Part 1604 of Title 29 of the Code of Federal Regulations as set forth below.

Signed at Washington. D.C., this 17th day of April, 1979.

Eleanor H. Norton,

Chair, Equal Employment Opportunity Commission.

1. 29 CFR 1604.10 is amended to read as follows:

§ 1604.10 Employment policies relating to pregnancy and childbirth.

(a) A written or unwritten employment policy or practice which excludes from employment opportunities applicants or employees because of pregnancy, childbirth or related medical conditions is in prima facie violation of Title VII.

(b) Disabilities caused or contributed to by pregnancy, childbirth, or related medical conditions, for all job-related purposes, shall be treated the same as disabilities caused or contributed to by other medical conditions, under any health or disability insurance or sick leave plan available in connection with employment. Written or unwritten employment policies and practices involving matters such as the commencement and duration of leave, the availability of extensions, the accrual of seniority and other benefits and privileges, reinstatement, and payment under any health or disability insurance or sick leave plan, formal or informal, shall be applied to disability due to pregnancy, childbirth, or related medical conditions on the same terms and conditions as they are applied to other disabilities. Health insurance benefits for abortion, except where the life of the mother would be endangered if the fetus were carried to term or where medical complications have arisen from an abortion, are not required to be paid by an employer; nothing herein, however, precludes an employer from providing abortion benefits or otherwise affects bargaining agreements in regard to abortion.

(c) Where the termination of an employee who is temporarily disabled is caused by an employment policy under which insufficient or no leave is available, such a termination violates the Act if it has a disparate impact on employees of one sex and is not justified by business necessity.

(d)(1) Any fringe benefit program, or fund, or insurance program which is in effect on October 31, 1978, which does not treat women affected by pregnancy, childbirth, or related medical conditions the same as other persons not so affected but similar in their ability or inability to work, must be in compliance with the provisions of § 1604.10(b) by April 29, 1979. In order to come into compliance with the provisions of § 1604.10(b), there can be no reduction of benefits or compensation which were in effect on October 31, 1978, before October 31, 1979 or the expiration of a collective bargaining agreement in effect on October 31, 1978, whichever is later.

(2) Any fringe benefit program implemented after October 31, 1978, must comply with the provisions of § 1604.10(b) upon implementation.

2. The following questions and answers, with an introduction, are added to 29 CFR Part 1604 as an appendix:

Questions and Answers on the Pregnancy Discrimination Act, Pub. L. 95–555, 92 Stat. 2076 (1978)

Introduction

On October 31, 1978, President Carter signed into law the *Pregnancy Discrimination Act* (Pub. L. 95–955). The Act is an amendment to Title VII of the Civil Rights Act of 1964 which prohibits, among other things, discrimination in employment on the basis of sex. The *Pregnancy Discrimination Act* makes it clear that "because of sex" or "on the basis of sex", as used in Title VII, includes "because of or on the basis of pregnancy, childbirth or related medical conditions." Therefore, Title VII prohibits discrimination in employment against women affected by pregnancy or related conditions.

The basic principle of the Act is that women affected by pregnancy and related conditions must be treated the same as other applicants and employees on the basis of their ability or inability to work. A woman is therefore protected against such practices as being fired, or refused a job or promotion, merely because she is pregnant or has had an abortion. She usually cannot be forced to go on leave as long as she can still work. If other employees who take disability leave are entitled to get their jobs back when they are able to work again, so are women who have been unable to work because of pregnancy.

In the area of fringe benefits, such as disability benefits, sick leave and health insurance, the same principle applies. A woman unable to work for pregnancy-related reasons is entitled to disability benefits or sick leave on the same basis as employees unable to work for other medical reasons. Also, any health insurance provided must cover expenses for pregnancy-related conditions on the same basis as expenses for other medical conditions. However, health insurance for expenses arising from abortion is not required except where the life of the mother would be endangered if the fetus were carried to term, or where medical complications have arisen from an abortion.

Some questions and answers about the *Pregnancy Discrimination Act* follow. Although the questions and answers often use only the term "employer," the Act—and these questions and answers—apply also to unions and other entities covered by Title VII.

1. Q. What is the effective date of the Pregnancy Discrimination Act?

A. The Act became effective on October 31, 1978, except that with respect to fringe benefit programs in effect on that date, the Act will take effect 180 days thereafter, that is, April 29, 1979.

To the extent that Title VII already required employers to treat persons affected by pregnancy-related conditions the same as persons affected by other medical conditions, the Act does not change employee rights arising prior to October 31, 1978, or April 29, 1979. Most employment practices relating to pregnancy, childbirth and related conditions—whether concerning fringe benefits or other practices—were already controlled by Title VII prior to this Act. For example, Title VII has always prohibited an employer from firing, or refusing to hire or promote, a woman because of pregnancy or related conditions, and from failing to accord a woman on pregnancy-related leave the same seniority retention and accrual accorded those on other disability leaves.

2. Q. If an employer had a sick leave policy in effect on October 31, 1978, by what date must the employer bring its policy into compliance with the Act?

A. With respect to payment of benefits, an employer has until April 29, 1979, to bring into compliance any fringe benefit or insurance program, including a sick leave policy, which was in effect on October 31, 1978. However, any such policy or program created after October 31, 1978, must be in compliance when created.

With respect to all aspects of sick leave policy other than payment of benefits, such as the terms governing retention and accrual of seniority, credit for vacation, and resumption of former job on return from sick leave, equality of treatment was required by Title VII without the Amendment.

3. Q. Must an employer provide benefits for pregnancy-related conditions to an employee whose pregnancy begins prior to April 29, 1979, and continues beyond that date?

A. As of April 29, 1979, the effective date of the Act's requirements, an employer must provide the same benefits for pregnancy-related conditions as it provides for other conditions, regardless of when the pregnancy began. Thus, disability benefits must be paid for all absences on or after April 29, 1979, resulting from pregnancy-related temporary disabilities to the same extent as they are paid for absences resulting from other temporary disabilities. For example, if an employee gives birth before April 29, 1979, but is still unable to work on or after that date, she is entitled to the same disability benefits available to other employees. Similarly, medical insurance benefits must be paid for pregnancy-related expenses incurred on or after April 29, 1979.

If an employer requires an employee to be employed for a predetermined period prior to being eligible for insurance coverage, the period prior to April 29, 1979, during which a pregnant employee has been employed must be credited toward the eligibility waiting period on the same basis as for any other employee.

As to any programs instituted for the first time after October 31, 1978, coverage for pregnancy-related conditions must be provided in the same manner as for other medical conditions.

4. Q. Would the answer to the preceding question be the same if the employee became pregnant prior to October 31, 1978?

A. Yes.

5. Q. If, for pregnancy-related reasons, an employee is unable to perform the functions of her job, does the employer have to provide her an alternative job?

A. An employer is required to treat an employee temporarily unable to perform the functions of her job because of her pregnancy-related condition in the same manner as it treats other temporarily disabled employees, whether by providing modified tasks, alternative assignments, disability leaves, leaves without pay, etc. For example, a woman's primary job function may be the operation of a machine, and, incidental to that function, she may carry materials to and from the machine. If other employees temporarily unable to lift are relieved of these functions, pregnant employees also unable to lift must be temporarily relieved of the function.

6. Q. What procedures may an employer use to determine whether to place on leave as unable to work a pregnant employee who claims she is able to work or deny leave to a pregnant employee who claims that she is disabled from work?

A. An employer may not single out pregnancy-related conditions for special procedures for determining an employee's ability to work. However, an employer may use any procedure used to determine the ability of all employees to work. For example, if an employer requires its employees to submit a doctor's statement concerning their inability to work before granting leave or paying sick benefits, the employer may require employees affected by pregnancy-related conditions to submit such statements. Similarly, if an employer allows its employees to obtain doctor's statements from their personal physicians for absences due to other disabilities or return dates from other disabilities it must accept doctor's statements from personal physicians for absences and return dates connected with pregnancy-related disabilities.

7. Q. Can an employer have a rule which prohibits an employee from returning to work for a predetermined length of time after childbirth?

A. No.

8. Q. If an employee has been absent from work as a result of a pregnancy-related condition and recovers, may her employer require her to remain on leave until after her baby is born?

A. No. An employee must be permitted to work at all times during pregnancy when she is able to perform her job.

9. Q. Must an employer hold open the job of an employee who is absent on leave because she is temporarily disabled by pregnancy-related conditions?

A. Unless the employee on leave has informed the employer that she does not intend to return to work, her job must be held open for her return on the same basis as jobs are held open for employees on sick or disability leave for other reasons.

10. Q. May an employer's policy concerning the accrual and crediting of seniority during absences for medical conditions be different for employees affected by pregnancy-related conditions than for other employees?

A. No. An employer's seniority policy must be the same for employees absent for pregnancy-related reasons as for those absent for other medical reasons.

11. Q. For purposes of calculating such matters as vacations and pay increases, may an employer credit time spent on leave for pregnancy-related reasons differently than time spent on leave for other reasons?

A. No. An employer's policy with respect to crediting time for the purpose of calculating such matters as vacations and pay increases cannot treat employees on leave for pregnancy-related reasons less favorably than employees on leave for other reasons. For example, if employees on leave for medical reasons are credited with the time spent on leave when computing entitlement to vacation or pay raises, an employee on leave for pregnancy-related disability is entitled to the same kind of time credit.

12. Q. Must an employer hire a woman who is medically unable, because of a pregnancy-related condition, to perform a necessary function of a job?

A. An employer cannot refuse to hire a woman because of her pregnancy-related condition so long as she is able to perform the major functions necessary to the job. Nor can an employer refuse to hire her because of its preferences against pregnant workers or the preferences of co-workers, clients, or customers.

13. Q. May an employer limit disability benefits for pregnancy-related conditions to married employees?

A. No.

14. Q. If an employer has an all female workforce or job classification, must benefits be provided for pregnancy-related conditions?

A. Yes. If benefits are provided for other conditions, they must also be provided for pregnancy-related conditions.

15. Q. For what length of time must an employee who provides income maintenance benefits for temporary disabilities provide such benefits for pregnancy-related disabilities?

A. Benefits should be provided for as long as the employee is unable to work for medical reasons unless some other limitation is set for all other temporary disabilities, in which case pregnancy-related disabilities should be treated the same as other temporary disabilities.

16. Q. Must an employer who provides benefits for long-term or permanent disabilities provide such bnefits for pregnancy-related conditions?

A. Yes. Benefits for long term or permanent disabilities resulting from pregnancy-related conditions must be provided to the same extent that such benefits are provided for other conditions which result in long term or permanent disability.

17. Q. If an employer provides benefits to employees on leave, such as installment purchase disability insurance, payment of premiums for health, life or other insurance, continued payments into pension, saving or profit

sharing plans, must the same benefits be provided for those on leave for pregnancy-related conditions?

A. Yes, the employer must provide the same benefits for those on leave for pregnancy-related conditions as for those on leave for other reasons.

18. Q. Can an employee who is absent due to a pregnancy-related disability be required to exhaust vacation benefits before receiving sick leave pay or disability benefits?

A. No. If employees who are absent because of other disabling causes receive sick leave pay or disability benefits without any requirement that they first exhaust vacation benefits, the employer cannot impose this requirement on an employee absent for a pregnancy-related cause.

18(A). Q. Must an employer grant leave to a female employee for childcare purposes after she is medically able to return to work following leave necessitated by pregnancy, childbirth or related medical conditions?

A. While leave for childcare purposes is not covered by the Pregnancy Discrimination Act, ordinary Title VII principles would require that leave for childcare purposes be granted on the same basis as leave which is granted to employees for other non-medical reasons. For example, if an employer allows its employees to take leave without pay or accrued annual leave for travel or education which is not job related, the same type of leave must be granted to those who wish to remain on leave for infant care, even though they are medically able to return to work.

19. Q. If state law requires an employer to provide disability insurance for a specified period before and after childbirth, does compliance with the state law fulfill the employer's obligation under the Pregnancy Discrimination Act?

A. Not necessarily. It is an employer's obligation to treat employees temporarily disabled by pregnancy in the same manner as employees affected by other temporary disabilities. Therefore, any restrictions imposed by state law on benefits for pregnancy-related disabilities, but not for other disabilities, do not excuse the employer from treating the individuals in both groups of employees the same. If, for example, a state law requires an employer to pay a maximum of 26 weeks benefits for disabilities other than pregnancy-related ones but only six weeks for pregnancy-related disabilities, the employer must provide benefits for the additional weeks to an employee disabled by pregnancy-related

conditions, up to the maximum provided other disabled employees.

20. Q. If a State or local government provides its own employees income maintenance benefits for disabilities, may it provide different benefits for disabilities arising from pregnancy-related conditions than for disabilities arising from other conditions?

A. No. State and local governments, as employers, are subject to the Pregnancy Discrimination Act in the same way as private employers and must bring their employment practices and programs into compliance with the Act, including disability and health insurance programs.

21. Q. Must an employer provide health insurance for the medical expenses of pregnancy-related conditions of the spouses of male employees? Of the dependents of all employees?

A. Where an employer provides no coverage for dependents, the employer is not required to institute such coverage. However, if an employer's insurance program covers the medical expenses of spouses of female employees, then it must equally cover the medical expenses of spouses of male employees, including those arising from pregnancy-related conditions.

But the insurance does not have to cover the pregnancy-related conditions of non-spouse dependents as long as it excludes the pregnancy-related conditions of such non-spouse dependents of male and female employees equally.

22. Q. Must an employer provide the same level of health insurance coverage for the pregnancy-related medical conditions of the spouses of male employees as it provides for its female employees?

A. No. It is not necessary to provide the same level of coverage for the pregnancy-related medical conditions of spouses of male employees as for female employees. However, where the employer provides coverage for the medical conditions of the spouses of its employees, then the level of coverage for pregnancy-related medical conditions of the spouses of male employees must be the same as the level of coverage for all other medical conditions of the spouses of female employees. For example, if the employer covers employees for 100 percent of reasonable and customary expenses sustained for a medical condition, but only covers dependent spouses for 50 percent of reasonable and customary expenses for their medical conditions, the pregnancy-related expenses of the

364

male employee's spouse must be covered at the 50 percent level.

23. Q. May an employer offer optional dependent coverage which excludes pregnancy-related medical conditions or offers less coverage for pregnancy-related medical conditions where the total premium for the optional coverage is paid by the employee?

A. No. Pregnancy-related medical conditions must be treated the same as other medical conditions under any health or disability insurance or sick leave plan *available in connection with employment*, regardless of who pays the premiums.

24. Q. Where an employer provides its employees a choice among several health insurance plans, must coverage for pregnancy-related conditions be offered in all of the plans?

A. Yes. Each of the plans must cover pregnancy-related conditions. For example, an employee with a single coverage policy cannot be forced to purchase a more expensive family coverage policy in order to receive coverage for her own pregnancy-related condition.

25. Q. On what basis should an employee be reimbursed for medical expenses arising from pregnancy, childbirth or related conditions?

A. Pregnancy-related expenses should be reimbursed in the same manner as are expenses incurred for other medical conditions. Therefore, whether a plan reimburses the employees on a fixed basis, or a percentage of reasonable and customary charge basis, the same basis should be used for reimbursement of expenses incurred for pregnancy-related conditions. Furthermore, if medical costs for pregnancy-related conditions increase, reevaluation of the reimbursement level should be conducted in the same manner as are cost reevaluations of increases for other medical conditions.

Coverage provided by a health insurance program for other conditions must be provided for pregnancy-related conditions. For example, if a plan provides major medical coverage, pregnancy-related conditions must be so covered. Similarly, if a plan covers the cost of a private room for other conditions, the plan must cover the cost of a private room for pregnancy-related conditions. Finally, where a health insurance plan covers office visits to physicians, pre-natal and post-natal visits must be included in such coverage.

26. Q. May an employer limit payment of costs for pregnancy-related medical conditions to a specified dollar amount set forth in an insurance policy.

collective bargaining agreement or other statement of benefits to which an employee is entitled?

A. The amounts payable for the costs incurred for pregnancy-related conditions can be limited only to the same extent as are costs for other conditions. Maximum recoverable dollar amounts may be specified for pregnancy-related conditions if such amounts are similarly specified for other conditions, and so long as the specified amounts in all instances cover the same proportion of actual costs. If, in addition to the scheduled amount for other procedures, additional costs are paid for, either directly or indirectly, by the employer, such additional payments must also be paid for pregnancy-related procedures.

27. Q. May an employer impose a different deductible for payment of costs for pregnancy-related medical conditions than for costs of other medical conditions?

A. No. Neither an additional deductible, an increase in the usual deductible, nor a larger deductible can be imposed for coverage for pregnancy-related medical costs, whether as a condition for inclusion of pregnancy-related costs in the policy or for payment of the costs when incurred. Thus, if pregnancy-related costs are the first incurred under the policy, the employee is required to pay only the same deductible as would otherwise be required had other medical costs been the first incurred. Once this deductible has been paid, no additional deductible can be required for other medical procedures. If the usual deductible has already been paid for other medical procedures, no additional deductible can be required when pregnancy-related costs are later incurred.

28. Q. If a health insurance plan excludes the payment of benefits for any conditions existing at the time the insured's coverage becomes effective (pre-existing condition clause), can benefits be denied for medical costs arising from a pregnancy existing at the time the coverage became effective?

A. Yes. However, such benefits cannot be denied unless the pre-existing condition clause also excludes benefits for other pre-existing conditions in the same way.

29. Q. If an employer's insurance plan provides benefits after the insured's employment has ended (i.e. extended benefits) for costs connected with pregnancy and delivery where conception occurred while the insured was working for the employer, but not for the costs of any other medical condition which began prior to

termination of employment, may an employer (a) continue to pay these extended benefits for pregnancy-related medical conditions but not for other medical conditions, or (b) terminate these benefits for pregnancy-related conditions?

A. Where a health insurance plan currently provides extended benefits for other medical conditions on a less favorable basis than for pregnancy-related medical conditions, extended benefits must be provided for other medical conditions on the same basis as for pregnancy-related medical conditions. Therefore, an employer can neither continue to provide less benefits for other medical conditions nor reduce benefits currently paid for pregnancy-related medical conditions.

30. Q. Where an employer's health insurance plan currently requires total disability as a prerequisite for payment of extended benefits for other medical conditions but not for pregnancy-related costs, may the employer now require total disability for payment of benefits for pregnancy-related medical conditions as well?

A. Since extended benefits cannot be reduced in order to come into compliance with the Act, a more stringent prerequisite for payment of extended benefits for pregnancy-related medical conditions, such as a requirement for total disability, cannot be imposed. Thus, in this instance, in order to comply with the Act, the employer must treat other medical conditions as pregnancy-related conditions are treated.

31. Q. Can the added cost of bringing benefit plans into compliance with the Act be apportioned between the employer and employee?

A. The added cost, if any, can be apportioned between the employer and employee in the same proportion that the cost of the fringe benefit plan was apportioned on October 31, 1978, if that apportionment was nondiscriminatory. If the costs were not apportioned on October 31, 1978, they may not be apportioned in order to come into compliance with the Act. However, in no circumstance may male or female employees be required to pay unequal apportionments on the basis of sex or pregnancy.

32. Q. In order to come into compliance with the Act, may an employer reduce benefits or compensation?

A. In order to come into compliance with the Act, benefits or compensation which an employer was paying on October 31, 1978 cannot be reduced before October 31, 1979 or before the expiration of a collective bargaining agreement in effect on October 31, 1978, whichever is later.

Where an employer has not been in compliance with the Act by the times specified in the Act, and attempts to reduce benefits, or compensation, the employer may be required to remedy its practices in accord with ordinary Title VII remedial principles.

33. Q. Can an employer self-insure benefits for pregnancy-related conditions if it does not self-insure benefits for other medical conditions?

A. Yes, so long as the benefits are the same. In measuring whether benefits are the same, factors other than the dollar coverage paid should be considered. Such factors include the range of choice of physicians and hospitals, and the processing and promptness of payment of claims.

34. Q. Can an employer discharge, refuse to hire or otherwise discriminate against a woman because she has had or is contemplating having an abortion?

A. No. An employer cannot discriminate in its employment practices against a woman who has had or is contemplating having an abortion.

35. Q. Is an employer required to provide fringe benefits for abortions if fringe benefits are provided for other medical conditions?

A. All fringe benefits other than health insurance, such as sick leave, which are provided for other medical conditions, must be provided for abortions. Health insurance, however, need be provided for abortions only where the life of the woman would be endangered if the fetus were carried to term or where medical complications arise from an abortion.

36. Q. If complications arise during the course of an abortion, as for instance excessive hemorraging, must an employer's health insurance plan cover the additional cost due to the complications of the abortion?

A. Yes. The plan is required to pay those additional costs attributable to the complications of the abortion. However, the employer is not required to pay for the abortion itself, except where the life of the mother would be endangered if the fetus were carried to term.

37. Q. May an employer elect to provide insurance coverage for abortions?

A. Yes. The Act specifically provides that an employer is not precluded from providing benefits for abortions whether directly or through a collective bargaining agreement, but if an employer decides to cover the costs of abortion, the employer must do so in the same manner and to the same degree as it covers other medical conditions.

[FR Doc. 79-12367 Filed 4-19-79; 8:45 am]

BILLING CODE 6570-06-M

Equal Employment Opportunity Executive Order 11246 As Amended By Executive Order 11375

U.S. Department of Labor
Employment Standards Administration
Office of Federal Contract Compliance Programs

OFCCP-4
November 1975

Under and by virtue of the authority vested in me as President of the United States, it is ordered as follows:

PART I — NONDISCRIMINATION IN GOVERNMENT EMPLOYMENT [1]

PART II — NONDISCRIMINATION IN EMPLOYMENT BY GOVERNMENT CONTRACTORS AND SUBCONTRACTORS

Subpart A — Duties of the Secretary of Labor

SEC. 201. The Secretary of Labor shall be responsible for the administration of parts II and III of this order and shall adopt such rules and regulations and issue such orders as he deems necessary and appropriate to achieve the purposes thereof.

Subpart B — Contractors' Agreements

SEC. 202. Except in contracts exempted in accordance with section 204 of this order, all Government contracting agencies shall include in every Government contract hereafter entered into the following provisions:

During the performance of this contract, the contractor agrees as follows:

(1) The contractor will not discriminate against any employee or applicant for employment because of race, color, religion, sex, or national origin. The contractor will take affirmative action to ensure that applicants are employed, and that employees are treated during employment, without regard to their race, color, religion, sex, or national origin. Such action shall include, but not be limited to the following: employment, upgrading, demotion, or transfer; recruitment or recruitment advertising; layoff or termination; rates of pay or other forms of compensation; and selection for training, including apprenticeship. The contractor agrees to post in conspicuous places, available to employees and applicants for employment, notices to be provided by the contracting officer setting forth the provisions of this nondiscrimination clause.[2]

(2) The contractor will, in all solicitations or advertisements for employees placed by or on behalf of the contractor, state that all qualified applicants will receive consideration for employment without regard to race, color, religion, sex, or national origin.[3]

(3) The contractor will send to each labor union or representative of workers with which he has a collective bargaining agreement or other contract or understanding, a notice, to be provided by the agency contracting officer, advising the labor union or workers' representative of the contractor's commitments under section 202 of Executive Order No. 11246 of September 24, 1965, and shall post copies of the notice in conspicuous places available to employees and applicants for employment.

(4) The contractor will comply with all provisions of Executive Order No. 11246 of September 24, 1965, and of the rules, regulations, and relevant orders of the Secretary of Labor.

---

[1] Secs. 101 through 105 of pt. I of Executive Order 11246 dealing with discrimination in Federal employment were superseded by Executive Order 11478. Executive Order 11478, which is concerned exclusively with Government employment, expanded considerably the obligation of the Government itself to undertake equal employment opportunity within its own organization. Executive Order 11478 was signed by President Richard Nixon on Aug. 8, 1969.

[2] Sec. 202, paragraphs (1) and (2) and sec. 203, subsec. (d) were amended by Executive Order 11375 to encompass sex discrimination. Executive Order 11375 was signed by President Lyndon B. Johnson on Sept. 24, 1965.

[3] Ibid.

370

(5) The contractor will furnish all information and reports required by Executive Order No. 11246 of September 24, 1965, and by the rules, regulations, and orders of the Secretary of Labor, or pursuant thereto, and will permit access to his books, records, and accounts by the contracting agency and the Secretary of Labor for purposes of investigation to ascertain compliance with such rules, regulations, and orders.

(6) In the event of the contractor's noncompliance with the nondiscrimination clauses of this contract or with any of such rules, regulations, or orders, this contract may be cancelled, terminated, or suspended in whole or in part and the contractor may be declared ineligible for further Government contracts in accordance with procedures authorized in Executive Order No. 11246 of September 24, 1965, and such other sanctions may be imposed and remedies involved as provided in Executive Order No. 11246 of September 24, 1965, or by rule, regulation, or order of the Secretary of Labor, or as otherwise provided by law.

(7) The contractor will include the provisions of paragraphs (1) through (7) in every subcontract or purchase order unless exempted by rules, regulations, or orders of the Secretary of Labor issued pursuant to section 204 of Executive Order No. 11246 of September 24, 1965, so that such provisions will be binding upon each subcontractor or vendor. The contractor will take such action with respect to any subcontract or purchase order as the contracting agency may direct as a means of enforcing such provisions including sanctions for noncompliance: *Provided, however,* That in the event the contractor becomes involved in, or threatened with, litigation with a subcontractor or vendor as a result of such direction by the contracting agency, the contractor may request the United States to enter into such litigation to protect the interests of the United States.

SEC. 203. (a) Each contractor having a contract containing the provisions prescribed in section 202 shall file, and shall cause each of his subcontractors to file, compliance reports with the contracting agency or the Secretary of Labor as may be directed. Compliance reports shall be filed within such times and shall contain such information as to the practices, policies, programs, and employment policies, programs, and employment statistics of the contractor and each subcontractor, and shall be in such form, as the Secretary of Labor may prescribe.

(b) Bidders or prospective contractors or subcontractors may be required to state whether they have participated in any previous contract subject to the provisions of this order, or any preceding similar executive order, and in that event to submit, on behalf of themselves and their proposed subcontractors, compliance reports prior to or as an initial part of their bid or negotiation of a contract.

(c) Whenever the contractor or subcontractor has a collective bargaining agreement or other contract or understanding with a labor union or an agency referring workers or providing or supervising apprenticeship or training for such workers, the compliance report shall include such information as to such labor union's or agency's practices and policies affecting compliance as the Secretary of Labor may prescribe: *Provided,* That to the extent such information is within the exclusive possession of a labor union or an agency referring workers or providing or supervising apprenticeship or training and such labor union or agency shall refuse to furnish such information to the contractor, the contractor shall so certify to the contracting agency as part of its compliance report and shall set forth what efforts he has made to obtain such information.

(d) The contracting agency or the Secretary of Labor may direct that any bidder or prospective contractor or subcontractor shall submit, as part of his compliance report, a statement in writing, signed by an authorized officer or agent on behalf of any labor union or agency referring workers or providing or supervising apprenticeship or other training, with which the bidder or prospective contractor deals, with supporting information, to the effect that the signer's

371

practices and policies do not discriminate on the grounds of race, color, religion, sex, or national origin, and that the signer either will affirmatively cooperate in the implementation of the policy and provisions of this order or that it consents and agrees that recruitment, employment, and the terms and conditions of employment under the proposed contract shall be in accordance with the purposes and provisions of the order. In the event that the union, or the agency, shall refuse to execute such a statement, the compliance report shall so certify and set forth what efforts have been made to secure such a statement and such additional factual material as the contracting agency or the Secretary of Labor may require.[4]

SEC. 204. The Secretary of Labor may, when he deems that special circumstances in the national interest so require, exempt a contracting agency from the requirement of including any or all of the provisions of section 202 of this order in any specific contract, subcontract, or purchase order. The Secretary of Labor may, by rule or regulation, also exempt certain classes of contracts, subcontracts, or purchase orders: (1) whenever work is to be or has been performed outside the United States and no recruitment of workers within the limits of the United States is involved; (2) for standard commercial supplies or raw materials; (3) involving less than specified amounts of money or specified numbers of workers; or (4) to the extent that they involve subcontracts below a specified tier. The Secretary of Labor may also provide, by rule, regulation, or order, for the exemption of facilities of a contractor which are in all respects separate and distinct from activities of the contractor related to the performance of the contract: *Provided,* That such an exemption will not interfere with or impede the effectuation of the purposes of this order: *And provided further,* That in the absence of such an exemption all facilities shall be covered by the provisions of this order.

Subpart C—Powers and Duties of the Secretary of Labor and the Contracting Agencies

SEC. 205. Each contracting agency shall be primarily responsible for obtaining compliance with the rules, regulations, and orders of the Secretary of Labor with respect to contracts entered into by such agency or its contractors. All contracting agencies shall comply with the rules of the Secretary of Labor in discharging their primary responsibility for securing compliance with the provisions of contracts and otherwise with the terms of this order and of the rules, regulations, and orders of the Secretary of Labor issued pursuant to this order. They are directed to cooperate with the Secretary of Labor and to furnish the Secretary of Labor such information and assistance as he may require in the performance of his functions under this order. They are further directed to appoint or designate, from among the agency's personnel, compliance officers. It shall be the duty of such officers to seek compliance with the objectives of this order by conference, conciliation, mediation, or persuasion.

SEC. 206. (a) The Secretary of Labor may investigate the employment practices of any Government contractor or subcontractor, or initiate such investigation by the appropriate contracting agency, to determine whether or not the contractural provisions specified in section 202 of this order have been violated. Such investigation shall be conducted in accordance with the procedures established by the Secretary of Labor and the investigating agency shall report to the Secretary of Labor any action taken or recommended.

---

[4] Ibid.

(b) The Secretary of Labor may receive and investigate or cause to be investigated complaints by employees or prospective employees of a Government contractor or subcontractor which allege discrimination contrary to the contractural provisions specified in section 202 of this order. If this investigation is conducted for the Secretary of Labor by a contracting agency, that agency shall report to the Secretary what action has been taken or is recommended with regard to such complaints.

SEC. 207. The Secretary of Labor shall use his best efforts, directly and through contracting agencies, other interested Federal, State, and local agencies, contractors, and all other available instrumentalities to cause any labor union engaged in work under Government contracts or any agency referring workers or providing or supervising apprenticeship or training for or in the course of such work to cooperate in the implementation of the purposes of this order. The Secretary of Labor shall, in appropriate cases, notify the Equal Employment Opportunity Commission, the Department of Justice, or other appropriate Federal agencies whenever it has reason to believe that the practices of any such labor organization or agency violate Titles VI or VII of the Civil Rights Act of 1964 or other provision of Federal law.

SEC. 208. (a) The Secretary of Labor, or any agency, officer, or employee in the executive branch of the Government designated by rule, regulation, or order of the Secretary, may hold such hearings, public or private, as the Secretary may deem advisable for compliance, enforcement, or educational purposes.

(b) The Secretary of Labor may hold, or cause to be held, hearings in accordance with subsection (a) of this section prior to imposing, ordering, or recommending the imposition of penalties and sanctions under this order. No order for debarment of any contractor from further Government contracts under section 209(a)(6) shall be made without affording the contractor an opportunity for a hearing.

Subpart D—Sanctions and Penalties

SEC. 209. (a) In accordance with such rules, regulations, or orders as the Secretary of Labor may issue or adopt, the Secretary or the appropriate contracting agency may:

(1) Publish, or cause to be published, the names of contractors or unions which it has concluded have complied or have failed to comply with the provisions of this order or of the rules, regulations, and orders of the Secretary of Labor.

(2) Recommend to the Department of Justice that, in cases in which there is substantial or material violation or the threat of substantial or material violation of the contractual provisions set forth in section 202 of this order, appropriate proceedings be brought to enforce those provisions, including the enjoining, within the limitations of applicable law, of organizations, individuals, or groups who prevent directly or indirectly, or seek to prevent directly or indirectly, compliance with the provisions of this order.

(3) Recommend to the Equal Employment Opportunity Commission or the Department of Justice that appropriate proceedings be instituted under Title VII of the Civil Rights Act of 1964.

(4) Recommend to the Department of Justice that criminal proceedings be brought for the furnishing of false information to any contracting agency or to

the Secretary of Labor as the case may be.

(5) Cancel, terminate, suspend, or cause to be cancelled, terminated, or suspended any contract, or any portion or portions thereof, for failure of the contractor or subcontractor to comply with the nondiscrimination provisions of the contract. Contracts may be cancelled, terminated, or suspended absolutely or continuance of contracts may be conditioned upon a program for future compliance approved by the contracting agency.

(6) Provide that any contracting agency shall refrain from entering into further contracts, or extensions or other modifications of existing contracts, with any noncomplying contractor, until such contractor has satisfied the Secretary of Labor that such contractor has established and will carry out personnel and employment policies in compliance with the provisions of this order.

(b) Under rules and regulations prescribed by the Secretary of Labor, each contracting agency shall make reasonable efforts within a reasonable time limitation to secure compliance with the contract provisions of this order by methods of conference, conciliation, mediation, and persuasion before proceedings shall be instituted under subsection (a)(2) of this section, or before a contract shall be cancelled or terminated in whole or part under subsection (a)(5) of this section for failure of a contractor or subcontractor to comply with the contract provisions of this order.

SEC. 210. Any contracting agency taking any action authorized by this subpart, whether on its own motion, or as directed by the Secretary of Labor, or under the rules and regulations of the Secretary, shall promptly notify the Secretary of such action. Whenever the Secretary of Labor makes a determination under this section, he shall promptly notify the appropriate contracting agency of the action recommended. The agency shall take such action and shall report the results thereof to the Secretary of Labor within such time as the Secretary shall specify.

SEC. 211. If the Secretary shall so direct, contracting agencies shall not enter into contracts with any bidder or prospective contractor unless the bidder or prospective contractor has satisfactorily complied with the provisions of this order or submits a program for compliance acceptable to the Secretary of Labor or, if the Secretary so authorizes, to the contracting agency.

SEC. 212. Whenever a contracting agency cancels or terminates a contract, or whenever a contractor has been debarred from further Government contracts, under section 209(a)(6) because of noncompliance with the contract provisions with regard to nondiscrimination, the Secretary of Labor, or the contracting agency involved, shall promptly notify the Comptroller General of the United States. Any such debarment may be rescinded by the Secretary of Labor or by the contracting agency which imposed the sanction.

Subpart E—Certificates of Merit

SEC. 213. The Secretary of Labor may provide for issuance of a U.S. Government certificate of merit to employers or labor unions, or other agencies which are or may hereafter be engaged in work under Government contracts, if the Secretary is satisfied that the personnel and employment practices of the employer, or that the personnel, training, apprenticeship, membership, grievance and representation, upgrading, and other practices and policies of the labor union or other agency conform to the purposes and provisions of this order.

SEC. 214. Any certificate of merit may at any time be suspended or revoked by the Secretary of Labor if the holder thereof, in the judgment of the Secretary, has failed to comply with the provisions of this order.

SEC. 215. The Secretary of Labor may provide for the exemption of any employer, labor union, or other agency from any reporting requirements imposed under or pursuant to this order if such employer, labor union, or other agency has been awarded a certificate of merit which has not been suspended or revoked.

PART III — NONDISCRIMINATION PROVISIONS IN FEDERALLY ASSISTED CONSTRUCTION CONTRACTS

SEC. 301. Each executive department and agency which administers a program involving Federal financial assistance shall require as a condition for the approval of any grant, contract, loan, insurance, or guarantee thereunder, which may involve a construction contract, that the applicant for Federal assistance undertake and agree to incorporate, or cause to be incorporated, into all construction contracts paid for in whole or in part with funds obtained from the Federal Government or borrowed on the credit of the Federal Government pursuant to such grant, contract, loan, insurance, or guarantee, or undertaken pursuant to any Federal program involving such grant, contract, loan, insurance, or guarantee, the provisions prescribed for Government contracts by section 202 of this order or such modification thereof, preserving in substance the contractor's obligations thereunder, as may be approved by the Secretary of Labor, together with such additional provisions as the Secretary deems appropriate to establish and protect the interest of the United States in the enforcement of those obligations. Each such applicant shall also undertake and agree: (1) to assist and cooperate actively with the administering department or agency and the Secretary of Labor in obtaining the compliance of contractors and subcontractors with those contract provisions and with the rules, regulations, and relevant orders of the Secretary; (2) to obtain and to furnish to the administering department or agency and to the Secretary of Labor such information as they may require for the supervision of such compliance; (3) to carry out sanctions and penalties for violation of such obligations imposed upon contractors and subcontractors by the Secretary of Labor or the administering department or agency pursuant to part II, subpart D, of this order; and (4) to refrain from entering into any contract subject to this order, or extension or other modification of such a contract with a contractor debarred from Government contracts under part II, subpart D, of this order.

SEC. 302. (a) "Construction contract" as used in this order means any contract for the construction, rehabilitation, alteration, conversion, extension, or repair of buildings, highways, or other improvements to real property.

(b) The provisions of part II of this order shall apply to such construction contracts, and for purposes of such application, the administering department or agency shall be considered the contracting agency referred to therein.

(c) The term "applicant" as used in this order means an applicant for Federal assistance or, as determined by agency regulation, other program participant, with respect to whom an application for any grant, contract, loan, insurance, or guarantee is not finally acted upon prior to the effective date of this part, and it includes such an applicant after he becomes a recipient of such Federal assistance.

SEC. 303 (a) Each administering department and agency shall be responsible for obtaining the compliance of such applicants with their undertakings under this order. Each administering department and agency is directed to cooperate with the Secretary of Labor, and to furnish the Secretary such information and assistance as he may require in the performance of his functions under this order.

(b) In the event an applicant fails and refuses to comply with his undertakings, the administering department or agency may take any or all of the following actions: (1) cancel, terminate, or suspend in whole or in part the agreement, contract, or other arrangement with such applicant with respect to which the failure and refusal occurred; (2) refrain from extending any further assistance to the applicant under the program with respect to which the failure or refusal occurred until satisfactory assurance of future compliance has been received from such applicant; and (3) refer the case to the Department of Justice for appropriate legal proceedings.

(c) Any action with respect to an applicant pursuant to subsection (b) shall be taken in conformity with section 602 of the Civil Rights Act of 1964 (and the regulations of the administering department or agency issued thereunder), to the extent applicable. In no case shall action be taken with respect to an applicant pursuant to clause (1) or (2) of subsection (b) without notice and opportunity for hearing before the administering department or agency.

SEC. 304. Any executive department or agency which imposes by rule, regulation, or order requirements of nondiscrimination in employment, other than requirements imposed pursuant to this order, may delegate to the Secretary of Labor by agreement such responsibilities with respect to compliance standards, reports, and procedures as would tend to bring the administration of such requirements into conformity with the administration of requirements imposed under this order: *Provided*, That actions to effect compliance by recipients of Federal financial assistance with requirements imposed pursuant to Title VI of the Civil Rights Act of 1964 shall be taken in conformity with the procedures and limitations prescribed in section 602 thereof and the regulations of the administering department or agency issued thereunder.

PART IV — MISCELLANEOUS

SEC. 401. The Secretary of Labor may delegate to any officer, agency, or employee in the executive branch of the Government, any function or duty of the Secretary under parts II and III of this order, except authority to promulgate rules and regulations of a general nature.

SEC. 402. The Secretary of Labor shall provide administrative support for the execution of the program known as the "Plans of Progress."

SEC. 403. (a) Executive Orders Nos. 10590 (Jan. 18, 1955), 10722 (Aug. 5, 1957), 10925 (Mar. 6, 1961), 11114 (June 22, 1963), and 11162 (July 28, 1964), are hereby superseded and the President's Committee on Equal Employment Opportunity established by Executive Order No. 10925 is hereby abolished. All records and property in the custody of the committee shall be transferred to the Civil Service Commission and the Secretary of Labor, as appropriate.

(b) Nothing in this order shall be deemed to relieve any person of any obligation assumed or imposed under or pursuant to any executive order superseded by this order. All rules, regulations, orders, instructions, designations, and other directives issued by the President's Committee on Equal Employment Opportunity and those issued by the heads of various departments or agencies under or pursuant to any of the executive orders superseded by this order, shall, to the extent that they are not inconsistent with this order, remain in full force and effect unless and until revoked or superseded by appropriate authority. References in such directives to provisions of the superseded orders shall be deemed to be references to the comparable provisions of this order.

SEC. 404. The General Services Administration shall take appropriate action to revise the standard Government contract forms to accord with the provisions of this order and of the rules and regulations of the Secretary of Labor.

SEC. 405. This order shall become effective 30 days after the date of this order.

LYNDON B. JOHNSON

THE WHITE HOUSE
September 24, 1965

FRIDAY, JANUARY 19, 1979
PART XI

EQUAL
EMPLOYMENT
OPPORTUNITY
COMMISSION

■

AFFIRMATIVE ACTION
GUIDELINES

Technical Amendments to the
Procedural Regulations

federal register

[6570–06–M]

Title 29—Labor

CHAPTER XIV—EQUAL EMPLOYMENT OPPORTUNITY COMMISSION

PART 1608—AFFIRMATIVE ACTION APPROPRIATE UNDER TITLE VII OF THE CIVIL RIGHTS ACT OF 1964, AS AMENDED

Adoption of Interpretative Guidelines

AGENCY: Equal Employment Opportunity Commission.

ACTION: Adoption of final Guidelines on Affirmative Action appropriate under Title VII of the Civil Rights Act of 1964, as amended.

SUMMARY: The Equal Employment Opportunity Commission wishes to encourage voluntary action to eliminate employment discrimination, and hereby publishes its final Guidelines on Affirmative Action. Proposed Guidelines were published on December 28, 1977 (42 FR 64,826) for public comment. The Commission has now analyzed those comments and taken them into consideration in preparing its final Guidelines. The Preamble, below, describes the Commission's purpose for issuing these Guidelines and explains how the issues raised by the comments have been addressed. These Guidelines clarify the kinds of voluntary actions that are appropriate under Federal law. They describe the action the Commission will take when the procedures outlined herein have been followed. By elucidating the standards for voluntary action in these Guidelines, the Commission encourages affirmative action without resort to litigation.

EFFECTIVE DATE: February 20, 1979.

FOR FURTHER INFORMATION CONTACT:

Peter C. Robertson, Director, Office of Policy Implementation, Room 4002A, 2401 E Street, N.W., Washington, D.C. 20506, (202) 254–7469, 634–7060

SUPPLEMENTARY INFORMATION:

An Overview of the Guidelines on Affirmative Action

The Equal Employment Opportunity Commission ("EEOC", "the Commission") enforces Title VII of the Civil Rights Act of 1964, as amended, ("Title VII," "the Act"), which makes it illegal to discriminate in employment on the basis of race, color, religion, sex, or national origin. The Act requires the Commission to investigate complaints and attempt to correct violations it discovers, informally and through conciliation, or, if necessary, through court action. The Act also authorizes private individuals to bring lawsuits if their complaints are not resolved to their satisfaction or within the statutory time period.

Since the enactment of Title VII of the Civil Rights Act of 1964, many employers, labor organizations, and other persons subject to the Act have altered employment systems to implement the purposes of Title VII by improving employment opportunities for previously excluded groups. Because of what Congress has called the "complex and pervasive" nature of systemic discrimination against minorities and women (see H.R. Rep. No. 92–238, 92nd Cong., 2nd Sess. 8 (1972)), these voluntary efforts often involve significant changes in employment relationships. Some of these actions have been challenged under Title VII, as conflicting with statutory language requiring that employment decisions not be based on race, color, religion, sex, or national origin considerations. Accordingly, the Commission believes it is important to announce the legal principles which govern voluntary affirmative action under Title VII and other employment discrimination laws, so that persons subject to the Act have appropriate guidance. These Guidelines constitute the Commission's interpretation of Title VII, harmonizing the need to eliminate and prevent discrimination and to correct the effects of prior discrimination with the need to protect all individuals from discrimination on the basis of race, color, religion, sex, or national origin.

Requests for guidance have been received by the Commission from persons subject to Title VII concerning the relationship between affirmative action and so-called "reverse discrimination." There is no separate concept under Title VII of "reverse discrimination." Discrimination against all individuals because of race, color, religion, sex, or national origin is illegal under Title VII. *McDonald* v. *Santa Fe Trail Transportation Co.*, 427 U.S. 273 (1976).

To clarify the relationship between affirmative action and a countervailing claim of discrimination, a new section 1608.1 of these Guidelines sets forth the historical and legislative foundation for the Commission's interpretation of Title VII. Section 1608.1(b) explains that Congress enacted Title VII in order to overcome the effects of past and present employment practices which are part of a larger pattern of restriction, exclusion, discrimination, segregation and inferior treatment of minorities and women in many areas of life. Congress sought to accomplish this objective by establishing a national policy against discrimination in employment and encouraging voluntary affirmative action to eliminate barriers to equal employment opportunity. It is the Commission's interpretation that appropriate voluntary affirmative action, or affirmative action pursuant to an administrative or judicial requirement, does not constitute unlawful discrimination in violation of the Act.

It is essential to the effective implementation of Title VII that those who take appropriate voluntary affirmative action receive adequate protection against claims that their efforts constitute discrimination. The term affirmative action means those actions appropriate to overcome the effects of past or present practices, policies, or other barriers to equal employment opportunity. Section 1608.3 of these Guidelines identifies circumstances in which voluntary affirmative action is permissible under Title VII. When such circumstances exist, and a plan or program otherwise complies with these Guidelines, the Commission will find that there is no reasonable cause to believe that the affirmative action plan or program violates Title VII. See § 1608.10(a). In addition, § 1608.10(b) provides that where the plan or program is in writing and was adopted in good faith, in conformity with, and in reliance upon these Guidelines, the Commission will provide the protection authorized under section 713(b)(1) of Title VII to the employer, labor organization, or other person taking the action. See *EEOC* v. *AT&T*, 419 F. Supp. 1022, 1055, n. 34 (E.D.Pa. 1976), *aff'd*, 556 F.2d 167 (3rd Cir. 1977), *cert. denied*, 98 S.Ct. 3145 (1978).

On December 28, 1977, at 42 FR 64826 the Commission published proposed "Guidelines on Remedial and/or Affirmative Action" in the FEDERAL REGISTER and invited comments from the public. Comments were received from almost 500 individuals and organizations. The paragraphs below summarize the major issues raised by the comments and indicate the way in which the final Guidelines address the concerns raised by the comments.

On December 11, 1978, the Commission voted to approve the Guidelines in final form. Pursuant to Executive Order 12067, the Guidelines were then distributed to all Federal agencies for their review. Comments received in this process are also reflected in the discussion below.

I. Change of Guidelines' Title

The proposed Guidelines were titled "Proposed Guidelines on Affirmative and/or Remedial Action" and the phrase "remedial and/or affirmative action" was utilized throughout the document. A number of comments questioned the difference, if any, between remedial action and affirmative action. The term "remedial" has been dropped because of the possible erroneous implication that a violation of the law was required before affirmative action could be taken.

II. THE COMMISSION WILL PROCESS COMPLAINTS ALLEGING DISCRIMINATION AGAINST ANY AGGRIEVED PERSON

Many of the comments interpreted the Guidelines as indicating a Commission position that whites or males are entitled to less protection against discrimination than minorities or females, and that the Commission would either ignore complaints filed by whites or males, or process them in a different manner from those filed by females and minorities. The Commission maintains its position, articulated prior to *McDonald* v. *Santa Fe Trail Transportation Co.,* 427 U.S. 273 (1976), that discrimination on the basis of race, color, religion, sex, or national origin, is prohibited under Title VII, regardless of the individual or class against whom such discrimination is directed. See, e.g., Commission Decision No. 74–31, 7 FEP Cases 1326, 1328, CCH EEOC Decisions, ¶6404, (1973). The Commission will follow the same procedures in processing complaints filed by all individuals, regardless of their race, color, religion, sex, or national origin.

To avoid any ambiguity on these issues, language in the proposed Guidelines suggesting that complaints filed by whites and males could be "dismissed" under certain circumstances has been amended. Proposed paragraph V stated that the Commission would "issue a notice of dismissal of the charge" when an affirmative action program conformed to the Guidelines' requirements. The word "dismissal" is a term of art used by the Commission in its procedural regulations to refer to all determinations other than "reasonable cause." Because its use was misconstrued in many comments, final sections have been amended by substituting the phrase "a determination of no reasonable cause" where such a finding is justified by the facts of the case.

III. CONSIDERATION OF RACE, COLOR, RELIGION, SEX, AND NATIONAL ORIGIN IN EMPLOYMENT DECISIONS

Some commentators objected to the draft Guidelines because of their belief that Title VII requires that all employment decisions be made without consideration of race, color, religion, sex, or national origin, regardless of the circumstances. This conclusion does not comport with United States Supreme Court decisions interpreting Title VII, nor with the recent decision in *Regents of the University of California* v. *Bakke,* 98 S. Ct. 2733 (1978) (discussed infra). In the Title VII cases, the Supreme Court has called upon

employers " '* * * to self-examine and to self-evaluate their employment practices and to endeavor to eliminate, so far as possible, the last vestiges of an unfortunate and ignominious page in this country's history.' " *Albemarle Paper Co.* v. *Moody,* 422 U.S. 405, 418 (1975). See also, *Griggs* v. *Duke Power Co.,* 401 U.S. 424 (1971).

Thus, the Supreme Court recognizes that persons subject to Title VII will consider race, sex and national origin in their analyses and evaluations. In addition, the Court has emphasized the concept of conciliation and voluntary action rather than litigation as the primary method of enforcing Title VII. See *Occidental Life Insurance Co. of California* v. *EEOC,* 432 U.S. 355 (1977). Voluntary action necessarily implies latitude to make a reasonable judgement as to whether action should be taken and the nature of such action.

At the same time, the Commission recognizes that considerations of race, color, religion, sex, and national origin are not permissible in other contexts. For example, in *McDonald* v. *Santa Fe Trail Transportation Co.,* 427 U.S. 273 (1976), the Court held that the antidiscrimination principle of Title VII could be invoked by white employees as well as minority employees. No question of affirmative action was involved. The Court held that disparate treatment violated Title VII, but specifically stated that its decision did not address any issues relating to affirmative action programs. *McDonald, supra,* at 280, n. 8. For the reasons set forth in § 1608.1, the Commission considers that these Guidelines are consistent with the statute, the Congressional intent behind it, and the decisions of the Supreme Court.

IV. TWO DIFFERENT JUSTIFICATIONS OF VOLUNTARY ACTION: THE RELATIONSHIP BETWEEN TITLE VII AND EXECUTIVE ORDER No. 11246, As Amended

A number of comments indicated uncertainty as to the relationship in the proposed Guidelines between the references to Title VII and the references to the Executive Order. These commentators apparently understood the Guidelines to mean that affirmative action required by Executive Order No. 11246, as amended, and its implementing regulations would be lawful under Title VII *only* where the contractor has a reasonable basis for concluding that such action is necessary under Title VII. The structure of the Guidelines has been changed to clarify the Commission's original interpretation that action taken pursuant to, and in conformity with the Executive order, as amended, and its implementing regulations, does not violate Title VII.

The legislative history of the Equal Employment Opportunity Act of 1972 shows that Congress repeatedly rejected limitations on affirmative action under the Executive Order, including the goals and timetables approach that had become by that time a central feature of the implementation of the Order. See, e.g., 118 Cong. Rec. 1385–1386 (1972) (remarks of Sen. Saxbe); 118 Cong. Rec. 1664–1665 (1972) (remarks of Sen. Javits); 118 Cong. Rec. 1676 (1972) (rejecting amendment offered by Sens. Allen and Ervin that would have prohibited requirements for certain types of affirmative action, including the goals approach, under the Executive Order); 118 Cong. Rec. 4918 (1972) (rejecting amendment offered by Sen. Ervin that would have applied section 703(j) of Title VII to the Executive Order).

The Commission concludes that Congress intended to permit the continuation of the Executive Order program which required affirmative action by government contractors. The Congress which acted to allow the Executive Order program to continue would not, in the same measure, invalidate it under Title VII. The statute should be construed to avoid such a contradictory conclusion, especially where such a conclusion would undermine the expressed Congressional purpose of opening employment opportunities to minorities and women who had in the past been denied such opportunities.

In the Equal Employment Opportunity Act of 1972, Congress recognized the contractor's right to rely on affirmative action plans that had been approved under the Executive Order. See section 718 of Title VII. Furthermore, Congress in section 715 established the Equal Employment Opportunity Coordinating Council (composed of the Secretary of Labor, the Chair of the EEOC, the Attorney General, the Chair of the U.S. Civil Service Commission, the Chair of the U.S. Commission on Civil Rights, or their respective delegates) "to minimize conflict, promote efficiency, and eliminate inconsistency – among * * * branches of the Federal Government responsible for the implementation and enforcement of equal opportunity legislation, orders, and policies." 42 U.S.C. 2000e–14. This coordination responsibility now rests in the Commission by virtue of 5 U.S.C. 901 et seq., as applied by Reorganization Plan No. 1 (1978), which was implemented by Executive Order 12067 (43 FR 28,967, July 30, 1978). In order to achieve the objectives of section 715 and Executive Order No. 12067, the Commission concludes that it must recognize compliance with the requirements of Executive Order No. 11246, as amended, and its implementing regulations, as a defense to a charge that the affirmative action compliance program is discriminatory. The Commission concludes that adherence to an affirmative action compliance program approved by an appropriate official of the Department of Labor or its authorized agencies is lawful under Title VII. This interpretation thus insures that government contractors will not be subject to inconsistent standards by the Equal Employment Opportunity Commission and the Office of Federal Contract Compliance Programs.

Thus, the Commission recognizes that affirmative action by government contractors may be lawful under Title VII for either of two distinct reasons: (a) Such efforts constitute reasonable action to implement the legislative purposes of Title VII, or (b) the action was taken pursuant to, and in conformity with Executive Order No. 11246, as amended, and its implementing regulations. The Guidelines have been revised to reflect these two independent justifications for affirmative action under Title VII. A separate § 1608.5 governs affirmative action under Executive Order No. 11246, as amended.

The three step analytical process required under § 1608.4., when action is being justified under Title VII, is not necessary under § 1608.5, when action is being justified as undertaken pursuant to an approved program under Executive Order No. 11246, as amended. The circumstances in which such affirmative action is required under the Executive Order and the nature of such affirmative action are established by the Department of Labor.

V. APPROPRIATE STEPS FOR TAKING VOLUNTARY ACTION

A number of comments suggested that the Guidelines did not clearly define the steps the Commission believes are appropriate in taking voluntary affirmative action. A new § 1608.4 has been added to explain the three step process applicable to action justified under Title VII: reasonable self analysis, reasonable basis for concluding that action is appropriate, and reasonable action to correct that situation. The process set forth in § 1608.4 should be utilized to determine whether the circumstances set forth in § 1608.3 are present. Section 1608.5 covers action pursuant to Executive Order No. 11246, as amended.

VI. REASONABLE SELF ANALYSIS

Some commentators requested further elaboration on the meaning of the term "self analysis." Section 1608.4(a) has been amended to make it clear that there is no single mandatory method of conducting the self analysis, and to refer to the method-

ology used by government contractors under Revised Order 4 as a model which employers and others may use in conducting a self analysis. Whatever method is used, the primary objective must be to determine whether the employment practices operate as barriers to equal employment opportunity.

Some commentators suggested that the Guidelines may be subject to abuse unless the self analysis is required to be in writing. The Commission believes that the protection from Title VII liability which may be available under section 713(b)(1) should only be recognized where the affirmative action plan or program has been carefully and consciously developed. Accordingly, the section 713(b)(1) defense will be recognized by the Commission only where the analysis and the affirmative action plan or program are in writing and are adopted in good faith, in conformity with, and in reliance upon these Guidelines. See §§ 1608.4(d) and 1608.10.

However, a respondent who has undertaken the analysis, self-evaluation, and development of an affirmative action plan of the type described in the Guidelines, but has not reduced the analysis and plan to writing, may assert these facts as a defense to a charge of discrimination. The analysis and plan need not be in writing because the Commission does not generally require that employer defenses be based on written documents. However, employers are encouraged to have written documentation since such written evidence would make it easier to establish that an analysis was conducted and that a plan or program exists. See § 1608.4(d)(2).

In response to comments which expressed concern that adoption of a plan or program might constitute an admission of discrimination, § 1608.4(d)(1) makes it clear that it is not necessary to state in writing the conclusion that a Title VII violation exists.

VII. THE GUIDELINES DO NOT APPROVE INADEQUATE REMEDIES

A number of commentators were concerned that violators of the Act could use the Guidelines and the section 713(b)(1) defense to shield themselves from liability for the underlying discrimination inadequately addressed by an affirmative action plan or program. The Guidelines do not lend themselves to this interpretation.

The proposed Guidelines stated in paragraph VII that the Guidelines were not intended to provide standards for determining whether voluntary action had fully remedied discrimination. The analysis and plan contemplated by these Guidelines will not establish whether discrimination

existed before the plan was adopted. Furthermore, the plan cannot determine whether discrimination might take place subsequent to its adoption. In addition, the judgment as to whether affirmative action is sufficient to eliminate discrimination is a complex one which may take into account circumstances that may not have been included in the analysis which underlies the affirmative action plan. For these reasons the existence of the plan cannot provide the basis for determining whether discrimination existed, or whether the plan itself provided an adequate remedy for such discrimination. Therefore, the Guidelines state that they do not apply to a determination of the adequacy of an affirmative action plan to eliminate discrimination against previously excluded groups. Furthermore, the section 713(b)(1) defense is not involved in a determination of the adequacy of such a plan or program. Section 1608.11(a) is intended to make it clear that employers, labor organizations, or other persons who take affirmative action may still be liable under Title VII if the plan or program does not adequately remedy illegal discrimination.

VIII. NO ADMISSION OF DISCRIMINATION REQUIRED

Another group of comments stated that, because the Guidelines do not require an admission or finding of discrimination, the Commission may thereby approve affirmative action which might constitute unlawful discrimination prohibited by Title VII. This interpretation is incorrect.

The proposed Guidelines stated in paragraph II that the lawfulness of affirmative action was not "dependent upon an admission, or a finding, or evidence sufficient to prove" that the person taking such action had actually violated Title VII. After careful analysis and consideration, the Commission is of the opinion that the statement, as amended, appearing in § 1608.4(b), represents an appropriate interpretation of Federal law and policy for the reasons set forth in § 1608.1(c).

These Guidelines provide a sufficient basis to determine whether affirmative action is appropriate. Persons subject to the Act should not, by taking reasonable affirmative action, be exposed to liability under the very Act they are seeking to implement. Similarly, the law should not force the employer or other person to speculate whether an arguable defense to a Title VII charge would be recognized by a court before taking affirmative action. Section 1608.4(b) makes it clear that this reasonable basis exists without regard to arguable defenses to a Title VII action.

IX. The Scope of Appropriate Voluntary Action

Several comments raised questions concerning the appropriate scope of voluntary affirmative action intended by the Guidelines. Some perceive the Commission's use of the words "ratios and other numerical remedies" in proposed Paragraph IV, in addition to the words "goals and timetables", as indicating that the Commission was endorsing "absolute quotas" or "fixed quotas" without regard to qualifications or the circumstances in which they were used. The words "ratios and other numerical remedies" have been omitted from these Guidelines in order to avoid ambiguity and to make it clear that any numerical objective is subject to the availability of sufficient applicants who are qualified by proper, validated standards.

Affirmative Action under these Guidelines must be reasonable and must be related to the problems disclosed by the self-analysis. A new § 1608.4(c) has been added to make this clear. Affirmative action under these Guidelines may include interim goals or targets. Such interim goals or targets for previously excluded groups may be higher than the percentage of their availability in the workforce so that the long term goal may be met in a reasonable period of time. In order to achieve such interim goals or targets, an employer may consider race, sex, and/or national origin in making selections from among qualified or qualifiable applicants. Courts have ordered actions of this kind in litigated cases and in consent decrees. *Carter v. Gallagher*, 452 F.2d 315 (8th Cir. 1972), *en banc*, *cert. denied* (98 S. Ct. 3145 (1978)); *U.S.* v. *Allegheny-Ludlum Industries, Inc.*, 517 F.2d 826 (5th Cir. 1975), *cert. denied*, 425 U.S. 944 (1976).

X. Relevance of Certain Court Cases

A number of comments indicated that there were court decisions rendering inappropriate the approach taken by the Commission in these Guidelines. Because the proposed Guidelines were issued for comment prior to the decision of the United States Supreme Court in the case of *Regents of University of California* v. *Bakke*, 98 S. Ct. 2733 (1978), a number of commentators suggested that either the Guidelines were inappropriate in light of the decision of the California Supreme Court in that case, or that the Commission should wait until the U.S. Supreme Court had issued its opinion. As recommended, the Commission awaited the action of the Supreme Court in that case before promulgating these Guidelines. The Commission has reviewed these Guidelines in light of the opinions of the Justices of the Supreme Court in *Bakke*. The Commission concludes that these Guidelines

are consistent with the action of the Supreme Court in that case.

In the *Bakke* case the university did not assert reliance on any detailed guidance and procedures for crafting an affirmative action plan. These Guidelines seek to provide such guidance and thereby to establish an appropriate legal foundation for voluntary action under Title VII.

Perhaps the case most frequently cited by the commentators as conflicting with the principles articulated in the proposed Guidelines was a split decision in *Weber* v. *Kaiser Aluminum Corp.*, 563 F.2d 216 (5th Cir. 1977), *cert. granted*, ── U.S. ──, *Weber*, however, was decided prior to *Bakke*, and therefore did not take into account the opinions in that case. In addition, it is fundamentally unfair to expose those subject to Executive Order No. 11246 to risks of liability under Title VII when they act in compliance with government requirements or when they act voluntarily and appropriately to achieve statutory objectives. Furthermore, the clarification provided by these Guidelines is necessary because the *Weber* decision may be interpreted to unduly interfere with the range of affirmative action which Congress intended to permit under Title VII.[1]

The Commission has examined all the decisions brought to its attention in the comments and other recent decisions of the United States Supreme Court and concludes that none of these decisions affect its interpretation of the circumstances in which affirmative action is lawful under Title VII.

By virtue of the authority vested in it by section 713 of Title VII of the Civil Rights Act of 1964, as amended, 42 U.S.C. 2000e–12, 78 Stat. 265, and after due consideration of all comments received, the Equal Employment Opportunity Commission hereby issues as new Part 1608 of Title 29 of the Code of Federal Regulations its "Guidelines on Affirmative Action Appropriate Under Title VII of the Civil Rights Act of 1964, as Amended" as set forth below.

Signed at Washington, D.C., this 16th day of January 1979.

For the Commission.

ELEANOR HOLMES NORTON,
Chair.

Sec.
1608.1 Statement of purpose.
1608.2 Written interpretation and opinion.
1608.3 Circumstances under which voluntary affirmative action is appropriate.

[1] The Commission has taken the position that the decision of the Court of Appeals is incorrect and that the affirmative action program there was lawful. The Solicitor General has taken the same position, and the Supreme Court has now granted petitions for a writ of certiorari.

1608.4 Establishing affirmative action plans.
1608.5 Affirmative action compliance programs under executive order No. 11246, as amended.
1608.6 Affirmative action plans which are part of commission conciliation or settlement agreements.
1608.7 Affirmative action plans or programs under State or local law.
1608.8 Adherence to court order.
1608.9 Reliance on directions of other government agencies.
1608.10 Standard of review.
1608.11 Limitations on the application of these guidelines.
1608.12 Equal employment opportunity plans adopted pursuant to section 717 of title VII.

AUTHORITY: Sec. 713 of title VII of the Civil Rights Act of 1964, as amended, 42 U.S.C. 2000e–12, 78 Stat. 265.

§ 1608.1 Statement of Purpose.

(a) *Need for Guidelines.* Since the passage of Title VII in 1964, many employers, labor organizations, and other persons subject to Title VII have changed their employment practices and systems to improve employment opportunities for minorities and women, and this must continue. These changes have been undertaken either on the initiative of the employer, labor organization, or other person subject to Title VII, or as a result of conciliation efforts under Title VII, action under Executive Order No. 11246, as amended, or under other Federal, state, or local laws, or litigation. Many decisions taken pursuant to affirmative action plans or programs have been race, sex, or national origin conscious in order to achieve the Congressional purpose of providing equal employment opportunity. Occasionally, these actions have been challenged as inconsistent with Title VII, because they took into account race, sex, or national origin. This is the so-called "reverse discrimination" claim. In such a situation, both the affirmative action undertaken to improve the conditions of minorities and women, and the objection to that action, are based upon the principles of Title VII. Any uncertainty as to the meaning and application of Title VII in such situations threatens the accomplishment of the clear Congressional intent to encourage voluntary affirmative action. The Commission believes that by the enactment of Title VII Congress did not intend to expose those who comply with the Act to charges that they are violating the very statute they are seeking to implement. Such a result would immobilize or reduce the efforts of many who would otherwise take action to improve the opportunities of minorities and women without litigation, thus frustrating the Congressional intent to encourage voluntary action and increasing the prospect of Title VII litigation. The Commission believes that it is now necessary to clarify and harmonize the principles of Title VII in order to achieve these Congressional objectives and protect those employers, labor organizations, and other persons who comply with the principles of Title VII.

(b) *Purposes of Title VII.* Congress enacted Title VII in order to improve the economic and social conditions of minorities and women by providing equality of opportunity in the work place. These conditions were part of a larger pattern of restriction, exclusion, discrimination, segregation, and inferior treatment of minorities and women in many areas of life.[1] The Legislative Histories of Title VII, the Equal Pay Act, and the Equal Employment Opportunity Act of 1972 contain extensive analyses of the higher unemployment rate, the lesser occupational status, and the consequent lower income levels of minorities and women.[2] The purpose of Executive Order No. 11246, as amended, is similar to the purpose of Title VII. In response to these economic and social conditions, Congress, by passage of Title VII, established a national policy against discrimination in employment on grounds of race, color, religion, sex, and national origin. In addition, Congress strongly encouraged employers, labor organizations, and other persons subject to Title VII (hereinafter referred to as "persons," see section 701(a) of the Act) to act on a voluntary basis to modify employment practices and systems which constituted barriers to equal employment opportunity, without awaiting litigation or formal government action. Conference, conciliation, and persuasion were the primary processes adopted by Congress in 1964, and reaffirmed in 1972,

[1] Congress has also addressed these conditions in other laws, including the Equal Pay Act of 1963, Pub. L. 88-38, 77 Stat. 56 (1963), as amended; the other Titles of the Civil Rights Act of 1964, Pub. L. 88-352, 78 Stat. 241 (1964), as amended; the Voting Rights Act of 1965, Pub. L. 89-110, 79 Stat. 437 (1965), as amended; the Fair Housing Act of 1968, Pub. L. 90-364, Title VII, 82 Stat. 73, 81 (1968), as amended; the Educational Opportunity Act (Title IX), Pub. L. 92-318, 86 Stat. 373 (1972), as amended; and the Equal Employment Opportunity Act of 1972, Pub. L. 92-261, 86 Stat. 103 (1972), as amended.

[2] Equal Pay Act of 1963: S. Rep. No. 176, 88th Cong., 1st Sess., 1-2 (1963). Civil Rights Act of 1964: H.R. Rep. No. 914, pt. 2, 88th Cong., 1st Sess. (1971). Equal Employment Opportunity Act of 1972: H.R. Rep. No. 92-238, 92d Cong., 1st Sess. (1971); S. Rep. No. 92-415, 92d Cong., 1st Sess. (1971). See also, Equal Employment Opportunity Commission, *Equal Employment Opportunity Report—1975, Job Patterns for Women in Private Industry* (1977); Equal Employment Opportunity Commission, *Minorities and Women in State and Local Government—1975* (1977); United States Commission on Civil Rights, *Social Indicators of Equality for Minorities and Women* (1978).

to achieve these objectives, with enforcement action through the courts or agencies as a supporting procedure where voluntary action did not take place and conciliation failed. See § 706 of Title VII.

(c) *Interpretation in furtherance of legislative purpose.* The principle of nondiscrimination in employment because of race, color, religion, sex, or national origin, and the principle that each person subject to Title VII should take voluntary action to correct the effects of past discrimination and to prevent present and future discrimination without awaiting litigation, are mutually consistent and interdependent methods of addressing social and economic conditions which precipitated the enactment of Title VII. Voluntary affirmative action to improve opportunities for minorities and women must be encouraged and protected in order to carry out the Congressional intent embodied in Title VII.[3] Affirmative action under these principles means those actions appropriate to overcome the effects of past or present practices, policies, or other barriers to equal employment opportunity. Such voluntary affirmative action cannot be measured by the standard of whether it would have been required had there been litigation, for this standard would undermine the legislative purpose of first encouraging voluntary action without litigation. Rather, persons subject to Title VII must be allowed flexibility in modifying employment systems and practices to comport with the purposes of Title VII. Correspondingly, Title VII must be construed to permit such voluntary action, and those taking such action should be afforded the protection against Title VII liability which the Commission is authorized to provide under section 713(b)(1).

(d) *Guidelines interpret Title VII and authorize use of Section 713(b)(1).* These Guidelines describe the circumstances in which persons subject to Title VII may take or agree upon action to improve employment opportunities of minorities and women, and describe the kinds of actions they may take which are consistent with Title VII. These Guidelines constitute the Commission's interpretation of Title VII and will be applied in the processing of claims of discrimination which involve voluntary affirmative action and programs. In addition, these

[3] Affirmative action often improves opportunities for all members of the workforce, as where affirmative action includes the posting of notices of job vacancies. Similarly, the integration of previously segregated jobs means that all workers will be provided opportunities to enter jobs previously restricted. See, e.g., *EEOC v. AT&T*, 419 F. Supp. 1022 (E.D.Pa. 1976); *aff'd*, 556 F. 2d 167 (3rd Cir. 1977), *cert. denied*, 98 S.Ct. 3145 (1978).

Guidelines state the circumstances under which the Commission will recognize that a person subject to Title VII is entitled to assert that actions were taken "in good faith, in conformity with, and in reliance upon a written interpretation or opinion of the Commission," including reliance upon the interpretation and opinion contained in these Guidelines, and thereby invoke the protection of section 713(b)(1) of Title VII.

(e) *Review of existing plans recommended.* Only affirmative action plans or programs adopted in good faith, in conformity with, and in reliance upon these Guidelines can receive the full protection of these Guidelines, including the section 713(b)(1) defense. See § 1608.10. Therefore, persons subject to Title VII who have existing affirmative action plans, programs, or agreements are encouraged to review them in light of these Guidelines, to modify them to the extent necessary to comply with these Guidelines, and to readopt or reaffirm them.

§ 1608.2 **Written interpretation and opinion.**

These Guidelines constitute "a written interpretation and opinion" of the Equal Employment Opportunity Commission as that term is used in section 713(b)(1) of Title VII of the Civil Rights Act of 1964, as amended, 42 U.S.C. 2000e-12(b)(1), and section 1601.33 of the Procedural Regulations of the Equal Employment Opportunity Commission (29 CFR 1601.30; 42 FR 55,394 (October 14, 1977)). Section 713(b)(1) provides:

In any action or proceeding based on any alleged unlawful employment practice, no person shall be subject to any liability or punishment for or on account of (1) the commission by such person of an unlawful employment practice if he pleads and proves that the act or omission complained of was in good faith, in conformity with, and in reliance on any written interpretation or opinion of the Commission * * *. Such a defense, if established, shall be a bar to the action or proceeding, notwithstanding that * * * after such act or omission, such interpretation or opinion is modified or rescinded or is determined by judicial authority to be invalid or of no legal effect * * *.

The applicability of these Guidelines is subject to the limitations on use set forth in § 1608.11.

§ 1608.3 **Circumstances under which voluntary affirmative action is appropriate.**

(a) *Adverse effect.* Title VII prohibits practices, procedures, or policies which have an adverse impact unless they are justified by business necessity. In addition, Title VII proscribes practices which "tend to deprive" persons of equal employment opportunities. Employers, labor organizations and other persons subject to Title VII may take affirmative action based on an analysis which reveals facts constituting actual or potential adverse impact, if such adverse impact is likely to result from existing or contemplated practices.

(b) *Effects of prior discriminatory practices.* Employers, labor organizations, or other persons subject to Title VII may also take affirmative action to correct the effects of prior discriminatory practices. The effects of prior discriminatory practices can be initially identified by a comparison between the employer's work force, or a part thereof, and an appropriate segment of the labor force.

(c) *Limited labor pool.* Because of historic restrictions by employers, labor organizations, and others, there are circumstances in which the available pool, particularly of qualified minorities and women, for employment or promotional opportunities is artificially limited. Employers, labor organizations, and other persons subject to Title VII may, and are encouraged to take affirmative action in such circumstances, including, but not limited to, the following:

(1) Training plans and programs, including on-the-job training, which emphasize providing minorities and women with the opportunity, skill, and experience necessary to perform the functions of skilled trades, crafts, or professions;

(2) Extensive and focused recruiting activity;

(3) Elimination of the adverse impact caused by unvalidated selection criteria (see sections 3 and 6, Uniform Guidelines on Employee Selection Procedures (1978), 43 FR 30,290; 38,297; 38,299 (August 25, 1978));

(4) Modification through collective bargaining where a labor organization represents employees, or unilaterally where one does not, of promotion and layoff procedures.

§ 1608.4 **Establishing affirmative action plans.**

An affirmative action plan or program under this section shall contain three elements: a reasonable self analysis; a reasonable basis for concluding action is appropriate; and reasonable action.

(a) *Reasonable self analysis.* The objective of a self analysis is to determine whether employment practices do, or tend to, exclude, disadvantage, restrict, or result in adverse impact or disparate treatment of previously excluded or restricted groups or leave uncorrected the effects of prior discrimination, and if so, to attempt to determine why. There is no mandatory method of conducting a self analysis. The employer may utilize techniques used in order to comply with

Executive Order No. 11246, as amended, and its implementing regulations, including 41 CFR Part 60-2 (known as Revised Order 4), or related orders issued by the Office of Federal Contract Compliance Programs or its authorized agencies, or may use an analysis similar to that required under other Federal, state, or local laws or regulations prohibiting employment discrimination. In conducting a self analysis, the employer, labor organization, or other person subject to Title VII should be concerned with the effect on its employment practices of circumstances which may be the result of discrimination by other persons or institutions. See *Griggs* v. *Duke Power Co.,* 401 U.S. 424 (1971).

(b) *Reasonable basis.* If the self analysis shows that one or more employment practices: (1) Have or tend to have an adverse effect on employment opportunities of members of previously excluded groups, or groups whose employment or promotional opportunities have been artificially limited, (2) leave uncorrected the effects of prior discrimination, or (3) result in disparate treatment, the person making the self analysis has a reasonable basis for concluding that action is appropriate. It is not necessary that the self analysis establish a violation of Title VII. This reasonable basis exists without any admission or formal finding that the person has violated Title VII, and without regard to whether there exists arguable defenses to a Title VII action.

(c) *Reasonable action.* The action taken pursuant to an affirmative action plan or program must be reasonable in relation to the problems disclosed by the self analysis. Such reasonable action may include goals and timetables or other appropriate employment tools which recognize the race, sex, or national origin of applicants or employees. It may include the adoption of practices which will eliminate the actual or potential adverse impact, disparate treatment, or effect or past discrimination by providing opportunities for members of groups which have been excluded, regardless of whether the persons benefited were themselves the victims of prior policies or procedures which produced the adverse impact or disparate treatment or which perpetuated past discrimination.

(1) *Illustrations of appropriate affirmative action.* Affirmative action plans or programs may include, but are not limited to, those described in the Equal Employment Opportunity Coordinating Council "Policy Statement on Affirmative Action Programs for State and Local Government Agencies," 41 FR 38,814 (September 13, 1976), reaffirmed and extended to all persons subject to Federal equal em-

ployment opportunity laws and orders, in the Uniform Guidelines on Employee Selection Procedures (1978) 43 FR 38,290; 38,300 (Aug. 25, 1978). That statement reads, in relevant part:

When an employer has reason to believe that its selection procedures have * * * exclusionary effect * * *, it should initiate affirmative steps to remedy the situation. Such steps, which in design and execution may be race, color, sex or ethnic 'conscious,' include, but are not limited to, the following:

The establishment of a long term goal and short range, interim goals and timetables for the specific job classifications, all of which should take into account the availability of basically qualified persons in the relevant job market;

A recruitment program designed to attract qualified members of the group in question;

A systematic effort to organize work and re-design jobs in ways that provide opportunities for persons lacking 'journeyman' level knowledge or skills to enter and, with appropriate training, to progress in a career field;

Revamping selection instruments or procedures which have not yet been validated in order to reduce or eliminate exclusionary effects on particular groups in particular job classifications;

The initiation of measures designed to assure that members of the affected group who are qualified to perform the job are included within the pool of persons from which the selecting official makes the selection;

A systematic effort to provide career advancement training, both classroom and on-the-job, to employees locked into dead end jobs; and

The establishment of a system for regularly monitoring the effectiveness of the particular affirmative action program, and procedures for making timely adjustments in this program where effectiveness is not demonstrated.

(2) *Standards of reasonable action.* In considering the reasonableness of a particular affirmative action plan or program, the Commission will generally apply the following standards:

(i) The plan should be tailored to solve the problems which were identified in the self analysis, see § 1608.4(a), supra, and to ensure that employment systems operate fairly in the future, while avoiding unnecessary restrictions on opportunities for the workforce as a whole. The race, sex, and national origin conscious provisions of the plan or program should be maintained only so long as is necessary to achieve these objectives.

(ii) Goals and timetables should be reasonably related to such considerations as the effects of past discrimination, the need for prompt elimination of adverse impact or disparate treatment, the availability of basically qualified or qualifiable applicants, and the number of employment opportunities expected to be available.

(d) *Written or unwritten plans or programs*—(1) *Written plans required for 713(b)(1) Protection.* The protection of section 713(b) of Title VII will be accorded by the Commission to a person subject to Title VII only if the self analysis and the affirmative action plan are dated and in writing, and the plan otherwise meets the requirements of Section 713(b)(1). The Commission will not require that there be any written statement concluding that a Title VII violation exists.

(2) *Reasonable cause determinations.* Where an affirmative action plan or program is alleged to violate Title VII, or is asserted as a defense to a charge of discrimination, the Commission will investigate the charge in accordance with its usual procedures and pursuant to the standards set forth in these Guidelines, whether or not the analysis and plan are in writing. However, the absence of a written self analysis and a written affirmative action plan or program may make it more difficult to provide credible evidence that the analysis was conducted, and that action was taken pursuant to a plan or program based on the analysis. Therefore, the Commission recommends that such analyses and plans be in writing.

§ 1608.5 Affirmative action compliance programs under Executive Order No. 11246, as amended.

Under Title VII, affirmative action compliance programs adopted pursuant to Executive Order No. 11246, as amended, and its implementing regulations, including 41 CFR Part 60-2 (Revised Order 4), will be considered by the Commission in light of the similar purposes of Title VII and the Executive Order, and the Commission's responsibility under Executive Order No. 12067 to avoid potential conflict among Federal equal employment opportunity programs. Accordingly, the Commission will process Title VII complaints involving such affirmative action compliance programs under this section.

(a) *Procedures for review of Affirmative Action Compliance Programs.* If adherence to an affirmative action compliance program adopted pursuant to Executive Order No. 11246, as amended, and its implementing regulations, is the basis of a complaint filed under Title VII, or is alleged to be the justification for an action which is challenged under Title VII, the Commission will investigate to determine:

(1) Whether the affirmative action compliance program was adopted by a person subject to the Order and pursuant to the Order, and (2) whether adherence to the program was the basis of the complaint or the justification.

(1) *Programs previously approved.* If the Commission makes the determination described in paragraph (a) of this section and also finds that the affirmative action program has been ap-

proved by an appropriate official of the Department of Labor or its authorized agencies, or is part of a conciliation or settlement agreement or an order of an administrative agency, whether entered by consent or after contested proceedings brought to enforce Executive Order No. 11246, as amended, the Commission will issue a determination of no reasonable cause.

(2) *Program not previously approved.* If the Commission makes the determination described in paragraph (a), of this section but the program has not been approved by an appropriate official of the Department of Labor or its authorized agencies, the Commission will: (i) Follow the procedure in § 1608.10(a) and review the program, or (ii) refer the plan to the Department of Labor for a determination of whether it is to be approved under Executive Order No. 11246, as amended, and its implementing regulations. If, the Commission finds that the program does conform to these Guidelines, or the Department of Labor approves the affirmative action compliance program, the Commission will issue a determination of no reasonable cause under § 1608.10(a).

(b) *Reliance on these guidelines.* In addition, if the affirmative action compliance program has been adopted in good faith reliance on these Guidelines, the provisions of section 713(b)(1) of Title VII and of § 1608.10(b), below, may be asserted by the contractor.

§ 1608.6 Affirmative action plans which are part of Commission conciliation or settlement agreements.

(a) *Procedures for review of plans.* If adherence to a conciliation or settlement agreement executed under Title VII and approved by a responsible official of the EEOC is the basis of a complaint filed under Title VII, or is alleged to be the justification for an action challenged under Title VII, the Commission will investigate to determine: (1) Whether the conciliation agreement or settlement agreement was approved by a. responsible official of the EEOC, and (2) whether adherence to the agreement was the basis for the complaint or justification. If the Commission so finds, it will make a determination of no reasonable cause under § 1608.10(a) and will advise the respondent of its right under section 713(b)(1) of Title VII to rely on the conciliation agreement.

(b) *Reliance on these guidelines.* In addition, if the affirmative action plan or program has been adopted in good faith reliance on these Guidelines, the provisions of section 713(b)(1) of Title VII and of § 1608.10(b), below, may be asserted by the respondent.

§ 1608.7 Affirmative action plans or programs under State or local law.

Affirmative action plans or programs executed by agreement with state or local government agencies, or by order of state or local government agencies, whether entered by consent or after contested proceedings, under statutes or ordinances described in Title VII, will be reviewed by the Commission in light of the similar purposes of Title VII and such statutes and ordinances. Accordingly, the Commission will process Title VII complaints involving such affirmative action plans or programs under this section.

(a) *Procedures for review of plans or programs.* If adherence to an affirmative action plan or program executed pursuant to a state statute or local ordinance described in Title VII is the basis of a complaint filed under Title VII or is alleged to be the justification for an action which is challenged under Title VII, the Commission will investigate to determine: (1) Whether the affirmative action plan or program was executed by an employer, labor organization, or person subject to the statute or ordinance, (2) whether the agreement was approved by an appropriate official of the state or local government, and (3) whether adherence to the plan or program was the basis of the complaint or justification.

(1) *Previously Approved Plans or Programs.* If the Commission finds the facts described in paragraph (a) of this section, the Commission will, in accordance with the "substantial weight" provisions of section 706 of the Act, find no reasonable cause where appropriate.

(2) *Plans or Programs not previously approved.* If the plan or program has not been approved by an appropriate official of the state or local government, the Commission will follow the procedure of § 1608.10 of these Guidelines. If the Commission finds that the plan or program does conform to these Guidelines, the Commission will make a determination of no reasonable cause as set forth in § 1608.10(a).

(b) *Reliance on these guidelines.* In addition, if the affirmative action plan or program has been adopted in good faith reliance on these Guidelines, the provisions of section 713(b)(1) and § 1608.10(b), below, may be asserted by the respondent.

§ 1608.8 Adherence to court order.

Parties are entitled to rely on orders of courts of competent jurisdiction. If adherence to an Order of a United States District Court or other court of competent jurisdiction, whether entered by consent or after contested litigation, in a case brought to enforce a Federal, state, or local equal employment opportunity law or regulation, is the basis of a complaint filed under Title VII or is alleged to be the justification for an action which is challenged under Title VII, the Commission will investigate to determine: (a) Whether such an Order exists and (b) whether adherence to the affirmative action plan which is part of the Order was the basis of the complaint or justification. If the Commission so finds, it will issue a determination of no reasonable cause. The Commission interprets Title VII to mean that actions taken pursuant to the direction of a Court Order cannot give rise to liability under Title VII.

§ 1608.9 Reliance on directions of other government agencies.

When a charge challenges an affirmative action plan or program, or when such a plan or program is raised as justification for an employment decision, and when the plan or program was developed pursuant to the requirements of a Federal or state law or regulation which in part seeks to ensure equal employment opportunity, the Commission will process the charge in accordance with § 1608.10(a). Other agencies with equal employment opportunity responsibilities may apply the principles of these Guidelines in the exercise of their authority.

§ 1608.10 Standard of review.

(a) *Affirmative action plans or programs not specifically relying on these guidelines.* If, during the investigation of a charge of discrimination filed with the Commission, a respondent asserts that the action complained of was taken pursuant to an in accordance with a plan or program of the type described in these Guidelines, the Commission will determine whether the assertion is true, and if so, whether such a plan or program conforms to the requirements of these guidelines. If the Commission so finds, it will issue a determination of no reasonable cause and, where appropriate, will state that the determination constitutes a written interpretation or opinion of the Commission under section 713(b)(1). This interpretation may be relied upon by the respondent and asserted as a defense in the event that new charges involving similar facts and circumstances are thereafter filed against the respondent, which are based on actions taken pursuant to the affirmative action plan or program. If the Commission does not so find, it will proceed with the investigation in the usual manner.

(b) *Reliance on these guidelines.* If a respondent asserts that the action taken was pursuant to and in accordance with a plan or program which was adopted or implemented in good

faith, in conformity with, and in reliance upon these Guidelines, and the self analysis and plan are in writing, the Commission will determine whether such assertion is true. If the Commission so finds, it will state in the determination of no reasonable cause and will advise the respondent that:

(1) The Commission has found that the respondent is entitled to the protection of section 713(b)(1) of Title VII; and

(2) That the determination is itself an additional written interpretation or opinion of the Commission pursuant to section 713(b)(1).

§ 1608.11 Limitations on the application of these guidelines.

(a) *No determination of adequacy of plan or program.* These Guidelines are applicable only with respect to the circumstances described in § 1608.1(d), above. They do not apply to, and the section 713(b)(1) defense is not available for the purpose of, determining the adequacy of an affirmative action plan or program to eliminate discrimination. Whether an employer who takes such affirmative action has done enough to remedy such discrimination will remain a question of fact in each case.

(b) *Guidelines inapplicable in absence of affirmative action.* Where an affirmative action plan or program does not exist, or where the plan or program is not the basis of the action complained of, these Guidelines are inapplicable.

(c) *Currency of plan or program.* Under section 713(b)(1), persons may rely on the plan or program only during the time when it is current. Currency is related to such factors as progress in correcting the conditions disclosed by the self analysis. The currency of the plan or program is a question of fact to be determined on a case by case basis. Programs developed under Executive Order No. 11246, as amended, will be deemed current in accordance with Department of Labor regulations at 41 CFR Chapter 60, or successor orders or regulations.

§ 1608.12 Equal employment opportunity plans adopted pursuant to section 717 of Title VII.

If adherence to an Equal Employment Opportunity Plan, adopted pursuant to Section 717 of Title VII, and approved by an appropriate official of the U.S. Civil Service Commission, is the basis of a complaint filed under Title VII, or is alleged to be the justification for an action under Title VII, these Guidelines will apply in a manner similar to that set forth in § 1608.5. The Commission will issue

regulations setting forth the procedure for processing such complaints.

[FR Doc. 79-2025 Filed 1-18-79; 8:45 am]

[6570-06-M]

PART 1601—PROCEDURAL REGULATIONS

Issuance of Interpretation or Opinion

AGENCY: Equal Employment Opportunity Commission.

ACTION: Final rule.

SUMMARY: The Commission is today publishing in final form a set of Guidelines on Affirmative Action (44 FR 4422), to encourage voluntary action to eliminate employment discrimination. Section 1601.33 of the Commission's regulations is being amended to reflect a new method, contemplated by these Guidelines, by which the Commission may issue an "interpretation of opinion" of the Commission within the meaning of Section 713 of Title VII of the Civil Rights Act of 1964, as amended.

EFFECTIVE DATE: February 20, 1979.

FOR FURTHER INFORMATION CONTACT:

Peter C. Robertson, Director, Office of Policy Implementation, 2401 E Street, NW., Room 4002A, Washington, D.C. 20506 (202) 254-7639.

SUPPLEMENTARY INFORMATION: The Commission's new Guidelines on Affirmative Action contemplate that in instances where a charge of discrimination has been filed and the Commission finds that the treatment complained of occurred as a result of affirmative action procedures consistent with its Guidelines on Affirmative Action, the Commission will issue a determination of no reasonable cause. This determination may contain language stating that it is "a written interpretation or opinion of the Commission" within the meaning of Section 713(b)(1) of Title VII of the Civil Rights Act of 1964, as amended. The respondent in such a case may rely upon this determination as a defense to any subsequent complaints of discrimination which involve similar facts and circumstances, if the subsequent actions complained of were also taken by the respondent under its affirmative action procedures.

Such language will also appear in no-cause determinations whenever the Commission finds that the action complained of occurred pursuant to an affirmative action plan adopted in good faith compliance with, and reliance upon, the Commission's Guidelines on affirmative Action.

The Commission's procedural regulations are accordingly revised to include this specific type of no-cause finding as a type of "written interpretation or opinion of the Commission."

Signed at Washington, D.C. this 16th day of January 1979.

For the Commission.

ELEANOR HOLMES NORTON,
Chair.

Therefore, 29 CFR 1601.33 is amended to read as follows:

§ 1601.33 Issuance of interpretation or opinion.

Only the following may be relied upon as a "written interpretation or opinion of the Commission" within the meaning of Section 713 of Title VII:

(a) A letter entitled "opinion letter" and signed by the General Counsel on behalf of the Commission, or

(b) Matter published and specifically designated as such in the FEDERAL REGISTER, including the Commission's Guidelines on Affirmative Action, or

(c) A Commission determination of no reasonable cause, issued under the circumstances described in § 1608.10 (a) or (b) of the Commission's Guidelines on Affirmative Action 29 CFR Part 1608, when such determination contains a statement that it is a "written interpretation or opinion of the Commission."

[FR Doc. 79-2026 Filed 1-18-79; 8:45 am]

Monday
December 29, 1980

Part VI

Equal Employment Opportunity Commission

Guidelines on Discrimination Because of
National Origin

387

388

EQUAL EMPLOYMENT OPPORTUNITY COMMISSION

29 CFR Part 1606

Guidelines on Discrimination Because of National Origin

AGENCY: Equal Employment Opportunity Commission.

ACTION: Final guidelines.

SUMMARY: The Equal Employment Opportunity Commission is revising its *Guidelines on Discrimination Because of National Origin* to clarify them and to specifically inform the public of unlawful employment practices which discriminate on the basis of national origin. These Guidelines reaffirm the Commission's position on national origin discrimination as expressed in Commission decisions and other legal interpretations.

EFFECTIVE DATE: December 29, 1980.

FOR FURTHER INFORMATION: Karen Danart, Acting Director, or Raj K. Gupta, Supervisory Attorney, Office of Policy Implementation, 2401 E Street NW., Room 4002, Washington, D.C. 20506, (202) 634–7060.

SUPPLEMENTARY INFORMATION:

I. Background

On January 13, 1970, (35 FR 421) the Commission adopted its *Guidelines on Discrimination Because of National Origin*. These Guidelines were issued as a result of charges filed by individuals alleging denial of equal employment opportunity because their last names suggested association with certain national origin groups, or because of their association with persons, schools, churches and other lawful organizations identified with certain national origin groups. The Guidelines were last amended on March 18, 1974, to conform to the Supreme Court decision in *Espinoza* v. *Farah Manufacturing Co., Inc.*, 414 U.S. 86, 92 (1973).

In order to allow interested persons an opportunity to participate in all stages of its guideline process and in compliance with Executive Order 12044 (43 FR 12661, March 24, 1978, as amended by E.O. 12221, 45 FR 44249, July 1, 1980), the Commission noticed its intent to review these Guidelines (45 FR 51229 at 51231, August 1, 1980). On September 19, 1980, 45 FR 62728, the Commission published a proposed revision of its current Guidelines which appear at 29 CFR 1606. The proposed Guidelines were published for public comment for 60 days. In compliance with Executive Order 12160 (44 FR 44787, September 26, 1979) and with the Commission's Final Consumer Program, (45 FR 38930, June 9, 1980), the Commission notified members of the public of their opportunity to comment on the proposed Guidelines by directly mailing them to various interested groups and individuals.

These Guidelines are a significant regulation under Executive Order 12044, (43 FR 12661, Mar. 24, 1978, as amended by E.O. 12221, 45 FR 44249, July 1, 1980). The Commission has determined that they will not have a major impact on the economy and that a regulatory analysis is not necessary.

In compliance with Executive Order 12067, (43 FR 28967, July 5, 1978), the Commission has consulted with representatives from the necessary federal departments and agencies on the revision of these Guidelines.

II. An Overview of the Guidelines and Public Comments

The Commission's main purpose in revising its Guidelines is to restructure and clarify the preceding Guidelines, and to incorporate into the Guidelines the Commission's major interpretations of Title VII discrimination on the basis of national origin. Therefore, each section of the Guidelines is based on existing policy which the Commission has stated in its Decisions, in the preceding *Guidelines on Discrimination Because of National Origin* or in other interpretations of Title VII.

During the 60 day comment period, the Commission received approximately 250 comments from individuals, civil rights organizations, business associations, educational institutions, and public and private employers. About two-thirds of these comments were general statements, either in support of, or against the Guidelines, and did not contain specific substantive comments on the Guidelines. Many of these commentators, focusing only on the section relating to the speak-English-only rules, incorrectly equated the Guidelines with the bilingual education programs and other bilingual programs. The Commission wants to emphasize that the Guidelines have no relationship to the bilingual education programs or other bilingual programs. The Commission also wants to emphasize that the Guidelines do not promote or require bilingualism in the workplace. The goal of the Guidelines is to protect employees from discriminatory employment practices and to remove unnecessary barriers, such as the broad speak-English-only rules, which result in the denial of employment opportunities to individuals on the basis of their national origin.

Many commentators strongly supported this revision of the Guidelines and indicated that these Guidelines would be beneficial in achieving equal job opportunities for all individuals regardless of their national origin, or their cultural or linguistic characteristics.

The following is an analysis of each section, the major comments received and the changes made to the proposed Guidelines.

§ 1606.1—Definition of National Origin Discrimination

This section is based on § 1606.1(b) of the preceding *Guidelines on Discrimination Because of National Origin*. It defines national origin discrimination broadly as including, but not limited to, employment discrimination because of an individual's, or his or her ancestor's place of origin, or because of an individual's physical, cultural or linguistic characteristics. As a result of the comments, the Commission has added physical characteristics to this definition. As several commentators noted, physical characteristics, such as facial features, are often the most obvious bases for national origin discrimination.

The Commission will carefully examine charges involving the denial of equal employment opportunity because of an individual's name, marriage to a person of a national origin group, or association with persons, organizations, schools or religious institutions identified with any national origin group. Some commentators suggested that the definition was too broad in extending protection to an individual merely because he or she is married to someone of a certain national origin or associates with institutions identified with a certain national origin. These comments are based on a misreading of the section. The section only states that such charges will be examined with particular concern to determine if, indeed, the alleged discrimination was based on national origin. To clarify this misunderstanding, the Commission has added a sentence stating that it will determine whether there has been unlawful national origin discrimination by applying general Title VII principles, such as disparate treatment and adverse impact. For example, it would be unlawful national origin discrimination for an employer to disparately treat an employee who it thought belonged to a certain national origin group because the employee's spouse had a pronounced foreign appearance or a foreign name.

A few commentators stated that the definition of national origin discrimination was too broad because it not only included minorities but also all white persons. National origin discrimination may often overlap with discrimination because of race or color. The Commission's definition of national origin discrimination is necessarily broad because Title VII protects all individuals from national origin discrimination regardless of their race or color.

Some commentators believed that the definition does not recognize national origin discrimination grounded in a person's manner of dressing, such as, the wearing of turbans or saris. If the facts of a case show that, under general Title VII principles, there has been discrimination on the basis of national origin, such discrimination would be covered under the definitional phrase "cultural characteristics of a national origin group."

Several commentators correctly noted that for an individual to be protected against national origin or his ancestors have their origins in a sovereign nation. See, for example, *Roach* v. *Dresser Industries*, 23 FEP Cases 1073 (W.D. La. 1980), where the court held that a person of Acadian descent ("Cajun") could sue under Title VII for national origin discrimination. Because the phrase "country of origin" may imply a reference to a sovereign nation, it has been substituted by the phrase "place of origin".

Also, the phrase "particular national origin" in the proposed Guidelines has been changed to "national origin group" throughout this section. In order to show that the alleged discriminator knew the *particular* national origin group to which the complainant belonged. To prove a national origin claim, it is enough to show that the complainant was treated differently than others because of his or her foreign accent, appearance or physical characteristics. See, for example, *Berke* v. *Ohio Department of Public Welfare*, 24 EPD ¶31,217 (6th Cir. 1980), which held that defendants had discriminated against Berke because of her accent which flowed from her national origin. The Court of Appeals, in a per curiam opinion, affirmed the unpublished district court opinion. The district court had held that it was immaterial that the employer could not have discriminated against the employee because she was of Polish origin; the employer did not know that the employee was Polish. It was sufficient that the employer treated

her differently because she had a "foreign" accent.

§ 1606.2—Scope of Title VII Protection

The first sentence of this section is based on § 1606.1(c) of the preceding Guidelines, and has been revised to conform with the coverage of Title VII. Section 1606.2 also recognizes that Title VII principles of disparate treatment and adverse impact equally apply to national origin discrimination.

One commentator suggested that the Commission clarify the responsibility of labor organizations regarding national origin discrimination. The last sentence has been restated to clarify that the Guidelines use the term "employer" to refer to all entities covered by Title VII. Therefore, the Guidelines apply to all entities covered by Title VII, including labor organizations, joint labor management committees controlling apprenticeship or other training or retraining, and public or private employment agencies.

§ 1606.3—The National Security Exception

Section 1606.3 is based on the exception in § 1606.1(d) of the preceding Guidelines. This Section recognizes the national security exception as it appears in Section 703(g) of Title VII.

The Commission did not receive any comments from the public on this section. However, as a result of interagency coordination under Executive Order 12067, a footnote has been added to refer to the national security provision for federal employment under 5 U.S.C. 7532.

§ 1606.4—The Bona Fide Occupational Qualification Exception

This section reiterates the last sentence in § 1606.1(a) of the preceding Guidelines and is based on the Commission's long held position that the bona fide occupational qualification exception under Section 703(e) of Title VII shall be strictly construed. Several commentators supported the Commission's strict construction of the BFOQ exception. There were no substantive comments on this section and no changes have been made.

§ 1606.5—Citizenship Requirements

This section is based on § 1606.1 (d) and (e) of the preceding Guidelines. In those circumstances where citizenship requirements have the purpose or effect of discriminating against an individual on the basis of national origin, they are prohibited by Title VII. See *Espinoza* v. *Farah Mfg. Co. Inc.*, 414 U.S. 86, 92 (1973).

Some commentators noted that the Guidelines do not indicate whether an employer would be liable under Title VII, if a State law prohibits the employment of illegal aliens and if the employer refuses to hire an "illegal alien" because of that State Law. The commentators mentioned twelve states which have laws prohibiting the employment of "illegal aliens". They also cited to the Supreme Court decision in *De Canas* v. *Bica*, 424 U.S. 351 (1976), which held that the State of California was not totally barred, by virtue of the Immigration and Nationality Act (INA), from regulating the employment of "illegal aliens" within its boundaries. However, the Court left the question open for the lower court to determine whether the California statute is too broad and therefore in conflict with the purposes and objectives of Congress in enacting the Immigration and Nationality Act. For example, the Court noted that the California statute prohibits the employment of aliens who are "not entitled to lawful residence in the United States"; and, that therefore, on its face, it appears to conflict with the INA which permits certain aliens, not entitled to lawful residence, to work in the United States. In *De Canas*, the Court was not presented with the issue of whether the California law was consistent with the purposes and objectives of Title VII. Similar analysis, however, would have to be made in determining whether a particular State law conflicts with Title VII. In Title VII, Congress only specifically excluded from coverage the employment of aliens outside the United States. See Section 702 of Title VII, 42 U.S.C. 2000e-1. Moreover, even if such a State law is found not to have been superseded under Section 708 of Title VII, 42 U.S.C. 2000e-7, as one of these commentators recognized, an employer may be liable under Title VII if it is shown that the employer treats applicants who look or speak like aliens differently than other applicants. Since the Commission has not been presented with charges involving respondent defenses based on such State laws, it has not developed policy in this area. If the Commission should receive such a charge, it will base its decision on the provisions of the State law involved and on the employer's application of the State law to its employment practices.

As a result of interagency coordination under Executive Order 12067, the Commission has added to footnote 2, a reference to Executive Order 11935, 5 CFR Part 7.4, and to 31 U.S.C. 699(b), which set forth citizenship requirements for certain types of Federal employment.

§ 1606.6—Selection Procedures

This section is derived from several of the concepts stated in § 1606.1(b) of the preceding Guidelines. As a result of the comments, this section has been revised. It affirms that in investigating selection procedures for adverse impact on the basis of national origin, the Commission will apply the principles of the *Uniform Guidelines on Employee Selection Procedures* (UGESP), 29 CFR Part 1607. As some commentators correctly noted, height and weight requirements are exceptions to the "bottom line" concept under Section 4C(2) of the UGESP. Section 1606.6(a)(2) now clearly states this. Some commentators also stated that the effect of § 1606.6(b) of the proposed Guidelines was to include fluency-in-English requirements and foreign training or education as exceptions to the "bottom line" concept. Section 1606.6(b) now clarifies that the Commission does not consider these selection procedures to be exceptions to the "bottom line" concept. However, this section emphasizes that fluency-in-English and foreign training or education requirements are other than the basis of national origin discrimination. Therefore, the Commission will carefully examine charges involving these requirements for evidence of discrimination under both the disparate treatment and adverse impact theories.

Some commentators were concerned with the lack of guidance on how to determine adverse impact and job relatedness for selection criteria identified in § 1606.6. They also wanted to know about the recordkeeping requirements for national origin groups. The Commission has given detailed guidance in the UGESP on how to determine adverse impact and on validation. Proposed § 1606.6(a)(1) has been revised to clarify that these are the standards which employers should apply in evaluating selection procedures for unlawful national origin discrimination. The UGESP, sections 4 and 15, specify the national origin groups for which employers are required to keep records in evaluating selection procedures for unlawful national origin discrimination. Those recordkeeping requirements apply to all the selection procedures mentioned in § 1606.6.

Most of the comments on this section concerned the selection procedures mentioned in §1606.6(b)(2), *i.e.*, the denial of employment opportunities because of an individual's foreign accent or inability to communicate well in English. An employer who considers a person's foreign accent or ability to communicate in English as one of its criteria in selecting applicants for a job or other employment opportunities, should examine these practices for evidence of disparate treatment on the bases of national origin, as well as for evidence of adverse impact under the UGESP. If there is adverse impact based on national origin, the employer must justify the use of the selection procedure by showing that it is job related or otherwise justified under Federal law. For example, knowing how to speak English could be job related for the job of selling shoes to English-speaking customers. However, if the employer required its sales people to speak without an accent or to have a certain degree of fluency in English, and if these requirements had an adverse impact based on national origin, the employer would have to show the job relatedness of the no-foreign-accent requirement, or of the degree of fluency in English which it required.

Several commentators were concerned about the liability under Title VII of employers who require their employees to be bilingual for certain jobs. A job requirement of bilingualism is a selection procedure under the UGESP, and employers should follow the principles of the UGESP in analyzing these jobs for adverse impact on the basis of national origin.

Some commentators were concerned that the Guidelines would discourage employees from improving their ability to speak English. A few employers mentioned that they had programs for their employees from non-English speaking backgrounds to study and improve their English language skills. The Commission strongly supports such programs, and nothing in these Guidelines precludes employers from encouraging their employees to improve their ability to speak English. Simply stated, the Commission's concern is that individuals are not deprived of employment opportunities on the basis of non-job-related language proficiency requirements which under the UGESP have an adverse impact on the basis of national origin, or which are used to disparately treat individuals because of their national origin.

Some commentators stated that it would be difficult and impractical to evaluate foreign training and education, especially in the professional fields, and that in some instances, a state licensing requirement for the job may treat foreign education or training differently. It is noted that an individual's foreign training or education is particularly susceptible to subjecting the individual to employment discrimination on the basis of national origin. Therefore, charges alleging discrimination on this basis will be carefully examined by the Commission for national origin discrimination. The Commission's investigation will focus on such questions as: does the employer treat all foreign training or education on the same basis, or does it discriminate between foreign training or education on the basis of an individual's national origin; although a job may ordinarily require a state license, does the employer uniformly and always require such license for the job. (For licensing or certification requirements that have an adverse impact, *inter alia*, on the basis of national origin, see also Sections 2B and 16W of the UGESP, 29 CFR 1607.2B and 1607.16W; and UGESP Questions and Answers #7, 44 FR 11996, 11997 (March 2, 1979).

§ 1606.7—Speak-English-Only Rules

This section recognizes that an individual's primary language is often an essential national origin characteristic. According to estimates from the Survey of Income and Education conducted by the U.S. Bureau of Census in Spring 1976, approximately 28 million persons in the United States (about 13% of the total U.S. population) have non-English language backgrounds and may be affected by an employer's speak-English-only rule. The survey identifies persons with non-English language backgrounds as persons whose mother tongue is not English, who normally use languages other than English, or who live in households where languages other than English are spoken. About 21 million, or seventy five percent, of this group are above the age of 18. The study shows the following approximate numbers for each of these language backgrounds: Spanish, 10.6 million; Italian, 2.9 million; German, 2.7 million; French, 1.9 million; Chinese, Japanese, Korean and Vietnamese, 1.8 million; Polish, 1.5 million. Approximately 2.4 million persons in the United States do not speak any English at all.[*]

An employer's rule which requires employees to speak English at all times, including during their work breaks and lunch time, is one example of an employment practice which discriminates against persons whose primary language is not English.

---

[*] See U.S. Department of Health, Education and Welfare, National Center for Education Statistics, Bulletin 78 B-5. August 22, 1978. "Geographic Distribution, Nativity, and Age Distribution of Language Minorities in the United States: Spring 1976"; Waggoner, Dorothy, "Non-English Language Background Persons: Three U.S. Surveys", TESOL Quarterly, vol. 12, No. 3 at 247–262, September, 1978.

Under § 1606.7(a), the Commission presumes that totally prohibiting employees from speaking their primary language, violates Title VII because it is a burdensome term and condition of employment which discriminates on the basis of national origin by disadvantaging an individual's employment opportunities and by creating a discriminatory working environment. Therefore, where such a rule exists, the Commission will closely scrutinize it. However, § 1606.7(b) also recognizes that an employer may require its employees to speak only in English at certain times and that this would not be discriminatory if the employer shows that the rule is justified by business necessity; for example, where safety requires that all communications be in English so that everyone can closely follow a particular task, such as, surgery or drilling of oil wells;** or where a salesperson is attending to English-speaking customers. When the employer believes that the rule is justified by business necessity, the employer should clearly inform its employees of the general circumstances under which they are required to speak only in English and the consequences of violating the rule. Notice of the rule is necessary because it is common for individuals whose primary language is not English to inadvertently change from speaking English to speaking their primary language. Any adverse employment decision against an individual based on a violation of the rule will be considered as evidence of discrimination when an employer has not given effective notice of the rule.

Most of the general, non-substantive comments were directed toward this section of the Guidelines. These comments reflected a misunderstanding of the Guidelines either by equating them with bilingual education and other bilingual programs or by concluding that their purpose is to promote bilingualism in the workplace. As we stated at the beginning of this analysis, the Guidelines are not concerned with bilingual education or other bilingual programs, and they do not promote bilingualism in the workplace. the purpose of the guidelines is to explain to employers, and other entities covered by Title VII, the Commission's interpretation of what constitutes national origin discrimination.

As the Court noted in *Garcia* v. *Gloor*, 618 F. 2d 264, 268 n.1 (5th Cir. 1980), the Commission's previous Guidelines did not give any standards for testing employer rules which prohibit the use of

** See for example, *Saucedo* v. *Brothers Well Service, Inc.*, 464 F. Supp. 919 (S.D. Texas 1979).

languages other than English. The purpose of § 1606.7 is to provide this guidance. The Commission's concern is to prevent employers from imposing speak-English-only rules, as arbitrary and oppressive terms and conditions of employment, on people who come from non-English-speaking backgrounds in order to deprive them of an equal employment opportunity for jobs they are otherwise fully qualified to perform. Section 1606.7 does not conflict with the *Gloor* decision. *Gloor* did not involve a speak-English-only rule which was applied at all times. Neither did the facts in *Gloor* involve a bilingual employee whose primary language was not English. In the Court's view, Mr. Garcia, who spoke both English and Spanish failed to prove that Spanish was his primary language

Several commentators objected to the presumption in § 1606.7(a) that a speak-English-only rule violates Title VII at all times, including break and lunch time, violates Title VII. The Commission believes that this would create such a burdensome term and condition of employment, for employees whose primary language is not English, that the mere application of such a rule would shift the burden to the employer. Therefore, the Commission believes it is necessary to closely scrutinize such an absolute prohibition. However, employers may require that English be spoken when it is justified by business necessity.

Section 1606.7(a) has been restructured, and the phrase "in the workplace has been added. The words "narrowly drawn" have been eliminated in § 1606.7(b) because they are redundant.

Some commentators stated that to notify employees of the "exact circumstances and times" of speak-English-only rules would be impractical for employers to implement. Therefore, the Commission has changed the phrase, "exact circumstances and times" in § 1606.7(c), to the more flexible concept of "general circumstances." The manner in which an employer notifies its employees does not matter. However, the notice must be effective, *i.e.*, the employee should know under what circumstances he or she is required to speak only in English and what will happen if he or she violates the rule.

Section 1606.8—Harassment

This section states that harassment on the basis of national origin is a violation of Title VII and that an employer has an affirmative duty to maintain a working environment free from harassment on the basis of national origin. Section 1606.8(c) applies general Title VII

principles to the issue of harassment and states that an employer is responsible for the acts of its supervisory employees or agents, regardless of whether the acts were authorized or forbidden by the employer and regardless of whether the employer knew or should have known of the acts. Section 1606.8(d) distinguishes the employer's responsibility for the acts of its agents or supervisors from the responsibility it has for conduct between fellow employees. This sub-section states that liability for acts of national origin harassment in the workplace between fellow employees exists only when the employer, its agents or supervisory employees, knows or should have known of the conduct, and the employer cannot demonstrate that it took immediate and appropriate corrective action. Section 1606.8(e) recognizes that in certain circumstances, an employer may also be responsible for the acts of non-employees with respect to harassment of employees on the basis of national origin.

Some commentators objected to the strict liability of an employer under § 1606.8(c) for the acts of harassment of its supervisory employees or agents. Other commentators objected to an employer's responsibility for the conduct of non-employees as set forth in § 1606.8(e).

This Commission has not made any change in this section. The principles of this section are the same as stated in the recently published Commission's *Guidelines on Sexual Harassment*, 45 FR 74676 (November 10, 1980). These principles have been carefully developed by the Commission and fully commented upon in the supplementary information to the Commission's final *Guidelines on Sexual Harassment*, 45 FR 74676, 74677.

Date: December 22, 1980.

Eleanor Holmes Norton,

Chair, Equal Employment Opportunity Commission.

Accordingly, 29 CFR Chapter XIV is amended by revising Part 1606 to read as follows:

PART 1606—GUIDELINES ON DISCRIMINATION BECAUSE OF NATIONAL ORIGIN

§ 1606.8 Harassment.

Authority: Title VII of the Civil Rights Act of 1964, as amended, 42 U.S.C. 2000e et seq.

§ 1606.1 Definition of national origin discrimination.

The Commission defines national origin discrimination broadly as including, but not limited to, the denial of equal employment opportunity because of an individual's, or his or her ancestor's, place of origin; or because an individual has the physical, cultural or linguistic characteristics of a national origin group. The Commission will examine with particular concern charges alleging that individuals within the jurisdiction of the Commission have been denied equal employment opportunity for reasons which are grounded in national origin considerations, such as (a) marriage to or association with persons of a national origin group; (b) membership in, or association with an organization identified with or seeking to promote the interests of national origin groups; (c) attendance or participation in schools, churches, temples or mosques, generally used by persons of a national origin group; and (d) because an individual's name or spouse's name is associated with a national origin group. In examining these charges for unlawful national origin discrimination, the Commission will apply general Title VII principles, such as disparate treatment and adverse impact.

§ 1606.2 Scope of Title VII protection.

Title VII of the Civil Rights Act of 1964, as amended, protects individuals against employment discrimination on the basis of race, color, religion, sex or national origin. The Title VII principles of disparate treatment and adverse impact equally apply to national origin discrimination. These Guidelines apply to all entities covered by Title VII (collectively referred to as "employer").

§ 1606.3 The national security exception.

It is not an unlawful employment practice to deny employment opportunities to any individual who does not fulfill the national security requirements stated in Section 703(g) of Title VII.[1]

§ 1606.4 The bona fide occupational qualification exception.

The exception stated in Section 703(e) of Title VII, that national origin may be a bona fide occupational qualification, shall be strictly construed.

[1] See also, 5 U.S.C. 7532, for the authority of the head of a federal agency or department to suspend or remove an employee on grounds of national security.

§ 1606.5 Citizenship requirements.

(a) In those circumstances, where citizenship requirements have the purpose or effect of discriminating against an individual on the basis of national origin, they are prohibited by Title VII.[2]

(b) Some State laws prohibit the employment of non-citizens. Where these laws are in conflict with Title VII, they are superseded under Section 708 of the Title.

§ 1606.6 Selection procedures.

(a)(1) In investigating an employer's selection procedures (including those identified below) for adverse impact on the basis of national origin, the Commission will apply the Uniform Guidelines on Employee Selection Procedures (UGESP), 29 CFR part 1607. Employers and other users of selection procedures should refer to the UGESP for guidance on matters, such as adverse impact, validation and recordkeeping requirements for national origin groups.

(2) Because height or weight requirements tend to exclude individuals on the basis of national origin,[3] the user is expected to evaluate these selection procedures for adverse impact, regardless of whether the total selection process has an adverse impact based on national origin. Therefore, height or weight requirements are identified here, as they are in the UGESP,[4] as exceptions to the "bottom line" concept.

(b) The Commission has found that the use of the following selection procedures may be discriminatory on the basis of national origin. Therefore, it will carefully investigate charges involving these selection procedures for both disparate treatment and adverse impact on the basis of national origin. However, the Commission does not consider these to be exceptions to the "bottom line" concept:

(1) Fluency-in-English requirements, such as denying employment opportunities because of an individual's

[2] See Espinoza v. Farah Mfg. Co., Inc., 414 U.S. 86, 92 (1973). See also, E.O. 11935, 5 CFR Part 7.4; and 31 U.S.C. 699(b), for citizenship requirements in certain Federal employment.

[3] See CD 71–1529 (1971), CCH EEOC Decisions ¶6231, 3 FEP Cases 952; CD 71–1418 (1971), CCH EEOC Decisions ¶5223, 3 FEP Cases 580; CD 74–25 (1973), CCH EEOC Decisions ¶6400, 10 FEP Cases 260. Davis v. County of Los Angeles, 566 F. 2d 1334, 1341–42 (9th Cir., 1977) vacated and remanded as moot on other grounds. 440 U.S. 625 (1979). See also, Dothard v. Rowlinson. 433 U.S. 321 (1977).

[4] See Section 4C(2) of the Uniform Guidelines on Employee Selection Procedures, 29 CFR 1607.4C(2).

foreign accent,[5] or inability to communicate well in English.[6]

(2) Training or education requirements which deny employment opportunities to an individual because of his or her foreign training or education, or which require an individual to be foreign trained or educated.

§ 1606.7 Speak-English-only rules.

(a) When Applied at all Times. A rule requiring employees to speak only English at all times in the workplace is a burdensome term and condition of employment. The primary language of an individual is often an essential national origin characteristic. Prohibiting employees at all times, in the workplace, from speaking their primary language or the language they speak most comfortably, disadvantages an individual's employment opportunities on the basis of national origin. It may also create an atmosphere of inferiority, isolation and intimidation based on national origin which could result in a discriminatory working environment.[7] Therefore, the Commission will presume that such a rule violates Title VII and will closely scrutinize it.

(b) When Applied Only at Certain Times. An employer may have a rule requiring that employees speak only in English at certain times where the employer can show that the rule is justified by business necessity.

(c) Notice of the Rule. It is common for individuals whose primary language is not English to inadvertently change from speaking English to speaking their primary language. Therefore, if an employer believes it has a business necessity for a speak-English-only rule at certain times, the employer should inform its employees of the general circumstances when speaking only in English is required and of the consequences of violating the rule. If an employer fails to effectively notify its employees of the rule and makes an adverse employment decision against an individual based on a violation of the rule, the Commission will consider the employer's application of the rule as evidence of discrimination on the basis of national origin.

§ 1606.8 Harassment.

(a) The Commission has consistently held that harassment on the basis of national origin is a violation of Title VII. An employer has an affirmative duty to

[5] See CD AL66–1–155E (1969), CCH EEOC Decisions ¶6008, 1 FEP Cases 921.

[6] See CD YAU9–048 (1969), CCH EEOC Decisions ¶6054, 2 FEP Cases 78.

[7] See CD 71–446 (1970), CCH EEOC Decisions ¶6173, 2 FEP Cases. 1127; CD 72–0281 (1971), CCH EEOC Decisions ¶6293.

maintain a working environment free of harassment on the basis of national origin.[6]

(b) Ethnic slurs and other verbal or physical conduct relating to an individual's national origin constitute harassment when this conduct: (1) Has the purpose or effect of creating an intimidating, hostile or offensive working environment; (2) has the purpose or effect of unreasonably interfering with an individual's work performance; or (3) otherwise adversely affects an individual's employment opportunities.

(c) An employer is responsible for its acts and those of its agents and supervisory employees with respect to harassment on the basis of national origin regardless of whether the specific acts complained of were authorized or even forbidden by the employer and regardless of whether the employer knew or should have known of their occurrence. The Commission will examine the circumstances of the particular employment relationship and the job functions performed by the individual in determining whether an individual acts in either a supervisory or agency capacity.

(d) With respect to conduct between fellow employees, an employer is responsible for acts of harassment in the workplace on the basis of national origin, where the employer, its agents or supervisory employees, knows or should have known of the conduct, unless the employer can show that it took immediate and appropriate corrective action.

(e) An employer may also be responsible for the acts of non-employees with respect to harassment of employees in the workplace on the basis of national origin, where the employer, its agents or supervisory employees, knows or should have known of the conduct and fails to take immediate and appropriate corrective action. In reviewing these cases, the Commission will consider the extent of the employer's control and any other legal responsibility which the employer may have with respect to the conduct of such non-employees.

[FR Doc. 80-41299 Filed 12–24–80; 8:45 am]

BILLING CODE 6570-06-M

[6] See CD CL66-12-431 EU (1969), CCH EEOC Decisions ¶6008, 2 FEP Cases 293; CD 72-0621 (1971), CCH EEOC Decisions ¶6311, 4 FEP Cases 312; CD 72-1561 (1972), CCH EEOC Decisions ¶6354, 4 FEP Cases 852; CD 74-05 (1973), CCH EEOC Decisions ¶6387, 6 FEP Cases 834; CD 76-41 (1975), CCH EEOC Decisions ¶6632. See also, Amendment to Guidelines on Discrimination Because of Sex, § 1604.11(a) n. 1, 45 FR 7478 ay 74677 (November 10, 1980).

Friday
October 31, 1980

Part XII

Equal Employment Opportunity Commission

Guidelines on Discrimination Because of Religion

EQUAL EMPLOYMENT OPPORTUNITY COMMISSION

29 CFR Part 1605

Guidelines on Discrimination Because of Religion

AGENCY: Equal Employment Opportunity Commission.

ACTION: Final guidelines.

SUMMARY: The Equal Employment Opportunity Commission is revising its *Guidelines on Discrimination Because of Religion* in response to public confusion concerning the duty of employers and labor organizations to reasonably accommodate the religious practices of employees and prospective employees. These Guidelines clarify this duty in an effort to protect employees and prospective employees from being discriminated against because of their religious practices or beliefs.

EFFECTIVE DATE: November 1, 1980.

FOR FURTHER INFORMATION CONTACT: Karen Danart, Acting Director, or Raj K. Gupta, Supervisory Attorney, Office of Policy Implementation, Room 4002, 2401 E Street, NW., Washington, D.C. 20506; (202) 634–7060.

SUPPLEMENTARY INFORMATION:

I. Background

Section 701(j) of Title VII of the Civil Rights Act of 1964, as amended, creates an obligation to provide reasonable accommodation for the religious practices of an employee or prospective employee unless to do so would create an undue hardship. In 1977, the Supreme Court rendered its decision in *Trans World Airlines, Inc.* v. *Hardison*, 432 U.S. 63 (1977). The Court's interpretation of an undue hardship led to much confusion in the employment sector. It left employers, employees and labor organizations unclear as to the extent of the statutory duty under Title VII to provide reasonable accommodation for the religious practices of an employee or prospective employee. The Commission held public informational hearings on this issue in April and May of 1978 in New York City, Los Angeles and Milwaukee. The hearings established that the public desired clarification of the Guidelines and that many employers had developed alternative methods for accommodating the religious practices of their employees and prospective employees which could generally be used by other employers.* To allow

*The transcript of the hearings can be examined by the public at: The Equal Employment Opportunity Commission, 2401 E Street, NW., Washington, D.C. 20506.

interested persons an opportunity to participate in all stages of its rulemaking process and in compliance with Executive Order 12044 (43 FR 12661, March 24, 1978, as amended by E.O. 12221, 45 FR 44249, July 1, 1980), the Commission noticed its intent to review its current *Guidelines on Discrimination Because of Religion* (44 FR 6200, January 31, 1979). On September 14, 1979, the Commission published a proposed revision (44 FR 53706) of its Guidelines which appear at 29 CFR 1605. The Proposed Guidelines were published for public comment for 90 days.

These Guidelines are a significant regulation under Executive Order 12044. There are no regulatory burdens or record keeping requirements necessary for compliance with the Guidelines. The Commission has determined that they will not have a major impact on the economy and that a regulatory analysis is not necessary.

In compliance with Executive Order 12067 (43 FR 28967, July 5, 1978), the Commission has consulted with the representatives of the necessary federal departments and agencies on the revision of its Guidelines.

II. An Overview of the Guidelines

A. *The Obligation to Reasonably Accommodate Religious Practices.* These Guidelines set forth the underlying principle of the Guidelines being superseded and of Section 701(j) of Title VII of the Civil Rights Act. The principle is: failure to reasonably accommodate the religious practices of an employee or prospective employee is an unlawful employment practice; and employers, labor organizations and other entities covered by Title VII (collectively referred to as "employer") have an obligation to accommodate religious practices, unless they can demonstrate that accommodation would result in undue hardship.[1]

The obligation to accommodate begins when an individual notifies the employer of the need for an accommodation. Once notified, the employer should consider the available alternatives for accommodating the religious practices of the individual involved. If there is more than one alternative available which would not cause undue hardship, the employer must offer the alternative which would least disadvantage the employment opportunities of the individual requiring the accommodation.[2]

B. *Alternatives for Accommodating Religious Practices.* The Guidelines include examples of alternatives which

[1] Section 1605.2(b).
[2] Section 1605.2(c).

an employer should consider when an individual's religious practices conflict with the employer's work schedule. The examples suggest the use of voluntary substitutes and swaps, flexible scheduling, lateral transfer and change of job assignment.[3]

The Guidelines specifically address the accommodation of religious practices which do not permit an individual to join or pay dues to a labor organization.[4]

The principles of the Guidelines also apply to the accommodation of other religious practices, such as practices concerning dietary requirements, dress and other grooming habits, observation of a mourning period for a deceased relative, and prohibition of medical examinations.[5]

C. *Undue Hardship.* If any employer refuses to accommodate an individual's religious practices, it must justify the refusal by demonstrating that undue hardship would in fact result from each available alternative.[6] In determining whether an accommodation would require more than a *de minimis* cost, and, therefore, constitute undue hardship, the Commission will give due consideration to the identifiable cost in relation to the size and operating cost of the employer, and the number of individuals who actually need the accommodation.[7] The Guidelines recognize that generally, under *Hardison*, the regular payment of premium wages would constitute undue hardship.[8] However, the Commission will presume that the infrequent or temporary payment of premium wages and the payment of administrative costs are not more than *de minimis* and do not constitute undue hardship.[9] A mere assumption that many others, with the same belief as the individual seeking accommodation, may also need an accommodation, is not sufficient to prove undue hardship in the case of that particular individual.[10]

In reference to the *Hardison* holding on seniority,[11] the Guidelines state that there would be undue hardship if an accommodation required a variance from a bona fide seniority system. They also make it clear that, under Title VII, employers and unions may include provisions in a collective bargaining agreement which allow for voluntary

[3] Section 1605.2(d)(1).
[4] Section 1605.2(d)(2).
[5] Section 1605.2(d)(1).
[6] Section 1605.2(c)(1).
[7] Section 1605.2(e)(1).
[8] *Hardison*, supra, 432 U.S. at 84.
[9] Section 1605.2(e)(1).
[10] Section 1605.2(c)(1).
[11] *Hardison*, supra, 432 U.S. at 80.

substitutes and swaps as a means of accommodating religious practices.

D. *Selection Practices.* The Guidelines address two selection practices which tend to exclude individuals from employment opportunities because of their religious beliefs: (1) the scheduling of tests and other selection procedures at a time when an individual cannot attend because of this or her religious practices;[12] and (2) inquiries which determine an applicant's availability to work during an employer's scheduled working hours.[13]

If an individual cannot take a test or comply with some other selection procedure because it is scheduled at a time which conflicts with his or her religious practices, the employer has an obligation to make a reasonable accommodation, for example, by allowing the person to take the test at another time.

Based on testimony from the hearings, discussions with representatives of organizations interested in the issue of religious discrimination, and comments from the public on the proposed Guidelines, the Commission concludes that the use of pre-selection inquiries which determine an applicant's availability has an exclusionary effect on persons whose religious practices conflict with an employer's working hours. An employer must, therefore, justify the use of these inquiries by business necessity.

E. *"Religious" Nature of a Practice or Belief.* The Guidelines do not confine the definition of religious practices to theistic concepts or to traditional religious beliefs. The definition also includes moral and ethical beliefs. Under the Guidelines, a belief is religious not because a religious group professes that belief, but because the individual sincerely holds that belief with the strength of traditional religious views. This definition is based on the Supreme court decisions in *Seeger*[14] and *Welsh*[15] and on the standard applied in Commission Decisions.[16]

III. Analysis of Public Comments and Changes to the Guidelines as Proposed

During the 90 day public comment period, the Commission received approximately 350 comments from employers, religious organizations, business associations, labor organizations, and private individuals. About one-half of the comments

[12] Section 1605.3(a).
[13] Section 1605.3(b).
[14] *United States* v. *Seeger.* 380 U.S. 163 (1965).
[15] *Welsh* v. *United States.* 398 U.S. 333 (1970).
[16] Section 1605.1.

supported the proposed Guidelines. Most of these comments were from individuals and organizations that observe the Sabbath from sunset on Friday to sunset on Saturday. These commentators described many personal experiences of alleged discrimination and emphasized that, if adopted, the proposed Guidelines would greatly decrease the incidence of religious discrimination in the future. In contrast, the criticism of the proposed Guidelines came mostly from employers and business associations.

The following is an analysis of the major comments received and the changes made to the proposed Guidelines because of these comments. For each section of the final Guidelines, the analysis describes the major public comments, the substantive changes and, finally, the structural changes, such as the incorporation of all substantive footnotes into the text of the Guidelines.

Section 1605.1—"Religious" Nature of a Practice or Belief. Some commentators criticized the definition of religious practices as being too broad and vague, and felt that determining whether a person's belief was sincerely held would be difficult. They also believed that the standard which the Supreme Court developed in the leading selective service decisions, *Seeger* and *Welsh*, was an inappropriate standard for Title VII. The Commission has not made any substantive changes to this section because the definition is well established by court decisions under Title VII and by Commission Decisions. (See *Overview* II E.)

Structural changes: proposed footnote 1 is now incorporated into the text as the last sentence of this section. Footnote 2 of the proposed Guidelines is now footnote 1.

Section 1605.2—Reasonable Accommodation Without Undue Hardship.

(a) *Purpose.* The Commission did not receive any comments on this sub-section. Therefore, no substantive changes have been made.

Structural changes: footnote 3 of the proposed Guidelines, quoting Section 701(j) of Title VII, has been eliminated as unnecessary. Footnote 4 of the proposed Guidelines is now incorporated into the text.

(b) *Duty to Accommodate.* No comments were received on this sub-section. Therefore, there are no substantive changes.

Structural changes: the two sentences of proposed § 1605.2(b)(1) are now sub-sections (1) and (2) respectively. Proposed footnote 5 is now footnote 2. Proposed footnote 6 is now incorporated into the text as sub-section (3).

(c) *Reasonable Accommodation.* This new sub-section combines § 1605.2(b)(2) and (c)(2) of the proposed Guidelines. Many commentators objected to the requirement in proposed § 1605.2(b)(2) that an employer must "explore all possible methods of reasonable accommodation." They felt that the word "explore" was vague and that the obligation "to explore all possible methods" was too onerous. The new § 1605.2(c)(1) clarifies the Commission's position that an employer's obligation to reasonably accommodate an individual's religious practices involves a consideration of available alternative methods of accommodation; and that where an employer refuses to accommodate, it must show that undue hardship would in fact result from each available method of accommodation.

Some commentators believed that the requirement in proposed § 1605.2(c)(2) to "adopt the alternative which least disadvantages the individual" would be inconsistent with *Hardison.* In response to these comments, § 1605.2(c)(2) has been revised. It now states the criteria the Commission will use to determine whether an accommodation is reasonable. It is consistent with *Hardison* and with general Title VII principles. the employer does not have to offer an alternative which would cause undue hardship. However, when there is more than one means of accommodation which would not cause undue hardship, the employer must offer the alternative which least disadvantages the employment opportunities of the individual being accommodated.

Some commentators thought the Guidelines should state that employees have a duty to cooperate in the making of a reasonable accommodation. Because neither Section 701(j), nor any other Section of Title VII, imposes such an obligation on the employee, the Commission does not deem it warranted.

(d) *Alternatives for Accommodating Religious Practices.* In response to the comments, the words "must explore" have been substituted by the words "should consider".

Some commentators objected to the use of the word "satisfactory" when referring to voluntary substitutes. Therefore, in place of "satisfactory", the final Guidelines now use the phrase "substantially similar qualifications", which is the same phrase as that used in the Commission's 1967 Guidelines at 29 CFR § 1605.1(b).[17] The word "swap" has been added to the subtitle "Voluntary

[17] 32 FR 10298 (July 13, 1967).

398

Substitutes" in response to the comments.

Structural changes: Proposed § 1605.2(c) is renumbered as § 1605.2(d). Footnote 7 of the proposed Guidelines is now footnote 4. Footnote 8 of the proposed Guidelines has been eliminated.

(e) *Undue Hardship.*

(1) *Cost*—Several commentators argued that the test of *de minimis* in *Hardison* is actual, not relative, cost and that factors such as the size and operating cost of the employer as stated in § 1605.2(e)(1), should not be considered in determining cost. The Commission has reviewed this sub-section in light of the comments and finds that it is consistent with the holding in *Hardison.* However, in response to comments, it has now been clarified that when investigating a charge, the Commission will presume that the infrequent or temporary payment of premium wages, and the payment of administrative costs do not constitute more than a *de minimis* cost. The language in the proposed Guidelines in this regard was misunderstood as suggesting that the incurring of these costs would always be viewed as *de minimis.*

(2) *Seniority.* Some employers mentioned that the unilateral implementation by the employer of suggested methods of accommodation, such as voluntary substitutes, flexible scheduling, lateral transfer and change of job assignment, could violate a seniority clause in a collective bargaining agreement. The language in this sub-section has been revised to make it clear that where such accommodation requires a variance from a bona fide seniority system, it would be considered as creating an undue hardship.

Structural changes: In the proposed Guidelines, this was sub-section (d) of § 1605.2. It is now sub-section (e).

Section 1605.3—Selection Practices. This section is derived from § 1605.2(e)(1) and (2) of the proposed Guidelines. Sub-section (a) is the same as proposed § 1605.2(e)(1). No comments were received on this sub-section, and no changes have been made.

Sub-section (b) was § 1605.2(e)(2) of the proposed Guidelines. This sub-section also incorporates the substance of footnotes 9 and 10. The sub-section has been rewritten to state the Commission's conclusion that the use of pre-selection inquiries into an applicant's availability has an exclusionary effect on the employment opportunities of persons with certain religious practices. The new language of this sub-section clarifies that unless an employer can show that its use of these inquiries, in fact, did not have an exclusionary effect on its employees or prospective employees, it must justify the use by business necessity. It also suggests an alternative selection procedure which would have a lesser exclusionary effect. Under this procedure, an employer could ask about an applicant's availability to work during the normal work hours apart from any required absences for religious needs; and after offering the position, but before hiring the applicant, it may inquire whether the applicant's religious practices would affect his or her availability in order to determine whether an accommodation is possible. Many employers objected to this alternative which was stated in footnote 10 of the proposed Guidelines. They emphasized their need to know, at the beginning of the selection process, when an individual is available to work. The Commission believes that this alternative is important and has left it in the final Guidelines. In an overwhelming number of cases, the decision by an employer to offer an employment opportunity is likely to remain unaffected by the post-offer information on the need for a religious accommodation. In those infrequent instances where the job is offered to an applicant who then states his or her need for a work schedule accommodation because of religious practices, an employer may be either able to accommodate the need or offer the job to another qualified applicant. Because of the infrequency of such situations and the minimal time required in offering the job to another applicant where the desired accommodation is not possible, the Commission believes that the suggested method would normally serve the employer's legitimate business interest, and also avoid unduly restricting the equal employment opportunities for the religious observers.

Appendix A to §§ 1605.2 and 1605.3—Background Information. No substantive changes to the appendix were necessary. Footnote 11 of the proposed Guidelines is now footnote 5 in the appendix.

Dated: October 28, 1980.

Eleanor Holmes Norton,

Chair, Equal Employment Opportunity Commission.

Accordingly, the Guidelines of the EEOC, 29 CFR Part 1605, are revised to read as follows:

PART 1605—GUIDELINES ON DISCRIMINATION BECAUSE OF RELIGION

Sec.
1605.1 "Religious" nature of a practice or belief.
1605.2 Reasonable accommodation without undue hardship as required by Section 701(j) of Title VII of the Civil Rights Act of 1964.
1605.3 Selection practices.
Appendix A to §§ 1605.2 and 1605.3 Background information.

Authority: Title VII of the Civil Rights Act of 1964, as amended, 42 U.S.C. 2000e et seq.

§ 1605.1 "Religious" nature of a practice or belief.

In most cases whether or not a practice or belief is religious is not at issue. However, in those cases in which the issue does exist, the Commission will define religious practices to include moral or ethical beliefs as to what is right and wrong which are sincerely held with the strength of traditional religious views. This standard was developed in *United States* v. *Seeger,* 380 U.S. 163 (1965) and *Welsh* v. *United States,* 398 U.S. 333 (1970). The Commission has consistently applied this standard in its decisions.[1] The fact that no religious group espouses such beliefs or the fact that the religious group to which the individual professes to belong may not accept such belief will not determine whether the belief is a religious belief of the employee or prospective employee. The phrase "religious practice" as used in these Guidelines includes both religious observances and practices, as stated in Section 701(j), 42 U.S.C. 2000e(j).

§ 1605.2 Reasonable accommodation without undue hardship as required by Section 701(j) of Title VII of the Civil Rights Act of 1964.

(a) *Purpose of this section.* This section clarifies the obligation imposed by Title VII of the Civil Rights Act of 1964, as amended, (sections 701(j), 703 and 717) to accommodate the religious practices of employees and prospective employees. This section does not address other obligations under Title VII not to discriminate on grounds of religion, nor other provisions of Title VII. This section is not intended to limit any additional obligations to accommodate religious practices which may exist pursuant to constitutional, or other statutory provisions; neither is it intended to provide guidance for statutes which require accommodation on bases other than religion such as § 503 of the Rehabilitation Act of 1973.

[1] See CD 76–104 (1976), CCH ¶6500; CD 71–2620 (1971), CCH ¶6283; CD 71–779 (1970), CCH ¶6180.

The legal principles which have been developed with respect to discrimination prohibited by Title VII on the bases of race, color, sex, and national origin also apply to religious discrimination in all circumstances other than where an accommodation is required.

(b) *Duty to accommodate.*

(1) Section 701(j) makes it an unlawful employment practice under § 703(a)(1) for an employer to fail to reasonably accommodate the religious practices of an employee or prospective employee, unless the employer demonstrates that accommodation would result in undue hardship on the conduct of its business.[2]

(2) Section 701(j) in conjunction with § 703(c), imposes an obligation on a labor organization to reasonably accommodate the religious practices of an employee or prospective employee, unless the labor organization demonstrates that accommodation would result in undue hardship.

(3) Section 1605.2 is primarily directed to obligations of employers or labor organizations, which are the entities covered by Title VII that will most often be required to make an accommodation. However, the principles of Section 1605.2 also apply when an accommodation can be required of other entities covered by Title VII, such as employment agencies (§ 703(b)) or joint labor-management committees controlling apprenticeship or other training or retraining (§ 703(d)). (See, for example, § 1605.3(a) "Scheduling of Tests or Other Selection Procedures.")

(c) *Reasonable Accommodation.*

(1) After an employee or prospective employee notifies the employer or labor organization of his or her need for a religious accommodation, the employer or labor organization has an obligation to reasonably accommodate the individual's religious practices. A refusal to accommodate is justified only when an employer or labor organization can demonstrate that an undue hardship would in fact result from each available alternative method of accommodation. A mere assumption that many more people, with the same religious practices as the person being accommodated, may also need accommodation is not evidence of undue hardship.

(2) When there is more than one method of accommodation available which would not cause undue hardship, the Commission will determine whether the accommodation offered is reasonable by examining:

---

[2] See *Trans World Airlines, Inc.* v. *Hardison,* 432 U.S. 63, 74 (1977).

(i) The alternatives for accommodation considered by the employer or labor organization; and

(ii) The alternatives for accommodation, if any, actually offered to the individual requiring accommodation. Some alternatives for accommodating religious practices might disadvantage the individual with respect to his or her employment opportunites, such as compensation, terms, conditions, or privileges of employment. Therefore, when there is more than one means of accommodation which would not cause undue hardship, the employer or labor organization must offer the alternative which least disadvantages the individual with respect to his or her employment opportunities.

(d) *Alternatives for Accommodating Religious Practices.*

(1) Employees and prospective employees most frequently request an accommodation because their religious practices conflict with their work schedules. The following subsections are some means of accommodating the conflict between work schedules and religious practices which the Commission believes that employers and labor organizations should consider as part of the obligation to accommodate and which the Commission will consider in investigating a charge. These are not intended to be all-inclusive. There are often other alternatives which would reasonably accommodate an individual's religious practices when they conflict with a work schedule.[3]

....ere are also employment practices ..esides work scheduling which may ..flict with religious practices and ..ause an individual to request an accommodation. See, for example, the Commission's finding number (3) from its Hearings on Religious Discrimination, in Appendix A to §§ 1605.2 and 1605.3. The principles expressed in these Guidelines apply as well to such requests for accommodation.

(i) Voluntary Substitutes and "Swaps".

Reasonable accommodation without undue hardship is generally possible where a voluntary substitute with substantially similar qualifications is available. One means of substitution is the voluntary swap. In a number of cases, the securing of a substitute has been left entirely up to the individual seeking the accommodation. The Commission believes that the obligation to accommodate requires that employers and labor organizations facilitate the securing of a voluntary substitute with substantially similar qualifications. Some means of doing this which employers and labor organizations

should consider are: to publicize policies regarding accommodation and voluntary substitution; to promote an atmosphere in which such substitutions are favorably regarded; to provide a central file, bulletin board or other means for matching voluntary substitutes with positions for which substitutes are needed.

(ii) Flexible Scheduling.

One means of providing reasonable accommodation for the religious practices of employees or prospective employees which employers and labor organizations should consider is the creation of a flexible work schedule for individuals requesting accommodation.

The following list is an example of areas in which flexibility might be introduced: flexible arrival and departure times; floating or optional holidays; flexible work breaks; use of lunch time in exchange for early departure; staggered work hours; and permitting an employee to make up time lost due to the observance of religious practices.[3]

(iii) Lateral Transfer and Change of Job Assignments.

When an employee cannot be accommodated either as to his or her entire job or an assignment within the job, employers and labor organizations should consider whether or not it is possible to change the job assignment or give the employee a lateral transfer.

(2) Payment of Dues to a Labor Organization.

Some collective bargaining agreements include a provision that each employee must join the labor organization or pay the labor organization a sum equivalent to dues. When an employee's religious practices to not permit compliance with such a provision, the labor organization should accommodate the employee by not requiring the employee to join the organization and by permitting him or her to donate a sum equivalent to dues to a charitable organization.

(e) *Undue Hardship.*

(1) Cost.

An employer may assert undue hardship to justify a refusal to accommodate an employee's need to be absent from his or her scheduled duty hours if the employer can demonstrate that the accommodation would require more than a *de minimis* cost.[4] The Commission will determine what constitutes "more than a *de minimis* cost" with due regard given to the

---

[3] On September 29, 1978, Congress enacted such a provision for the accommodation of Federal employees' religious practices. See Pub. L 95-390, § U.S.C. 5550a "Compensatory-Time Off for Religious Observances."

[4] *Hardison, supra,* 432 U.S. at 84.

identifiable cost in relation to the size and operating cost of the employer, and the number of individuals who will in fact need a particular accommodation. In general, the Commission interprets this phrase as it was used in the *Hardison* decision to mean that costs similar to the regular payment of premium wages of substitutes, which was at issue in *Hardison*, would constitute undue hardship. However, the Commission will presume that the infrequent payment of premium wages for a substitute or the payment of premium wages while a more permanent accommodation is being sought are costs which an employer can be required to bear as a means of providing a reasonable accommodation. Further, the Commission will presume that generally, the payment of administrative costs necessary for providing the accommodation will not constitute more than a *de minimis* cost. Administrative costs, for example, include those costs involved in rearranging schedules and recording substitutions for payroll purposes.

(2) Seniority Rights. Undue hardship would also be shown where a variance from a bona fide seniority system is necessary in order to accommodate an employee's religious practices when doing so would deny another employee his or her job or shift preference guaranteed by that system. *Hardison, supra,* 432 U.S. at 80. Arrangements for voluntary substitutes and swaps (see paragraph (d)(1)(i) of this section) do not constitute an undue hardship to the extent the arrangements do not violate a bona fide seniority system. Nothing in the Statute or these Guidelines precludes an employer and a union from including arrangements for voluntary substitutes and swaps as part of a collective bargaining agreement.

§ 1605.3 Selection practices.

(a) Scheduling of Tests or Other Selection Procedures. When a test or other selection procedure is scheduled at a time when an employee or prospective employee cannot attend because of his or her religious practices, the user of the test should be aware that the principles enunciated in these guidelines apply and that it has an obligation to accommodate such employee or prospective employee unless undue hardship would result.

(b) Inquiries Which Determine An Applicant's Availability to Work During An Employer's Scheduled Working Hours.

(1) The duty to accommodate pertains to prospective employees as well as current employees. Consequently, an employer may not permit an applicant's

need for a religious accommodation to affect in any way its decision whether to hire the applicant unless it can demonstrate that it cannot reasonably accommodate the applicant's religious practices without undue hardship.

(2) As a result of the oral and written testimony submitted at the Commission's Hearings on Religious Discrimination, discussions with representatives of organizations interested in the issue of religious discrimination, and the comments received from the public on these Guidelines as proposed, the Commission has concluded that the use of pre-selection inquiries which determine an applicant's availability has an exclusionary effect on the employment opportunities of persons with certain religious practices. The use of such inquiries will, therefore, be considered to violate Title VII unless the employer can show that it:

(i) Did not have an exclusionary effect on its employees or prospective employees needing an accommodation for the same religious practices; or

(ii) Was otherwise justified by business necessity.

Employers who believe they have a legitimate interest in knowing the availability of their applicants prior to selection must consider procedures which would serve this interest and which would have a lesser exclusionary effect on persons whose religious practices need accommodation. An example of such a procedure is for the employer to state the normal work hours for the job and, after making it clear to the applicant that he or she is not required to indicate the need for any absences for religious practices during the scheduled work hours, ask the applicant whether he or she is otherwise available to work those hours. Then, after a position is offered, but before the applicant is hired, the employer can inquire into the need for a religious accommodation and determine, according to the principles of these Guidelines, whether an accommodation is possible. This type of inquiry would provide an employer with information concerning the availability of most of its applicants, while deferring until after a position is offered the identification of the usually small number of applicants who require an accommodation.

(3) The Commission will infer that the need for an accommodation discriminatorily influenced a decision to reject an applicant when: (i) prior to an offer of employment the employer makes an inquiry into an applicant's availability without having a business necessity justification; and (ii) after the

employer has determined the applicant's need for an accommodation, the employer rejects a qualified applicant. The burden is then on the employer to demonstrate that factors other than the need for an accommodation were the reason for rejecting the qualified applicant, or that a reasonable accommodation without undue hardship was not possible.

Appendix A to §§ 1605.2 and 1605.3—Background Information

In 1966, the Commission adopted guidelines on religious discrimination which stated that an employer had an obligation to accommodate the religious practices of its employees or prospective employees unless to do so would create a "serious inconvenience to the conduct of the business". 29 CFR 1605.1(a)(2), 31 FR 3870 (1966).

In 1967, the Commission revised these guidelines to state that an employer had an obligation to reasonably accommodate the religious practices of its employees or prospective employees, unless the employer could prove that to do so would create an "undue hardship". 29 CFR 1605.1(b)(c), 32 FR 10298.

In 1972, Congress amended Title VII to incorporate the obligation to accommodate expressed in the Commission's 1967 Guidelines by adding section 701(j).

In 1977, the United States Supreme Court issued its decision in the case of *Trans World Airlines, Inc.* v. *Hardison,* 432 U.S. 63 (1977). *Hardison* was brought under section 703(a)(1) because it involved facts occurring before the enactment of Section 701(j). The Court applied the Commission's 1967 Guidelines, but indicated that the result would be the same under Section 701(j). It stated that Trans World Airlines had made reasonable efforts to accommodate the religious needs of its employee, Hardison. The Court held that to require Trans World Airlines to make further attempts at accommodations—by unilaterally violating a seniority provision of the collective bargaining agreement, paying premium wages on a regular basis to another employee to replace Hardison, or creating a serious shortage of necessary employees in another department in order to replace Hardison—would create an undue hardship on the conduct of Trans World Airlines' business, and would therefore, exceed the duty to accommodate Hardison.

In 1978, the Commission conducted public hearings on religious discrimination in New York City, Milwaukee, and Los Angeles in order to respond to the concerns raised by *Hardison.* Approximately 150 witnesses testified or submitted written statements.[5] The witnesses included employers, employees, representatives of religious and labor organizations and representatives of Federal, State and local governments.

The Commission found from the hearings that:

---

[5] The transcript of the Commission's Hearings on Religious Discrimination can be examined by the public at: The Equal Employment Opportunity Commission, 2401 E Street NW., Washington, D.C. 20506.

(1) There is widespread confusion concerning the extent of accommodation under the *Hardison* decision.

(2) The religious practices of some individuals and some groups of individuals are not being accommodated.

(3) Some of those practices which are not being accommodated are:

—Observance of a Sabbath or religious holidays;

—Need for prayer break during working hours;

—Practice of following certain dietary requirements;

—Practice of not working during a mourning period for a deceased relative;

—Prohibition against medical examinations;

—Prohibition against membership in labor and other organizations; and

—Practices concerning dress and other personal grooming habits.

(4) Many of the employers who testified had developed alternative employment practices which accommodate the religious practices of employees and prospective employees and which meet the employer's business needs.

(5) Little evidence was submitted by employers which showed actual attempts to accommodate religious practices with resultant unfavorable consequences to the employer's business. Employers appeared to have substantial anticipatory concerns but no, or very little, actual experience with the problems they theorized would emerge by providing reasonable accommodation for religious practices.

Based on these findings, the Commission is revising its Guidelines to clarify the obligation imposed by Section 701(j) to accommodate the religious practices of employees and prospective employees.

[FR Doc. 80-34046 Filed 10-30-80; 8:45 am]

BILLING CODE 6570-06-M

New York City 150
    political status 152
    public utilities 117, 123, 672
    recruitment (see heading)
    seniority (see heading)
    sex discrimination 223
    southern women 242, 932
    testing 130, 181, 638-639, 644, 648, 651, 656, 661, 663-664
    underemployment 3, 60
    unemployment 3, 60, 137, 147, 854
    wages 41, 398, 402, 946
    white-collar positions 118, 672, 824, 946
    women 194-195, 223, 242, 932

Nashville Gas Co. v. Satty 257

National Labor Relations Act 64, 98, 105, 126, 143-144, 151, 445

National Labor Relations Board 8, 68, 98, 110, 144

National origin discrimination:
    arbitration (see heading)
    cases 182, 1060
    citizenship 185, 188
    complaints (see heading)
    English Only Rule 179-180, 185, 187
    guidelines 120, 177, 180-181, 184-185, 1060
    harassment 180-181, 185
    testing 186
    Title VII 3, 61, 151, 177-179, 183, 970

Native Americans (see American Indians heading)

Negroes (see minorities)

New York City Transit Authority v. Beaver 491

New York Times Co. v. Sullian 368

New Orleans Police Department 87

Newport News Shipbuilding and Dry Dock Co. v. EEOC 264, 271

Norris v. Arizona 251

Occupational Safety and Health Act 64

Office of Federal Contract Compliance Program:
    enforcement powers 33, 62, 82, 96, 112, 114, 143, 242, 324,
        497, 763, 1014, 1026-1027

Ohio Civil Rights Commission 95

Ohio Fair Employment Practices Law 68, 95

Quotas (see preferential treatment heading)

Race discrimination:
    America 137, 147, 149, 152-153, 407, 748, 778
    arrest records 132
    assessment centers 833
    corporations 131, 134, 136, 141
    employment 61, 116, 133, 137, 153, 219, 223, 607, 817, 921,
        963, 970, 1041-1042, 1060, 1070, 1094, 1127
    historical development 149
    labor unions 783, 787 (also see heading)
    laws 151, 968
    litigation (see heading)
    minorities (see heading)
    preferential treatment 744, 747, 751, 763, 765, 778, 1101-
        1103, 1114 (also see heading)
    recruitment (see heading)
    remedies 143-144
    statistics 818
    testing 186, 638, 645, 654-656, 661, 664
    Title VII 132

Railway Labor Act 98

Recruitment:
    affirmative action (see heading)
    American Indians 856 (also see heading)
    handicapped applicants 537, 855, 866, 891
    Hispanics 856, 871, 875 (also see heading)
    law firms 858
    minorities 62, 67, 133, 136, 142, 638, 854, 856, 858, 860-
        864, 869-870, 872-874, 876, 878, 896, 903, 908, 963, 993
    networking 863
    requirements 19, 43, 62, 136, 635, 945
    Title VII 19, 854, 867
    women 62, 191, 422, 857, 859, 862-865, 868, 870, 872, 874,
        876-877, 896, 903, 908, 917, 993

Rehabilitation Act of 1973:
    administrative procedure 491, 507, 510
    amendments 519, 521-522, 526
    coverage 43, 466, 475, 478, 484, 486, 489-491, 493-495, 498,
        501, 503, 510, 513, 517-521, 525-526, 528, 532, 534, 536,
        539-540, 543, 549-556, 929, 956, 1013
    effectiveness 506, 511, 534
    enforcement 472, 484, 491, 497, 517
    handicap discrimination (see heading)
    HEW 475
    historical background 491
    litigation (see heading)
    remedies 490, 506, 525
    Section 503 463, 477, 481-482, 489, 503, 513, 517-518, 525,
        848
    Section 504 460, 466-467, 472, 475, 481, 488, 492-494, 503,
        507, 509, 526, 528-529, 532, 535-536

Religious discrimination:
    accommodation 58, 116, 154-176, 635, 929, 970
    arbitration (see heading)
    broadcasting 170
    collective bargaining agreement (see seniority heading)
    complaints (see heading)
    EEOC decisions 157
    EEOC guidelines 120, 154-156, 159-160, 163, 165-166, 174, 929
    employer's responsibilities 10
    Establishment Clause 154, 159-160, 165, 169, 174
    Federal Communication Commission 170
    general 120, 173
    history 154-155, 173
    litigation (see heading)
    seniority (see heading)
    Title VII 61, 144, 151, 154-155, 159-162, 165, 167-168, 172,
        174, 970
    Retaliation (see complaints heading)
    Reverse discrimination (see preferential treatment)
    Revenue Sharing Act 53
    Revised Order No. 4 928
    Ricks v. Delaware State College 1047

Schomer v. Smidt 368

Sears Roebuck Co. 1051

Seniority (layoffs):
    adverse impact 113, 137, 701, 704, 723
    affirmative action (see heading)
    age discrimination 573
    arbitration 104
    bonafide 1, 19, 62, 79, 82, 85, 113, 148, 227, 700-702, 704-
        705, 709-712, 715, 718-719, 722-723, 725-726, 732-733,
        735-736, 738, 909, 930, 1008, 1079
    Civil Rights Acts of 1866 and 1871 718
    departmental 63, 702
    EEOC 707, 730, 909
    Executive Order 11246 712-713, 719, 722
    federal employment 701, 722
    labor unions (see heading)
    litigation (see heading)
    minorities 133, 137, 148, 699, 700-701, 704, 707, 710-711,
        716-718, 720-722, 726-729, 736, 945
    plant-wide 699, 737
    preferential treatment (see heading)
    religious discrimination 66, 155, 167-168, 176
    remedies 704, 706, 708, 710, 725, 727, 729, 731, 734
    retroactive 706, 717
    sex discrimination 191
    statistics 814
    testing 703
    Title VII 29, 40, 47, 701-702, 704, 706, 709-711, 714-719,
        722, 725, 728, 733-736, 1008, 1079
    Women 236, 702, 704, 710-711, 718, 729, 731

definition 279, 305, 307-308, 331, 334, 338-339, 343, 346,
      356, 367, 375, 389, 929
Department of Education, Office for Civil Rights 280
effects 232, 277, 293-294, 297, 300-303
extent 281, 289, 316-318, 320, 323, 327, 343, 349, 353-355,
      357-360, 362, 364, 367, 375, 377-378, 382, 388
factory workers 375
female lawyers 384
guidelines 245, 289, 294-295, 299, 303, 313, 320, 323-324,
      329-332, 334, 337, 342-345, 348, 354, 370-371, 375, 380,
      383, 929
homosexuality 313
hospitality industry 278
historical development 284, 392
labor unions (see heading)
liability 283, 290, 299-300, 330, 334, 346, 366-367, 371-
      373, 385, 387, 391
litigations (see heading)
Marriott Corporation 278
Merit System Protection Board 315, 379
Michigan Task Force 334
OFCCP 324
Occupational Safety and Health Act 279
prevention 33, 279, 284, 286-287, 290, 296-299, 304-305, 307,
      311-312, 315, 322, 325-326, 346, 352, 356-358, 360, 362-
      363, 367, 371, 375, 378, 380-381, 385-386, 940
public sector 310, 343, 377
remedies 277, 279, 281, 287, 290-291, 296, 301-304, 306, 317,
      333-334, 342, 349, 356, 358, 378-378
secretaries 288, 318, 376
state government 289, 354, 378
survey 279, 282, 294, 297, 308, 315, 320, 322, 342, 351,
      360, 367, 379, 390
Title VII 279, 295, 305, 311, 312, 324, 332, 334-335, 341-342,
      349, 354, 361-362, 368, 370, 375, 385-386, 388, 391
Title IX 279-280, 356
tort action 335, 347, 368, 391
unemployment insurance 279, 292, 369, 374
waitresses 376
Washington, D.C. 298, 340
worker's compensation 277, 347
Working Women's Institute 317

Shultz v. Wheatson 407

Southbridge Plastics v. Local 759, Rubber Workers 719

Statistics:
    adverse impact 809
    affirmative action (see heading)
    age discrimination 568
    availability 807, 820-823 (also see labor market heading)
    chi-square 809
    defending discrimination claims 806
    litigation (see heading)